Understanding China

The series will provide you with in-depth information on China's social, cultural and economic aspects. It covers a broad variety of topics, from economics and history to law, philosophy, cultural geography and regional politics, and offers a wealth of materials for researchers, doctoral students, and experienced practitioners.

Renshan Zhang

Traditional Legal Culture in China

Springer

南京大學出版社
NANJING UNIVERSITY PRESS

Renshan Zhang
School of Law
Nanjing University
Nanjing, Jiangsu, China

ISSN 2196-3134 ISSN 2196-3142 (electronic)
Understanding China
ISBN 978-981-95-4696-1 ISBN 978-981-95-4697-8 (eBook)
https://doi.org/10.1007/978-981-95-4697-8

Jointly published with Nanjing University Press
The print edition is not for sale in Mainland China. Customers from Mainland China please order the print book from: Nanjing University Press.

978-7-305-20067-0

Translation from the Chinese Simplified language edition: "《中国法律文明》" by Renshan Zhang, © Nanjing University Press 2018. Published by Nanjing University Press. All Rights Reserved.

This work was supported by Chinese Fund for the Humanities and Social Sciences (18WFX001).

This Springer imprint is published by the registered company Springer Nature Singapore Pte Ltd.
The registered company address is: 152 Beach Road, #21-01/04 Gateway East, Singapore 189721, Singapore

Preface

The Chinese title of this book is *Zhongguo Falü Wenming* (*Chinese Legal Civilization* as the literal translation). Here, the term "civilization" actually carries a meaning closer to "culture" in this context. Thus, "Chinese legal civilization" essentially refers to the traditional legal culture in China. A fundamental distinction between the concepts of "legal civilization" and "legal culture" is that legal civilizations converge while legal cultures diverge. The standards for legal civilization are objective, measurable against benchmarks such as humanism versus barbarism, progress versus backwardness, liberty versus constraint, equality versus oppression, openness versus closedness, and democracy versus autocracy. Legal culture, by contrast, is quite inclusive, containing both commendable and undesirable aspects. Only a legal culture that is open and impartial, respectful of human nature, and inclusive can turn into a constituent piece in the mosaic of legal civilization.

Legal culture is inherently pluralistic. Throughout human history, diverse legal models have emerged. On a macro level, a number of major legal systems have been formed, such as the Civil Law system, the Anglo-American Law system, the Hindu Law system, the Islamic Law system, and the *Zhonghua Faxi*（中华法系）, manifested primarily in the traditional Chinese legal system. These law systems have continuously demonstrated profound legal wisdom and have propelled historical progress. On a micro level, each legal system encompasses a variety of legal forms shaped by distinct regions, administrative levels, and beliefs. Together, these manifold legal cultures compose a richly varied legal knowledge graph, rendering human life multidimensional, meaningful, vibrant, and fascinating.

Conflicts are inherent in legal culture. Human history has witnessed incessant and enduring clashes between different legal cultures, intertwined with acts of conquest and resistance, colonization and decolonization, assimilation and dissimilation. Such conflicts can arise between nations, ethnic groups, and regions, as well as between the state and its people, among families, and within neighborhoods. To prevent and resolve these conflicts, it becomes necessary to establish relatively fair and just public rules, i.e., law, or to devise mechanisms for settling and mediating disputes, termed "administration of justice." Legal culture has always advanced with difficulty through various forms of conflicts, which, in turn, has compelled the continuous development and refinement of the means of resolving disputes.

Legal cultures are capable of fusion. During the process of prolonged conflicts, pluralistic legal cultures are engaged in continuous comparison, mutual absorption, and competitive selection, and eventually, the most quintessential elements are often adopted by the majority and thus preserved and handed down. The process of conflict and fusion can be at times rapid, at times gradual, and can even be reversed sometimes, yet the primary trend toward fusion remains largely unchanged. It is through this fusion that legal cultures supplement each other and retain the essential, advancing the progress of legal civilization.

Legal cultures develop at various paces across different epochs. However, the disparity of development paces cannot negate the fundamental homogeneity of legal civilization. This shared foundation is reflected in the principles as follows: A sound legal system must recognize every individual as a "person," safeguarding their "personal" rights to life, liberty, property, equality, and dignity. Public power must derive from the populace, serve private rights, and be subject to stringent constraints; No one shall exercise their freedoms and rights in a manner that infringes upon the freedoms and rights of others. Virtues such as benevolence, righteousness, propriety, wisdom, fidelity, truth, goodness, beauty, friendship, and love should form the essential public morality of a healthy society.

Legal cultures develop with regional variations. However, regional differences cannot be indiscriminately overemphasized, under the pretext of preserving regional characteristics to justify adherence to legal-cultural practices that history has proven backward or even barbaric, including rigid hierarchies, male supremacy, inhumane chastity and filial piety rituals, interrogation by torture, and judicial injustice. Rejecting the fruits of advanced legal civilization under this guise is equal to fundamentally denying the universal applicability of legal civilization itself.

Traditional Chinese legal culture holds a unique position in the world's legal systems and has made profound contributions to the advancement of global legal civilization. Its finest elements, no matter whether in the past, at present, or in the future, remain treasures within the long river of world legal heritage, shining brilliantly across time and space. Conversely, those dross elements that fall out of step with the progress of contemporary legal civilization demand critical reflection and deliberate abandonment.

It is the foundational purpose of this book to enable traditional Chinese legal culture to achieve renewal through inheritance and purification, thereby continuing to contribute to the continuous advancement of human legal civilization.

Lastly, I wish to express my profound gratitude to Ms. Wang Haiping for her diligent translation efforts. With her assistance, a number of errors in the original manuscript have been corrected.

Nanjing, Jiangsu, China
October 8th, 2025

Zhang Renshan

Contents

Chapter 1
The Culture of Rites and Etiquettes

礼*Li* (rites), in Chinese traditional legal culture, is undoubtedly one of the most important concepts. The Chinese nation known as a "land of ceremony and decorum" is also named after the advancement of rites. The origin and development of rites have differentiated Chinese traditional legal culture from that of other nations and made Chinese legal system more diverse, hierarchical, and ethical. It has also shaped the pluralistic legal concepts or legal beliefs of the Chinese people and played a guiding role in the national governance model, the forming of the social order, and the orientation of the social life style in later generations. More specifically, rites and etiquettes determine the status of social members; rites and morality stipulate social morality and ethics; and rites and ethics guide social customs. Integrating ritual propriety, etiquettes, morality, and ethics, the system of rites has been central to Chinese culture, guiding behavior across all social strata, from the imperial court down to the countryside. The flourishing or decay of these rites was often seen as directly reflecting the nation's destiny, embodying the traditional belief: "Rise of rites leads to national prosperity and fall of rites results in national decline."[1] Hence, in order to understand the traditional legal culture in China, we need to start with the origin and development of rites.

1.1 Banquet Manners

1.1.1 Feasts Celebrating Bumper Harvests

When it comes to food, possibly no people in the world can approach food like the Chinese whose abilities and skills are fully showcased in the catering industry. "Have you eaten yet?" as a common greeting in China might be considered to pry

[1] Sima, Q., *Historical Records,* vol. 23.

R. Zhang, *Traditional Legal Culture in China*, Understanding China,
https://doi.org/10.1007/978-981-95-4697-8_1

into the privacy of others in other countries, whereas in China, it expresses friendliness and concern with good nature. It has been a long history since Chinese ancestors started to sit around the table, enjoying food and sharing food vessels together. The attentive people may find that at a relatively formal party, seating arrangements for everyone would be slightly different, and the order to speak and propose a toast varies with diners. Who is the host; who is the major guest and who is the minor guest—everything is evident, including each diner's social status and identity. Circumstances change with the passage of time, yet banquet manners remain as the legacy of traditional rites and etiquettes. Currently, those banquet manners are not imperative, but the role of rites is indispensable in the developing process of traditional legal culture in China.

Here is a quote from the classic *The Book of Rites:Qu Li* concentrated on rites in early China:

In the highest antiquity, they prized virtue; in the time next to it, giving and repaying was the thing attended to. What the rules of rites value is reciprocity. If one gives a gift and nothing comes in return, that is contrary to rites; if something comes to one in return, but he gives nothing, that also is contrary to rites. If one observes the rules of rites, he is in a condition of security; if he does not, he is in one of danger. Hence there is the saying, "The rules of rites should by no means be left unlearned."

"Reciprocity" is emphasized in the practice of rites. No reciprocity, no rites. In ancient China, people who did not follow rites were not secure. Modern interpersonal relationship will not be jeopardized if people do not follow rites, and at most, they will not be good friends. Why would people feel insecure when they did not follow rites in ancient China? The answer lies in the origin of the character "礼"(rites).

礼*Li* (the modern simplified form of 禮), according to its explanation from *Analytical Dictionary of Characters*, means: "*Li (rites)*, the principle of behavior, is just like shoes that people stand in and follow to walk. The rise of rites stems from the worship of gods, serving gods with rituals for gods' blessings. Based on the rule of ancient writing, the glyph combines "the meaning of示and 豊," with "豊" as the sound radical. That is to say, rites originated from religious rituals. *Notes on Analytical Dictionary of Characters* explains: "There are five types of rites, with the most important type as offering sacrifice, so the glyph of "禮"(rites) adopts "示" as the left radical. The right radical "豊" can be visualized as a sacrificial vessel." As was researched by Chinese archeologists, *Li*(rites) was written as "豊" in oracle bone inscriptions, symbolizing vessels full of jade and other treasures as sacrifice to gods and ancestors, and therefore the process of offering sacrifice and adopted rituals during the process is called "rites." This explanation emphasizes the relationship between rites and gods, but in human societies, does interpersonal interaction precede man-god contact or vice versa? To atheists, it is self-evident that interpersonal interaction precedes man-god contact. *Analytical Dictionary of Characters* was written during Han Dynasty in which the explanation on豊 is close to offering sacrifice. The radical豊in *Analytical Dictionary of Characters* symbolizes a vessel containing sacrifice using the豆pictograph. Characters in the category of indexing component豊all adopt this radical. Whereas the function of 豊is different from the original meaning of rites, the origin of rites should be explored from the early interpersonal activities.

Those who have failed to fulfill the obligation of repaying the host of a banquet after receiving his gift may be punished immediately for giving nothing in return. In minor cases, they could be left out of discussions on public affairs; more seriously, they could face retaliatory consequences, which poses a risk. Such cases are recorded in the history, and therefore rites encompass etiquettes, etiquettes encompass power, violation of etiquettes results in punishment, and absence of rites leads to jeopardy.

1.1.2 Rules of Reciprocities

In primitive societies, when barter behavior is rendered as ceremonial exchange, limited by materials, crops in exchange, especially in agriculture-based ethnic groups, might be the early gifts. That is to say, materials contained in vessels could be crops such as cereals instead of treasures like jade.[2] Researches of anthropologists and sociologists prove that primitive rites include gifts and etiquettes. Inside primitive societies, there is no commercial transaction but a friendship-based or coerced loan system. The loan system stipulates what is supposed to be given must be given and what is supposed to be accepted must be accepted; the recipient should pay the giver back even after quite a long time. The act of giving, receiving, and repaying is carried out in grand banquets and fetes celebrating harvests. In the process of exchange, people behave in humble manners, offer feasts, and stress etiquettes; attendants maintain order and there might be songs and dances. Seemingly, gifts and repayments are offered voluntarily, but in fact, they are compulsory in strict terms, whose binding force is either negotiated in private or settled by war in public.

People's social status is decided by their roles in a banquet: the host of a banquet must be the one with most power in the clan or the neighboring clans, reflected by his build, wisdom, wealth, and so on; the invited qualified guests must be the most prestigious and powerful in the clan or the neighboring clans. Certain etiquettes are applied to those invited guests, including their dressing codes, the number of their attendants, modes of transport, when to take their seats and which one to take at the table upon arriving, when to withdraw from the table, the order of withdrawal at the end of the banquet, and so on and so forth. Specification of rites and etiquettes is hereby demonstrated.

When the banquet is processed to a certain extent, the guests and the host rejoice with cheerful songs and dances, and then the music and dance etiquettes follow. This is also the reason why in traditional China, rites and music coexist as norms. In

---

[2] Jiang, S. (1998). On rites. *Tsinghua Law Review* (1).

social life, types of music and scale of dance vary with people, events, and places, and they have formed a binding system of specifications, combined with rites, penalties, and decrees.

A banquet is a place where important events are announced and titles are bestowed. If one's title or name was announced in private without being witnessed by public at a banquet, it would be considered thoughtless conduct, shameful and presumptuous, and might degrade his status as well. To guests, a banquet functions the same. The one with the highest status in a clan shall be invited first, receiving his share, and the rest shall then be distributed among the other guests according to seniority. Wealth is thus circulated in a compulsory manner: either bestowed as gifts or received as tributes. Those who are entitled to give possess wealth as well as a noble position and spirit; those who receive gifts accept both materials and spirit, and therefore, they repay the giver with materials and spirit. The spiritual repayment embodies thankfulness and faithfulness as coercive obligation. Once the repayment is not considered adequate, it entails violation of rites and of the de facto law. It is the reason and process of giving and repaying that can convert material force into spiritual burden and spiritual burden into material force once more, including gifts and etiquettes.[3] Gifts refer to gift-giving while etiquettes refer to fetes or activities where gifts are given and repayments are made. To sum up, rites mainly adjust the relationship between givers and repayers.

Giving and repaying of this kind, in Chinese tradition, is what the rules of rites value most—reciprocity. After a state came into being, rites turned into the privilege of the privileged class as a self-evident label of social status. The right to give and bestow is gradually centralized in the hands of rulers, and hence they are entitled to host ceremonies, bestow gifts, and demand those who have received their gifts to fulfill the obligation to repay. They shall establish all the specifications of etiquettes. Therefore, rites have been more and more hierarchical, and those among materials and ceremonies serve as binding social conduct for all social members. "Rites" embody both spiritual and material forces, rich in coercive nature as law. It has become increasingly easier to observe that "rites are adopted to emphasize distinctions."

In brief, primitive rites center upon food and banquets, and a large number of unearthed sacrificial vessels support the meaning of pictograph "礼"*Li* (rites).

1.1.3 Legacies of Hierarchical Consumption

Details of propriety in the later generations mostly exist in banquet etiquettes, ranging from greetings at the meeting, identity at a banquet, codes of dressing, drinking, and eating to order of seats, dancing, housing, etc. Banquets will be held at wedding and funeral ceremonies, encompassing ostentation and extravagance, and eating and

[3]The well-known French sociologist Mauss Marcel initiated the concept of Potlatch first that means a ceremony in which gifts are bestowed upon guests, published in *Sino-French University Monthly* 1933(1), quoted from a second source: Yang, X. (1986). Issues on the origin of "Rites"—On "Potlatch". *Journal of Hebei Normal University* (3).

drinking to define everybody's identity. Chinese food culture is so rich that eating almost extends to every corner of social life: job-hunting is called "searching for a rice bowl"; a stable job is called "iron rice bowl"; barely understanding something once unknown is "swallow raw and whole"; having a thorough grasp of something is "eat through"; not being certain is "eat without accuracy"; being sure is "take a reassurance pill"; more examples are silkworms' bites and a whale's gulp, big-pot rice, strangers, that is, *Shengren* (*Sheng* means raw), and acquaintances, that is, *Shuren* (*Shu* means cooked); what is done cannot be undone (literal translation: raw rice fully cooked); one cannot make bricks without straw (literal translation: the cleverest housewives cannot cook a meal without rice); revolution is not to treat guests to dinner; and practice makes perfect, making chop suey and so on and so forth.

Legacies to the present could be detailed specifications on the following things: "How many dishes and a soup" to cater for officials of different ranks? Should wine be available for official receptions? What types of cars should officials of different ranks deserve? What is the size of housing for officials of different ranks? What level of medical insurance is applied? And there are more to enumerate. Once those specifications are breached, including overstandard reception, oversize of housing, overstandard car use, and so forth, it leads to violation of rules and regulations. The people concerned need to correct their behavior and those who make serious mistakes would suffer punishment. Material and spiritual identity and status are consequently mirrored.

On the condition that the level of banquet etiquettes has been raised, only powerful and rich people can afford delicate food and dresses and offer sacrifices to gods or ancestors, which in turn has been the exclusive right of the privileged class. If the rites and etiquettes enjoined by the privileged class are copied by the ordinary people, that might be regarded as arrogation or breach of rites, namely, absence of rites, which would spell criminal or administrative penalties on them in terms of law, and their being expelled from the community in terms of spirit.

Rites as the label of social status have gradually gained greater influence in class-based societies. The right to give and bestow is totally at the hands of the ruling class of aristocrats who have the exclusive right to host ceremonies, bestow gifts, and demand those who have received the gifts repay them unconditionally. They further host ceremonies to share with deities and define all the specifications of etiquettes. Therefore, rites have been more and more hierarchical. Material rites and ceremonial rites both have binding force to regulate people's social conduct equipped with coercive nature like law.

1.2 The Divinity of Rites

1.2.1 The Making of Deities

Why is it that rites, commonly associated with food and banquets, imply the meaning of offering sacrifice to gods according to the early *Analytical Dictionary of Characters*? This connection highlights the long-term evolution of the concept within human social life.

Do deities create the world or human beings create deities? In the eyes of theists, the answer is the former, and to the believers of God, all the more so, for they believe God is the only true god, the Creator of everything. While to atheists, images of deities are all imagined and created by human beings, and hence it is the human beings who created deities. The divinity of rites is illustrated from the perspective of atheists as follows.

After the clan society evolved into the class society, deities were created and mythological consciousness became the mainstream worldview. Rites and the implication of sacrifice were connected. In primitive clans, those who were entitled to host banquets and bestow gifts gradually turned into a more powerful group with their biological features remaining the same as those of the ordinary. They, too, would grow old in appearance, yet their minds remained distinct. For the purpose to ensure their noble position in the clan, they set off a new round of apotheosis movement, cover their ordinary flesh with the halo of god, and make themselves the immortal idol the masses worship.

The more primitive humans are, the more ignorant they are of natural phenomena and the greater awe they have. However, the wiser group who stands out from the clans manages to grasp the right to interpret anomalies of nature. As they have occupied the respectable position in the clan, they might employ intellectuals such as recorders, sorcerers, and Confucian scholars to form a "think tank" to interpret certain natural phenomena through divination and other special rituals. What ordinary people cannot understand is believed to be mastered by the supernatural gods and heaven. When gods and heaven need to have their intention realized in the secular world, they must find a spokesperson or an agent. Those who are respected by the clan can be justified to act as the spokesperson or the agent.

There is a famous saying in *Zuozhuan: Commentary on the "Spring and Autumn Annals:13th Year of Duke Cheng's Rule*: "祀*Si*(sacrifice) and 戎*Rong*(warfare)are the two most critical state affairs." *Rong* refers to military power, while *Si* deals with the provision and interpretation of rules. These rules can not only restrict the behavior of the people but also some of the behavior of the rulers themselves and influence their political decisions, for example, to determine the feasibility of political activities via fortune-telling through divination. During Xia, Shang, and Zhou Dynasties, the monarchs wielded military and political power, and the power to enact and interpret laws and record cases was controlled by groups of the officers of prayers, diviners, recorders, sorcerers, Confucian scholars, and so forth authorized by monarchs. Due to their propaganda, many social rules, such as "rites," were constantly deified, and the halo of god was gradually formed and worn on the monarch's head.

1.2.2 Worships and Sacrifices

By continuous brainwash and indoctrination upon the people, apotheosis has become more and more deeply rooted. Those in power often elevate themselves to divine status by deifying certain natural phenomena. Ordinary people first worship heaven and gods and then respect those who have created and interpreted spirits and gods. Much of the original totem worship is the expression of the worship of gods. Take the origin of the Chinese "法"(the modern simplified form of灋), for example, it appears to be similar to totem worship. The earliest form of trial might be deemed as an ordeal. According to *Analytical Dictionary of Characters*, the character "法" *Fa* (law), particularly understood through its older form 灋, derives its meaning from its components: "Law, as penalties, symbolized by flat surface of water, should be level, just, and fair, and then "氵" (water) is adopted as the left radical. The right side incorporates "廌" *Zhi*, a mythical and single-horned creature likened to an ox or a sheep, used in ancient trials or ordeals to identify, strike, and remove the guilty party, so the character also adopts the radical of "去" (remove). "廌," an ox or a sheep with a single horn, was used to strike the guilty party during a trial in ancient times. It is a pictograph." What kind of animal is廌 or獬豸 *Xiezhi* used by later generations? It is likened to an ox, a sheep, a deer, a kylin, a bear, or even a David's deer, but all of them fall into a mythical category with ancient religious traces. As for the dragon totem, it invariably symbolizes Chinese emperors.

Because the ancient people revere heaven, the rulers try their utmost to take the will of heaven as the criterion in dealing with social affairs. The essence of heaven is order, so under the heavenly gods, there is the god of land; other gods like the god of the sun, the moon, and the stars, gods of mountains and rivers, and animals such as cats and mice all belong to heaven. Heaven and earth and order of precedence are all heavenly ways. If applied to human society, it is immoral to apply anything that is not in line with order. Therefore, the only thing that functions in the field of morality is "中"*Zhong* (The concept that individuals of various social statuses and positions have the appropriate morals suitable for their respective time and place is referred to as "the just".), which is the foundation of morality, and the patriarchal system is the fundamental element that contributes to its formation.[4] Patriarchs and clan leaders upgraded from patriarchs naturally become the leaders of their own clans. By apotheosis, they fuel their power with super legitimacy and continue to strengthen such public consciousness: the worship of their power is the same as the worship of heaven, god, and emperor. After the formation of the state, this trend has been increasingly strengthened. There are many such records during the pre-Qin era, such as the birth of Shang Dynasty, accompanied by advent of God Bird. According to *The Classic of Poetry:Ode of Shang:Swallow*: By Heaven sent down, the swallow came to earth and gave to our great 契Qi his mystic birth. The sire of Shang and his children long abode in Yin-land, waxing great. Zheng Xuanjian said: Heaven sent a swallow and it dropped an egg, which Jian Di, the daughter of *Rong*Tribe, took and swallowed; and from this came the birth of Qi. A legend about the manner of Qi's conception is that Jian Di, Emperor Ku's (an ancient legendary emperor) minor concubine, the daughter of *Rong* Tribe, was bathing with others in an open place and saw an egg that dropped by a swallow and swallowed it. Afterward, she was pregnant and gave birth to Qi, who was the ancestor of Shang. Hence,

[4] Cai,Y. (1998). *The History of Chinese Ethics*, The Commercial Press, 8–9.

Shang Dynasty has the tradition of worshiping gods. *The Book of Rites*:*Biao Ji* records, "the king of Yin (Shang) worshiped ghosts and gods, lead the people to serve ghosts and gods, value ghosts and gods and despise rites." Zhou's ancestor, Hou Ji, was also the son of deity. "And thus she bore her son, Hou Ji…Once in a narrow lane exposed, the sheep and oxen round him closed, and sheltered with their loving care. Again the woodman found him, where in a wide forest he was placed, and bore him from the darksome waste. On the cold ice exposed once more, a bird, beneath the child and over, stretched its great wings. When it took flight, how Ji began to wail in fright."[5] *Historical Records* also recorded: "The ancestor of Zhou Dynasty was called *Qi* (abandon). His mother is the daughter of "*Youtaishi*" Tribe leader, named Jiang Yuan. Jiang Yuan was the first spouse of Emperor Ku. When Jiang Yuan went to the wild and saw the footprint of a giant. She flipped and hence stepped on the footprint. As soon as she stepped on it, she felt something moving in her womb, as if she were pregnant. When she gave birth to the baby with full term, she felt unlucky, and therefore she left the baby in a narrow lane, but the horses and cows that passed by avoided stepping on him; and then she abandoned him in the woods, only to find that there were too many people. Afterward, she left him on the ice of the ditch, birds came and covered or supported him with their wings to protect him. Jiang Yuan thought it was a miracle, and hence brought him back and raised him. Because she wanted to abandon the child at the very beginning, she named him *Qi* (abandon)."[6] Since *Hou Ji*as Zhou's ancestor was born after his mother stepped on a giant's footprint and thus conceived, wherever he showed up, he was sheltered.

Class societies emerged during Xia, Shang, and Zhou Dynasties. It is not until Shang and Zhou Dynasties that礼(rites) truly became rich in meaning as interpreted by *Analytical Dictionary of Characters*. Similar to this is帝(emperor), meaning the dead ancestors. As is explained in *Analytical Dictionary of Characters*: "帝equals 谛, the name called to rule the world." The ancient meaning, on the other hand, was that帝adopts the radical of木(wood) and of束(a referential symbol meaning to tie up). So tie up the firewood and sacrifice it to god as a whole in meaning is the composition of the character帝. The emperor thereafter presides over the sacrificial rituals to heaven, ghosts, gods, and so on, acting as the supreme "ruler" who takes charge of everything in the world, such as logging, hunting, production, construction of cities, disasters, and so forth. On behalf of god's will, he exercises the unanimous power in the world. Whoever disobeys his orders is against the will of heaven, and he has the ultimate right to punish those people. Such discourses read everywhere in early kings' speeches (to the army), instructions, counsels, and so on.

From this, we may think of the traditional deities in China, who are most often the personified idols. Since they are anthropomorphized, those deities must experience human emotions and desires. They also need basic necessities of life such as food, clothing, shelter, and means of transport. Additionally, they might seek companionship: a grandfather gnome should be paired with a grandmother gnome; gods

---

[5] The Classic of Poetry:DaYa:Shengmin.

[6] *The Records of the Grand Historian*, Vol. 4, Annals of Zhou Dynasty, Chap. IV.

and goddesses appear in pairs, for example, Jade Emperor is matched with the Queen Mother. The Goddess of Mercy can appear as a masculine, robust man, or a plump and gentle woman.

Since god is incarnation of humans, he will hold banquets and sacrifice regularly to provide good food and wine. Similarly, there are descriptions of sacrificial rituals in the Bible: Sunday is designated by God as the "Sabbath Day." As is narrated in *Exodus*, God has sent a message to Moses: Make for me an altar of earth, offering on it your burned offerings and your peace-offerings, and your sheep and your oxen. Sacrifices are in need of fixed altars, vessels, and time; the power to preside over sacrifices to gods belongs exclusively to rulers, many of whom are early "kings." On the one hand, they fear gods; on the other hand, they want to put the halo of gods on their own heads and show the orthodoxy and supremacy of their status. A man who has the power to create gods and the halo of gods can not only manipulate the property and even lives of ordinary people while he himself is alive but also pass down the halo to his son when he dies; after the son is gone, he can again move it to the next generation. In short, once a ruler, always a ruler, generation after generation. Upon entering the class society, these individuals became the so-called kings, Sons of Heaven, and emperors, superior to all common people.

1.2.3 Mandate of Heaven on Rulership

According to oracle bone inscriptions, heavenly gods are supreme who have the absolute authority and take charge of wind, rain, thunder, lightning, and other natural phenomena. They are omnipotent. Gods are created by humans, and the creator is the model of god; hereafter, "kings," the agent of gods on earth, often emphasize "do by god's will," through which they can do anything, such as making rules, interpreting rules, and implementing rules. All in all, it is they who decide everything.

During Shang and Zhou Dynasties, the idea that the king's power was "ordained by god" was popular in the mainstream worldview. Rulers must make believe that they do everything according to the will of god, either petty or big. They often legitimize their behavior and intention by claiming that's god's will. The war waged against the enemy can be described as a "divine punishment" or "nemesis." When King Tang of Shang crusaded against King Jie of Xia, he claimed: "but for the many crimes of the sovereign of Xia, Heaven has given the charge to destroy him." "The sovereign of Xia is guilty, and as I fear God, I dare not but punish him."[7] So everything is done in accordance with the God's will, that is, "Now, I, Fa, am simply executing, respectfully the punishment appointed by Heaven."[8] The king of Shang crusaded against Xiais to enforce justice on behalf of Heaven, and therefore the subordinates had to obey and follow his orders; otherwise, the king would punish

[7] *The Book of Historical Documents*:The Books of Shang:The Speech of Tang.

[8] *The Book of Historical Documents*:The Books of Zhou:The Speech at Mu.

them. Before the late Shang Dynasty, God seemed to be a supernatural commander-in-chief, and King Yin was also dominated by Him. King Yin was then the agent of God on earth.

Worship of ancestors was also popular during Shang Dynasty. Ancestors were regarded as heavenly gods who took charge of every worldly thing, and hence King Yin needed to inquire about everything from ancestors by practicing divination, a set of very complicated and tedious rituals. In the late Shang Dynasty, a dead king was called "emperor," "king emperor," and "上帝God." Nevertheless, "God" here is not the Creator God in the Chinese version of the *Bible* but a personified god. A king is opposite to God and is thus called the Lower Emperor. In this way, the king and God are emperors and they commence to integrate. The king is rendered opposite to all the people and becomes superior to them in the position of carrying out the God's will, inheriting the ancestors' career, and saving the lives of the people; God is supreme, but only the king has the authority to inherit the destiny of God in the embodiment of Him; the ancestors are gods too, but only the king is their heir. All men are saved and dominated by the king.[9] *Pan Geng I of The Book of Documents* states: "Heaven will perpetuate its decree in our favor in this new city--the great inheritance of the former kings will be continued and renewed, and tranquility will be secured to the four quarters (of the kingdom)." Similar records can be found in *Pan Geng II of The Book of Documents*: My measures are forecast to prolong your (least of) life from Heaven; do I force you by the terrors of my power? My object is to support and nourish you all." The literal translation could be: Your lives are passed on to me from God. How dare I press you by force! All that I want to do is to support you!

Since the king is the symbol of God, in justice practice, the king also has supreme power. *Pan Geng I of The Book of Historical Documents* records: "Do not you despise the old and experienced, and do not make little of the helpless and young. Seek every on long continuance in this (new city), which is to be your abode…and listen to the plans of me, the One man. I will make no distinction between men as being more distantly or more nearly related to me--the criminal shall die the death, and the good-doer shall have his virtue distinguished. The prosperity of the country (ought to) come from you all. If it fail in prosperity, that must arise from me, the One man, erring in the application of punishment. Be sure, all of you, to make known this announcement. From this time forward, attend respectfully to your business; have (the duties of) your offices regularly adjusted; bring your tongues under the rule of law:--lest punishment come upon you, when repentance will be of no avail." The announcement simply means: since your lives have been renewed from heaven by me, all your actions have to completely conform to my orders and you need to be utterly faithful to me without having a second thought; nothing will go right without my decisions and orders; from now on, everyone should behave themselves; do not speak or act in an unruly way; if you disobey my orders, you are just making a rod for your own back; do not regret it if punished by me. To those who

---

[9] Liu, Z. (1992). *Chinese Ancient History of Political Ideas*.Nankai University Press. 2–3.

disobeyed his orders, the king of Yin also threatened not only to kill them but also to let them die without descendants—"I shall execute all of them and cut off their family lines." The king of Shang has completely held the power of enforcing criminal law in his own hands. He has not only pulled "Heaven" to make the flag of command but also employed their dead fathers and grandfathers as gods to strengthen his own voice: "Of old, my royal predecessors made your ancestors and toil (only for their good). You are equally the people whom I (wish to) cherish. But your conduct is injurious--it is cherished in your hearts. Whereas my royal predecessors made your ancestors and fathers happy, they, your ancestors and fathers, will (now) cut you off and abandon you, and not save you from death. Here are those ministers of my government, who share with me the offices (of the kingdom)--and yet they (only think of hoarding up) cowries and gems. Your ancestors and fathers earnestly represent (their course) to my high sovereign, saying, 'Execute great punishments on our descendants.' So do they advise my high sovereign to send down great calamites (on those men)."[10] And he added: "long ago, our predecessor, King Tang, contributed much more than his predecessors to our country and reduced the possibility of natural disasters by moving his subjects to the mountains. Now that my subjects have been displaced by floods and have no stable settlement, you ask me why I want to move in large numbers. This is because God will renew the virtue of our ancestors and well govern our kingdom. I eagerly and respectfully abide by the will of God to save my subjects and live forever in the new kingdom. Therefore, I, a young man, dare not give up my great strategy of moving our capital to a new place, for God's will has been conveyed through messengers; I dare not go against the result of divination and must carry forward the will of God."[11] Brainwashed continuously for a long term, ordinary folks have gradually accepted the trinity status of Heaven, Emperor, and King. It is entirely ordained by God that all the power under heaven is mastered in the hands of the king and the people shall never doubt it.

King Wu of Zhou Dynasty crusaded again King Zhou of Shang Dynasty also claimed that he followed God's will, "The iniquity of Shang is full. Heaven gives the command to destroy it. If I did not obey Heaven, my iniquity would be great."[12] King Wu's conquest of King Zhou obeyed heavenly order. Most of later emperors were keen on deifying themselves, and examples like "follow God's will and inherit

[10] *The Book of Historical Documents*:The Books of Shang:Pan Geng II.

[11] *The Book of Historical Documents*:The Books of Shang:Pan Geng III: "Of old, my royal predecessor, (Tang), that his merit might exceed that of those who were before him, proceeded to the hill-site. Thereby he removed our evils, and accomplished admirable good for our country. Now you, my people, were by (your position) dissipated and separated, so that you had no abiding place. (And yet) you asked why I was troubling your myriads and requiring you to remove. But God, being about to renew the virtuous service of my high ancestor, and secure the good government of our kingdom, I, with the sincere and respectful (of my ministers), felt a reverent care for the lives of the people, and have made a lasting settlement in (this) new city. I, a youth, did not neglect your counsels; I (only) used the best of them. Nor did any of you presumptuously oppose the decision of the tortoise-shell;—so we are here to enlarge our great inheritance."

[12] *The Book of Historical Documents*:The Books of Zhou:The Great Declaration I.

a new fortune," "a Son of Heaven," "wisdom endowed by God," and "incarnated by the holy Dragon" were all duplicates of early apotheosis. *The Records of the Grand Historian* records: after drinking some wine, Liu Bang was crossing over a swampy land, while suddenly, a giant snake appeared; he drew his sword and chopped it. Afterward, he met a granny crying over her son moaning that her son was the son of the White Emperor, incarnated as a snake, but got killed by the son of the Red Emperor when he stood on the road. She then disappeared all of a sudden. On hearing this, Liu Bang was delighted, believing he himself was the son of the Red Emperor. When he escaped and hid himself in the wild between Mang and Yang mountains, "a number of mysterious things did happen one after another. After people of Pei County heard about it, they wanted to follow him."[13] *Zi Zhi Tong Jian* (The Comprehensive Mirror to Aid in Government) records: "Liu Bang, with courtesy name Ji, had a high nose and distinct features that had some resemblance to that of a dragon. He also had 72 dark spots all over his left leg." Liu Bang was born to be an emperor. As the founding emperor of Han Dynasty, he was widely depicted as a deity. The *History of the Ming Dynasty* records: "When Zhu Yuanzhang's mother was pregnant with him, one night in her dream, a fairy gave her a pill. She put the pill in her palm and found the pill shed light. She then swallowed it and when she woke up, there was still fragrance in her mouth. When Zhu Yuanzhang was born, red light filled the room." Since then neighbors have often seen the Zhu's family on fire, only to find nothing wrong when they ran over to help. "The Queen Mother often dreams of a Taoist priest coming from the northwest to Shenan wheat field, putting a pill of white medicine in the hands of the Queen Mother. It shed light and turned bigger." The fairy explained that the precious pill was edible. She swallowed the pill and woke up. She retold the dream to her husband and could still smell the fragrance vaguely. The next day, Zhu Yuanzhang was born.[14] Apotheosis of this kind is not uncommon even in the modern times. Stories that shed light upon "immortality," "long live (the king)," "shine forever like the moon and the sun," and so forth still occur from time to time as traces of deification of ancient rites.

1.3 The Secularities of Rites

1.3.1 Fitness with Rites

The rulership is strengthened by theocracy, and it is easy to be extremely cruel because of the latter, which is not restricted by rules and often makes the national policy lose room for adjustment and go to extremes, proved with evidence by King Zhou of Shang Dynasty. In the end, he bemoaned: "Alas, isn't my life at the hand of

[13] *The Records of the Grand Historian* Vol. 8, Annals of Gaozu the 8th.

[14] *The History of Ming Dynasty*, Vol. 1, Annals 1, *Records of Taizu* Vol 1; *Records of Taizu of Ming Dynasty*, Vol 0.1.

God?"[15] Therefore, some people start to question the role of deified monarchy, trying to find a lubricant between God's will, rulership, and law to ensure the flexibility and continuity of national policy.

In the process of regime change, it is often necessary to answer some questions on "fitness with rites": since the rulership is bestowed by God, then how can we explain the relationship between the overthrow of the old dynasties by "Tang &Wu Revolution" and the violation of God's will? King Zhou also claimed to be the embodiment of God, whereas the people of Zhou Dynasty overthrew him. Isn't it tantamount to offending God? This requires the people of Zhou Dynasty to find a theoretical basis to take off the crown of God from the head of the king of Shang Dynasty and put it on the head of the king of Zhou Dynasty. Therefore, representatives such as Zhou Gongdan thoroughly revised the concept of God and made a timely interpretation of "fitness with rites," based on the experience and lessons from the vicissitudes of Xia and Shang Dynasties.

People of Zhou Dynasty, like those of Shang Dynasty, worshiped God as well but solved the contradiction between man and God: on the one hand, God cannot be abandoned; on the other hand, God's will might change. For example, the worldly fate bestowed by God is not immutable. "Only fate is fickle" is what we are saying. What does Heaven refer to when bestowing humans with fate? That depends on the performance of them, especially that of the king: good performances fetch blessings and good fortune; bad performances fetch ill omens and bereavement. This is the rule of regime change in Xia, Shang, and Zhou Dynasties. As is known to people of Zhou Dynasty, "God's will is never constant" is a fit explanation.[16] Then "the virtuous occupy rulership," for "the doings of High Heaven have neither sound nor smell. Take your pattern from King Wen, and the myriad regions will repose confidence in you." God only choose those with a high virtue. Who has got a high virtue? Certainly they refer to the founders of Zhou Dynasty represented by King Wen, for "think of the virtue of King Wen, and enter greatly into his boundless anxieties."[17] Since everything is the will of God, there is no choice but to accept it. "The thing was from Heaven; do not offer resistance"[18]; therefore, King Wen, King Wu, and so forth helped to strengthen small states such as Zhou, and such was also the result of people's efforts of Zhou. What evidence can prove the rulers are virtuous? It lies in the feelings of the people to reflect God's will that they are the leaders truly devoted to the people wholeheartedly. It was stated in *The Book of Historical Documents:The Books of Zhou:The Announcement to the Prince of Kang* that "Awful though Heaven be, it yet helps the sincere. The feelings of the people can for the most part be discerned." It means that awfulness and sincerity of Heaven can be reflected by the feelings of the people and thus arose the thought that the people were closer than

---

[15] Liu, Z (Ed.) (1992). *History of Ancient Chinese Political Thought.* Nankai University Press, 6; *The Book of Historical Documents:The Books of Shang:The Chief of the West's Conquest of Li.*

[16] The Classic of Poetry:DaYa:Wen Wang.

[17] The Book of Historical Documents:The Books of Zhou:Prince Shi.

[18] The Book of Historical Documents:The Books of Zhou:The Numerous Officers.

Heaven and it was not necessary to speculate on God's will without understanding the feelings of the people. If the rulers fail to make the people sensible and lead them to a state of peace and well-being, they are not commensurate to understanding God's will. Therefore, in political life, adhering to "following God's will and protecting the people" is the key. In *The Book of Historical Documents:The Announcement about Drunkenness*, it warns "let not people look into water; let them look into other people as a mirror" reflecting foresight and insight.

The exact wisdom of Duke Zhou and others rulers lies in their preservation of the concept of "God" and explanation of the necessity of regime change. They not only regard ghosts, gods, emperors, and heaven as spiritual "umbrellas" but also put forward the idea of being reality-oriented and human affairs-based, so as to meet the requirements of both humans and gods. The systemized version of this thought is the legislative principle of "matching heaven with virtue, following God's will and protecting the people" and the judicial principle of "promoting morality and being prudent in infliction of punishment."[19] From this formed the philosophy of rites and laws under the unique patriarchal system of the Western Zhou Dynasty. The rulers of the Zhou Dynasty were more reality-oriented, paid due attention to human affairs, revised the concept of God, and realized the change from emphasizing God-related affaires to emphasizing human affairs.

1.3.2 The System of Ritual Codes

1.3.2.1 Establishment of the System of Ritual Codes

Western Zhou Dynasty lasted from the eleventh-century BC to 771 BC. In order to strengthen rulership, the rulers of the early Zhou Dynasty carried out the policy of "enacting the system of enfeoffment and building the same surname," enfeoffing the aristocrats of the Zhou royal family with pieces of land throughout the country to found vassal states. On the basis of "the founding of vassal states," Duke Zhou distilled the inherited systems of former dynasties and established a systematic set of rules related to "rites and music." *Shangshu Dazhuan* (The Annotations on *The Book of Historical Documents*) records: "While Duke Zhou acted as regent, he ended chaos the first year, conquered Shang Dynasty the second year, recovered the rebellious state Yan the third year, enacted the system of enfeoffment the fourth year, established Luoyi as the capital of the East to strengthen the central rulership there the fifth year, established a systematic set of rules related to "rites and music" the sixth year, and finally returned his power to King Cheng the seventh year." It took Duke Zhou 6 years to help the Zhou Dynasty complete the system of rites and music, and he became a "saint" worshipped by Confucians in later generations. Rites, originated from etiquette and custom, started to shift to the secular system of

[19]The Book of Historical Documents:The Books of Zhou:The Announcement to the Prince of Kang.

rites. Based on the patriarchal clan system, this shift is closely related to the formation of social structure of the Zhou Dynasty featuring home-country integration.

The system of enfeoffment is a major measure for the Western Zhou Dynasty to fulfill the establishment of its political power and consolidation of its rule. Western Zhou used to be a "small vassal state" in the northwest of Shang Dynasty. How could it now control the vast territory of the country? Especially how could it accommodate the old aristocrats of Shang Dynasty who just failed and still have the idea of restoring their rulership? All these are urgently awaiting the new regime to cope. The two measures that the new regime Western Zhou has taken are "move the numerous officers who remained from the Yin (Shang) Dynasty to Chengzhou (Luoyang)" and "enact the system of enfeoffment." The system of enfeoffment enfeoffs the brothers, uncles, and nephews of the Zhou royal family, aristocrats with the same surname, relatives with different surnames, and founding members of the Zhou Dynasty, with varied pieces of land. These newly established vassal states serve as a new system of rulership over the newly occupied land and function as the protective defense for the rule of the Zhou Dynasty, that is, "enfeoffing relatives with land, establishing vassal states to defend Zhou" or "enfeoffing princes and establishing defensive vassal states."

According to basic statistics, there were 71 vassal states at the beginning of the Zhou Dynasty, from which 40 states were ruled by princes of surname Ji. Rites were adopted as the only criteria for enfeoffment. The size of enfeoffed lands, varied ranks of title, and grades of service systems of enfeoffed lands were all determined by the distance and proximity from the king of Zhou. Generally speaking, there were five hierarchical ranks of title as Duke, Marquess, Count, Viscount, and Baron and five hierarchical grades of the service system (*Wu Fu*), that is, Dian, Hou, Sui, Yao, and Huang from the highest to the lowest. Ranks of title determine social statuses and grades of the service system determine levels of tributes. Enfeoffment by the king of Zhou is called "construction of vassal states." Every time a Hou (Marquess) state is enfeoffed, the king of Zhou issues a message to the enfeoffed person, which is called a "*CeMing*" (Appointment), providing information on the boundary of the state territory, the population of the jurisdiction, the size of the land, and the subordinate officials, servants, slaves, and sacrificial vessels, flags and attires, etc., so as to indicate the ruling power over the vassal state and rank of power of the enfeoffed one. The enfeoffed state princes also followed the same pattern to enfeoff their ministers and senior officials with feoffs within the vassal state.

The king of Zhou had the right to enfeoff princes, and the vassal states must do their duty to the king of Zhou, so as to conform to the reciprocal circle of "giving and repaying." The rights of princes were such as to decide everything in their own vassal state, including taxes, land use, city construction, and so on, to establish their own army, and to let their descendants inherit the vassal state. Those who were enfeoffed should do their duties. The duties of the princes were as follows: to serve the king of Zhou as their joint ruler, pay respects to him, render tributes to him, provide corvee and military assistance, defend the royal family of the king of Zhou, and so forth. The king of Zhou enfeoffed the princes with land and people, not only fulfilling the obligation to protect the rights of the princes but also possessing the power to deprive the princes of their titles, cut down their lands, and lower their ranks. To those princes, the king of Zhou had the power to either reward or punish them. The king of Zhou also inquired about the succession and abolition of the rulership of princes and even the appointment and removal of ministers or senior officials of vassal states. Some princes of vassal states also hold the post of ministers serving the royal family of Zhou. In this way, the political ties between the royal family and princes of vassal states would be closer. Therefore, the circular etiquette and custom of giving and repaying at the original banquet was upgraded into rites and etiquettes at the national level. The royal family of Zhou was the giver, the vassal state was the repayer, and thus the value of reciprocity was redefined. If the vassal state fails to fulfill its obligations, such as failure to render tributes including local products to the king of Zhou on time, it will be deemed as violation of rites and etiquettes. The king of Zhou can send a punitive expedition to the vassal states based on this reason, which is the essence of "if one doesn't observe the rules of rites, he is the one in danger." According to this system of enfeoffment, the king of Zhou enfeoffed those who were close to him with vassal states, and they were then called princes; the princes thereafter enfeoffed their relatives and meritorious officials with pieces of land within the vassal state who then became ministers and senior officials in the vassal state. Those ministers and senior officials could also divide and give some proportion of their land to their sons who then became masters of their feoffs. The king of Zhou is the greatest suzerain and the princes become vassals. Each layer below the princes constitutes suzerains and vassals alternately, and the vassals must obey the command of the suzerains.

Specifications of enfeoffment:

Ranks of title: Duke, Marquess, Count, Viscount, and Baron

Grades of the service system, that is, Dian, Hou, Sui, Yao, and Huang (each grade of service covers 500 li)

Specifications of rites and etiquettes: land, music, servants, palace, carriages, etc.

Relationship of administrative subordination: suzerain-vassal, rituals-loyalty, and rights-duties.

The enfeoffment system further expanded the patriarchal clan system centered on the surname of Ji. The Western Zhou Dynasty was a typical patriarchal society. The entire society was established on the patriarchal hierarchy, forming the hierarchical relationship between the king, princes, ministers, senior officials, and so on. The king of Zhou was the greatest patriarch, and the throne was inherited by the eldest son, and the rest were princes, that is, lesser patriarchs; the princes' ranks of title were also inherited by the eldest sons, and there were again differences between the greatest and lesser patriarchs and so did the aristocrats. The princes and aristocrats with different surnames practiced the same patriarchal system, and the princes and aristocrats with the surname of Ji and those of different surnames usually constructed their alliance by marriages. In this way, a huge kinship network centered on the king, spread by various ranks on the hierarchy such as princes, ministers, senior officials, and so on. In the network, kingship power and clan power merge together, and the aristocratic class guarantees the inheritance of its status through this system.

"Rites" fit well to maintain and protect this system. The principles of law and rites based on "kinship" and "hierarchy" started to take form.

During the Middle Ages, Europe also carried out a system of enfeoffment: the suzerain handed over territory to the vassals, who had to fulfill certain obligations in return for the suzerain. In his own vassal state, the vassal minister has absolute authority. In this way, layers of enfeoffments finally form a pyramid structure, as was the case in the feudal society of the Middle Ages in the West. The academic circles generally called this system the "feudal system." It has been accepted by many scholars that the Western Zhou Dynasty was in the feudal period of Chinese history.

1.3.2.2 Rites and Music

The five main aspects of the ritual codes of the Western Zhou Dynasty are known as "five rituals": *Ji Li* (sacrificial ceremonies), *Xiong Li* (burial rites), *Jun Li* (army etiquettes), *Bin Li* (hospitality etiquettes), and *Jia Li* (wedding ceremonies). The function of those rites is to maintain social hierarchy, preventing "arrogation." The ritual codes of the Western Zhou Dynasty stipulate the number of tripods and the types of meat therein for different classes in aristocratic banquets: nine tripods for kings (beef, lamb, piglet, dried fish, dried meat, tripe, pork, fresh fish, fresh dried meat), seven tripods for princes (beef, lamb, piglet, dried fish, dried meat, tripe, pork); five tripods for ministers (lamb, piglet, dried fish, dried meat, tripe); and three tripods for aristocrats (piglet, dried fish, dried meat). The number of music and dance performers also varies with classes. Take dance for example: ceremonial dance of the highest level consists of 8 佾*Yi* (lines, 1 *Yi* equals 8 and 8 times *Yi* equals 64), 64 dancers; inferior levels are reduced to 6 lines, 4 lines, and 2 lines in turn, with 8 dancers per each line. If someone does not follow the specifications, he is about to be punished for violation of rites.

Western Zhou's system of rites and music is part of social super structure. "Rites" emphasizes "differentiation" between classes, meaning "respecting those who deserve to be respected"; the central problem to be solved by "rites" is to distinguish between the high and low of social status, for the establishment of patriarchal clan system or the system of succession. Derived from the patriarchal clan system is the ritual law that defines and maintains the strict hierarchical relationship between father and son, among brothers and princes, as the embodiment of relationship of subordination. On the other hand, rites play a role in consolidating the patriarchal clan system to safeguard it and maintain the rule of the king of Zhou. Whoever violates the ritual law that has specified etiquettes, housing, clothing, utensils, etc. will be regarded as violation of rites or arrogation. Music has the function to harmonize and to "keep relatives and friends close." It is stated in *The Book of Rites: Yueji: Yuelun* that "music comes from within, and rites derive from the external. Music comes from within, so it influences minds without being noticed; rites derive from the external, so they constitute the system of rites." It is written in *Yueji: Yuehua* that music cultivates the mind and rites correct behavior. Zheng Xuan in the Eastern Han

Dynasty who annotated *The Book of Rites* explained: "Music is from within so harmony rests in mind; rites are external and therefore reflect respect in appearance only." Wang Yinzhi, a scholar in Qing Dynasty, believed that music generates from within and is sincere and true while rites reflect the external human behavior and they are dynamic, hence not necessarily sincere from the heart. Sun Xidan, from the Qing Dynasty as well, added: "I believe the nature of music and rites rests in the heart. Nevertheless, music is used to harmonize the rule of the king, attained by the agreeable hearts; therefore, music generates from within. Rites are used to differentiate degrees of kinship and stratify classes of people, realized by restricting people's external behavior; therefore, rites derive from the external. Music comes from within, hence exempt from stratification of social classes, which aims to influence without being noticed, while rites derive from the external, hence defined in great detail, which help constitute a system."[20] Music is part of rites in a broader sense. Music and rites, aiming at harmony and differentiation, are the two ways to consolidate the internal solidarity of the Zhou people. The king of Zhou can enfeoff his land on the premise of nationalization of land, for "All the land under heaven belongs to the king and all within the land are the king's subjects."[21] It is stated in *The Analects* that "in the normal state of the king's rule of a kingdom, the initiative and final decision in matters of rites, music, recruitment of soldiers and declaration of war rest with the supreme prerogative of the king; during abnormal conditions without the king's rule of a kingdom, the prerogative passes into the hands of the princes." These remarks reflect the absolute power the king of Zhou had. Later generations named the social cultural state shaped by the system of rites and music as "rites and music culture" or "rites and music civilization." Confucian scholars regard it as a prototype of a "civilized" society, which has cast a huge and far-reaching impact on Chinese culture in later generations. Confucius has pursued a perfect society with orderly rites and music through all his life, who sang high praise of Zhou repeatedly: "the rule of rites in the Zhou Dynasty features great diversity, and I advocate it."

1.3.2.3 Evolution of Rites

Later generations might fail to follow "five rites" initiated by the Zhou Dynasty, but Zhou's ritual system has been an original template for the following dynasties in making their ritual codes in a long run. *Taibao Tongli* (Rituals of Taibao), *Da Ming Jili* (Rituals of the Great Ming), *Da Qing Tongli* (Rituals of the Great Qing), and so on basically take the Zhou system of rites as the prototype. Let us take the ritual codes of Qing Dynasty for a brief illustration.

---

[20] Su, Y. (2015). Dialectical understanding of the status and function of "rule of law," *Shandong Social Sciences*. Vol. 12.

[21] The Book of Songs:Xiaoya:Beishan.

Emperor Qianlong of the Qing Dynasty pointed out the main reason for the reestablishment of rites was that the former ritual system had rather limited regulation on people's basic material and spiritual life that covers clothing, food, housing, transportation, wedding, funeral, offering sacrifice, etc. In his view, the purpose of establishing the ritual system is to "keep the people in order, prevent extravagance and save them from decay." After the Qin and Han Dynasties, the ritual system only "roughly prepared rituals on offering sacrifices to heaven and earth and ancestors, and presenting the imperial court's authority. The sacrificial vessels were all labeled and stored in the relevant ministry and used occasionally when necessary." Consequently, even ministers and scholars might not have a thorough knowledge of ritual codes. As for the rituals of mode of transport, clothing, housing, wedding ceremonies, funeral, and sacrifice of the common people, their corresponding specifications have not been regulated yet so that people compete for extravagance from which exhaustion results. Therefore, we need to customize the specific rituals for the common people to stop waste. To fulfill that, we shall "collect all the books of rites of the past dynasties. In combination with the Huidian (jurisdictional corpus on administrative matters) compiled during Qing, all the rites of passage, wedding, funeral and sacrifice are specified and considered prudently of which a book of rites should be compiled" so that scholars and people can easily abide by it.[22] *Qianlong* stressed that rules of rites be made not only followed by the upper social class but also by the middle and lower classes; the past convention that rules of rites formulated and collected by the government should be changed in order to make rites approachable among the vast number of nobles and common people. Ritual law should function as household rules, followed by people of their own will, and thus the purpose of rites to "stabilize the country and rule the people" can be realized.

The format of *Da Qing Tongli* is also composed of five parts: *Ji Li* (sacrificial ceremonies), *Xiong Li* (burial rites), *Jun Li* (army etiquettes), *Bin Li* (hospitality etiquettes), and *Jia Li* (wedding ceremonies). Details of rituals are stipulated explicitly, ranging from higher rituals as offering sacrifice to heaven and ancestors by the royal family to lower rituals detailing weddings clothes for nobles and common people. Sacrifices are also graded explicitly. Take sacrifices for ancestors as an example: first- to third-class ministers can offer a whole sheep and a whole pig; fourth- to seventh-class officials can only offer a whole pig; officials beneath the eighth class do not need to offer a whole pig. Sacrificial vessels: ministers above the third class may use two meat tables, six split-bamboo food baskets, and six stemmed bowls; officials above the seventh class may use four split-bamboo food baskets and eight stemmed bowls, and ranks below have fewer vessels in turn. Seasonal sacrifices include four kinds of fresh fruit, four dishes, four bowls of rice or soup per tray pertaining to first- to third-class ministers, and three kinds of fresh fruit per tray for fourth- to seventh-class officials. Low-rank officials offer seasonal sacrifices to ancestors in spring, autumn, and winter that may include two bowls of rice and four

[22] Holy Sermons by Emperor Gaozong of Qing Dynasty. Vol. 251. Develop Rites and Music. First year of Qianlong Reign. June 22.

kinds of dishes: meat, fruit, vegetable, other solid food, and two kinds of thick soup. The common people may even offer less: no more than four kinds including rice, vegetable, and fruit per table.[23]

The ritual system of Qing Dynasty as the standard of material life was protected by legal provisions, which made the ritual system more rigorous and serious. Hierarchical specifications of housing, clothing, and food stipulated by the ritual system only allows top-down practice (higher classes practice rituals of lower classes), but forbids bottom-up arrogation (lower classes practice rituals of higher classes). Those officials who violate the stipulated rituals would be sentenced 100 strokes of beating with the heavy bamboo stick and removed from office. The common people would be sentenced 50 strokes of beating with the light bamboo stick. Their parents suffer collective punishment, and the associated craftsmen are sentenced 50 strokes of beating with the light bamboo stick. If either officials or common people use the prohibited dragon and phoenix patterns in their rituals, all would be sentenced 100 stokes of beating with the heavy bamboo stick and 3-year imprisonment. Officials would be removed from office.[24] Through the enforcement of law, the implementation of the ritual system can be further guaranteed.

The impressive volume number, much-detailed content and wide range of coverages of *Da Qing Tongli,* is unprecedented on the whole in the history, compared with any other book on rites. In the early period of Qianlong, *Da Qing Tongli, Da Qing Huidian Zeli (Precedents Added to the Jurisdictional Corpus on Administrative Matters Compiled during Qing),* and *The Great Qing Code* constituted strict and severe rules and regulations of rites. The process from creation to perfection of *Da Qing Tongli* is consistent with the gradual consolidation of Qing's rule and the strengthening of its autocratic rulership. The strengthening of Qing's rulership is the basis of the detailed preparation of ritual law, and the perfection of ritual law is on the other hand an important symbol of the strengthening of Qing's rulership.

After the compilation of *Da Qing Tongli* was continued during Dao Guang's reign, the Qing court did not organize any kind of revision of it. In the late Qing Dynasty, in order to prepare for the establishment of constitutional monarchy, in June of the 33rd year of Guang Xu's reign (1907), the Qing court set up a college of rites affiliated to the Ministry of Rites to draft the statutes, hire consultants, and collect books on rites. On September 29th in the 34th year during Guang Xu's reign (1908), the Qing court assigned the Ministry of Rites to "further develop rites and change the custom." On February 17th of Xuan Tong's first year, Chen Baoshen, the secretary of the Grand Secretariat, presided over the opening ceremony of the College of Rites. Left prime minister, member of the royal clan, Ying Mian, right prime minister Liu Guo, left Can Yi (a type of official who reviews relevant ministerial decrees), Liang Kui, and right Can Yi Cao Guangquan held a concurrent post as coordinator, responsible for revision of *Da Qing Tongli*. The court also demanded

[23]Comprehensive Canon on Rituals of the Great Qing. Vol. 16. Family Sacrifice Rituals for Different Ranks of Officials:Family Sacrifice Rituals for Low-rank Officials.

[24]The Great Qing Code. Vol. 17. Ritual Codes:Ceremonies:Housing and Clothing.

that the three colleges of constitutionalism, law, and rites should collaborate with each other and that the two colleges of rites and law should agree on a plan for revision first and then the plan be reviewed by the college of constitutionalism.

However, the revision of *Da Qing Tongli* at the end of Qing Dynasty cannot catch up with the codification of the criminal law: the former aims at restoring and perfecting the old ritual system while the latter targets the establishment of a new system and eradication of the old. Since the purpose of revision and codification is diametrically different, there would be nothing in common. Furthermore, *The Great Qing Code* itself is a mixture of rites and laws where law substantially embodies and protects rites. In light of this, rites and law are actually separated in form after the revision. The codification of criminal law was completed by promulgation of *New Criminal Code of Qing Dynasty.* The revision of *Da Qing Tongli* began late, and within the 3 years from the very beginning of revision, Qing Dynasty was terminated. The revision of *Da Qing Tongli* was, as it were, left half-done and abolished naturally with the decline of Qing Court.

1.3.3 Codes of Rites and Governments

Western Zhou's emphasis on "law of rites" permeated every corner of the society and played a significant role in ruling the country. The system of rites per se can be regarded as a system with property of constitution in ancient China. It is stated in *The Book of Rites*:

They are the rules of rites, that furnish the means of determining the observances towards relatives, as near and remote; of settling points which may cause suspicion or doubts; of distinguishing where there should be agreement, and where difference; and of making clear what is right and what is wrong...The course of duty, virtue, benevolence and righteousness cannot be fully carried out without the rules of propriety; nor are training and oral lessons for the rectification of manners complete; nor can the clearing up of quarrels and discriminating in disputes be accomplished; nor can the duties between ruler and minister, high and low, father and son, elder brother and younger, be determined; nor can students for office and other learners, in serving their masters, have an attachment for them; nor can majesty and dignity be shown in assigning the different places at court, in the government of the armies, and in discharging the duties of office so as to secure the operation of the laws, nor can there be the proper sincerity and gravity in presenting the offerings to spiritual Beings on occasions of supplication, thanksgiving, and the various sacrifices.

Since the rules of rites furnish the means of determining the observances toward relatives, as near and remote, of settling points which may cause suspicion or doubts, of distinguishing where there should be agreement and where difference, and of making clear what is right and what is wrong, they dominate and stipulate social ethics and morality, conventionality, administration, military affairs, justice, religion, education, marriage, family life, etc. People's conduct pertaining to clothing, food, housing, travel, marriage, mourning, sacrifice, music and dance, social intercourse, and so on should be strictly stratified in accordance to the rule of rites. No arrogation is allowed, or penalties shall be imposed and law enforced. At this point, rites, from the primitive time, to Xia, Shang, and Zhou Dynasties, have developed successively and completed the progress from ritual convention, sacrifice, etiquette, and then ritual system and eventually official codes of rites.

Among the "three classics on rites,"[25] *The Rites of the Zhou* was recognized as one of the most detailed official codes of governments. In the Qing Dynasty, Sun Dairang called it "the law of governments." *The Rites of the Zhou* was not written during the Western Zhou Dynasty, nor written by the Duke of Zhou, but compiled during the warring States period or even later; nevertheless it did preserve a large number of historical records of Western Zhou. More than one-fourth of the official posts in *The Rites of the Zhou* can be confirmed by the bronze inscriptions during the Western Zhou Dynasty. *The Rites of the Zhou*, as an official code, involves politics, economy, justice, military affairs, culture, planning, and design and many other administrative fields, affecting the next hundred generations. The judicial system, criminal litigations all derive from the rites of the Zhou Dynasty. *The Rites of the Zhou* does not rule out death penalty, because "due punishment of the people prohibits violence." Penalties are imposed as one of the means to edify the populace with the purpose to "quell lawsuit and prevent people from committing crimes." Even though the populace is not yet edified and files lawsuits, it should be the local officials of civil ministries that were in place to settle them. Only under the condition that the criminal law is violated would the lawsuits be transferred to scholar-bureaucrats and settled by officials for autumn. Officials for autumn have close contact with local officials in charge of justice and the chief responsibility to prevent and mediate lawsuits. "Ministers of justice as officials for autumn are employed to be in charge of national legal prohibitions and assist the king in punishing the vassal states (if they violate the law)." "Those involved in criminal lawsuits must swear. If the two parties involved in a criminal case are tried, they must first swear. The party without good faith naturally does not dare to swear and get past the preliminary examination; therefore, in this way, the number of lawsuits can be reduced. In the aspect of punishing crimes, theft, homicide, and wounding people with the sight of blood and intimidating them from filing a lawsuit are all key objects of punishment. In *Autumn Officer:Minister of Justice V*, the judicial administrative system, composed of varied levels of office such as "minister of justice," "vice minister of justice," "director of corporal punishments," "director of contract management," "sanctifier of covenants," "dissemination and inquiry officials," "justiciar of the inherited region," and so on, provides reference for later generations.[26]

---

[25] "三礼"(The three classics on rites)refers to *Rites of the Zhou*, *Etiquette and Rites* and *The Book of Rites*.

[26] Chen, G. (1937). The Judicial System Described in the Rites of Zhou Dynasty. *The Journal of Chinese Law*, New Volume 1, No. 5, No. 6, Zheng Zhong Publishing House, (Special Issue on Judicial Systems).

The law of ruling the country derived from "*The Rites of the Zhou*" is summarized in its chapter *Official in Heaven:Minister of State I* as Ten canons: six codes, eight laws, eight rules, eight tactics to dominate officials, eight tactics to rule the populace, nine official positions, nine taxes, nine etiquettes, nine tributes, nine tactics to unite the populace. The ten canons provide a systematic detailed prototype of administration for later dynasties. For example, the "six ministries" in the administrative system of "three provinces and six ministries" implemented by the Sui Dynasty was modeled after the "six officials" in *The Rites of the Zhou.* In Tang Dynasty, the six ministries were defined as the Ministry of Personnel, the Ministry of Revenue, the Ministry of Rites, the Ministry of War, the Ministry of Punishments, and the Ministry of Works, which served as the main body of the central official system and were followed by later dynasties until Qing. Later dynasties continued to revise codes of rites and governments, including "*Tang Liudian,*" "*Da Qing Huidian,*" basically derived from *The Rites of the Zhou* as the original prototype. Criminal codes developed from codes of governments are all born from the rites of Zhou Dynasty, such as "*Great Code of Ming Dynasty*" and "*Great Code of Qing Dynasty,*" which classified six sections of laws by relatedness to Personnel, Revenue, Rites, War, Punishments, and Works. Therefore, the system of rites can be deemed as the most "fundamental" law of the traditional society.[27]

1.4 Hierarchies in Rites and Statues

1.4.1 Hierarchies in Rites and Penalties

It is one of the main functions of rites to distinguish different classes. Different people, because of their different backgrounds, enjoy different rights and obligations. Stratified identity is mainly reflected by rites and etiquette. In ancient times, many ritual instruments, music and dance, the guard of honor, and so on are all symbols of rank and status. Identity difference leads to differentiated legal treatment. Different punishments might occur to the same crime. The most familiar to the Chinese would be "the rules of rites do not go down to the common people"; "the penal statutes do not go up to the nobles and senior officers"; "men who have suffered punishment should not (be allowed to) be by the side of the ruler," etc.[28] Though in academia, different schools of thought have rather different views on the original meaning of those quotes and are able to support their respective arguments with evidence, there will not be any divergence in the common people's understanding: the nobles and senior officers are not shackled by punishments, and the common people are not treated with rites and etiquettes. Nevertheless, it is not equal to "the common people do not need to follow rites and the nobles and senior officers

[27] Zhou, G. http://www.haretu.com/guwen/article_21421.html.

[28] The Book of Rites:Qu Li I.

do not need to be punished." The crux comes with the question to what extent the rules of rites do not go down to the common people and to what extent the penal statutes do not go up to the nobles and senior officers.

"The rules of rites do not go down to the common people" actually means the rites of the nobles do not go down to the common people and nor are the common people allowed to use the rites of the nobles. "Rites cannot reach the common people, because they have to toil day and night to make a living and hence they are not ready to fully abide by the rites in all aspects" (Zheng Xuan's notes). Even if they are allowed to enjoy the rites of a higher standard, they might not have the ability to do so. "The common people do not practice temple sacrificial ceremonies which in turn do not reach them; the common people walk on foot and then the courtesy of commuting does not reach them; the common people do not meet the nobles with the purpose to be accepted and then there is no need to perform the ceremony of the court. That the rules of rites do not go down means they cannot extend to the common people (You Gui's notes).

It is for sure that those who do not observe the rites or arrogate to themselves superior rites must be severely punished. That is to say, in terms of the definition of "rites," there is a difference between the senior officers and the common people, and the "rites" that should be followed by the two classes are different as well. In terms of detailed systems of rites, except the national ceremonies such as the court, the military, and guest-greeting ceremonies, ancient codes and records, for example, *The Book of Rites, Discourses of the States*,[29] and the alike all specified detailed "rites" that the common people must observe related to almost every aspect of life including funeral, offering sacrifice, greeting, child birth, etc. "Rites," as the fundamental of the patriarchal clan system in Western Zhou, stipulated the entire social life and was enforced by the strong and severe coercive force of the country. "Rites" as the norm of social conduct must be learned and observed by everyone; neither the nobles nor the common people are of exception. The so-called rules of rites that "do not go down to the common people" merely refer to the rites that are confined to the nobles and intended to consolidate solidarity among the nobles. Rites emphasize differentiation of ranks, and therefore "the emperor has his own system of rites, the princes have the rites for the princes, senior officers have the rites for senior officers, and the common people have the rites for the common people, which means different classes have their own class-specific rites." Generally speaking, higher classes are allowed to observe lower rites if they wish to while lower ranks are forbidden to follow higher rites; otherwise they commit arrogation. All those conduct that violate or arrogate rites shall be severely punished.

What the so-called "The penal statutes do not go up to the nobles and senior officers" practically means is that some of the penal statutes do not go up to the nobles and senior officers in order to maintain the dignity and decency correlative

[29] Guo, Y. "Discourses of the states" is a collection of anecdotes and discourses, mostly between rulers and ministers, from the Spring and Autumn period 春秋 (770–fifth-century BCE). Zuo Qiuming 左丘明 (around 500) was formerly believed being the author of the collection, but his authorship of the book cannot be attested.

to their status. It is not true that the nobles and senior officers are exempt from any legal liability if they commit a crime. During Zhou Dynasty under the rule of rites, any violation of rites was to be severely punished. No specific article in criminal codes ever stipulates how senior officers should be punished if they commit a crime, but the sections that mention crimes committed by senior officers and royal nobles are not rare in "the three classics on rites" and they suffer punishment as well.

However, some penalties are not applicable to ranks above *Dafu (Grand Mast, a rank of senior officer)*, for example, castration. It is stated in *The Book of Rites:Wenwang Shizi*: the nobles of the royal lineage that face death penalty shall be hanged secretly by *Dianren* (an ancient official title, mastering affaires in the countryside and the nobles' execution) and the nobles of the royal lineage that are sentenced corporal punishment shall suffer tattooing, amputation of nose, amputation of foot, or removal of the kneecaps handled by *Dianren*. The nobles of the royal lineage are exempt from castration. The nobles of the royal lineage cannot avoid corporal punishment, and the privilege they enjoy is the exemption of castration. If they ever commit a crime that results in castration, shaving the head is imposed instead.

Why is castration not inflicted on the nobles? According to *The Book of Rites*:*Wenwang Shizi:* "The nobles of the royal lineage are exempt from castration so that they might not die without descendants." Since castration terminates reproduction, the clan temple of the royal family will be cut off if it is inflicted on the nobles, and the reproduction of the royal family and other noble families of Zhou Dynasty will be diminished. Therefore, shaving head takes place of castration. Shaving head (shaving hair on the temples) is not even considered as a punishment now, but it was a severe humiliating punishment in ancient China where people had a strong conviction that "the whole physical body, with skin and hair, was bestowed from the parents and should never be damaged, which is the basics of filial piety."

The nobles could enjoy quite a few privileges in litigation rights, suffer partial punishment, and also be executed in secrecy without public exposure to preserve face when they commit a crime. *The Rites of The Zhou:Autumn Office Minister of Justice* states: "The job of vice minister of justice is to settle people's lawsuits with five penalties…Those命夫(*mìngfū*: the nobles and higher officers above the rank of *Grand Master*) and 命妇 (*mìngfù*: wives of the nobles and higher officers above the rank of *Grand Master*) may not appear in person for trial. When the nobles of the royal lineage commit a crime, their execution is not exposed to the public." "Not appearing in person for trial" here means they need not appear in court personally to face officials of justice and their relatives and disciples can do it instead. The so-called 命夫*mìngfū* and命妇*mìngfù*, noted by *Zheng Xuan* who quoted from Mourning Attire, are *Grand Masters* and their wives. Secret execution of the nobles of the royal lineage has a long history. When they commit a capital crime, they will not be executed in a downtown area, or the populace sees it and the nobles suffer disgrace, which might even affect the dignity and reputation of the whole royal family. In the aspect of custody and shackles of prisoners, the nobles and common people are also treated differently. According to *The Rites of The Zhou:Autumn Office Minister of Justice*, "For all the prisoners in captivity, those who commit felonies are shackled by wooden handcuffs

(拲*Gong*: hands fixed in a piece of wood),a pillory(梏*Gu*: a wooden frame with a hole for the head or holes for the head and hands) and wooden fetters (桎*Zhi*: wooden fetters); Those who commit a crime between a felony and a misdemeanor have a pillory and fetters; those who commit a misdemeanor wear a pillory. The nobles of the royal lineage should be shackled by wooden handcuffs and those with the rank of nobility should wear wooden fetters, waiting for sentencing or execution." Ordinary prisoners are usually taken into custody with a pillory and fetters or a pillory only while member of the royal family and the nobles are granted some preferential treatment.

"The rules of rites do not go down to the common people and the penal statutes do not go up to the nobles and senior officers" has laid down the guiding principle for the political and legal system at that time and of later generations. In particular, the "Babi Libang Law" (the eight conditions for mitigating punishment) directly leads to the system of "Shang Qing" (asking for instructions from the emperor) or "Xian Qing" (asking for instructions from the emperor in advance) in the Han Dynasty, that is, when the nobles and senior officials commit a crime, officials handling the case must ask for instructions from the emperor on how to punish them. "Qing" means asking the emperor for instructions on the punishment in order to make a decision of mitigating it, which is designed to protect the privilege of the nobles and high-rank officials. The judicial result is that the nobles and the common people have different punishments for the same crime, which embodies an important part of codified rites and morality.[30] After *Wei* of the Three Kingdoms' period, some criminal legal systems have continued to remain in criminal codes of later dynasties, such as "Guan Dang" (deprivation of office in exchange for punishment mitigation) and "Ba Yi" (eight privileged groups of people whose cases are to be especially deliberated): those who were the relatives of the sovereign, those who were old acquaintances of the sovereign, those who were of great virtue, those who were of great ability, those who were meritorious, those who were high officials, those who were exceptionally zealous of government duties, those who were the guests of the sovereign, those eight groups of people enjoy the privilege of mitigated punishment or exemption therefrom); etc. Although Emperor *Yongzheng* of the Qing Dynasty once called for the abolition of 八议"*Ba Yi*" system (eight privileged groups of people whose cases are to be especially deliberated), the system remained (not applicable), and it was not until the end of the Qing Dynasty that the system was finally abolished.

1.4.2 Determination of Crimes by the Five Mournings in Family Relations

1.4.2.1 The Ritual System of Five Mournings

The origin of China as a state was based on the gradual expansion of clan-based organizations with strong emphasis on clan kinship. After the state was established, the feudal system was adopted to delineate the boundaries of the vassal states. Nevertheless, the function of maintaining blood ties was not weakened by the

[30] *The History of the Former Han Dynasty* Vol. VIII, Chapter VIII. The Annals of Emperor *Xuan*.

formation of the state but was instead integrated with the state machinery. The rules of patriarchal clan kinship were inclined to be unified with the legal system of the state, and then rites began to contain laws that were stipulated within the framework of rites. After the collapse of the feudal system from the Qin and Han dynasties, the patriarchal clan system did not weaken but was strengthened by the trend of plebification. The institutionalization of rituals and ethics was given new life in its development full of twists and turns. Meanwhile, legalization of the system of rites has become more and more prominent, such as the system of "first-born succession," the "six etiquettes" of a traditional Chinese wedding ceremony, and the "five mournings" system. Penalization according to "five degrees of mourning" is considered the most representative among all, which means "someone is penalized based on his/her degree of mourning." This system represents one of the most important impacts of rites on the legal system.

According to *The Book of Rites:Mournings*, the classification of five degrees of mourning rests upon degree of kinship—"In the system of kinship mourning, closeness extends from three to five generations, and from five to nine. It diminishes upward and downward to distant ancestors and descendants and diminishes laterally to collateral relatives, until the ties of kinship are exhausted.[31] (See Table 1.1 of Five Degrees of Mourning for reference.) The three closest degrees of kinship refers kinship that extends from self (in the middle) to his father (upward) and son (downward), that is, the scope of three 族*Zu* (degrees of kindred). The scope is then extended from father to grandfather (upward) and from son to grandson (downward), forming the scope of five *Zu*. Thus, the scope of kinship can be extended to seven *Zu* from grandfather to great grandfather (upward) and grandson to great grandson (downward) and to nine *Zu* from great grandfather to great great grandfather (upward) and great grandson to great great grandson (downward). These nine generations form the lineal kinship. "杀"(Sha) equals "衰" (Cui), meaning decline and weaken. In lineal kinship, the degree of kinship descends gradually upward from self till great great grandfather and descends gradually downward from self till great great grandson. The collateral branches also descend from self to brothers, first cousins, second cousins, and finally *Zu* brothers/third cousins (rightward). The so-called nine *Zu* kindred comes to an end as 缌麻*Sima* (lowest degree of mourning). Those beyond nine *Zu* are not kindred.

Generally, the kindredship-based degrees of mourning attire is called "formal clothes." Chinese kinship is patrilineal, and maternal relatives are called "outside" relatives, inferior to one's patrilineage. In either *Statutes of the Yuan Dynasty* or *Collected Statutes of the Ming Dynasty*, it is stipulated that wives should conform to their husbands' relative degree of mourning and count in their husbands' nine *Zu* as their relatives, with their mourning attire the same as their husbands' for lower generations and a degree less than their husbands' for higher generations (except parents). *The Great Qing Code* stipulates that aunts, sisters, daughters, and granddaughters who are not married or return home after divorce wear the same

[31] Sun,X. (1989). *Annotations to the Book of Rites II*. Zhonghua Book Company., 1376.

Table 1.1 *Wufu* (five degrees of mourning)

				Great great grandparents *Zicui* 3-month mourning					
			Great grandaunts Unmarried *Sima*, Married *mourning attire not applicable*	Great grandparents *Zicui* 5-month mourning		Great granduncles and their wives *Sima*			
		First cousins twice removed Unmarried *Sima*, Married *mourning attire not applicable*	Grandaunts Unmarried *Xiaogong*, Married *Sima*	Grandparents *Zicui* *Buzhangqi* 1-year mourning with a staff		Granduncles and their wives *Xiaogong*	First cousins twice removed and their wives *Sima*		
	Second cousins once removed Unmarried *Sima*, Married *mourning attire not applicable*	First cousins once removed Unmarried *Xiaogong*, Married *Sima*	Aunts Unmarried *Jinian*, Married *Dagong*	Parents *Zhancui* 3-year mourning		Uncles and their wives *Jinian*	First cousins once removed and their wives *Xiaogong*	Second cousins once removed and their wives *Sima*	
Third cousins Unmarried *Sima*, Married *mourning attire not applicable*	Second cousins Unmarried *Xiaogong*, Married *Sima*	First cousins Unmarried *Dagong*, Married *Xiaogong*	Sisters Unmarried *Jinian*, Married *Dagong*	Self (male)+wife		Brothers *Jinian* Their wives *Xiaogong*	First cousins *Dagong* Their wives *Xiaogong*	Second cousins *Xiaogong* Their wives *mourning attire not applicable*	Third cousins *Sima*, Their wives *mourning attire not applicable*
	Second cousins once removed Unmarried *Sima*, Married *mourning attire not applicable*	First cousins once removed Unmarried *Xiaogong*, Married *Sima*	Nieces Unmarried *Jinian*, Married *Dagong*	Other sons *Jinian* Their wives *Dagong*	Eldest son and his wife *Jinian*	Nephews *Dagong* Their wives *Xiaogong*	First cousins once removed *Xiaogong*, Their wives *Sima*	Second cousins once removed *Sima* Their wives *mourning attire not applicable*	
		First cousins twice removed Unmarried *Sima*, Married *mourning attire not applicable*	Grandnieces Unmarried *Xiaogong*, Married *Sima*	Other grandsons *Dagong* Their wives *Sima*	Eldest grandson *Jinian* His wife *Xiaogong*	Grandnephews *Xiaogong*, Their wives *Sima*	First cousins twice removed *Sima* Their wives *mourning attire not applicable*		
			Great grandnieces Unmarried *Sima* Married *mourning attire not applicable*	Great grandsons *Sima* Their wives *Mourning attire not applicable*		Great grandnephews *Sima*, Their wives *mourning attire not applicable*			
				Great greatgrandsons *Sima* Their wives *Mourning attire not applicable*					

Notes on the degrees of mourning attire:
*Zhancui*斩衰: coarse hemp with frayed edges (3 years).
*Zicui*齐衰: less coarse hemp (1 year).
*Zhangqi*杖期: wear a mourning staff (1 year).
*Buzhangqi*不杖期: not wear a mourning staff (1 year).
*Jinian*期年: 1 year.
*Dagong*大功: coarse hemp fabric (9 months).
*Xiaogong*小功: lightly processed hemp (5 months).
Sima 缌麻: fine hemp (3 months).
All the relatives in Table 1.1 *are from the paternal side. Females are all in the left wing and males in the right.*

mourning attire as males do, but if married, they must wear a degree less within their own patrilineage and follow their husbands' degree of mourning.[32] The following table may simplify the system for the convenience of readers:

According to Table 1.1, there are at most nine *Zu* (generations) based on kinship in a family genealogy. Within the nine *Zu* vertically, there are great great grandparents, great grandparents, grandparents, parents, self, sons, grandsons, great grandsons, and great great grandsons; horizontally, there are self, brothers, sisters, first cousins, second cousins, and third cousins. All the relatives in the nine *Zu* are assigned with different degrees of mourning attire, thus forming the genealogical system of five degrees of mourning, with higher generations including uncles and their spouses, first cousins once removed and their spouses, second cousins once removed and their spouses, granduncles and their spouses, first cousins twice removed and their spouses, great granduncles and their spouses, great great grandparents, aunts, first cousins once removed (female), second cousins once removed (female), grandaunts, first cousins twice removed (female), great grandaunts and lower generations including nephews and their spouses, first cousin once removed and their spouses, second cousins once removed and their spouses, nieces, first cousins once removed (female), second cousins once removed (female), grandnephews and their spouses, first cousins twice removed and their spouses, grandnieces, first cousins twice removed (female), great grandnephews and their spouses, and great grandnieces.

Wufu (five degrees of mourning) can also be referred to as five generations, including self, and great great grandfather, great grandfather, grandfather and father higher than self, or including self, and sons, grandsons, great grandsons, great great grandsons lower than self. Either kinship relations within the higher five generation or lower five generations are considered relatives, namely, all the kinship relations descending from the same great great grandfather are relatives. The higher five generations are counted from great great grandfather to self, forming *Wufu* system, and people outside the system are not considered relatives but available for marriage.

1.4.2.2 Conviction Based Upon Five Mourning Attire System

The development and perfection of Five Degrees of Mourning Attire System inevitably reflects the combination of rites and law, stratifying individuals' genealogical positions discreetly. In terms of kinship, people within the Five Degrees of Mourning group are close while those outside it are considered distant. Within the system, the closer she/he is to Self, the heavier the mourning, and the more distant she/he is from Self, the lighter the mourning.

Since the Jin Dynasty (265–420 AD), Five Degrees of Mourning has been written in law. Recorded in *The History of Jin:Criminal Law*, Wen Emperor

[32] Ding, L. (2000). *Chinese History of Mourning Attire*, Shanghai People's Publishing House. 216–217.

(211–265 AD) of Jin Dynasty promulgated a new law to "to strengthen rites and morality and convict a person of a crime based on Five Degrees of Mourning system" and thus establish a social order that makes "hierarchy reinforced, benevolence and righteousness thrive, the nine *zu* harmonized, and the King's rule stable and peaceful." The mourning degrees are integrated with criminal law so that any infringer within the Five Degrees of Mourning group shall be convicted according to his or her relative degree of mourning. In short, the degree of punishment is determined in relation to the corresponding degree of mourning. The Figure of Five Degrees of Mourning Attire tops a criminal code in order to clarify the degrees of relatives and convict an offender of his/her crime at the discretion of it. Concrete principles are as follows:

First, different litigation status. Laws since Han Dynasty stipulated that there should be concealment of a crime among relatives, and informing the authorities of a senior's crime was forbidden. Criminalization of reporting a senior's crime varies with the offender's degree of mourning.

Second, different punishment for the same crime. Officials' decision of a case was generally based on the relationship between the plaintiff and defendant. They should clarify whether the plaintiff and defendant were relatives; if so, they must make sure to which degree of mourning the plaintiff and defendant should be assigned and finally decide the related conviction and sentence. The Ministry of Justice emphasized that for the cases involving people within the Five Degrees of Mourning group, their related degrees of mourning must be located first based on which a conviction should be entailed.

Third, 连坐*Lianzuo* (collective punishment/liability) and 荫庇*Yinbi* (hereditary system). The abominations related to upheaval of the sovereign were to incur extremely cruel punishments such as 缘坐*Yuanzuo* and *Lianzuo*. Involvement of the Nine *Zu* (the whole Five Degrees of Mourning genealogy) in a criminal case is called *Yuanzuo*, and involvement of colleagues, teachers, and students is called *Lianzuo*. *Yuanzuo* passed down to being written in the criminal code at the end of the Qing Dynasty, and as for *Lianzuo*, it was never repealed in practice.

Fourth, conviction of incest. Criminal codes stipulated that illicit intercourse between members of the Five Degrees of Mourning group was considered incest which must be forbidden in order to maintain the ethical social order and avoid confusion of the genealogical bloodline.

1.4.3 The Legalization of Mourning Rituals

In a funeral, younger generations wear mourning attire for the deceased senior to express filial piety and grief. The mourning rite of wearing mourning attire originated in the rites of Zhou Dynasty. Generally, wearing worst clothes made of coarse materials and leading a hard life for the deceased senior equals to "Mianzui" (a remission of sins) for the deceased so that they would suffer less in the underworld. The detailed style of every family member's mourning attire is decided by their relation with the deceased complying with traditional rites.

1.4.3.1 Rites-Based Mourning Attire

For thousands of years, Chinese mourning attire has undergone minor changes but remained stable in terms of the basic format, classified into five degrees as *Zhancui*, *Zicui*, *Dagong*, *Xiaogong*, and *Sima* (see Table 1.2).

Table 1.2 has been part of the legal codes up till the Qing Dynasty since *Song Lian* et al. researched the degrees of mourning attire of previous dynasties and compiled *Xiaocilu* (an instructive book on rites) during the Ming Dynasty. According to Table 1.2, mourning terms vary from 3 months, 5 months, 9 months, and 1 year to 3 years that match differentiated degrees of mourning attire from the lightest to the heaviest: *Sima*, *Xiaogong*, *Dagong*, *Zicui*, and *Zhancui*. Then, what is the function of the Five Degrees of Mourning Attire? It is stated in the *Book of Rites:Dazhuan XVI* that there are six principles of formulating the Mourning Attire system, *Qinqin* (degree of kinship), *Zunzun* (social status), *Ming* (a married woman's status in the husband's family who is from a different genealogy), *Churu* (a woman's marital status who is from the same genealogy), *Zhangyou* (whether the deceased is an adult), and *congfu* (wearing mourning attire for relatives of spouses/in-laws and relatives of a king/regional ruler). There are six types of occasions to wear *Congfu*: *Shucong* (mourning for the deceased because of indirect kinship), *Tucong* (mourning for nonkinship), *Cong youfu er wufu* (mourning attire not applicable because of special taboos), *Cong wufu er youfu* (mourning attire from not applicable to applicable following husband's genealogy), *Congzhongerqing* (mourning attire changed from a heavy degree to a light degree), and *Congqingerzhong* (mourning attire changed from a light degree to a heavy degree). Therefore, the formulation of mourning attire degrees can clarify kinship, status, adulthood, and primary and secondary relations based on恩*En* (affection), 理*Li* (reason), 节*Jie* (principles), and 权*Quan* (flexibility), namely, 仁*Ren* (benevolence), 义*Yi* (righteousness), 礼*Li*

Table 1.2 The Five Degrees of Mourning Attire

*Zhancui*斩衰 (three years)		Mourning robe, made of coarse or raw hemp without seam binding at the edges of the cloth
*Zicui*齐衰	*Zhangqi*杖期 (1 year) With a mourning staff	Mourning robe, made of coarse hemp with seams felled with close, even-leveled stitches
	*Buzhangqi*不杖期 (1 year) Without a mourning staff	
*Dagong*大功 (9 months)		Mourning robe, made of coarse hemp fabric
*Xiaogong*小功 (5 months)		Mourning robe, made of lightly processed hemp
*Sima*缌麻 (3 months)		Mourning robe, made of fine hemp

The Ming Code: Tables and The Great Qing Code: Tables

(rites), 智*Zhi* (wisdom), and hence人道具矣*Rendaojuyi*[33] (people's moral character building could be complete). These principles provide practice of ritual law with customary rules, which has made it possible for a personal intention to override law.

There are four types of mourning attire:正服*Zhengfu* (the regular mourning attire), 义服*Yifu* (ritual mourning attire), 加服*Jiafu* (the upgraded mourning attire), and 降服*Jiangfu* (the downgraded mourning attire). *Zhengfu*, the regular mourning attire, should be worn for affection, for example, sons wearing *Zhancui* to mourn their parents. *Yifu*, the ritual mourning attire, should be worn by ministers for a deceased ruler or women for in-laws in a ritual mode, for example, daughters-in-law wearing *Zhancui* to mourn their parents-in-law. *Jiafu*, the upgraded mourning attire, should be worn by the people for in a ritual mode who need not wear this degree of mourning attire in the first place, for example, the eldest grandson wearing *Zhancui* for his paternal grandparents. *Jiangfu*, the downgraded mourning attire, should be worn by women who are married with the kinship degree to the deceased kept the same, but the degree of the mourning attire could be downgraded, for example, women wear the downgraded mourning attire for their parents after being married off.

Zhancui is the heaviest degree of mourning attire, worn by princesses for kings, ministers for emperors, sons and unmarried daughters for a father, daughters-in-law for parents-in-law, the eldest grandson for his grandfather, and wives and concubines for their husband. During the Ming and Qing Dynasties, 3 years of *Zicui* was upgraded to *Zhancui* which should be worn by sons and unmarried daughters for their mother, the eldest grandson for his paternal grandmother, and the daughter-in-law for her mother-in-law. Women who wear *Zhancui* must use raw hemp to wear the hair in a mourning bun. The period of mourning in practice is more than 2 years, mostly 25 months, that is, "three years of mourning completed after 25 months."

Zicui is less heavy than *Zhancui*, made of undyed raw hemp, and the period of mourning varies from 3 years, 1 year, and 5 months to 3 months. *Zhangqi* means one-year mourning with a mourning staff (*Zhang*), and *Buzhangqi* means one-year mourning without a mourning staff (*Zhang*). *Qingshigao:Li XII* (*Draft to a history of the Qing:Rites XII*) states that *Zicui* with a mourning staff should be worn by the eldest son and his wife, other sons and their wives for their father's concubines, sons for their remarried or divorced birth mother, a husband for his wife, and the eldest grandson for his paternal grandmother when his paternal grandfather is alive; *Zicui* without a mourning staff should be worn by the nephews for their paternal uncles and their spouses, for brothers, for brothers' sons or unmarried daughters, sons for their cohabiting stepfathers without any relatives within the *Dagong* mourning obligation (or closer), and so on and so forth.

Dagong is less heavy than *Zicui*, made of treated hemp, coarse hemp fabric, and finer than *Zicui*. The period of mourning is 9 months. *Dagong* should be worn for one's paternal uncles and their spouses, paternal male cousins, unmarried paternal

[33] Book of Rites:*SangfuSizhi*(mourning attire):No. 49.

female cousins, married aunts or sisters, daughters who have been married off for their mother, their paternal uncles and spouses, or their brothers.

Xiaogong is less heavy than *Dagong*, made of lightly processed hemp. The period of mourning is 5 months. *Xiaogong* should be worn for one's paternal great grandparents, paternal granduncles, first male cousins once removed and their wives, unmarried grandaunts, unmarried first female cousins once removed, married paternal female cousins, brothers' wives, second male cousins, unmarried second female cousins, and one's maternal grandparents, maternal uncles, maternal aunts, etc.

Sima is the lightest mourning attire, the lowest degree of mourning attire, made of finer hemp than *Xiaogong*. The period of mourning is 3 months. Take the Qing Dynasty, for example, *Sima* should be worn by males for their paternal great great grandparents, great granduncles and their wives, first cousins twice removed and their wives, second cousins once removed and their wives, and third cousins and maternal grandsons, sons-in-law, wife's parents, maternal cousins, etc.

Traditional mourning rituals vary in the length of term, and the kind of material different degrees of mourning attire is made of to determine the status and degree of relationship.

The core of Five Degrees of Mourning system is to maintain patrilineage dominated by males, whereas females and matrilineage are dependent upon males and patrilineage. The principles of ritual law during the Qing Dynasty fully demonstrate the ultimate goal of maintaining the patriarchal system.

In modern and contemporary China, influenced by the Western culture, the mourning rituals have witnessed a noticeable change. Urban people mourn the dead and bid farewell by wearing a white/yellow flower on the left side of the chest or a piece of black silk around the upper left arm, much simplified compared with the traditional mourning attire. However, in the rural areas, traditional mourning rituals as Five Degrees of Mourning Attire have handed down to the present, and wearing mourning attire made of raw hemp is still an indispensable mourning rite in a funeral, which maintains as a "custom" instead of a state-mandated system nor a legal requirement.

1.4.3.2 Mourning Rituals Stipulated by Law

Keeping Vigil Beside the Coffin

Shousang, keeping vigil beside the coffin, is also called *Jusang*, *Shouzhi*, *Dingyou*, etc., rendered as a custom to extend mourning to the deceased. *Shousang* system is an important embodiment of the Confucian concept filial piety, underscored and advocated by the ruling class of traditional China and upgraded to the level of being written in legal codes to ensure its implementation in social life by coercive power.

Shousang system, as a mandatory rule, started from the Qin Dynasty under highly centralized power, and the first emperor *Qin Shi Huang* promulgated *Shousang* system in the decree and forced his subjects to implement it in the national mourning and it was then passed down to the Han Dynasty. Since Emperor Wu of the Han Dynasty adopted the policy of "dismissing the hundred schools and revering only Confucianism," Confucian rituals were tremendously promoted and integrated into the legal system. As a mandatory rule, *Shousang* system was first enforced in the upper social class. Legal codes during the Tang Dynasty have managed to absorb the experience and lessons passed down by previous dynasties since the Qin and Han Dynasties, with Confucian philosophies as the guiding principles, that is, "morality and ethics serves as the foundation of governance while penalty is the tool of governance." Among a considerable number of Confucian doctrines integrated into law, *Shousang* system was fully established in *The Tang Code*, which symbolized completion of its legalization and reached maturity during the Ming and Qing Dynasties.

Penalization of Concealing the Occasion of Mourning

In *The Tang Code:Administrative Regulations*, the article "concealing and evading mourning on hearing of the deaths of parents or husband" stipulated: those who upon hearing of the deaths of parents or husband but conceal it and absent themselves from mourning rituals shall be sentenced to life exile of 2000 *Li* (1000 km); those who take off the mourning attire and put on daily clothes before the period of mourning is completed or neglect mourning by making music (by oneself or having it played) shall be sentenced to three-year penal servitude; those who entertain themselves with variety plays during the period of mourning shall be sentenced to one-year penal servitude; those who chance upon music and partake of feasts shall be sentenced to a hundred blows with a heavy stick; and those who do not mourn for second-degree relatives whose period of mourning equals a year shall be punished likewise but a degree less. One must wear the mourning attire on his/her parent's death and absent himself/herself from any form of social or political activities, for example, Confucian scholars are not allowed to attend the Civil Service Exam during the period of mourning. In December of the 13th year of Yongzheng's reign (1735) during the Qing Dynasty, Zou Kaishu, director of the provincial education commission of Henan province, proposed: Confucian scholars, martial students, recommended candidates, or students from *Guozijian* (highest official school during the Ming and Qing Dynasties) should neither attend the qualification tests for the Civil Service Exam nor the provincial and metropolitan levels of the Civil Service Exam during the mourning year. Neither should Confucian apprentices attend a district exam, a prefectural exam, nor a commission exam. The emperor granted the proposal immediately and institutionalized it afterward, and it was eventually stipulated in the legal code in the fifth year of *Qianlong*'s reign (1740).[34]

On the other hand, those who falsely allege the pretext of mourning, while their parents are actually still living, or after they are so long dead that the period of

[34] Veritable records of *Qianlong* Vol. IX, December, the 13th year of *Yongzheng*'s reign; *The Great Qing Code* Vol. XVII, *Ritual Code:Administration of Rites:Concealing the Occasion of Mourning*.

mourning had expired, for the purpose to evade civil service, shall be liable to due punishment. During the period of mourning, officials should not change their mourning attire when offered official posts, present gifts, or partake of feasts, and the offenders shall be downgraded three ranks when filling official posts.[35]

Marriage During the Period of Mourning

Penalizing marriage during the period of mourning refers to the following three conditions: arrange for one's own marriage, officiate at a marriage, or act as a go-between. *The Tang Code:The Household and Marriage* stipulates: All cases of marrying during the period of mourning for parents or husband result in being punished by 3 years of penal servitude. If a person takes or becomes a concubine during the period of mourning, the punishment is reduced by three degrees. The relationship must be terminated in each case. Those who have known the circumstances but decide upon marriage shall be punished with five degrees reduced in each case, whereas those who have no knowledge of the circumstances shall not be punished. The article of *Acting as Officiant of the Marriage during the Period of Mourning for Parents* in *The Tang Code:The Household and Marriage* stipulates: Those who act as officiants of the marriage during the period of mourning for parents for others who are allowed to marry are punished by 100 blows with the heavy stick. Those who act as officiants of the marriage during the period of mourning for parents in cases where the couple is not allowed to marry will inflict punishment heavier than 100 blows with the heavy stick. Though *The Tang Code* has no specific provision where a wife during the period of mourning for her husband acts as the officiant of the marriage for people who are allowed to marry, the punishment should be heavier for doing what ought not to be done, that is, eighty blows with the heavy stick. Those who act as a go-between during the period of mourning for parents in cases where the couple is allowed to marry shall result in heavier punishment for doing what ought not to be done, that is, eighty blows with the heavy stick. For the same offense during the period of mourning for husband, the punishment is lighter for doing what out not to be done, that is, 40 blows with the light stick. Practicing mourning rituals according to ritual codes is vigorously promoted by the government and coerced by law in traditional China so that filial piety is advocated and the folk custom developed.

Dingyou System

Dingyou system (civil officials' leaving their duty and mourning for their parents) targets officials of government. The period of mourning might not matter a lot to a commoner but must be taken seriously be civil officials who are concerned about

---

[35]Veritable records of *Qianlong* Vol. XXXVIII, March of the second year of Qianlong's reign (1737), Clause XXXIII.

Qifu (the restoring of official posts after the period of mourning is completed). *Dingyou* means sons or grandsons go back home to follow the mourning rituals on hearing of parents' or paternal grandparents' death. *Qifu* means after the end of the period of mourning; the officials' posts will be restored. *Dingyou* covers mourning for four generations under great grandparents. Both *Dingyou* and *Qifu* require a *Ganjie* (a written promise of fulfilling duties) issued by the mourner's family.

Complying with the ritual law, civil officials should retire from their posts and go back home for mourning the next day after hearing of their parents' deaths. During the period of mourning, they shall not resume office, get married, partake of feasts, sit the Civil Service Exam, or expose themselves in public places and associate with colleagues. Only when the period of mourning is completed can they be restored to official posts. During the period of mourning, the mourners' posts will be filled by others. If the officials, during the period of mourning, do not comply with mourning rituals, show reluctance to retire from their posts and cling to fame and wealth, devise ways to gain benefits and neglect mourning, they shall end up in serious trouble. In a word, the time effect of mourning shall never be neglected, and the stipulation on Five Degrees of Mourning in the ritual law is important, though.

The article related to *Dingyou* in *The Qing Code* follows that in *The Ming Code*, on hearing of the death of his parent, the civil official is bound to retire from office during the period of mourning; if he does not do so in order to avoid such retirement, he shall inflict the punishment of 100 blows of the heavy stick, be deposed from office and rendered incapable of again entering into the public service. If, before the end of the lawful term of absence in consequence of the loss of a parent, any official returns to and resumes his office, he shall be deprived thereof and punished with 80 blows. If the superiors in the same department have known the prematurity of the mourner's return and let him resume his office, they shall suffer equal punishment. Compared with the Ming Dynasty, the Qing Dynasty implemented *Dingyou* System more strictly. Emperors of the Qing Dynasty were convinced that "it is of universal value to mourn for parents, and it is the representation of a son's affection toward his parents to abide by the mourning rituals." *Dingyou* System was in line with the policy of advocating filial piety; if the officials cannot complete the period of mourning for 3 years, then "all moral characters are rendered rootless."[36] In special cases where those officials were urgently needed, they shall resume their office and need not retire from their duty to go back home mourning, only under the emperor's order of commanding them to remain in employment in the name of "Duoqing" (reducing sorrow during the period of mourning). Nevertheless, they shall not reveal joy in the face at the emperor's offer for him to stay but to decline several times with sorrowful feelings till reluctantly agree to. Meanwhile, they must comply with the mourning rituals while resuming their office, that is, their daily life should agree with the simple and coarse style for the period of mourning. All social activities such as various forms of entertainment and plays were forbidden, and the

[36] Wang,X. &*DonghuaL.* the 40th year of Kangxi's reign (1701), August of the 25th year of Kangxi's reign (1686), Article XXXXIIII; *Qinggaozong Shilu* (Veritable records of *Qianlong*) Vol. IV, October of the 13th year of *Yongzheng*'s reign (1735), Article XII.

offenders shall suffer punishment. The Buddhist plays performed with traditional stringed and woodwind instruments were forbidden by local magistrates either.[37] If, during the period of mourning, families practice abstinence and arrange sacrifices and libations for the deceased, and men and women mix together, drinking wine and eating meat, the head of the household shall suffer 80 blows of the heavy stick, and a Buddhists or Taoists monk involved shall be punished and defrocked.[38]

Strict practice of the *Dingyou* system often deprives civil officials of their opportunities of timely promotion in the case of completing the period of mourning. By the end of the period of mourning, they might have missed the golden age for promotion and public service, which limits their contribution to the society. Many officials could have entrusted their elderly parents to their sisters at home or married or their reliable neighbors and focused on their duties, but because of the ritual law, they had to retire from office and return home, causing a huge waste of talent.

In addition, there are many factors pertaining to the *Zongfa* (patriarchal/lineage) system influencing the official personnel system, such as *Tongzong Huibi* (avoid employment of candidates from the same lineage in the same department or avoid employment of candidates from the same lineage that may cause conflict of interest) system, *Zhongyang* (retire from office and perform the duties of filial piety after parents/grandparents are over 70 years old) system, *Huiji Shiyang* (similar to *Zhongyang*, return to the native place and support and serve the aging parents) system, *Fengzeng* (the emperor bestows honorific titles to officials, their ancestors and family members) system, *Yinxi* (if an official has an inheritable title, the eldest son or son's son of the official wife will be designated to inherit it) system, *Chuji Guizong* (adopted by others as a son and afterward return to his original lineage to inherit official ranks/posts) system, *Gengming Fuxing* (similar to *Chuji Guizong*, renamed after adoption but then restore the original surname and return to the original lineage to inherit official ranks/posts) system, etc. All the above-mentioned personnel regulations implement and reflect the Five Degrees of Mourning system. The elements of the patriarchal clan system are integrated into the official personnel system, which serves as an important congruence between the official personnel system and the patriarchal clan system and clearly shows the patriarchal concepts and ethics.

1.5 Cultivation of Rites at the Grassroots Level

Traditional Chinese eat and drink not only for the purpose of solving the problem of food and clothing but also for the purpose of cultivating the masses and keeping social order, among which is the grassroots education via 乡饮酒礼*Xiang Yin Jiu Li* (village wine-drinking rituals).

---

[37] *The Great Qing Code* Vol. XVII, *Ritual Code:Administration of Rites:Funerals,* Clauses II and III.

[38] *Glossary Ming Code:RitualCode:Administration of Rites;The Great Qing Code* Vol. XVII, *Ritual Code:Administration of Rites:Funerals.*

1.5.1 Moral Demonstration

乡饮酒礼*Xiang Yin Jiu Li*, by its name, means a type of wine-drinking rituals in the village, recorded as the rituals of wine-drinking in the village by historical documents. In practice, this type of rituals was not so much as confined to the rural area but adopted as a prevailing ritual mastered by hosts at all levels where only the elderly and higher generations were invited. By the regular organization of this ritual, the status and role of the host, the seniority and reputation of the invited, positioning of seats, specifications of drinking vessels, music-making and dancing, doctrines of moral teaching at the ceremonies, and so forth are clarified, and hence the ritual concepts such as revering the senior, the old, the virtuous, and the able and observing rites can be deeply rooted in villagers and the moral atmosphere be formed where the old are respected and the young taken good care of and the virtuous valued and the guests cherished.

Among the three classics on rites, *Xiang Yin Jiu Li* IIII in *Ceremonial Etiquette* and *Xiang Yin Jiu Li* XXXXV in *The Book of Rites* both manage to specify procedural etiquettes of the ritual which tend to follow the natural way that harmonizes the heaven and earth, *Yin* and *Yang*, the Five Elements, four seasons, superiors and inferiors, the old and the young, opposite (all) directions, and the sun, the moon, and the stars.

Various groups and social classes of people are cultivated to different degrees via *Xiang Yin Jiu Li*. If this drinking ritual can be carried out regularly, guests and hosts abide by rites without failing any detailed etiquette, and the daily life will be rendered orderly this way; therefore, the social order can attain the height of differentiating the noble and humble, ceremonious and simple; being harmonious and happy but not vulgar; respecting the elderly entirely; enjoying leisure without confusion. These five principles being fulfilled, "everyone is able to cultivate his/her moral character and the state is then stabilized." *Xiang Yin Jiu Li* covers all social communities and all levels of social order, related to individuals, the state, and all under heaven, which symbolizes whether the rule of virtue is realized. There is no wonder that Confucius once said, through *Xiang Yin Jiu Li*, people come to understand "the ease of the rule of virtue," and then the rule of virtue can be realized.[39]

Xiang Yin Jiu Li is a comprehensive system of activities aiming at inculcation of filial piety and implementation of ritual laws, including demonstrating the hierarchy in the classification of the senior and young through the rituals that underscore the respect for the elderly and the senior, announcing decrees as a way of disseminating legal knowledge, organizing the drinking rituals in the rural communities to socialize lineage ethics, and inviting the senior and virtuous at the drinking rituals who will be more disciplined and diligent after returning home and set an example of serving the local authorities and cooperating with them to effectively rule the village.

---

[39] *Book of Rites:Xiang Yin Jiu Li XXXXV.*

1.5.2 Popular Indoctrination of Laws

During the Warring States Period (476–221 BC) and Qin Dynasty (221–207 BC), the rites and music were in ruins, the legalist school of thought prevailed and Confucianism waned, and eventually the related rites and etiquettes were rendered obsolete. During and after the Han Dynasty (202 BC–220 AD), rites and etiquettes were restored gradually, and they were formalized during the Tang Dynasty (618–907), detailedly stipulated in legal codes during the Song (960–1279), Yuan (1271–1368), Ming (1368–1644), and Qing (1636–1912) Dynasties. Up until the revision of law at the end of Qing Dynasty, rites and etiquettes were no longer put in legal codes.

As time passed by, *Xiang Yin Jiu Li* witnessed changes concerning participants and proprieties. In the Tang Dynasty (618–907), for example, there were two types of drinking rituals: the first type called *Zhengchiwei* was normally organized during every December in order to clarify the senior and junior positions. Local officials would invite the renowned guests to demonstrate their reverence for the virtuous and seize the opportunity to disseminate the ritual law and keep morality from declining; the second type was also the most popular where the hosts would invite the successful candidates at various screening levels of the Civil Service Exam and moral models who fully fulfilled the duty of filial piety and fraternal love.[40] Local authorities would express their volition to respect the wise and talented and award virtues of filial piety and fraternal love by organizing community drinking rituals and thus create a positive atmosphere that underlined cultivation of moral character and filial piety to the senior. During the Song Dynasty (960–1279), more drinking rituals were held. The local authorities were so keen on organizing those rituals that they not only planned and mastered the rituals but also revised treatises on them.

The Ming Dynasty (1368–1644) witnessed both centralization of power in the hands of the sovereign and control over the literati and the masses. *Xiang Yin Jiu Li* converted to a means as authorities' coercive instruction ceremonies to the people for inculcation of differentiating the senior and the junior, the elderly and the young, and the virtuous and vicious and of loyalty to the sovereign and filial piety to the senior, from a way of educating the Confucian literati. The ritual law of the Ming Dynasty specifically stipulated that wrongdoers must stand in shame at the ceremony, hearing the instructions and reflecting on their misconduct. In the 22nd year of Hongwu's reign (1390), it was stipulated in a decree that those wrongdoers should sit in the outer ring and not mix with the virtuous.[41] *Xiang Yin Jiu Li* was widely practiced in the rural area by the means of promulgating *Jiaomin Bangwen* (Placard of Instructions to the People) that repeatedly underlined the significance of organizing *Xiang Yin Jiu Li*. *Jiaomin Bangwen* Article 27 stated: *Xiang Yin Jiu Li* aims at differentiating the senior and the junior, the elderly and the young, and the virtuous and vicious, and it has been practiced by all communities as good law that

[40] *New Book of the Tang* Vol. XVIIII, Treatises VIIII, *Treatises on Rites and Music* VIIII.

[41] *The History of the Ming Dynasty* Vol. XXXXXVI, Treatises XXXII, Rites X.

underlines good custom. It is hereby stated once more that specifications of the ritual must be complied with to ensure orderly seating of the senior and the junior, the elderly and the young, and no mixture of the virtuous and nonvirtuous. When the practice is routinized, people naturally come to discern good from evil and behave law-abidingly.[42] That is to say, as long as people abide by the ritual law, organize drinking rituals accordingly, and distinguish between the elderly and the young and the virtuous and nonvirtuous, the custom can be purified and the moral character molded.

The Qing Court started the momentum of learning from the culture of Han nationality as soon as their military power reached the capital city Beijing through Shanhai Pass. In terms of *Xiang Yin Jiu li*, they inherited the rituals from the Ming Dynasty and made the rituals more standardized and systemized. In the first year of Shunzhi's reign (1644), every January 15th and October first, *Xiang Yin Jiu li* was organized in the capital city, provincial capitals, prefectures, and counties, setting seats (please refer to Fig. 1.1) such as 宾*Bin* (the most virtuous guest), 介*Jie* (the second virtuous guest), 主人*Zhuren* (the host), and 众宾*Zhongbin* (the rest three virtuous guests). Chiefs of the capital city, provincial capitals, prefectures, and counties served as hosts. 大宾*Dabin* (the most virtuous guest) was chosen from the senior and virtuous of the village and was seated in the northwest; *Jie* (the second virtuous guest) was seated in the southwest, and the rest three guests took their seats in turn by age on the west side, between *Dabin*and *Jie*. 司正*Sizheng* (ritual director), usually occupied by instructors from the official school, held up the wine vessel and announce punishment for those who failed to abide by rites, with the purpose to "advocate rites and announce ordinances," that is, to "announce statues and ordinances promulgated by the royal court and instruct people to respect seniority." In the second year of Shunzhi's reign (1645), it was stipulated that statutes and ordinances must be announced at the ritual: *Xiang Yin Jiu Li* was organized to disseminate law and respect the senior, the virtuous, and the talented. The senior and virtuous should be seated at the upper position and the rest seated in turn by age. The offenders should be punished according to specific rituals by the ritual director. *Xiang Yin Jiu Li* continued throughout the Qing Dynasty and was the most systemized in the mid-Qing. In the second year of Qianlong's reign (1737), it was confirmed that the seats at *Xiang Yin Jiu Li* should be set by rituals. In order to regulate the specific procedures of the drinking ritual, *Xiang Yin Jiu Li:Yi Zhu* (annotations of the drinking ritual) was printed in advance and distributed to the guests and helpers so that they would practice the ritual precisely. The statutes and ordinances to be announced were enclosed to *Yi Zhu* (annotations of the drinking ritual) and later read to all at the ritual. In provincial capitals, higher-rank officials were appointed to supervise the ritual, and local officials were summoned to organize it cautiously. Those who failed to observe *Xiang Yin Jiu Li* shall be punished accordingly.

Xiang Yin Jiu Li:Yi Zhu has recorded the detailed specifications of the ritual, among which two procedures are the most important: 司正*Sizheng* (the ritual

[42] See *Jiaomin Bangwen (Placard of Instructions to the People)*.

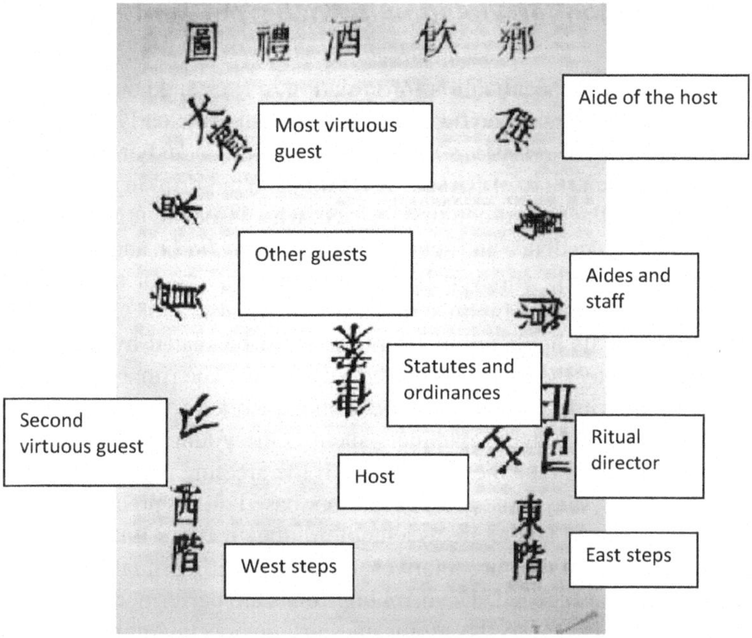

Fig. 1.1 *The Seating Map of Xiang Yin Jiu Li* (Huo, M. Y., Guo, H. W. 2009. *Qinding Xuezheng Quanshu Jiaozhu*. Wuhai University Press. 298)

director) (please refer to Fig. 1.1) holds up the wine vessel and address the audience on the purpose of organizing the drinking ritual—respectfully support the royal court, follow up the conventional specifications, and revere rites and ethics rather than merely eat and drink. All the elderly and young should be supportive to each other and form a society where ministers are loyal to the sovereign and sons are filial to the parents; people revere seniority; brothers show love and respect to each other; members foster harmony within a clan; and villagers are friendly to one another in the neighborhood. Do not abandon these virtues, and be worthy of the parents' love and care. In a word, the purpose of organizing *Xiang Yin Jiu Li* is not to provide food but to advocate the subjects to practice rites and ethics such as loyalty, filial piety, fraternal love, and so forth. The other important procedure is announcing statutes and ordinances. The Qing Dynasty emphasized not only the enactment of laws but also their dissemination, with the regular practice of *Xiang Yin Jiu Li* serving as an institutionalized mechanism for public legal education.

1.5.3 Penalization for Violation in Xiang Yin Jiu Li

Xiang Yin Jiu Li reflects penalization for violation in rites and etiquettes during the Ming and Qing Dynasties. Specifications of the ritual are clearly stipulated in the section of "ritual law" of *The Ming Code* and *The Qing Code*. For example, both of the codes contain the article of Ritual Law:Village Wine-drinking Rituals: Among the inhabitants of villages and country districts who associate together, there is an established rule of precedence and seniority at *Xiang Yin Jiu Li*, and there are certain specifications prescribed; whoever disregards either the one or the other shall be punished with 50 blows for his misconduct. The ritual law of Qing enlarged the object and scope of its application: people need to be seated by precedence and seniority prescribed by the ritual law in their daily life. The ritual law has also prescribed the greeting rituals when scholars, farmers, workers, businessmen, and others meet each other and attend banquets such as the young perform the greeting ritual first and the senior take the upper seats. If the greeting parties are not equal in terms of social status, they must greet each other based on the precedence of seniority. For example, when a tenant greets a landlord, the greeting ritual from the junior to the senior is a must. If they are relatives, only the greeting ritual based on seniority in the family/clan is needed. The drinking rituals are performed to revere seniority and underscore virtues, so the senior and virtuous occupy upper seats, and the senior and law-abiding take equal seats to honor precedence and seniority. Those who once violated law must be stationed backward and not be allowed to take any formal seat; offenders will be punished accordingly. If the hosts are not cautious and mix the virtuous with nonvirtuous to sabotage the right order of the ritual, or their misconduct is exposed by those seated, they shall be punished with 50 blows.[43]

The royal court set a very high standard of choosing representatives to attend *Xiang Yin Jiu Li*, and those who fail to observe the rituals shall suffer punishment. The specifications of *Xiang Yin Jiu Li* were set by the royal court during the first year of Shunzhi's reign (1644). In the second year of Yongzheng's reign (1724), Emperor Yongzheng seriously criticized the officials who failed to organize the drinking ritual properly and then dispatched head of the Ministry of Rites to 顺天府*Shuntian* Prefecture for supervision of the ritual. In the second year of Qianlong's reign (1737), the royal court again emphasized the rigorous screening process of the guests invited to the ritual and the cases where local authorities recommended unsuitable candidates for private reasons or the nonvirtuous replaced and defamed the chosen candidates and created impediments to the holding of the ritual would all be thoroughly investigated. Local authorities must supervise the selection of candidates in person. Where there was no suitable candidate, the ritual could be temporarily suspended, but the circumstances should specially be reported to the royal court. In addition, specific formal attire was required of all that participated in the

[43] *Comprehensive Canon on Rituals of the Great Qing* Vol. XXXVIII, Jia Li; Huo, M. Y., Guo, H. W. (2009). *Qinding Xuezheng Quanshu Jiaozhu*. Wuhai University Press.295–296; *The Great Qing Code* Vol. XVII, Ritual Code:Administration of Rites.

ritual without any misuse.[44] The practice of *Xiang Yin Jiu Li* makes the abstract code of ethics tangible and visible to the ordinary people, and it can be passed down through generations. The formation of such a long-lasting ritual is not accidental but intrinsic, which is very much worth further investigation.

The rule of rites is not equivalent to the rule of man. The rule of law in traditional China differs from the rule of law in modern China. The rule of rites in traditional China is justifiable in modern terms: it provides an alternative set of regulations for behavior besides the rule of law, by which people abide of their own accord and are subtly inculcated. In this way, people's moral standard and spiritual taste can be promoted so that they are willing to maintain social order, foster harmonious relationships, cultivate their own moral character, and positively influence others, thereby revitalizing the overall atmosphere of society.

[44] Precedents of the Jurisdictional Corpus on Administrative Matters Vol. 408, The Ministry of Rites:Feng Jiao:Xiang Yin Jiu Li.

Chapter 2
Penal Culture and Practice

2.1 Origins of Penalties

Since the late nineteenth and the early twentieth century, after the word "law" in English was translated into Chinese "法" and introduced in China, the concept of law used by the Chinese people was borrowed from Western legal language. The terms in legal text books and monographs were unexceptionally constitution, criminal law, civil law, civil procedure law, criminal procedure law, administrative law, etc. centering upon conceptions such as legal system, freedom, equality, and rights. Therefore, discussions related to law could barely be carried out without using Western legal discourse. Therefore, the following arguments were triggered: China lacked constitution, the rule of law, democracy, human rights, and civil law; China combined various laws together and failed to make a clear distinction between civil law and criminal law; China's judiciary was not independent; China's criminal law was far too cruel and so on and so forth. Since then, when talking about Chinese traditional legal issues, we would always use the modern Western legal concepts to explain and resolve them, and the issues for which no proper counterparts can be found and applied would be criticized, as if the Western legal culture were of good nature while China's legal culture had been of bad nature since ancient times. In fact, each legal culture has been rooted and developed in its own path due to its own economic, social, and cultural backgrounds. Without considering these backgrounds, it would be difficult to explain the diversity of human legal culture by selecting several preset formats and applying them roughly. In a broader sense, law should be understood as a set of social norms that have binding force on the behavior of members of the society.

Concepts as rites, codes, decrees, and punishments from ancient China are closely related to the modern concept of law but not simply equivalent to law. The characteristics of traditional Chinese legal concepts are as extensive and general as those typical of Chinese culture. Concepts ranging from written law, unwritten law,

R. Zhang, *Traditional Legal Culture in China*, Understanding China,
https://doi.org/10.1007/978-981-95-4697-8_2

state law, and family law to ritual codes can be covered by the legal concepts we now use, collectively referred to as "ritual law."

In traditional Chinese society, social norms were generally perceived as broad concepts, whereas law was predominantly associated with "penalization"—often being equated with punishment. The definition of "law" in Chinese phrases such as "no laws, no boundaries" or "violating the law of the land" mostly refers to criminal law for punishment. Criminal law is prioritized over other types of law in traditional China, which is attributed to the origin and functions of penalties. In Chinese history, criminal codes have been fully developed, whereas traditional law covers a much wider range, far more than penal codes.

2.1.1 Penalties Incurred by War

Similar to rites, laws of early China also experienced a process from secularization to apotheosization and then back to secularization. One of the ways to decide a case in ancient China was by ordeal. It is said that Shun, the leader of ancient Chinese tribes, appointed Gao Yao as judge. Gao was very fair and impartial upon law enforcement. When deciding cases, he would use a divine animal named *Xie Zhi* to help him find the real sinful person. According to *Analytical Dictionary of Characters* compiled by Xu Shen in the Han Dynasty, "Law, as penalties, should be like flat surface of water, just and fair, and then '氵' (water) is adopted as the left radical. "廌", an ox or a sheep with a single horn would strike the guilty and remove it during a trial, so the character also adopts the radical of '去' (remove)" on the right. Being flat surface of water means equality, fairness, and impartiality; "廌" is a kind of divine animal shaped like a unicorn. Legends say it was born to know who is guilty and who is not, and it would strike and remove the guilty with its horn. Therefore, the radical "去" is beneath the radical "廌." "廌" is a pictograph that symbolizes how the ancient divine animal decides a case, a legacy of totem worship. It expresses people's fine wishes of upholding justice and eradicating crimes, reflecting ancient people's strong dependence on divine forces.

In fact, apotheosized law was imagined by later generations. Similar to the origin of rites, law was undoubtedly rooted in secular life before it was apotheosized. The Chinese character "法" can be traced back to the legendary period of Cang Jie's creation of Chinese characters. It exclusively referred to the concept of punishment imposed on criminals, which prevailed during pre-Qin era. It is not true that civil regulations did not exist in traditional China. But from the perspective of rulers, it is the hierarchical social order that needs to be maintained. Therefore, inevitably the legal system in traditional China renders a strong impression of punishment. Most of the laws in ancient China were called "criminal laws." For example, The *Book of Historical Documents: Da Zhuan* stated that "there are over three thousand kinds of punishments in the Xia Dynasty (2070-1600 BC)." And *The Book of Documents: Book of Punishments* by Lü also stated that "Marquis Lü, assigned by King Mu, followed Shu Xing (redeemed from punishment by paying a fine in lieu) from the

Xia Dynasty, and then compiled the penal code named Lü Punishments." Judging from the content, crimes are catalogued by punishments. "Of crimes that may be redeemed by the fine in lieu of tattooing (tattooing the face with the black ink) there are 1000; and the same number of those that would otherwise incur nose amputation. The fine in lieu of foot amputation extends to 500 cases; that in lieu of castration is three hundred and that in lieu of death is two hundred. Altogether there are three thousand crimes set against the five punishments." The number of punishments is decided by crimes and these punishments are the core of the legal structure. During the Spring and Autumn Period (770–476 BC), Zi Chan, a legalist in ancient China, inscribed *The Book of Punishments* on a tripod, which is not called criminal penalty or penal code.

Law, before it is deified, is generally interpreted by scholars as punitive expedition, equivalent to punishments incurred by war. War functions as a means to treat different races. *The Book of Documents: Books of Zhou: Book of Punishments* by Lü stated that "The people of Miao ethnic group did not use the power of goodness, but resorted to the restraint of punishments so five cruel punishments were initiated as engines of oppression and were called laws. They slaughtered the innocent and were the first also to go to excess in amputation of nose or ears, castration, and tattooing. All those liable to the punishments were dealt with without distinction and no remission would be given to those who could offer excuses." Different races usually refer to ethnic groups and clans other than the majority. It is possible that punishments may be used as the earliest way of the conquest and rule of one ethnic group over another.

The evolution of the Chinese character 国 (guó, state) reveals the intrinsic connection between punishments and state formation.

Figure 2.1 shows the earliest form of the Chinese character "国" is written as "或" which symbolizes a person holding a dagger-axe "戈" to safeguard a vast area of territory and this territory stands for a state. Weapons, as the name suggests, are used to guard against foreign enemies rather than direct the spearhead at people on one's own side. Only when the collective interest of a clan is threatened and there comes to a life-death moment will weapons be used to fight with life against those offenders and keep them outside the territory. Any Chinese character that adopts "戈" as a radical part is related to warfare or weapons such as "战 (war)", "戟 (halberd)", etc.

What is exactly the connection between punishment and war? Punishment, according to its explanation from *Analytical Dictionary of Characters*, means, "punish criminals." It adopts "井" and "刀" as its radicals. Changes state that "井" means law. "辠" means crimes, so 刑 equals to punishments on crimes. With

Fig. 2.1 *The evolutionary forms of the Chinese character* "国"

radicals of "井" and "刀," a more direct interpretation could be law enforced by weapons. Shen Zi states that "punishment means amputation of limbs and cuts on the skin," which is very consistent with the basic sprit of punishment in ancient times. The explanation appears more direct in Han Fei Zi: "punishment is execution." In *Books of Han: Penal Code*, "刑" is defined as "punishment to the cruelest degree is to execute death penalty by tearing a person asunder by five carts, a less cruel one is to behead a criminal with axes; Medium-level punishment could be amputation of limbs with a sword and tattooing of the skin with a chisel; and the lightest level of punishment is to flog with whips" Lü Simian, a master of Chinese literature history, wrote in his book Pre-Qin History: "'刑', since its birth, symbolized the way we treated different races, and the connotation then is different from today's. People in Han dynasty would say: 'once the punishment is executed, it is irreversible'; therefore, at that time, when it comes to punishment, it must refer to the five cruel punishments that leave irreversible harm, and punishments such as penal servitude with heavy labor cannot be included. "[1] Lü's understanding of "刑" of that time refers specifically to corporal punishment and death penalty, for example, the five punishments are recorded in the *Book of Punishments by Lü*: tattooing, amputation of nose, amputation of feet, castration, and capital punishment. Hard labor, exile, and penal servitude in imprisonment executed by later generations are only regarded as "penalties" instead of punishments.

The legal systems of later dynasties are deeply imprinted with traits of war and punishment, for example, the judicial officers among autumn officers of justice of Zhou Dynasty were called "Sikou" (officers in the Ministry of Punishment) and "Shishi" (law enforcement officers), and Chief Justice was called "Da Sikou" (Minister of Justice). In Qin Dynasty, Chief Justice was called "Tingwei" (Commandant of Justice), and the supervisory officials were called "Yushi" (Imperial Counsellor) based on military ranks as a prototype. As for the grassroots judicial organizations, they also originated from ancient military units. For example, as is described in *Rites of the Zhou Dynasty: Di Guan* (officials of earth): "five households form a '*bi*', ten households form a '*lian*', five people form a '*wu*', ten people form a '*lian*', four '*lü*'s (25 families as a '*lü*') form a '*zu*'(clan), eight '*lü*'s form a '*lian*' so that they may be entrusted with mutual security, and that they may receive and share punishments and rewards." In fact, it is the precedent of the later generations' "baojia" (collective neighborhood guarantee system) and "lianzuo" (collective punishment) systems similar to those in military law.[2]

---

[1] Lü, S.(1982). *Pre-Qin History*. Shanghai Classics Publishing House, 425.

[2] Chen, G. (1937). The judicial system described in the rites of the Zhou Dynasty, *The Journal of Chinese Law*, New Volume 1, No. 5, No. 6, Zheng Zhong Publishing House (Special Issue on Judicial Systems).

2.1.2 *Penalties Determined by Crimes*

Zhou Dynasty ruled the country with rites, but penalties also played a part. The guiding principle was that rites were prioritized and penalties were imposed where rites could not be applied. Rites prevented crimes from happening while penalties punished crimes that were already committed. Therefore, penalties were usually the last choice, which pertained to the patriarchal integration as the social structure during the Western Zhou Dynasty. Ordained by rites and law, the emperor enjoyed the power of "rites, music, warfare, and expedition," and thus the social order remained stable and the emperor was of supreme status.

The transition from lists of penalties to law equals a transition from crimes catalogued by penalties to penalties catalogued by crimes. In other words, the emphasis started to be placed on the right and wrong of people's behavior and standardization of their behavior. Lǜ (legal code) originally referred to notes of melody. In *Analytical Dictionary of Characters*, it meant "tuner," which symbolized a feature of uniformity. This was exactly the legalists' ideal during the pre-Qin period when they declared "everyone be equal before law." Then Shang Yang's revision from "fa" (law) into "lǜ" (legal code) might be attributed to that. The relationship between rites and penalties was defined as "the behavior that goes beyond rites falls into the jurisdiction of penalties; penalties can only be applied when the behavior goes beyond rites; rites and penalties supplement each other."[3] From the Spring and Autumn and Warring States periods to the Qin and Han Dynasties, to a large extent, rites evolved from a rigid normative form (rites and etiquettes) into a flexible standard of judgment (rites and morality), while penalization evolved from a simple toolkit of penalties into a complex code of conduct (law), thus forming a new system that adopted penal law as a code of conduct, rites, and morality as the standard of judgment to ultimately enhance the emperor's rule of the society.

The transition from penalty to law and then to codes represents a trend that law began to be independent. The argument that "crimes were catalogued by penalties" in "the book of punishments compiled in the Xia Dynasty" and "the book of punishments by Lü" is not completely right, which is simply based on the paradigm of criminal law from modern Western countries. Since penal law was affiliated to rites then, the so-called crime actually referred to the violation of rites. Penalty in this ruling system was merely a corrective tool to complement rites and only when people violated rites would penalty be imposed on them. Even if certain penalties should be imposed, they must conform to the system of rites. For example, "castration should not be imposed on the aristocrats to preserve the function of generating offspring," "if a senior official is deposed and his post can't be restored for the rest of his life, he can still receive burial rituals as a senior official." In this way, rites and penalties complement each other.

Rites and law (penalty) jointly constitute the elements of ruling a state in the early stage of a class society: rites are the cornerstone in peacetime while penalties

[3] *Book of Later Han*, Vol. 76, Biography 36,Chen Chong.

are essential in turbulent times; and they highlight different aspects. "The most important affair for a state is offering sacrifices and waging wars," which gradually evolves into rites and law, morality, and penalty. Rites are mainly applied among the internal tribes while penalty is used mainly in punitive expedition as a way to fight external ethnic groups; rites are applied to the higher rank in the tribes and penalty to the lower rank. These stratifications already appeared in the early formation period of ritual law. Sayings as "inculcate the aristocrats with rites and music and regulate the common people with laws and regulations[4]; the rules of rites do not go down to the common people; the penal statutes do not go up to the nobles and senior officers[5]" all reflect the hierarchy of rite and penalties. As is stated in *The Book of Rites*, "If one observes the rules of rites, he is in a condition of security; if he does not, he is in one of danger." It is the cooperation and transition between the two ways as offering sacrifices and forging wars, rites and law, virtues, and penalties that help rule a state.

There was a legal system in traditional China but it does not equal the one in constitutionalism era. Some scholars reckon that the term "legal system" in modern times did not originate in China but a borrowed word from Japan. Traditional Chinese law can be regarded as punitive expedition, punishment, war, etc. Law interpreted as punitive expedition and conquering is similar to the integration of punishment and war. All regulations with orders and prohibitions as the content are laws, besides penalties. Laws here become a general term of the code of conduct in our daily life. For example, the First Emperor of Qin ordained that "the emperor's commands are imperial decisions and decrees are imperial instructions," a legal system did not only include legal cases but also the summary of the ruler's will.[6] Although law contains the nature of violence, it is by no means punishments only but also the general concept of laws and regulations. These codes and regulations are rather the codified rites and morality, which include rites and etiquettes, ritual systems, and ritual codes evolved from the early concept of propriety than penalization.

2.1.3 The Diversity of Penal Laws

2.1.3.1 Multiethnic Penal Culture

In the later stage of clan society, conflicts between clans prevailed; therefore, penal law came to achieve full development. In the *Book of Documents*, war-related language such as clan chief's orders, instructions, and vows were pervasive. *Book of Punishments by Lü*, the earliest written penal law, was therefore compiled during the conquest of Miao ethnic group. Most of Miao's penal laws were corporal

[4] Xunzi: Fuguo (the wealth of nations).

[5] The Book of Rites: Qu Li I: First.

[6] Cai, S. (1983). *History of Chinese Criminal Law*, Guangxi People's Publishing House, 4–5.

punishments, reflected by the story of how they invented the penal law. The *Book of Documents: Book of Punishments by Lü* stated that "The people of Miao ethnic group did not use the power of goodness, but resorted to the restraint of punishments so five cruel punishments were initiated as engines of oppression and were called laws. They slaughtered the innocent and were the first also to go to excess in amputation of nose or ears, castration, and tattooing. All those liable to the punishments were dealt with without distinction and no remission would be given to those who could offer excuses... The great emperor compassionated the innocent multitudes that were in danger of being murdered, and made the oppressors feel the terror of his majesty. He restrained and extinguished the people of Miao, so that they should not continue to future generations." It means penal law was neither created by the civilized Han ethnic group nor by a sage emperor but by the barbaric Miao ethnic group. Miao's punishments made innocent people slaughtered mercilessly, which astonished the God of heaven who sympathized them and sent a sage emperor, the emperor of Xia dynasty, to conquer and suppress the Miao ethnic group. After the conquest, Miao's corporal punishments were reserved for the Miao ethnic group who had already been degraded to slaves. Since the period of Sanhuang Wudi (Three Sovereigns and Five Emperors), wars between different ethnic groups never ceased, which gradually made it a tradition that the victors became rulers and the losers the ruled class. Punishments presented themselves as punitive expeditions during wars and as the means of controlling prisoners after wars. Military forces made the change of dynasties possible: earlier examples included Xia's conquest of Miao, Shang's conquest of Xia, Zhou's conquest of Shang, the scrambling for hegemony during the Spring and Autumn Period, the emergence of the seven powerful states during the Warring States Period, and the unification of the whole nation by the First Emperor of Qin; later events included the fight between Chu and Han, Three Kingdoms' Tripartite Confrontation, and Qing's conquest of Ming. Competition between military forces continued throughout the history, thus rendering punishment the integration of the legal culture from multiethnic groups.

The saying that traditional Chinese penal law derived from the art of war could explain the advanced development of the art of war in ancient China. Frequent wars generated a multitude of penal laws as well as the art of war. Those who were knowledgeable and of higher social status were all keen to study the art of war. In the Spring and Autumn period, there were already a series of books on the art of war, such as *Guan Zi*, *Sun Zi*, *Weiliao Zi*, *Sima Fa* (Methods of the Minister of War), etc. These books all descended to later generations. Sun Zi was known as "the sage of war" around the globe, which gave a glimpse of the status of Chinese art of war in the world. Accordingly, Chinese penal law was also advanced. The *Book of Punishments by Lü*, *Canon of Laws*, *The Tang Code*, *The Ming Code*, and *The Great Qing Code* were all representative samples in the world history of penal law.

2.1.3.2 The Highlighted Function of Public Law

When wars ceased, the function of punitive expedition and corporal punishment was reserved. Since the written law already appeared, the content of punishment was expanded, including not only corporal punishments but also written prohibitions. Where someone violated those prohibitions, she/he must be punished. Punishment was still the main function of law, and therefore law appeared in a form of coercive regulations to maintain the internal social order.

With the development of the concept of law after the Spring and Autumn Period and Warring States Period, more and more written laws were established successively and as factors affecting law multiplied, forms of law also became various. In particular, the First Emperor of Qin ordained that "the emperor's commands are imperial decisions and decrees are imperial instructions," and thus the forms of law were diversified. But we could still confirm that penal law held a dominant position in traditional Chinese legal system. Public law invariably played an absolutely predominant role in social life, while private law did not occupy much space in national laws and regulations.

In the entire penal law system, everything was related to the state power, which proves the mainstay is a public law rather than private law. The concept of "punishment" was most frequently used in early legal literature and almost replaced law. A fixed concept was generated in the ancient people's mind: law was equivalent to punishment and vice versa. The initial meaning of written law pertained to penal law whose characteristics that penal law and public law were more emphasized than civil law and private law never changed ever since the written law was created. China's highest legal institution was invariably called the "Ministry of Punishment" before the political reform during the late-Qing dynasty in 1906 can be seen as an illustration. The general principles and 11 books in The Tang Code which represented the complete legal system of China were all related to penal law. After the Ming Dynasty, the structure of legal codes was transformed. *The Ming Code* and *The Great Qing Code* cover general principles and six divisions pertaining to the Ministry of Personnel, the Ministry of Household Registration, the Ministry of Rites, the Ministry of War, the Ministry of Justice, and the Ministry of Works accordingly where criminal punishments served as the final treatment for most cases.

Since the Spring and Autumn Period and Warring States Period, political and legal scholars began to interpret the concept of law in a new way. The function of punishment was rendered as internal punishment rather than external expedition. In the same process, the concept of awards was introduced to complement punishment. There were also disputes between Confucianism and legalism over the role of penal law and moral teaching, but this type of disputes was limited only to the order and status of law instead of the necessity of law, which will be further discussed in the next chapter on the view of law of Confucianists and legalists.

2.2 Caution and Leniency in Penalization

2.2.1 Caution in Penalization

Penal law was deemed as "ominous" under most circumstances, and therefore rulers generally placed the concept of "rule by punishment" after "rule of rites" in their promotion of the ruling policies. Collection and assortment of penal codes received less attention than other sorts of books. For example, there were 10,246 kinds of copied and reedited manuscripts and archival book abstracts recorded in the *Summary of the Catalogue of Si Ku Quan Shu (Complete Library in the Four Branches of Literature)* compiled by Ji Yun in the Qing Dynasty, of which, however, there were only two kinds of copied and reedited manuscripts and five kinds of archival book abstracts on law.[7] Ji Yun explained that "penalties can neither be abolished nor advocated in flourishing ages, so what recorded just serves as the gist of the content." The chief editor's attitude toward penal law was rather aloof.[8] The idea that "ruling by penalties" prevailed in some periods; nevertheless, caution in penalization was still the mainstream thought and never changed fundamentally.

Caution in penalization entails cautious, careful, and restrained application of penal law. First, penalties should not be imposed easily; moral teaching goes first and then penalties; abuse of penalties must be prohibited. Second, implementation of penalties should be lenient and humane, not abusive. Third, penalties should be imposed in accordance with law; penal law must be "fair and just"; that is, implementation of penalties shall be impartial, moderate, and under control. In sum, in the process of formulating penal laws, legislators must narrow down the application scope of penalties, tighten the net of justice, and reduce the applicable amount of penalties. When penalties must be implemented, a cautious attitude is needed, and reckless and abusive use of penalties is not acceptable.

2.2.1.1 Implementation of Punishment Based on Motivation

In traditional China, the idea of caution in penalization was the mainstream in most periods. Officials had long realized that the implementation of penalty is in need of deliberation, and abusive penalty should be prohibited to avoid hurting innocent people. The *Book of Documents: The Canon of Shun* states that "Common punishments are carved on utensils in the form of graphics; exile serves as a mitigation for the five corporal punishments." It means in the cases of common punishments, convicts fit for five punishments can be sentenced to exile as a substitute with leniency. In terms of motivation and subjective mentality, individual criminals should be treated case by case. It was argued in *The Book of Documents: The Announcement*

[7] Xie, G. (2013). *Preface* & Wang, J. (2013). *Republican Judicial History*. The Commercial Press, 22.

[8] Han, D. (1946). What we need is "Rule of Law," *The Observation*, 1(10).

to the Prince of Kang that those who have caused harm to the society due to negligence, even if the crime is serious, shall be treated leniently and even be pardoned and those who have deliberately endangered the society and do not repent of the crime, even if the crime is minor, shall be sentenced with heavy punishment. In addition, some concepts were very progressive at that time such as the attempt to restrain family annihilation and collective punishments, the emphasis on the idea that "punishments should end with the convict," and "individuals bear the consequence of their own crime and do not entangle others even between father and son or brothers."

2.2.1.2 Prevention of Mistakes in the Implementation of Punishment

In the Middle Western Zhou dynasty, King Mu ordered Marquis Lü to compile the *Book of Punishments by Lü*, from the entire content of which "fair and just" was emphasized. This means penalties must be sanctioned in a proper way, neither too heavy nor too light, "with deliberation before each punishment." In other words, punishments should be inflicted properly based on the circumstances of each case. In the early period of Zhou Dynasty, rulers concluded from the historical lessons that the heavy punishment in Shang Dynasty made it meet its doom. Therefore, they proposed a series of ideas related to caution in penalization. For example, they realized the importance of the people's support and emphasized that punishments should conform to the public opinions, such as "the ministers and magistrates should fairly inflict punishment on people in exact adaptation to each offence"; "the clear adjudication of punishments effected the fair regulation of the people"; "examine the penal code carefully, and deliberate with all about it so that your decisions may be fair and just"; "it is not Heaven that does not deal impartially with men, but men ruin themselves"; and "all crimes related to five punishments were dealt with fairly and moderately and hence worth praise." "Punishments and fines should vary with different ages" means severity of punishment should be decided in adaptation to different situations. The theory on "punishments and fines should vary with different ages" and the principle on "San Guo San Dian" (the severity of punishment is decided in accordance with the public security of the state) are further development of the idea of "revering illustrious virtue and being cautious in inflicting a punishment." "Revering illustrious virtue" requires rulers in two aspects: first, it requires the rulers to restrain their excessive desires and eliminate perverse acts; second, it requires the rulers to be concerned about people's sufferings, reduce their burden, and let them live and work in peace and contentment. The common goal of both aspects is to obtain the support from the people to maintain the ruler's virtue, through which the ruler could be blessed by the God of Heaven, that is, to attain the threshold of "having virtues that match the status of rulership bestowed by God." Only those who are virtuous could properly exercise the idea of "revering illustrious virtue and being cautious in inflicting a punishment," as is stated in *TheBook of Documents: TheAnnouncement to the Prince of Kang* that "it was your greatly distinguished father, the king Wen, who was able to illustrate his virtue and be careful in the use of punishments." "Being cautious in inflicting a punishment" means punishments should be sanctioned with great care instead of abusing and slaughtering the innocent people.

For the convicts sentenced to capital punishment, they should be treated with more caution. Here is the guiding principle: "instead of killing the innocent, we'd rather make mistakes in law enforcement." Between the choices of executing an innocent person wrongfully and acquitting a guilty person by mistake, the latter is preferred, for the result of the case could be reversed if a guilty person is acquitted by mistake while the result will be irreversible if an innocent person is executed wrongfully. The idea of caution in penalization has not only won the people's support but also achieved positive social effect. A historical book stated, "The ruler's concern about the people's welfare is welcomed and therefore, people do not offend him." It should be noted that being prudent in ruling the people is not only acceptable to the rulers but also beneficial to them as it could alleviate class contradictions to a certain extent.

2.2.1.3 Light Punishment Preferred

Consistent with the concept of "caution in penalization," "light punishment" refers to mitigation of punishment in sentencing a convict. If one's guilt is considered excusable, punishment for him can be appropriately mitigated in order to prevent severe punishment. In *The Book of Documents: The Canon of Yao*, before the introduction of five punishments, lenience is highlighted, which is termed "宥 *You*" (tolerance). It also proposed that negligent offenders shall be probated or pardoned. In his elaboration of the idea of light punishment, Gao Yao believes that the emperor shall be brief and approachable to his ministers and be tolerant and lenient to his people; the sentence of convicts shall not implicate their offspring while rewards to the meritorious can benefit their servants. For negligent offenders, even if his/her negligence causes serious consequences, lenient punishment shall be considered; however, for those deliberate offenders, even if the offense is minor, corresponding punishment shall be inflicted. For those whose offense is not beyond doubt, they shall be given light punishment while for those whose facts of merit are not verified, light as the merit may be, they shall still be rewarded. Valuing prevention of crimes, avoiding execution of innocent people, and not fearing releasing a convict by mistake and then the recapture of him/her all reflect the concept of light punishment. Prevention of wrongfully executing innocent people conforms to the will of the people and is conducive to the development of productivity and social progress. This is the reason why Guan Zhong in the Spring and Autumn Period praised that "Shun didn't impose severe punishments and injunctions, whereas people all supported him."

What lies behind the concept of caution in penalization and light punishment is the ruler's wish of "nonpunishment." It means "the ultimate goal of punishment is to create a society without the need of it."[9] In other words, rulers impose punishments to eradicate crimes so that no punishment is needed. The prospect of penalization is to make people behave in the righteous way, thus realizing the purpose of governance. It should be noted that the goal of "nonpunishment" is one of the important aspects pertaining to Chinese primitive penal thought.

2.2.1.4 Nonpunishment as the Ultimate Goal of Penalization

Theories as caution in penalization and light punishment in the early period, developed by traditional Confucianists, have gradually become the cornerstone of traditional Chinese penal policies. Confucius states in *The Analects: On Government* that: "If a ruler adopts the rule of virtue, he will be deemed as the polestar; wherever the polestar is, it will be surrounded by multitudinous stars." Confucius believed moral education served an important way to prevent crimes, arguing that moral education was realized on the basis of material prosperity; punishment should be implemented if moral education failed and direct punishment without centralized correction in advance was not accepted. The concepts proposed by him concerning the hierarchy of administration, penalty, morality, and rites in their regulating effect of the public conduct has always been regarded as the motto for governance by the later generations: "Govern the people by regulations, keep order among them by punishments, and they will flee from you, and lose all self-respect. Govern them by moral force, keep order among them by rites and they will keep their self-respect and come to you of their own accord." It means that the ruling class has two ways to rule people: one is by decrees and penalties while the other is by rites and morality. The former uses decrees to coerce people and penalties to drive them and people have to follow in order to avoid punishments without knowing that committing crimes is disgraceful; the later uses virtues to influence people and rites and morality to cultivate them, and therefore, people feel deeply grateful and establish moral sense the same time. They will be able to distinguish good from evil and refrain themselves from committing crimes of their own accord.

Most of the Christians in Western countries are aware of the original sin, and they believe that everyone is sinful before God and therefore they shall repent of the original sin. Only those with a strong conviction and purified mind can go to heaven after death, while sinful people can only go to hell. The implication of the word sin is different from that of guilt. In spite of daily prayers and atonement, no one knows to what extent is his/her sin, for nothing will be known until the Judgment Day with the final verdict given by God. Confucianists emphasize this life instead of afterlife and they believe that everything can be verified in real life. If the differentiation between the two concepts of "sin" and "guilt" in the Bible is applied to the explanation of Confucius' philosophy, punishment and laws can only induce people's

[9] *The Book of History*: Yushu: Counsels of the Great Yu.

shame through guilt while morality and rites make people feel ashamed through a sense of "sin."

Confucianists inherited Confucius's idea of light punishment and continued to advocate cautious penalization such as "spare penalties," "penalties shall not be extended to one's wife and children," etc. The so-called spare penalties opposes severe punishment and abusive execution of innocent people. The argument that "penalties shall not be extended to one's wife and children" means that penalties are imposed on the convict only and shall not entangle the innocent. Mencius opposes Legalists' extreme practices of "extending punishment to one's kindred," and he believes that entangling the innocent is a vicious institution. Mencius said: "if a ruler is not inclined to kill, people will all look up to him and follow him." "With a single piece of misconduct or a single innocent person killed, even if one finally rules the whole country, he is not considered righteous."

For sure, the Confucian advocates as caution in penalization and light punishment do not equal abolishment of punishment; instead, they emphasize the credibility of it. This point is revealed in Hsun Tzu's theory. He proposed that "both rites and law should be valued," opposed to ruling by punishment and force. He believed that it is to attend the trifles and neglect the essentials that strict decrees and complicated punishments are applied without emphasizing virtues and rites. But he also believes that "rewards and punishments" are important ruling tools. Rulers need to formulate and publish written law, and in this way, "people all over the world will clearly know that it is impossible to get rich by stealing, to live a long life out of robbery and murder, to stay safe while violating the ruler's decrees." Moral education should precede punishment, and decrees and punishment should be implemented as the backup for "rule of virtue" and "rites and ethics." In the aspect of punishment, he advocates that punishment should be proportional to the crime that is committed by the individual. It is stated in *Hsun Tzu: Zheng Lun* (rebuttal) that "if the individual who commits a severe crime only receives a very light punishment, the public will know nothing about the harm of committing crimes, and thus the society will be chaotic. Therefore, nothing is more unfortunate than the scenario where one's morality doesn't match his/her status; one's ability doesn't match his/her post; one's reward is not proportional to his/her credit; one's punishment is not proportional to his/her crime." The conclusion is that "a country can be well ruled if a convict's punishment is proportional to his/her crime and the converse only leads to chaos. Confucianism advocates non-punishment through moral education while legalism believes in non-punishment through strict law and severe punishment. Nevertheless, Hsun Tzu combines morality and punishment and proposes the idea of "laying equal emphasis on morality and penalty."

2.2.2 Leniency in Punishment

2.2.2.1 Punishment Meted Out with "Mercy"

"Leniency in penalization" can be incorporated into "caution in penalization," but the former is considered to be more pro-people and humane compared with the later. Leniency in penalization, opposite to cruel punishment, means that punishment should be meted out with mercy, so as to reflect the principle of the ruler's "solicitude for his subjects." Only when caution in penalization is indeed practiced in real life can the principle of the ruler's "solicitude for his subjects" be realized, which is more vividly embodied in the Confucian theories concerning criminal penalty.

Leniency in penalization originated as early as in *The Book of Documents: The Canon of Shun*: "Let me be reverent! Let me be reverent! Let leniency rule in punishment." Leniency in penalization also emphasizes the reversal of miscarriage of justice and makes it possible for the bottom-up transmission of voices. The *Book of Documents: The Canon of Shun* mentioned "forgiveness" as well: Shun enacted banishment as a mitigation of the five punishments, which means those who should be inflicted with the punishments as tattooing, amputation of nose, amputation of feet, etc., if the circumstances are considered excusable, and then the original punishment can be replaced by banishment as a way of mitigation.

Influenced by the Confucian idea that "morality is given priority over penalty," orthodox legal theorists of the later generations confirmed that law enforcement officials should be restrained by "mercy" and value the principle of leniency and probation in penalization. Only in this way will penalty be meted out with the best effect. The story of "Ji Gao saved by a person whose toes were amputated" recorded in the *Family Analects of Confucius* highlighted "leniency and probation in penalization" by law enforcement officials under the guidance of orthodox legal theorists. Ji Gao, the judicial officer of Wei state, often sentenced convicts to the amputation of toes. Later, insurrection occurred and Ji Gao abandoned the city and fled. When he reached the outer gate of the city, he was saved by a prisoner gatekeeper who had once been sentenced to the amputation of toes by him. Ji Gao wondered why the prisoner would save him and thus inquired: "I once sentenced you to the amputation of toes and now I am in distress, it is high time for you to take revenge, why have you repeatedly saved me instead of seeking revenge?" The prisoner responded: "when you were deliberating on my case and finally rendered the judgment, you convicted others ahead of me and I thought that you were attempting to find an opportunity to exempt me from punishment; when it came to the conviction and moment of amputation, your face was clouded by merciful sorrow. Therefore, I recognized that you were an impartial judge with a noble character and a kind heart and it is the reason why I want to save you." Confucius thought that Ji Gao's handling of cases and application of law had already reached a high level of professionalism, for he had not only applied law but also integrated mercy into it. When applying law, the law enforcement official should know leniency and mercy in penalization, casting unconscious influence on people's character building; however, if he blindly abuses cruel punishment, hatred will arise.[10]

Most of the conventional ruling class was aware that if they inflicted punishment without mercy and leniency, people would not support them. For example, in the 16th year during the Reign of Zhenguan (642 AD), Emperor Taizong of Tang dynasty pointed out in one of his conversations with Sun Fujia, chief minister of大理寺*Dali Si* (The Court of Judicial Review), on law enforcement that the common problem of judicial officials was "they strive to leave profound impressions, take death penalty as advantageous," manipulate statutes, sabotage the rule of law, and all these reflected Emperor Taizong's concerns in this regard.[11] Wei Zheng also detested those practices such as "striving to leave profound impressions," not strictly following the law and abusing punishment, so he asked Emperor Taizong of the Tang Dynasty to "inflict punishment with caution and follow the penal code with leniency" and demanded judicial officials be cautious in infliction of punishment and execution of criminals and decide cases in accordance with law. In Ming Dynasty, Qiu Rui compiled *Caution in Penalization* and systematically explained the concept of caution and leniency in penalization and the purposes such as "petition for miscarriage of justice," "being compassionate," "preventing mistakes of imprisonment," etc. He also listed a series of theories from important codes and attached his elaborations and those of the scholars from different dynasties as appendixes in his book.

2.2.2.2 Punishment Meted Out with Compassion

In Chinese traditional penal history, leniency in penalization was widely put into practice, such as applying corresponding punishment to specific groups of population.

First, minors, seniors, and the diseased. For people below or above a certain age, they can be exempt from punishment or their punishment can be mitigated if they have done something harmful to endanger the society. This principle is reflected by the age threshold for criminal responsibility in modern criminal law. In ancient China, legislation concerning the age for criminal responsibility had long been established. In the Western Zhou period, the law of "三赦*San She*" (exemption of punishment for three specific groups of people) was stipulated in legal system: minors, seniors, and the retarded (*Rites of the Zhou Dynasty: Autumn Officials: Sici* (Judicial officials in charge of criminal penalty)). Those who have the rank of nobility, aged over 70 or minors with temporary teeth, will be free of being slaves (*Rites in the Zhou Dynasty: Autumn Officials: Si Li* (Judicial officials in charge of thieves and confiscating their weapons and property)). It is also stated in *The Book of Rites: Qu Li* that "people aged eighty and ninety are said to be very old and children aged

[10] *Family Analects of Confucius.*

[11] Yang, H.(2000). *Legal Thoughts in Chinese History*, Qunzhong Publishing House, 259.

seven could be an object of pitying love. Such children and those who are very old, though they may be chargeable with crime, are not subject to punishment." In other words, if minors, seniors, and the retarded violate law, they could be exempt from punishment, or their punishment can be mitigated. During the Spring and Autumn Period and the Warring States Period, it was stipulated in the article *Mitigation of Punishment* of *Canon of Laws* by Li Kui that "For criminals under fifteen years old, if they are convicted of felony, their punishment can be mitigated by three grades; or if they are convicted of misdemeanor, their punishment can be mitigated by one grade." The principle of leniency in penalization is mainly formulated according to one's physiological characteristics such as age and mental status. The law of Qin Dynasty adopted height as the standard to decide whether a convict should bear criminal responsibility. For example, it was stated in *Question and Answers on Law* that "a child less than 6 Chi (in the Qin Dynasty, 1 Chi equals to 23.1cm) owned a horse and raised it by himself. By accident, the horse suddenly got frightened and ate up around one Dan (1 Dan equals 61.58 Jin, 30.79 kg in the Qin Dynasty) of crops in others' field. Here comes the question. Is the child guilty or not? The answer is that the child is not guilty and does not need to compensate for the crops. People shorter than 6 Chi shall not bear criminal responsibilities even if they commit crimes. If males taller than 6 Chi but shorter than 6.5 Chi and females taller than 6 Chi but shorter than 6.2 Chi commit crimes, their punishment can be mitigated and they can only be sentenced to penal servitude. In the Western Han Dynasty, when emperor Hui came into power, he promulgated the imperial decree: if those who aged over 70 or below 10 commit crimes and need to be punished, the punishment is merely shaving their sideburns and beard shaved, with their hair kept intact. That is to keep them from suffering the hair-cut punishment. In the third year of post Yuan years, emperor Jing of the Western Han Dynasty promulgated a similar decree: "People aged over 80 or below 8, pregnant women, blind musicians or dwarfs can be imprisoned without wearing wooden handcuffs and fetters."[12]

Article 30 of *The Tang Code: General Principles* establishes a three-tiered classification of criminal responsibility based on age: Category 1, individuals above 90 or below 7 years of age; Category 2, individuals between 7 and 10 (inclusive) or between 80 (inclusive) and 90; and Category 3, individuals above 70 or below 15 years of age. It specifies different punishments for different situations from lesser punishment and mitigated punishment to exemption of punishment and demonstrates a clear system. Besides, The Tang Code also stipulated how to identify the age of minors. *Tang Code with Commentaries* stated that "if a seven-year-old commits capital offence while the crime is discovered at the age of eight, he is still exempt from death penalty; if an offender commits murder at the age of ten, while the crime is discovered at the age of eleven, then the case needs to be reported to the higher authorities for instructions; if an offender steals at the age of fifteen, while the offense is discovered at the age of sixteen, it can be redeemed with money." This means when an offender commits a crime at a younger age but the crime itself is

[12] *Book of Han*, Vol. 23, Zhi (Treatises) III, Criminal Law.

discovered at an older age, the younger age shall be taken as the standard of the age for deciding the criminal responsibility.

In the Yuan Dynasty, it was stipulated that "For criminals aged above seventy or below fifteen as well as the disabled, punishments for them could be redeemed with money. Each flogging could be redeemed with one Guan (a specific denomination of Yuan Dynasty paper currency) of Zhong Tong (the Central Treasury Bureau) notes."[13] This stipulation makes it possible for the old, sick, weak, disabled criminals to redeem their crimes and use economic penalty to replace corporal punishment such as flogging.

In Ming Dynasty, criminals of minors and seniors will be imprisoned separately. It is recorded in *Collected Regulations of the Ming Dynasty* that in the first year during the reign of Hong Wu emperor in Ming Dynasty (1368), "criminals aged over seventy or below fifteen as well as the disabled should be imprisoned separately and those with varying degrees of severity. Mingling of prisoners is prohibited." The *New Criminal Code of the Great Qing Dynasty* absorbed the execution concept of modern western countries and exhibited a more scientific approach in the process of conviction and sentencing as well as the selection of subjects for correction. For example, article 11 stipulates that those aged below 12 years old will not be punished for their criminal acts, but they should receive correction education in accordance with their circumstances of crime. In the first section of article 12, those with mental illness will not be punished for their criminal acts, but they should be subject to detention in accordance with their circumstances of crime. Article 50 further stipulates that those who commit a crime aged below 16 or over 80 may have their sentences reduced by one or two degrees.

Second, women, and pregnant women. Considering the vulnerable position of women relative to men and the special protection for fetuses and infants, Chinese penal law legislators of past dynasties have formulated some lenient provisions on the application and execution of penalties for women and pregnant women involved in crimes, and these provisions are constantly being improved.

According to Shen Jiaben's textual research, in ancient times, "based on the execution system, female criminals' bodies shall not be exposed in public after execution. In Tang Dynasty, if a female criminal was not to be beheaded, she shall be hanged in privacy, which means women shall not be executed in public. This indicates the basic concept of the execution system of the Qin Dynasty."[14] In the fourth year of Yuan Shi reign of Emperor Ping of the Han Dynasty, there was a decree: "If women do not personally commit crimes and their families do not act wrongly, those named for investigation shall not be detained. If an interrogation needs to be conducted, it should be conducted at their residence." For women who do not personally commit the offense, only those who have committed serious crimes shall be detained, and if interrogation is necessary, it should be conducted at their place of

[13] *The History of Yuan*, vol.105, Zhi (Treatises) LIII, Criminal law IV.

[14] Shen, J. (2010). *Historical Investigations of Penal Systems: Execution Systems*, in Xu Shihong (ed.) *The Complete Works of Shen Jiaben*, Vol. 4, China University of Political Science and Law Press.

residence. During Han Dynasty, many methods for redeeming crimes were specifically prescribed for female offenders. For example, one method called "Gushan" for female offenders was a form of redeeming crimes. It means that female offenders, even though convicted, could return home without serving the sentence personally and hire someone else with 300 copper coins to serve the sentence on her behalf. The *Jin Code* also stipulated that all female offenders sentenced to penal servitude can redeem them with money.

In the third year of Hou Yuan reign of Emperor Jing of Han Dynasty, pregnant women can serve their sentence without wearing fetters.[15] As is recorded in *The History of Wei:Chapter of Criminal Law*, during the reign of emperor Tai Wu in North Wei Dynasty, if a pregnant woman is sentenced to death, she shall be executed 100 days after delivery. It reflects an institution that could temporarily suspend the execution of death sentences for pregnant women who had committed capital crimes in North Wei Dynasty, which has a great influence on the legal practices of Sui and Tang Dynasties. As is recorded in *Criminal Law of Northern and Southern Dynasties*, during the reign of Emperor Wu of Liang Dynasty of Southern Dynasties, it was provided that pregnant women should not be sentenced to punishment. Execution of the prescribed penalties was prohibited for women who were currently pregnant.

Article 26 in *Adjudicating Cases on the Tang Code with Commentaries* stipulates that "if a pregnant woman is sentenced to death, she shall be executed until 100 days after delivery. If a pregnant woman is executed before delivery, the law enforcement official shall serve a two-year sentence. If a pregnant woman is executed within 100 days after delivery, the law enforcement official shall serve a one-year sentence. If a pregnant offender flees, the law enforcement officials shall be punished in accordance with the foregoing provisions with two grades of commutation. If a pregnant offender is not executed after 100 days after delivery, the law enforcement officials shall report the reasons for not executing the offender to the upper levels of authorities stepwise." Pregnant women who have committed capital crimes shall be executed until 100 days after delivery. If a pregnant offender is executed before delivery or within 100 days after delivery, the responsibility of the relevant officials shall be investigated. "For minor offenses and those aged from under ten to over eighty, the disabled, dwarfs, and pregnant women, leniency shall be applied... For travelers who are sick on the road, pregnant women, those whose grandparents or parents have passed away, and those whose male and female servants have died, all are granted leave and provided with food rations."[16]

In the Yuan Dynasty, criminals such as pregnant women, the old, the weak, and the disabled will be given a certain preferential treatment. "If a pregnant woman committed crimes, she could be sentenced until hundred days after delivery. She can be bailed out during the month of awaiting delivery and then detained again until twenty days after the delivery. But those who have committed capital punishment

[15] *Book of Han*, Vol. 23, Zhi (Treatises)III, Criminal Law.

[16] *Old Book of Tang*, vol. 50, Zhi (Treatises) XXX, Criminal Law.

shall not be bailed out. During the delivery, a midwife would be arranged to offer assistance".[17] It reflects the humanitarian spirit of postponing the adjudication date based on the special circumstances of the pregnant woman and arranging a midwife to take care of the one who is about to give birth. For offenders hard to be convicted due to the lack of evidence or those who cannot be convicted after being detained for 5 years, they can be released when there is an amnesty in order to show the judicial principle that "it is better to handle the case by violating the conventional law rather than to wrongly kill an innocent one."[18]

The implementation of leniency in penalization reflects the "benevolent rule" of the ruling class, which can alleviate the conflicts to a great extent during periods of tense social contradictions and provide the successor with caution during the transition from dynasty to dynasty: leniency in penalization can win people's support while excessive punishment will only do the opposite.

2.2.3 Kind Treatment of Prisoners

Another representative practice derived from leniency in penalization is 录囚*Luqiu* (detained prisoners' case review system) and 悯囚*Minqiu* (humane treatment of prisoners). Detained prisoners' case review system is an important judicial and prison management system in ancient society. It is often a system in which the emperor or superior officers inquire about the situation and conviction of prisoners, redress miscarriage of justice, rectify wrongful convictions, or supervise long-pending cases, also called "虑囚*Lüqiu*" sometimes. In Western Zhou Dynasty, there were judicial officers inspecting prisons on a regular basis to review detained prisoners' cases. It is recorded in *The Book of Rites:Monthly Ordinances* that "In second and third months of spring, officials are recorded to inspect the prisons." In later dynasties, the *Luqiu*system had never ceased. In the Han Dynasty, *Luqiu* system not only prevailed but also became institutionalized as a regular practice in prison management. Historical records mention that in the Western Han Dynasty, Juan Buyi was appointed as magistrate of the prefecture of Jing Zhao. "Each time Juan returned from inspecting the prisons, his mother would ask him with certainty: How many wrongful convictions have been rectified and how many lives have been spared?"[19] He Wu served as magistrate of Yangzhou, who would review the cases of detained prisoners in their jurisdictions in August.[20] There are also other records of "magistrates of provinces and prefectures reviewing the cases of detained prisoners in August."[21] In the Western Han Dynasty, officials of all levels reviewed the cases of

[17] *The History of Yuan*, vol.105, Zhi (Treatises) LIII, Criminal Law IV.

[18] *The Book of History*: Yushu: Counsels of the Great Yu.

[19] *Book of Han*, Vol. 71, Biographies No. 41, Jun Buyi.

[20] *Book of Han*, Vol. 86, Biographies No. 56, He Wu.

[21] *Book of Later Han*, Vol. 38, Zhi (Treatises) XXVIII, Officials V.

detain prisoners in order to rectify wrongful convictions, thus gaining the approval of the people.

Since Eastern Han dynasty, the emperors would review the detained prisoners' cases in person, making it an important system in the aspect of judicial and prison management. Historical records state "During the resurgence of Han Dynasty under the reign of Emperor Guang Wu, the emperor paid attention to penal cases and often heard proceedings and decided the pending cases in person."[22]After the Emperor Ming of Eastern Han Dynasty ascended the throne, the son of Emperor Guang Wu, Prince Ying of Chu, was deposed due to charges of rebellion and committed suicide in the thirteenth year during Yongping period. Then Emperor Ming imprisoned thousands of people who were convicted of rebellion. Later, when the Imperial Censor Han Lang was reviewing those old cases, he discovered many miscarriages of justice and then submitted a written statement to the higher authority to defend the innocent, which aroused Emperor Ming's attention. Subsequently, "the emperor went to the prison in Luo Yang personally and a thousand people were released after investigation."[23]

During the Wei Jin and Southern and Northern Dynasties, the *Luqiu* system developed a lot and became a stable institution during Liang and Chen Dynasties of the Southern Dynasties. For example, in Chen Dynasty, in order to interrogate the prisoners and redress the wrong cases, a special institute called *Luyuanju* (Bureau of Rectifying Wrongful Convictions) was established. Emperors' reviewing of detained prisoners' cases became regular. As is recorded in the *Book of Sui:Penal Code*, Emperor Wen of Sui Dynasty "interrogated the prisoners personally every season and checked claimed convictions of each province before autumn equinox. In three years, he reviewed thousands of cases submitted by the Ministry of Punishment and realized that many people had been convicted because the penal statutes were too strict and meticulous. Therefore, he ordered Su Wei and Niu Hong to stipulate new statutes." The emperor took *Luqiu* system as an important way of inspecting prison conditions and supervising the judiciary. Considering the wide use of torture instruments and cruel treatment of prisoners in Southern and Northern Dynasties, he made unified provisions on the specifications of prison facilities so as to "uniformly standardize the size and quality of all the shackles and punishing rods."

In the Tang Dynasty, the *Luqiu* system was further advanced, and it became a normal institution to officials of various levels and was greatly valued by Li Yuan, the first emperor of Tang Dynasty and Li Shiming, Emperor Taizong. In the sixth year during the reign of Taizong, "The emperor interrogated the prisoners personally, temporarily released home all together three hundred and ninety prisoners who had been sentenced death penalty and ordered them to return next autumn for execution. When the agreed time came, all prisoners returned and no one broke the rule.

[22] *Book of Jin*, Vol. 30, Treatises of Criminal Law.

[23] *Book of Later Han*, Vol. 10I, Consorts, No.10I, Empress Dowager Deng of He Xi.

The emperor appreciated their keeping the promise and pardoned all of them."[24] Except the regular inspection of prisons himself, the emperor also ordered that "superintendents of all prisons should inspect prison conditions every five days. In summer, prisoners should be provided with cold beverage and be given the chance to take a bath once a month. Once ill, they should be given medical treatment. In cases of severe diseases, they should be exempted from wearing fetters and one of their families could be designated to take care of them. For convicts ranked above third class of official positions, two family members could be summoned to provide care,"[25] standardizing the system of inspecting prison conditions. The practice of the *Luqiu* system could help discover judicial problems, revise outdated laws, and in turn promote legal reform. For example, thanks to emperor Taizong's compassion, collective penalty lessened in the Tang Dynasty. Although the number of individuals who benefited from this was unclear, it was stated in relative documents that "compared with the past dynasties, the number of convicts sentenced to death reduced in half."[26] The *Luqiu* system in the Tang Dynasty was consistent with Tang's legal principles of tolerance and caution in penalization. During Emperor Taizong's reign in the Tang Dynasty, "the cases of convicts imprisoned in the capital would be reported to the emperor by the Ministry of Punishment once a month and reviewed by Imperial Censors.[27] Undecided cases would be deliberated jointly by officials in Shangshu Sheng (Department of State Affairs) and forwarded to the Secretariat. The Ministry of Punishment dispatched officials annually in the first month of the year to inspect the prison conditions and review cases of the detained prisoners and rectify any deviations from law."[28] Afterward, it is then stipulated in the law of the Yuan Dynasty: "among all the suspicious cases where defendants had been detained for over five years while their guilt was not established beyond reasonable doubt, they could be released when there was an amnesty."[29]

By the Ming Dynasty, the system of collegial panel trial was applied, and emperors no longer reviewed detained prisoners' cases in person but entrusted the three judicial ministries (Ministry of Punishment, Court of Judicial Review, Ministry of Censorate) and the eunuchs of Directorate of Ceremonials to preside over the review of prisoners' crimes. "The collegial panel system was started from thirtieth year during Hongwu's reign." The summer and winter assizes started from Yongle's reign by Emperor Chengzu of Ming Dynasty. In the third year of Yongle's Reign, Emperor Chengzu of Ming Dynasty started to establish summer assizes to "review and settle misdemeanors." Soon, it expanded to the scope where "the punishments below penal servitude and exile were all included." All capital punishment convicts would be executed after autumn and misdemeanors settled immediately. For those

[24] *New Book of the Tang,* Vol. 56, Zhi (Treatises) XLVI, Criminal Law.

[25] *Old Book of the Tang,* Vol. 50, Zhi (Treatises) XXX, Criminal Law.

[26] *Old Book of the Tang,* Vol. 50, Zhi (Treatises) XXX, Criminal Law.

[27] *New Book of the Tang,* Vol. 56, Zhi (Treatises) XLVI, Criminal Law.

[28] *Old Book of the Tang,* Vol. 50, Zhi (Treatises) XXX, Criminal Law.

[29] *History of Yuan* Vol.105, Treatises of Criminal Law LIII, Criminal Law.

who could not be convicted immediately, they needed to wait outside the prison for final decisions. During the Chenghua reign of Emperor Xianzong in Ming Dynasty, the summer assizes system was further refined, stipulating specific regulations such as "treating serious crimes with suspicion, reducing punishments for minor offenders, loosening prisoners' shackles and fetters, etc."[30] Winter assizes system started from the fourth year of Yongle during the reign of Chengzu in Ming Dynasty. Given that many noncapital offenders may freeze to death in the cold weather, Chengzu ordered that "of the two hundred mixed offenders subject to capital punishment, all be allowed to redeem their sentences through banishment."[31] Since then, the winter assizes system has come into being. "After Frost's Descent every year, the three judicial chief ministries, together with dukes, marquises, and earls, should jointly try criminals who had committed felonies, which was known as court assizes.[32] Though Ming Dynasty initiated the system of collegial panel for reviewing prisoners' cases including winter assizes, summer assizes and court assizes, with the gradual decline of the political and judicial systems of the Ming Dynasty, these systems often existed in name only."

In Qing Dynasty, there existed summer assizes but no winter assizes. Autumn and Court assizes were further developed. In the 13th year during the reign of Emperor ShunZhi, the emperor's edict was issued to the Ministry of Punishment that "the court assizes and autumn assizes were crucial systems concerning criminal cases, and hence I shall review the details of the cases to ensure justice and prevent wrongful death penalties." Since then, emperors thereafter all had a cautious attitude toward the autumn assizes and diligently reviewed the cases. The systems of autumn assizes and court assizes originated in Ming Dynasty and were perfected in Qing Dynasty. "For over two hundred years, the Ministry of Punishment has meticulously handled autumn and court assizes, ensuring thoroughness and precision."[33] The *Luqiu* system gradually developed into a form of being conducted collectively by judicial officials under the supervision of the emperor.

Minqiu system is similar to *Luqiu* system, meaning that compassion should be extended to the detained prisoners, and if possible, their requests, especially capital offenders' and their families' desperate requests, should be met, such as the provision that "capital offenders' wives could be allowed to stay in jail under petition", which means for a childless married capital offender, his wife could be allowed to stay in the jail until pregnant before the offender was executed. Other examples included "releasing the prisoners to return home" during the Han and Tang Dynasties to show the emperor's "mercy" and "forgiveness." The emperors' and local officials' regular or irregular inspection of prisons and their supervision and inquiry about the prison conditions and prisoners' case decisions advocated the establishment of a benevolent government. These judicial measures of reviewing pending

[30] *History of Ming* Vol. 2, Zhi (Treatises) LXX, Criminal Law II.

[31] *History of Ming* Vol. 2, Zhi (Treatises) LXX, Criminal Law II.

[32] *History of Ming* Vol. 2, Zhi (Treatises) LXX, Criminal Law II.

[33] *Draft History of Qing* Vol.144, Zhi (Treatises) CXIX, Treatises of Criminal Law III.

and settled cases of detained prisoners prevented the occurrence of wrongful imprisonment and prolonged detention. Luqiu and Minqiu systems are unique judicial systems in traditional Chinese legal culture. They also embody the Confucian philosophy of "caution in penalization," which was conducive to the high centralization and uniformity of judicial power.[34]

Whether many laws might not be strictly observed in practice, at least, it is sure that from central to local levels, there remains caution in penalization. Preventing "abusive punishment" is also a reflection of leniency in penalization. Considering the existence of the creed that "confession is of paramount importance" and the fact that a county magistrate is a one-man court and single judge, abuses of punishment in local places are unavoidable, resulting in the inevitability of coerced confessions. Generally, leniency in penalization can be well implemented in the earlier and middle stages of a dynasty while it may deteriorate in the later or final stages. Because abuses of punishment can accelerate the collapse of a regime, in the early stages of the successive dynasties, lessons from former dynasties are learned, and punishments are reduced to relieve some pressure on the people. Although there may have been some deviations in practice, the concept of caution and leniency in penalization has been advocated in traditional Chinese legal culture and also played a significant role in advancing criminal law civilization.

Although the concepts of "Luqiu" and "Minqiu" do not exist in modern society, to them, the modern establishment of relevant systems can be connected. For example, the implementation of the "retrial" system and the establishment of the death penalty review system as well as the accountability system for misjudged cases can to a large extent prevent and redress the wrongful convictions. These modern systems can be regarded as the continuation of the traditional system of leniency in penalization and therefore the unfailing value in some aspects of the traditional legal civilization still hold relevance in modern society.

2.3 Penal Amnesties

2.3.1 Extrastatutory Leniency

Punishment, in the eyes of Chinese people, is deemed as warfare, some ominous symbol, an omen of misfortune or a deadly weapon; therefore, rulers usually keep a cautious, compassionate, and restrained attitude toward enforcement of penal law. Sometimes, in order to mitigate the "ominous" nature of penal law, people may instead refer to it as "祥刑 fair and just penalization" or "详刑cautious penalization." Although harsh punishments and strict laws, even abusive punishments were advocated and encouraged in sporadic dynasties by certain rulers, generally

[34] Wan, A. (1997). A preliminary study on the evolution of prison system in the early period of Chinese feudal society, *Social Sciences in Guangdong*, (3).

speaking, in traditional China, advocates and policies as leniency and caution in penalization were still the mainstream. Penal amnesty system is considered representative, serving as one of the important features of traditional Chinese penal culture.

Amnesty belongs to the system of leniency and it is an act of state forgiveness, specifically manifested as the exemption or reduction of punishment for offenders. In ancient China, this system was referred to as "赦宥pardon and leniency," "赦 pardon," or "赦免exempt offenders from punishment." For example, offenders who cause damages because of negligence should be on probation, pardoned or released. In ancient China that featured the rule of man and the integration of morality into law, amnesty was frequently implemented by rulers of successive dynasties that contributed to stabilizing regimes, reducing cruel punishments and promoting benevolent governance.

Amnesty had long been recorded in *The Book of Historical Documents: Shun Code* as "enacting banishment as a mitigation of the five punishments" and "inadvertent offences and those ascribed to misfortune to be pardoned." It means when offenders were subject to five punishments as tattooing, amputation of the nose, amputation of feet, castration, and capital punishment, if their circumstances were excusable, then the ruler might enact banishment as a mitigation of those punishments,[35] of which banishment was used as the replacement for capital punishment, exempting the offender from death. After the Spring and Autumn and Warring States Periods, amnesty was quickly developed, and when it came to the Wei, Jin, and Northern and Southern Dynasties, since the national political situation stabilized, emperors' use of amnesty dropped. Especially during the golden age of Tang Dynasty, most rulers took a cautious attitude toward amnesty: "Amnesty edicts shall not be issued arbitrarily." Even for rulers in Ming and Qing Dynasties who rarely issued amnesty edicts, amnesty was still considered as a form of "extrastatutory leniency" during the enforcement of strict laws in chaotic times.

Emperors in ancient China granted amnesty for many reasons. During Han Dynasty, for example, regular occasions for a general amnesty included "the great mourning events," "enthronization of the emperor," "annual suburban sacrificial ceremonies," "the Mingtang[36] sacrificial ceremonies," "the emperor's visit to Piyong,"[37] "offering sacrifices to Heaven and Earth on Mount Tai," "establishing temples for offering sacrifices to ancestors," etc. Later, reasons for granting amnesty

---

[35] Guo, J. & Miao, M. (2003). *An Overview of the Amnesty System in China and Abroad*, Qunzhong Publishing House, 4.

[36] The "Bright Hall" (Mingtang 明堂) or "Hall of Distinction" was the most grandiose structure built by ancient emperors. It was used for holding meetings with vassal lords, issuing royal decrees, conducting grand autumn ceremonies to worship Heaven, and offering sacrifices to ancestors.

[37] Piyong (辟雍) was the highest educational institution established by emperors in ancient China. It was initiated during Zhou Dynasty as part of the Imperial Academy (Taixue), serving as an important place where emperors gave instructions and conducted ceremonies. The structure was surrounded by water, symbolizing a place of scholarly pursuit and education on rites. It also reflected Zhou Dynasty's emphasis on education and ritual ceremonies.

became ubiquitous and extended to various occasions as a new emperor's coming to power, the change of reign title, discovery of rare animals, rivers turning clear, engraving of imperial seals, the establishment of an empress or crown prince, quelling a rebellion, expanding territories, suffering natural disasters, the affliction of plagues, and offering sacrifices to Heaven and Earth and grand ceremonies. Amnesty was also granted for major royal celebrations or mourning events, encountering plagues and calamities such as solar or lunar eclipses, the turbidity of rivers, earthquake and landslide, and auspicious events like good harvests and appearances of auspicious signs, for example, the acquisition of treasures such as jade artifacts and the imperial seal or rare creatures such as Ganoderma, phoenix, kylin, black hare, etc. Amnesty was granted to honor gods and seek blessings through offering sacrifices and holding ceremonies and for significant national affairs like change of reign title, the empress' accession to the throne and establishment of the capital, etc. Regular amnesty, general amnesty, special amnesty, amnesty of grace and amnesty for eight special groups—八辟之赦 (Bapi Zhi She), which is granted to eight privileged groups—specifically as the "relatives, old acquaintances, the virtuous, the capable, the meritorious, the noble, the diligent, and guests.[38] Besides, there were also "德音*De Yin*" (a form of amnesty broader than special amnesty but narrower than regional amnesty), "曲社*Qu She*" (regional amnesty), and "郊赦*Jiao She*" (a general amnesty granted by the emperor after offering sacrifices to Heaven and Earth at the southern and northern suburbs), which all fall under the category of amnesty.

The imperial court also attached great importance to amnesty ceremonies and stipulated them specifically. As is recorded in *The History of Ming: Rites X*, "amnesty ceremonies" belong to auspicious ceremonies. Ceremonies for enactment of amnesty were held by the imperial court, and those for reception of amnesty were held by local governments. In Qing Dynasty, systems related to amnesty became more complete because the emperors' edicts and decrees were usually very simple but difficult to apply specifically; therefore, detailed "provisions of amnesty" needed to be issued by related institutions after the proclamation of these edicts and decrees. At that time, there were strict requirements for the formulation and review of the amnesty provisions, and the law was more rigorous than that of other dynasties.

2.3.2 Leniency as a Principle of Government

2.3.2.1 Ruling a Country on the Basis of Leniency

Most of amnesties were deeply influenced by theocracy, Confucianism, and religious concepts. For example, in Yuan Dynasty, the amnesty system was influenced both by Confucianism and Buddhism. During the reign of Emperor Chengzong of Yuan Dynasty, Buddhists once requested the emperor to release the prisoners

[38] *The Book of Rites*: Wangzhi (Royal Regulations): No.5.

because of Buddhist events. Thereafter, once Buddhists held grand religious ceremony, major criminal offenders would be released at large. This kind of amnesty happened in every dynasty, though the frequency varied with some dynasties granting more amnesties and others fewer. Song and Qing Dynasties, for example, had relatively more amnesties. The Song Dynasty established itself on leniency as a principle of rule and followed the ancestral laws to maintain the reputation for being "benevolent and generous," resulting in frequent and widespread amnesties. The Song Dynasty granted various types of amnesties including general amnesty, special amnesty, regional amnesties, *De Yin*, and so on. It is recorded in *The Book of Penal Law*: "the system of imperial benevolence and leniency involved granting amnesty to all criminals under its jurisdiction, releasing those convicted of various offenses except for capital crimes, and to those guilty of unforgivable crimes. All special amnesties were restricted to particular areas. When the emperor's amnesty edict was issued, capital and exile sentences would be reduced and convicts of other offenses would be released. Occasionally, even those sentenced to exile were released." This showed that although *De Yin*, general amnesty, and special amnesty all belonged to amnesty system, there were obvious differences between them. According to the textual research of *On Penal Codes of Successive Dynasties* by Shen Jiaben, in the 316th year of Song Dynasty, except *De Yin*, special amnesty, and regular amnesty, there were 144 times of general amnesty and 105 times of regional amnesty. Amnesties were granted almost every year.[39] During the reign of Emperor Guangxu in the late Qing Dynasty, the number of provisions on amnesty increased to 20. The Qing Dynasty had a greater number and richer content of amnesty provisions than any previous dynasty. Before the middle period of Guangxu's reign, amnesty was still a part of the traditional amnesty system, while amnesty from the late Qing Dynasty to the early Republic of China marked the beginning of the modern amnesty system.

The amnesty system has been questioned ever since its emergence. The reasons are as follows: leniency toward criminals would do further harm to victims and injustice to law-abiding people. It may provide evil people chances to commit crimes. Criminals get away with punishments and victims suffer injustice. Particularly in Song Dynasty when a general amnesty was a triennial event, it became hard to carry out death sentences in remote regions, because in Song Dynasty, the imperial court had the final decision on death penalty, and it took too much time on procedures; therefore, criminals were likely to be released or their sentences commuted when there was a general amnesty. Wang Anshi even criticized this as "irresponsible rule," meaning that the rule of the country did not adhere to proper regulations.

There are also criminologists in Western countries who oppose the amnesty system. Cesare Beccaria specially wrote a chapter named "amnesty by grace" in his book *On Crimes and Punishments* to explain the unnecessariness of amnesty:

---

[39] Shen, J. (2010). *Historical Investigations of Penal Systems: Amnesty* Vol.12, Investigation on Amnesty V: Song Dynasty, Xu Shihong (ed.) *The Complete Works of Shen Jiaben,* Vol. 3, China University of Political Science and Law Press, 410,433.

As punishment is inflicted with more leniency and mercy, it seems tolerance is no longer necessary. Hence, mercy becomes the noblest prerogative of an emperor and the most precious nature of monarchical power. It is the silent repudiation of a flawed code by philanthropists who bestowed public good. Mercy is the virtue of law makers rather than the virtue of law executors. It should be shining in the code, rather than being exhibited in an individual trial. If people see that their crimes might be tolerated or punishments might not necessarily be the inevitable result of their crimes, then it will foster the illusion that crimes can go unpunished. Since criminals could be given leniency, people may believe that harsh punishments are not the manifestation of justice but rather an act of tyranny. Law should be just and impartial, so should the law executors in each case. However, it is the law makers that should be gentle, tolerant and humane.[40]

But for the ancient Chinese rulers, the establishment of the amnesty system was not entirely a means of establishing a persona or winning over the subjects but also revealed their own reflections on the nature of punitive justice.

2.3.2.2 Reverence for Nature

Natural disasters impact the daily life and even the survival of the people. Rulers of successive dynasties have always taken them seriously. In response to disasters, rulers would extend their benevolence and compassion and promote relief policies through various forms of amnesty. It is recorded in Volume 27, *The Book of Celestial Bodies*, in *Records of the Grand Historian* compiled by Sima Qian: "when the Yang star is prominent, there is a sudden increase of imprisonment and when the Sun is prominent, it indicates severe drought and widespread death and disaster."[41] It suggests that in the mind of ancient people, the sign of drought was related to unjust imprisonment. Many historical records stated that when faced with drought, emperors would send officials to review detained prisoners' cases and release those with minor offences. The emperor or empress would also occasionally review detained prisoners' cases in person. For example, in the Eastern Han Dynasty, amnesties by grace increased to as many as 16 times in the face of drought. This shows that the rulers believed that drought is closely related to injustice of imprisonment.

During times of drought, rulers advocated for reviewing detained prisoners' cases to relieve Heaven's punishment on them so as to restore harmony with the environment. For example, in the Eastern Han Dynasty, some attributed the recurrent droughts to the widespread imprisonment since the reign of Yong Ping, which prevented the emperor's benevolence from reaching the common people, as the misery and sorrow of those involved in the widespread imprisonments were profound enough to move Heaven and Earth, causing the disorder of Yin and Yang (a

[40] Cesare Beccaria (2008), *On Crimes and Punishments*, translated by Huangfeng, Peking University Press, 110–111.

[41] *Records of the Grand Historian*, Vol. 27, Eight Books V, The Book of Celestial Bodies.

disruption of the natural order).[42] Some officials argued in their written statements that it was the increasing number of prisoners as well as the deaths of some inmates due to the poor conditions in the prison that led to the Heaven's punishment-drought. In the face of such written statements, emperors would accept and implement them actively.[43] In the Eastern Han Dynasty, during times of drought, amnesty was considered as an effective way of mitigating natural disasters. The cultural imagery of imprisonment and drought were gradually integrated into the cultural framework of Yin, Yang, and Five elements by the literati. The arguments advocated by the literati during the Western and Eastern Han, especially during the Eastern Han, on the relationship between drought and the penal system, were undoubtedly inherited by the literati and emperors during Wei, Jin, and Northern and Southern Dynasties. As a result, during times of drought, more amnesties and reviews of detained prisoners' cases would be carried out.[44] The emperors and senior officials would consciously take such measures as reviewing detained prisoners' cases and hearing grievances to avoid miscarriage of justice and reduce the punishment of prisoners. In this way, they expected rain from Heaven. At the same time, they also regarded the number of imprisonments as a reflection of their benevolent rule.

2.3.2.3 Reflection on Ruling a Country

The emperor is regarded as the symbol of the nation and the primary constraint of imperial power stems from ritual law. Ministers can also effectively restrict imperial power through remonstrations and court deliberations. However, fundamentally, the restrictions on the imperial power are limited. Compared with the remonstrations from the ministers, the moral standards of a "sage monarch" might be more effective. There is also the will of Heaven. Since the emperor is revered as the Son of Heaven, he should embody the will of Heaven. Heaven's different emotions such as joy, anger, and sorrow can be manifested by through natural anomalies, and hence people should never offend Heaven. For example, in the Northern Zhou Dynasty, when the drought occurred, emperor Wu regarded "the misapplication of penal law" as one of the important reasons for the occurrence of it.[45] A corrective action corresponding to amnesty, aimed at redressing mistakes in the rule of the country, was to issue "edicts of self-reproach" occasionally so as to achieve the goals of criticism and self-criticism. According to historical records, this practice began with Yu and Tang. Since then, emperors such as King Cheng of Zhou Dynasty, Duke Mu of Qin Dynasty, Emperor Wu of Han Dynasty, Emperor Dezong of Tang Dynasty, Emperor Huizong of Song Dynasty, and Emperor Shunzhi of Qing Dynasty had all issued

[42] *Book of Later Han* Vol. 78, Biographies XXXVIII, Yangzhong.

[43] *Book of Later Han* Vol. 61, Biographies LI, Huangqiong.

[44] *Book of Wei* Vol. 62, Biography of Li Biao.

[45] *Book of Zhou* Vol. 5, Records of Emperor Wu (Emperor Yong) I; History of Northern Dynasties Vol. 10, Zhou Gaozu Emperor Wu Yuwen Yong II.

"edicts of self-reproach." These edicts were usually issued during times of frequent natural disasters, severe social conflicts, and crises that threatened the ruling authority. The rulers would review their successes and failures in ruling the country and adjust their policies accordingly, including the criminal policies, and reduction of punishments, in order to eliminate the public grievances and quell people's rebellious sentiments.

According to preliminary statistics, there have been over 1200 general amnesties in the more than 2000-year history since Qin Dynasty. The total number of amnesties would exceed 2000 if regional amnesties, special amnesties, commutations, and *De Yin* (similar to commutations where death penalty is reduced to exile, exile to penal servitude, and all lesser punishments are pardoned) are all included. It is considered a natural way of upholding justice and gratifying the public to sentence those who have committed crimes, so why would amnesties be granted to those who deserve punishments? Does it create a paradox between amnesty and punishment? We could not come to a hasty conclusion. Because law is the product of a civilized society, the purpose of punishment in a civilized society is no longer the same as a simple revenge in a primitive society. Instead, it serves multiple functions as a mechanism to realize effective social control. The rulers gradually came to understand that punishment should not be an end, which leads to an opposite practice—amnesty. Although amnesty is issued by the ruler, it reflects people's sense of compassion. From the Confucian perspective, it manifests benevolence and compassion in a patriarchal system.[46] From the religious perspective, it is potentially inspired by the concepts of karma and retribution. From the need of secular governance, the exercise of the centralized power cannot be separated from the appropriate adjustment of the rule, so as to align with the will of Heaven and the sentiments of the people as much as possible. The system of amnesty undoubtedly reflects these various demands mentioned above.

2.3.3 Moralization and Persuasion

In a centralized regime, no matter what the reason is, the moderate and reasonable use of amnesty would undoubtedly let the highest authority be aware of self-restraint in the application of penal law, and it also renders certain compassion to inauspicious punishments. In special periods, it also helped rulers win support from the people and eased the tension between the ruling class and the ruled class.

Law is a set of rules, and as a result, it should be objective, rigid, and not subject to arbitrary changes or violations. In many countries including China, there exists the phenomenon of penal amnesty. Even in a highly technologically advanced "rule of law" society where everything can be quantified, judicial procedures and

---

[46] Wang, X. (2010). Advantages and Disadvantages of traditional Chinese amnesty system, *Nanfang Metropolis Daily*, December 5.

outcomes may not necessarily withstand a scientifically quantified test. "Law should not be an object of ridicule, but what consoles people may not be law." "How vast is the distance between the rigid legal rules and their formalistic shell, and the human heart and sprit!" Jurists have passed down accurate and precise systems and regulations for generations, but "no matter how splendid the amour is, without the soul of justice, it may just be a killing machine."[47] The system of amnesty can be regarded as the embodiment of the highly centralized power of rulers, and to some extent, it is against the rule of law. Nevertheless, before the philosophers invented a sound system of checks and balances, rulers, by complying with dynamic situations and appropriately reducing punishments, could moderate the political climate of the country and alleviate the severity of harsh punishments, which is conducive to making up for the deficiency of the law and maintaining the ruling order. By granting amnesty, "the limits of the law can be remedied."[48]

From this point of view, if the system of amnesty is applied properly, it indeed has the potential to address the rigidity of the law and its lack of flexibility. By balancing rigidity with flexibility and combining authority and benevolence, the system of amnesty, simultaneously with the deterrent effect of the penal law, can comfort people, increase the labor resources, ease the social conflicts, and reduce social pressure. Max Weber once remarked that "Amnesty is a miracle of benevolence in ancient as well as modern times. It normally coexists with rigid penalties, thus showing the power of moralization and persuasion in the worldly rule of man." The effect of moralization and persuasion is not necessarily inferior to that of harsh punishment. From the perspective of sociology, amnesty not only helps to reduce the use of death sentences, resolve special conflicts, and save judicial resources, but more importantly, it can comfort people and thus showcase the benevolence of the state (or region).

The traditional Chinese penal law values harmony between nature and society. It may not withstand the scrutiny of modern reasoning nor sustain the test of modern science and technology, but the fact that it had certain positive effects in specific periods should not be easily denied.

2.4 Trends in Death Penalties

China is often criticized for the large number of death sentences each year, and many scholars advocate that China abolish death penalty immediately. They tend to hold discussions on death penalty from a modern perspective of "human rights." In fact, the attitude toward death penalty is not so much a reflection of human rights as one of the phenomena in the evolution process of legal civilization. Discussing

---

[47] Chen, G. (2012). The beginning is one-way love; the end is double-sided guilt, *Reading*, (1):151.

[48] Yang, H. (1998). *The History of Chinese Legal Thoughts II*, China University of Political Science and Law Press, 248.

death penalty outside the context in which legal civilization exists and evolves often fails to provide a convincing explanation.

Both Chinese and Western penal laws have gone through the process from barbarism to less barbarism, from cruelty to less cruelty, and from uncivilized practices to more civilized ones. The execution of death penalty in the history of penal law in China is unique in the global progress of legal civilization.

2.4.1 Resubmission of Death Penalties

Caution in penalization is often reflected in traditional Chinese judicial practice, and the institutional systems such as the resubmission of death penalties, the joint adjudication of death penalties, and the review of detained prisoners' cases can all be taken as the further reflection of caution in penalization.

Death penalty has long been regarded as the heaviest punishment. The ancient people gradually came to realize that death penalty is irreversible while executing it; therefore, it was implemented with more caution. In another word, the concept of executing death penalty is being redressed continuously through recurrent lessons. "Resubmission" of death penalty refers to the system that the decision to execute a criminal should be resubmitted to the emperor before it is actually carried out. The system of resubmission of death penalty was established in the Northern and Southern Dynasties. Though entrusting the ultimate decision on death penalties to the highest authority of the state is not explicable through the independence of the judiciary, it at least indicates a cautious attitude toward death penalties. For example, in Sui Dynasties, every death penalty case should be resubmitted three times, known as "three resubmissions." It is stated in *The Book of Sui Dynasty: The Book of Criminal Law* that "In the fifteenth year during the reign of Emperor Kaihuang, it was decreed that for those sentenced to capital punishment, the cases should be resubmitted to the emperor three times before execution." In Tang Dynasty, the number of resubmissions increased to five, known as "five resubmissions," reflecting Emperor Taizong's cautious attitude toward death penalty. During Emperor Taizong's reign, Zhang Yungu, a judicial officer, was wrongfully executed by the emperor, for he was suspected of sheltering a hysterical convict called Li Haode while handling his case. Emperor Taizong deeply regretted it later. Another case was the wrongful execution of Lu Zushang (a meritorious general), which led to the remorse of Emperor Tai Zong who finally realized that "human life is of utmost value and death is irreversible" and insufficient caution would result in wrongful executions. Consequently, he changed three resubmissions to five resubmissions except for the cases in local areas. When it comes to the execution date, wine and meat were not served and music and dance were suspended, which was consistent with the rites of reducing music and food to reflect respect for life. The system of resubmissions of death penal cases was therefore increasingly perfected.[49]

From "three resubmissions" to "five resubmissions," the reinforcement of the review system of death penalty was an important reflection of "the trend of avoiding the use of punishments" and "lenience and simplification in penalization" valued by Emperor Taizong in Tang Dynasty. In the early period of Tang dynasty, the judicial system was already relatively perfect. The phrase "all the cases should be handled by officials of SanhuaiJiujing (high-ranking and upright officials responsible for important administrative and judicial duties)" reflects Emperor Taizong's cautious attitude toward adjudication. However, after killing Li Haode from Henei and hence regretting it, and executing Lu Zushang, the Governor of Jiaozhou, for defying imperial orders and subsequently feeling remorse, Emperor Taizong was forced to decree that "all the death penalty cases, even those to be executed immediately, must still be resubmitted three times." His rationale was that "human life is of utmost value and death is irreversible." He also remarked, "Although the current practice is three resubmissions, the decision is still made in a short time without due deliberation. What is the benefit of three resubmissions? Henceforth, there should be five resubmissions for death penalty cases within the capital area and three resubmissions for those cases in the local areas." However, he also stipulated that "only those who commit abominations shall be subject to just one resubmission."[50]

2.4.2 *Joint Adjudication of Death Penalties*

2.4.2.1 The Autumn Assizes of Death Penalty Cases

Joint adjudication is the main representative practice of the traditional Chinese review system of death penalty. During Ming and Qing Dynasties, the Autumn Assizes further refined the system of caution in penalization. In the third year of Tianshun during the reign of Emperor Ying Zong in Ming Dynasty, "After the Frost's Descent every year, the three judicial chief ministries review serious criminal cases together with the dukes, marquises and earls, known as the Court Assize".[51] "At the time of Frost's Descent, serious criminal cases were reviewed by officials from the Five Departments, the Nine Ministries, and the Censorate. Cases with doubt were set aside, those with legal arguments were referred back to the relevant authorities for further investigations, and those who were convicted were held for execution".[52] This established the system of joint adjudication for death penalty cases. The joint adjudication is usually scheduled for the late autumn, during the

---

[49] Ou Yangxiu: *New Book of Tang*, Vol. 62, Zhi (Treatises) XLVI, Criminal Law.

[50] *Old Book of Tang*, Vol. 50, Zhi (Treatises) XXX, Criminal Law.

[51] *History of Ming*Vol. 94, Zhi (Treatises) LXX, Criminal Law II.

[52] *History of Ming* Vol.72, Zhi (Treatises) XLVIII, Officials I.

season of withering and chill. This reflects the traditional Chinese view of human and nature that associates the end of life with the decline of nature.

The global penal system has witnessed few countries treating the joint adjudication of death penalty cases with the same level of caution as traditional China, especially the Autumn Assize system in Qing Dynasty. The system of reviewing death sentence cases of different provinces in autumn by court officials in Qing Dynasty followed the Court Assize system in Ming Dynasty and made it more systematic, holding the Court Assize first and then the Autumn Assize. In *The Great Qing Code* categorized death penalty into two types: "immediate execution" and "detention with postponement"; the former would not be affected by Autumn Assizes and only the latter would be incorporated into the process of Autumn Assizes. Cases involving decapitation and strangulation of a criminal in detention with postponement were often those of brawling leading to death and thefts, which had relatively less severe consequences. For these cases, the duty of a local magistrate was to conduct investigations, performing autopsies, fill out corpse examination reports, apprehend the suspects, record confessions, reserve witness statements, and prepare all necessary documents with judicial officers and coroners. These materials were then compiled into case records by local jurisdictions and sent to higher authorities for review. Subsequently, they were reported to the Ministry of Justice at the specified time. After the provincial governor's initial decisions and the submission of these records to the emperor, the Ministry of Justice reviewed and prepared the cases for the Autumn Assize. The Ministry of Personnel, the Ministry of Household Registration, the Ministry of Rites, the Ministry of Warfare, the Ministry of Justice, and the Ministry of Works would organize the biggest collegial panel of the country with officials of the Court of Judicial Review and the Censorate and chief officials of other departments to review the death penalty cases reported from the capital and local provinces. Since the collegial panel was composed of officials from the nine most important departments of the imperial court, it was called "round adjudication by the nine ministers" in the Ming Dynasty and "joint adjudication by the nine ministers" in the Qing Dynasty. Not all of the officials involved in the joint adjudication were specialized in judicial practice, and their involvement in reviewing death penalty cases could be criticized for lacking judicial professionalism. Nevertheless, the system of extensive consultation can help minimize wrongful convictions and undoubtedly reflect the judicial spirit of keeping a cautious attitude toward capital punishment.

2.4.2.2 The Procedure of Joint Adjudication

The steps as follows are to illustrate the strictness and prudence in the joint adjudication process in Qing Dynasty:

I. Deadline

Cases involving death penalties reported from the local, after the examination and approval from the Ministry of Justice, were submitted to the emperor, and there was a fixed deadline for each step whether the cases shall be incorporated to the Autumn Assizes of the year. Provinces such as Yunnan, Guizhou, Sichuan, Guangdong, and Guangxi adopted the end of the year as the date to store away official seals; Fujian province used January 30th of the Chinese lunar new year as the date to store away official seals; the three northeastern provinces of China (Heilongjiang, Jilin, Liaoning), Shaanxi, Gansu, Hunan, Hubei, Zhejiang, Jiangxi, Anhui, and Jiangsu regarded February tenth of the Chinese lunar new year as the date to store away official seals; Henan, Shandong, and Shanxi took the first ten days of the new year as the dates to store away seals; and Zhili (Hebei) province took March 30th. Those serious cases newly closed beyond the sealing date shall be included into the next year's Autumn Assizes. If officials guilty of serious corruption and bribery or negligence of their basic duties were sentenced to capital punishment as decapitation or strangulation and their cases were closed before the execution date, those cases could still be submitted for review. Even if the submission already exceeded the execution date, the execution could still be carried out. Other cases closed after the sealing date should be included into the registration of new matters of the next year.

II. Provisions

Provisions of Autumn Assizes were divided into five categories: hierarchical official duties, cases involving human lives, cases of adultery, theft and robbery, miscellaneous crimes, and leniency in penalization. There were three ways of handling cases: serious crimes were included in the confirmed category, minor crimes in the probation category, and those with extenuating circumstances in the doubtful category. Although there were lots of cases every year, less than one-tenth eventually fell into the confirmed category.

III. Case Briefing

During the days when official seals were stored away, the Autumn Assize Ministry drafted the personnel list in charge of the initial and secondary reviews for this year's Autumn Assizes and distributed it to various departments for posting. After unsealing of the seals, Guangxi Department compiled the annual list of criminals, transcribed and briefed the relevant cases in accordance with the format, and then submitted them along with the original reports to the initial and secondary reviews. The initial reviewer used blue ink and the secondary reviewer used purple ink. They both needed to write corrections in neat regular script with close spacing. Once there were corrections to be made, whether of one character or multiple characters, reviewers needed to follow standard modification formats without random points or alterations. Cases in need of further deliberation were marked by the reviewers with comments. When the secondary review was finished, the documents would be sent to the Autumn Assize Ministry for another round of review, again divided into initial and secondary reviews. The initial reviewer labeled the documents and the chief was responsible for making final decisions. Case briefs were composed of two parts: the first part includes the reasons for the original suspicion and conviction of the suspects and the applicable legal articles. The second part was the facts and reasons given by the Ministry of Justice and the judicial reviews. The additional important facts were written on a separate piece of paper, and the review decisions were appended at the end, such as "confirmed," "probation," or "doubtful," known as the "ministry's conclusion," actually representing the legal opinions from the Autumn Assize Ministry. The Court Assizes were handled by Fujian Department.

IV. Meetings

The procedure of case briefing was determined by the Ministry of Justice, and all case briefs were delivered for printing after they were completed. And the investigation departments of each province also added their "exterior conclusion" that needed to be submitted to the Ministry of Justice before May. The "exterior conclusion" was similar to the "ministry's conclusion" and only differentiated between the confirmed cases and probation cases. The documents prepared by the local departments were not as rigorous and refined as those of the Ministry of Justice. The "exterior conclusion" was appended after the "ministry's conclusion." The Autumn Assize Ministry included the cases that differed in legal opinions and expressions into the category of "inconsistent cases." The Ministry of Justice would organize three types of meetings:

First, the ministry deliberation venue was set at the Autumn Assize Ministry, presided over by the chiefs from both Man and Han ethnic groups. At the scene, a book of inconsistent cases from the Court and Autumn Assizes and a set of a writing brush, an ink stick, and an ink stone were distributed. A scribe would read aloud the facts and annotations marked in blue and purple ink. Discussants respectively wrote down "confirmed," "probation" or "changed to confirmed," "changed to probation," "record truthfully as decided," and "doubtful" and submit these to "Hall Deliberation" for further discussion.

Second, the "hall deliberation" venue was at Baiyun Pavilion. The ministers and deputy ministers of Man and Han ethnic groups jointly held the "hall deliberation." The procedure was the same as that at the Autumn Assize Ministry. Decisions were made on the basis of the majority opinion of the ministry deliberation: severity of the sentence was decided by the presiding official, and then the decisions would be compiled into the yellow register. Except the confirmed and probation cases, the results of the meeting would be transcribed on small tags and stuck them on the top section of each document. At this stage, the review process of the Ministry of Justice came to a temporary end.

Third, the "reexamination" followed the "hall deliberation." The printed Autumn Assizes registers were delivered to each office above the imperial secretary, the intendance-general of the heir-apparent, the censorate, and the nine ministers, for all the chiefs of these offices had the right to report to the emperor independently. When it came to August, the Ministry of Justice would petition the emperor to appoint imperial ministers to conduct the "reexamination" of the cases. The location of "reexamination" lay in the southwestern room of the Jinshui bridge. Autumn and Court Assizes would be organized in two separate days. The Court Assize involved officials from the department of prison administration, and they came to the room to hear the decisions of this year's cases in the capital city. The scribe loudly announced whether each prisoner was confirmed or deferred, and the officials should hear the announcements on knees. They departed immediately after the announcements were made. On the second day, all the opinions of the joint adjudication were collected and reported to the emperor, resulting in collective decisions. Only after the Frost's Descent in August can prisoners be executed.

V. The Yellow Register

Collective opinions were written on the white Xuan paper with red grids in the neat regular script. There were eight lines every half page and 20 characters in each line. And the register was bound with mounted yellow silk and hence called "yellow register."

VI. Tick to Confirm Execution in Red Ink

The results of the reexamination were then reported by the imperial ministers; after which the Ministry of Justice proposed the deadline for the cases to be reviewed be the emperor, generally starting with distant provinces and then moving to nearby provinces. Within the review period, the Grand Secretary and officials from the Ministry of Justice must participate. If there were Mongolian prisoners involved, the Ministry of Minorities Affairs was also required to participate. Censors from various provinces also took part. The Court Assizes were organized with the help of capital district's censors. The Grand Secretariat submitted the list of the reviewed cases to the emperor for the final confirmation which were categorized as "confirmed" or "changed to confirmed." Emperors Kangxi and Qianlong frequently identified errors in the previous review processes and personally changed decisions, holding officials of the Ministry of Justice or participating officials in the collegial panel accountable. Once the execution orders were issued, the Ministry of Justice informed the local provinces to carry out the executions and the deadlines of executions varied based on the distance from the capital. Prisoners whose names were not ticked by the emperor in the current year were then included in the next year's imperial review list. For death penalty cases involving familial violations (e.g., an inferior killing a superior), immediate execution was mandated unless the crimes were specific exceptions as regulated as "unintentional" and were considered "pardonable." Special labels with initial decisions of "detention with postponement" were applied to such cases which were specially presented in a yellow booklet, and despite being categorized as "confirmed," generally, they were exempted from immediate execution. Only on the condition that officials who had committed crimes were not confirmed by the emperor to be executed after ten reviews and ordinary prisoners after two reviews, may their sentences permanently alter to "deferred execution."[53]

The Autumn Assizes aimed to realize caution in penalization and execution, and hence the system of joint adjudication became a major event in the country's

[53] Dong, K.(1935). The judicial system of the pretreaty Qing, *Journal of Law*, 8(4).

political life. From Emperor Shunzhi in Qing Dynasty, it was greatly valued by the successive emperors, especially Emperors Kangxi and Qianlong. Not only did they revise the sentences personally, but they also held the officials who originally adjudicated the cases accountable. While handling Autumn Assize cases, Emperor Shunzhi's attitude was rather rigorous. "Emperor Shunzhi often carefully examined the details of each case to ensure the deceased suffered no injustice and doubtful cases were not overlooked." Emperor Kangxi "reviewed each case repeatedly in person until he confirmed those beyond any doubt as definitely unforgivable and eligible for execution." Emperor Qianlong "formulated forty articles for examining and reviewing cases in person, distributing them among various departments and provinces as the criteria for case review."[54] The continuous improvement and perfection of the Autumn Assize system greatly reduced the occurrence of wrongful convictions. Judging from the above, it can be seen that in the Qing Dynasty, to sentence a person to death needed at least six levels of review until the final verdict was made: the county head magistrate, magistrate of a prefecture, the provincial governor, the Ministry of Justice, the Nine Ministers, and the emperor. Additionally, the joint adjudication process involved six procedures: reporting before the deadline, case briefing in accordance with the law, holding joint adjudication meetings, drafting the yellow register, and the final confirmation by the emperor. Although the death sentence cases reported from the local authorities were initially proposed for deferred decapitation or strangulation, only 10% of them were eventually confirmed for execution by the autumn assizes. This demonstrated that the trial and execution of death penalty cases was a very complex and cautious process.

From the modern perspective of judicial independence, the collegial panel of Autumn Assizes does not only include judicial officials but also other administrative officers. The emperor has no law background but plays a role as that of the "supreme court." All these are not consistent with the principle of judicial independence. But judging from the emphatic attitude toward death penalty cases, no other country in the world history can compare to traditional China. Traditional China managed to minimize the likelihood of wrongful convictions and executions.

It is certain that in terms of the process of execution, "summary execution" is not uncommon in the Chinese history. However, these typically happened during the time when the country was in a state of emergency, such as during peasant uprisings and rebellions. In such cases, the imperial court bestowed the local authorities the power to suppress rebels immediately without going through the formal judicial procedures. For example, during the period of Taiping Rebellion, the imperial court once delegated the right of "summary execution" to senior generals who were quelling the rebellion. Once the uprising was suppressed, the imperial court then revoked these generals' power of "summary execution" and restored the power of making final decisions of death penalty to the imperial court.

---

[54] *Drafts of Qing History*, vol. 144, Annals119, Criminal Law III.

2.4.3 Legal Regulations on Punishment

It is recorded that there was death penalty as early as the time of the legendary Yellow Emperor period, called Ji Xing (殛刑), meaning to be killed. According to the legend, in the war between Yellow Emperor (mythological emperor of China) and Chiyou (legendary creator of metalwork and weapons), Chiyou was defeated, and then the Yellow Emperor implemented Chizhi punishment on Chiyou. Chi (蚩) refers to Chiyou and Zhi (支) means to kill or execute. Subsequently, "political disorder in Xia Dynasty brought about Yu's punishments, political disorder in Shang Dynasty lead to Tang's punishments, and political disorder in Zhou Dynasty brought resulted in Nine Punishments." Among them, each form of punishment was established on capital punishment as a foundation to maintain the ruling order. It could be concluded that early capital punishment was not only derived from the simple sense of "life for life" but also served the ruler's need to suppress external wars and internal rebellions.

Before Qin and Han Dynasties, death penalty in China was mostly called *Da Pi* (大辟), but how to implement *Da Pi* lacked statutory requirements, resulting in various forms of death penalty and abusive extrajudicial punishment, such as炮烙*Pao Luo* (execution by scalding on a heated bronze pillar) in Shang Dynasty, 戮*Lu* (decapitation), 腰斩*Yaozhan* (waist chop), 车裂*Chelie* (being dismembered by five chariots), 枭首*Xiaoshou* (public display of severed heads), 弃市*Qishi* (public execution with mandatory corpse exposure), and extermination of three types of kindred in Qin Dynasty, among which "simultaneous five punishments" was the heaviest. It involved amputation of one's nose, left and right toes, flogging to death, beheading, and dismembering the bones and flesh in public. During the process, those who insulted the sovereign or uttered curses would have their tongues cut out and hence the name "simultaneous five punishments." Other forms of death penalty included chiseling the head, extracting ribs, boiling alive, and throwing into the deep water to be drowned to death.

After Wei, Jin, and Southern and Northern Dynasties, forms of death penalty were gradually unified into two: decapitation and strangulation. After the Southern Song Dynasty, "The imperial edict prisons" (involving high-rank officials who could only be imprisoned upon the issuance of an imperial edict) became prevalent, and *Lingchi* (death by a thousand cuts) gradually became a statutory death penalty.

In Chinese historical records, *Chelie* (dismembered by chariots) and *Lingchi* (death by a thousand cuts) were the cruelest among all the death penalties, deterring people even when they talked about it. Shang Yang was the chief contributor to the unification of the whole country under Qin's rule. After the old emperor passed away, Shang Yang's political enemies instigated the new emperor to take revenge on him. King Huiwen of Qin State sent troops to attack Shang Yang and killed him at Mianchi in the territory of Zheng State and then dismembered him by chariots. The edict said "Take for example the case of Shang Yang's rebellion whose entire kindred was exterminated".[55] Shang Yang was first executed and then his corpse was dismembered by chariots.

Lingchi (death by a thousand cuts) is the most brutal form of punishment in China since the Middle Ages, commonly referred to as "death by thousands of cuts and slices," "death by a thousand cuts," or "death by fish scales slicing." According to historical records, Liu Jin, the head of secret police during the Ming Dynasty, notorious for his countless crimes and atrocities, was sentenced to *Lingchi* after he lost power, as his political opponents sought revenge. In accordance with Emperor Zhengzong's imperial edict, Liu Jin was to be executed in the form of *Lingchi* for 3 days, with his body dismembered and his head displaced. The number of cuts was initially set at 3357, but he eventually died before the 3-day torture was completed after just over 3000 cuts.[56] Another convict subjected to this sort of punishment was Cheng De (or Chen De) during Jiaqing's reign in Qing Dynasty. He was charged with plotting to assassinate the emperor and was sentenced to death by fish scales slicing.

He had his ears, nose, breasts cut off, followed by fish scales slicing on his left arm, right arm, chest and back. At first, each cut drew blood, but eventually, there was no blood left, only yellowish fluid. After his upper body was sliced, suddenly, he said: "Hurry up!" As soon as his voice stopped, an official from the execution platform descended and told him, "The emperor has decreed to let you suffer more." Hearing this, he closed his eyes and said nothing. Finally, he died after his whole body was sliced.[57]

In Western history, there were also brutal punishments such as execution by fire, water torture, and impalement. Compared to China's *Chelie* (dismembered by chariots) and *Lingchi* (death by a thousand cuts), the cruelty of some Western punishments did not fall behind. Around the same time as the Qing Dynasty in China, there was also a similar form of death penalty that quartered a person alive by horses. This is evidenced by the case cited in Michel Foucault's *Discipline and Punish*.

Here's the detailed description of the execution of Robert-François Damiens in 1757 (The 22nd year of Qianlong's Reign in Qing Dynasty): On 1 March 1757 Damiens the regicide was condemned "to make the amende honorable before the main door of the Church of Paris", where he was to be "taken and conveyed in a cart, wearing nothing but a shirt, holding a torch of burning wax weighing two pounds"; then, "in the said cart, to the Place de Grève, where, on a scaffold that will be erected there, the flesh will be torn from his breasts, arms, thighs and claves with red-hot pincers, his right hand, holding the knife with which he committed the said parricide, burnt with sulphur, and, on those places where the flesh will be torn

---

[55] *Records of the Grand Historian* Vol. 68, the Biography of Shangyang, Eighth.

[56] *Zhang Wenlin Duan Yan Gong Nianpu (Zhang Wenlin's Chronicle)*, Chen Qiyuan: *Notes on Yong Xianzhai*, cited in Zhu, An (1988). *A Series of Talks on People, Customs and Institutions: Liu Jin*, Shanghai Bookstore Publishing House, 197–198.

[57] *Zhang Wenlin Duan Yan Gong Nianpu (Zhang Wenlin's Chronicle)*, Chen Qiyuan: *Notes on Yong Xianzhai*, cited in Zhu, An (1988). *A Series of Talks on People, Customs and Institutions: Liu Jin*, Shanghai Bookstore Publishing House, 197–198.

away, poured molten lead, boiling oil, burning resin, wax and sulphur melted together and then his body drawn and quartered by four horses and his limbs and body consumed by fire, reduced to ashes and his ashes thrown to the winds". "Finally, he was quartered," recounts the Gazette d'Amsterdam of 1 April 1757. "This last operation was very long, because the horses used were not accustomed to drawing; consequently, instead of four, six were needed; and when that did not suffice, they were forced, in order to cut off the wretch's thighs, to sever the sinews and hack at the joints...[58]

The quotation of Foucault's description of the death penalty aims to conduct a comparative analysis of China's death penalty in the context of the global penal civilization. *Lingchi* (death by a thousand cuts) itself was a statutory punishment, and its execution followed a certain statutory procedure: The process started from cutting off the two breasts first and then two arms and opening the chest to remove the organs, making three incisions and finally decapitating the convict. For those who were sentenced to *Lingchi* twice or additional cuts, the two rib sides were scrapped before death. In Ming Dynasty, executions were carried out at the Western Sipailou, and in Qing Dynasty, the execution cite was changed to Caishikou.[59] As for *Lingchi*, the number of cuts during the execution must strictly stick to the statutory procedure, and the executioner had no right to alter it arbitrarily.

The punishments imposed on Liu Jin and Cheng De were special cases belonging to extrastatutory *Lingchi* instead of regular punishments, which were subject to the emperor's personal will. In contrast, the scene of Damien's execution described by Foucault, with the presence of formal court officials and the cooperation of the priest, conformed to a complete judicial procedure and could be considered as a statutory form of torture. The severity of the torture on the convict was no less than the regular form of *Lingchi* in China. Moreover, during the European Middle Ages, the Inquisition often sentenced those deemed heretics to burning at the stake, some of whom merely explored the natural sciences and presented their scientific discoveries unknown to the majority at that time. This kind of punishment is almost undocumented in the history of Chinese penal law. In addition, punishments such as impalement and water torture are also extremely rare in Chinese penal history.

In terms of regular punishments, the phenomenon of torture exists in both China and the West. This is also a common phenomenon in the development of the world's criminal law civilization. However, influenced by the traditional thoughts of caution and leniency in penalization, China has generally maintained a cautious attitude toward the death penalty and would not easily impose it, except the cases involving certain tyrants or special crimes.

---

[58] Foucault, M. (1999). *Discipline and Punishment.* Joint Publishing Company, 9.

[59] Dong, K.(1935). The judicial system of the pretreaty Qing, *Journal of Law*, 8(4).

2.4.4 Sites of Deterrence

Death penalty also serves as a cultural phenomenon in traditional China. Concepts that law refers to penal law and penal law is equivalent to punishments are universally recognized legal values in the society. Although there are legal thoughts such as "morality given priority over penalty," "penalty applied in cases beyond the jurisdiction of rites," "indoctrinate people by punishments," and the punitive and deterrent functions of penal law have always been the mainstream in the penal culture. The legal idea of eliminating the need for punishments through the imposition of them equates to the concept of "implementing punishments in an expectation of removing them" advocated by the legalists. Thus, the death penalty, as the cruelest form of punishment, has been diversified in its forms by those who formulate, interpret, and enforce it, and it has been vigorously and spectacularly carried out in real practice.

The reason for the death penalty designed to be extremely cruel is that the ruler follows retributive justice of penal law. For legislators and law enforcement, the more they torture the condemned, the more it demonstrates the public power. Therefore, the death penalty is not only a kind of punishment but also a cultural and information symbol. The suffering of the condemned serves as a spectacle for the onlookers who consciously or unconsciously receive the cultural message. The death penalty is not only aimed at ending the life of the condemned but also conveys a powerful message to the living through the bloody and cruel execution scene that people who commit such crimes will result in deserved retribution. For example, in Ming Dynasty, when Zheng Man was going to be executed in the form of *Lingchi* (death by a thousand cuts), "suddenly, the imperial edict was pronounced in the noisy crowd that there should be three thousand and six hundred cuts. Hundreds of executioners responded to the edict in a thunderous roar, causing widespread fear amongst the onlookers. After the cannon was fired (execution signal), the crowd surged forward... Shortly after, a small red flag swiftly carried the message eastward, moving with the speed of wind and lightning, reporting the number of cuts to the imperial palace."[60] In ancient times, the death penalty was called *Qishi* (public execution with mandatory corpse exposure), referred to as the social effect generated by "executing the condemned in public" and "discarding the condemned with all onlookers." In the late Ming and Qing Dynasties, the executions were all carried out in bustling downtown areas, such as the Western Sipailou and Caishikou in Beijing and the Yudao street in Nanjing. Modern executions continue this tradition by posting death penalty notices publicly in the pursuit of generating a sensation. The larger the audience witnesses the execution and reads the death penalty notices, the greater the effect is.

However, can the "performance" style of death penalty really achieve the purpose of intimidation, deterrence, and "eliminating the need for punishments

[60] Indirectly cited from Chen, D., *Old News of National History*. Also in Jin, L. (1996). *Torture and Chinese Society*, Zhejiang People's Publishing House, 16.

through the imposition of them?" In a certain period of time, it may bring about the above effects, but in a long run, the effect does not seem obvious. The prevalence of torture did not necessarily synchronize with low crime rates. Most of the audience did not take it seriously. On the one hand, the scene of death penalty was terrifying; on the other hand, criminals still desperately took risks. For example, emperor Hongwu of the Ming Dynasty did not manage to deter or eliminate corruption by punishing the corruptive officials with "flaying their skins and stuffing them with straw." The audience was undoubtedly fearful of the bloody scenes of the death penalty, but they were also notably fascinated and indifferent, viewing the executions as spectacles. Some even joined the crowd with a rather utilitarian mind. During Ming Dynasty, public executions such as *Lingchi* (death by a thousand cuts) in the capital city would attract large crowds, not only showing the scenes that "after the cannon was fired (execution signal), the crowd surged forward" but also the phenomena that "pharmacists would gather to collect the flesh and blood of the condemned as the treatment of ailments like choking or hiccup, making it into thousands of medicinal pills".[61] For ordinary people, the deterrence brought by death penalty was temporary, but followed by prolonged nonchalance."

Can harsh death penalty really intimidate and deter people from committing crimes and thus reduce crime rates? Would light punishment or probation indulge and tolerate criminals and thus increase crime rates? Is the social function of the criminal law to deprive the criminals of their lives to achieve the retributive justice, or to rehabilitate them from "abnormal people" to "normal people" through reformative education? Opinions vary throughout the history and across countries. Due to different cultural backgrounds, life values, and customs, there are great differences in the understanding of the function of the death penalty among various countries and ethnic groups, and this divergence will continue for a long time. But it is certain that the overall future trend of penal law will approach leniency, emphasis on humanity, civilized execution, and focus on rehabilitation.

Merely intensifying the death penalty and enforcing retribution is not necessarily the best way to eradicate major crimes and realize the goal of "eliminating the need for punishments through the imposition of them." Durkheim, a sociologist, once said: "The emphasis of legal development is laid upon society." If the underlying conditions that lead to vicious crimes are not fundamentally improved, then no matter how severe the death penalty is, it cannot achieve the permanent effect of killing one to deter hundreds. It is impossible to expect a society with extreme polarization to be free of theft and crime where the majority of people are living in extreme destitution that they have to chew the tree bark, eat soil, and even exchange their offspring for food. It is equally impractical to expect a highly autocratic regime with no checks and balances to cultivate honest and incorruptible officials.

The death penalty in history is a means of retributive punishment for criminals and consolation to the victims and their families, but for most of the "outsiders," it is merely a cultural symbol, but their responses often do not conform with the

[61] Dong, K.(1935). The judicial system of the pretreaty Qing, *Journal of Law*, 8(4).

purpose of law makers and executioners. As early as 1764, Beccaria pointed out that "extremely horrific murders are reenacted with indifference and nonchalance," and that "public executions create a mixed terror that envelops both the executioner and the criminal. This process often transforms the shame suffered by the condemned into a sort of sympathy or even admiration from the public, and it turns the executioner's lawful violence into disgrace." "Public executions are seen as a hearth reigniting the flames of violence." This is considered the greatest failure of the death penalty.[62] Foucault has made a similar argument that this form of punishment appears no less or even more barbaric than the crime itself. It habituates the audience to the crimes it intends to deter them from. It becomes a means of displaying crimes to the audience, transforming the executioners into criminals and the judges into murderers, and in the end, all the roles are reversed, turning the condemned into objects of pity or praise.[63]

2.4.5 Becoming Civilized Over Time

In the process of social development, the implementation of the death penalty has become less frequent and more civilized. The practice of Lingchi (death by a thousand cuts) in China started from the Southern Song Dynasty and continued to the late Qing Dynasty. In April of 1905, Wang Weiqin was executed in the form of Lingchi because he and his soldiers exterminated Li Jichang's family of 12, including a 3-year-old child. His Manchu servant, Fu Zhuli, was the last person to suffer Lingchi, whose execution date was April 9, 1905. This date marks a significant moment in Chinese legal history as Lingchi was permanently abolished from the Qing's legal system in the following months. Although over a thousand people were executed in the form of Lingchi during the 200-odd years of Qing Dynasty, this torture ceased to exist thereafter.[64] This change can be attributed to the legal reforms at the end of the Qing Dynasty.

In the legal reforms during the late Qing Dynasty, reformist officials represented by Shen Jiaben advocated a more humane and compassionate approach to penal law through studying and referring to modern Western criminal law theories. They proposed and implemented several reforms to realize the evolution from the traditional thought of caution in penalization to the modern civilized penal system. Shen Jiaben's main thoughts on death penalty are as follows: first, reducing the number and types of death penalty provisions and narrowing the scope of its application, and second, abolishing brutal punishments such as *Lingchi* (death by a thousand

[62] Beccaria, C. (2008). *On Crimes and Punishments*, Peking University Press, 112; *Crimes and Punishments*, 101.

[63] Foucault, M. (1999). *Discipline and Punishment*, translated by Liu Beicheng and Yang Yuanying, Joint Publishing Company, 9–10, 372–374.

[64] Brook, T., Bourgon, J., & Blue, G. (2013). *Death by a Thousand Cuts* (Zhang Guangrun et al., Trans.). The Commercial Press, 3–6.

cuts), *Xiaoshou* (public display of severed heads), and *Lushi* (dismemberment and deformation of the corpse), replacing them with more humane methods like decapitation and hanging, advocating for a singular form of execution. Wu Tingfang also supported benevolent governance and light punishment, believing that "Benevolence is the priority of ruling a country. Those who discuss criminal law invariably advocate for justice with righteousness and execution with leniency. Therefore, it is imperative today to shift from severe punishments to more lenient ones, making benevolence the priority of governance." The purpose of punishment is to "maintain the state rights and protect public security" rather than revenge or severe deterrence. The severity of punishment should be based on "balancing individual interests and social interests"; therefore, punishments should neither be too harsh nor cruel, corporal punishment and torture must be abolished, and the emphasis should be laid on investigation of evidence and improvement of prison conditions. The legal thoughts of caution in penalization of Shen Jiaben and Wu Tingfang were implemented in the criminal codes mainly revised by Shen Jiaben, such as *The Existing Criminal Code of the Great Qing Dynasty*, *The New Criminal Code of the Great Qing Dynasty*, and others. In the newly revised penal codes, punishments including *Lingchi* (death by a thousand cuts), *Xiaoshou* (public display of severed heads), *Lushi* (dismemberment and deformation of the corpse), collective punishment, and tattooing were all abolished.[65] Hanging remained as the only form of execution and decapitation was also largely abolished.

Since the Republic of China, execution by shooting was implemented and lethal injection followed. The calls for the abolition of the death penalty were also strengthening. Although the death penalty still exists at present, its frequency has been greatly reduced, and China's execution system has gradually been aligning with the modern penal practices of the world. All the efforts to achieve a more civilized approach to the death penalty in traditional China are undoubtedly important elements in the global development of penal civilization.

2.5 An Analysis of Penal Codes

2.5.1 Harsh Penalties Hurt People

Views such as severe punishment for minor offences and rule by punishments were created by legalists and prevailed during the Warring States Period. Legalists such as Shang Yang and Han Fei were known for advocating severe punishments, and they believed that "the way to establish a ruler's authority is through the enforcement of the law; the key to law enforcement is eliminating villainy and the

[65] Yang, Y,(1937). The longitudinal observation of China's judicial system, *The Journal of Chinese Law*, New Volume 1, No. 5, No. 6, Zheng Zhong Publishing House, (Special Issue on Judicial Systems).

foundation of eliminating villainy is severe punishments."[66] "There is no better way to prohibit villainy and prevent crimes than heavy punishments."[67] Shang yang's concept of "heavy punishment" had its specific meanings. First, it contrasted with rewards and he believed that "punishments should outnumber rewards"; second, it was intended to increase the punishment for minor offences, and he put forward the theory of "eliminating the need for punishments through the imposition of them." He argued that "by heavily punishing minor offences, people would neither commit minor offences nor major crimes."[68] This would eventually render criminal law unnecessary, as the fear of punishment would deter people from committing crimes entirely. Thus, the use of severe punishments for minor offences and the call for equal justice under the law would help achieve the goal of "eliminating the need for punishments through the imposition of them" and "eliminating murder through execution."

Han Fei, the leading legalist philosopher, who synthesized legalist theories inherited and developed Shang Yang's theory of "heavy punishment." He fully endorsed and supported the ideas of "imposing severe punishment on light crimes" and "eliminating the need for punishments through the imposition of them." In *Han Fei Zi: The Seven Strategies for the Ruler to Control His Ministers*, he stated: "The Law of Gongsun Yang (Shang Yang) punishes minor offences seriously. Major crimes are hard for people to commit and minor offences are easy to avoid. To let people avoid what is easy and stay away from what is difficult is the right way of ruling the country. In this way, neither minor offences nor major crimes would occur, resulting in a stable social order." Han realized that minor faults were easy to correct, and by imposing severe punishments on minor offences, it is possible to deter major crimes. When people no longer commit minor offences, they would certainly avoid committing major crimes. Han's theory of "heavy punishment" was established on an analysis of human psychology, particularly the understanding that "people chase benefits and avoid harms." It is further elaborated in *Han Fei Zi: Six Contradictions*:

Crimes that could be deterred by heavy punishments might not necessarily be deterred by light punishments. However, crimes that can be deterred by light punishments would definitely be deterred by heavy punishments. Therefore, if the ruler's imposition of heavy punishments could eliminate all the villainy, how could this harm the common people? By imposing heavy punishments, criminals suffer severe affliction for trivial benefits, and since people are not willing to suffer severe punishments in exchange of small benefits, all the villainy can be prevented. By imposing light punishments, criminals could gain relatively large benefits while the punishments imposed on them are light. Therefore, people may seek large benefits without being afraid of committing crimes and the villainy cannot be prevented.

Han Fei Zi believed that people are naturally benefits-driven, and they may commit major offences merely for small gains. Instead of allowing people to commit

[66] *Shang Jun Shu (Book of Shang Yang)*: Kai Sai (initiation and abolition).

[67] *Shang Jun Shu (Book of Shang Yang)*: Rewards and Punishments.

[68] *Shang Jun Shu (Book of Shang Yang)*: Strict Orders.

major crimes for small gains, it is better to prevent these crimes by imposing severe punishments when they seek small benefits. In this way, heavy punishments would deter people from testing the law easily and the number of offenders would decrease accordingly. The rapid rise of Qin Dynasty was attributed to the legalist philosophy of harsh punishments and strict laws. During Qin Dynasty, anything however trivial should be decided by the law. Collective punishment was prevalent, and severe punishments such as amputation of foot and castration were widely applied, for example, full carts of amputated feet and over 700, 000 afflicted with castration all reflecting the rule by severe punishment.

The governance of a country cannot solely depend on punishments. Law was merely one of the methods of governing a country, not the entire or the only means of it. The Qin Dynasty's exclusive reliance on punishments, along with its authoritarian practices, treated punishments as the sole method of its rule. This rule led to the burning of books and the burial of Confucian scholars alive to realize the autocratic control of the populace's intellectual and cultural life. The legal system of Qin Dynasty was so intricate and oppressive that it was compared to "white flowers of reeds for its quantity and congealed fat for its tightness." Within the oppressive legal system, the populace was viewed as mere objects rather than living, feeling individuals. Consequently, since "people had long suffered the cruel rule of Qin," Chen Sheng and Wu Guang's uprising which lead to the overthrow of Qin Dynasty was an inevitable outcome.

Song Dynasty also implemented *Heavy Penalties on Burglary* and *Heavier Punishments in Specific Jurisdictions*. The former targeted collective incidents with more severe punishments. The latter designated specific jurisdictions where more strict laws and heavier punishments should be implemented. As a result, these severe punishments not only failed to alleviate social conflicts and promote social stability but also constantly exacerbated the tensions and led to frequent uprisings among the populace.

In the early Ming Dynasty, severe punishments also prevailed. At its establishment, Ming Dynasty confronted sharp social conflicts and the destruction brought forth by continuous wars, so the social economy declined and the political situation was unstable. Faced with such a grim reality, Emperor Zhu Yuanzhang drew lessons from the rise and fall of previous dynasties, especially the downfall of the Yuan Dynasty. He attributed Yuan's failure to its lax laws and therefore advocated strict laws at the outset of Ming Dynasty to restore social order. He put forward concepts such as "save the country with strict laws" and "severe punishment is a must in chaotic periods."[69] Compared with the Tang code, the Ming code featured "severe punishments on major crimes and light punishments on minor offences." It means punishments would generally be heavier on crimes that directly threatened the political regime. For instance, in terms of "plotting rebellion" and "plotting great sedition" of the ten abominations, the Tang code stipulated that the offenders, be they principal or accessory, would equally be sentenced to decapitation, while their

[69] *The Annals of the Ming Dynasty* Vol.14; History of Ming Vol. 93, Criminal Law I.

fathers or sons aged over 16 would be sentenced to strangulation and other kindred exempt from death penalty. However, the Ming code prescribed *Lingchi* (death by a thousand cuts) for offenders of the same crimes, and their parents, grandparents, children, grandchildren, brothers and cohabiting relatives regardless of their surnames, uncles, and brothers' children aged over 16, regardless of their status or heath conditions, would all be sentenced to decapitation. Additionally, punishments for robbery were more severe in the Ming code than in the Tang code. However, after the Ming regime was stabilized, the severity of punishments was somewhat alleviated, and less harmful offences were punished more leniently compared to the Tang Dynasty.

Generally speaking, after Han Dynasty, criminal theories such as "morality given priority over penalty," "virtues and rites as the foundation of governance, punishments as its tool," and "strictness of the law as the foundation, supplemented by leniency" were the mainstream official beliefs. Despite the recurring instances of harsh punishments throughout history, such practices were generally viewed negatively. Rulers did not want to be labeled as tyrants, and the populace always detested tyrannical rule. Therefore, rulers often implemented the criminal law under a cloak of the Confucian principle of caution in penalization to soften its harsh image.

2.5.2 Excessive Use of Penalties

Excessive use of penalties means arbitrary use of them which often results in extrastatutory punishments or penalties. The term has two main implications: first, it involves applying punishments that are not prescribed in the legal code; second, it refers to the executioner's heavier implementation of the punishment within the same category prescribed in the law during execution. In traditional China, aside from regular punishments, there was also excessive use of extrastatutory torture. Emperor Zhou of Shang Dynasty invented *Pao Luo* (execution by scalding on a heated bronze pillar). In Qin Dynasty, there was "simultaneous five punishments" which involved amputation of one's nose, left and right toes, flogging to death, beheading, and dismembering the bones and flesh in public. The reign of Empress Wuzetian of Tang Dynasty witnessed the torture of "letting the offender step into a vat heated by fire." *Lingchi* (death by a thousand cuts) was invented after Song Dynasty and Ming Dynasty had the punishments of "flaying the skins and stuffing them with straw," "extermination of ten types of kindred," and "official to be beaten with a large rod in front of the imperial court. During Qing Dynasty, there were harsh punishments such as "death by fish scales slicing," "two dragons spitting whiskers" (being starved before the execution, the offender was forced to eat half raw noodles and was then turned upside down to let the noodles be squeezed out from his nostrils, even more torturous than *Lingchi*), "first-rank official dress" (the offender was wrapped up in a burned hot iron robe), and "dragon crossing the mountain" (with the clothes stripped off, the offender was wrapped with an over 6-meter tin tube, leaving only the chest and the lower part of the body unwrapped, and then the boiling water was poured into one side of the tube and then flowed out from the other side of the tube). In addition to physical abuse, there was also psychological abuse, such as beating the close relatives of the person involved to force confessions.[70] Torture could be in various forms, too many to list exhaustively.

Penal law is crucial to the formation and security of a country. Although ranked lower in the ritual system, its function is the most significant. Law often manifests itself by the means of penal law which is implemented in the form of punishments and penalties. The guiding principle of penal law varied across different dynasties: some adhered to severe punishments as the guideline and imposed severe punishments on light crimes, such as Qin Dynasty; others prioritized morality over punishment and advocated to reduce penalties, such as early Han and Tang Dynasties. Ming Dynasty implemented the policy of "indoctrinating people by punishments" and adopted punishments as priority. However, the main purposes of penal law were typically retribution, deterrence, and suppression so as to maintain the hierarchical ethics and consolidate the autocratic monarchy. The judicial process often followed presumption of guilt instead of the principle of legality, and many punishments were inhumane, disregarding individual rights and dignity. Penal law profoundly influenced Chinese legal consciousness with its violence, and under most circumstances, law was often equated to punishment.

The Western criminal law philosophy has long advocated the principle of legality and opposed the implementation of extrastatutory punishments. For example, Cesare Bonesana Beccaria argued that "In order that punishment should not be an act of violence perpetrated by one or many upon a private citizen, it is essential that it should be public, speedy, necessary, the minimum possible in the given circumstances, proportionate to the crime, and determined by the law."[71] According to Beccaria, punishment should only be applied when necessary and, under established conditions, should be as mild as possible, which he considered an axiom. Another famous jurist, Jeremy Bentham argued that punishment should not be imposed under the following circumstances:

(1) Punishment is groundless: When there is no harm that requires prevention, meaning the action in question is not harmful overall.
(2) Punishment is inefficacious: When the punishment cannot prevent the harm
(3) Punishment is unprofitable: When the harm caused by the punishment exceeds the harm it prevents.
(4) Punishment is needless: When the harm can be prevented by other means at a lesser cost.[72]

Due to traditional China's emphasis on law being enforced through military power, its function in national political life was to "suppress chaos and stop

[70] Lü, B. & Meng, X. (1995). *Lawsuits and Judgments in Traditional China*, The Commercial Press, 95–98.

[71] Beccaria, C. (2008). *On crimes and punishments*. Peking University Press, 112.

[72] Bentham, J. (2000). *An Introduction to the Principles of Morals and Legislation*. The Commercial Press, 122–123.

violence." This tool was under the control of the leaders of primitive tribes and later by autocratic rulers after the formation of the state, such as the "Son of Heaven," "king," or "emperor." All citizens were their subjects, with their persons and land belonging to the ruler alone. As was recorded in *The Book of Songs*, "All the land under heaven belongs to the king and all within the land are the king's subjects." Everything under heaven belonged to the king. Later theories were based on this view as the keynote. No matter it was the Confucianism, Legalism, or Taoism, they all taught rulers how to rule the people and taught the people how to be compliant subjects. People were instructed on what to do without needing to know the reasons behind it. Theories as "people can be made to follow, but they cannot be made to understand," "comply with the way of Nature; yet everything is accomplished," "universal love," "aloofness," and "rule a large country as cooking a small fish" all supported centralized autocracy rather than harm it. Group violence such as theft and banditry and other actions that would destruct feudal ethics and patriarchal authority and post threats to monarchy power were thus seriously prevented and harshly suppressed by law. From this point of view, law was a tool to prevent people from rebellion. The rule of man across dynasties directly led to the continuous excessive use of punishment.

2.5.3 *Fear of Punishment and Law*

The frequent use of cruel and excessive punishments directly resulted in people's lasting misunderstanding and fear of the law. This has caused them to keep a respectful distance from the law, adhering to the belief that "I cannot afford provoking the law, but I can afford avoiding it" and thus fostering the attitude of fearing and despising punishments simultaneously.

When do people come into contact with law? It happens when they are punished for acts that are detrimental to the ruler. Therefore, common people consider law as something horrible, an ominous encounter to be avoided. They believe "bringing a case to the court" should be a dreadful experience. Given the law's formidable power, local magistrates often tend to criminalize civil disputes. When people have to seek the help of the local authorities to protect their rights, they will always exaggerate the acts of the opposing party in order to attract the magistrate's attention and secure a favorable judgment. For example, in Ming and Qing Dynasties, the format of the petition statement with "four-character pearl phrases" was quite prevalent. If the plaintiff and defendant did not use the format of "pearl phrases" when stating the reason for their complaint, the local magistrates would not hear the case. "Pearl phrases" refer to concise four-character sentences that summarize the complaint. By the Ming and Qing Dynasties, these phrases had become an officially recognized format for summarizing case briefs. Seeing these phrases almost immediately allowed one to infer the nature of the case and make decisions of "fault" or even "guilt."

Some scholar found in the Qing Dynasty litigation archives in Huang Yan that complaint documents had preprinted sections reserved for "four-character pearl phrases" when printed. As a result, these four-character pearl phrases were adopted to state the reasons of the complaints. For common civil disputes, since "pearl phrases" were used, the issues then turned into sensational major cases. For example, the complaint documents consisted of two parts, "the content of disputes" and "pearl phrases." The content included "disputes over water: bailing water into the pond by force," "inheritance dispute: forcibly seizing inheritance," "debt dispute: forcibly seizing debt," "theft case: nighttime burglary," "inheritance dispute: inciting crowds to obstruct burial," and "contract disputes: being harmed in mediation or falsely accused of defrauding." Additional "pearl phrases" included "adultery causing bankruptcy," "relying on force to deceive," "conspiracy in sales," "forcible possession by wife or adopted son," etc. These "pearl phrases" were constantly updated, often creating a sense of alarm and shock.

Actually, most of the contents of the complaints is trivial civil matters, including conflicts among siblings, debt disputes, or even misunderstandings of contracts. However, it seems that unless the issue was exaggerated as significant, it might not attract the attention of the officials. It can be observed that the plaintiffs were unaware of their civil rights at the beginning of the complaints when they decided to "Da Guansi" (file a lawsuit). The word "打 (*Da*)" is a specific and vivid character in Chinese which means "hit" or "attack." "官司 (*Guansi*)", a lawsuit, literally means relying on the officials to handle it. Therefore, asserting one party's civil rights often involves portraying the other party in the dispute as a criminal or a villain, so that his or her rights can be upheld through the intervention of the "parent-like magistrates." The widespread use of "four-character pearl phrases" in complaints was an inevitable product of the historical conditions at that time, as every civil case needed the guarantee of "public power" to be asserted.[73] Hence these civil cases were initially classified with the criminal tendency; corporal punishments such as slapping in face, finger clamps, or confinement were unavoidable when the parties came to the court regardless of the validity of the claims. Therefore, litigation naturally became "Da Guansi" (file a lawsuit) or preparing for "being beaten" by a lawsuit. Occasionally, a few upright officials emerged, and they were deemed as the saviors of the common people. They were revered as "Masters of the Blue Sky" (honest and impartial officials), worshipped both during their lifetimes and posthumously, like Bao Gong and Hai Rui.

The state and the monarch do not emphasize equality, freedom, and rights of the people but stress the obligations of each member to maintain the established order and harmony. Patriarchs are small-scale monarchs and own their children. In the larger society, patriarchs are subject to the monarch as servants, so do their children. Law or punishment is the weapon in the monarch's hands. Whether in times of prosperity or decline, the law is indispensable. The ruler can rise above the law, and

[73] Wang, H. (2004). *Introduction to Huangyan Litigation Archives*. In Tian Tao, Xu Chuanxi, Wang Hongzhi (Eds), *Huangyan Litigation and Investigation Report I* (pp. 62–67). Law Press.

even a forced suicide decreed by the emperor should be referred to as a "bestowed death." The recipient must express gratitude such as "Thank you, Your Majesty, for your grace." The traditional monarch's approach to law is merely a matter of degree—whether more or less severe—but remains fundamentally unchanged regardless of necessity.

The legal function influences people's attitude toward litigation which in turn shapes the public legal consciousness. The perception of law as merely a tool for punishing villains and suppressing riots casts a shadow over the people. People initially viewed the law with obvious hostility, considering it not only a violation of human morality but also a disruption of the higher cosmic order. This shows that from the beginning, the populace treated criminal law with disdain and condemnation. After the written law emerged, people's attitude toward law did not change and almost everyone feared the law, turning pale at its mention. People deemed punishment and military force as two inauspicious things. Phrases very familiar to people are "using military force in times of chaos, using law in times of peace," "military force is ominous," and "military conflicts bring disasters." Whenever a ruler advocated for lenient, mild, or reduced punishments, the populace would praise him as a wise and enlightened monarch. It is a long tradition of the public's fear of the law.

In ancient Greek and Roman legal concepts, private law emerged very early to safeguard the property rights of citizens. In China, the concept of private law remained obscure until the late Qing Dynasty. Why is there such a significant difference? The main reason lies in the distinct problems confronted by the West compared to those faced by the ancient Chinese society. In the West, there was no interclan warfare but fierce fights between social groups. Although these conflicts also involved intrigue and hidden dangers, it had not come to the point of life-and-death struggles that must be resolved through warfare. These social groups were divided based on interests rather than race or clan, and they sought to determine how to distribute the interests among the groups and find a mutually acceptable principle that could take into account the interests of all parties. This required a middle ground, an authoritative clause, to define the rights and obligations of all parties. The Solon Reforms in Athens were the result of this need, leading to the emergence of political law. Besides, civil law was developed separately from the political life of a country, and it only focused on the exchange of property, debt relations, and inheritance among individuals. The decisive factor was the free will of individuals rather than the coercive administrative orders of the country. Transactions were determined by contracts with private property at their core. Members of the society might dislike a specific law, but they could not violate it. The law was an overarching regulation, protecting both the national order and individual rights and property. In contrast, early Chinese laws rarely covered these contents with the primary focus being on the regulation of interstate warfare (external conquests) and the maintenance of domestic social control (internal suppression) through penal law.

Chapter 3
Legal Philosophies

Law, fundamentally, is the epistemic domain for elites or for the "jurists." Without legal elites, law may only function as orders, instructions, or policy provisions in the customary, political, or military spheres, and hence law can neither be universal nor mandatory social norms. Just as Max Weber put it, "Law can never come into existence without the great minds of jurists."[1] The legal elites are the architects of law, continually contemplating, creating, interpreting, and refining it. They also preserve and pass down legal traditions through history. Their contributions ensure the continuity and evolution of law.

The development of law is not independent of society which embodies social life, social customs, social structures, and social psychology. Legal rules are derived from social lifestyles; the system of law is designed to maintain the stability of the social structure or social order; legal philosophies are based on the shared psychological identity among social groups; and the evolution of law is subject to the general trend of social change. Society itself is intuitive, perceptual, and realistic, and life experience per se is rich, fresh, and dynamic, while legal rules are general, abstract, rational, and universal. Hence the society itself and the state of life per se cannot generate legal rules. It is a group of people in society with a keen insight and rigorous thinking ability that have abstracted the mandatory binding norms of social conduct, namely, law, through observation of social life and summarization of social experience. This group of people from masses yet superior to them has made law, thus belonging to the "legal elites." Legal philosophies refer to a thinking mode to guide creation, practice, and supervision of law and should be positioned as the mainstream mindset. Legal philosophies in the modern history highlight the rule of law and recognize that sound laws, based on equity and justice, bring convenience to the public. Under the guidance of the philosophy of the rule of law, the ideal of

[1] Weber, M. (2005). *A Collection of Works by Max Weber IV: Sociology of Law*. Trans. Kang, L. & Jian, H. M. Guilin: Guangxi Normal University Press.

R. Zhang, *Traditional Legal Culture in China*, Understanding China,
https://doi.org/10.1007/978-981-95-4697-8_3

the rule of law equals the motive and behavioral orientation to depict or construct the social model embodied by the rule of law.[2]

Several major legal transformations in Chinese history were initiated and promoted by legal elites. The transformation from customary law to theocratic law cannot be independent of the early interpretations of celestial phenomena, geology, yin and yang, and five elements by sorcerers, historiographers, Confucian scholars, and so forth. They recorded such kind of interpretation by means of astrology, divination, and other methods and then formed relatively fixed rules, which monopolized the voice of theocratic law for those in power, and hence justified the political power in the name of God. The transformation from theocratic law to secular law has been completed in the hands of a group of political and legal elites, represented by Duke Zhou. Legal power has turned from divine affairs to secular affairs: principles such as respecting nature and protecting the people, advocating virtue and being prudent in punishment, situations of the people reflecting the enforcement of the Mandate of Heaven, and so forth have become the mainstream philosophy for the legal elites. The construction of the rites-and-law system is produced under the influence of the legal elite culture. The transformation from unwritten law to written law was mainly realized by the aristocrats during the Spring and Autumn and Warring States periods. The transition of Chinese traditional law to modern law was completed by new legal elites in late Qing Dynasty. Similar to the West, Chinese people understand law in either broad or narrow perspective, with vigorous debate between various schools of legal thoughts. Although there was no such social class as jurists in Rome, statesmen, thinkers, and so on all discussed law in Chinese history.

There were more than one school of legal thought presenting their ideas of legal rules, and this phenomenon was called "the Contention of a Hundred Schools of Thought," which refers, in a general sense, to the diversity of Chinese legal philosophies including those originating from Confucianism and Legalism that have the most profound influence on later generations. As one of the pre-Qin schools of thought, the extensive and profound Confucianism has played an important role in the promotion of social propriety and imperial governance. Besides Confucianism, however, there were many other self-justified schools of thought which were ideological products and cultural source initiated by ancestral Chinese; therefore, we should neither solely focus on Confucianism nor ignore the other schools of thought when tracing origins of the Chinese culture.[3] Similarly, Chinese legal culture is not just the "Confucianized" legal culture but also a pluralistic system of legal cultures. Objectively speaking, it is undeniable that Confucianism and Legalism, the two most popular schools of thought among rulers, have made the greatest contribution to the development of the legal system, which is based on the ruling principle that a ruler should rule his country by integrating rites and laws, virtue, and punishment.

---

[2]Zhang, R. (2007). *The Perspective of the History of Legal Society*. Beijing: Law Press of China.

[3]Xiao G.Q. (1936). Holy Doctrine and Heterodoxy—On the Status of Confucius in the History of Chinese Culture in terms of Political Thoughts (Vols. I,II, and III). *Views*, *1*(10,11,12).

In a word, compared with other schools of thought, Confucianism and Legalism constitute the dual foundational pillars of traditional Chinese legal philosophies, serving as complementary yet competing frameworks for imperial governance. This chapter mainly discusses the formation and evolution of legal concepts since the Spring and Autumn and Warring States periods.

3.1 Conflicts Between Confucian and Legalist Philosophies

3.1.1 The First Legal Debate

Throughout Chinese history, only two legal debates could be regarded as truly free debates. The first one on law was known as "the Contention of a Hundred Schools of Thought" in the Spring and Autumn period and the Warring States period, and the second one was called "the Debate between Rites and Law" during the course of legal revision in the late Qing Dynasty. Both of them generated new legal systems in the context of drastic social transformations. Here, we will focus on the first debate in the period of "the Contention of a Hundred Schools of Thought," when the legal elites represented by Confucian and Legalist scholars debated on how to rule a country.

The fall of Western Zhou marked the beginning of the Spring and Autumn and the Warring States periods (770–221 BC). With the declining power of the emperor of Western Zhou, social contradictions increasingly sharpened, various social forces opposing traditional social order emerged. As a result, the harmonious and well-developed hierarchy of the patriarchal clan system collapsed. This historical period witnessed the chaos in the original political order; *Li Beng Yue Huai* (the system of rites collapsed and ritual music corrupted) and *Dao Shu Jiang Wei Tian Xia Lie* (academic evolution from the general to the specific, from the learning of the aristocrats to the flourishing of a hundred schools of thoughts) and *Zhu Hou Fen Qi* (independence of vassal states). Dedicated to obtaining regional autonomy, increasingly more dukes and princes defied the waning imperial rule and waged wars against each other to expand their sphere of influence. For this purpose, there emerged a need for a spiritual weapon to control people's thought, and the weapon of law became the first choice.

Since the Spring and Autumn period, scholars of different schools of thought have been playing a constantly changing role in the formation of Chinese legal system. During the Spring and Autumn period, the system of rites gradually broke down and the whole country split apart. With no restrictions on travel, scholars at that time could freely express their views, thus achieving particularly lofty social status. As strong advocates for the rule of Confucian orthodoxy and the rule of virtue instead of the rule of hereditary monarchy and the rule of law, they gave thought-provoking remarks, either positive or negative, over the emperors' behavior, showing their deepest concerns about national affairs. Through their inspiring and noble remarks such as "My doctrines make no way. I will get upon a raft, and float about on the sea" and "Riches and honors acquired by unrighteousness are to me as floating cloud," these scholars resolved to serve as advisors to the emperors, assisting them in ruling the country and maintaining a stable hierarchical social order. Thanks to the "Contention of a Hundred Schools of Thought," scholars basically enjoyed equal political, legal, and social status. Although they opposed each other's arguments, they were not rivals in the political arena. By fully tapping into their wisdom and imagination, they were all striving to construct social rules.

The "Contention of a Hundred Schools of Thought" trend sparked a heated debate over the legal philosophy. Various schools competed with their own principles and proposals on governing and controlling a society. Some of them were opposed to one another, but some others were complementary. Over rounds of debate and deliberation, Confucianism and Legalism came to prominence with far-reaching historical significance.

With alternation of dynasties, people were faced with quite a number of challenges, such as which political structure would replace the "one-ruler-of-All-under--Heaven" structure, what social order should be established after the old one under the rule of virtue had been disrupted, what could be done to put an end to the era when individuals' social status and rights were determined by their consanguinity identity, how to establish secular beliefs by rational thinking after the mythological ideas had been brought into question, etc., With regard to legal philosophies, especially those of Confucianism and Legalism, the key issues centered upon how people should view the role of rites and laws and how a state could preserve its strength and defeat others, so as to accelerate its development to the utmost in fierce competition and then unify the whole nation to realize the rule of rites or the rule of law and then manage to maneuver the relationship between the emperor and his people, resulting in the establishment of a new social order. Confucian scholars and legalists also advocated and put into practice the two major modes of national governance—the rule of rites and the rule of law (i.e., the rule of punishment). "The Contention of a Hundred Schools of Thought" directly contributed to the first national debate on law.

3.1.2 The Showdown Between Confucian and Legalist Conceptions of Rite and Law

3.1.2.1 Rule of Rites Advocated by Confucian Scholars

Liang Qichao summarized Confucian concepts of politics and law as "the rule of man," "the rule of virtue," or "the rule of rites" in his *History of Political Thoughts in the Pre-Qin Period*. The three long-standing terms have been used by almost all researchers working on Chinese legal history. Wu Jingxiong (John C.H. Wu) pointed out in his *Evolution of Legal Philosophies* before the Tang Dynasty that it was before the fifth-century BC that the rule of rites had prevailed with the integration of law and ethics and "the creed was that rites are all it takes to rule the country without the need for law as a benevolent and ethical ruler can exert a positive influence on his people." In his view, Confucian ideas were dominant throughout the rule-of-rites period.[4] In *The History of Chinese Legal System*, Chen Guyuan holds that the core of Confucian views on politics and law is to establish a kingly form of government by promoting the rule of rites, the rule of virtue, and the rule of man.

In the Spring and Autumn period, Confucian legal philosophies were continuously developed by generations of Confucian scholars represented by Confucius, Mencius, and Xunzi. Their understandings of these philosophies, such as the rule of virtue, benevolent governance, the theory of good human nature, and the theory of evil human nature, though, to some extent, might vary from each other, but they shared some fundamental characteristics: they were all dedicated to singing odes to the great deeds of ancient sages including Emperor Yao, Emperor Shun, King Wen of Zhou, King Wu of Zhou, and the Duke of Zhou, valuing virtues of these sages as the beacon, prop, or even "umbrella" for their thoughts; followers of Confucius tended to honor him as their mentor; these Confucian scholars all strove to rebuild social order under the patriarchal clan system in the Western Zhou Dynasty, and as Confucius put it, "the rule of rites in the Zhou Dynasty features great diversity, and I advocate it." They all upheld the idea of maintaining a hierarchically stable social order through the rule of rites and were opposed to the principle of being fair in rewards and punishments; they suggested the people excel in Six Arts; they attached great importance to benevolence, righteousness, wisdom, honesty, filial piety, loyalty, love, and the golden mean as the Confucian basic ethical concepts and practices; these scholars were strong advocates for governing a country by the rule of virtue instead of the rule of punishment; they refused and resisted legal reforms; they approved of unwritten law and disapproved of written law; they advocated rites given priority over penalty and expressed their disapproval of punishing without prior education, and if punishment was unavoidable, a lesser punishment should be imposed instead of a heavy one, and they suggested to quell litigation. Overall, Confucius supported the political order under the patriarchal clan system in the Western Zhou Dynasty, and under this guidance, his legal theories led people to the comment on the reality to maintain a hierarchically harmonious society.

3.1.2.2 "Rule by Law" Advocated by Legalists

The Warring States period was an era in which the new landlord class was in a dominant position in society. Since the Spring and Autumn period, hereditary aristocrats gradually lost their exclusive privileges and high social status in fierce wars, facing the trend of even being eliminated by the society. Meanwhile, some other social classes that were not closely related to the ruling family by blood became powerful

---

[4]Wu, John C.H. (2005). *Research in the Philosophy of Law*. Beijing: Tsinghua University Press, 74–75.

political forces as a result of their growing economic and military strength and political talent. With the collapse of the patriarchal clan system and the increasingly fierce military competition, these emerging classes began to demonstrate their remarkable strength and entrepreneurial spirit. To seek their own interests, they stood firmly against the traditional unjust social order and proposed new political, economic, and legal systems. Consequently, after the middle of the Spring and Autumn period, a group of legal reformers dedicated to creating new laws emerged with the calling to implement new legal systems and advocate reforms of the old legal system. Among these reformers, Guan Zhong, Li Kui, Wu Qi, Shang Yang, Han Fei, and Li Si were the most outstanding representatives, and they were called "Legalists" by the succeeding generations. They frequently used some concepts and terms to illustrate their political theories and paradigms, including law, tactic, power, punishment, reward, penalty, interest, public, private, farming, and war. Pillared on these concepts, Legalists gained a strong and unique presence in Chinese history. At the beginning of the Warring States period, their legal philosophies were mostly adopted by the rulers who newly came into power which played a prominent role in the national political life and became the mainstream legal philosophy with real positive effects in practical wars. It is undeniable that the triumph of Qin state, to some extent, equals the triumph of Legalist thought.

The main characteristics of Legalism include the following:

1. Emphasizing the rule by law. In legalists' view, everything should be determined by law and "a great ruler relies on law to govern instead of on righteousness, and law must be impartial and strictly enforced."[5] They believe that law is the best tool to run a country and rulers must ensure that all the matters should be handled by law.
2. Highlighting written law. It is necessary to familiarize the people with laws to make sure all the rules are well understood and strictly observed. In this way, ideally everyone in the country would commit no crime. If an innocent person suffers false accusations, he may go to government offices to seek a statement.
3. Using rewards and punishment fairly. Under the premise that the interests of the state and its ruler have been guaranteed, law should be applied without discrimination to ensure that all people are equally bound by law regardless of their social status. This philosophy is clearly expressed in Han Fei's words, "nobility should not be exempted from punishment and rewards should not leave out the ordinary people." Some famous sayings by other legalists also embody a similar idea: Li Kui's proposed that "the principle of ruling is to provide laborers with food, contributors with their due salaries, and capable talents with government positions, and to be discriminating in rewards and punishment."[6] Shang Yang pointed out that "a saintly ruler establishes standardized systems of rewards,

[5] Shang Yang. (1974). *The Book of Lord Shang: 18 Charting the Policies*. Shanghai: Zhonghua Book Company.

[6] Liu X. (2013). *The Garden of Stories: Political Theories*. Shanghai: Zhonghua Book Company.

punishment, and education"[7] and "a prince who commits a crime will be punished the same way as ordinary people."
4. Tendency toward severe punishment. They upheld the belief that severe punishment was imposed for people's sake. If the punishment is severe enough, people would be deterred from committing crimes.
5. Legislative power in the hands of dictatorial rulers. To rule and unify a country, the ruler must have good command of power, law, and tactics, and hence only dictatorship can make the ruler a real king of the world.[8]

3.1.2.3 The Rule by Law Giving Rise to Criminal Laws

These legal reformers embody the knowledge and views on law of the emerging landlord class during the Warring States period. The legal concepts were elaborated and put into practice by legalists, which profoundly affected the development of the legal system during the Warring States period and had far-reaching impact on later development of law. The concept of rule by law, as the budding concept of integrating individual rights with obligations in law, reflects the desire of the emerging landlord class to abolish the patriarchal clan system and the hereditary nobility and to protect personal interests by law. Compared with legal ideas in the era of the patriarchal clan system, the rule by law was a fresh idea for the legal elites, let alone the public, who had difficulties accepting it and could only be enlightened through some primitive and most direct methods. For example, Li Kui adjudicated pending cases according to relevant parties' archery levels, and Shang Yang honored his commitment by awarding the man who carried a piece of wood from the south gate to the north gate, which laid the foundation for his credibility.

In order to apply law as a social norm, Li Kui drew on the codes and decrees of various states and systematically compiled the Canon of Laws on the basis of the written law in the Spring and Autumn period. Then, Shang Yang brought it to the state of Qin and changed the law into code. This is the first relatively systematic and complete code of written law in Chinese history. It epitomizes written law since the Spring and Autumn period and the Warring States period, occupying an important position in the legislative history of China. The *Cannon of Laws* comprised six chapters, *Treason Law*, *Theft and Robbery Law*, *Prisoner (Extent of Justice) Law*, *Law of Arrest*, *Miscellaneous Law*, and *Law of Possession*, which were inherited directly by the Qin and Han Dynasties as the main pillar of Qin and Han Codes. Based on these six chapters, Xiao He, a Chinese statesman of the early Western Han dynasty, added another three chapters of legal code covering family register, conscription, and livestock in his time-honored work, namely, the Nine Chapter Law. After the Wei and Jin Dynasties, legal scholars facilitated the further development

---

[7] Shang Y. (1974). *The Book of Lord Shang: 17 Rewards the Punishments*. Shanghai: Zhonghua Book Company.

[8] Han Fei, Inner Congeries of Sayings: First Series; Outer Congeries of Sayings: Upper Right Series.

of legal code system in which the Terminology of Precedents and Laws serves as the general guidance and the other chapters as specific provisions. The relatively thorough political reform in the Qin State leads to its rapid economic and military development. Under the guidance of the principle, a series of harsh penalties were imposed, including familial exterminations and collective punishment whereby a suspect's family members, colleagues, and neighbors were targeted and punished as well.

Legalists attached great importance to the rule by law and favored it over other philosophies, among whom Han Fei inherited the theory of evil human nature from Xunzi and firmly believed that an evil man could never become a decent one through moral education. As a strong advocate for dictatorship, he viewed all the people as enemies and insisted that rulers should rest their hope of ruling the country well on the strict enforcement of law. The core legal philosophy of legalism was the alleged rule by law while that of Confucianism was the rule of rites.[9]

3.1.3 The Actual Process of Confucian and Legalist Conflicts

3.1.3.1 Dictatorship with the Form of Democracy

The conflict between "the rule of rites" and "the rule by law" actually showcases the rivalry between Confucian and Legalist philosophies of ruling a country. During the Spring and Autumn period and the Warring States period, especially the late Warring States period, the irresistible rise of Legalism dwarfed Confucianism and other schools of thought. In the pursuit of finding a new model of monarchy, legalists deliberately marginalized Confucian scholars, with a determination to exclude Confucianism from the orthodox thought. The transformation from unwritten law to written law was carried out by several legal elites including Zichan, Deng Xi, and LiKui. Then, legalists, such as Shang Yang, Han Fei, and Li Si, in line with the principles of the rule by law, punishment regardless of social status, severe punishment for minor offences, and making the law known to the public, separated law from the system of rites established during the Western Zhou Dynasty. "Ruling a country by law" has become the fundamental legalist ideal. Moreover, legalists mobilized the public opinion that people must abide by laws and regulations when expressing their views and learn the laws from legal officials while all the other schools of thought should be abolished. They attempted to eliminate Confucian scholars who preferred "the rule of rites" to "the rule by law." Thus, Confucianism was gradually eclipsed by Legalism. Legalists who advocated the rule of law neglected its real connotation and were finally trapped in the idea of the rule of man, which entails that "people can be made to follow, but they cannot be made to understand." Legalists dominated, manipulated, and controlled people by imposing law on them

[9] Liang, Qichao. *The History of Chinese Jurisprudence. The Well-Selected Works of Yinbingshi* (Vol. 5).

regardless of whether people really know or understand law or whether they are truly convinced.[10]

The "Contention of a Hundred Schools of Thought" seems to epitomize the idea of democracy. Nevertheless, most scholars were true defenders of monarchy dictatorship. They favored their own thoughts only and rejected others' thoughts, vying for autocratic monarchy of their own design. The freedom of thoughts has its boundary though, which is determined by the interests of the ruling class. The contrasting approaches of Zheng statesmen—Zichan's preservation of village schools as public forums versus Sichuan's execution of the famous legalist Deng Xi—epitomize this dialectic in pre-Qin governance.[11] As the prime minister of Zheng State, Zichan spoke out against the destruction of a village school in order to hear voices from the general public. Nevertheless, Deng Xi, the earliest folk legal practitioner in China, disapproved of Zichan's legal thoughts of ruling and caused the public opinion of Zheng State to be in an uproar. To eliminate potential worries, the successor of Zichan, Sichuan, eventually executed Deng Xi so that he could no longer teach the ordinary people to challenge the authority.[12] Therefore, the "Contention of a Hundred Schools of Thought" could bring neither democracy nor the freedom of thought but only served as a powerful driving force to improve and intensify dictatorship. The sharp contrast between the democratic form and dictatorial nature constitutes the distinct feature of the "Contention of a Hundred Schools of Thought."

3.1.3.2 Role Exchange Between Rites and Laws

The conflicts between rites and laws equal the temporary role exchange between the two as the policy to rule a country in different historical contexts. In terms of the understanding of the importance of virtue and punishment, legalists denied the rule of virtue, reckoning that the central political issue is power and the rule of virtue played a complementary role or was even considered useless, while Confucian scholars held an opposite view, regarding punishment as a subordinate to the rule of virtue. As Confucius put it, "If the people are led by laws, and uniformity is sought to be given them by punishments, they will try to avoid the punishment, but have no sense of shame. If they are led by virtue, and uniformity is sought to be given them by the rules of rites, they will have the sense of shame, and moreover will become good."[13] In other words, virtue and rites enable the people to actively pursue the spiritual enlightenment while law and punishment just physically restrain the behavior of the people. The difference between these two ways of ruling coincides with that between guilt and sin in the *Bible*. Guilt is an external behavior, and anyone

[10] Chen, L. (1929). *Legalist Political Philosophy.* Shanghai: Huatong Book Company.

[11] *Zuozhuan (Zuo's Commentary): Duke Xiang, 31st year.*

[12] *Lü's Commentaries of History: Words Against Actions.*

[13] *The Analects of Confucius: The practice of government.*

who is guilty should be punished by commandments, while sin refers to internal confession and sinners must confess to God from the bottom of their hearts.

When different attitudes of legalists and Confucian scholars toward rites and laws were applied to practice, legalists gave first priority to punishment while Confucian scholars preferred moral education. In the long run, Confucian scholars are more farsighted, who have raised fundamental questions, such as how to educate people, how to behave oneself and treat others, and what qualifications a ruler should have to rule a country and so forth.

Attaching great importance to self-control, self-retrospection, self-discipline, and self-accusation, early Confucianism advocated that a person should know themselves. As Confucius put it, "When you know a thing, to hold that you know it; and when you do not know a thing, to allow that you do not know it - this is knowledge." There are other principles of proper conduct, such as "Let those who can serve as teachers." "Acting in a perfectly justifiable manner," "The person of perfect virtue, wishing to be established themselves, seeks also to establish others; wishing to be developed themselves, seeks also to develop others," and "One should not impose on others what they themselves do not desire." Confucian scholars also proposed that a gentleman should be compassionate, charitable, and forgiving to others. With regard to education, they were strong advocates of the principle that students should be taught in accordance with their aptitude and be treated equally without discrimination. Furthermore, acting bravely for a just cause and putting oneself in others' shoes are basic elements of moral virtue, and as the saying goes, "caring for others' elders and children as one's own," Confucian scholars put forward the theory of the original goodness of human beings, reckoning that a person can eventually be a good one through moral education. A person of great virtue can be considered as a sage; a sage is capable of extending the benevolence to others and fairly ruling a country through prioritizing the people, adhering to the principle of "the people are more important than the ruler." The sage ruler can uphold the way of the golden mean, equity judicature, and just governance; thus wining the people's hearts and minds by virtue and all under heaven turns to them for their perfect righteousness.

Since greediness, selfishness, and so on are deeply rooted in human nature and these sins breed various weaknesses in human beings, it is in the firm belief of Confucian scholars that human beings have a good nature with less evil thoughts, self-discipline is superior to heteronomy, and a country can be governed well through the rule of virtue instead of the rule by law. Therefore, the ideal world would remain unattainable until a significant advancement of human civilization is realized, that is, until the advent of a world of universal harmony.

The first generation of Confucian scholars, dedicated to singing odes to the great deeds of ancient sages including Emperors Yao and Shun and to appreciating the rule in the Xia, Shang, and Zhou Dynasties, indeed drew the future landscape of a society in Great Harmony from the perspective of historical overview. The lofty Confucian ideals, with the pursuit of universal values, are comparable to the principles of confession, introspection, and love for others advocated in the *Bible*. Thus, early Confucianism was not conservative and instead boasted a strong universal appeal. It is even difficult to realize many Confucian visions in today's world, let alone in the Spring and Autumn and the Warring States periods. Later Confucian doctrines, such as "the interaction between Heaven and humanity," "三纲*Sangang* (the three cardinal guides: the ruler rules and sets an example for his subjects; the father leads and is a model for his son; the husband guides and is a prime example for his wife) and五常*Wuchang* (five constant virtues: benevolence, righteousness, propriety, wisdom and fidelity)", "upholding heavenly principles, annihilating human desires," and "starving to death is a small matter while losing chastity is an extremely great matter" are far from the original intentions of early Confucianism. Furthermore, their idea of deifying Confucius and Mencius as "supreme sages and masters" is contrary to Confucius' attitudes toward spirits and ghosts, reflected by what he said such as "if one is not able to serve humans, how can they serve ghosts and spirits," and "focusing on human affairs and respecting ghosts and spirits but keeping a distance from them." However, while Confucius himself did not believe in the existence of ghosts and spirits, so how could he possibly approve of being worshipped as a deity? Confucius himself would have been rendered speechless with complex feelings if he had been still alive.

In the short run, however, Legalism played a more prominent role in ruling a country. The competition between different schools of thought can be likened to a horse race, where players have to spur their horses to win. The victory of Legalism in the Warring States period was made possible by the win-or-die stress overwhelming all the states. To defeat other states, the rulers had to keep moving toward the final triumph. As for whether the horse could withstand such high pressure for a long time, the rulers could not and would not bother to consider as survival was all that mattered. Legalists are a group of interest-driven scholars who emphasize practicality and visible effects in a short term. By contrast, Confucian scholars advocate moral education and insist that punishment should be imposed on people who misbehave only when moral education fails. It takes a long time and persistent patience to achieve the goal of moral education. Therefore, legalists are akin to 100-meter dashers with explosive strength while Confucian scholars resemble marathon runners with immense endurance. The Warring States period, however, necessitated the former.

The Warring States period marked a significant milestone in China's legal development: Li Kui from the Wei State wrote the *Canon of Laws*; Wu Qi from the Zhao State launched a legal reform; and Shang Yang of the Qin State developed law into "code." All these efforts were made to keep up with the emerging situation so that their mother states could remain intact and undefeated in the fierce competition. What is different is that Confucian scholars led by Confucius honored only kings of the Zhou Dynasty as true rulers and demanded everyone's obedience to the kings of Zhou Dynasty; legalists, however, aimed to crown new rulers regardless of their surnames. Thus, their conflict did not rest on monarchy but on the monarch's surname. They all agreed that the hierarchical social order underlying the monarchy could never be replaced but had different opinions on how to maintain the order. Confucianism upheld the patriarchal clan system while Legalism preferred the hierarchical system based on military merits. At this point, the conflict between the rule of virtue and the rule by law was no longer a matter of ideological contention but became the temporary shift of their roles in line with the times. The relation between rites and laws resembles that of the "carrot and stick"—law is the stick, indispensable, and crucial for a particular period, while rites can serve as both the stick and the carrot. Clearly, the Warring States period was a time when all the states were in greater need of the stick. Nevertheless, it does not mean that carrot is unnecessary, and when to apply both the stick and the carrot is determined by the development trend of the situation. The goal set by Confucian scholars was too lofty to achieve in the short run. Yan Zi once pointed out that Confucian scholars were masters of flexibility so that legal rules could hardly impose restrictions on them; they were too arrogant to serve the rulers; they advocated mourning to the utmost through an extravagant funeral, which should not be encouraged as a custom; they travelled through various states seeking high positions and generous salaries but were not suitable for employment in ruling a country. Confucius paid excessive attention to formalities, etiquettes, and even the walking postures during the morning court sessions. All the etiquettes were so complicated that it would take more than one year to learn. Such customs are not suitable for the common people. As Yan Zi put it, "the philosophy of Confucius is not worth spreading and it is impractical to edify people through it."[14] Confucius almost starved to death during his five-day siege in the State of Wey, and he was derided as a bookworm who could neither do physical work nor distinguish rice from wheat. Admirably, despite enduring numerous trials and tribulations, Confucius remained steadfast in his mission, dedicating himself to the preservation and dissemination of ritual civilization throughout his life.

Modern scholars have discussed a lot on the differences and relations between Confucianism and Legalism in the Chinese legal history. Several mainstream opinions are as follows:

Firstly, Confucianism is equivalent to Legalism. "In Chinese history of legal system and legal philosophy, Confucian scholars played the role as legalists or jurists in the ancient agricultural civilization." "The core principles of Confucianism included: human beings should fulfill their duties without entitlement to their rights and sacrifice their individual interests for the sake of their families; they should possess no freedom but accept unlimited interference from the superiors; there is no equality between different classes; harmony is highlighted rather than competition and so on. These philosophies bred legal principles including the rule of virtue, the rule of rites and differential liabilities in compliance with the autocratic monarchy against the background of the agrarian society, and they gave rise to the old legal system when applied to law.[15]

Second, legalists and Confucian scholars have different interpretations of the rule of law. The former advocated that the government or the ruler should enact harsh legal rules and regulations and impose cruel punishments on the people to realize the hegemony's military ambitions. Their philosophy is harsh and merciless, shortsighted, ruthless, and unreasonable. By contrast, Confucian scholars' rule of

---

[14] *The Eighth chapter* of *The Spring and Autumn Annals of Master Yan.*

[15] Cai, S. H. (1942), *Comments on Chinese Legal System.* Zhengzhong Book Company.

law entails the all-inclusive philosophy, with the rule of law and the rule of rites, law and morality, and law and humanity complementary to each other.[16]

Third, legalist laws and Confucian rites actually serve the same purpose. "Legalism was a subbranch of Confucianism. The laws advocated by legalists are indeed the rites advocated by Confucian scholars. Though different in naming, the two philosophies share core principles of maintaining the same hierarchical social system—ruler guides subject, father guides son and husband guides wife." Confucianism and Legalism stemmed from the same source of thought.[17]

Fourth, there is a debate between the differentiation and identity in behavior norm. "The so-called conflict between Confucianism and Legalism mainly revolves around the contention between the rule of rites and the rule by law. More specifically, it is a debate over differential behavior norms versus uniform behavior norms. The conflict among the rule of virtue, the rule of man and the rule of punishment is secondary. The primary issue lies in the type of behavior norms to be adopted while the promotion of virtue or punishment to enforce these norms is a secondary consideration."[18]

Fifth, Confucian scholars did not utterly deny law and penalties while legalists did not resist filial piety either. For example, Qin Shi Huang, in the field of cultural theories, first drew inspiration mainly from legalist philosophy and the practices of some other schools of thought. The School of Yin and Yang (Zhou is a dynasty of fire and Qin of water), Confucianism (Confucian scholars serve as officials in charge of historical documents), Taoism, and the religious theology (immortality) all played a role in the rule the country. Duke Xiao of Qin authorized Shang Yang to conduct a series of drastic reforms but was given the posthumous title of "Xiao" (filial piety). Emperor Qin Shi Huang started the inspection tour of his new territory from Mount Yi where he brought together Confucian scholars to discuss on rites. He placed stone tablets on high mountain tops to record his reign, and one of the inscriptions claimed, "The way of filial piety stands and shines!" When in Kuaiji Commandery, he ordered Li Si to erect inscribed stelae to change local customs and advocate both men and women to observe loyalty and filial piety. Therefore, the pressure of public opinion forced Emperor Qin Shi Huang to welcome his mother back who had an infamous reputation. Filial piety, only strictly observed in the aristocratic families, was equivalent to decency at that time.[19]

In conclusion, whether Legalism and Confucianism are different or from the same source of thought, their general principles for the rule of the country vary a little, that is, rites and laws play their respective roles and complement each other, so do virtue and punishment. In terms of weight, the rulers preferred rites to penalties.

---

[16] He, L. (1941, August). New Development of Confucianism. *Mind and Times*.

[17] Chen, D. X. (1937). Confucius and China. *Eastern Miscellany*, *Vol. 34* (18, 19).

[18] Qu, T. Z. (1998). Confucianization of Chinese Law. *Collection of Qu Tongzu's Theories on Law* (pp. 362). Beijing: China University of Political Science and Law Press.

[19] Fu, S. N. (1997). On Social factors in Confucianism Adapting to the Qin and Han dynasties. *On the Problems of Life: Fu Sinian's Academic Articles* (pp. 129–139). Shanghai: Academia Press.

3.1.3.3 Legalism Provisionally Wins Out

The conflict between the rule of rites and the rule by law reveals the collision between different political factions, rather than the conceptual conflict between Confucianism and Legalism. Legalists had shaped extreme autocracy, which led to the expansion of centralized power and the wider application of heavy penalties. Hence Confucian scholars were temporarily frustrated.

Confucianism survived the Spring and Autumn and the Warring States periods and was then improved by Xunzi. Among the great changes that Confucianism has undergone, the most prominent change is the enhancement of its feasibility. In particular, Xunzi proposed the theory of integrating the rule of rites and the rule by law, but a group of his students, for example, Han Fei and Li Si, preferred laws to rites. They blindly pursued the philosophy of rewards and penalties and were thus appreciated by Emperor Qin Shi Huang.

Supported by the effective legalist reforms, Emperor Qin Shi Huang conquered the other six states and established a unified autocratic empire. However, this majestic empire was remarkably short-lived. Surviving only 15 years, the Qin Dynasty was eventually overthrown by masses uprisings. The glories and tragedies of Qin have left future generations with many issues worth contemplating, especially its legal philosophies.

Legal philosophy proposed by legalists has ignited many far-reaching impacts, of which the most prominent one is the establishment of autocratic regimes. By defending the principles of "supremacy of imperial power" and severe punishment, their legal philosophy constitutes the cornerstone of autocracy. Li Si, a well-known legalist of the Qin Dynasty, once denounced those scholars who advocated frugality and brave exhortation as obstacles to realizing autocracy and claimed that all these scholars should be eliminated. He also conveyed his idea to Hu Hai, the second emperor of the Qin Dynasty in person, "The only way to maintain an emperor's supreme power lies in autocracy and severe punishment. An autocratic ruler who closely supervises all the officials and sentences the guilty with maximum punishment can intimidate all his enemies." Consequently, Hu Hai implemented Li Si's theory, resulting in a situation where "officials who killed more were regarded more loyal to the throne, and executioners were lining up while the dead piled up in the marketplace day by day."[20] The extreme desires and harsh punishments of Emperor Qin Shi Huang and his son created a vicious cycle, which was one of the reasons for the dramatic collapse of the Qin Dynasty.

The coexistence of diversified philosophies was able to sustain the rule of Qin Empire but may also cause conflicts with Qin Shi Huang's ambition for centralized authority, thus intensifying contradictions between the emperor and scholars. As one of the mainstream schools of thought, Confucianism emphasizing the rule of virtue, bore the brunt, and was fatally devastated, which could be best exemplified by the "Burning of books and burying of scholars." Let us start with the burning of

[20] *Comprehensive Mirror for Aid in Government*, Volume 8, Chap. 3 of the Qin Dynasty.

books. In 213 BC, 70 official scholars gathered in Xianyang Palace to celebrate the birthday of Qin Shi Huang and expressed political advice on how to rule the empire. Some scholars represented by Zhou Qingchen were strong advocates of the system of prefectures and counties, while some others including Chun Yuyue preferred the patriarchal clan system and reverting to the old ways. Generally speaking, Confucian scholars engaged themselves in state affairs through remonstrance and criticism, and it could be beneficial to a wise ruler who might grasp some valuable insights for the rule of the empire. However, some "military counsellors," such as Li Si, deliberately misinterpreted these scholars' comments and suggested to Qin Shi Huang that these scholars disparaged the present by extolling the past and deceived the people with an attempt to overturn the regime. They added that the freedom of speech was the root cause of a split country. In their option, though Qin Shi Huang unified the whole country, his laws and decrees were widely discussed by scholars in private schools, who they thought only paid lip service to the emperor without taking any actions. If such phenomenon was not prohibited, cliques would emerge among officials and the people, weakening the imperial power. According to them, it was urgent to burn books in order to prevent the spread of free speech. Fusu, the eldest son of Qin Shi Huang, counseled his father: "As the country was just unified and the territory afar was not yet stabilized, such a harsh punishment imposed on those who respect Confucius would cause the fall of the whole nation into chaos and disorder." On hearing that, Qin Shi Huang burst into outrage and then sent Fusu in exile to the northern frontier where Meng Tian was stationed. Fusu was thereafter away from the core circle of power.[21]

The burying of scholars features complicated plots. In 211 BC, two years after the burning of books, learning that Qin Shi Huang feared death and was a firm believer in immortality, alchemists including Lu Sheng and Hou Sheng suggested the construction of a palace of 270 rooms where the emperor could sleep in a different room every night to hide from assassinators, but they spoke ill of the emperor behind his back. Xu Fu, an alchemist who volunteered to find elixir for the emperor, squandered a vast sum of money and carried on a sea voyage eastward but never came back. The feeling of betrayal served as a catalyst to the burying of 460 Confucian scholars.

It remains uncertain whether Qin Shi Huang intended to launch the burning of books. Actually, not only Confucian classics such as *Classic of Poetry* and *Book of Documents* were burned, but the writings of the hundred schools of thought also suffered a great damage. As for the burying of scholars, the emperor was not infuriated by Confucian scholars but by the betrayal and deception of alchemists. Furthermore, there also remained a great number of Confucian classics during that period, and many scholars delved into Confucianism at the same time. These Confucian scholars including Fu Sheng and Shusun Tong recruited students to spread Confucianism immediately after the fall of the Qin Dynasty. Therefore, the burying of scholars could not be defined as the direct conflict between rites and

[21] Records of the Grand Historian Chap. VI, *Basic Annals of Qin Shi Huang, Section 6.*

laws. However, as an intellectual catastrophe in Chinese cultural history, it unprecedentedly intensified cultural autocracy, serving as an evil start of prohibiting the exchange of thoughts and free speech through violent means, and thus it created opportunities for unbridled power.

Confucianism, suppressed by Qin Shi Huang, was ignored from the Warring States period to the Qin Dynasty. Rites and laws, temporarily in conflict with each other in mere formality, would come into harmonious coexistence when the time comes and restore the situation before the Spring and Autumn period. Qin Shi Huang and his son believed in Legalism, but their autocracy made it impossible to let serious legalists deliberate on their policies. It is undeniable that Legalism was harshly blamed for the rapid fall of the Qin Dynasty. However, despite the fall of the Qin Dynasty, those principles of autocratic monarchy proposed by legalists were rather improved and carried forward instead of being abandoned. Furthermore, the fall of the Qin Dynasty also marked the revival of Confucianism, which adapted to the times and subsequently integrated itself with Legalism.

The establishment and consolidation of the Qin Dynasty marked the exclusive domination of Legalism in the first legal debate instead of "the Contention of a Hundred Schools of Thoughts." In the Spring and Autumn period and the Warring-States period, the princes that first advocated the rule by law and carried on political reforms established their own states one after another and vied for supremacy. Eventually, the State of Qin, which completed the most thorough legalist reforms, conquered all of the other states and unified China, laying a solid foundation for China's centralized autocratic system which lasted for about 2000 years.

Legalism and Confucianism, both striving to manifest the value of law through their distinct models, are fundamentally incompatible. This incompatibility was so profound that legalists derived immense satisfaction from the eradication of Confucianism. The establishment of the Qin Dynasty and the tyranny of Qin Shi Huang both heralded the downfall of Confucianism. Nevertheless, as the social order designed by legalists propelled autocracy toward its peak, legalists also lost their room for any flexibility. The fixed mindset featured by "everyone has to make their comments in accordance with the law" and "learn the laws from legal officials" led to the breakdown of the platform allowing legal elites to think independently and debate freely on the ruling system. Scholars, who used to enjoy the freedom of speech, were faced with increasingly strict restrictions. Consequently, the first Golden Age of free legal debate came to an end.

3.2 The Reconciliation Between Confucian and Legalist Philosophies

3.2.1 The Evolution of Confucianism

After the intense legal debates in the Spring and Autumn period and the Warring States period, the relative standings of Confucianism and Legalism were made apparent. The Confucian school, facing a competition that was not purely academic, was nearly obliterated, while legalists with their legal philosophy were foregrounded in Chinese history. Undoubtedly, the most prominent achievement of legalists' philosophy was the design of the supremacy of imperial power and the advocacy of harsh laws and severe punishments with the purpose to secure the autocratic monarchy. Supported by legalists' effective legal reforms, the Qin State annihilated the other six states and established a unified autocratic empire.

The fall of the Qin Dynasty led legalists' "cruel and merciless" legal purposes to a dead end. Renowned representatives of Legalism such as Shang Yang were doomed to tragedy. Despite the extensive criticism, the legalist philosophy was not entirely abandoned after the fall of Qin Dynasty. Instead, it was further developed and refined. Similarly, Confucianism experienced a revival following the collapse of the Qin Dynasty. Under the reign of Emperor Wu of Han Dynasty, the two once irreconcilable schools made peace with each other and jointly worked out a unified legal philosophy. The outcome was made possible due to two factors: on the one hand, Confucian scholars in the early Han Dynasty could adapt to the prevailing circumstances; on the other hand, Emperor Wu of Han Dynasty had a clear understanding of the essence and value of both schools' legal philosophies.

The early period of the Han Dynasty is the golden age for the rejuvenation of Confucianism. Surviving the ruthless reign of the Qin Dynasty and the chaos following its fall, Confucian scholars learned the lesson at the cost of blood and lives. After the Han Dynasty was established, several Confucian scholars that survived the hard times represented by Shusun Tong decided to adapt themselves to the society and act in accordance with the needs of the time. They no longer dared to offer advice as the bookish advisors to the ruler; instead, they lowered the moral standard of the "rule of virtue" and proactively persuaded the rulers to integrate moral education into punishment. Thus, they viewed themselves more as servants than teachers to the emperor. In doing so, they managed to reillustrate Confucian beliefs to the ruling class. There are some well-known stories, such as Liyiji persuaded Liu Bang, Emperor Gaozu of the Han Dynasty, to respect Confucian scholars and the elders; Lu Jia encouraged Liu Bang to read the *Book of Songs* and *Book of Documents*; Shusun Tong introduced rituals to the new Han empire to transform Liu Bang's rowdy generals into obedient participants of the court; and Jia Yi interpreted the relationship between rites and laws while prioritizing the former.[22] Gradually, the

[22] The Biographies of Liu Jing and Shusun Tong. *Records of the Grand Historian (Vol. 99)*; The Biography of Master Jia. *Records of the Grand Historian (Vol. 84).*

theoretically ideal theory of "the rule of virtue" proposed by Confucian scholars was put into practice. Through the establishment of the system of rites in the Han Dynasty, Confucian scholars, represented by Shusun Tong, rebuilt their confidence in ruling the country by rites.

In the early Han Dynasty, although Liu Bang changed his perception of Confucianism, legal philosophies in Confucianism were still far from being the guiding principle for national laws, and different schools of thought still maintained momentum of development. In fact, the rulers, such as Emperor Wen of Han Dynasty and his wife—Empress Dou, and Emperor Jing of Han Dynasty, all preferred the Huang-Lao philosophy (combining the teachings of the Yellow Emperor and elements of Taoism) or Legalism to Confucianism. Yuan Gu Sheng, a Confucian scholar-official, told Empress Dou that *Tao Te Ching* was a book of words from the inferior class and narrowly escaped being fed to pigs. Consequently, a group of Confucian scholars' lives were endangered, and they then underwent many hardships and much suffering.[23]

The status of Confucianism was elevated under the reign of Emperor Wu of Han Dynasty, Liu Che. Ascending to the throne at the age of 17, Liu Che was one of the most ambitious and wise emperors in Chinese history. In the sixth year after his succession, Empress Dou died and Emperor Wu was then able to realize his ambitions. As the Han Dynasty had been established for more than 60 years, the Taoist principle of "无为*Wu Wei*," meaning inaction and letting things take their own course, no longer served its purpose of ruling, which required the ruler to play a more active role. What is the principle of ruling the country? He believed that Confucianism, which had then been reinterpreted by Confucian scholars, was more practical and more suited to his needs than the Huang-Lao philosophy. Confucianism was revived due to the support of Emperor Wu. Tian Fen, with the title of Marquis of Wu'an, was appointed counselor-in-chief. He dismissed hundreds of schools of thought including the Huang-Lao philosophy and Legalism but advocated Confucianism. Gongsun Hong, who was born a commoner, was conferred the title of "Marquis of Pingjin" as he was well known for his research on the history of the Spring and Autumn period and was then promoted to counselor-in-chief. Both of them were good at reading the mind of Emperor Wu, making neither bold decisions on their own nor personal judgments. They implemented extremely practical strategies to maintain the status of Confucianism. For instance, every time Gongsun Hong made some recommendations at the imperial court, he always suggested Emperor Wu should make his own decisions without any refutation with him. Thus, he was highly regarded by Emperor Wu. He was harsh-hearted but outwardly friendly. In addition, he studied the Spring and Autumn Annals, but he also mastered the practice of laws and administrative duties and enhanced them with Confucian principles.[24] In fact, he was integrating Confucianism with Legalism.

[23] Annals of the XiaowuEmperor. *Records of the Grand Historian (Vol. 12).*

[24] The Biography of Gongsun Hong, *Book of Han (Vol. 58).*

As the status of Confucianism was dramatically raised, Confucian scholars across the country all expected to seek the opportunity of personal achievements in the political arena. Emperor Wu of Han Dynasty frequently sought advice on maintaining the great unity of the empire. Dong Zhongshu, a master of The Gongyang Commentary on the *Spring and Autumn Annals*, was asked to find a solution to it. He said, "The great unity in the *Spring and Autumn Annals* is the constant principle of Heaven and Earth, and the common understanding of ancient and modern times. Nowadays, there are various schools of thought and opinions and their intentions point to different directions. Accordingly, there is no longer a unified way to maintain unity. The laws and systems have undergone frequent changes, and the ruled do not know what to follow. I recommend that any methods that are not included in the Six Arts and teachings of Confucius should be excluded from the discourse, and not be allowed to progress. Once the heretical and deviant theories are eradicated, academic standards can be unified, laws and regulations can be clarified, so that the people will know what to follow."[25] In his view, chaos in thinking would inevitably lead to political turmoil. The deviant theories of the hundred schools of thought were detrimental to the stability of the great unity of the Han Dynasty and must be eliminated from the political arena. The slogan of "dismissing the hundred schools of thought and exclusively revering Confucianism" was proposed in this context. Although Dong Zhongshu emphasized the decisive role of Confucianism, he did not deny the role of law; rather, he regarded the domination of Confucianism as the prerequisite for "unified academic standards and clarified laws and regulations, so that the people will know what to follow." Emperor Wu accepted Dong's suggestions and replaced "the Huang-Lao school of thought" with Confucianism as the official ruling thought.

Confucian principles such as respect for authority, hierarchical rites, and the values of loyalty and filial piety help maintain the authority of the ruler. Strict control of the people's mind and constraints on their behavior are equally important. Confucian theories on the rule of virtue and benevolent rule provide refinements and supplements to the ruler's political approach. The Confucian rules and regulations on rites can disguise the autocratic rule as benevolent governance. Confucian ideas on hierarchy and interpersonal relationships act as a lubricant for harmonious and inclusive social interactions. Since then, after the adoption of this ruling thought by successive ruling classes, Confucian legal concepts, at least on the surface, became the mainstream of the traditional legal theories, having a great influence on the development of Chinese law. The official endorsement of Confucianism is both the result of its timely adaptation to the dynamic situation and its absorption of scholarly achievements from other schools, especially those of Legalism. The so-called exclusive reverence for Confucianism is not merely reverence for the theories developed by Confucius and Mencius but also refers to the modified version of Confucianism.

[25] The Biography of Dong Zhongshu, *Book of Han (Vol. 56)*.

3.2.2 Statesmen Involved in the Reconciliation Between Confucianism and Legalism

The growing status of Confucian scholars gave rise to the revival of Confucianism, and these scholars finally attained the recognition and honor they have long been yearning for. However, Emperor Wu's reverence for Confucianism did not lead to his adoption of Confucian doctrines as the foundation for all his policies. Instead, he valued the decorative function of Confucianism. "Although he favored Confucianism, he preferred its name to its essential values,[26] admired its surface glamour while neglecting its inherent substance." It was Confucianism in appearance but Legalism in practice. Emperor Wu never forgot the punitive and restrictive functions of the law to restrain people's behavior and preferred punishment and law to virtue and rites, which was evident in his political practices.

During the reign of Emperor Wu of Han, the study of Confucian classics allowed Confucian scholars to attain a higher social status with great power. However, officials dedicated to techniques of the law and advocating harsh punishment were also holding high positions. In historical records, the term "cruel officials" includes those who adhered to laws and regulations and ruled with integrity and those who manipulated legal principles and deliberately misinterpreting laws to condemn innocent people. Nevertheless, during the reign of Emperor Wu of Han, cruel officials enjoyed an equally high social status as Confucian scholars did and shared the legalists' qualities of the Warring States period and the Qin Dynasty—a thorough and tactful command of laws, strategies, and power. Notable cruel officials including Ning Cheng, Zhou Yangyou, Zhao Yu, Zhang Tang, and Du Zhou became very powerful at that time. Among them, Zhang Tang and Du Zhou were the most representative. Known as a cruel man for his severity, Zhang Tang was a master in reading the Emperor's mind. He exploited his subordinates and decided cases merely based on the Emperor's preferences instead of strictly following the law. For example, learning that Emperor Wu was interested in literature, Zhang Tang would select a Confucian scholar-official proficient in *Spring and Autumn Annals* and *Book of Documents* to assist him in interpreting and deciding complex cases; if Emperor Wu intended to release a suspect, Zhang Tang would try every means to prove the accused innocent; otherwise, he would spare no efforts to condemn the accused and even sentenced them to death. He would claim credit for cases the emperor approved and shift blame for those without the emperor's approval onto his subordinates. Unexpectedly, such a calculating, deceptive, and indecent official would befriend Confucian scholar-officials on purpose. Even Gongsun Hong, the Chancellor, who rose to power through Confucianism, spoke well of him in front of the emperor. As a result, Zhang Tang was promoted from Commandant of Justice (Chief Justice) to Imperial Counsellor (Chief Censor).

Du Zhou, another cruel official who had a close relationship with Zhang Tang. With Zhang's endorsement and recommendation, Du rose to high positions as

---

[26] *Anthology of Sima Guang*, vol. 12.

Commandant of Justice (Chief Justice) and Imperial Counsellor (Chief Censor), wielding considerable power for a time. His style of handling cases closely mirrored Zhang Tang's, adeptly acting according to Emperor Wu's preferences. "For those who the ruler disfavored, he would fabricate charges to entrap them; for those who the emperor intended to release, he would detain them for a long time and subtly present their grievances." He would let the cases he handled implicate thousands of people covering hundreds of miles. Someone once questioned him, "As the Commandant of Justice, you never decided any case by law but by the emperor's intentions only. How could you defend real justice?" Du Zhou replied, "Where does the law come from? Previously affirmed things by the emperor were codified into law, and presently affirmed things are formulated into decrees. With the assent of our emperor, why should I bother to comply with the outdated laws?"[27] Apparently, Du Zhou regarded the emperor's orders as the law. In his view, all the laws were determined and then utilized by the ruler.

Emperor Wu of Han favored Confucianism on the one hand and endeavored to practice Legalism on the other hand. In doing so, he reconciled Confucian and Legalist scholars after the long-standing enmity between the two schools of thought. With his exceptional skills in managing his officials, he made Confucian and Legalist scholars coexist harmoniously and willingly serve his interests. Although Legalism was ill-reputed after the fall of the Qin Dynasty, during Emperor Wu's reign, whether they were dutiful or cruel officials, Confucian scholars, or legalists, as long as they served his purposes and upheld his authority, they were considered good officials and scholars. Confucianism and Legalism each had their place and coexisted peacefully. Thereafter, in China's judicial system, there was a fusion of Confucianism and Legalism, with elements of each influencing and complementing each other, and they jointly constituted the cornerstone of Chinese legal system with equally high status.

The legal elites represented by Confucian scholars in the Han Dynasty realized the revival of Confucianism, which was made possible because of their adaption to the situation.[28] In the Spring and Autumn period and the Warring States period, Confucian legal philosophy was once suppressed by legalists and stricken with burning satire and freezing irony. Through the strenuous efforts of later generations, Confucian philosophy of law came back to life, and Confucian masters including Confucius, Mencius, and Xunzi achieved eternal glory posthumously, unexpected while they were alive. Confucian scholars also made some attempts to eradicate the remnants of Legalism among whom Dong Zhongshu was the most active in this effort, strongly advocating "dismissing the hundred schools of thought and exclusively revering Confucianism." However, just as legalist elites could not completely eradicate Confucian legal elites, it was impossible for Confucian scholars to wipe out the deep-rooted Legalism overnight. Furthermore, even Qin Shi Huang, known

[27] Article 62 of the "Biographies of Upright Officials," *Records of the Grand Historian*, Vol. 122.

[28] Article 39 of the "Biographies of Liu Jing and Shusun Tong," *Records of the Grand Historian*, Vol. 99.

for his iron-fisted rule and despotic nature, could not entirely eradicate Confucian legal elites. As the ruler that supported Confucian scholars such as Dong Zhongshu, Emperor Wu of Han "favored Confucianism, but he preferred the name to the essential values, and admired its surface glamour while neglecting its inherent substance."[29] He was actually a political strategist who "practiced Legalism in the name of Confucianism" and thus was unlikely to ruthlessly eliminate Legalism. Instead, the emperor allowed Legalism to seek refuge under the guise of Confucian legal culture, skillfully integrate its principles of "law" and "punishment" into Confucian rites, and hence receive tacit approval from the emperor. This way not only thoroughly "washed away" the negative reputation of Legalism as being "cruel and merciless" which was to blame for the rapid fall of the Qin Dynasty but also allowed legalist ideas to blend seamlessly into the Chinese legal cultural system, thus shaping the legal system featured by integration of rites and laws and exerting a profound influence on traditional Chinese legal spirit and legal psychology for thousands of years.

3.2.3 Basic Trends in the Integration of Rites and Laws

The basic trends in traditional Chinese law are characterized by the coexistence of virtues and punishments and the integration of rites and laws. Emperor Wu of Han played a crucial role in promoting Confucianization of the legal system. Before the reign of Emperor Wu of Han, Confucian scholars were rarely engaged in judicial practice. However, this situation changed during the reign of Emperor Wu when Confucian scholars gradually infused Confucianism into judicial practice and legal interpretation, pioneering in the Confucianization of the legal system and the integration of rites and laws.

According to Dong Zhongshu's conceptual framework, for a sage to rule a country, the first step must be to establish a rigid hierarchy of social ranks so that the Confucian tradition of rites reflected the way of Yin and Yang. The hierarchical system is essential for the survival of monarchy. Dong Zhongshu provided a more elaborate theory to strengthen the hierarchical system, namely, 三纲*Sangang* (the three cardinal guides: the ruler rules and sets an example for his subjects; the father leads and is a model for his son; the husband guides and is a prime example for his wife) and五常*Wuchang* (five constant virtues: benevolence, righteousness, propriety, wisdom, and fidelity), and guided judicial practice with Confucian classics. The most prominent judicial practice was "judging cases by Confucian classics" or "adjudicating cases according to doctrines in *the Spring and Autumn Annals*" with the core principle of "conviction based on motives and circumstances."

Dong Zhongshu was just a senior Confucian scholar. However, Zhang Tang, Commandant of Justice, though cruel and merciless, condescended several times to

---

[29] *Anthology of Sima Guang*, vol. 12.

consult Dong for his opinions on cases. Zhang Tang was motivated to do so entirely due to Emperor Wu's reverence for Confucianism. Dong Zhongshu proactively made suggestions and applied Confucian classics to analyze the cases. He even compiled the *Precedents based on the Spring and Autumn Annals*, which included 232 cases. The principle of "conviction based on motives and circumstances" involved understanding of the background of the cases, investigating the motives of the criminals, and emphasizing the distinction between good and evil motives. The motives that conformed to Confucian principles from *The Spring and Autumn Annals* were good, while otherwise evil. Those with good motives shall be punished lightly while those with evil motives shall be severely punished. Confucian scholars, who reformed the law of the Han Dynasty in line with the *Spring and Autumn Annals*, were not aiming at replacing the law with Confucian principles. Such a replacement was impossible at that time as the majority of cases were still judged according to the law. The attempt to adjudicate cases according to doctrines in *The Spring and Autumn Annals* marked the beginning of the Confucianization of Chinese law. Emperor Wu of Han initiated the fusion of Confucian principles and judicial practice. From then on, Confucianism was gradually integrated into the legal system, leading to its eventual transformation. The establishment and enforcement of *The Tang Code in the Tang Dynasty* marked the full integration of the legal system and Confucianism, and the conviction based on rites and laws replaced the legal practice of adjudicate cases according to doctrines in *The Spring and Autumn Annals*, guiding judicial practice with Confucian classics and even replacing laws with these classics as the basis of conviction aimed at aligning the legal system with the unity of rites and laws. After the reign of Emperor Wu of Han, the traditional Chinese law developed along the lines of internal Legalism under the guise of Confucianism.

A comprehensive legal code embodying the integration of rites and laws did not emerge throughout the entire Han Dynasty. However, undergoing changes during the Wei, Jin, and Southern and Northern Dynasties, the concept of combining virtues and punishments and integrating rites into laws was gradually formalized into legal codes in the Sui and Tang Dynasties. This tradition continued through the Ming and Qing Dynasties and underwent successive generations. Therefore, the foundation for the coexistence of virtues and punishments, and the integration of rites and laws in traditional Chinese law, can be said to have been established during the reign of Emperor Wu of Han.

Under the advocacy of Dong Zhongshu, the legal philosophy of Confucianism had gradually been recognized or accepted by the society, and the Confucianization of principles of legal application began to take shape, such as "reporting cases to the emperor," "leniency in penalization," and "permitting covering minor crimes for relatives." After the Cao Wei period, the pace of Confucianization of the Chinese law was accelerated. During the Cao Wei period, the八议*Ba Yi* (eight privileged groups of people whose cases are to be especially deliberated) system was officially incorporated into the law. The *Northern Wei Code* and *Chen Code* legalized 官当*Guan Dang* (deprivation of office in exchange for punishment mitigation). The *Jin Code* introduced the concept of "punishment according to 五服*Wu Fu* (the Five degrees of Mourning)." The *Northern Qi Code* stipulated "Zhongzui Shitiao" (Ten Articles of Felonies), including rebellion (to overthrow the current regime), great sedition (to damage or destroy royal temples, tumuli, or palaces), treason (to betray the regime), surrender (to defect to an enemy state), parricide (to harm or murder one's relatives of higher generations), depravity (to mercilessly murder others), great irreverence (to steal the royal household items and display irreverence to the emperor), lack of filial piety (to maltreat one's parents or not to mourn for one's parents after their deaths according to the ritual code), unrighteousness (to murder local magistrates or one's tutors), and incest (to have illicit sexual intercourse within prohibited mourning degrees). Emperor Wen of the Sui Dynasty formulated *Kaihuang Code*, revising the Ten Articles of Felonies into the Ten Abominations as follows: plotting rebellion, plotting great sedition, plotting treason, parricide, depravity, great irreverence, filial impiety, discord, unrighteousness, and incest.

3.3 The Integration of Rites and Laws

3.3.1 The Establishment of Morality as Foundation and Punishment as Methods

Ever since the Tang Dynasty, the legal system has gradually come into being on the basis of rites as the content and laws as the form that are integrated under the guiding principle that "morality is the foundation of political moralization; punishment and chastisements are the instruments of political moralization. Like night and day, the *yang* of spring and the *yin* of autumn, they are mutually dependent on each other to bring completeness."[30] Confucianism and legalism eventually came to a truce after the principle of "morality as foundation and punishment as instruments" was adopted in the Tang Dynasty and the legal system that embodied the unity of rites and laws was thus established.

Tang Code with Commentaries sets a typical example of the unity of rites and laws: guiding principles of rites serve as the foundation, for example, 三纲*san gang* (the three cardinal guides: the ruler rules and sets an example for his subjects; the father leads and is a model for his son; the husband guides and is a prime example for his wife) is the foundation of the legal system and core content of the legal codes. The naming of the Ten Abominations is derived from the three cardinal guides that govern the most important social relations. Many laws are developed from ritual rules, for example, *Ba Yi* (eight privileged groups of people whose cases are to be especially deliberated) is derived from *Rites of Zhou*. "七出*Qi Chu*" (seven conditions under which the wife could be repudiated by the husband and the marriage dissolved), "三不去*San Buqu*" (three conditions under which the wife could not be repudiated by the husband), etc. are derived from *Da Dai Liji* (*Records of*

[30] Zhangsun Wuji, et al. (1983). *The Tang Code: General Principles*. Zhonghua Book Company.

Ritual Matters by Dai the Elder). *Tang Code with Commentaries* is generally based on the repertoire of rites, including quotes from 20 Confucian classics and references from 100-odd works on Confucianism. Besides, statutes, regulations, and ordinances during the Tang Dynasty are related to rites more or less.[31] *The Tang Code* has thus become China's traditional legal classic. The integration of rites and laws embarked on the way from the Three Kingdoms, the Two Jin Dynasties, and the Southern and Northern Dynasties and took shape during the Sui and Tang Dynasties. In a word, the Tang Dynasty consummated the unity of rites and laws. *Siku Quanshu Tiyao (A Compendium of Complete Library of Four Treasures)* stated "*The Tang Code* was established upon rites and encompassed justice crystallized throughout the history; therefore, it was applied in the Song Dynasty and referred to in rulings of cases during the Yuan Dynasty; Hongwu Emperor of the Ming Dynasty appointed the officials well-versed in Confucianism to teach the officials of justice *The Tang Code* and later assigned Liu Weiqian and other officials the task of making *The Ming Code* with the table of contents following that of *The Tang Code*." Later dynasties scrupulously honored the guiding principles from *The Tang Code* that law assisted moral education and legal codes were made to restore rites, thus merely revising the detailed articles with the guiding principles intact.[32] A more complete comment would be *The Tang Code* is formulated upon rites and laws, for it has resulted from the integration of Confucianism and Legalism, morality and punishment, rites, and laws ever since the Han Dynasty. Later dynasties inherited the legal spirit of the Tang Code and developed and perfected it continuously. "*Li*" (rites) that covers the basic principles for families, ethics, and social stratification has become the core content of laws. The traditional feudal rulers' way of ruling lies in the "*Li-Fa*" unity (the fusion of rites and laws), which is not only rendered as rites and laws as a whole in ancient times, but also the binding force of rites that prevents depravity and discord. *Li-Fa* unity, regarded as moral law or legislation of morals, is the combination of laws and morals encompassing all social conduct and social relations and the reflection of fundamental feudal ethics featuring social hierarchy. The social order it maintains is called "*Li-Fa* order."

Since the Qin and Han Dynasties, with the integration of Confucian orthodoxy and hereditary monarchy, Confucianism, and Legalism, the demarcation between Confucian scholars and officials has blurred, and centralization of autocratic power has been reinforced. Diverse schools of thoughts, including Confucianism and Legalism, almost sought the similar legal system that worked for Chinese traditional society. Legal elites tended to locate harmony between the legal pattern and political pattern although the conflicts between the legal pattern, political pattern, and thought pattern were inevitable. On the other hand, legal elites put the right of legislation in the sovereign's hands and justified "laws enacted by the sovereign." The earlier Confucian natural ethics was quite universal; however, the Confucian political ethics advocated the sage's rule, that is, all the power being put in the hands

[31] Zhangsun Wuji, et al. (1983). *The Tang Code*. Zhonghua Book Company.

[32] *Qing Shi Gao* (*History of the Qing Dynasty*) Vol. 141, Treatises 117, Criminal Law I.

of a sage was the way. The statement that "in the normal state of the king's rule of a kingdom, the initiative and final decision in matters of rites, music, recruitment of soldiers and declaration of war rest with the supreme prerogative of the king while during abnormal conditions without the king's rule of a kingdom, the prerogative passes into the hands of the princes" evidenced Confucian orthodoxy. But the fundamental flaw with Confucian orthodoxy is that it failed to work out the mechanism to correct the sage's mistakes in case he made one. Legalist proposed core concepts such as 法*Fa* (laws or decrees), 术*Shu* (the sovereign's strategies to control his subjects), and 势*Shi* (the ruling power of the sovereign) and advocated centralized power in the hands of the sovereign as well, only to leave the same problem unsolved that there was no mechanism to prevent and correct the sovereign's mistakes. To some extent, the jurisprudence of Confucianism and Legalism was more or less the same. It is no wonder that legalists worked as the suitable designers for centralized politics and Confucianists were called "sages of autocracy."[33]

The ruling class sang high praise of the legal elites' achievements. The legal elites were then set in the paradox: on the one hand, they need to formulate law as the tool to maintain public power, especially the sovereign's autocracy, and thus the criminal law that mainly protected public power was quite developed. While on the other hand, civil and commercial law, economic law, and other laws that were closely related to people's daily life were never the mainstream national laws, even if those laws took shape, they were only folk customs or ritual customs in form which might have had some binding force to regulate social members' social conduct but were rendered far from the legal concept and value in modern terms.

3.3.2 The Making of Neo-Confucianism

The formulation and enactment of *The Tang Code* resulted from the evolving traditional legal philosophy since the Shang and Zhou Dynasties and symbolized its maturity. However, the formal appearance of the legal system featuring *Li-Fa* unity was not made during the Tang Dynasty but after the Song and Yuan Dynasties. With the full development of traditional legal philosophy, autocratic politics of feudal China also reached its peak. Therefore, the pace of development of the traditional legal philosophy coincided with that of autocratic politics.

Confucianism experienced a doctrinal revival following the Han Dynasty, ultimately attaining the status of state orthodoxy, it was not popular with the masses and rites, and etiquettes were only applied to the upper social class without influence upon the lower social class.

In a word, antagonism between rites and laws during the Spring and Autumn Period and Warring States Period gradually declined after the Han Dynasty and nearly dissolved through the Wei, Jin, and Northern and Southern Dynasties till the

[33] Liu, Y. (1992). *History of Ancient Chinese political thought*, Nankai University Press, 50.

Tang Dynasty. On the other hand, feudal ethics and rites were not fully inculcated until the Song Dynasty. Before the Song Dynasty, the spirit of rites did not permeate through social life and ethics, and people's daily life and ethical concepts were not heavily influenced: the intellectuals were quintessentially liberal-minded during the Wei and Jin Dynasties; Mulan defied traditional customs and laws by disguising herself as a man to join the army in place of her father; Cao Cao, the seminal warlord-statesman of the late Eastern Han dynasty, behaved unrestricted by rites; the dressing style in Tang was considered bold and resplendent; couples married without considering each other's social status during the Northern Song Dynasty; etc. Those may not conform to the code of ethics and spirit of rites in the later dynasties. Emphasis on women's chastity embodies the spirit of rites, but before the Song Dynasty, there was no prejudice against remarriage of widows: before the Northern Song Dynasty, remarriage of a woman not only happened to women in aristocratic families but also to royal princesses, and such the Han and Tang Dynasties witnessed the most.[34] The so-called Han-Tang style, to some extent, refers to a liberal and open style. Prevalence of *Cheng-Zhu Lixue* (the neo-Confucianism or School of Universal Principles, often called the Cheng-Zhu school after its leading philosophers, Cheng Yi and Zhu Xi) that reinterpreted Confucianism occurred after the Song and Yuan Dynasties.

Since the Song and Yuan Dynasties, there have been two levels of rites: one as the system of rites and laws and the other as the code of ethics. Rites and laws served as the mechanism of national regulations while the code of ethics emphasized spiritual cultivation of the masses. The integration of the two levels constituted a complete system for the autocratic ruling and the neo-Confucianism functioned as the theoretical cornerstone.

The Song Dynasty witnessed the prime age of the neo-Confucianism which, however, remained less than a mainstream philosophy. Zhu Xi's theory was even considered pseudolearning in the later Southern Song Dynasty (forbidden in 1196's "Qingyuan Dangjin" political event—the The Prohibition of Court Factions during the Qingyuan Reign) and likened to a secret cult called "Shi Cai Shi Mo." Zhu Xi's annotations to the Four Books on Confucianism were banned, for the ruling class feared his "aggressive" political programs as his alleged "wise emperor" did not appear yet. However, since the Yuan Dynasty, Cheng Yi's and Zhu Xi's legal thoughts became popular and were adopted as the official philosophy as they catered for the momentum of reunification of the whole nation. Zhu Xi prioritized *Great Learning* as the first of the Four Books, which directly speaks of the way of great learning, that is, "the great learning lies in building up a good moral character and renewing one's spirit. It means a peaceful world is premised on a well-governed country or nation, which starts with cultivating the ethical self and having one's family organized." Zhu Xi's school of thought emerged during the process from division to unity when economy developed across different localities and people

[34] *Qiyi Wencun* Vol. III, Speeches: Speeches of the Wedding Officiant of Remarried Women, *Lidai Xingfa Kao* (On Criminal Laws in Ancient Dynasties), Zhonghua Book Company, 1985, P2116.

from different nationalities and localities could not bear a divided country and yearned for unity where materials and spiritual resources could be circulated countrywide. Therefore, the momentum from division to unity when Zhu Xi's thought was born was the general trend somewhat like the end of the Warring States Period before the Qin Dynasty. "Morality" in Zhu Xi's mind means "conscience," underscoring Confucian orthodoxy. During the period when the country was divided, the so-called Confucian orthodoxy was by no means marketable. Zhu Xi's thought did not reach the North until early Yuan Dynasty. After more than 70 years (1313), Zhu Xi's disciple called Xiong He made great efforts in disseminating neo-Confucianism and recommended Zhu Xi and his new-Confucianism to the imperial court. From then on, Zhu Xi's neo-Confucianism started to attract the sovereign's attention. During Renzong's reign (1311–1320) of the Yuan Dynasty, the Four Books annotated by Zhu Xi et al. were listed as compulsory reference books for the Keju Exam (the Civil Service Exam), symbolizing that neo-Confucianism came to be an official political philosophy and started to influence the legal system.[35] Zhu Xi's memorial tablet was erected in the Confucius Temple where Zhu Xi was offered sacrifices and worshiped more during the Ming and Qing Dynasties.

The neo-Confucianism developed over 700 years of which "human nature and the way of Heaven" is the core content. The initiator Cheng Yi once argued "relationships between fathers and sons, subjects and the sovereign all belong to theorems under heaven that are not supposed to elude universality."[36] The heavenly theorem (principle) is the foundation from which the myriad things of the universe evolve. Cheng Yi believed that as long as *Sangang Wuchang* (the three cardinal guides and five constant virtues) were followed, all other truths of life could be applicable as well, and he emphasized the way of heaven that further rendered his theories on cardinal guides and constant virtues a mysterious touch. Zhu Xi argued that the heavenly principle was dynamic and perpetual, connoting "the unity of human nature and the heavenly principle"[37] embodied by the three cardinal guides and five constant virtues. Ethical relationships between the sovereign and subjects, fathers and sons, siblings, husbands and wives, and friends are all embodiment of the heavenly principle. Since the heavenly principle remains constant, the three cardinal guides and five constant virtues should be followed permanently as prescriptive ethical rules. Nobody should evade those ethical rules and nobody should doubt the heavenly principle. Those who offend three cardinal guides and five constant virtues intrinsically violate the heavenly principle, and they are considered possessive of "selfish desires." The purpose of disseminating neo-Confucianism is to "存天理灭人欲"*Cun Tianli Mie Renyu* (support heavenly principles and suppress human desires).

The neo-Confucianism has reinterpreted Confucianism to the extreme, adopted Confucianism as the mainstay and absorbed Buddhist and Taoist ideas

[35] Jin, K. (1986). Application of Thematology, *Reading*, Vol. III.

[36] *Er Cheng Yishu* (Remnant Books of the Two Cheng brothers): *Yulu* (Discourses).

[37] *Zhuzi Yulei* (A Collection of Conversations of Master Zhu) Vol. I.

simultaneously. In the intellectual history, the neo-Confucianism is a new development stage after a hundred schools of thoughts once flourishing before the Qin Dynasty, the study of Confucian classics during the Western and Eastern Han Dynasties, the focus on metaphysics during the Wei and Jin Dynasties, and the thriving Buddhism during the Sui and Tang Dynasties. The neo-Confucianism is a school of philosophy, related to jurisprudence, politics, ethics, education, religion, and other fields of study.

Up to the Ming Dynasty, the neo-Confucianism initiated by Cheng Yi and Zhu Xi was developed into *Xin Xue* (study of the heart and mind). The neo-Confucianism mainly advocated moral education and opposed law and punishment, regarding law and punishment external and a last resort. Neo-Confucianists also inherited Dong Zhongshu's theory of "天人感应"*Tian Ren Gan Ying* (interactions between Heaven and Man), attributing any kind of change in the natural environment to human affairs and emphasizing being scrupulous in human affairs to follow the way of Heaven, such as the "permanent" rules of ethics on cardinal guides and constant virtues initiated by Cheng Yi and Zhu Xi. In essence, the purpose of the theories by Dong Zhongshu, Cheng Yi, and Zhu Xi was the same as to maintain the Confucian ethics, to observe "the guides and virtues and the Confucian ethical code." They supported legislation adaptable to time and circumstances; they argued there was no priority between morality and punishment because they supplemented each other and formed a unity; they advocated proper and timely rewards and punishments to enforce law. With the development of neo-Confucianism, Confucianism, as a school of thought, has eventually evolved into a system of feudal ethics.

3.3.3 The Legalization of Confucian Doctrine

3.3.3.1 Reinforce Ethics of Hierarchy

The neo-Confucianism developed by Zhu Xi embraced unprecedented reverence during the Ming and Qing Dynasties. In the legal history, the legal concepts initiated by Zhu Xi were thoroughly implemented in legislation. *The Ming Code*, *The Great Qing Code*, and *Comprehensive Canon on Rituals of the Great Qing* all signified the full implementation of ritual law. Those legal concepts were not only applied in judicial practice but also popular with the ordinary people. During the Qing Dynasty, the neo-Confucianism was further advanced and there emerged a group of neo-Confucianism advocates and practitioners. Emperor Kangxi and Emperor Qianlong during the Qing Dynasty adopted filial piety as the ruling thought.

At the level of the code of ethics, the sovereign made great efforts to inculcate Confucian ethics. Emperor Kangxi paid multiple visits to Mansion of Confucius for reverence; Emperor Yongzheng firmly believed in Confucianism and selected candidates from the Civil Service Exam by reading their responses to the Four Books, requiring candidates to comment only on the annotations made by Zhu Xi. Emperor Qianlong followed suit and further commented: "I read and recited the abridged edition of Confucian classics and looked up to Confucius from the bottom of my heart. Everything I say and Everything I do all follow Confucius instructions as prescriptive rules."[38] Good education equipped Emperor Qianlong with enough knowledge to study and comment on Confucian classics, which provided him with the necessary premise to form the ethics of hierarchy. Under the condition of inheriting Confucian ethics, Emperor Qianlong made his own innovations as well. On the other hand, local officials spared no effort to implement Qianlong's ruling thoughts, including competent neo-Confucianists such as Li Guangdi, Lu Longqi, Tang Bin, Lan Dingyuan, and Zhang Boxing, to name just a few. On the one hand, they disseminated the spirit of Confucian ethics; on the other hand, they implemented ritual law to order people's social life.

In virtue of the efforts of three generations of emperors from Shunzhi, Kangxi, to Yongzheng, the social status of Confucius and his descendants ascended quickly and reached its peak during Qianlong's Reign, that is to say, the status of Confucius even topped "the Son of Heaven" (the emperor). In order to demonstrate his determination of following the Confucian instructions, Emperor Qianlong visited Mansion of Confucius nine times, performing the etiquette of kneeling three times and kowtowing nine times (formal etiquette on meeting the emperor) in front of the Confucius memorial tablet. The ceremony was grandiose and unprecedented. As for the patriarchal clan of Confucius, Qianlong was generous enough to confer special protections and favors. In the ninth year of Qianlong's Reign (1744), a mine was opened up, but Qianlong was afraid that opening the mine would disturb Cemetery of Confucius and hence ordered to terminate the project. Every time he visited Mansion of Confucius, Qianlong would bestow upon the patriarchal clan of Confucius generous rewards.

The reason why the sovereigns preferred Confucianism was that they realized "all wise emperors from ancient times inculcated people when they claimed the throne. Confucius epitomizes the essence of ethics, providing the rulers three cardinal guides as the foundation, five constant virtues to regulate human relations, eight aspects of ruling a country, nine standard rules to follow for governance, five types of rites and six forms of ritual music. As long as Confucian ethics is followed scrupulously, the way of ruling remains constant, humanity will never dissolve."[39] In a word, social stratification based upon ethics is the core of Confucianism, and therefore, only through advocating Confucianism can the ruling class maintain the feudal way of "ruling" and "humanity."

Emperor Qianlong believed ethics of hierarchy could guarantee stability of the society and the way of ruling depended upon instruction and inculcation. The function of instruction and inculcation was reflected inside a family: whoever was docile to the parents must be filial and whoever was reverent to the elder must be fraternal. Therefore, those who observed ethics of hierarchy must have possessed virtues as

---

[38] *Qing Gaozong shilu* (Veritable Records during Qianlong's Reign of the Qing dynasty, 1735–1799). Vol. 292, June, 12th year of Qianlong's Reign (1747).

[39] *Qing Gaozong shilu* (Veritable Records during Qianlong's Reign of the Qing dynasty, 1735–1799). Vol. 309, March, 13th year of Qianlong's Reign (1748).

filial piety and fraternity. On the condition that everyone had the virtues, social customs could be purified; as the result of lack of filial piety and fraternity, people would misbehave and even commit crimes. With ethics of hierarchy available, "peace and happiness fills a family and grand harmony dominates the universe."[40] National stability rests with the extent to which people follow Confucian ethics. On the other hand, disturbance in the society results from people's violation of Confucian ethics and thereafter the disorder in social hierarchy.

Emperor Qianlong theoretically elaborated on the ethics of hierarchy and pointed out stable social stratification was the premise of peaceful national order. According to his point of view, everyone should be content with his/her position and not arrogate to himself/herself anything beyond his/her status. In order to practice his ethics of hierarchy, Qianlong took practical measures to regulate the words and deeds of his subjects within the framework of his views adaptable to time and contexts in reality.

3.3.3.2 Rites and Laws That Maintain the Code of Ethics

The ruling class managed to imprint the code of ethics in people's deep soul via disseminating three cardinal guides and five constant virtues and male superiority over females. Confucianism has always attached great importance to spiritually strengthening women's obedience to their husbands. Mencius's "body contact is not allowed in passing objects between men and women," Dong Zhongshu's "three cardinal guides and five constant virtues," chastity-related concepts strengthened by Confucianists during the Song Dynasty such as "starvation to death is minor and loss of chastity is major" and the saying on filial piety that "amongst all evils lewdness is the first, and amongst all virtues filial piety is the first" all target women. In the early Qing Dynasty, the public opinion on women's chastity and faithfulness to men was more closely related to ritual law than in previous dynasties. The ritual law restricted women's behavior in their material, spiritual, and social lives and further stipulated detailed reward and punishment provisions for women who followed or violated traditional "women's morals."

In *The Great Qing Code: CriminalLaws: Incest and Adultery*, Criminal intercourse by mutual consent was still listed as the first article under the crime "incest and adultery" based on The Ming Code: criminal intercourse by mutual consent with an unmarried woman shall be punished with 80 blows of the heavy stick; if with a married woman, the punishment shall be 90 blows of the heavy stick.[41] Both men and women who commit criminal intercourse by mutual consent should be punished. Private love affairs were absolutely not allowed by feudal ethics. Even the couples who were not officially wedded, that is, those couples who cohabited

---

[40] *Qing Gaozong shilu* (Veritable Records during Qianlong's Reign of the Qing dynasty, 1735–1799). Vol. 130, November, fifth year of Qianlong's Reign (1740).

[41] *The Great Qing Code,* Vol. XXXIII, *Criminal Laws: Incest and Adultery.*

without going through official wedding ceremonies shall be punished in the name of the crime of criminal intercourse by mutual consent. Though the crime itself neither interfered with others' interests nor endangered the society, it was forbidden by law for the sake of protecting the traditional "social morals." In a criminal intercourse, to women, they lost chastity, and to men, they were rendered promiscuous. The public opinion and the code of ethics were more critical of the women's loss of chastity than men's lewdness.

The code of ethics during the Qing Dynasty generally punished women more severely than men for the same conduct. The focus of ethics lay in maintaining women's chastity, embodied by the recognition of chastity. During the Qing Dynasty, *Jiefu* (virtuous women) referred to the women who never remarried after their husbands' deaths. There were certain standards for commending virtuous women which varied with different emperors. For example, in the sixth year of Kangxi's Reign, the standard was set that "women who kept chaste after their husbands' deaths before the age of 30 till the age of 50 could be commended as virtuous women." In the first year of Yongzheng's Reign (1723), the standards for commending virtuous women were relaxed, considering the local wealthy families were able to report cases of virtuous women; however, chaste women from poor families in rural areas were even unnoticed who were in need of local officials' thorough investigations. "In order to let the chaste women in poverty-stricken families enjoy the emperor's grace equally, those women who passed away over 40 years old and remained chaste for more than 15 years after their husbands' deaths should all be commended as virtuous women."[42] Later, women who remained chaste for 15 years without remarriage after their husbands' deaths and were over 40 years old could be recognized as virtuous women. The government would then award the virtuous woman's family 30 taels (one tael approximately equals 1.3 ounces) of silver for the construction of a chastity archway.

In the early Qianlong's Reign, the standards for recognition of virtuous women were further relaxed, but the requests upon officials responsible for commending virtuous women were more rigorous. Up to the 14th year of Qianlong's Reign (1749), the scope of recognition of virtuous women was expanded to the women after their husbands' deaths who continued to take care of their parents-in-law, who raised children alone, who were killed in rape cases in order to protect chastity, who kept chaste and did not remarry despite harsh conditions, etc. The responsibility for related local officials was clarified: those who misreported or failed to report the candidates for recognition as virtuous women shall all be penalized regardless of their ranks. Recognition of chastity and filial piety at that time became a system reflecting coercive ritual law. In real practice, besides the afore-listed general principles, more supplementary information was added to quite a few cases of

[42] Guangxu. *Da-Qing Huidian Shili* (The Jurisdictional Corpus on Administrative Matters in the Qing Dynasty, Guangxu Version). Vol. 403. *The Ministry of Rites: Customs Education: Recognition of Chastity and Filial Piety.*

recognized virtuous women, which made the system more regular and detailed.[43] In order to prevent women from committing criminal intercourse, the ritual law in the Qing Dynasty had more rigorous rules to punish those women than previous dynasties. Under the condition of official dissemination and severe enforcement of the ritual law, women were shackled by the suppressing code of ethics, such as 三从四德 San Cong Si De (the three obediences: to her father before marriage, to her husband during married life and to her sons in widowhood and four virtues: fidelity, physical charm, propriety in speech, and efficiency in needle work). Gradually, women became appendages to men and many were even deprived of their lives by the invisible sword called "ritual law."[44]

3.3.4 *The Solidification of Rites and Laws*

3.3.4.1 Rites and Laws Promoting Unification

The concept of "ritual law" underscores "ritual politics" as the mainstay and "criminal politics" as the supplementary. Feudal emperors preferred the rule of rites as the foundation for the ruling thought. Take Zhu Yuanzhang, for example, he hated Mencius' arguments, such as "the priority of the people, the state being the inferior and the ruler rendered the least important"; "if a sovereign treats a minister with brotherhood, the minister will consider him trustworthy; if a sovereign treats a minister like a dog/horse, i.e. like a slave, the minister will treat him as a stranger; if a sovereign treats a minister like dirt, the minister will regard him as a bandit or enemy." He even for a time removed *Mencius*' memorial tablet from the Temple of Confucius. Nevertheless, considering the cumulative impact of Confucianism, he finally restored Mencius' memorial tablet in the Temple of Confucius. At most, Zhu Yuanzhang cut 85 sections from the original *Mencius*, leaving merely 100-odd sections compiled as *Abridged Texts of Mencius* which was later published and popularized to ensure predominance of Confucianism represented by Confucius and Mencius.

During the late imperial period, the Qing Dynasty adopted Confucianism as the ruling thought, further elaborated on the Confucian points of view concerning rites and laws, and proposed feasible concepts on the rule of rites. Emperor Kangxi believed the priority of an emperor's rule lay in maintaining social customs and stratification, advocating thriftiness instead of extravagance; if officials and commoners all led a lavish life and refused to adhere to their social positions and if the rich craved for luxuries and the poor kept up with the Joneses, the society would be inflicted by thefts and frauds out of poverty, people would be aggressive and

[43] *Qing Gaozong shilu* (Veritable Records during Qianlong's Reign of the Qing dynasty, 1735–1799). Vol. 344, Early July, 14th year of Qianlong's Reign (1749).

[44] Zhang, R.(2013). *Rites: Laws: Society—Legal Transformation and Social Changes in the Qing Dynasty*. The Commercial Press.

arrogant, and social customs would deteriorate. All these were closely related to the rule of the country and inculcation of customs.[45] Emperor Yongzheng once instructed: in order to pacify the people, the priority should be given to inculcation of customs; in order to prioritize inculcation of customs, the focus should be placed upon advocation of thriftiness. *The Rites of Zhou* institutionalized sumptuary regulations as a cornerstone of social stratification: because of limited resources, overstepping one's status privileges should be prevented, lavishness forbidden.[46] Following suit, Emperor Qianlong also pointed out: prioritizing frugality and rejecting lavishness is the key to inculcation of customs.[47] The aforementioned emperors' instructions can be summarized into three key points: first, the system of rites is closely related to material life. In order to stabilize social stratification, people must abide by the sumptuary hierarchy, with material consumption rigorously commensurate with their social positions. Frugality must be promoted to suppress people's desires for consumption. If people follow a luxurious lifestyle, their consumption life would overstep their positions. Second, the system of rites determines social customs. The fundamental purpose of Qing's rule is to realize simple and honest folk customs. "The real essence of the statement that governance of a state prevents unrest of it and averts danger by preparedness lies in the foundation of social customs, i.e. people are honest and the customs must be uncorrupted; the royal court is upright, and the fortune of the state must last long."[48] Third, the system of rites is associated with autocracy. Emperor Kangxi said: "if the sovereign implements the rule of virtue, he must prioritize maintenance of social customs and distinguish social classes." The emperor himself is the symbol of supreme autocratic power erected on a rigorous hierarchical system. Once the demarcation between social classes and positions is blurred, it leads to loss of the supreme power and failure of the emperor's rule. To ensure stability of the supreme power, a powerful political tool is needed to maintain a hierarchical social system; coincidentally, the system of rites serves the function of distinguishing social statuses and positions.

The rulers of the Qing Dynasty summarized theories on the association between the system of rites and social life into frugality, social stratification, social customs, and the rule of virtue. Frugality prevents lavishness and leads to distinction of social statuses; people's adhering to their positions and duties can purify social customs; pure social customs can help implement the rule of virtue. Frugality is the foundation without which the system of rites would be rootless. Therefore, Emperor Qianlong pointed out the reason why *Comprehensive Canon on Rituals of the Great Qing* should be revised was that the previous system of rites failed to sufficiently

[45] *Qing Shengzu Shilu* (Veritable Records during Kangxi's Reign of the Qing Dynasty, 1661–1722). Vol. 39, 11th year of Kangxi's Reign (1672), Article 50.

[46] *Qing Shizong Shilu*. (Veritable Records during Yongzheng's Reign of the Qing Dynasty, 1722–1735). Vol. 10, sixth year of Yongzheng's Reign (1728), Article 56.

[47] *Qing Gaozong shilu* (Veritable Records during Qianlong's Reign of the Qing dynasty, 1735–1799). Vol. 245, July, tenth year of Qianlong's Reign (1745).

[48] Wang Xianqian. *Dong Hua Lu* (A Chronicle of the Qing Dynasty 1644–1911). Qianlong XIIII, July, sixth Year of Qianlong's Reign (1741). Article 8.

regulate people's daily life. The purpose of the system of rites is to "regulate people's behavior, prevent lavishness and save them from poverty." However, after the Qin and Han Dynasties, the system of rites only provided for basic sacrificial and court rituals and the detailed sacrificial vessels and specifications collected by officials of related departments were only displayed when utilized. Even scholar officials were not well-versed in the system of rites, not to mention distinction of rituals and etiquettes of transportation, clothing, shelter, weddings, funerals, and offering sacrifices from stratified social classes. Emperor Qianlong then instructed that a succinct and clear summary based on the books concerning rites from previous dynasties, integrated with *The Jurisdictional Corpus on Administrative Matters in the Qing Dynasty*, should be compiled so that previous rituals of capping, wedding, funeral, and sacrificial ceremonies were perfected to let everyone follow.[49] Qianlong particularly emphasized there must be specified rites not only for the middle and upper social classes but also for the lower social class. He changed the original situation of the ritual provisions from formulated and collected by officials into applied by the majority of people so that common people familiarized themselves with those ritual provisions which could substantially play the role of "empowering the emperor and ruling the people."

The Qing Dynasty comprehensively inherited and developed the traditional Chinese culture with Confucianism as the mainstay and skillfully integrated and hid Manchu's ruling tactics in the traditional Han culture. Meanwhile, the emperors of the Qing Dynasty carried forward previous emperors' thoughts on diligence, benevolence, and filial piety so that the relevant concepts of rites and laws in the Confucian classics were successfully changed into real ruling practical and the Qing Dynasty therefore became the epitome of traditional ritual culture.[50] Mid-Qing was the peak period of political development in traditional China and the prime time embracing combination of ritual law, code of ethics, and ritual righteousness in Chinese history, which regulated social life comprehensively, including material life, spiritual life, concepts, and thoughts, conducive to the consolidation of the autocratic monarchy. The detailed perfection process of the ritual system in the Qing Dynasty was consistent with the growing process of the autocratic imperial power. The strengthening of the imperial power is the basis of the perfection process of the ritual system while the perfection process of the ritual system and its function of maintaining social hierarchy contributed to the strengthening of the imperial power and promoted unification of the empire.

---

[49] *Qing Gaozong Shengxun* (Emperor Qianlong's Instructions), Vol. 251, Xing Li Yue (Make Rites and Music Thrive), June, the first year of Qianlong's Reign, Article 22.

[50] Chang, J. (2006). *Studies on the State and Society of the Qing Dynasty*. People's Publishing House, 2.

3.3.4.2 Consolidation of Concepts on Rites and Laws

Inculcation of rites into people was conducive to the consolidation of autocratic imperial power and the formation of a unified nation, but the unification under autocratic imperial power prevented the society from reforming, centralizing people's thoughts and behavior under the rule of the emperor. Through standardization of the system of rites, people have formed the political ideas of advocating authorities and the ethical ideas of worshipping ancestors and developed the closed and rigid conservative mindset and the value system that emphasized agriculture and suppressed commerce; in practice, people became content with their positions without cultivating the enterprising spirit. This is what we often consider as the negative effects of Confucian culture on Chinese society. During the May fourth Movement, revolutionists proposed slogans to overthrow Confucianism and criticize the code of ethics that "eats" people and started the trend of overturning the ethics of cardinal guidelines and constant virtues. Their real target was the neo-Confucianism interpreted and explicated by Zhu Xi.

The situation deserved to be called "legal debate" was merely a flash in the pan during the Spring and Autumn Period and Warring States Period. In terms of form, the atmosphere was democratic and liberal during the contention of a hundred schools of thoughts, and the elites that represented a hundred schools of thoughts fully demonstrated their spiritual pursuits in a comparatively more relaxed environment. In fact, in that seemingly democratic and liberal environment, even the legal paradigm designed by the legal elites would never allow the existence of real democratic and liberal spirit.

Since the Qin and Han Dynasties, the legal debate similar to the one that occurred during the Spring and Autumn Period and Warring States Period never happened again. To some extent, it reflected the strong stability and continuity of Chinese legal tradition, but the function of law was mainly reflected in the aspects such as highlighting public power, inhibiting private power, maintaining autocracy, rejecting democracy, etc. The task of legal elites was to try every means to justify the existence of autocratic power, and they themselves became the appendage to the autocratic power and sacrifice to the rule of man. From then on, the legal elites either focused on traditional jurisprudence or engaged themselves in studying Confucian classics to attain official posts through the Civil Service Exam or became intoxicated with textual criticism and immersed in adding annotations to the Confucian classics. They lost the opportunity and courage to discuss the following topics such as value of law, the function of law, the restriction of public power and the guarantee of private rights by law, the balance of power, judicial independence, basic human rights, equality before the law, rule of law, freedom of speech, and many other issues related to the rule of law. What they did at best was relevant discussions on severity of punishment, abolition of corporal punishment, simplification of legal articles, or whether the sovereign was sober-minded or muddle-headed. Their ideal of the "rule of law" equaled the ideal of a sage emperor's rule, the ideal of autocratic and centralized imperial power and the ideal of the "rule of man." On the other hand, the independent and distinct personality legal elites were supposed to have was not successfully cultivated. "In terms of individuals' independent personality in Chinese inherent culture, except the aspect of morality and ethics highlighted by Confucianism, other aspects, such as the legal aspect, political aspect, and social aspect of individuals' independent personality were not virtually realized."[51] The advocated "Civil officials should try to admonish the emperor even at the risk of being executed" and "Military generals should fight desperately on the battlefield to serve the country" entailed death that was only meant for the exclusive autocratic monarchy, instead of the ideal of the rule of law. Even if the existing political order was questioned and challenged, the challenge was conducted on the premise that justification of the current "monarchy" was recognized and maintained. Take Hai Rui (a famous minister in the Ming Dynasty for his morality, honesty, and bluntness) for example, even though he hated what the emperor did, all he did was carrying a coffin with him to the court to admonish the emperor at the risk of death without considering restricting the imperial power by legislation or removing the imperial power through legal procedures. The other way of challenging the imperial power was "replacement," for example, Zhao Kuangyin (the first emperor of the Song Dynasty) was draped with the imperial yellow robe by his supporters and claimed himself the emperor of a new dynasty; peasants' uprisings were represented by Chen Sheng and Wu Guang at the end of the Qin Dynasty. These became normal transitions of power in the autocratic society, and therefore legal elites could not develop independently in such a political and social environment.

3.4 The Separation of Rites from Laws

3.4.1 New Challenges to Rites and Laws

From the later Qianlong's reign to the early twentieth century, the traditional Chinese autocracy declined from maturity to decay. Due to the invasion of foreign forces, the nature of Chinese society also changed. At the turning point, the legal philosophy also witnessed new changes. During Qianlong's, Jiaqing's and Daoguang's Reigns, various social conflicts intensified, the political entities on which law rested upon were on the wane, and the changing social life impacted on the traditional system of rites in many aspects and the social order relying upon the ritual system and concepts to maintain began to collapse. Many people of insight constantly questioned the rationality of the traditional legal philosophy and criticized its negative effects, represented by Dai Zhen, Yu Zhengxie, Gong Zizhen, and Wei Yuan, just to name a few. However, their critique remains confined to traditional legal philosophy, failing to articulate substantive pathways for reforming China's jurisprudential heritage.

[51] Zhang, D. (1998). *Thoughts and Society*. Liaoning Education Press, 235.

After the Opium War, Chinese traditional social order was assaulted by external forces; hence the national crisis was deepened, represented by the loss of extraterritorial jurisdiction. In 1843 (23rd year of Daoguang's Reign), *General Regulations under Which the British Trade Is to Be Conducted at the Five Ports of Canton, Amoy, Foochow, Ningpo, and Shanghai and Treaty of Bogue* stipulated: "where the litigation involves the British and Chinese, how to convict the British shall be based on the British law by the British consulate; how to convict the Chinese shall be based on the Chinese law." In the next year, in addition to the above provisions, *Treaty of Peace, Amity, and Commerce, between the United States of America and the Chinese Empire* also stipulated: "where the people of the United States at all ports of China are involved in litigations over property, how to convict them shall be decided by the American consulate; where the people of the United States in China are involved in litigations with people from countries other than China, those involved shall be convicted based on the treaties made by respective countries and Chinese officials are not entitled to those cases." Later, France, Russia, Japan, and so forth grabbed such privileges as well. Finally, for all those countries that enjoyed extraterritorial jurisdiction in China, if their emigrants in China committed crimes and became defendants in criminal proceedings, they may not be punished by the Chinese law.

The Infiltration of foreign forces forced people to open their eyes to the outside world. People of insight first saw the advanced military forces and gradually sought to reform the political, military, and legal systems. On the one hand, they criticized the system of traditional legal philosophies, and on the other hand, they put forward some legal concepts to adapt to the new era. At the beginning of the twentieth century, the Qing Court was in a difficult situation under the assault of large-scale mass movements and the oppression of the imperialist powers. In the difficult political situation, officials inside and outside the court generally called for new policies, and hence terminating the chaos, defending against invasions, and advocating establishment of the constitution and commitment to reform became the main theme of the zeitgeist. Abolishment of the old law and compiling and promulgating the new law was rendered one of the strongest notes in the "main theme." With the rise of the constitutional movement, the evolution of Chinese legal concepts entered a new stage, that is, separation between the ritual system and legal system was realized on the basis of modern jurisprudence.

After 1901, the 27th year of Guangxu's Reign, the call for the revision of law became stronger and stronger; many people began to criticize the old law and revealed the merits and demerits of the old law with reference to the Western law. On September 27 of the same year, Zhang Zhidong, Liu Kunyi, and others mentioned in a package of proposals concerning the reform of law that compared with the law of Han, Sui, Tang, and Ming Dynasties, *The Great Qing Code* was generous and just, while compared with the Western criminal law, there were flaws in implementing the Qing Code, so the General Administration can call diplomatic envoys to invite famous lawyers from various countries to China who may act as legal trainers and help China formulate similar laws with reference to laws on mining, railway, commerce, and criminality from various countries. They even predicted that if the above four laws could be formulated earlier, "they were not specifically meant to make money, but to prevent disasters."[52] Zhang Zhidong and others were soon approved by the highest authorities, and the royal court then appointed them as ministers responsible for the revision of laws and ordered Shen Jiaben and Wu Tingfang to revise the current laws based on real situations of trade negotiations with reference to the laws of other countries so that the revised laws could be applicable at home and abroad and be beneficial to governance. The Ministry of Punishment also embarked on revision of the criminal law in the same year. Afterward, law revisers focused on abolishment of the extraterritorial jurisdiction.[53] Thereafter, the revision of law at the end of the Qing Dynasty entered a new stage when legal elites were assigned the task.

3.4.2 The Birth of New-Type Legal Philosophy

The modern legal elites, on the one hand, boldly explored the advanced Western law. The translation hall was dedicated to the introduction and translation of Western legal works. Foreign legal experts such as Okada Asatarō (1868–1936) and Matsuoka Yoshimasa (1870–1939) and Ogawa Sigejirou (1861–1915) from Japan came in person to explain the Western law. Therefore, the legal elites were heavily influenced by the Western legal concepts, and they were determined to reform the traditional Chinese legal philosophy, but on the other hand, they were also able to treat the Chinese legal tradition in a correct way without blindly worshiping them, and instead, they proceeded from reality, retained the useful, and rejected the futile based on national conditions.

Jurists at the end of the Qing Dynasty believed there were three important stages in the governance of a country: legislation, justice, and observance of law. In terms of legal theories, they highlighted the study on legal science. In the aspect of the legislative guiding principle, they advocated nationalism instead of familism. As for judicial principles, they supported a break with the traditional ritual principles, such as the reform of punishment from being heavy to being lenient, all ethnic groups being equal before the law, opposing hierarchical punishment, the abolition of slave trade and human trafficking, equality between men and women, conviction and sentencing being based on formal articles of the criminal law instead of reasoning by analogy or comparison to the relevant circumstances, etc. There was no distinction between criminal law and civil law in the old code; legislation, administration, and justice were all in the hands of the emperor, and in provinces and counties, both

[52] *Guangxu Chao Donghua Lu* (Records of the Eastern Flower (Gate), a chronicle of Guangxu's Reign of the Qing Dynasty), Sep. 27th, 1901, 27th year of Guangxu's Reign, Article 4744, 4763–4764.

[53] *Guangxu Chao Donghua Lu* (Records of the Eastern Flower (Gate), a chronicle of Guangxu's Reign of the Qing Dynasty), Article of May 13th, 1902, 28th year of Guangxu's Reign; *Qing Shi Gao* (Draft History of the Qing Dynasty), Vol. 142, *Zhi* (Record) 117, Criminal Law I.

administration and justice were placed upon local authorities; when different members of the society committed crimes, the corresponding conviction should comply with the offender's social status and kinship factors that involved affection, reasoning, and righteousness; and different social identities and statuses would lead to different litigation rights. Even the effectiveness of the evidence in litigation should be determined by the social status of the evidence provider. Parents enjoyed the right of direct action concerning their family members without any litigation procedure, and they could directly send their children to local authorities for conviction. Other litigation systems such as "violating the code of ethics and offending justice," "children or grandchildren violating parents' or grandparents' instructions and orders," "mutual concealment between relatives," "women's committing crimes," "conviction based on Five Degrees of Mourning," and "eight privileged groups of people whose cases are to be especially deliberated" all derived from the ritual law, served the ritual law, and completely ruled out the openness of litigation proceedings, independence of justice, and the equality of civil rights and interests. All these became the object of legal reform for jurists.

The revision of law at the end of the Qing Dynasty resulted in *The Draft Criminal and Civil Procedure Law of the Great Qing Dynasty*, *Draft Criminal Code of the Great Qing Dynasty*, *The Existing Criminal Code of the Great Qing Dynasty*, *The New Criminal Code of the Great Qing Dynasty*, *The Maritime Law*, etc. But the only law promulgated by the Qing Court was *The New Criminal Code of the Great Qing Dynasty*, which was rendered a symbol of the modernization of China's legal system.

3.4.3 The Second Legal Debate

3.4.3.1 The Upgraded Contention Between Rites and Laws

During the Spring Autumn Period and Warring States Period, Confucianists and Legalists once had the first round of contention between "the rule of rites" and "the rule of law." The contention between rites and laws occurred again at the end of the Qing Dynasty. The first contention aimed at the means used to shape the autocratic order. The second contention, on the other hand, focused on the revision of laws, with the purpose to either realize the modern Western legal order or maintain the traditional Chinese Confucian ethics. Therefore, this is an upgraded version of the contention between rites and laws.

The road to the modernization of Chinese law was not smooth. The purpose of revising the law in the late Qing Dynasty was to abolish the extraterritorial jurisdiction. But there emerged a fierce dispute over the guiding legal principles and legal technical issues. The debate was carried out between the school of jurisprudence and the school of feudal ethics, mainly centering upon the guiding legislative concepts and specifications of the new criminal code. Fundamentally speaking, the essence of the debate lay in how to treat the traditional legal philosophy centering upon the unity of rites and laws and the traditional legal system.

The proposal written by Shen Jiaben and other jurists and *Draft Criminal and Civil Procedure Law of the Great Qing Dynasty* (1906) placed themselves against *The Great Qing Code*. Shen Jiaben's procedure law called for the introduction of modern Western jury system and lawyer defense system into China, which would naturally encounter the obstruction from the "ritual law" doctrine. Therefore, as soon as the jurists proposed to the royal court, Zhang Zhidong led the school of feudal ethics to strike back against the jurists. *Draft Criminal and Civil Procedure Law of the Great Qing Dynasty* was rejected without publication. This is the first stage of the contention between rites and laws. However, the impact forged by the draft further expanded the contention in the discussions on the revision of *Draft Criminal Code of the Great Qing Dynasty* and *The New Criminal Code of the Great Qing Dynasty* and formed a surging tide afterward, with a thousand spinning vortexes, which lashed the embankment of the traditional law.

Local authorities had strong reaction toward two points in the new criminal code when they endorsed the draft: one was the absence of the article "children or grandchildren violating parents' or grandparents' instructions and orders," and the other was the article on "adultery" and "illicit intercourse committed by an unmarried woman." Jurists further checked that "children or grandchildren violating parents' or grandparents' instructions and orders" was different from "filial impiety" of Ten Abominations. Based on this factor, it was stipulated in the new code that the corresponding punishment was the fourth grade (100 blows of heavy stick) at the heaviest. The previous cases of this type were usually filed because the children or grandchildren led an idle life without fulfilling their filial duties, and the current articles in the draft concerning police offense and loitering were explicated and could be cited for conviction and sentencing. If there were cases, where children assaulted and failed to support their parents, the article of coercing by force and abandoning senior relatives in the manuscript of *The New Criminal Code of the Great Qing Dynasty* and the article intended to add to the new code as the insult of senior relatives could all be cited. On the other hand, the punishment for "violating the code of ethics and offending justice" was also rendered heavier. Eventually, crimes such as jeopardizing the security of the royal family, internal riots (to subvert the government), treason (collusion with other countries), offense against senior relatives, robbery, tomb robbery, illicit intercourse committed by an unmarried woman, and the fifth supplementary provision became the five articles in the *Provisional Act*, which was a compromise and consolation to the school of feudal ethics so as to establish communication between the new and the traditional and facilitate implementation of the new law. When the national education, police, and prison systems were more prepared, new revisions of law could be on the way.

3.4.3.2 The Contention Between Familism and Nationalism

The school of feudal ethics demanded that all the supplementary provisions be written in the main body of the code, which was rejected. The amended *Draft Criminal Code of the Great Qing Dynasty* was later *The New Criminal Code of the Great*

Qing Dynasty. The school of feudal ethics was not content with the work done by the Constitutional Compilation Bureau, and they were not to give up. The leading representative of the school Lao Naixuan unexpectedly launched the campaign of collecting 100 people's signatures at the Advisory Council and formulated *The Amendment to the New Criminal Code*, making revisions, changes, and additions to *The New Criminal Code of the Great Qing Dynasty*, with the focus still on the articles concerning rites and ethics.

While *Draft Criminal Code of the Great Qing Dynasty* was endorsed, the arguments made by the school of feudal ethics had been active for a while and caused a rising clamor. Since the court issued a decree on 27th of the first month of the first year of Xuantong's Reign (February 17, 1909), the school of feudal ethics treated it as the imperial sward to guard their stance as they advanced step by step and nearly overthrew *The New Criminal Code of the Great Qing Dynasty*. On the other hand, the school of jurisprudence would not be content with arguments only and began to take actions. They resolutely stood up to refute the criticisms set forth by the school of feudal ethics. While the school of jurisprudence formulated *Revised Draft Criminal Code of the Great Qing Dynasty*, the school of feudal ethics responded with a recommendation on *Revised Draft Criminal Code of the Great Qing Dynasty*; while the school of jurisprudence compiled the recommendation on discretionary approach to the new law, the school of feudal ethics responded with a statement of opinion; while the school of jurisprudence completed *The New Criminal Code of the Great Qing Dynasty*, the school of feudal ethics made the rebuttal by formulating *The Amendment to the New Criminal Code*. The two sides disagreed with each other, and the middle forces and foreign legal circles also participated in the debate. The debate gradually converged on the ethical dogmas related to the status and stratification of family members.

In order to accommodate the school of feudal ethics, the school of jurisprudence had regressed while compiling *Draft Criminal Code of the Great Qing Dynasty* and *Revised Draft Criminal Code of the Great Qing Dynasty*; nevertheless, their concessions soon became the "spear" and "shield" the same time that seemed to be contradictory, which was seized by the school of feudal ethics who pointed out that part of the content in *Draft Criminal Code of the Great Qing Dynasty* was quite different from the criminal law of other countries. For example, Article 82 defined the scope of senior relatives; Article 311 stipulated that those who committed the crime of murdering the senior relative shall be sentenced to death; Article 316 stated those who assaulted the senior relative but did not cause the injury of the latter shall be sentenced to the imprisonment of the third to fifth grade or be fined from 50 to 500 Yuan (a type of monetary unit during the Qing Dynasty); Article 289 prescribed that the illicit intercourse by mutual consent with a married woman shall be sentenced to imprisonment of the third to fifth grade; and so on and so forth. The school of feudal ethics was concerned whether the articles of the new criminal law were the same as their counterparts of criminal laws of other countries. "It was impossible and irrational that all of the articles were the same as those of criminal laws of other countries and therefore they could be observed by the foreign residents. If this was the way to abolish the extraterritorial jurisdiction, the whole approach was doomed."

The so-called revision of the old law should aim at general consistency between the Eastern law and the Western law, such as aspects of operational proceedings and prison conditions. It was not necessary to make all the types of crimes and the related articles the same as those in the criminal laws of other countries. As long as other countries considered the revision appropriate, extraterritorial jurisdiction was expected to be abolished. Therefore, the argument that the purpose of abandoning the code of ethics and customs was to help abolish extraterritorial jurisdiction was untenable.[54] With the submission, discussion, and vote of *Draft Criminal Code of the Great Qing Dynasty*, the debate on how to frame the criminal law system in modern China became more intense. The contention between familism and nationalism was one of the foci.

Those who supported familism elaborated on the necessity of it in the following aspects: the school of feudal ethics believed law derived from the form of government; the form of government derived from the code of ethics; the code of ethics derived from the social customs; and the social customs derived from the means of livelihood. Family disciplines were the foundation of the customs of an agrarian country; besides, the code of ethics and form of government were built upon family disciplines too. The emperor to ministers was the father to sons, which demonstrated distinct statuses as well as intimate relationships. "Law is made to maintain the significance of family disciplines. If all the families govern themselves well, the country can also exhibit sound governance." "If everyone loves their relatives and respects their elders, then the world will be peaceful and harmonious." On the other hand, those who supported nationalism attributed the disadvantages of China at that time to the regime based on family disciplines and argued that the fellow countrymen only had their families in mind instead of their nation. Therefore, the rule of family disciplines should be abandoned, and the Western policies based on commercial law that advocated equality and rights should be adopted instead. The school of feudal ethics did not agree. They pointed out it was not the family disciplines that caused Chinese to love their families but not their nation. Before the Qin Dynasty, everybody learned to love their motherland, but after the Qin Dynasty was established, an autocratic regime was formed and it implemented obscurantist policies. Thus the political power was manipulated by the ministers, and the people only learned to pay taxes but had no concept of the nation. Their affection was limited to their families only and they were not aware of the nation. In a word, people's lack of affection for their nation originated from their attachment to their families. It was untenable that people would automatically love their nation on the condition that they were forbidden to love their families. Furthermore, the school of feudal ethics argued that if the current family system was sabotaged, the old and weak would not be taken care of and their bodies be dumped outdoors. In the stage when the old social foundation was destroyed but the new social foundation was not yet established, there must be prudent policies that managed to connect the old and new

[54] Lao Naixuan. *Xiuzheng Xinglü Cao'an Shuotie* (Recommendation on Revised Draft Criminal Code of the Great Qing Dynasty); *Xin Xinglü Xiuzheng An Huilu* (Collections on *The Amendment to the New Criminal Code of the Great Qing Dynasty*).

systems at the turning point and could truly take effect and avoid the fall of the nation. In the aspect of economics, collective ownership of the senior members of the family could dissolve disputes over property. Denying familism did not conform to economic policies. In the aspect of religion, Chinese revered Confucianism, with filial piety and loyal at the core, and the nation and the family were considered as unity. As Confucianism was not abandoned yet, denying familism was contrary to the national religion. In the aspect of politics, China then was prepared for constitutionalism. The immediate sabotage on familism was not absolutely correct, and denying it was a political phenomenon not suitable for China. In the aspect of population, the rise and fall of a country can be reflected by the fertility of its people, and hence abandoning familism would necessarily decrease fertility of the people. To sum up, the school of feudal ethics believed the reason why people lacked the concept of the nation lay in the autocratic regime instead of the family system, and therefore denying familism was inconsistent with the national conditions in the aspects of politics, economics, religion, population, and so forth.[55]

The two schools' arguments were incompatible as fire and water. The nationalists argued that familism only catered for autocracy; since the era was transformed, the guiding legal principles should be reformed accordingly.[56] China must survive the law of the jungle by evolving from familism into nationalism. When China was in the phase of preliminary constitutionalism, the guiding legal principle could be neither familism nor familism plus nationalism. Only on the condition that nationalism alone was adopted as the guiding legal principle and all the senior and junior family members of the whole nation were responsible for it could 400 million people be 400 million "national citizens" and could China be prosperous and powerful. To sum up, the new criminal code was consistent with the spirit of nationalism, namely, the spirit of constitutionalism, so it must literally be abided by without being added anything to against the spirit of constitutionalism.

3.4.3.3 The Contention on the Relationship Between Morality and Law

Another focus of the contention between the school of jurisprudence and the school of feudal ethics was on how law and morality were reflected in the new criminal code. The school of feudal ethics firmly believed law and rites were supplementary to each other. A noticeable dispute was over detailed articles in the criminal law concerning illicit intercourse with an unmarried woman and the positioning of seniors and juniors. The school of jurisprudence argued that illicit intercourse by mutual consent would not disappear by prohibition. Even if the article of it was made explicit, it was still merely a literal legal article. Only by means of popularizing education, purifying family atmosphere, and

---

[55] ßLin Zhiping. *Bianming Guojia Zhuyi Yu Jiazu Zhuyi Burong Liangli Shuo* (Clarifying the Dispute between Nationalism and Familism); *Xin Xinglü Xiuzheng An Huilu* (Collections on *The Amendment to the New Criminal Code of the Great Qing Dynasty*).

[56] *Guanyu Xiugai Xinglü de Yanjiang* (Speeches on Revising the Criminal Code).

empowering the media to let people grow with a sense of shame could the obscene lifestyle be lessened. It was not law but education needed to prevent the shameful conduct from occurring. On the other hand, law and morality were different but complementary to each other in fact; separating law and morality was absurd. Therefore, the articles in the old criminal code pertaining to feudal ethics such as violating the code of ethics and offending justice, putting culprits on probation to support lineal elders, fornication between relatives, theft between relatives, exchange of blows between relatives, husband and wife striking each other, tomb robbery, fornication (fornicating with a married woman or fornicating with an unmarried woman), fornication with force, and children or grandchildren committing crimes should all be listed in the main text of the new criminal code. All in all, revision of the criminal code shall never go against the traditional code of ethics and the public mood. Abolishment of extraterritorial jurisdiction was not dependent upon the revision of articles concerning the feudal code of ethics.

The school of jurisprudence held the opposite opinion, advocating separating morality from law. They believed the conduct violating moral rules should be rectified by education while criminal offenders must be punished according to the law. They refused the request issued by the school of feudal ethics to include ethics-related articles such as violating the code of ethics and offending justice, putting culprits on probation to support lineal elders, fornication between relatives, theft between relatives, exchange of blows between relatives, intentionally killing a son or son's son, killing juniors within the five degrees of mourning, husband and wife striking each other, fornicating with an unmarried woman, and children or grandchildren violating parents' or grandparents' instructions and orders in the new criminal code.[57]

Westernization of the legal system at the end of the Qing Dynasty proposed by the school of jurisprudence was an attempt to reform the society at the institutional level, representing the jurists' state of mind of learning from the advanced and their acquired inspiration by examining the outlook of the world. Take Japan, for example, before Meiji Restoration, Japan copied statutes from China, while after Meiji Restoration, Japan started to borrow laws from France and then directly duplicated laws from Germany, which played an important role in the abolishment of extraterritorial jurisdiction.[58] The school of jurisprudence translated a large volume of Japanese laws during the revision of the criminal code

[57] Shen Jiaben. *Shu Lao Tixue Xin Xinglü Cao'an Shuotie Hou*, The Postscript of *Jiyi Wencun* (Shen Jiaben's Collected Works) Vol. VIII, *Lidai Xingfa Kao* (Studies on Criminal Laws of Past Dynasties), Zhonghua Book Company, 1985, pp. 2283–2286. Also named *Shen Dachen Zhuoni Banfa Shuotie* (Shen Jiaben's Recommendation on Discretionary Approach to the New Law), See *Xin Xinglü Xiuzheng An Huilu* (Collections on *The Amendment to the New Criminal Code of the Great Qing Dynasty*).

[58] *Deguo Fake Jinshi Heshanxinshi Yu Jiang Yuanwai Kai Wenda*, *Xin Xinglü Xiuzheng An Huilu* (Collections on *The Amendment to the New Criminal Code of the Great Qing Dynasty*).

which directly involved jurists from Japan in the compilation of it. And the criminal code of Japan after Meiji Restoration was taken as the template for the new criminal code of the Qing Dynasty compiled by the school of jurisprudence.

3.4.3.4 The Realization of Separation Between Rites and Laws

Strong political pressure eventually realized the legal dream of the school of the jurisprudence. On November 11 of the second year of Xuantong's Reign (1910), the school of feudal ethics submitted *A Recommendation on Revised Draft Criminal Code of the Great Qing Dynasty* to the Advisory Council. At the meeting held on December 6, the attempt to revise offending the senior relatives into the type of cases that was not applicable to justifiable defense was not approved. At the meeting held on January 8 afterward, the majority approved the article on illicit intercourse by mutual consent, but it was still suspended for the vote of it did not pass on January 9; there were too many bills to discuss with no time left for the article on January 10, and the meeting was closed before the topic was adopted again. On December 25, the Qing Court enacted *The New Criminal Code of the Great Qing Dynasty*, and all the recommendations on revision of it were pending for discussion in the following year.[59] Till then, all the efforts that the school of feudal ethics made for years with the purpose to revise *The New Criminal Code of the Great Qing Dynasty* ended up in vain because of an imperial decree. Their reputation also plunged. Various newspapers were sarcastically opposing the new Criminal Law.[60] After many twists and turns, the new criminal code which was guided by nationalism and distinct from the traditional law that embraced unity of rites and laws finally came into being.

The traditional Chinese legal philosophy centering upon the unity of rites and laws suffered unprecedented impacts during Shen Jiaben's revision of the criminal code, which paved the way for the renewal of China's legal concepts and the enhancement of people's awareness of the rule of law. It was for the first time that the new code reflected direct application of the Western legal concepts to China's legislative practice and the establishment of the modern legal model, which updated the traditional studies of legal texts to jurisprudence, and made jurisprudence a formal academic study and a significant element in the national political life. Shen Jiaben, who had made outstanding contributions in the process of revision of the criminal code, was named "the first go-between who made the Chinese legal system and western legal system unite in marriage" by Yang Honglie, a renowned expert in Chinese legal history.

There were three main features of the evolution of legal concepts in modern China. First, the modern legal concepts came into being in the process of criticizing

[59] *The Amendment to the New Criminal Code of the Great Qing Dynasty, Xin Xinglü Xiuzheng An Huilu* (Collections on *The Amendment to the New Criminal Code of the Great Qing Dynasty*).

[60] *The Amendment to the New Criminal Code of the Great Qing Dynasty.*

and absorbing Western legal concepts. Schools of legal thoughts presented diversity. The process of the evolution of legal concepts in modern China was virtually the process of confrontation between the Western legal concepts and the traditional Chinese legal concepts and the continuous transplantation of the Western legal concepts into the Chinese legal system. Second, the level of prudence in law exhibited a spiral upward trend with the deepening of the national crises. Every national crisis triggered deep thoughts of legal issues, and the latter innovation of the legal concepts was invariably generated upon the previous one. Third, the modern legal concepts were mainly generated by legal elites without extensive social foundation, led by the national fate and political movements of modern China. The urgent need for national salvation was prioritized over social enlightenment, so the extent of social enlightenment was rather limited. Due to the lack of an extensive social foundation, the democratic and legal consciousness of the ordinary people was not substantially awakened.

3.4.4 Repercussion of the Debate on Rites and Laws

3.4.4.1 The Foundation of the Resilience of Ritual Law

As the pillar of the traditional legal philosophy, the concepts of ritual law have lasted continuously for quite a long time, and the resilience of it is rare in the world. There are two main reasons as follows:

First, the ritual law system is supported by the traditional society and economics.

The patriarchal clan structure is the social foundation of the ritual system. Inside the patriarchal clan structure, the family or clan is the basic unit, the patriarchal spirit that features ethicized law and legalized ethics permeates everything, such as hierarchy of emperor and ministers, father, and son, the three cardinal guides and the five constant virtues, heavenly principles and human desires, filial piety and fraternal love, and loyalty and forgiveness, all guided by the patriarchal spirit. Maintaining stratification of upper and lower social classes is the main purpose of discussions on law by both Confucianists and legalists. Peoples' eating, clothing, housing, transportation, marriages, funerals, and interpersonal communication etiquettes and so on and so forth all need to comply with corresponding degrees beyond arrogation. In terms of the function of law, it emphasizes too much on the obligations of the people and ignores their personal rights, requires the people to obey the existing social order, and insists individuals should not be independent. This is reflected in the following examples: "if the king orders the minister to die, the minister must die"; children must be filial to their parents and parents have the right of the family property, the right to control their children's marriage, and the right of instructing their children, the five degrees of mourning system, the responsibility toward the country and family and self-cultivation, substitute of filial piety with loyalty to the country, etc. All these reflect the low status of individuals. The high status of senior relatives, the substitute of filial piety with loyalty to the country, the integration of nation and family, laws being orders from emperors, monarchial power being legal power, and so forth all have been the main fulcrum of the ritual law system. Legal ideas are developed during rounds of debates, suffocated in suppression, dependent upon whether the atmosphere of legal discussion is relaxed or not. The development of legal ideas has been negatively correlated with the rise and fall of autocratic politics: when centralization of power is relatively weak, legal ideas become active; when centralization of power is reinforced, legal ideas are kept from developing.

Second, the ritual law system is maintained by the traditional politics and culture.

The political model with power as the core and bureaucratic system are the political foundation of the ritual law system. In Chinese history, the strong autocracy and bureaucratic system with power at the core have stifled people's thoughts. The reform of legal philosophy cannot escape the control of the system and can only circulate within the system with the purpose to maintain the system. Reforms of the legal system are nothing more than mitigation of punishment, reducing the burden of corvee and taxation, expecting sober-minded emperors and upright officials, etc. which have not escaped the presented system track. The autocratic government has vigorously promoted moral instruction. The moral power based on Confucianism has always maintained the overall operation of the civil official system. As the institution is too mature, individual freedom is then restrained, not able to make the consciousness of Natural Rights and equality before the law advocated by the West deeply rooted in China.

The thinking model dominated by Confucianism and legalism is the cultural foundation of the ritual law system. The essence of Confucianism is conservative, hierarchical, ethical, and authoritarian. Though in different periods, Confucianism is treated in different ways; its trajectory within China's ideological landscape demonstrates a consistent ascent, progressively evolving into state orthodoxy that has shaped the national cognitive frameworks and governed the social conduct. Legalism and Confucianism are consistent in the pursuit of autocracy and play the role of maintaining the centralized political order together under the cover of Confucianism after the Han Dynasty without suffering too much blame. But at some critical moments, Confucianism becomes the object of criticism, especially in modern times: every enlightenment is accompanied by the criticism of Confucian ethics; it is true during the legal reform in the late Qing Dynasty and the May fourth Movement.

3.4.4.2 Awkward Separation Between Rites and Laws

The abnormity of Chinese social transformation in modern times lies in the coercion of the outside. The transformation of Chinese legal philosophy is the result of gradual transformation of Chinese social transformation as well as the coercion from the Western powers: the West seized the "extraterritorial jurisdiction" in China through unequal treaties. To reclaim judicial sovereignty, China had to revise the traditional laws. The question lay in the standard, which was undoubtedly determined by the Western powers. But jurists were not very sure about which Western standard to adopt. In the urgent situation, they randomly selected Western legal concepts wherever they deemed suitable for China and preserved some local legal concepts simultaneously. Thus, the modern Chinese legal system was born.

The modernization of China is a passive process by nature, coerced into the modernization vortex. Law, as a part of politics, has naturally embarked on the same path. Legal elites have come to be awaken under the political and social pressure, review the traditional Chinese legal model, and contact the foreign legal ideas. In the whole trend of political modernization, the modernization of China's legal system is arguably a "tide rider." In the judicial practice, due to the lack of the coordinated social environment, the legal system is often deformed in practice, which does not result from the legal system itself but from the restriction of politics, economics, and public consciousness of the whole society. The transformation of the legal system from traditional to modern times is realized under the pressure of national salvation and restoration of sovereignty, a movement that is not active enough but excessively passive.

Law guides social development while social development determines the future direction of law. Modern philosophers have produced many insightful arguments on the relationship between the two. Montesquieu pointed out in *The Spirit of the Laws* that "the law drafted for the people of one country should be very suitable for the people of that country." "Law should have relation to the degree of liberty which the constitution will bear; to the religion of the inhabitants, to their inclinations, riches, population, commerce, manners, and customs."[61] In short, law should be developed in harmony with politics, society, and customs. Renowned jurists or legal sociologists such as Durkheim, Henri Lévy-Bruhl, and others also argued that law is as dynamic and diverse as social groups and it more or less expresses the will of social groups; it is the reflection of social life like language, art, religion, etc. Law can never be separated from the social phenomena closely related to it.[62] They all regard law as the reflection of the society and consider law should be "suitable" for people's social life.

Voltaire made an analogy while discussing law, "law is like our customs. People in Constantinople must wear Turkish robes, while in Paris they wear knee-length tunics." He also said, "Law and customs are not contradictory to each other. If customs are good enough, then law becomes useless."[63] Lao Naixuan, who never went abroad and was totally immersed in traditional Chinese culture all his life, clearly put forward his argument that customs is the mother of law in the discussion on the innovation of the legal system in the late Qing Dynasty:

[61] Montesquieu. (1994). *The Spirit of the Laws*. (Translated by Zhang Yanshen). The Commercial Press, 6–7.

[62] Henry Lévy-Bruhl.(1987). *Sociologie du droit*. (Translated by Xu Jun). Shanghai People's Publishing House, 98.

[63] Voltaire. (2008). *Philosophical Dictionary*. (Edited and translated by Xu Jianguo). Beijing Publishing House, 141–143.

Where is law derived from? From the form of government. Where is the form of government derived from? From the code of ethics. Where is the code of ethics derived from? From customs. Where is customs derived from? From the means of living. The means of living can mainly be classified into three categories: farming and sericulture, hunting and husbandry, industry and commerce.

Customs is the mother of law. If the law is not established upon customs, it is like the tenon not conforming to the mortise. China relies on farming and sericulture and therefore should be based on family disciplines; the north is dependent upon hunting and husbandry, so they need to adopt the rule of military law; Europe and America feature industry and commerce and hence they are in need of commercial law. If Chinese family disciplines are used to rule the north and the military law in the north is adopted to rule Europe and America, ordinary people are able to know the infeasibility of this kind of practice. Today, we plan to adopt the commercial law in Europe and America to rule China. Isn't it deemed malpractice? Law shall never be incompatible with the customs. It should be practiced for thousands of years and proved effective; however, only empty ideals and pure speculations are by no means helpful.

The jurisprudence of the so-called new law should reinforce what we used to protect, revising what is corruptive and improving its adaptability. There is no need to seek truth from the outside and actually the truth belongs here. Why should we be intimidated by others and abandon our own learning?

How should we reform our law today? The answer is to revise law and clarify it on the basis of familism and substantiate and develop it into nationalism step by step, and then we can double the achievements with half the efforts.[64]

In fact, customs and laws are not equivalent to each other. New customs can adapt to new law while old customs may be contradictory to new law; nevertheless, old customs cannot be used as an excuse to reject new law. However, at the beginning of the revision of laws in the late Qing Dynasty, the school of jurisprudence did not take the changes of the traditional Chinese social customs as the main rationale for legal revision. On the contrary, they overemphasized the importance of the abolishment of extraterritorial jurisdiction which was by nature a problem that could not be solved by law itself. The flaw of their argument was easily seized by the school of feudal ethics that then heavily attacked the school of jurisprudence. When the school of feudal ethics put forward the argument on the unchanging customs and habits of China, the school of jurisprudence failed to list the various phenomena of social life changes in time to refute the argument of the school of feudal ethics that social customs and habits remained constant from the ancient times, and accordingly, law should maintain the original appearance.

[64] Lao Naixuan. The Prelude to *Xin Xinglü Xiuzheng An Huilu* (Collections on *The Amendment to the New Criminal Code of the Great Qing Dynasty*); *Xin Xinglü Xiuzheng An Huilu* (Collections on *The Amendment to the New Criminal Code of the Great Qing Dynasty*) edited by Lao Naixuan; *Tongxiang Laoxiansheng Yigao* (Posthumous Manuscripts by Lao Naixuan from Tongxiang), Tongxiang Lushi Jiaokeben (proofread by Lu).

3.4.4.3 Repercussion of the Debate on Rites and Laws

The debate on rites and laws is the contention on the guiding principles of the legal code revision between the school of jurisprudence and the school of feudal ethics at the end of the Qing Dynasty. The focus of the debate centers upon how China should learn from the advanced legal culture in the world and maintain the traditional code of ethics and national customs simultaneously. In essence, the debate focuses on how to cope with the relationship between the advanced legal system introduced into China and the local social and culture traditions.

In modern China, masters in legal science came out in succession, such as Shen Jiaben, Wu Tingfang, Dong Kang, Wang Chonghui, and so on in earlier times and Wu Jingxiong, Wang Shijie, Zhou Gengsheng, Qian Duansheng, Yang Zhaolong, Zhang Junmai, and so forth in later times. Most of them are legal elites who have studied both home and abroad, accumulated a thorough knowledge of both Western and traditional Chinese legal science, and successfully established their academic reputation in the world legal academic community. In the process of introducing and formulating the modernized legal system, they made immeasurable contributions, but in terms of the way of adapting an advanced legal system to Chinese local society, they failed to work out a suitable strategy. In legal practice, if the transplanted legal texts cannot be compatible with the local conditions, then nobody could put forward a detailed solution. Only a few masters in legal science, after the introduction of the western legal system on a large scale, calmed down and began to reflect on the negative effects brought forth by the complete dependence on transplanting foreign laws and abandoning local legal traditions.

Dong Kang, a senior expert in the legal academic community, drew multiple lessons from the contempt of the legal tradition and ignorance of social reality during the transformation of the legal system in modern China. He summarized a bitter lesson from the past experiences: "all laws are contingent upon social conditions and societies are established upon national customs." Our legal system is based upon our oriental nation, which has endured retaining and reforming for successive dynasties. "Only laws related to international affairs should comply with the international conventions and the left should not." He commented on the revision of the legal code: "With explicit references to legal texts and books, the implicit guiding principles were destructive which triggered the debate between the old and new parties. Considering how fierce the contention used to be at present, it turns meaningless." "We adopted the continental law to reform our own law and then suffered blames of 'cutting the feet to fit the shoes' for long. We need to seize the right time to change the direction." Since the Republic of China was founded more than a decade ago, "the new legal system was implemented and case files were piled up. I began to realize the malpractice of adopting the continental legal system: the procedures were refined, and the process would stagnate, for law and customs ran in opposite directions. I visited Britain and America in the past and did field studies there that proved the argument was not misleading." Dong Kang also admitted that he used to be "the fiercest debater" against the code of ethics. After more than 30 years, he felt "his previous proposals were no more than digging up one's own fences and breaching one's own embankment. His sense of shame pushed him to repent what he did." His reflection resulted from his practice of the revision of laws for decades, his visits to the West, and his careful comparisons between the judicial practices of various countries. He clearly pointed out while revising the traditional laws, jurists discarded traditional things like a broken broom, thus losing the line of "inherited learning." In consequence, the more dense the law, the more disturbed the public. For example, civil cases settled in accordance with law only occupied no more than "one to two percent" in the past, while now, civil regulations have been perfected, various costs are rising, and the litigation process is prolonged. The judge at least fulfills his/her duty after the judgment of final instance, but "the people's pain is deepened." Therefore, advocating rites prioritized over laws, morality over penalty, and moderating laws with customs to reduce the number of lawsuits is not contradictory to judicial independence:

All in all, those which cannot be settled by rites should be covered by penalty. Penalty is the last resort, inferior to inculcation of rites. The legal talents we develop need to learn how to moderate laws with customs to attain the optimal state "free from litigation." If they only view law as a social ladder to reach a higher rank or a means to make money, it means we have missed the purpose of advocating judicial independence.[65]

After reflection, Dong Kang seems to return to the legal idea of "moderating laws with customs to attain the optimal state of no lawsuit" and "advocating the original purpose of judicial independence." This is not a setback of Dong Kang's legal philosophy; on the other hand, he has compared the legal system and the social reality witnessed how the judicial system and the social reality have parted and cautioned those who had ignored compatibility between law and society. However, it is rather a pity that Dong Kang was just a minority, inconsistent with the popular trend of earnestly imitating the West at that time. Most people were still content with transplanting Western legal systems mechanically.

At present, China still meets the contradiction between learning from the Western legal system and maintaining Chinese own characteristics in terms of legislation and justice. It is infeasible to either completely copy the Western legal system or to utterly stick to the traditions. How to find the optimal balance between the two rather than simply despise the tradition and look up to the West or indulge in self-admiration and reject advancement? It requires going beyond the cultural boundaries to make a highly wise answer. In this sense, the difficult problems that emerged during the debate between rites and laws a hundred years ago have not been completely solved. The discussion of the relationship between rites and laws in the new era will continue. The less developed countries should establish the consciousness of learning all the advanced laws and should not be complacent; in the process of learning, it is important to enlighten the legal consciousness of the public and promote the consciousness of the rule of law in the whole society. While learning

[65] Dong, K. (1925). Reflecting 13 years of judicial practice in the republic of China. *Law Quarterly*, (2)3; Dong, K. (1924). Summary of justice in the pre-treaty Qing Dynasty. *Law Quarterly*, (2)2; Dong, K. (1935). The judicial system in the pre-treaty Qing Dynasty. *Journal of Legal Studies*, (8)4.

advanced foreign legal cultures, attention should be paid to the inheritance of the excellent local legal cultural heritage. Legal reforms should synchronize with social reforms; otherwise, no matter how advanced the law is, it is difficult to take root, blossom, and bear fruit in the conservative and backward soil. The reform of the political system needs to provide conditions and a guarantee for the reform of the legal system; political democratization is the premise of legal modernization; politics should provide the necessary free atmosphere for the contention of legal concepts, to ensure the fair and efficient enforcement of laws.

Chapter 4
The Culture of a Legal System

Though the formation of legal systems in most countries and regions is much later than the emergence of laws, influenced by ethnic, national, and geographic factors, certain features of legal systems have already revealed themselves in early laws.

Historically, there were five major legal systems across the world, the imperial Chinese legal system, the Hindu legal system, the Islamic legal system, the Continental legal system, and the Anglo-American legal system, among which 中华法系*Zhonghua Faxi* (the imperial Chinese legal system) outlasted the other four and influenced all of East Asia.

Available evidence shows that the imperial Chinese legal system first appeared in pre-Qin days and was further developed during Qin and Han Dynasties. It then entered into a formative phase during Sui and Tang Dynasties before reaching perfection in Ming and Qing Dynasties.

In modern times, the Western legal concepts flooded into China, along with their merchandise, warships, and cannons. To maintain their dying regime, as well as abolish extraterritorial authority by foreign powers, the rulers of the waning Qing Dynasty were forced to introduce the Western legal system while overturning the imperial legal system, which resulted in the traditional Chinese legal system teetering on the brink of collapse.

When it comes to social norms, the public perception is that there should not be just one single set of norms in the world but a spectrum of norms ranging from laws enacted by rulers, moral standards, and social conventions to religious rules, sacred and ancestral teachings, clan and family rules, customary law, and articles of association and contracts, to name but a few.[1] In this chapter, the approach of exemplification is adopted to examine both the constituents of the imperial Chinese legal system and its evolution.

[1] Zhang, W. (2011). The Heaven Eye and the Scale-Different Symbols of Law in the Eyes of Chinese and Western Jurists, edited by *Chinese Legal History Society* and *Institute of History and Philology, Academia Sinica*. *Chinese Legal History*, 20: 196.

R. Zhang, *Traditional Legal Culture in China*, Understanding China,
https://doi.org/10.1007/978-981-95-4697-8_4

4.1 Evolution of the Legal System

In addition to legal code, which was the most significant form of imperial Chinese law, other forms of law also emerged in every dynasty. One of the earliest forms was imperial edicts, which consisted of *shi* (oaths), *mo* (plans), *gao* (announcements), *ming* (mandates), *yu* (orders), and *ling* (decrees). In a society ruled by man, imperial edicts, though not in written form, still had the force of law.

The Qin legal system encompassed *lü* (statutes), *ling* (decrees), *tingxingshi* (legal precedents), *weilizhidao* (a way of becoming a good official), and *falüwenda* (questions and answers on laws); the Han legal system comprised *lü*, *ling*, *ke* (rulings), and *bi* (comparisons); the Wei and Jin legal system added *ge* (regulations) and *shi* (specifications); the Sui and Tang legal system was built upon *lü*, *ling*, *ge*, and *shi*, and the Song law added *bianchi* (collections of imperial edicts), *duanli* (precedents), and *zhihui* (imperial edicts).

The legal system of Yuan Dynasty was dominated by *tiaoge* (itemized regulations) and *bianchi*. The Ming legal system included *dagao* (grand announcements), *zhizhang* (handbooks of government posts), *zuxun* (emperor's admonitions), *jili* (collected rites), *xian'gang* (regulations for the censorial system), *tiaoli* (regulations), and *shilei* (classified legal clauses). The Qing legal system added *shili* (general precedents), *zeli* (rules), *tiaoli*, and *zhangcheng* (articles of association).

4.1.1 The Emergence of the Legal System

Imperial Chinese jurisprudence exhibited dynamic legal pluralism, with each dynasty featuring its unique normative frameworks. The earliest legal frameworks consisted of刑*xing* (penal codes), such as *Yuxing* (*Penal code of Yu*) in the Xia Dynasty (2070–1600 BCE), *Tangxing* (*Penal Code of Tang*) in the Shang period (1600–1046 BCE),[2] and *Jiuxing* (*Nine Punishments*) and *Lüxing* (*Penal Code of Marquis Lü*) in the Western Zhou period (1046–771 BCE). In the Zhou Dynasty (1046–256 BCE), a system of rules dominated by礼*li* (rites) and 刑*xing* (punishments) began to take shape. While *li* is an overarching framework for all codes of conduct and regulations in the Zhou Dynasty, representing a system of moral cultivation, *xing* refers to corporal penalties imposed on offenders. As *li* was comprised of most laws (though not all of them) of Zhou Dynasty, it played an instrumental role in controlling society and people's behavior. It dealt with a wider range of subject matters than *xing* did.

In the Spring and Autumn period (770–476 BCE) and the Warring States period (475–221 BCE), *xing* played an increasingly crucial role in society. It was

[2]The Volume the Sixth Year during the Reign of Duke Zhao of Lu in the book *Commentary of Zuo* documented that "*Penal Code of Yu* was enacted amidst a turmoil during the Xia period while *Penal Code of Tang* was also enacted amidst a turmoil during the Shang period."

beginning from this period that the Imperial Chinese law was inclined to the nature of being mostly penal. Written laws were enacted at the end of the Spring and Autumn period, so the populace could observe them and oversee their enforcement. The State of Zheng's carvings of legal texts into bronze vessels and announcement of *Punishments Carved on Bamboos* as the state law and the State of Jin's completion of *Penal Code Carved on Tripods* marked the birth of written laws in Imperial China.

As the codification of written laws was quite favored by rulers in the Warring States period, newly established economic and political systems were also codified into the law. Xing was replaced by fa which became the official name for law. Produced by Li Kui (a legalist scholar during the Warring States period), Fajing (*Canon of Laws*) is considered to be China's first written law. Despite what the name suggests, the canon is a penal code for all its six chapters are about rules of punishment, as is recorded in *The Book of Jin: Chapter of Treaties on the Penal Law*.

Based on the belief that cracking down on crimes against law and order was the prerequisite of the rule of the state, Li Kui started to write the code on assault and the code on robbery. To provide guidance on how to punish suspected criminals, he then wrote the code on arrest and the code on incarcerated persons. The code on miscellaneous matters meted out punishments for a series of offenses, including deceitful behaviors, scaling city walls, gambling, men sleeping over at houses of non-related women, taking bribes, extravagant lifestyles, and breaking the hierarchical order.

The *Cannon of Laws* serves the needs of the kings to rule the state, so it is by nature a public law. Since the six chapters are all about rules of punishment, it is fair to say that it is in essence a penal code.

4.1.2 The Development of the Legal System

Li Kui's *Canon of Laws* served as the foundation for subsequent reforms of Shang Yang, an influential statesman in the Qin state who produced *Qin lü* (*Qin Statutes*) by revising and enriching the *Canon of Laws*. He transformed the six codes of the canon (i.e., the code on assault, code on robbery, code on incarcerated persons, code on arrest, code on miscellaneous matters, and code on the composition of judgments) into six statutes and added some new content into it based on the actual conditions in the Qin state. The *Shuihudi Bamboo Slips* recorded that there were over 30 titles of statutes in the state of Qin, and these statutes remained effective throughout Qin Dynasty, the first imperial empire in China established by the Qin state after its unification of the warring states in 221 BCE.

Based on the *Qin statutes*, Han Dynasty (the second imperial Chinese empire) enacted Jiuzhanglü (*Nine Chapter Statutes*), which comprised nine chapters, six of which were adapted from Shang Yang's six statutes, and the other three chapters regarding households, conscription, and livestock were produced by Xiao He, a high-ranking official in the early Western Han Dynasty.

The *Nine Chapter Statutes*, as the mainstay of the Han legal system, along with the Bangzhanglü (*Statutes on Ritual Propriety*) (in 18 chapters), Chao lü (*Statutes on Court Audiences*) (in 6 chapters), and Yuegonglü (*Statutes on Court Guards*) (in 27 chapters), formed the Han Code of 60 chapters. Some other statutes were also enacted in Han Dynasty, covering a wide range of topics including administration, economy, ceremony, and jurisdiction.

A scrutiny of the codification of both Qin and Han laws shows that statutes and other forms of law in the two dynasties were either codified laws or individually enacted laws. In the Qin Dynasty, forms of law included *lü* (statutes), *ming* (orders), *ling* (decrees), *zhi* (imperial decisions), *zhao* (imperial instructions), *cheng* (administrative norms), *shi* (procedural templates), *ke* (performance evaluations), *falüwenda* (questions and answers on laws), and *tingxingshi* (judicial precedents), while in the Han Dynasty, there were *lü*, *ling*, *ke*, *pin* (graded regulations), and *bi* (case analogies).

Legal codes in Qin Dynasty (221 BCE–207 BCE):

Statutes in the Qin Dynasty are divided into two categories, the codified Qin Statutes (in six chapters, that is, statutes on robbery, statutes on assault, statutes on incarcerated persons, statutes on arrest, statutes on miscellaneous matters, and statutes on the composition of judgments) and other individually enacted statutes, such as Statutes on Official Conduct (Zhililü), Statutes on Administrative Accountability (Xiao lü), Statutes on Food Rations at Conveyance Stations (Chuanshi lü), Statutes on the Transmission of Documents (Xingshulü), Miscellaneous Statutes Concerning the Ministry of Finance (Neishizalü), Statutes on Fiefs (Shubanglü), Statues on Dismissal of Officials (Chulilü), Statutes on Dismissed Retainers (Chudizilü), Statutes on Itinerant Functionaries (Youshilü), Statutes on Fields (Tian lü), Statutes on Livestock (Jiuyuanlü), Statutes on State Granaries (Cang lü), Statutes on Finance (Jinbulü), Statutes on Customs and Markets (Guanshilü), Statutes on Corvée Labor (Yao lü), Statutes on Property Ownership (Ji lü), Statutes on the Imperial Stables and Hunts (Gongchesimalie lü), Statutes on the State Treasury (Cang lü), Statutes on Conscription Registration (Fu lü), Statutes on Military Ranks (Junjuelü), Statutes on Military Services (Zhonglaolü), Statutes on Garrison Soldiers (Shu lü), Statutes on Frontier Defenses (Tunbiaolü), Miscellaneous Statutes of the Commandant (Weizalü), Statutes on Artisans (Gong lü), Statutes on Artisan Quotas (Jungonglü), and Statutes on Conscripted Labor (Sikonglü).[3]

Qin decrees include Decrees on Burning Books (Fenshu ling), Decrees on Fields (Tian ling), and Decrees on Collective Liability (Lianzuo ling).[4]

Enacted in parallel with statutes and decrees were norms [Personnel Norms on Artisans (Gongrencheng)], models [Models for Litigation and Trial (Fengzhenshi)], evaluations [Evaluations on Raising of Cattle and Sheep (Niuyangke)], imperial orders [Speech Documents (Yu shu)], and Questions and Answers on Laws.

Legal codes in the Han Dynasty (206 BCE–220 CE):

---

[3] *Shuihudi Bamboo Texts*.

[4] *Shuihudi Bamboo Texts*, and Volume 6 "Biography of Emperor Qinshihuang" and Volume 87 "Biography of Politician Lisi" in the book *Records of the Grand Scribe*.

Statutes in Han Dynasty consist of (1) codified statutes, Nine Chapter Statutes (Jiuzhanglü), Statutes on Ritual Proprieties (Bangzhanglü) (in 18 chapters), Statutes on Court Audiences (Chao lü) (in 6 chapters), Statutes on Court Guards (Yuegonglü) (in 27 chapters), and Statutes and Decrees of the Second Year (Ernianlüling) (in 28 chapters during the reign of Empress Lü), and (2) individually enacted miscellaneous statutes, Statutes on Rites and Music (Dayuelü), Statutes on the Commandant of Justice (Wei lü), Statutes on the Annual Forwarding of Accounts (Shangjilü), Statutes on Paying Gold Tribute (Zhoujinlü), Statutes on Cash (Qian lü), Statutes on Fields (Tian lü), Statutes on Agricultural Fields Taxes (Tianzushuilü), Statutes Concerning Officials Charged With Wrongdoings (Zuoguanlü), and Statutes on the Concealment of Books (Jiashulü).[5]

There are four types of decrees:

(a) Named by ordinal (collectively codified): Decrees A, Decrees B, and Decrees C.
(b) Named by administrative divisions (collectively codified): Decrees on the Essential Points for the Commandery of Lelang (Lelang qieling) and Decrees on the Essential Points for the Northern Border (Beibian qieling).
(c) Named by officer titles (collectively codified): Decrees on the Essential Points for the Chamberlain for Attendants (Guanglu qieling), Decrees on the Essential Points for the Chief Justice (Tingwei qieling) (carved on planks), Decrees on the Essential Points for the Chief Justice (Tingwei qieling) (written), Decrees on the Essential Points for the Chamberlain for Dependencies (Dahonglu qieling), and Decrees on the Essential Points for Royal Scribes (Yushi qieling).
(d) Named by subject matters (mostly individually enacted): on management of officers [Decrees Concerning Officers' Salaries (Zhilu ling), Decrees Concerning the Palace's Boundary Gates (Gongwei ling), Decrees on the Selection of Officers (Pin ling), Decrees on the Appointment of Sons (Renzi ling), Decrees Concerning the Granting of Leave (Yugao ling), Decrees on the Selection and Evaluation of Scholars (Gong ling), and Decrees on Bribery (Shousuojianlin ling)]; on economy [Decrees on Fields (Tian ling), Decrees on Waterworks (Shui ling), Decrees on Horses (Mafu ling), Decrees on Finance (Jinbu ling), and Decrees Concerning Strung Cash (Minqian ling)]; on ritual proprieties [Decrees Concerning Sacrifices (Cisi ling) and Decrees Concerning Fasting (Zhai ling)]; on military affairs [Decrees on Garrison Conscripts (Shuzu ling), Decrees on the Major of the Gate Traffic Control Office (Gongchesima ling) and Decrees on the Sale of Offices (Maijue ling)]; on judicial matters [Decrees on Prisons (Yu ling) and Decrees on Proceedings (Yanyu ling)]; and on care for pregnant women and senior subjects [Decrees on Pregnancy (Taiyang ling) and Decrees on Care for the Elderly (Yanglao ling)].

---

[5] *Book of Han: Chapter of Treaties on Penal Law*, *Book of Jin: Chapter of Treaties on the Penal Law*, *Zhangjiashan Bamboo Texts*, *Book of Han: Biography of Emperor Zhao*, *Comments to Rites of Zhou: Chapter of Spring Offices Regulators of Chariots*, *Continued Book of Han: Chapter of Rites*, *Records of the Grand Scribe: List of Chief Officers*, *Book of Han: List of Dukes*, and *Book of Han: Biography of Emperor Hui*.

Lists of rules include the List of Ritual Proprieties (Yi pin), List of Equipment for Defense (Shouyuqipin), List of Conscripted Labor for Convicts (Fuzuo pin), List of Redemption (Shu pin), and List of Agreed-upon Fire Signals Atop Frontier Defenses (Fenghuo pin).

Rulings include the Rulings on Harboring Criminals (Shounike), Rulings on the Granting of Bereavement Leave for Officers (Ninggaoke), Rulings on Fugitives (Wangtaoke), Rulings on Heads of Household Registry (Yizike), and Rulings on Public Executions of Criminals Charged with Menacing (Toushuqishike).[6]

The legal codes mentioned above are by no means an exhaustive list of all the legal codes enacted in Qin and Han Dynasties, as legal systems in the two dynasties included highly sophisticated categories, structures, and subject matters. For example, Han Dynasty issued both codified and individually enacted miscellaneous statutes, most of the latter focusing on single subject matters. Specifically, the Statutes on Rites and Music governed matters that related to temple sacrifices and the inauguration of officers, while the Statutes on Fields governed agricultural activities and fields taxes.

As an important form of law second to statutes, decrees were either enacted individually or in codified form, based on their different structures and substance.[7]

4.1.3 The Maturity of the Legal System

Historical records document that hundreds of new decrees, including Decrees for Regions and Commanderies (Zhoujun ling) (in 45 chapters), Decrees for the Office of the Imperial Secretariat (Shangshuguan ling), and Decrees for the Army (Junzhong ling) (approximately 180 chapters), were issued in parallel with the New Statutes (Xin lü) (in 18 chapters) in the Wei Kingdom. Jin Dynasty recorded more than 2306 articles of decrees that continued in effect in the later Liu Song and Southern Qi periods of the Southern Dynasties. While the Liang and Chen periods produced 30 volumes of decrees, the Northern Qi introduced a 40-volume New Decrees (Xin ling) and a 2-volume Supplementary Decrees (Quan ling). Sui Dynasty published the Kaihuang Code (Kaihuanglü) and Decrees of the Daye Era (Daye Ling) (both in 30 volumes). Tang Dynasty witnessed frequent revisions of previous decrees and codes, as well as the creation of new legal texts, among which the Decrees of the Zhenguan Era (Zhenguan Ling) (in 30 volumes with more than 1590 articles) is the best-known. The following are some of the most important statutes and decrees.

Legal codes in the Wei Kingdom:

[6]Yang, Y. (2002). A Major Misunderstanding in the Imperial Chinese Legal System Research Work: Questions on the Theory Advocating the Dominance of Penal Law over Civil Law and Blurry Boundaries Between All Fields of Law. *Social Sciences in China*, 78–94.

[7]Yang, Y. (2002). *Rethought on the Imperial Legal System*and*Criticism and Reconstruction: A Reflection on the Research of Chinese Legal History*. Law Press.

The New Statutes was organized in the following 18 chapters: (1) statutes on criminal punishments, (2) statutes on robbery, (3) statutes on intimidation and kidnapping, (4) statutes on assault, (5) statutes on fraud and deceit, (6) statutes on damage and loss, (7) statutes on accusations and impeachments, (8) statutes on detention and interrogation, (9) statutes on judgments and prison, (10) statutes on soliciting of bribes, (11) statutes on unauthorized conscription levies, (12) statutes on matters left undone, (13) statutes on emergencies, (14) statutes on the restoration of illicit goods, (15) statutes on households, (16) statutes on arrest, (17) statutes on miscellaneous matters, and (18) statutes on exemption of collective liability.[8]

Decrees include Decrees for Regions and Commanderies (in 45 chapters) and Decrees for the Office of the Imperial Secretariat and Decrees for the Army (in about 180 chapters).

Legal codes in Jin Dynasty (265–317 CE):

Jin Code was organized in 20 chapters: (1) statutes on criminal punishments, (2) statutes on rules of application of criminal punishments, (3) statutes on theft, (4) statutes on robbery, (5) statutes on fraud and counterfeit, (6) statutes on soliciting bribes, (7) statutes on accusations and impeachments, (8) statutes on arrest, (9) statutes on detention and interrogation, (10) statutes on judgments and prison, (11) statutes on miscellaneous matters, (12) statutes on households, (13) statutes on unauthorized conscription levies, (14) statutes on damage and loss, (15) statutes on court guards, (16) statutes on flood and fire relief, (17) statutes on livestock, (18) statutes on passes and markets, (19) statutes on disobeying regulations, and (20) statutes on feudal lords.

Jin Decrees (Jin ling) had a total of 40 chapters organized as follows: (1) households, (2) schooling, (3) gongshi (nominees for offices), (4) official ranks, (5) government officers, (6) salary standards, (7) dress codes, (8) sacrifices, (9) poll taxes, (10) agricultural fields, (11) exemption from taxes and conscripted labor, (12) passes and markets, (13) arrests and fugitives, (14) prison officers, (15) floggings, (16) medicine and illness, (17) funerals, (18) miscellaneous matters (I), (19) miscellaneous matters (II), (20) miscellaneous matters (III), (21) cavaliers under the Chancellery and the Palace Secretariat, (22) the Imperial Secretariat, (23) the secretaries under the Censorate, the Outer Bureau, and the Intermediate Bureau, (24) feudal lords, (25) military officers, (26) the selection of officers, (27) the selection of military generals, (28) the selection of miscellaneous scholars, (29) court guards, (30) redemption matters, (31) the army and ground warfare, (32) the navy and naval warfare, (33–38) military affairs; and (39–40) miscellaneous decrees.

Legal codes in Sui Dynasty (581–618 CE):

Kaihuang Code was organized in 12 chapters: (1) definitions and general principles, (2) imperial guards and prohibitions, (3) administrative regulations, (4) household and marriage, (5) stables and storehouses, (6) unauthorized conscription

[8] *Six Statutes of Tang Dynasty* and *Treaties on the Penal Law of All Dynasties*. The General Public Press. 1988.

levies, (7) theft and violence, (8) assaults and accusations, (9) fraud and deceit, (10) miscellaneous matters, (11) arrests and fugitives, and (12) judgments and prison.

Kaihuang Decrees (Kaihuang ling) comprised 30 volumes: (1) official ranks (I); (2) official ranks (II); (3) officers in government agencies; (4) officers in charge of all courts; (5) officers in charge of imperial procession guards; (6) officers in the Eastern Palace; (7) officers in charge of outer branches of the Imperial Secretariat; (8) officers in prefectures, commanderies, counties, townships, and garrisons; (9) noblewomen; (10) sacrifices; (11) households; (12) schooling; (13) the selection of government officials; (14) bestowal of noble titles and salary standards; (15) the annual evaluation of officials; (16) court guards and the military defense; (17) dress codes; (18) the imperial entourage (I); (19) the imperial entourage (II); (20) ritual proprieties; (21) writing of government documents (I); (22) writing of government documents (II); (23) agricultural fields; (24) taxes and corvee labor,;(25) granaries and livestock; (26) passes and markets; (27) the granting of leave; (28) prison officers; (29) funerals; and (30) miscellaneous matters.

Legal codes in Tang Dynasty (618–907 CE):

The traditional Chinese law was getting increasingly mature during Tang Dynasty as the forms and structures of law became highly standardized. There were four major forms of law: lü (statutes), ling (decrees), ge (regulations), and shi (specifications). As stated in the sixth volume of the Tang liudian (Six Statutes of Tang Dynasty), "Statutes are issued to determine punishments of crimes, and decrees to establish hierarchy and administrative rules. Regulations are provisional edicts issued by emperors to clamp down on evildoing, and specifications are detailed rules governing state affairs and writing of government documents."[9]

To be more specific, statutes applied exclusively to criminal offenses and served to determine crimes and punishments, while decrees established hierarchy and specified administrative rules. Regulations represented collections of provisional imperial decrees and edicts issued by emperors to decide particular cases. Specifications are detailed rules for managing state affairs and writing official documents.[10] Complicated and massive as the imperial decrees and edicts were, there might be circumstances where similar cases ended up with different rulings. To address this concern, the Three Departments and Six Ministries of Tang Dynasty would periodically codify regulations, which became known as "fixed regulations" (yongge). Regulations were classified as either "sanbange" (universal regulations) or "liusige" (exclusive regulations) in terms of the scope of their application. Universal regulations were applied to the general public and exclusive regulations to government officials.

Statutes and decrees enacted in Tang Dynasty included Statutes of the Wude Era, Statutes of the Zhenguan Era, the Yonghui Code, Decrees of the Wude Era, Decrees of the Zhenguan Era, Decrees of the Yonghui Era, and Decrees of the Kaiyuan Era. Regulations included First Regulations of the Zhenguan Era (in 7 volumes), Later

[9]Volume 6 "The Ministry of Justice" in the book *Six Statutes of Tang Dynasty*.

[10]Penal Law in the Volume 56 in the book *Xin Tang Shu* (*New Book of Tang*).

Regulations of the Zhenguan Era (in 18 volumes), Exclusive Regulations of the Yonghui Era (in 18 volumes), Universal Regulations of the Yonghui Era (in 7 volumes), Exclusive Regulations of the Chuigong Era (in 6 volumes), Universal Regulations of the Chuigong Era (in 3 volumes), Universal Regulations of the Shenlong Era (in 3 volumes), Imperial Regulations of the Taiji Period (in 10 volumes), First Regulations of the Kaiyuan Era (in 10 volumes), New Regulations of the Kaiyuan Era (in 10 volumes), and Later Regulations of the Kaiyuan Era (in 10 volumes). Specifications were Specifications of the Wude Era (in 14 volumes), Specifications of the Zhenguan Era (in 33 volumes), Specifications of the Yonghui Era (in 14 volumes), Specifications of the Chuigong Era (in 20 volumes), Specifications of the Shenlong Era (in 20 volumes), and Specifications of the Kaiyuan Era (in 20 volumes).

Statutes, decrees, regulations, and specifications were applied nationally during Tang Dynasty.[11] While statutes were mostly penal and decrees were administrative rules, specifications were created to ensure the enforcement of statutes and decrees, and regulations were largely revisions and amendments to statutes, decrees, and specifications. The four forms of law constituted integral parts of the Tang legal system, each playing an indispensable as well as supplementary role and acting as the backbone of the Imperial Chinese Legal System which exerted especially great influence over the whole East Asia.

The following are details of some of the most important legal codes.

The Yonghui Code with Commentaries (Yonghuilüshu), historically known as Tang Code with Commentaries, offered detailed explanations on every article of the Yonghui Code (Yonghuilü) which consists of 30 volumes arranged in the following 12 chapters: (1) general principles, (2) the imperial guards and prohibitions, (3) administrative regulations, (4) households and marriages, (5) public stables and warehouses, (6) unauthorized conscription levies, (7) theft and robbery, (8) assaults and accusations, (9) fraud and counterfeit, (10) miscellaneous matters, (11) arrests and escapes, and (12) judgments and prison.

The Decrees of the Kaiyuan Era (Kaiyuan ling) comprised 1546 articles that were grouped in 33 chapters. The titles were (1) official ranks (I, II); (2) the three preceptors, the three dukes, and officers of the department of state affairs; (3) supervisors of the courts; (4) guards in the generals' residences; (5) officers in the Eastern Palace and the princely residences; (6) officers in prefectures, counties, townships, garrisons, prisons, canals, passes, and fords; (7) noblewomen; (8) sacrifices; (9) households; (10) the selection of government officials; (11) the annual evaluation of officials; (12) the imperial palace and guards; (13) the military defense; (14) dressing codes; (15) ritual proprieties; (16) the imperial entourage (I, II); (17) writing of government documents (I, II); (18) agricultural fields; (19) taxes and corvee labor; (20) warehouses; (21) livestock; (22) passes and markets; (23) medicine and illness; (24) prison officers; (25) civil engineering; (26) funerals; (27) miscellaneous

[11] Penal Law in the Volume 50 "Zhi" in the book *Jiu Tang Shu* (*Old Book of Tang*).

matters; (28) schooling; (29) bestowal of noble titles; (30) salary standards; (31) music; (32) arrests and escapes; and (33) the granting of leave.[12]

The Regulations of Tang Dynasty (Tang ge) comprised 24 chapters that were named after state offices. The titles of the chapters were (1) the Ministry of Personnel, (2) the Bureau of Honors, (3) the Bureau of Rewards, (4) the Bureau of Evaluations, (5) the Ministry of Revenue, (6) the Bureau of Taxes, (7) the Bureau of Treasury, (8) the Bureau of Granaries, (9) the Ministry of Rites, (10) the Ministry of Sacrifices, (11) the Bureau of Catering, (12) the Bureau of Receptions, (13) the Ministry of War, (14) the Bureau of Territories, (15) the Bureau of Equipment, (16) the Bureau of Arsenals, (17) the Ministry of Justice, (18) the Criminal Administration Bureau, (19) the Bureau of Review, (20) the Bureau of Customs, (21) the Ministry of Works, (22) the Bureau of Agrarian Colonies, (23) the Bureau of Forestry, and (24) the Bureau of Water.

Specifications (Shi) issued in the Kaiyuan era had a total of 33 chapters, 24 titles of which were the same as those of Tang ge, while the 9 nine were (1) the Palace Library, (2) the Court of Imperial Sacrifices, (3) the Court of National Granaries, (4) the Court of Imperial Entertainments, (5) the Court of Imperial Carriages and Horses, (6) the Court of Imperial Treasury, (7) the Directorate for Imperial Manufactories, (8) the Imperial Bodyguard, and (9) the Accounting.

Codified by a team of state officials, the Six Statutes of Tang Dynasty (Tang liudian), an administrative law by nature, was a detailed compendium of central state offices and their evolution, including the Three Preceptors, the Three Dukes, the Department of State Affairs, the Ministry of Personnel, the Ministry of Revenue, the Ministry of Rites, the Ministry of War, the Ministry of Justice, the Ministry of Works, and the Department of Chancellery.

Legal codes in Song Dynasty (960–1279 CE):

The Penal Code of Song Dynasty (Song xingtong) was organized into 12 chapters: (1) definitions and general principles, (2) imperial guards and prohibitions, (3) administrative regulations, (4) household and marriage, (5) stables and storehouses, (6) unauthorized conscription levies, (7) theft and violence, (8) assaults and accusations, (9) fraud and deceit, (10) miscellaneous matters, (11) arrests and fugitives, and (12) judgments and prison.

Decrees:

The Tiansheng Decrees (Tiansheng ling) had 30 volumes in total, yet only the last 10 volumes survived: (21) decrees on fields, (22) decrees on tax and corvee, (23) decrees on warehouses, (24) decrees on livestock, (25) decrees on passes and markets, (26) decrees on curing illness, (27) decrees on the administration of prisons, (28) decrees on civil engineering, (29) decrees on funeral and burial, and (30) miscellaneous matters. The Clauses from the Legal System of the Ministry of Personnel (Libutiaofa) is a decree about the recruitment and management of officials in Southern Song Dynasty (1127–1279 CE), covering the appointment of local

[12] Noboru, N. (1989). *Toryo shui* (*Addenda and Corrigenda to the Remnants of Tang Decrees*). Changchun Press.

officers by the Ministry of Personnel (chaizhu), appointment by recommendation (zoupi), appointment through imperial examination (kaoren), the management of Buddhist Temples and Taoist abbeys (gongguanmiao), official performance records (yinzhi), recommendation and promotion (jianju), promotions (guansheng), changing office (gaiguan), and performance review (mokan).[13]

Bianchi (collections of imperial edicts) are collections of regularly compiled imperial rulings with legally binding effect. Song Dynasty issued over 80 collections of imperial edicts. In fact, imperial edicts and statutes worked in parallel as two legal forms of Song Dynasty, with the former taking precedence over the latter in terms of applicability. This order of applicability was observed in Song Dynasty ever since it was first specified in the Penal Code of Song Dynasty (Song Xingtong):

Any criminal case shall be decided in accordance with articles from lü (statutes), ling (decrees), ge (regulations), shi (decrees), and bianchi (collections of imperial edicts). If applicable articles can be found in collections of imperial edicts, the case shall be decided in accordance with collections of imperial edicts. If no applicable articles can be found in collections of imperial edicts, the case shall be decided in accordance with ge (regulations). If no applicable articles can be found in ge, the case shall be decided in accordance with lü (statutes).[14]

Duanli (precedents): court decisions based on previous rulings. Precedents played a significant role in deciding cases in Song Dynasty. They were important supplements to or sometimes substitutions for written law.

Zhihui (imperial edicts): issued by the Imperial Secretariat (Shangshu sheng) and given to its six subordinate ministries, including the Ministry of Personnel, the Ministry of Revenue, and the Ministry of Justice.

Tiaoli (regulations): a collection of regulations issued or approved by the emperors.

Tiaofa Shilei (classified legal clauses): including edicts, decrees, and specifications. The classified legal clauses effective in the Qingyuan era (Qingyuan Tiaofa Shilei) offer a good example. The surviving parts of it covered the following topics: officialdom, recruitment of officials, documentary processes, proscribed and monopolized goods, finance, warehouse management, agriculture and sericulture, Buddhists and Taoists, clerks, criminal justice, sumptuary and ritual affairs, tribal groups, livestock raising, and miscellaneous matters.

4.1.4 The Perfection of the Legal System

Legal codes and forms of law in Yuan Dynasty (1271–1368 CE):

---

[13] *The Rehabilitated Ming Copy of Tensheng Decrees*. Beijing: Zhonghua Book Company, 2006. The copy is housed at Tianyige Museum.

[14] Volume 30 "Statutes on Deciding Legal Cases: Order of Applicable Statutes, Decrees, Regulations and Specifications" in the book *Penal Code of Song Dynasty*.

Tiaoge (legislative articles): a collection of emperors' edicts or administrative decrees issued by emperors or central governments to lower-level departments, covering a wide range of topics including civil affairs, administration, and finance.

Duanli (precedents): precedents cited from previous emperors' or judges' rulings, most of which were about criminal cases. Duanli were not as formal as written law in wording as they were usually provisional decrees or previous rulings.

The legal system of the Mongol Empire was dominated by customary law, while after its founding of Yuan Dynasty, the rulers began to enact written laws. The most important legal codes of Yuan Dynasty are as follows:

The New Code of the Zhiyuan Era (Zhiyuan Xinge) is a comprehensive legal code with administrative law as the mainstay issued by Kublai Khan, the Emperor Shizu of Yuan. It is the first written law of Yuan Dynasty.

The Comprehensive Regulations of the Great Yuan Dynasty (Dayuantongzhi) is a collection of regulations issued by Gegeen Khan, the fifth emperor of Yuan Dynasty. Adapted from the statutes of Tang and Song Dynasties, it consists of zhaozhi (imperial edicts), tiaoge (legislative articles), duanli (precedents), and bielei (categorized articles), four essential forms of law during Yuan Dynasty.

The Itemized Regulations of the Zhizheng Era (Zhizhengtiaoge) is a comprehensive administrative code issued during the reign of Emperor Shun. The code, consisting of zhaozhi, tiaoge, and duanli, was a supplement to the Dayuantongzhi.

The Statutes of Yuan Dynasty (Yuan Dianzhang) was a collection of laws compiled from the beginning to mid-Yuan, coproduced by local officers and private publishing houses. For a long period of Yuan Dynasty did not enact any code, their administrative and judicial practices were largely based on past regulations, decrees, and precedents. As the quantity of those documents increased, however, it became necessary to collect, categorize, and compile them for more convenient reference. This was the purpose of compiling the Yuan Dianzhang, which falls into eight categories: state laws, court principles, the Ministry of Personnel, the Ministry of Revenue, the Ministry of Rites, the Ministry of War, the Ministry of Works, and the Ministry of Justice. As a supplement to the official historical documents, the civil and criminal cases cataloged in Yuan Dianzhang provide an insight into disputes in daily life in Yuan Dynasty.[15]

Legal codes in Ming Dynasty (1368–1644 CE):

The Great Ming Code (Daminglü) is a penal code enacted in 1398 (the 30th year during the reign of Emperor Hongwu). The Code consists of 30 volumes with 460 articles. It falls into seven parts: general provisions, personnel, revenue, rituals, military affairs, penal affairs, and public works.

The Imperial Statutes and Announcements (Qindinglügao) consists of 147 articles on capital offence, including 111 articles from the Great Ming Code (102 on

[15] *Preface to the Statutes of Yuan Dynasty*. Tianjin Classics Press. 2011.

irredeemable conditions and 9 on redeemable conditions) and 36 announcements (12 on irredeemable conditions and 24 on redeemable conditions).[16]

The Grand Ming Pronouncement (Ming dagao) is a collection of 236 imperial decrees issued by Emperor Hongwu. It consists of Dagao Yibian (Grand Pronouncements), Dagao Xubian (Supplement to the Grand Pronouncements), Dagao Sanbian (Further Supplement to the Grand Pronouncements), and Dagao Wuchen (Grand Pronouncements to Military Officials).

The *Handbook of Government Posts* (Zhusizhizhang) specifies the roles and duties of the six ministries (viz., the Ministry of Personnel, the Ministry of Revenue, the Ministry of Rites, the Ministry of War, the Ministry of Justice, the Ministry of Works), the Censorate, the Court of Judicial Review, and other government agencies.

The Great Ming Decrees consists of decrees on personnel, decrees on revenue, decrees on rites, decrees on war, decrees on justice, and decrees on works.

Tiaoli (regulations): Regulations on Judicial Interrogation (Wenxingtiaoli), first issued during the reign of Emperor Hongzhi and revised during the reign of Emperor Jiajing and Emperor Wanli, Regulations on Military Exile (Chongjuntiaoli), Regulations on Capital Crimes by Descending Degrees (Zhenfanzafansizuitiaoli), and Code of the Great Ming With Collected Commentaries and Appended Substatutes (Daminglüjijiefuli), which is the first legal code that included both statutes and regulations.

The Collected Statutes of Ming Dynasty (Daminghuidian): a collection of official statutes of Ming Dynasty. It introduces the administrative system of Ming Dynasty and the duties of all its administrative bodies, including the Court of the Imperial Clan, the Ministry of Personnel, the Ministry of Revenue, the Ministry of Rites, the Ministry of War, the Ministry of Justice, the Ministry of Works, and the Censorate.

Zhuanmenguizhang (special laws): Information on Heads of Circuits in Charge of Collecting Taxes, Revised Regulations on Taxes and Corvee (Chongdingfuyichenggui), Imperial Orders on Officials Who Fail In Their Duties of Collecting Taxes (Cuizhengqianliangjiangfashili), Regulations on Salt Trade (Yanfatiaoli), Articles of Encouraging Private Donations for Public Projects (Released by the Ministry of Public Works), Information on Factories and Storehouses of the Ministry of the Public Works (Gongbuchangkuxuzhi), and Regulations on Tribute Grain Transport (Caoyunyidan).

Jiaominbangwen (Proclamation of Instructions for the People): minor disputes such as fights, quarrels, or those related to households, marriage, and fields shall be decided by the village elder or the Lijia, the lowest administrative level in Ming Dynasty. Serious incidents such as rape, theft, fraud, and life-threatening cases shall be reported to law enforcement officers.

Legal codes in Qing Dynasty (1636–1912 CE):

---

[16]Yang, Y. (1984). *An Examination of Severe Punishments in the Early Ming Dynasty*. Hunan People's Publishing House 9.

Lüli (statutes and regulations): Statutes of the Great Qing with Collected Commentaries and Appended Substatutes (Daqing lüjijiefuli) and the Great Qing Code (Daqing lüli). The latter (based on the structure of Daminglü) includes both statutes and regulations. Issued in 1740 (the fifth year of the reign of Emperor Qianlong), the code was the best example of having statutes and regulations in one. It was revised on a regular basis and continued in effect until 1911. It is a landmark code representing that the Imperial legal system reached perfection.

Zeli (regulations and rules): Administrative Regulations of the Six Ministries (the Ministry of Personnel, the Ministry of Revenue, the Ministry of Rites, the Ministry of War, the Ministry of Justice, the Ministry of Works), Regulations and Rules of the Court of Imperial Clan (Zongrenfu Zeli), Regulations and Rules of the Grand Secretariat (Neige Zeli), Regulations and Rules of the Court of Colonial Affairs (Lifanyuan Zeli), Regulations of the Ministry of Personnel for the Selection and Appointment of State Officials (Libuquanxuan Zeli), Regulations and Administrative Punishments for the Board of Civil Officials (Libuchufen Zeli), Regulations and Rules of the Bureau of Appointments (Yanfengsi Zeli), Regulations and Rules of the Bureau of Records (Jixunsi Zeli), Laws on Supervision and Arrest (Dubu Zeli), Regulations and Rules of the Eight Banners (Baqi Zeli), Regulations and Rules of the Green Standard Army (Lüying Zeli), Weapons and Military Equipment Regulations (Junqi Zeli), and Complete Book on School Administration (Xuezhengquanshu).

Huidian (jurisdictional corpus on administrative affairs): Collected Statutes of the Great Qing was revised five times, during the reigns of Emperor Kangxi, Emperor Yongzheng, Emperor Qianlong, Emperor Jiaqing, and Emperor Guangxu. The versions issued during the reigns of Emperor Qianlong and Emperor Jiaqing were called Huidianzeli, and the version issued during the reign of Emperor Guangxu called Huidianshili.

Tiaoli (regulations): Regulations of Government Departments and Imperially Commissioned Examinations Regulations.

Lizhi (rites): Comprehensive Rites of the Great Qing (Daqing tongli) and Illustrated Regulations for Ceremonial Paraphernalia of Qing Dynasty (Huangchaoliqitushi).

Zhuanmenguizhang (special laws): Imperially Endorsed Compendium of Educational Administration (Qindingxuezhengquanshu), Complete Tax Registers (Fuyiquanshu), A Complete Book on Tax Exemption (Fuhuiquanshu), and A Complete Book of the Grain Tribute Transport (Hubucaoyunquanshu).

Zhaoling (imperial instruction): Imperial Rules for Learning, Sacred Edicts of the Kangxi Emperor (Yuzhixuegui), Sixteen Maxims (Shengyushiliutiao), Sacred Edicts (Shengyuguangxun), Essentials of Prefectural and County [Government] (Zhouxiantigang), and Guidelines on Local Administration (Qinbanzhouxianshiyi).

Shengli (provincial regulations): Armed Feuds Prevention Regulations (Jiangxi Province), Brigands Prevention Regulations (Caozhou Prefecture and Yanzhou Prefecture), Sworn Brothers Prevention Regulations (Sichuan Province and Shaanxi Province), and Kidnapping and Extortion Prevention Regulations (Guangdong Province and Guangxi Province).

Most of the extant legal codes from Ming and Qing Dynasties pertain to crimes, administration, economy, military affairs, and rites, with hundreds of them being individually enacted regulations. As an important form of law and supplement to Lü during Ming and Qing Dynasties, individually enacted regulations played a significant role in perfecting China's imperial legal system.[17]

4.1.5 The Transformation of the Legal System

In 1901 when the Qing Government implemented the Late Qing Reform, Chinese legal specialists embarked on a decade-long journey to reform the existing legal system. The earliest reform led by Shen Jiaben and Wu Tingfang, two prominent figures in the legal history of the late Qing Dynasty, was designed to break from China's imperial legal tradition and promote the modernization of Chinese law. An important part of the legal reform was to revoke the extraterritorial privileges of foreign powers in China.

In 1906, the Qing Government issued an imperial decree announcing the constitutional campaign. After that, it enacted the *Outline of a Constitution by Imperial Decree* and *The Nineteen Major Articles of the Constitution*, which represented China's earliest constitutional documents, marking the beginning of China's constitutional history.

Reviewing the imperial legal system in the backdrop of an ever-changing world, the reformists found it urgent to align the Chinese law with the global trend. They focused their efforts on amending laws, aiming to create a brand-new legal system. In this period, a number of legal codes were amended and drafted, including the *New Criminal Code of the Great Qing*, *Great Qing Commercial Code*, *Great Qing Newspaper Code*, *Bankruptcy Law*, *Law of Criminal and Civil Procedure* (draft), and *The Draft Civil Code of the Great Qing Dynasty*.[18]

Between 1912 and 1928 when the Republic of China was in chaos and turmoil, the ruling Beiyang government was unable to keep up with the agenda of legislation for lack of legal professionals and financial resources. In addition, a regional division led to diverse legal practices nationwide, making it difficult to standardize the legal system of the country. For these reasons, there were no nationally applicable written laws ever enacted. The missing of a comprehensive written code helped create a legal system dominated by case law. It is worth noting that the case law mentioned here was not the same as today's case law; instead, it referred to legal precedents made by the Dali Yuan (which was renamed as the Supreme Court in 1927).

As the Nationalist government restored its central authority in 1927, legislative reforms were back on the nation's agenda. In the same year, the *Criminal Code of*

[17] Dong, K. (1935). The judicial system of the early Qing Dynasty. *Law Science*, no. 4.

[18] *New Code of Qing Dynasty*. The Commercial Press. 2011.

the Republic of China and the *Criminal Procedure Law of the Republic of China* were enacted. Between 1929 and 1930, the Nationalist government stepped up its effort to fill the gap in civil law after the dissolution of the Shanghai Mixed Court. After two years of endeavors, it published the *Civil Code of the Republic of China* which fell into five parts, namely, general principles, obligations, rights in rem, family, and succession. The first three parts are precisely borrowed from models of Germany, Switzerland, and Japan, and the last two parts were based on China's traditional legal practice.

In 1931, the Nationalist government enacted the *Civil Procedure Law of the Republic of China,* and the *Organic Law of the People's Courts of the Republic of China* was passed in the following year and was introduced on July 22th of 1935 after amendment. The year 1935 witnessed the amendment and enactment of the *Criminal Code of the Republic of China* (also known as the *New Criminal Code*) and the issuance of a series of administrative regulations. In 1947, the Nationalist government enacted the *Constitution of the Republic of China*, whose draft version was introduced on May fifth of 1936, establishing a comprehensive legal system supported by constitution, criminal code, criminal procedure law, civil code, civil procedure law, and administrative regulations. From the *Collection of Laws and Regulations in Republican China*, we can learn that the legal system of the Republic of China covered laws in various fields with complete topics and a well-organized structure that could match the continental legal system.[19] The modernization of China's legal system was near to completion at this time.

Upon establishing the People's Republic of China in 1949, the Communist Party systematically dismantled the Nationalist government's legal framework including the six codes and criticized the Nationalist government's legal system as a "reactionary legal system." All levels of judicial bodies were banned from invoking articles of the Nationalist legal system in deciding cases.[20] Having done away with the Nationalist legal institutions, the new government began to follow the Soviet pattern. Since then, China has embarked on a bumpy path of legislation reform.

4.2 Characteristics of the Legal System

4.2.1 The Diversity of Legal Forms

Contemporarily, legal pluralism refers to the coexistence of different domains of law, such as criminal law, administrative law, civil law, and economic law. Yet in Imperial China, legal pluralism refers to the coexistence of multiple forms of law

[19] *Collection of Laws in the Republic of China*. Huangshan Publishing House. 1999.

[20] "Abolishing Kuomintang's Six Codes and All Reactionary Laws" in the book *Legal Thought of Dong Biwu*, pp. 14–15. Law Press, 2001. The document was an order signed by Dong Biwu and jointly executed by Dong Biwu, Bo Yibo, Lan Gongwu, and Yang Xiufeng under the title of President and Vice-President of the North China People's Government.

including ritual norms, statutes, and decrees. A closer examination of the imperial codification of laws reveals that these forms were not created to constitute a unified system but established to be separate from one another. Though decrees, regulations, and specifications cover different legal domains, none of them cover penal law (apart from regulations issued by the Ministry of Justice), as penal law was defined by statutes.[21] It is thus fair to say that legal pluralism in Imperial China is quite different from the concept of contemporary legal pluralism.

Legal pluralism has existed worldwide throughout time. Throughout the entire human history and prevalent across nearly every nation, formally enacted laws have consistently been accompanied by several customary laws. Even in today's most developed countries, state law is by no means the only enacted law.[22] This was also the case in Imperial China, where multiple forms of law coexisted and where public laws, such as the two most developed fields of penal and administrative law, made up a largely disproportionate portion of the Imperial legal system. This system was dominated by a highly centralized government and greatly influenced by the complexity of social organizations.

In Imperial China, the penal law invariably prevailed over other laws when deciding legal cases due to the centuries-old absolute monarchy system and the profound influence of Confucianism. The penal law was so sophisticated that there were situations where civil, administrative, and even economic disputes were decided by penal law. This, however, does not mean that there were no civil and administrative laws in Imperial China. The two primary ways of codifying laws during Imperial China included either codifying laws on paper as written codes or inscribing laws on metal or stone tablets. For example, penal codes in early Imperial China were carved onto bronze vessels. After Han Dynasty, rulers increasingly favored inscribing laws on stone tablets, a practice that gained popularity during Ming and Qing Dynasties.

Inscribing agreements or prohibitions on stone tablets had a long history in Imperial China. During Han Dynasty, Wang Jing, the Governor of the Lujiang Commandery (today's Hefei, Anhui), reportedly called upon local officials and farmers to reclaim farmland from large tracts of wasteland, teaching farmers how to use plows to increase their productivity. Thanks to these efforts, the area of reclaimed farmland in the commandery doubled, leading to bumper harvests. He then ordered to inscribe prohibitions onto stone tablets for public inspection. Wang also taught the locals how to rear silkworms and weave silk and ordered the inscribing of instructional guides on all pavilions in the commandery.[23]Inscribing on stones did not gain widespread popularity until Tang and Song Dynasties, when the highest authorities began carving Imperial decrees, laws, regulations, and official documents onto stone tablets as a way of formally enacting them, which explained the

[21] Li, Y. (2004). Studies on the Tang Legal System. *The Jurist*. (5).

[22] Liang Z. (1996). *Customary Law of Qing Dynasty: Society and the State*. China University of Political Science and Law Press, 32.

[23] Volume 76 "Xunli liezhuan" (The Collective Biography of Benevolent Officials) in the *Book of the Later Han*.

surge of stone tablets inscribed with Imperial orders and edicts, admonitions to state officials, and promissory notes during these two dynasties.

Song and Yuan Dynasties continued to see rapid growth in the number of steles engraved with Imperial bans and government orders. The inscriptions on most of these government tablets were specific regulations from Imperial edicts and decrees. The growing use of these steles highly influenced the use of Imperial steles engraved with laws describing prohibited actions in the successive Qing and Ming Dynasties, during which the system of Imperial steles matured. Imperial prohibition steles refer to those carved with Imperial edicts and decrees that contain laws prohibiting certain actions. These steles fall into two categories: the first are those carved with national laws and the second are those with laws applying only in specific cases or to specific communities.[24] Though these laws are inscribed on stones, their legal authority is no different from that of codified laws, both of which need to be followed.

Furthermore, Imperial edicts, decrees, and governmental prohibitions were also displayed in Pavilions for Explicating Clarity (Shenmingting), which were often set up at crowded places near government offices or on high streets. At a time when information could not be quickly shared via the Internet, displaying laws and regulations using these pavilions was the major way to familiarize the general public with codified laws.

4.2.2 The Continuity of the Penal Codes

Laws and regulations on administrative, civil, and economic issues, ritual propriety, and military matters were enacted as early as Xia, Shang, and Zhou Dynasties. Succeeding imperial dynasties introduced more laws and codes, as well as many other forms of law. Legal texts produced after Tang Dynasty were relatively well-preserved, but many before this time are lost to history.

Every Imperial dynasty features a cornerstone code, such as the *Canons of Law* of the Warring States period, the *Nine Chapter Statutes* of Han Dynasty, the *New Statutes* of the Kingdom of Wei, the *Jin Code* of Jin Dynasty, the *Northern Qi Code* of Northern Qi Dynasty, the *Kaihuang Code* of Sui Dynasty, the *Yonghui Statues with Commentary* of Tang Dynasty, the *Penal Code of Song Dynasty,* the *Comprehensive Regulations of the Great Yuan Dynasty,* the *Great Ming Code,* and the *Great Qing Code.* These codes mostly concerned penal law. For example, the *Yonghui Statutes* was comprised of 502 articles organized into the following 12 chapters: (1) general principles, (2) Imperial guards and prohibited actions, (3) administrative regulations, (4) households and marriages, (5) public stables and warehouses, (6) unauthorized levies, (7) theft and robbery, (8) assaults and

[24]Ye, C. (1995). *Yushi jiaozhu* (*Analyses on the Discussions of Stones*), Beijing: China Today Press. 1995. 335–336.

accusations, (9) fraud and counterfeiting, (10) miscellaneous matters, (11) arrests and escapes from the law, and (12) judgments and imprisonment. While Chapter one covered the general principles of the penal system (including the Five Punishments, the Ten Abominations, and the Eight Deliberations) and how these laws are to be applied, the later 11 chapters, which at first appeared to include non-penal provisions judging by the chapter titles, actually extensively described specific criminal offenses and laws. It was said that the Tang people knew very clearly that the main purpose of the *Yonghui Statutes* was to determine guilt and punishment. Thus, it can be safely concluded that the *Yonghui Statutes* was a code dedicated to defining crimes and imposing punishments.

Both the *Great Ming Code* and the *Great Qing Code* comprise the following seven chapters: (1) general principles, (2) statutes on personnel, (3) statutes on revenue, (4) statutes on rituals, (5) statutes on military affairs, (6) statutes on penal affairs, and (7) statutes on public works. Some of the topics covered in these two codes, however, do not concern what we contemporarily think of as penal law. For example, a few of the articles in chapter two actually concern what is considered administrative law today, while several other articles on marriages and farmland in chapter three would fall under civil law today. However, these were all actions that threatened social stability during those time periods and so were deemed as criminal offenses and tried under penal law, despite not being issues that fall under penal law today.

In pre-Imperial China, penal laws were undeniably the focus of the legal system: the *Penal Code of Yu,* the *Penal Code of Tang,* and the *Nine Punishments* were all dedicated to defining laws for punishments. Though other forms of law such as "canons" and "statutes" emerged in the Spring and Autumn periods, irreversibly changing the legal landscape, they were still penal in nature. This legal tradition largely defined the penal focus of legal codes in later imperial dynasties.

The same "penal-focused" approach is found in almost all other countries in the early stages of their legal history. Henry Sumner Maine once observed that "the more archaic the code, the fuller and the minuter is its penal legislation."[25]Furthermore, Max Weber clearly specified that "even in the late stages of otherwise complex legal developments, every action was simply looked upon as sounding in tort."[26] The Imperial Chinese legal system was dominated by the penal law for a much longer period compared to the Western legal system, which can be attributed to its highly centralized political system, low social mobility, and economic stagnation.

---

[25] Maine, H. J. S. (2011). *Ancient law* (M. Gao & H. Zhai, Trans.). China Social Sciences Press. 281–282.

[26] Max, W. (1998). *Economy and Society II*. The Commercial Press.7.

4.2.3 The Full Development of Administrative Laws

In addition to civil laws, Imperial rulers also issued volumes of administrative regulations specifying the structure of government agencies, their rights and responsibilities, and their management system, requiring officials at all levels to fulfill their responsibilities and act in a disciplined manner to rule the state more efficiently. As an integral part of China's Imperial legal framework, the administrative law became increasingly systematic and standardized, representing one of the most effective and comprehensive laws of its kind in the world.[27] Noticeably, there were no procedural or licensing laws under the administrative system of Imperial China, unlike modern China. With its many laws on organizational structure and bureaucratic system regulations, the Imperial administrative law put more emphasis on regulating the operation of government agencies.

With a long history of centralized imperial rule, China had a unique administrative system during the dynastic period. Traditionally, capable rulers ruled over people through governing officials, and so the selection, appointment, supervision, and management of these officials were important issues that needed to be addressed, as the systems for doing so served as the foundation for enforcing the rulers' authority and ensuring social stability. In Imperial China's long history, its bureaucratic system became increasingly comprehensive with more and more sophisticated administrative laws, which became a distinct feature of China's traditional legal culture.

The creation of administrative agencies and a bureaucratic political system dates back to Xia Dynasty. It has been reported that there were nearly 100 state official positions in Xia Dynasty, including the Chezheng (in charge of coach manufacturing), Muzheng (in charge of livestock management), and E'zheng (in charge of Imperial meals) roles,[28] indicating that the Xia kings already ruled through a bureaucratic system where state officials were selected. Shang Dynasty introduced penalties to crack down on official misconduct and began purges of administrative institutions.[29]

Western Zhou Dynasty implemented a civil service system to support the kings in ruling the state, according to the *Rites of Zhou*, which stated "Govern the country by setting up official positions and specifying administrative duties." The *Rites of Zhou* contain a systematic list of bureaucrats, as well as details on the functions of each office. It is divided into six chapters: offices of heaven (on general governance), offices of the earth (on taxation and division of land), offices of spring (on education as well as social and religious institutions), offices of summer (on military affairs), offices of autumn (on justice), and offices of winter (on population, territory, and agriculture management). These chapters each described the six

---

[27] Zhang, J. (1999). *Evolution of the Chinese Legal Civilization*. China University of Political Science and Law Press.8.

[28] *Book of Rites: the Position in the Hall of Distinction.*

[29] Shen, J. (1985). "Book of documents: the instructions of Yi" in *Examination on the Penal Law of All Dynasties*. Vol. 2 Offical penal code of the Shang Dynasty. Zhonghua Book Company.

ministries that were in charge of affairs concerning personnel, revenues, rites, war, justice, and public works. Edited by government agencies, the *Rites of Zhou* is also known as the "*Officers of Zhou.*" As one of the important Chinese classics, the *Rites of Zhou* consists of six chapters corresponding to the six government ministries, and while it might not be completely credible, it does provide us with a broad outline of China's Imperial administrative system.[30]

Imperial Administrative legislation has a long history and features a comprehensively developed system. From Xia Dynasty to Tang Dynasty, a complete system of administrative law was gradually developed, featuring many different types of law covering a wide range of activities, as recorded in the *Six Statutes of Tang Dynasty*. Zhang Taiyan, a philologist from the late Qing Dynasty, once commented on the Tang legal system, "Tang Dynasty enacted the *Six Statutes of Tang Dynasty* and the *Kaiyuan Period of the Great Tang*, which proves that statutes are penal (not administrative) in nature."[31] Decrees from Tang and Song Dynasties, such as the *Tiansheng Decrees*, brought the codification of administrative laws to new heights. Qing Dynasty enacted many volumes of collected statutes, regulations on government ministries, including Collected Statutes of the Qing Dynasty, Precedents and Regulations of the Collected Statutes, Case Precedents of the Collected Statutes, and ministry-specific regulations and provincial administrative rules and regulations, further perfecting the Imperial China's administrative legal system.

Imperial administrative laws were largely focused on the operation of government agencies. When the Continental legal system was introduced to China in the late Qing Dynasty, especially after a legal system based on the six codes was implemented by the Nationalist government, China began to develop a modern administrative legal system with a more well-organized structure.

4.2.4 The Incipiency and Ambiguities of Private Laws

The Imperial Chinese civil law distinguished itself from other civil laws of the world with a unique system for resolving disputes.

Private law is rarely found in Imperial law codes, not even in the most developed and detailed codes such as the *Tang Code* and the *Great Qing Code*.[32] Some scholars hold that there were no civil laws in Imperial China at all, as the populace understood little about individualism, rights-based principles, and private autonomy, the three elements considered by Westerners as the most fundamental elements of society. However, it is undeniable that people in the Imperial period were also involved in social activities such as marriage, starting families, trading, leasing, and loaning.

[30] Zang, Y. (1987). *An Explanation Table of the Office Systems, Military Systems and the Imperil Exam Systems of All Dynasties*. Jiangsu Ancient Book Press. 2.

[31] Volume 3 "An Examination of the Han Law" in the book *Collective Books of Zhang Taiyan*.

[32] Liang, Z. (1996). *Customary Law of Qing Dynasty: Society and the State*, China University of Political Science and Law Press.31.

If these activities were not governed by civil law, what else could they be governed by? They had to have been governed by civil law.

Though no civil code was ever enacted in Imperial China, some penal laws governed civil matters. Many criminal offenses in the past are simply considered to be civil matters today but were defined as criminal matters at that time as they either directly or indirectly threatened the political order of the Imperial era.

A major part of this civil law was regulation on social status, a core subject that needed to be defined by law (especially civil law) in a society governed by an absolute monarchy through patriarchal and hierarchical systems. For example, the law clearly defines the hierarchical relationship between rulers and ministers, masters and servants, and the social status of scholars, farmers, artisans, and merchants. Regulations on family relations were also very sophisticated, with laws defining the relationships between father and son, husband and wife, grandparent and grandchild, siblings, uncle and nephew, concubines, the eldest son of one's wife, sons of concubines, the first son and second son, stepchildren, illegitimate children, posthumous children, foster children, and matrilocal husbands. The law also included regulations for marriages, covering a wide range of topics such as the six rituals of marriage, marriage contracts, matchmakers, the seven conditions under which a man can divorce his wife and the three conditions in which he cannot, prohibitions on marriages between individuals who share last names, prohibitions on marriages between individuals of different social classes, prohibitions on marriages between cousins, contested and uncontested divorces, and concubines. In addition, regulations on other family issues were also included in the law, such as laws on parent-child relationships, children being disobedient to their parents, and even laws specifying appropriate mourning dress and attire. There were also regulations governing inheritance, such as laws on primogeniture, the order of succession, testate succession, and who can inherit property left without an heir.

The Imperial law provided equally sophisticated property ownership regulations. Historical documents record that as early as the Western Zhou period there were already agreements on and precedents for legally assigning property, based on inscriptions found carved onto bronze vessels. The huge cost of creating such carvings hints at the fact that property ownership was an important concern during those times. Customary law played a significant role in Jin Dynasty where it was regarded as having the same legal effect as statutes and decrees. In the dynasties following Jin Dynasty, regulations on property ownership and the concept of rights in personam advanced even further, constituting unique property laws governing sales agreements, loan agreements, real estate agreements, the pawning of items, mortgage, preferential purchase rights granted to relatives and neighbors, creditors and debtors, and the rights of permanent tenants.

China's vast territory, hugely different social conventions, lineage systems, deep-rooted systems of rites and moral ethics, and the practice of there being unofficial civil mediator made it difficult and unnecessary for the central government to introduce a standard civil code applicable to the entire nation. Less important criminal cases in the eyes of local officials were mostly considered civil disputes, and the parties involved would not turn to a far-away court but instead rely on mediation carried out by family clans or local communities.

Though no civil code was ever enacted in Imperial China, there was a complete system for resolving civil disputes. Civil regulations such as the *Administrative Regulations of the Ministry of Revenue,* customary law, and family rules all served to support social harmony, which demonstrates the crystallized wisdom of China's age-old legal tradition.

4.3 Local Prohibitions

Local prohibitions refer to a series of prohibitions issued by local governments based on local conditions. They could be government notices posted in Pavilions for Explicating Clarity (Shenming ting) or instructions engraved on metal materials or stone tablets and displayed in public, which were more authoritative than the former and had a lasting effect.

Engraving prohibitions on stone tablets was an age-old practice in Imperial China. As stated in the *Book of Rites: Monthly Decrees* (chapter: Early Winter), "Engrave the craftsman's name on the artifacts to clarify his accountability." Additionally, Ouyang Xiu, a Chinese essayist during Song Dynasty, wrote in the *Account of the Daytime Brocade Hall in Xiangzhou*, "Merits be inscribed on stone tablets and poems of praise be celebrated everywhere." All these show that engravings were formal notices and had a lasting effect.

Early prohibitions engraved on bronze vessels had a higher level of legal force and wider coverage. Generally, only the lords of states were eligible to engrave notices on bronze vessels. By comparison, it was easier and more cost-effective to engrave notices on stone tablets, and all local officials (typically county, prefectural, and provincial governors in the late Qing Dynasty) were eligible to engrave notices on stone tablets. During Han Dynasty, Governor Wang Jing, of Lujiang Commandery (Hefei, Anhui) was reported to have called upon local officials and peasants to reclaim farmland from wastelands, teaching farmers how to use plows to increase their productivity. As a result, the area of reclaimed fields in the commandery doubled, leading to bumper harvests. He then issued an order to engrave preventative laws on stone tablets for public display. Wang also taught the locals to rear silkworms and weave silk and ordered engraved instructions to be displayed on all commandery pavilions.[33]

However, stone engravings were not a common practice until Tang and Song Dynasties, when the highest authorities began engraving imperial decrees, laws, and official documents on stone tablets, which explains the surge of stone tablets engraved with imperial orders and edicts, admonitions to state officials, and promissory notes during the two dynasties. In the Ming and Qing Dynasties, many stone

[33] Volume 76 (The Collective Biography of Benevolent Officials in the book *Book of the Later Han.*

tablets carried the inscription, "The prohibition shall take immediate effect upon the stele being erected" or "this stele is erected pursuant to imperial orders," meaning that the prohibitions were engraved on imperial orders. This practice represented a legislative model led by local governments while involving the participation of local residents, especially the gentry. The stone tablets were typically engraved with a paragraph stating that the prohibitions were displayed at the request of the gentry. Nevertheless, it was the governments that ordered engravings specifically banning detrimental local practices.[34]

Most local prohibitions were enacted to ban regional group activities that might threaten public safety and rights, while some served to improve public order and overall social conduct.

4.3.1 Protection of Common Resources

Rulers of Imperial China have always valued the preservation of natural resources throughout history. As recorded in the *Discourses of the States*, on a summer day, Li Ge, a scholar-official of the State of Lu in the Spring and Autumn Period, ripped apart the Duke of Lu's fishing net to stop him from fishing. He then reminded the Duke of the importance of protecting fishes and allowing them to breed and thrive. The Duke of Lu commended Li for giving honest advice and decided to stop fishing from then on.[35]

The central government during the Qin Dynasty enacted the *Decrees on Fields,* banning unauthorized logging and fishing to protect the natural ecosystem. The practice was later adopted by many local governments in subsequent dynasties. For example, the Wuyi Mountain Nine-bend River was well protected by local governments of all dynasties. During the reign of Emperor Kangxi of the Qing Dynasty, the Jianning Prefecture government improved its legislation to protect the Nine-bend River, engraving prohibitions on stone tablets banning pollution and fishing. The prohibition has since remained a local regulation, allowing locals or monks to bring any violators to the local court to face a public trial.[36]

Some local officials also enacted stone prohibitions to protect trees believed to be auspicious under the traditional Chinese practice fengshui. For instance, at the Xichang County, Sichuan Province government and local villagers erected a stone tablet displaying prohibitions against cutting down auspicious trees. The

[34] Li, X. (2015). *The Tradition of Carving Laws on Bronzes and Stone Tablets: Stone Prohibition Systems in Ming and Qing Dynasties*. Zhonghua Book Company. 343. Li, X. (2009). *An Examination of Historical Legal Texts Carved on Stone Tablets*. Social Sciences Academic Press.

[35] *Discourses of the State: Discourses of the Duke of Lu: Li Ge Ripping Apart Duke Lu's Fishing Net to Help Him Become a Better Official.*

[36] *Stone Prohibition on Polluting Fishing Activities*. The prohibition, carved on the rocks in the Xiao jiuqu valley in Wuyi mountains, Fujian Province, was issued by Chong'an County, Jianning Prefecture. See Zhu Ping'an. *Studies on the Texts Carved on Rocks in Wuyi Mountains and on the Wuyi Culture*, 479. Xiamen University Press. 2008.

inscriptions on the tablet read, "It is hereby announced that the public is no longer permitted on the mountain to prevent the felling of auspicious trees. Break the rule at your own peril."[37]

Many ancient water engineering projects affected several regions, so it was unfeasible for local governments to create individual rules. In most cases, rule planning required a legislative panel consisting of officials from different governments to coordinate the rule-making process so that all stakeholders could observe the rules and utilize water resources in a coordinated manner, instead of going their own way for their own interests. In this sense, stone prohibitions played a prominent role in water conservation, as recorded in *Stele Listing Anti-Unauthorized Construction Projects Policy over the Lake Xiang*. In terms of regional disputes over water utilization, local governments were supposed to reach a compromise through negotiation to ensure the disputes were properly resolved. The compromise would then be inscribed onto the stone tablet and served as a prohibition. The *Stele Inscribed with the Solution to the Irrigation Dispute between Zhaocheng County and Hongdong County* mentions that a stone tablet was erected in 1139 to settle water disputes between Hongdong County and Zhaocheng County.

In Chengdu County, Sichuan Province, a man enrolled at the national school occupied a local temple and took temple property as his own, sparking complaints from temple donors. To settle the disputes, the government issued a stone prohibition which read, "Built on public funds, the temple is public property and shall be managed by the monks and the nuns. No donor is allowed to sell temple property. Local officials who violate the prohibition shall be punished in accordance with the law, and the precedent shall be inscribed on the tablet to serve as an example."[38]

4.3.2 Ban on Government Officials' Disturbance Against the People

Throughout history, it was not uncommon for a few local government officials to disturb or exploit the people under color of official duty. Therefore, local governments often enacted prohibitions to nip these vices in the bud.

Take Ding Baozhen, the Fuzhou Maritime Administration Grand Minister and Fujian Province Patrol Officer, as an example. After being informed that the local authorities in Taiwan Prefecture were lining their pockets with money from local farmers when purchasing grain to replenish government granaries, he imposed a

[37] *A Stele Displaying the Prohibition Against Felling Trees in Xichang County*. The prohibition was jointly carved by both local people and officials in Xichang county, Sichuan Province, in the 13th year during the reign of Emperor Tongzhi. *Texts of Stone Prohibitions of All Dynasties, Housed in the Capital Library*, 77.

[38] *Stone Prohibition against National School Enrollments Taking Temple Property*, issued on April eighth in the 31st year during the reign of Emperor Qianlong. The stele is housed in the Zhangliang Temple in Liuba County.

prohibition against such misconduct: "Any government official and their subordinates who attempt to extort money from the public or burden them with extra field taxes shall be held accountable and caned to death. This prohibition shall be enforced immediately. All officials shall act accordingly and must not violate it."

In February of the second year during the reign of Emperor Guangxu, this prohibition was inscribed on a stele which was later erected in Fengshan County, Taiwan Prefecture, by County Magistrate Sun Jizu. The tablet served as a constant reminder of the deadly consequences (being held accountable and caned to death) faced by any official who dared violate the prohibition.

There were also prohibitions against corruption when transporting grain tributes via canals. For instance, the Qing Circuit Intendant responsible for grain transportation in the four prefectures of Suzhou, Songjiang, Changzhou, and Zhenjiang once erected a stone tablet with a paragraph that read, "All acts of corruption involving the transportation of grain tribute via canal have been prohibited and abolished under my watch. I swear that I did not take a grain of rice during the entire process. My subordinates, however, were accused of extorting taxes from local residents through violence, resulting in a financial loss. This tablet is hereby erected today to warn officials who violate this prohibition that they will be dismissed. Every circuit or prefecture shall send intendants to independent departments and counties to supervise the transportation of grain, and the selected intendants shall not deliberately cover up any acts when performing their duties. If discovered doing so, they shall be sentenced to death."[39]

Many other steles carved with similar prohibitions and rules were also erected. For instance, a stele titled *Stele Displaying the Rule of Submitting Ten Households' Guarantees to Clamp Down on Police Officers Who Harbor Robbers and Thieves* was found in Nanxiang Town, Jiading County, with its year remaining unknown.

Others include the *Stele Displaying Prohibitions Against Vicious Officials Who Tamper With Judicial Dossiers to Frame Up Innocent Salt Merchants under Color of Official Duty* (created during the 12th year of the of Emperor Shunzhi), *Stele Displaying Jiading County's Permanent Prohibitions Against Law Enforcement Officers Who Force Innocent People to Get Implicated in Crimes* (created in November of the 31st year of the reign of Emperor Qianlong), *Stele Displaying Changshu County's Permanent Prohibitions Against the Practice of Government Officials Who Overcharge Taxes from Fishmongers* (created during the ninth year of the reign of Emperor Kangxi), *Stele Displaying Yuanhe County's Prohibitions Against Government Officials' Disturbance of Commercial Tenants And Passenger Boats in the Hushan and Shantang Areas* (created during the 11th year of the reign of Emperor Jiaqing), *Stele Displaying Yuanhe, Changzhou and Wusan Counties' Permanent Prohibitions Against Government Officials' Racketeering of Commercial*

---

[39] *Stone Prohibitions Against Any Corruption Found in Grain Tribute Transport in the Four Prefectures of Suzhou, Songjiang, Changzhou and Zhenjiang*. The stele is now housed in the Changshu Beike Museum. The text can be found in page 657 of the collection *Selected Stone Texts Found in the Jiangsu Province since Ming and Qing Dynasties*, compiled by the Jiangsu Museum and published by the Joint Publishing in 1959.

Ships (created during the 15th year of the reign of Emperor Jiaqing), *Stele Displaying Jiading County's Prohibitions Against Soldiers Who Bully Commercial Tenants in Collusion with Hooligans* (created in May of the 24th year of the reign of Emperor Kangxi), *Stele Displaying Suzhou and Songjiang Counties' Prohibitions Against the Sale of Counterfeit Textiles by Cloth Brokers* (created in April of the 12th year of the reign of Emperor Shunzhi), *Stele Displaying Songjiang County's Prohibitions Against the Extortion of Tea Merchants by Devious Yamen (local magistrate's office) Runners and Traders* (created in November of the 12th year of the reign of Emperor Kangxi), *Stele Displaying Shanghai County's Prohibitions Against the Exaction of Various Dues and Fees from Ningbo Candle Merchants by Shanghai Candle Tycoons* (created in June of the seventh year of the reign of Emperor Tongzhi), *Stele Displaying Jiading County's Rule of Redemption and Release of Bondservants* (created in the fourth year of the reign of Emperor Qianlong), and *Stele Displaying Jiading County's Prohibitions Against the Practice of Sending Orphanage Staff to the Junhe River Area As Conscripted Labor* (created in August of the 23rd year of the reign of Emperor Qianlong).[40]

4.3.3 Ban on Collective Actions

People residing in Jiangnan (south of the lower reaches of Yangtze River) during Ming and Qing Dynasties usually joined large processions to pay tribute to gods and deities. Some criminals would see such gatherings as good opportunities to enrich themselves. In light of this, local governments introduced a prohibition to crack down on such incidents. A prohibition was inscribed stating that "Hereafter, no large gatherings, processions, or the practice of illegally amassing fortunes shall be permitted. Anyone who is caught violating the prohibition either explicitly or implicitly shall face severe punishments, and the main culprits involved shall be punished without mercy."[41]

The employment of artisans was not unheard of during these two dynasties, especially in the more developed industrial and commercial regions. The wide gap between the shortage of skilled artisans and the high demand for them inevitably rendered employers susceptible to frequent strikes, more often triggered by

[40] Pages 453, 454, and 457 in the collection *Selected Stone Texts Found in Shangha*, compiled by the Shanghai Museum and published by the Shanghai People's Press in 1980.*Collection of Stone Texts Regarding Industry and Commerce in the Suzhou Province in Ming and Qing Dynasties*, jointly compiled by the Suzhou Museum, the School of History in the Suzhou Normal University, and the Research Center of the History of Ming and Qing Dynasties in the Nanjing University, and published by Jiangsu People's Press in 1981.

[41] *Stone Prohibition on the Main Halls in Changzhou County, Suzhou Prefecture*, issued on March 28th in the seventh year during the reign of Emperor Tongzhi. The stele is now housed in the Suzhou Police Museum.

unsatisfactory salaries. This, in turn, would lead to the sluggish growth of the traditional craft industry.

With legal protection, employers often suffered huge economic losses whenever faced with a strike. As a result, they petitioned local governments to ban strikes to ensure the operation of the industry.

The governments approved their requests and issued prohibitions criminalizing artisan strikes. For example, in Qing Dynasty, the Changzhou County government of Suzhou Province erected a stone prohibition that read, "To all artisans: anyone who attempts to initiate a strike shall be tried under the statute of market manipulation and pilloried in public. All artisans shall abide by this prohibition and carry out their work in earnest."[42]

On one hand, this prohibition encouraged local residents to report "lawless gangs" who dared go on strikes or abet others to do so to local governments. On the other hand, it also set punitive measures for offenders by drawing on judicial precedents in penal cases. It only applied to local artisans and could not be extended.

Steles inscribed with similar prohibitions include the *Stele Displaying Yuanhe County's Prohibitions Against Strikes Launched by Riotous Textile Artisans* (created during the second year of the reign of Emperor Daoguang), *Stele Displaying Suzhou Prefecture's Permanent Prohibitions Against Protest Marches Launched by Fabric Artisans Asking for Unreasonable Salary Increase* (created during the 32nd year of the reign of Emperor Kangxi), *Stele Displaying Suzhou Prefecture's Restrictions on Fabric Artisans* (created during the 40th year of the reign of Emperor Kangxi), *Stele Displaying Yuanhe, Changzhou and Wusan Counties' Prohibitions Against Strikes Launched by Paper-producing Artisans Asking for Unreasonable Salary Increase* (created during the 21st year of the reign of Emperor Qianlong), and *Stele Displaying Wusan County's Permanent Prohibitions Against Strikes Launched by Foil-producing Artisans* (created during the 17th year of the reign of Emperor Daoguang).

4.3.4 Maintenance of Local Security

Local governments were responsible for ensuring public safety, so it was necessary for them to enact targeted prohibitions to maintain public order. As public safety could vary from area to area and encompass almost every facet of daily life, prohibitions on issues related to public safety varied significantly in different areas. Some prohibitions were against the practice of disturbances at burials or robberies aimed at widows, while some were against gambling or the illegal sale of salt. These incidents were a constant threat to public order and social stability.

[42] Stone Prohibitions Against Artisans Initiating Strikes, collected in the *Collection of Stone Texts Regarding Industry and Commerce in the Suzhou Province in Ming and Qing Dynasties*, jointly compiled by the Suzhou Museum, the School of History in the Suzhou Normal University, and the Research Center of the History of Ming and Qing Dynasties in the Nanjing University, and published by Jiangsu People's Press in 1981.

For example, the Magistrate of Qingpu County joined forces with the Prefect of Songjiang Prefecture and ordered the erection of the "Stele Displaying Qingpu County's Prohibitions against Activities of Local Hooligans" in Jinze Town. The stele read, "Hereafter, whenever a hooligan deliberately breaks the law or causes harm to others, all people are empowered to arrest him and bring him to justice. With clear evidence, the hooligan shall be tried under the penal law and be severely punished."[43]

This stele was jointly erected by Songjiang and Qingpu Prefectures, which evidently revealed the severity of the harm to local order caused by activities such as obstructing burials, kidnapping widows, organizing gambling, and trafficking salt. In Songjiang Prefecture, traveling muleteers and trumpeters posed potential threats to society, as they were known to gang up and extort their employers whenever they had issues with their salaries. To address this concern, the government enacted several prohibitions and ordered their inscription on steles, such as the *Stele Displaying Songjiang Prefecture's Regulations of Salary Standards for Traveling Muleteers* (created in February of the 22nd year of the reign of Emperor Kangxi), *Stele Displaying Jiading County's Prohibitions Against Protest Marches by Traveling Muleteers* (created during the 25th year of the reign of Emperor Kangxi), *Stele Displaying Huating County's Prohibitions Against the Practice of Traveling Muleteers Creating Disturbances at Weddings And Funerals* (created in October of the 20th year of the reign of Emperor Qianlong), *Stele Displaying Shanghai County's Prohibitions Against Forcing Local Area Residents Into Free Labor* (created in November of the sixth year of the reign of Emperor Jiaqing), and *Stele Displaying Regulations of Salary Standards for Trumpeters And Prohibitions Against the Extortion by Them* (created in May of the eighth year of the reign of Emperor Tongzhi). Another significant headache for local governments was beggars and crooks, who often gathered together to make trouble wherever they went. They were considered "blots on the landscape." Governments issued several prohibitions and steles to deal with these street gangs, including the *Stele Displaying Shanghai County's Prohibitions Against the Practice of Beggars Creating Disturbances* (created in June of the second year of the reign of Emperor Daoguang), *Stele Displaying Qingpu County's Permanent Prohibitions Against Beggars Creating Disturbances* (created in July of the 23rd year of the reign of Emperor Daoguang), *Stele Displaying Songjiang Prefecture's Prohibitions Against Extortion and Robbery by Beggars And Crooks* (created in August of the 25th year of the reign of Emperor Daoguang), *Stele Displaying Prohibitions Against Extortion of Local Residents by Beggars And Crooks* (created in November of the 12th year of the reign of Emperor Tongzhi), and *Stele Displaying Songjiang Prefecture's Permanent Prohibitions Against Evil Acts Committed by Vicious Crooks* (created in March of the 41th year of the reign of Emperor Kangxi).[44]

---

[43] Pages 449–451 in the collection *Selected Stone Texts Found in Shanghai*, compiled by the Shanghai Museum and published by the Shanghai People's Press in 1980.

[44] *Selected Stone Texts Found in Shanghai*, compiled by the Shanghai Museum and published by the Shanghai People's Press in 1980.

Prohibitions inscribed on steles were the most authoritative of all local prohibitions. There were also written prohibitions displayed in public places to keep the populace informed. For example, the government of Guangning County in Guangdong Province once enacted a ban to prevent local people from stealing bamboo rafts owned by merchants from rivers:

> Hereafter, all shall abide by the law and shall not drag bamboo rafts belonging to merchants from rivers. Should storms scatter the rafts; nobody is permitted to drag them and sell stray rafts. Anyone who purchases stolen rafts shall be held responsible and be punished accordingly. Men of prestige that dare harbor the lawbreakers or are suspected as accomplices shall also be held responsible and be severely punished. All shall abide by this prohibition.
> March, 17th Year of the Reign of Emperor Jiaqing.[45]

There were many similar prohibitions. Governments sometimes even had to issue prohibitions on trivial matters, such as people anchoring boats loaded with manure along wharves, which often upset local fishermen and farmers. A good example was the *Stele Displaying Changshu and Zhaowen Counties' Prohibitions Against the Occupancy of Wharves by Boats Loaded with Feces Which Has Created Disturbances Among Local Fishermen and Farmers* (created in the 28th year of the reign of Emperor Guangxu).

The local prohibitions discussed here only applied to a particular group of people in a given period. They served to supplement the national legal system.

4.4 Local Regulations and Community Conventions

Conventions are a set of social norms passed down from generation to generation in a group or community. They are derived from everyday life and seen as a set of common practices. These practices are generally accepted by members of a community and help govern human relations and settle disputes, protecting the interests of community members. Systematically recorded in writing, conventions may evolve into rules and regulations and gain stronger legal authority over time. Unlike imperial edicts issued by emperors or laws enacted by legislatures, they are created by members of a community through discussions and usually have a long history. Even before the introduction of written laws, conventions already served to govern the social conduct of members within a community and have evolved into "customary law" as referred to by modern people.

The modern meaning of "law" is utterly understood by all, yet it is arguable whether the modern concept of "law" exists in the folk community. Just like the term "契*Qi*" (contract), our ancestors came up with impressive customary law concepts, including village regulations and community agreements, family and clan rules, and industry regulations. To avoid ambiguity in the use of the term "law" in

[45] *Stele Displaying Guangdong Provincial Surveillance Commission's Prohibition on Stealing Drifting Bamboo Rafts on Rivers*, issued in December in the ninth year during the reign of Emperor Tongzhi, was a copy of official prohibitions.

both modern and ancient contexts, the direct use of "folk conventions" is more suitable, which encompasses the concepts of village regulations and community agreements, family and clan rules, and industry regulations. Folk conventions come from customs and habits, but not all customs and habits can eventually turn into folk conventions: they are two different but closely related concepts.

4.4.1 Village Regulations

In the feudal society of the Western Zhou Dynasty, a feudal system defined the ruling class consisting of the rulers, feudal lords, high ministers, and great officers, with subordinate officers under them to govern the nation. The Qin and Han Dynasties adopted the Junxian (commanderies and counties) system and began governing the country by appointing bureaucrats to every commandery and county. Later, the imperial examination system was implemented, striking a blow against the hereditary aristocracy system. Apart from a few groups of people that were prohibited from taking exams, every man (there was also a brief period when women were allowed to take the exams) could become an official as long as he passed the exams. Those who passed the Palace Examination would be awarded the title "Jinshi" and registered as a qualified official by the Ministry of Personnel. The civil service system was composed of nine ranks (seven ranks in some periods) of civil officials, with the ninth rank (seventh rank in some dynasties) being the lowest. As the largest group making up these ninth-rank officials, a county governor was considered a low-level civil official.

Generally, imperial examinations were only used to select government officials at the county level or above. This meant that the civil service system, with the county governor role being the lowest level of official within that system, did not concern itself with the administration of individual villages. Maintaining regional order, collecting taxes, providing labor for national projects, and handling criminal cases were the responsibility of county governors, yet almost all other issues were handled by village residents themselves. In some areas where with no applicable national or local laws, village residents would make their own rules enforced in only a particular group or area. These generally accepted rules specified rights and obligations and protected village residents while not contradicting national law.

Different places have unique customs. As part of the community, every member was obliged to follow the rules to ensure that everyone in the community got along well with each other and lived in harmony. Village regulations played an important role in governing the behavior of village residents. There were many types of village regulations, including signed written agreements and signed agreements inscribed in the stone tablets. Village regulations also addressed many issues important and related to the interests of the majority of village residents, such as fulfilling official duties, environmental protection, auspicious *Feng Shui* arrangement, maintenance of social order and security, and the management of ancestral shrines in the whole village.

4.4.1.1 Fulfilling Official Duties

One of the earliest agreements written in stone was the *Binding Stone Agreement for the Purchase of Fields of the Fulao and Dan Association of Shiting Li* created in 77 CE (second year of Emperor Zhang's reign during Eastern Han Dynasty). *Dan* refers to an administrative region at the village or subvillage level. In Han Dynasty, *li* referred to an administrative unit smaller than a village or county consisting of 100 households. The term *Fulao* referred to the head of a *li* who manages public affairs together with local governments. Generally, *Fulao* were reputable and wealthy local elders. Widely respected within the community, they assisted local governments in handling public affairs without pay, which meant that the role was a financial burden. The *Fulao Dan* was created to address the problem. According to the inscriptions of *On the Binding Stone Agreement for the Purchase of Fields of the Fulao Dan Association of Shiting Li*, 25 village residents from the community would pool money to purchase 82 *mu* (about 5.5 hectares) of land, and the income from this land would be used to defray their obligations for serving as heads of *Shiting Li*. The stone contract also included rules on the rights to use and inherit this land and issues concerning land return, assignment, and lease. It is worth mentioning that the *Fulao Dan* operated differently from the *Zheng Dan*. It can be inferred from the inscriptions of the *Liu Xiong Stele* that the *Zheng Dan* was a village association in charge of statute labor and run by the local people but, in reality, the association was controlled by the government.[46] The existence of the *Fulao Dan* shows that village communities maintained a certain degree of autonomy.

The *Baojia* system operated without government intervention, despite being a traditional system of community-based management introduced and advocated by the government. Under this system, local residents were responsible for governing and keeping order in their communities. Specifically, every household signed and complied with a *Baojia* agreement which specified the purpose for setting up a *Jia* (a unit consisting of ten households), the rights and obligations of each household, and tax rules. However, it is noteworthy that Baojia agreements varied from village to village as they took into account local conditions. For example, in Qing Dynasty, a *Jia* in Yingjiapeng village, Fenghua County, Zhejiang Province, adjusted its Baojia agreement reasons specific to the region. When the head of the *Jia* resigned as he was unable to handle the administrative work due to family reasons and there were no qualified candidates to fill the vacancy and take on the responsibilities of the role, this led to a new agreement requiring each household to contribute and share the responsibilities of the position, ensuring that administrative tasks were still being effectively carried out within the community.

> The clans of Ying, Chen, and Jiang jointly decided to contribute funds to set up a "Yunshan Jiazhong," an organization designed to assist with tax collection and maintain order in the community, with different members taking turns in serving as the community head. The income generated from their contributions would be used to pay taxes. With competent heads and well-established rules, the community can achieve long-term stability. The

[46] Gao, W. (1997). *Han Steles with Comments*, Henan University Press. 11.

contract is hereby made in four copies, of which three copies are kept by the Ying, the Chen and the Jiang, and one copy by other clans. The terms (10 in total) are listed as follows.
April, 15th year of the reign of Emperor Guangxu.[47]

The contract was signed by every household in Yingjiapeng Village of Fenghua Countyand provided detailed rules on a wide range of issues. For example, it specified who was qualified for the post of the head (those in mourning and widows were not eligible) and laid out that each individual could serve in the post for three years. It also provided the fees that members were required to pay, mortgage requirements, and also who was responsible for collecting taxes and what their specific duties were. With these specified provisions, the contract was approved by the community in Yingjiapeng Village, which did not have direct connections with the national law.

4.4.1.2 Protection of Natural Resources

People cared about protecting the environment as much as they did about their livelihoods. In addition to the general regulations outlined by national laws on the conservation of natural ecological resources, there were also rural agreements with detailed and protective provisions for the living space in which villager residents were born and grew. Drawing upon generations of experience, village residents had clear ideas on what they had to protect and how to go about it. For example, during the reign of Emperor Qianlong of Qing Dynasty, a village in Ruyuan County of Guangdong Province issued the *Stone Prohibition against Agricultural Activities to Facilitate Afforestation,* comprising of ten provisions. Below is an excerpt from this inscription.

Anyone who acts against this prohibition shall be punished. Those who refuse to accept these penalties shall be brought to court for trial and shown no mercy. This stele is hereby set up to keep village residents informed of these regulations.
Early winter, 21st year of the reign of Emperor Qianlong.[2]

The signatures on the stele show that 22 families participated in the creation of this law, and it applied to everyone living in the village, including both locals and new residents, the Han, and ethnic minorities. With the prohibitions detailing a series of ten provisions, including against cutting down trees and stealing crops, the stele is a typical example of village regulations. Violators shall first be punished based on the regulations, and in cases of severe violations beyond the scope of the regulations, offenders shall be punished harshly by the official courts. It is clear that these village regulations possessed at least some authority, with the national law only being applied for particularly serious violations.

Many other villages also traditionally set rules to protect natural resources. These rules usually applied to particular groups concentrated in a small community, such as to those of the same clan (some villages consisted solely of members of the same

[47] Zhang R. (2010). *Selected Documents on Zhedong Agreements in the Qing Dynasty*. Zhejiang University Press.105.

clan) or those who worshiped at the same ancestral temple. Some villages also enforced rules to protect trees thought to be auspicious according to Feng Shui beliefs. For example, a clan in Encun Village, Renhua County, Guangzhou, set up a stele inscribed with prohibitions against cutting down trees to protect the Feng Shui of the village. Below is a paragraph from these inscriptions:

> It is prescribed here that village residents are banned from cutting down trees ... Anyone who is caught breaking these rules will be punished heavily with no mercy. Those who dare to resist shall be restrained and tried. Everyone must respect and observe these rules, and no violations are allowed.
>
> Patriarch Meng Chenrui& other elders of high prestige.
>
> Autumn, 15th year of the reign of Emperor Guangxu (Year of the Ox).[48]

It is clear that these prohibitions served the purpose of protecting the village's *Feng Shui* (Chinese traditional practice of harmonizing individuals with their surrounding environment by using energy forces "*Qi*"). It was believed that trees guaranteed good Feng Shui for the village and that cutting down these trees would lead to bad Feng Shui. For this reason, rules were made which stated "Cutting down trees, even if just a branch, is prohibited. Violations will lead to heavy punishment, and anyone who reports these violations or helps capture offenders will be rewarded." It can be inferred from the inscribed signatures that this agreement was jointly created by Patriarch Meng Chenrui and other highly respected seniors in a village mainly inhabited by members of the Meng clan. Deeply influenced by Feng Shui, people in Huizhou (modern-day Anhui Province) were keen on protecting trees near sources of water and on hills with cemeteries. In February 1767 (the 32nd year of the reign of Emperor Qianlong), the Huang family in Tafang Village, Qimen County, created a prohibition banning people from damaging the surroundings of hill cemeteries, with the first two articles of this prohibition detailing the penalties to be imposed.

Article 1 Cutting down trees on hill cemeteries is prohibited. Violators shall pay for a public show.

Article 2 Anyone who sets the mountainside on fire, burns down forests or digs out the stumps of pine or fir trees shall pay for a public show.[49]

Another example was the prohibitions inscribed in stone produced in Huansha, Penglong Village, Qimen County, in 1797 (the second year of the reign of Emperor Jiaqing). The inscriptions highlighted the hazards of deforestation and the importance of prohibiting acts of deforestation, outlawing actions such as cutting down trees, burning down forests, or converting forests to farmlands to protect natural forests. It also specified incentives and penalties to ensure that these laws were followed and implemented.

[48] *Villagers Are Banned from Cutting Tress*, issued in the 15th year during the reign of Emperor Guangxu. The stele is now housed in the Encun village in Renhua xian in Guangzhou. The text can be found on page 112 in the *Collection of Guangding Stone Texts*.

[49] Chen, Q. (2006). The Tradition of Sponsoring a Public Show When Violate the Rule of Protecting Trees in Past Huizhou. *Anhui Linye*, (4).

Anyone who sets mountainsides on fire or burns down forest shall pay for a public show and would be liable for any damage caused. Anyone who digs out the stumps of pine or fir trees shall sponsor a Doutai (drama competition). Anyone who chops down pine or fir trees for wood (dry or wet) to build a fire shall pay for a public show.[50]

Today, the well-preserved Shuikou trees in Qimen County remain a wondrous sight to behold, due in no small part to the social agreements created and strictly enforced by the ancestors of locals living in the region.

Village regulations generally include both penalties and incentives. For example, while violators were punished by being forced to pay for a public show, village residents were rewarded by being able to watch and enjoy a play. The rules that violators should pay for a public show were usually inscribed on stone tablets. Clans were required to draft an agreement and announce it by including it in their clan genealogy, posting it in public places, and organizing a public show. While costly, doing so had a community-wide impact. Once the date of the performance was set, clan members would slaughter pigs for a feast and invite the gentry in neighboring villages to come and watch the performance. Before the performance, they would read out the agreement and warn local and neighboring village residents not to break it; otherwise, they would have to pay for a public play themselves. Besides watching the play, the invited gentry would also take on the role of ensuring that the agreement was followed.[51]

Penalizing violators by asking them to pay for a public show was a mild penalty, serving as a deterrent to village residents and a way to penalize violators while entertaining local residents at the same time. *The Defendant*, a Chinese movie released in 1994, reproduced how this punishment system worked in rural China. In the movie, the protagonist Shangang Ye, the chief of Duiduiping Village, gathers village residents together to punish Qiangying, Shanwa's wife, for abusing her elderly mother-in-law. He demands that Qiangying pay the money for screening a movie for the entire village and creates a new rule that anyone who abuses the elderly shall be punished by being forced to pay the money for screening a movie for the village. This new rule, unanimously accepted by the whole village, is an example of village regulations in traditional China.

Some villages traditionally worshiped deities at ancestral temples. Based on the belief that trees near ancestral temples were the guardians for these deities, rules were made to prevent village residents from cutting down these trees. For instance, village residents in Daxili Village, Shangshe Town, Yu County, Shanxi Province, worshiped deities at Sanguan Temple and Xiama Temple. To protect the trees surrounding the temples, they created prohibitions inscribed in stone banning the practice of cutting down trees.

---

[50] Chun, Y. (2009). *Studies on the Civil Mediation System in the Late Qing Dynasty*. Beijing University Press. 212.

[51] Chun, Y. (2009). *Studies on the Civil Mediation System in the Late Qing Dynasty*. Beijing University Press. 211.

> Anyone who burns trees down shall be fined a dan (equivalent to about 133 pounds) of grain.
>
> July, 32nd year of the reign of Emperor Qianlong.[52]

The inscriptions also stated that these prohibitions be enacted after discussion among the whole village, granting the agreement more authority and indicating that all village residents must follow these rules. This shows that these village regulations were not just statements inscribed on stone tablets or printed on papers; they were rules that every village resident must strictly observe.

4.4.1.3 Maintaining Order in the Community

Despite the ancient Chinese statement that all lands under heaven fall within the domain of the emperor and all people living on this land are subject to his rule, it is doubtful whether the power of the emperor can be so extensive. Indeed, in rural China, the proverb that Heaven is high and the emperor is far away is more realistic. Village residents rarely dealt with the government at all in their lifetime, unless they committed serious crimes such as murder, arson, theft, and robbery or failed to pay taxes. Public security was maintained by village residents with a high degree of autonomy. In many rural areas, public security regulations reflect the image of rural social organizations and self-governance. For example, 34 representatives from 20 villages in Anning County, Yunnan Province, gathered together to discuss how to maintain the public security and signed a joint agreement specifying the rules. To ensure peace and security in all 20 villages, the agreement required village residents to stay on guard against any local troublemakers, criminals from outside the county, and *Yamen* (local magistrate's office) clerks and runners who disturbed the local people. Village residents were supposed to turn to the government for anything beyond the scope of the agreement. Interestingly, the signatures on the agreement were in the shape of radial concentric circles,[53] symbolizing the determination of these village residents to follow the rules and emphasizing the fact that the agreement was signed voluntarily by representatives of the 20 villages.

An ideal rural society features down-to-earth and honest people. Village residents would try to prevent any harmful practices that were believed to have negative impacts on their lives or society at large: they would sign an agreement after resolving a matter. Once the agreement was entered into effect, each one of them would ensure that the agreement was implemented and followed by all members of the village. For example, in Qing Dynasty, the Wang family from a village contributed to the signing of an agreement that aimed to ban gambling in the community. As

[52] Stone Prohibition Against Felling Trees Surrounding Sanguan Temple. The stele is now housed in the Hama Temple in Daxili village, Yu county, Shanxi Province. The text can be found on page 296 in the collection *Collection of Stones Texts Found in Shanxi Province: Volume of Yu County in Yangquan City*, compiled by Liu Zemin and Li Yuming and published by Sanjin Press in 2010.

[53] Wu, X. & Xu, Z. (2013). *Collection of Documents of Agreements Housed in Yunnan Museum*. Volume 3. People's Publishing House. 270.

gambling was ubiquitous in the village and accounted for unemployment and poverty, the Wang family called upon all other village residents to enact an agreement against the evil practice so as to avoid possible crises invoked by it. Including both national laws and local prohibitions, the agreement specified penalties for gamblers and those aiding and abetting them, with an aim to restoring good family values and helping people get back on the right track. It also clarified what purpose the agreement served, what grounds the penalties were based on, and how the document should be preserved so that it could be referenced in the future, keeping all village residents informed of every detail. The agreement was backed by authority and had legal power, requiring all village residents to strictly follow its rules.[54]

To ensure that all village residents were of good moral character, some villages enacted agreements banishing slaves bought by local residents; some villages even inscribed these agreements on stone tablets. For example, in Panyu County of Guangzhou, four influential clans proposed to create prohibitions inscribed in stone determining how slaves belonging to local families were to be treated. Below is a paragraph from the inscriptions.

> Our village stresses the hierarchical differences between masters and slaves. In general, slaves of local village residents shall be expelled from the village. If they have to stay for some reason, they shall strictly observe this hierarchy from generation to generation, including when it concerns coming-of-age and marriage ceremonies, funeral ceremonies, housing arrangements, and dress codes. They are permanently banned from building ancestral halls. The local gentry shall not cover for and keep slaves who break these rules, and village residents are encouraged to report slaves who violate these rules. If they are found guilty, the Bureau will expel them immediately and expropriate their houses and fields with proper compensation. These permanent prohibitions are hereby enacted when the Chen Yazhan (a slave of the Wang family) case is handled by the Bureau.
>
> Clans of Wang, He, Lí, Lǐ, Renrang Bureau.
>
> Mid-May, 11th year of the reign of Emperor Guangxu.[55]

The inscribed agreement was highly discriminatory and exclusive, but despite that, it was accepted by the local people and had the force of law. Village regulations of fundraising for sacrificial events and praying for blessings and disaster prevention played a prominent role in uniting people of an acquaintance society and enriching village culture. They vary from village to village, due to the differences between these villages (between the deities people worshiped, economic conditions, the scale of sacrificial events, the funds needed to establish She (sites of sacrifice or societies)), but once an agreement was created by a village, signatories had to observe the rules. For instance, in Tang and Song Dynasties, the Dunhuang region had a tradition of establishing societies. To regulate the establishment of those societies and their activities, village residents would sign bylaws laying out the detailed rules and membership requirements. Below are a few examples of these bylaws: *Bylaws Enacted by the Xixiang Society in Rufeng Fang during the Reign of Emperor*

---

[54] Chu, Y. (2009). *Studies on the Civil Mediation System in the Late Qing Dynasty*, Beijing University Press. 209–210.

[55] *Stone Prohibition Enacted by Four Clans*, enacted in May in the 11th year during the reign of Emperor Guangxu. The text can be found on page 74 in the *Collection of Guangding Stone Texts*.

Xuan of Tang Dynasty, Bylaws for the Buddhist Grotto Construction Project Led by the Monk Fuhuiin the Year 970, Bylaws of Societies in Dunuhangjun, Bylaws of Society Establishment, Ancestral Bylaws, Bylaws Enacted by the Society Organized By Wang Wu in the Year 855, Bylaws of the Jingfangxiang Women's Society Enacted in the Year 968, Bylaws of A Society Enacted in the Year 894, Bylaws of the Women's Society Enacted in the Year 968, Buddhist Society's Revised Bylaws Enacted by Wang Nuzi and Members of other Buddhist Societies in the Year 828, Society Bylaws Enacted in February of the Year 983, and *Buddhist Temples Renovation Association Bylaws Enacted in the Year of 1004.*

In traditional China, village residents had the custom of establishing religious societies and holding religious events. To ensure the smooth operation of these societies, they would enact bylaws on various topics, such as how society leaders should be chosen, how expenses would be allotted, and what the membership requirements were. For example, in the Qing Dynasty, residents of a village in Eastern Zhejiang Province signed a bylaw titled *Yingyoukan Society* specifying the purpose and event time of their society, the rights and obligations of the heads and members, and the membership fees. The bylaw was jointly formulated by all members and everyone should abide by it. The society also needed to host large meetings frequently (e.g., the annual Yingyoukan meeting was held three times a year), so village residents needed to pool their money, organize the meetings collectively, and elect a head to be responsible for the arrangements. Organizing meetings was considered a "public welfare event" for the entire village, the operation of which was ensured by the bylaw specifying the rights and obligations of village residents.[56]

4.4.2 Trade Regulations

In late imperial China, merchants from the same industry tended to unite together to start a *hui-guan* (the most common term at this time for merchant associations as well as for the buildings that housed them) and make regulations within the associations (known as articles of association in modern times) to maintain their trade reputation and allow for members to help each other out.

These established regulations, which would be inscribed on stone tablets and announced to all merchants, played an instrumental role in governing trading activities and shaping a healthy environment for both sellers and consumers. As the cornerstone of trade and a way to ensure the smooth operation of trading activities, the rules dealt with a broad range of topics, including how to maintain business reputation and engage in fair trades, how merchants who cheated consumers should be

[56] *Bylaw of the Yingyou Kanhui*, enacted in the fourth year during the reign of Emperor Guangxu. The text can be found on page 110 in the collection *Selected Documents on Zhedong Agreements in the Qing Dynasty*, compiled by Zhang Jieren and published by Zhejiang University Press in 2010.

treated, and how merchants who sold stolen goods or evaded taxes should be punished.

Take the *Newly Established Stele Displaying the Rules of the Leather Industry* in Beijing as an example. The stele clearly lays out rules against the purchase (or reselling) of stolen goods. It provides that "All merchants in the leather industry are prohibited from purchasing stolen leather patches, boiled or raw. Violators shall be fined according to the number of patches they had purchased, as well as taking into account the majority opinion of all other merchants. Those who refuse to pay fines shall be regarded as thieves and be punished accordingly." "Anyone who witnesses a purchase of stolen or lost leather patches and reports this to the head of the leather association shall be awarded two liang (100 g) of silver."[57] The rules include both penalties for purchasing stolen leather and rewards for those who report thieves or offer assistance with identifying the rightful owners and are a good example of the rules for merchant associations at that time.

Trading principles such as "honesty is the best policy," "selling without cheating," and "harmony brings wealth" were upheld by Chinese merchants in imperial times. Though there were also phrases such as "no merchant is not self-seeking," "self-seeking" here did not mean that a merchant would do anything to cheat his consumers to earn unlawful income but that he simply wanted to make more money by persuading customers to buy more of his goods. The practice of a merchant selling counterfeit goods or tarnishing the reputation of others was banned not only in the leather industry but in all other industries.

For example, the *Agreed-upon General Rules of the Anhuai Silverware Association* provides that "Anyone caught selling silver of inferior quality or cheating consumers through theft or copying the work of other shops shall be fined or brought to justice depending on how severe the damages are."[58] From this text, it can be inferred that a merchant who commits a minor offense would be fined and punished internally, while one who commits a serious offense would be brought before local government courts and be punished under national law.

Competition was a fact of life for merchants in the same industry. Assuming that no rules were made to manage their actions, unhealthy competition would inevitably arise, leading to disorder. As such, many merchant associations would make rules based on how markets operated and their actual conditions to better govern the merchant behavior and ensure healthy competition.

Take the Shanxi Grocery Stores Association as an example. During the reign of Emperor Qianlong, the Association passed a set of rules for grocery stores inscribed on stone tablets on September 17, 1785.[59] The rules detailed what merchants should

---

[57] Peng, Z. (1997). *Collection of Stone Texts Regarding Industry and Commerce in the Qing Dynasty*. Zhongzhou Classics Publishing House. 24.

[58] Peng, Z. (1997). *Collection of Stone Texts Regarding Industry and Commerce in the Qing Dynasty*. Zhongzhou Classics Publishing House. 117.

[59] *Agreed-upon Rules of the Grocery Businesses*. The stele was erected in the 50th year during the reign of Emperor Qianlong and is now housed in the west hall of Shanshan huiguan in Sheqi County, Henan Province. The text can be found on pages 379–380 in the collection *Selected Stone*

know before opening a store, the principles underlying the normal functioning of a store, what to avoid when doing businesses, how to better treat customers, and how to compete with other stores fairly. In addition, it also laid out what penalties should be imposed on rule-breakers. These rules, though not submitted to the government, still had legal power over all merchants in the grocery store industry.

Another indispensable part of the rules for associations was to promote an environment where association members could mutually help each other out. Mutual aid relief would be set up to guarantee that every member could have all the necessities they required; emergency aid relief would also be provided to encourage members to fight in unity against threats from outsiders. United actions, however, were taken cautiously as they involved the overall interests of the entire industry. A good example would be the *Agreed-upon Rules of Zhengyici Silverware Association* (created in 1721), which stipulates:

It is inevitable that unexpected troubles or disasters may strike at any time to any member of our association. When that happens, all other members shall assist the troubled member and help him overcome his struggles. This aid scheme, however, should not be used for outsiders or members who invite trouble upon themselves. However, if an outsider who is in the right finds himself in trouble, all members of our association shall come to their assistance regardless of the danger. Members who refuse to help be fined 10 liang of silver.[60]

The text describes how emergency aid relief would be granted to both association members and morally righteous persons but denied to idlers and those who commit evil.

Some merchant associations would constantly make revisions to their rules after the first version has been created, so as to constantly adapt to change. For example, the *Newly Established Rules of the Suzhou Ruyi Association* expounded on the reasons why a new set of rules had to be established: the past rules were "out of date and disorganized" and possessed numerous loopholes even after multiple revisions. That was why a new and better-organized set of rules were necessary.[61]

Replacing "outdated" rules was not something new to the craft and commercial industries, as the government also ordered steles with outdated rules and regulations to be dismantled. The emergence of a new industry or the expansion of a small industry would be almost certainly accompanied by a new or revised set of rules. For example, the *Stele Displaying the Agreed-upon Rules of the Sesame Industry in Shanghai County* (created in 1871) specified that "no rules were ever established for the sesame industry before 1856, as there were only a few sesame stores with little custom." Entering 1861, however, "stores began to proliferate and trades volume

Texts Found in Shanxi Province in the Ming and Qing Dynasties, compiled by Zhang Zhengming, Ke Dawei, and Wang Yonghong and published by the Shanxi Publishing Group in 2009.

[60] Peng, Z. *Collection of Stone Texts Regarding Industry and Commerce in the Qing Dynasty*. 35–36.

[61] Wang, G. *Selected Stone Texts Regarding the History of Suzhou City since the Ming and Qing Dynastie*. 323.

quickly grew." Under these conditions, the establishment of a sesame association and of a set of rules needed to be prioritized.[62]

In order to protect their common property, many merchant associations would inscribe common property contracts on stone tablets (as "copies") and request support from the government to protect these tablets.[63] This practice complied with national law and was instrumental in preventing the destruction of common property. In these cases, rules for merchant associations were in line with national law. For example, under the sixth section of the articles on illegal selling of common property in the *Statutes on Revenue of the Great Qing Code*, "descendants who illegally sell their ancestral lands or charitable fields that are part of common property… shall be punished pursuant to regulations."

4.4.3 Regulations of Societies

In Imperial China, there was a myriad of self-governing societies that would establish rules independently to deal with a broad range of internal issues.

Charitable activities were mostly carried out by individual clans, charity organizations and houses, private schools, and academies and were supported by the government.

The government also recognized administrative rules established for charity work by organizations to encourage charitable activities and ease the burden on government agencies. *Deyilu,* a book compiled by Yu Zhi during the reign of Emperor Tongzhi, details rules for more than 60 charitable organizations. The names of some of these organizations are listed here for readers to have an idea of what these organizations were:

Rules of the Fan Lineage Charitable Estate, Rules of the Society for Sharing Goodness, Rules of the Society for Supporting New-born Infants of Poor Families, Articles of Infant Orphanages, Rules of the Society for the Care of Widows, Articles of the Society for the Care of Young Widows, Articles of the Society for the Care of the Homeless Elderly, Rules for the Adoption of Orphans in the Eleventh Lunar Month, Rules for the Care of Beggars in the Eleventh Lunar Month, Articles of the Life-saving Society, Articles of the Firefighting Society, Articles of the Pharmaceutical Society, Articles of the Society for Helping Refugees, Articles of Charitable Granaries, Articles for Combating Famines, Articles for Distributing Charitable Porridge During Famines, Rules of Supporting New-born Infants in Poor Families in Famine Times, Articles of the Sericulture Society, Rules for Combating Floods, Articles for Catching Locusts, Rules of the Society for Promoting Frugality, Articles of the Society for Freeing Captive Animals, Rules for Freeing Captive Animals to

---

[62] Peng, Z. *Collection of Stone Texts Regarding Industry and Commerce in Qing Dynasty*. 75.

[63] Li, X. (2010). Industrial and commercial norms as customary law in the Qing Dynasty: Centering on the jurisprudential analysis of guild stone inscriptions, *Legal Science*, (6).

Rivers Governed by the State, Rules of the Society for Raising Funds from the Rich During Festivals, Articles of Sowing, Rules of the Society for the Care of the Poor During Cold Times, Rules of the Society for Aiding in Burying Deceased Family Members, Rules of the Society for Ensuring Burials of the Deceased, Rules for Protecting Graves, Rules for Collecting and Burying Unidentified Corpses, Articles of Morgues' Expenditure, Rules for Obtaining Loans to Buy Given Coffins, Rules for Teaching How to Have Filial Piety, Yimen Clan Rules, Rules of Sacrificial Halls, Household Rules, School Cleaning Rules, Rules of Academies, Articles of the Studying Society, Rules of Yuedong Charitable Kindergarten, Articles of Biantong Charitable Primary School, Rules of Kindergartens, Articles of the Society for Collecting and Disposing Erotic Books, Articles of the Book Society for Encouraging Virtue, Rules of the Society for Encouraging the Recycling of Waste Paper, Rules of the Society for Encouraging the Cherishing of Grains, Articles of the Society for Encouraging Goodness, Rules of Encouraging Virtue, Rules of the Education Society, Rules of the Lantian Lü Clan, Articles of the Baojia System, Rules of the Society for the Care of the Homeless, Rules of the Landed Gentry, Rules of Teachings for the Masses, Articles of Prison Labor, and *Rules of Doing Charities Without Donating Money*.

The rules mentioned above largely focused on charitable activities but also covered issues including education, rehabilitating offenders, the *Baojia* system, and campaigns for informing commoners of the law.

In addition, different groups would also make rules for their own groups independently. For example, the literati established societies and made rules for these societies; the names of their societies sounded more elegant than those founded by farmers and village residents and were thus also known as "elegant societies." There were *Rules of the Grace Society, Rules of Charitable Schools, Rules of the Archery Society, Rules of the Jishan Academy, Rules of the Chilu Academy, Rules of the Donglin Academy, Explanations For Clan Rules, Rules of the Zhengren Society, Revised Rules of the Zhengren Society, Rules of the Shenglian Society, Rules of the Studying Society, Rules of the Zhenshuai Society, Rules of the Guhuan Society, Rules of School Lecturing, Rules of the Zhongshan Academy, Rules of the Reading Society, Rules of the Society for Freeing Captive Animals, Rules of Monthly Gatherings,* and *Rules of Gatherings on the Date of Confucius' Birthday.*

Comprehensive village regulations were created by families and clans, specific regions, or activity types, such as the *Village Regulations of the Lü Clan, Revised Village Regulations of the Lantian Lü Clan, Nangan Village Regulations, Taiquan Village Ritual Proprieties, Compiled Village Regulations, Village Regulations on the Baojia System, Community Governance Rules, Agreed-upon Rules of the Same Li,* and *Currently Effective Village Regulations.*[64]

In summary, village regulations and community agreements in traditional China fall into four categories, which are administrative or natural village regulations, clan

[64] *Customary Law in the Imperial China* is considered as the most comprehensive collection of civil agreements in Imperial China. It was compiled by Yang Yifan and Liu Ducai and published by Social Sciences Academic Press in 2014

village regulations, society village regulations, and group village regulations. They touch upon numerous different topics, including family and clan rules, forest protection, common clan property, cemeteries, agreements, gambling, the establishment of schools, promotion of education, and methods of mediation. The agreements both provided information and described prohibitions and specified both penalties and incentives. They were either written down or inscribed on steles and planks. Paper agreements were easy to carry around and were accessible by every household for later reference, while agreements were inscribed on steles or temples to inform the general public of their provisions and as a symbol of their importance and permanence.[65]

National law and social agreements support each other and serve the shared purpose of maintaining social stability and harmony. While national law provides broad guidelines governing the actions of everyone, social agreements specify detailed rules regulating people's behavior. The latter is both more acceptable and familiar to the local populace, as it deals with issues closely related to their daily lives.

4.5 Family Regulations and Clan Rules

A family is the basic unit of a society, and a clan is the extension of a family. The supreme power of emperors is the best representation of patriarchy, a social system that highlights the power of the male heads of a family. As family structure has a direct bearing on the stability of the society at large, the Chinese imperial legal system served the primary function of maintaining a patriarchal clan system based on bloodlines. The term "clan" referred to the royal family in the pre-Qin days, after which its definition extended to any group of people united by kinship bonds.

Clan affairs involved government participation but were primarily managed by the clan members themselves. The system of self-governance was mainly supported by a variety of family-based normative documents and codes of conduct, which were divided into family codes, family rules, family warnings, clan admonitions, clan rules, rules for ancestral halls, and rules for charitable estates. Some family rules were made independently while some were added to genealogy books. With rules covering many aspects of family life, including those that guided people to treat family and clan members, friends, emperors, state, and law in a proper manner, family rules that had the force of law represented the highest moral standard as well as the basic norm of clan members' behaviors. They were highly practical and conformed to the traditional Chinese moral system, emphasizing filial piety, loyalty toward rulers, and respect for national law. The academic community tends to refer to them as "clan laws" and regarded them as part of the "community-based laws." Family rules and national laws were independent of each other, though they were

[65] Chun, Y. (2009). *Studies on the Civil Mediation System in the Late Qing Dynasty*, Beijing University Press. 208.

also closely related in terms of functions and forms. Sometimes they contradicted each other but in most cases intertwined with and complemented each other, playing an indispensable role in guaranteeing community order. With the participation of local people and support from the state, family rules developed diverse and unique characteristics.

4.5.1 Guidelines on Personal and Family Disciplining

As the Chinese proverb goes, "sweep your own house before you sweep the world." Simply put, it means that anyone aspiring to contribute to society should organize their own matters first, as expecting someone who cannot even manage their own family affairs to achieve something big is ultimately quixotic. According to Confucianism, self-development is a prerequisite for family management, state rule, and world harmony. It represents a fundamental principle that guides people to behave appropriately, do the right things, and serve their country. This shows that families in traditional China valued moral development and order and explains why many families, especially the families of scholar-officials, created family rules and passed them down generation after generation. Some rules were passed down verbally and gradually became part of the family culture. Generally, family rules were created by the most prestigious and respected clan members and inherited through generations. As a code of family conduct, family rules served to provide moral guidance, while other community agreements served to bind people's behavior.

Why was it important to create family rules? The preface to the *Family Rules* (*Genealogy of the Wang Family in Aotai*) explains the significance of family rules, stating, "It is thus important to respect your ancestors' instructions and create family rules by collecting words of wisdom. As indispensable as clothes and food, family rules regulate family members' moral conduct and relationships. Just like a plumb line is used to cut wood straight, family rules guide members to behave themselves." This shows that people created family rules as a sign of respect for their ancestors and to regulate family members' behavior. As written in the genealogy of the Zhang family in Wujin County, Jiangsu Province, "Emperors enact the state law to ensure the rule of the state, and in the same vein, heads of families create rules to regulate family members' behavior. Without laws, a country would descend into disorder; without rules, a family would fall into disunity."[66] In other words, family rules played an important role in uniting the entire family. Without generally accepted rules, it was impossible for family members to recognize the authority of the heads and build a united community.

The Yang family in Keqiao, Shaoxing City, Zhejiang Province, also emphasized the importance of family rules. "A man must know how to manage his family before

[66] Volume 2 "Clan Rules" in the *Genealogy of the Zhang Family in Piling County*, created during the Republic of China.

he rules a country. If a ruler learns how to rule a country from his family, he must heed the helpful advice from his fathers and brothers to nurture his kindness and wash the evil from him. Not every member of a family develops good moral character. Without honest advice from elders, those family members with moral failings would be at loss and wouldn't know how to do right things. In turn, those with better morals may lose self-discipline and slack off. Over time, the entire family would be prone to bad habits, lose all sense of shame and propriety, and downplay filial piety, codes of friendship, and marriage, thus causing great harm to the existing relationships and social stability. It is necessary that family rules be stipulated."[67]

The Yang family in Jimo, Shandong Province, believed that it was necessary to improve moral education and that family rules had an important role to play in such, as reflected in the family genealogy that states, "The morally superior know how to behave themselves without being taught, while the morally inferior may fail to do so even with external assistance. Yet people with high or low moral character are in the minority, while the majority possesses average moral character. Therefore, whether they can move closer to goodness depends on their moral education. This is why moral education is a permanent task."[68] Based on the Confucian belief that self-development and family management are fundamental for national rule and world harmony, it is necessary to create family rules that help control people's behavior at the family level.

Imperial China witnessed the creation of countless family regulations and rules, among which the *Family Instructions of Mister Yan*, *Family Discussions of Zhu Xi*, and *Family Letters of Zeng Guofan* are best known. Written by Yan Zhitui during Sui Dynasty, *Family Instructions of Mister Yan* was based on his personal experience and knowledge. Yan recommended practical approaches to moral education to instruct his descendants on how to develop their personalities and manage certain issues. In line with the purpose of Confucianism defining the five cardinal relationships (between ruler and subject, father and son, husband and wife, older and younger brothers, and friends)—and the traditional educational philosophy that self-development is a prerequisite for family management, national rule, and world harmony, *Family Instructions of Mister Yan* emphasized the importance of the core function of learning and advocated that a good book should instruct people to practice filial piety and mind their words and action. It also guided family members to look up to take men of great virtue. Since its publishing, the book has served as a respected family education model and won the support of imperial rulers, who even celebrated it as "the best example of family rules." It provided a reference for and had a far-reaching influence on dozens of family rules produced during the Tang and later dynasties, including the *Family Rules of Zhu Xi* (Song Dynasty), *Family Instructions of Zhu Xi* (late Ming Dynasty), and *Rules on Proper Upbringing* (by Chen Hong Mou, Qing Dynasty). Family rules consisted of a variety of helpful

[67] Volume 1 "Family Rules" in the *Genealogy of the Yang Family in Shanyin County*, created during the reign of Emperor Guangx in Zhejiang Province.

[68] *The Genealogy of the Yang Family: Family Rules*, created in Shandong Province.

instructions, guiding family members to develop good habits, improve cultural literacy, conduct themselves around others, develop personality, and respect the law.

For example, the *Family Instructions of Zhu Xi* set standards for daily conduct; guided people on how to treat their spouse, elders, children, and teachers; and emphasized the importance of learning, morality, and law. Many aphorisms in the book are celebrated as words of wisdom even to this day, such as "Do not do evil things, though they may seem petty. Do not give up good things, though they may seem minor," "Do not let personal prejudices affect personal and family matters," and "Do not pursue personal gains at the expense of others and do not be jealous of others' talents." *Family Instructions of Zhu Xi*, with self-development and family management as its fundamental purposes, provided instructions in many aspects of life, including choosing partners and marriage, amending genealogy, sacrificial rituals, how to treat others, education, and political careers, and guided people on how to resolve disputes and abide by the law. Respected as the model family instructions by scholar-officials, it provided a reference for the *Du Family of Xianyuan County Genealogy* (during the reign of Emperor Guangxu) and *Fourteen Family Rules*. The following rules are direct quotes from the *Family Instructions of Zhu Xi*: secure the solemnity of ancestral temples, sincerely perform sacrificial rituals, treat sacrificial utensils with care, look after properties in ancestral temples, regularly revise its genealogy good housewives, clarify the rules for rewards and punishments, minimize unnecessary expenses, maintain the hierarchical relationship between masters and servants, and keep everything well-managed.[69] Similar family rules include the following:

Family Rules (*Genealogy of Family Wang in Aotai*) in Baoan County, Guangdong Province: develop filial piety and perform fraternal duties; respect rituals; show care for neighbors; pay taxes on time; build roads; improve scholars' moral conduct; get married on auspicious days; do not become involved in the opium trade; do not avoid drafts; resolve disputes peacefully; do not sell stolen goods; do not commit any evil acts; do not gamble; and do not privately occupy public property.

The *Revised Genealogy of Family Xiong* in Yiyang City, Hunan Province during the reign of Emperor Guangxu listed roughly 20 family rules: develop filial piety; perform fraternal duties; get along well with friends, clan members, and neighbors; keep family well-managed; follow elders' advice; practice frugality; learn from mistakes; be considerate; do good and help others; give helpful advice; do not drown baby girls; avoid alcoholism; overcome lust; overcome greed; overcome irritability; and resolve disputes peacefully.

The first volume of the *Genealogy of the Xu Family in Yunxi County* created during the reign of Emperor Jiaqing sets out clan rules: abide by state laws; respect hierarchical relationships among family members; get along well with family members; supervise children's behaviors; value moral integrity; women should stay

[69] "Fourteen Family Rules" in the *Genealogy of Du Family of Xianyuan County*, created during the reign of Emperor Guangxu.

home as housewives; practice frugality; resolve disputes peacefully; respect elders' advice; and respect well-educated men.

The *Rules of the Hu Family* (Weichuan, She County, Anhui Province): take good care of ancestral temples; protect ancestral temple property; build tombs; practice filial piety; perform fraternal duties; improve moral conduct; get along well with family members; respect the patriarchal clan system; remain committed to marriage; work hard; practice frugality; pay taxes on time; maintain self-discipline; and resolve disputes peacefully.[70]

The family rules section in the *Genealogy of the Lang Family* (Hebei Province) required clan members to follow the ten instructions: respect Confucianism, develop moral integrity; focus on fundamental issues; study hard; perform marriage and funeral ceremonies properly; carefully fulfill official duties; sincerely perform sacrificial ceremonies; do the right things; show empathy for servants; and honor loyalty. According to the *Genealogy*, the ten instructions helped develop virtues (loyalty for men and obedience for women), which were prized treasures for a family. It also encouraged family members to reward those who respected elders and supported the young to "facilitate the development of talents that may bring grace upon the family name."

The *Family Letters of Zeng Guofan* (Qing Dynasty) was regarded as instructions for the Zeng family.

Some families made rules based on actual family conditions. For instance, the Bian family in Renqiu County during the reign of Emperor Qianlong required members to align their behaviors to the general principle: In dealing with people and other matters, one should remain sober-minded and always stay humble. If people judge you, it is due in no small part to your own fault, so you must learn from mistakes and try to be more considerate and thoughtful. In addition to the general principle, it also brought forward dozens of specific instructions: regularly conduct self-reflection; do good deeds and you will be sent to heaven after death, or you will end up in hell; contribute your wisdom to society; never take noble connections as a display of virility, or you may be despised; do not feel obliged to befriend those who do not have much in common with you; do not brag about your knowledge of poetry and writing at dinner parties or you might attract envy and hatred from guests ashamed of their inferiority; do not joke with wicked men; do not complain of being hard up before others to avoid disdain; develop a generous and forgiving soul; perform filial duties, especially when parents are old, sick, widowed, or poor; husbands should lead by example in performing filial duties; and the law is as important as Confucian classics in education, as it helps settle disputes and protect individuals' rights and interests.[71] Simple and practical, all of these exemplify the rules for established and noble families.

[70] Volume 2 "Clan Rules" in the *Genealogy of the Hu Family in Weichuan,* created in the fourth year of the Republic of China.

[71] *The Genealogy of the Bian Family: Family Rules,* completed by Bian Yuanhou on March 13th in the Bingzi year during the reign of Emperor Qianlong. A copy was created in the 35th year during the reign of Emperor Qianlong and is now housed in Hebei University Library.

The rules for established families became increasingly systematic after revisions over generations. For example, Qian Liu, a warlord in the late Tang Dynasty and founder of the Wuyue kingdom, promulgated *Eight Directives* in 912 CE and *Ten Admonitions* on his deathbed in 932 CE, reminding descendants to stay loyal, perform filial piety, love the people, be hardworking and frugal, and pursue either education or farming. These instructions were passed down throughout generations and refined by Qian's descendants, who produced the *Genealogy of the Qian Family in Wenlingong* in the seventh year during the reign of Emperor Guangxu. The *Genealogy* incorporated *Rules of Family Qian*, which were divided into eight parts, that is, filial piety, fraternal duties, loyalty, honesty, rituals, integrity, rectitude, and sense of shame. In Ming and Qing Dynasties, Qian's descendants produced the *Genealogy of Family Qian*. Family instructions in the *Genealogy* covered issues related to individuals, family, society, and states. The following are excerpts from the family instructions: do not entertain evil thoughts and do not say or do things against your conscience; heaven and earth would forgive you if you learn from your mistakes and amend your ways, and spirits would never bother you if you behave righteously; create family rules that help keep the house tidy and maintain hierarchical relationships among family members to create a sound family environment; be devoted to friends, be nice to neighbors, be sympathetic toward widows and orphans, show respect for the elderly, and care for children; respect the law, maintain moral integrity, love your subjects as a man loves his own children, show no mercy for evil forces, be strict about subordinate supervision, and treat people with empathy; and place public interest before personal concerns and wait for bigger gains instead of seeking immediate benefits.[72]

To sum up, family rules and instructions covered a wide range of topics, including ethical issues, occupation, financial management, marriage, the principles of making friends and dealing with people and other matters, the law, and recreational activities. They were quite similar when it comes to the basic principles, such as practicing filial piety and loyalty and respecting rituals and laws, but were different in terms of details, quality, and length.

4.5.2 Filial Piety as Ethnic Code

Predicated on the substance of "the three cardinal guides and five constant virtues," a core Confucian philosophy, family, or clan rules are made to cover a myriad of subjects, with its main priority to focus on ensuring all its members show filial piety to their parents.

This priority of putting filial piety first is shown by an article from the *Family Rules of Yang Jie,* which was written by Yang Jie during the reign of Emperor

[72] Pages 6–8 in the *Genealogy of the Qian Family in Wenlingong* included in the collection *the Genealogy of the Qian Family*, housed in Yi Zhuang.

Kangxi, a magistrate born in Jimo, Shandong Province. The rules read: "one must show respect and deference to his parents, loyalty to his ruler, kindness to his brothers, and righteousness to his community members. He must also aspire to become a sage and earnestly study the classics." The very first sentence of this article stresses children's duty to show filial piety.[73]

As for how to show filial piety, members of the Yang clan believed that "while a child owes a great debt of gratitude to his parents, it is better for him to settle his affairs first before exhibiting deference to his parents. If he is a scholar, he needs to study his books hard; if he is a farmer, he needs to farm conscientiously; if he is an artisan, he needs to hone his skills and do his job well. A child shall resolve his personal matters first, and then show filial piety to his parents. When a child has the thought of doing a good deed, he must do it without hesitation knowing that his practice will manifest the teachings of his parents. Contrarily, if he intends to commit an evil deed, he must refrain from carrying it out, knowing that it will tarnish the honor of his parents. Furthermore, a child shall not show sadness or negative emotions in front of his parents, nor shall he hurt his parents' feelings. He should show filial piety throughout his entire life. Nowadays, many children tend to hurt their parents' feelings due to trivial matters. Aren't they shameful?" Members also held that "a child shall show filial piety as early as possible." As the old saying goes, "Just as the tree longs for stillness but the wind refuses to stop, so too does a child longs to care for their parents, only to find it is too late."

To summarize, the Yang clan set out four requirements for children. First, a child needs to have a steady job to put his parents' mind at ease; second, he needs to be prudent when making decisions, since what he does largely relates to his parents' reputation. Good deeds are encouraged because they are vital to family honor. Third, he should never let his parents down. Finally, he needs to show filial piety throughout his life and do it in a consistent, timely manner.

The Xie clan in Yihuang, Jiangxi Province, once expounded why filial piety matters in its clan rules: "A mother suffers great physical pain in labor, and the level of pain continues as she breastfeeds her baby for a year or two. When the baby grows up, he should treat his parents with kindness, support them when they get older, talk with them patiently, and greet them every morning and night. He should be grateful that his mother has brought him up. Hereafter all children of the clan shall be aware of this."[74]

The Ye clan in Pingjiang, Hunan Province, required children to show respect and deference to their parents in three aspects. First, they need to not only fulfill their parents' needs but also maintain a good reputation and comply with their parents' teachings. Second, they need to earn enough money as either scholar-officials or

[73] *Genealogy of the Yang Family: Family Rules*, created in Shandong Province.

[74] *Sixth Revised Genealogy of the Xie Family in Yiyi: Family Rules*, created in Yihuang during the reign of Emperor Tongzhi.

farmers to financially support their parents. Third, those who choose to be artisans or merchants need to live a frugal life to have extra money to support their parents."[75]

In almost all clans, showing filial piety was seen as the most fundamental element of becoming a good man. It was no less important than paying tribute to the gods or avoiding evil forces. There was also a hierarchical structure of how dutiful a child can be. On the basic level were moderately dutiful children, who were able to support their parents' basic needs. On the next level were good dutiful children, who could not only afford to support their parents' basic needs but also do things that pleased their parents, such as offering something that their parents never asked for or expected. On the top level were greatly dutiful children, who would both support their parents and reinforce the family honor by doing good deeds for society or the country at large.[76]

At home, a child was required to show filial piety to his parents; in the clan, he needed to show deference to ancestors and clan chiefs while maintaining harmonious relationships with all other clan members. These requirements were included in almost all family or clan rules.

4.5.3 Ties to Bring a Clan Together

4.5.3.1 Maintaining Harmony in the Clan

Every member was expected to show respect to their elders, love to the younger members, and improve their relationships to achieve clan harmony. The *Clan Rules of the Genealogy of the Yao Clan in Wangchuanli* had a total of eight articles, one of which provided that harmony was the key for the clan to last. To achieve harmony required all members to carry out "three musts" and "four duties." The "three musts" were (1) show deference to the venerable, (2) show filial piety to elders, and (3) show respect to the wise. The "four duties" were (1) have compassion for the vulnerable, (2) help orphans and widows, (3) give alms to the poor, and (4) mediate disputes. Outstanding members of the clan were expected to do much more than just the "three musts" and "four duties": they were expected to donate fields to the clan for public use, set up charitable granaries for times of poor harvest, set up charitable schools for families with children unable to afford high tuition costs, and build charitable cemeteries for the burial of unidentified corpses. If every member kept in mind how their ancestors had formed the clan with solidarity in the first place, they would know that maintaining harmony within the clan was the key to its survival.[77]

---

[75] Volume 1 "Five Family Rules" in the *Genealogy of the Ye Family in Pingjiang*, created during the reign of Emperor Guangxu.

[76] Feng, E. (2006). State law, family Rules and the society. *Nanjing University Law Review*, Autumn Issue.

[77] Wooden movable type printing edition, revised by Yao Menglian, 1873

The fourth volume of the *Genealogy of the Zhu Family in Zijiang*, Guizhou Province, during the reign of the Republic of China contained the *Twelve Articles of Family Rules of the Old Genealogy* that specified:

Showing deference to our ancestors represents our overall respect for the clan, and respect underpins the unity of the clan. If a member is unable to afford the costs involved in his coming-of-age ceremony, his wedding, the funerals of his parents, or sacrifices, families with stronger finances shall help him, either independently or collectively, to cover the costs. If a skilled member is unemployed, richer families shall help him find a job or rent him land to farm so that he can support himself and not become an idler or a thief. If a smart child is unable to afford tuition at school, richer families shall also financially aid him in finishing his schooling, as if the child becomes prominent when he grows up, he can enhance the honor of the clan.[78]

The duties of showing filial piety and maintaining clan harmony were emphasized here. This is also the case with the Hong family in Jiayingzhou, Guangdong Province, the first article of whose family rules provided "to all members: a child must show respect to his parents, and a little brother must do the same to his elder brothers. The young must show respect to their elders, and an inferior must do the same to his superiors. Harmony and respect are the cornerstones of the clan, and all members are expected to be honest and loyal."

The seventh article, titled "Maintaining the Harmony of Both the Clan and the Town," pointed out that "though some of our members may feel close only to their families but distant to the clan as a whole, we are all our ancestors' descendants, and on that point, we are the same."[79]

The family rules of the Wu family in Shaoxing, Zhejiang Province, once explained why harmony was crucial to the clan: "All members of the clan are descendants of a common ancestor. Though they are different in terms of social status, each is an integral part of the clan. When a member is unfortunately stuck in poverty and misfortune or falls ill, other members are expected to lift him out of the situation. When a member plans on starting a career, others are expected to give him helpful advice. When a member makes mistakes, others are expected to correct his wrongful behavior. All members are encouraged to share their personal possessions and food with others. If all these rules can be observed, our kinship will be so reinforced that the spirits of our deceased ancestors may rest in peace."[80]

The rules of the Yang family in Qingjiang County, Jiangxi Province, emphasized a bond among its members: "All members have the same roots. Though personal finances vary from member to member, all are expected to help each other. If any dispute arises among the members, it shall be settled in accordance with the opinion

[78] Movable type printing edition, revised by Zhu Qiling, housed in Nankai University Library.

[79] *Continued Genealogy of the Hong Family: Ancestors' Instructions*. Zhejiang: Zhengjiang People's Publishing House, 1982.

[80] Volume 1 "Family Rules" in the *Genealogy of the Wu Family in Tangpu (Shaoxing, Zhejiang Province)*.

of the clan's venerable elder. Any member who dares bully others and bring shame to the clan shall be punished accordingly."[81]

The rules of the Xu family in Qingjiang, Jiangxi Province, promoted mutual assistance among members: "All our members come from a common bloodline and shall be treated equally. When a member has spare cash or possessions, he is expected to share them with those in need. When a member holds a wedding or funeral, all others are expected to be present at the event. The philosophy of sharing and mutual assistance is attributed to people living in the past who, as neighbors, shared common wells, a practice that demonstrated their bonds and closeness."[82]

As can be seen above, families and clans highly valued the concept of common descent and bloodline (no matter how many generations had passed).

4.5.3.2 Genealogical Purity

A prominent feature of traditional Chinese society is the kin groups based on male descent lines, which predicated the structure of genealogy books. Revisions to the books could ensure the continuity of the male bloodline, reinforcing the kinship solidarity. As genealogy played such a crucial role, clans were all highly attentive to their genealogical purity, staying alert to the invasion of non-kin members. They would repeatedly examine the identity of every member recorded in their genealogy books. Moreover, some charitable estates' rules emphasized the importance of the protection of genealogy books and inheritance.

For example, the *Clan Rules of the Genealogy of the Yao Clan in Wangchuanli* particularly emphasized the importance of genealogical records, specifying that genealogical records shall be kept confidential for generations by designated members of each kin group. They shall take the original genealogical records to annual sacrificial ceremonies and return them home at the end of the ceremonies. Should one member not properly manage the records, by staining them or allowing them to be damaged by mice, he shall be punished in the shrine before the ancestral spirit tablets under the watch of the shrine head and all other members. He shall no longer be trusted with the records, and another capable member in his kin group shall be elected for the management. The new elected member's information shall be recorded by the clan for later inspection. If any member dares betray the ancestors by selling the genealogical records or defile the clan by making profits through selling the copies of the records, even if he does not harm the interests of clan members, he has harmed the honor of ancestors and shall not be allowed to enter the shrine again. If he insists on entering the shrine, he shall be brought to government courts and tried under the law. He who randomly revises or falsifies records shall be punished under both clan rules and national law."

[81] *Third Revised Genealogy of the Yang Family in Yongbin (Jiangxi Province): Clan Rules.*

[82] *Genealogy of the Xu Family in Yunxi (Qingjiang County, Jiangxi Province): Clan Rules.*

The *Rules of the Yanling Charitable Estate* provided that "inheritance matters are the most important part of genealogy. If a member has no children as heir to his estate, the eldest son of his closest relative shall become the legal heir. If his closest relative has only one son, they shall become legal heir entitled to two or three inheritances. If the eldest son of his closest relative refuses the inheritance, the member shall gather all clan members in the charitable state to decide who shall be his legal heir in front of the local deity spirit tablets. Chosen heirs that still refuse the inheritance shall be removed from the genealogical records, and their younger brothers shall not be entitled to the inheritance to prevent the genealogy from being disturbed. Anyone who gives his inheritance to outsiders with different surnames will have their rights to grain from the charitable estate revoked. Anyone who attempts to allow the outsiders to inherit will have their right to grain from the charitable estate revoked. If a member's son becomes the legal heir to another member's inheritance, the son is not permitted to squander the inheritance, or it shall be confiscated by the clan."[83]

The *Family Rules in the Genealogy of Li Family* in Jiaohe, Hebei Province, provided that "if a member marries a woman with sons, the sons shall not be recorded in the clan's genealogy book as this disturbs the clan structure. If the eldest child of a member's wife is a female, the eldest son of his first concubine shall be the legal heir to his inheritance. If the member's concubines have no sons, the younger son of his wife shall be the legal heir. If the member has no heir, he shall select a son of his close relatives to be the legal heir. If the selected son refuses to inherit, the member shall instead select a son of his distant relatives to inherit. If both selected sons refuse to inherit, he may select an outsider to inherit, but this has to be officially approved by the clan. The outsider approved by the clan shall be recorded in the genealogy book." These words are a telling clue to the fact that clans restricted disturbance of the structure of the clan by outsiders.

After the collapse of the Qing government, the idea of genealogical purity continued to exist in society, supported by governments in both legislation and judicial processes. For example, in the early days of the Republic of China, the Supreme Court of Justice (*daliyuan*) issued a series of judicial interpretations on the issues of maintaining the stability of clans by rejecting outsiders with different surnames. The Court held that the "New Code of the Great Qing specified that the structure of a clan shall not be disturbed by outsiders. If an old genealogy book records an outsider, it shall stay that way and not be changed arbitrarily" (No. 1271, Third Year of the Republic of China) and that "the persons in charge of revising a genealogy book have the right to refuse the addition of an outsider, but if an outsider was previously admitted, then the revisers have no right to refuse his addition. Other members of the clan shall not dissent" (No. 916, Ninth Year of the Republic of China).[84]

[83] *Selected Stone Texts Regarding the History of Suzhou City Since Ming and Qing Dynasties*, pages 276–281. Suzhou: Suzhou University Press, 1998. The collection is now housed in Suzhou Beike Museum.

[84] *Collection of Civil Laws*, page 1, compiled in the 13th year of the Republic of China and published by Shanghai Shijie Shuju.

Clan rules included in genealogy books had the force of law, as evidenced in this judicial interpretation: "since a clan's rules included in its genealogy book are passed by all the members through discussion and negotiation, revisions of the rules shall also be made in the same way. Certain exceptional issues may be exempt from the rules. If the rules adhere to moral standards, they shall have the force of law" (No. 531, Seventh Year of the Republic of China). According to Case No. 940 made by the Supreme Court of Justice in the Seventh Year of the Republic of China, "a clan's rules included in its genealogy book are, in effect, a kind of agreement. If they do not violate national law or moral standards, then they shall have the force of law over the members."[85]

During the reign of the Republic of China, the Judicial Court often issued interpretations as a fix to the loopholes of civil law. For example, an interpretation made in 1928 provided that "the genealogy book of a kin group records the facts of all its members. Unless they contradict the law or party guidelines, the rules in this book shall be considered legally binding on the members." Another interpretation made in 1929 provided that "a clan's rules included in its genealogy book are essentially a kind of agreement. If they do not violate state law or moral standards, the rules shall have the force of the law on the members."

Furthermore, an interpretation made in 1930 provided that "the genealogy book of a kin group records details on all its members." Another two interpretations made in the same year provided that "the genealogy book of a clan is used to study the clan lineage. Despite the fact that the book may not be completely accurate, members are not expected to sue other members with malicious intent, unless such inaccuracies materially infringe upon their rights" and that "renewals to the rules in a clan's genealogy book or the creation of new rules shall be approved by all clan members. No family or clan shall unilaterally change the rules."[86]

Judicial interpretations clearly specified that as long as the rules in genealogy books did not contradict the law, the party's guidelines, or moral standards, then were of great value and needed to be supported by the judiciary.[87]

Judges during the Republic of China were expected to rule in a fair, cautious manner based on the premise that the system of clan rules was effective. They were to make the right decisions without going against the spirits of both new law and traditional laws, allowing family rules as a supplement to civil law. It is fair to say that the effect of clan rules was extended to the state's legislation and judiciary system.

---

[85] Guo, W. (1931). *Collection of Supreme Court Cases*. Shanghai: Shanghai Huiwentang Xinji Shuju. 206.

[86] *Essentials on Cases Ruled by the Supreme Court 1927–1998,* 589, compiled by the Editorial Board of Precedents of the Supreme Court and published by Wanxing Xingye Co., Ltd. in 2001.

[87] See the *Supreme Court Archives,* housed in the Second Historical Archive Museum of China, no. 1137, no. 1136, and no. 9.

4.5.3.3 Protection of Ancestral Shrines

A clan's ancestral shrine was the place where all its members could offer sacrifices to their ancestors and settle disputes under the family justice system. Therefore, it was all members' duty to protect the shrine and its property from being damaged and uphold its dignity and grace. The shrine, similar to a church in a Western community, pulled together all members. Though shrine rules varied from clan to clan, they had certain similarities: all members were required to protect their shrine, offer sacrifices to their ancestors, safeguard the clan's honor, and follow the shrine's internal rules.

For example, the Shao clan in Huayang, Jixi, Anhui Province, provided for the protection and conservation of their shrine in the first section of their shrine rules. The rules also covered topics including the cleaning of the shrine, stewardship of keys, opening of the gate, sacrifice dates and the preparation of sacrificial offerings, aid to the vulnerable, hanging of plaques, what to do with stillborn babies, and what should follow during ghost weddings. The rules provided that four groups of people were not allowed to enter the shrine: monks, prostitutes, women whose husbands move into their houses after marriage, and those who placed too much value on a person's success and accomplishments when choosing partners. The rules also forbade defiance of the venerable elder, bullying, slandering, theft, illegal occupancy of others' property, and all illegal acts. Members also had the duty to protect their ancestors' coffins and graves. They were not allowed to indulge in gambling or drinking, as these vices would bring shame to the clan. Loyalty, filial piety, and moral integrity were encouraged. In addition to setting requirements for the creation of genealogy records and their subsequent revisions, the rules also regulated the election of the shrine head and the learning and studying of the rules by all members.

According to the 1850 *Agreed Rules of the Yuzhang Ancestral Shrine in the Fourth Revision Genealogy of the Huang Clan*, the ancestral shrine should be managed by specially designated members and should be kept clean both inside and outside, with the gate especially clean so that the shrine would not be disdained by whoever passes it. Members who reside in the shrine are not allowed to gamble, drink, or fight nor lease their residence to others. The rules shall be submitted to the Nanchang County Censorate for the record.[88]

The *Family Rules in the Genealogy of Li Family* provided that the ancestral shrine shall be managed by specially designated members. The gate shall only be opened during sacrificial ceremonies. Anyone who does not dismount their horse or cart when arriving at the gate shall face severe punishment.

Some clans set special rules for protecting the *Feng Shui* of their shrine and inscribed these rules on steles to inform the public. For example, in 1768, the venerable elder head of the ancestral shrine of the Fu clan in Nan'an, Fujian Province, passed the "five prohibitions" concerning the shrine: (1) it is forbidden to build

---

[88] Edited by Huang Zuluo and Huang Zhensheng, 1899 edition, housed in the National Library of China.

latrines on the holy grounds of the shrine; (2) it is forbidden to grow trees both in front and behind the shrine; (3) it is forbidden to dry clothes on the roofs of the shrine; and (4) it is forbidden to store objects and dry grain in the shrine or rent out its desks and chairs. "He who dares break these rules shall be punished in front of all members."

The continuous existence of a clan was dependent on the efforts of the clan head, the dignity and assets of the ancestral shrine, and the genealogy books. As the top manager, the clan head had the right to control all clan members' behavior and to manage clan affairs. The ancestral shrine was where members could offer sacrifices to their ancestors and where public and large events were held. The genealogical records detailed the history and the bloodline of the clan, while the assets of the clan were used to ensure the regular function of clan affairs and for the payment of public utilities and relief for the vulnerable. These were all provided in the internal clan rules.

4.5.3.4 Regulations of Charitable Estates

A clan was required to establish charitable estates to provide financial support for its members and keep the bloodline pure. The establishment of a charitable estate was inevitably accompanied by the introduction of a set of rules to ensure proper management, including how to distribute relief and who was entitled to such relief.

Earlier similar rules were the *Regulations of the Fan Lineage Charitable Estate*, which specified how the estate should be managed and who was entitled to relief. Moreover, the Regulations also contained articles on managing the conduct of members who broke the rules and specified penalties for such (including without limitation fines and the cancellation of entitlement to relief). In some cases, they would even be sent to government courts for trial. The Regulations included both rules for charitable matters and restrictions for the member actions. The structure and substance of the subsequent regulations of charitable estates often predicated the Fan Regulations or improved upon them.

The size of charitable estates varied from clan to clan, and the regulations were made by the clan itself to be followed by all clan members. For example, *Regulations of the Longzhitang Charitable Estate of the Zou Clan in Changshu* (approved by the government) during the reigns of Emperors Daoguang and Xianfeng provided that charitable estates include fields, shrines, local deities, schools, and burial grounds built using member donations. The Regulations described many issues, including renting of fields and the amount of distributed grain. They also specified who was entitled to relief, such as the vulnerable, widows, and those who could not afford to pay school tuition or wedding and funeral costs.

Those who were not entitled to relief included: those who owned fields, those who owned businesses, those looked after by their family members, and members who left the clan to make a living. Hooligans, monks, and butchers were also denied relief. Additionally, relief was not granted to those members who did not show filial piety to their parents, indulged in gambling or drinking, or squandered their ancestors' inheritance. Nevertheless, there were exceptions. Those who realized their mistakes and corrected their wrongful behavior could regain their entitlement to relief with the unanimous agreement of other members.

To maintain the purity of the clan lineage, the Regulations also provided that adopted outsiders, parents who abandoned their children to the care of others with different surnames, and women who lived with their parents even after marriage (excluding those who lost husbands) were not entitled to relief. The charitable estate also had a president and a vice-president elected by all the members. A clan's venerable elder was not to intervene in the estate's affairs, which fell completely under the remits of the president and vice president. Key estate issues were to be reported to the presidents and the directorate of ceremonies, who then needed to gather together with other members for further discussion. No one was permitted to create an affray in violation of the rules. The set of rules officially passed would be submitted to both the Confucian schools at Changshu county and the local government for approval to obtain official binding effect.[89]

Similarly, the *Regulations of the Jiyang Charitable Estate* provided that relief was granted to both vulnerable clan members and members who suffered from unexpected losses and was denied to those who bequeathed their assets to outsiders or adopted children with different surnames. The ones who gave up their inheritance were also denied charitable money or grain nor could they be recorded in the genealogy book. All these rules were created to ensure the purity of the clan lineage. Anyone who commits wrongdoings (such as not showing filial piety, becoming corrupt or a slave, selling his daughters as concubines, or slandering his ancestors) shall be removed from the genealogy book, and he and his wife shall be deprived of their entitlement to charitable grain. Should he correct his behavior the entitlement may then be reclaimed. Estate employees shall regularly verify the eligibility of the members receiving relief and shall not hide those who are no longer eligible.[90] Regulations of charitable estates were not just for improving mutual aid within clans: they were also intended to control members who acted inappropriately.

Regulations of the Yanling Charitable Estate also had punitive measures for its members acted inappropriately: any member who did not exhibit filial piety to his parents, became corrupt, or committed crimes and other acts that humiliated the ancestors shall be removed from the genealogy book (but his wife and children shall remain in the book). In the worst circumstances, he shall be expelled from the clan entirely together with his wife and children.[91]

---

[89] Wang, G. (1988). *Selected Stone Texts Regarding the History of Suzhou City Since Ming and Qing Dynasties*. Suzhou: Suzhou University Press. 230–235. The collection is housed in Suzhou Beike Museum.

[90] Wang, G. (1988). *Selected Stone Texts Regarding the History of Suzhou City Since Ming and Qing Dynasties*. Suzhou: Suzhou University Press. 258–263. The collection is housed in Suzhou Beike Museum.

[91] Wang, G. (1988). *Selected Stone Texts Regarding the History of Suzhou City Since Ming and Qing Dynasties*. Suzhou: Suzhou University Press.276–281.The collection is housed in Suzhou Beike Museum.

All issues within a charitable estate shall be resolved by the presidents and the directorate of ceremonies together with the members, and venerable clan members shall not intervene. Presidents shall perform their duties in a transparent manner to ensure the implementation of the estate's regulations.

4.5.4 Duties to Serve the Ruler and the State

Family rules embodied the essence of state laws—filial piety laid the foundation for the rule of the state and equal importance was given to filial piety and loyalty.

4.5.4.1 Enforcement of Imperial Edicts

Some families used the simplest possible language to make their own rules, while others decided to borrow from imperial edicts, which represented the most authoritative kind of family instructions. For example, some inscribed the six maxims written by Emperor Hongwu (practice filial piety, respect elders, get along well with neighbors, serve as a role model to children, work for a living, and never commit evil) on a plaque, which was displayed in the main hall as a reminder to descendants. Some Quanzhou families during Qing Dynasty made small changes to the six maxims of Emperor Hongwu and inscribed them on carved wood, dragon-patterned plaques. They changed the Chinese character "毋" to "莫," likely because they thought "莫" was easier to understand, yet the meaning of the maxims remained unchanged. Other than that, the modified version was exactly the same as the original version.

Some family instructions were based on imperial edicts. For example, Gao Panlong (1562–1626), a politician during Ming Dynasty, wrote in *Family Instructions*, "Those who do not receive education should at least follow the six maxims of Emperor Hongwu…" Compared with reciting classics, remembering the six maxims would be more productive, helping you develop goodness and atone for sins. People should resist evil practices, especially prostitution, gambling, and snitching. The uneducated are most inclined to commit these three offenses, which are a bane for both individuals and families.[92]

Yao Shunmu (1543–1627), a Ming Dynasty scholar, wrote in his family instructions that the six maxims of Emperor Hongwu were enough for ordinary people to develop goodness. Imperial edicts were also displayed in ancestral halls, as evidenced in the first article of the *Genealogy Book of Family Yao in Wangchuan: Clan Rules*:

Everyone shall respect and observe imperial edicts. "Practice filial piety, respect elders, get along well with neighbors, prioritize moral instruction for children, work

[92] Gao Panlong. *Gao Panlong's Works.*

for a living, and never do evil." Emperor Hongwu's six maxims concisely communicate the principles of life, helping develop loyal ministers, martyrs, and devoted children. Despite everyone knowing the six maxims are helpful instructions, some refuse to follow them and therefore plunge into the abyss of evil. The tragedy is something that our ancestors would not bear to see. For this reason, it was decided to model after the announcement of community agreements and communicate imperial edicts in ancestral halls. On the first day of every month, heads of families shall take members to ancestral halls to learn about imperial edicts.[93]

It can be determined that imperial edicts and community agreements were regarded as the primary principles of family instructions and were to be observed by all family members.

Venerable elders at clan gatherings would give a lesson on family instructions, typically centered on the emperors' imperial edicts, so that family members could follow the guide and behave themselves appropriately. For example, the 16 maxims of Emperor Kangxi and the sacred edicts of Emperor Yongzheng were frequently quoted in the family instructions in genealogy books. To add authority to it, some clans even created positions of lecturers and associate lecturers, who instructed members not to do evil or associate with evil people and guide them to report any suspicious figures noticed to county officers. In this sense, promoting clan rules and imperial edicts was conducive to the maintenance of local order and security, as it not only informed clan members of what to do and what not to do but also facilitated uniform doctrine.

Some clans even asked governments to help extend outreach and supervise implementation to add more authority to family instructions. For example, the Liang family in Dongyu Village (Huanggang District, Zhaoqing, Guangdong Province) produced the *Collection of Advice for Men and Women* during the Qing Dynasty and reported it to the county officers, as evidenced by the paragraph, "The family instructions were approved by Officer Jiang, Officer Dai, and Officer Yang, and it has now been decided to inscribe them on stone tablets." The *Admonitions* consisted of ten maxims for men (practice filial piety, respect elders, get along well with neighbors, prioritize moral instructions for children, work for a living, never do evil, farm hard, pay taxes on time, develop endurance, and enjoy doing good deeds) and six maxims for women (take good care of parents-in-law, respect husbands, get along well with female relatives, be devoted to your husbands, sleep late and get up early, and be a dedicated housekeeper).

Each clan family head was to keep one copy of the *Admonitions* to instruct family members and record members' merits and demerits in a separate book. Clan mediators would take turns collecting record books and presenting them at sacrificial ceremonies. "Rewards and punishments will be given accordingly. Those who commit lesser offenses shall first be recorded in the book. They shall then kneel before the statue of Emperor Hongwu at the sacrificial ceremony and listen to the family instruction lecturer before receiving punishment." Family instruction itself

[93] Wooden movable type printing edition, revised by Yao Menglian, 1873.

was dedicated to controlling members' conduct through moral education, yet when it involved the participation of governments and was inscribed on stone tablets, it became a mandatory code of conduct to be strictly followed.

4.5.4.2 Loyalty to Emperors

The first article of the *Family Instructions of Hong Zhongming* (*Duxun*), written by Hong Zhongming, a Jinshi degree holder in Jiaying Prefecture, during the first year during of the reign of Emperor Jiaqing, was about loyalty toward rulers: "The grace of emperors overweighs the grace of parents. As the proverb goes, a man can live without a father, but a state cannot survive without a ruler. We are now living in a peaceful world, and it is because we have a wise ruler who reduces penalties, cuts taxes, and encourages society to respect its ancestors and intellectuals. We should remember this for the rest of our lives."[94] Hong believed that a peaceful world was due in no small part to the emperors' hard work and wise policies, so everyone should be grateful to emperors and show loyalty in return.

Instructions of the Ye family in Pingjiang County: *A primary purpose of family instructions is to define social relations, among which the relationship between rulers and subjects is the most important. Rulers lay the foundation for family management, family education, and inheritance of family culture. Generally, ordinary people concern themselves with agricultural activities instead of state affairs. If they are not regarded as subjects of the emperor, it is meaningless to talk about loyalty. Nevertheless, it is important to acknowledge that "all lands under heaven fall within the domain of the emperor and all people on this land are his subjects" and that the subjects of His Majesty are not limited to ministers at court. All men who inherit the virtues of ancestors and work hard on farmlands within the state territory are subjects of His Majesty. To show loyalty towards His Majesty, they do not need to give their all; they just need to keep families well-managed, ensure family members are well-educated, pay taxes on time, and abide by the law. This is how they should repay His Majesty, without whom they and their ancestors would not be able to live in a peaceful world. The Sacred Edicts of the Kangxi Emperor provides many wise instructions. It is advised that family members set a day to gather together to learn sacred edicts. They can write down the most helpful and practical instructions and put them up on doors as a reminder for everyone. This is also a way to show their loyalty towards His Majesty. It is hoped that we can all take heart from it.*[95]

The instructions reminded clan members that, ordinary as they are, their life is inseparable from the rulers. They should feel grateful for the rulers for enabling them to work and live in a peaceful world and should abide by the law and show loyalty to repay the favor.

[94] *Genealogy of the Hong Family: Ancestors' Instructions.*

[95] *Genealogy of the Ye Family in Pingjiang: Five Family Rules.*

The Gao family in Wujin County, Jiangsu Province, also emphasized the relationship between commoners and emperors in their family instructions, "Every subject should feel indebted to their emperors. Common folk who do not need to worry about shelter and can farm for a living owe their happiness to the emperor, who worksaround the clock to ensure all his subjects can live in contentment."[96] Likewise, the Xu family in Qingjiang County, Jiangxi Province, wrote in their clan instructions, "Rulers provide food and shelter for subjects, thus enabling them to live in contentment. To repay the grace, all subjects should show loyalty and remain obedient."[97]

4.5.4.3 Loyalty to the State

Clan instructions had specific requirements for those who held political office: fulfill duties with dedication; serve people with clean hands; support rulers; and do not shift blame on rulers. The Yang family in Jimo County, Jiaozhou Prefecture, amended their genealogy during Qing Dynasty. In the new version, they added instructions to guide family members to be good officers by modeling after ancestors who held political office in Ming Dynasty. The following are some quotes from the amended genealogy.

"The only purpose of being an official is to repay His Majesty by assisting him in ruling the state." (Lord Taiyuan, during the reign of Emperor Jiajing).

"As role models to their fellow men, civil servants should abide by the primary principle of honesty and keep themselves away from corruption." (Lord Peigong, during the reign of Emperor Wanli).

"People called officials "ye", another way of addressing their father, implying that they see officials as their "fathers." Generally, however, a father gives his all to love his children. Can I live up to this name and treat the people the same way I treat my children? Every day I have to reflect on myself whether I perform my official duties with as much dedication as my family matters." (Lord Yunhe, during the reign of Emperor Wanli).

Based on ancestors' instructions, the Yang family specified three requirements for members that held political office:

1. Show loyalty and commitment towards rulers:

"An official should be loyal to his ruler, otherwise he is just a glory hound, independent of his achievements. On the one hand, ghosts, and spirits despise his vanity. On the other hand, even with great achievements, he is not a qualified official and is doomed to failure, as was always the case throughout history."

"An official should have a strong sense of responsibility when assisting rulers and should step up at critical moments without hesitation. An indecisive official

[96] *Genealogy of the Gao Family in Piling: Family Rules.*

[97] *Genealogy of the Xu Family in Yunxi (Qingjiang County, Jiangxi Province): Clan Rules.*

cannot achieve anything significant." (Officials should take the blame for anything that went wrong instead of shifting blame to emperors, and should take any necessary decisive action instead of being overcome by misgivings.)

2. Remain honest and stand against corruption:

"Greed is a taboo quality for officials. Admittedly, an important motivation for becoming an official is to bring glory to the family name. However, once an official was convicted for corruption, far from bringing glory to the family name, he would face impeachment and be bombarded with criticism, bringing huge disgrace on his ancestors and descendants even after death."

3. Remain sober-minded and do not gang up to seek personal gains.

"An official should never seek personal gains by flattering those high up or forming cliques. He should think twice about wearing the official robe but should not hesitate to remove it when it is time to do so. After all, it is not a good idea to remain in a political circle, an arena of temptation and vanity, for a long time. A gentleman shall never have an insatiable desire for promotion, which is nothing short of moral decay."[98]

4.5.5 *Duties to Abide by Law and Rites*

4.5.5.1 Compliance with Law and Rites

To ensure their members abide by state law and government mandates (the most basic requirements for people), many clans included some articles of state law in their genealogy books, such as *The System of Mourning Garments*, *Family Pedigrees*, *The System of Mourning Garments for Three Fathers and Eight Mothers*, and *Prose-Poem on the Penal Code*. They wanted their members to follow rites and law by keeping these rules in mind. Some of them also particularly emphasized bans on gambling and theft.

The family rules of the Yang kin group in Qingjiang required its members not to gamble or commit theft: "Gambling violates the law. It is undeniable that people who indulge themselves in gambling are more inclined to become thieves. Therefore, measures shall be taken to help the unemployed get jobs. If a good person abandons his home or becomes a thief because of gambling, he shall be punished under the law for bringing shame upon his family."[99]

The family rules of the Xiong kin group in Yiyang, Hunan Province, also banned gambling: "Owners of the gambling houses often set traps for good people, enticing them to gamble while offering good food and sometimes even beautiful women. If they become addicted to this vice, the people would lose their money and, even

[98] *Genealogy of the Yang Family: Family Rules*, created in Shandong Province.

[99] *Third Revised Genealogy of the Yang Family in Yongbin (Jiangxi Province) Clan Rules.*

worse, their jobs, which could be detrimental to their families. Recently, some men and women in the gambling houses even drifted into prostitution, which is a real shame. Members of our group are forbidden to take part in these immoral acts."[100]

In the heyday of the Qing government, a period that witnessed the prevalence of speech crimes, many clans purposefully revised their rules to avoid falling victim to the inquisition. For example, the Huang clan in Lingan, Shandong Province, passed a special rule declaring the invalidity of its old, outdated rules in violation of state law. The new rule specified that "ambiguous wording in our old, outdated family rules need to be revised under the current law. Therefore, the old rules shall be made obsolete and a new set of new rules is necessary."[101]

Some families required their members to read both the classics and law codes, for "the majority of people nowadays consider studying the penal law useless, but when they come up against trouble, none of them know how to deal with the problem. Some people even repeatedly make the same mistake simply because they do not know it violates the law. There are traditional laws and new laws that both need to be studied. Law plays a crucial role in the rulers' governance of the country. We cannot dare ignore it!"[102]

This rule provided guidelines for its members on how to maintain good relationships with each other through mutual respect and also encouraged them to study law codes so that they would know how to defend themselves when facing legal problems.

4.5.5.2 Obligations to Pay Taxes

Paying taxes on time is an obligation of every subject, as well as a way to directly show loyalty toward rulers and make contributions to the country. The Xu family in Qingjiang County, Linjiang Prefecture, Jiangxi Province, wrote in their family instructions, "Abiding by the law: The state needs to collect field taxes every year. All subjects must pay taxes on time, an important way to repay His Majesty and show people's loyalty towards rulers and respect for the law. Everyone in the family should remember this and respect it as the primary principle. Laws are fundamental to the rule of the state. If subjects abide by laws and stay obedient to His Majesty, they can avoid many mistakes and lead a much better life."[103] The Nie family in Qingjiang also instructed members to pay taxes on time, as was written in their family instructions, "In accordance with laws, every subject is obliged to pay field taxes, which resemble a kind of tribute that subjects dedicate to rulers. As the proverb goes, you can lead a peaceful life free of government disturbance if you pay taxes

---

[100] *Continued Genealogy of the Xiong Family (Yiyang, Hunan Province).*

[101] *Revised Genealogy of the Huang Family in Lingan (Jiangxi Province): Rules.*

[102] *Genealogy of the Bian Family: Family Rules,* completed by Bian Yuanhou on March 13th in the Bingzi year during the reign of Emperor Qianlong. A copy was created in the 35th year during the reign of Emperor Qianlong and it is now housed in Hebei University Library.

[103] *Genealogy of the Xu Family in Yunxi (Qingjiang County, Jiangxi Province): Clan Instructions.*

on time. All family members shall pay off taxes as early as possible before tax collectors become involved and cause a disturbance. It is hoped that family members of all generations never fall behind on paying taxes."[104]

The Huang family in Jiangxi Province also instructed family members to "pay taxes on time to avoid unnecessary disturbances from tax collectors," as was written in their family instructions, "Agricultural taxes are the most important source of state revenue and people of all social classes shall pay taxes on time without being prompted. If a man paid his fair share of taxes as required, he and his family members would be able to live in reassurance. Otherwise, he would have to endure being disturbed by tax collectors, who might ask for taxes higher than the share they are liable for and even try to torture him. Instead of being tortured into yielding, the wise decision is to be a law-abiding person and pay taxes on time."[105] Instructions of this kind could be found in the *Genealogy of Family Wang in Aotai* and also in the *Instructions for Family Hu in Wujin County of Jiangsu Province*.

"As subjects of the country, all shall pay taxes on time to support rulers' effort in managing state affairs. To avoid falling behind on taxation, everyone shall ensure they pay half of their taxesin April and the full payment is made before August. Those who fail to pay taxes on time shall be subject to reprimand and warning in ancestral halls." (*Genealogy of Family Wang in Aotai*).

"Taxes shall be paid on time and corvee work shall be performed as required." (*Instructions for Family Hu in Wujin County of Jiangsu Province*).

There are four main ideas that can be summarized from the family instructions on taxation. First, every subject was obliged to pay taxes, independent of social class. Second, a law-abiding man shall pay taxes on time to live with reassurance. Otherwise, he might be disturbed or tortured by tax collectors, thus bringing disgrace to his family name. Third, every subject should fulfill the duties of paying taxes and performing corvee labor to show gratitude for his country. Fourth, paying taxes on time was a yardstick for law-abiding subjects. All in all, taxation was the economic foundation for state revenue, and paying taxes on time was the obligation of every farmer, representing a way to show loyalty toward rulers and states.

Family instructions provided a set of criteria for the settlement of family disputes. (See Chap. 6.)

Given the roles of *The Bible* in developing public legal awareness, it is claimed that Christianity helped guide Western people to abide by law. Unlike Western society, China was not dominated by monotheism, and there were diverse religious beliefs. People tended to believe in what served their interests best and were more concerned with issues related to humanity itself, including social status, individuals' reputation, and social relations. In essence, all these issues had much to do with the bloodline, moral rules, and the philosophy of life. While the influence of Christianity in developing public legal awareness was society-wide, the influence of

[104] *Fourth Revised Genealogy of the Nie Family in Huzhuang (Qingjiang County, Jiangxi Province: Eight Clan Rules.*

[105] The *Revised Genealogy of the Huang Family in Lingan (Jiangxi Province): Rules.*

family instructions that arose from the closed system of clan autonomy was community-based. Fortunately, Confucianism and Legalism aligned family instructions with state laws in core values, helping avoid the fragmentation of family instructions.

Family rules and the state legal system were independent of but closely related to each other in terms of form and function. They might conflict in particular situations, but in general, they went hand in hand and were complementary to each other, constituting an integral part of the system that helped maintain community order. Thus, families and clans, the basic units of China's traditional society, were where people began to learn about rules, and family instructions played a prominent role in developing public legal awareness.

Chapter 5
Contractual Culture

In terms of legal theories, contract theory in Western countries is more systematic than that in China. Popular sayings in the Western culture have persisted for a long time, such as "consent makes the law," "agreements constitute the law of contract," "the agreement of parties overrides the law," etc. However, tracing back to its origin, the concept of契约*Qiyue* (contract) was not initiated by Westerners only. Throughout the long history of civilization, the people in China have developed a complete set of rules for resolving civil disputes. Among the rules, 契*Qi* (Chinese traditional contract) embodies the rights, obligations, and the spirit of contract of the traditional Chinese people. The term *Qiyue* used in contemporary China is equivalent to *Qi* in traditional China or 合同*Hetong* in modern China. For the sake of consistency, we adopt the term *Qiyue* (contract) in most cases.

There was no unified civil code in ancient China. Many criminal codes included certain aspects of civil law. Thus, a popular argument in the legal academia is that "there was no distinction between civil law and criminal law, and the history of Chinese legal system is equivalent to the history of criminal law." In that case, people cannot help wondering: during thousands of years, how did the ancient Chinese deal with civil disputes without a dedicated civil code? What principles and rules did they use to settle these disputes? It is hard to imagine a civilization can last for thousands of years without rules to help resolve disputes. The concept of "civil law" that Chinese scholars have been using since contemporary times was translated from its English counterpart, which derived from "jus civile," the civil law in a Civil Society. However, the traditional Chinese society was not a Civil Society judged by the Western criteria, and the civil legal relationship in the traditional Chinese society cannot be paired with its counterpart in a Civil Society. Therefore, further elaboration on the civil legal relationship in traditional China within the Western "civil law" umbrella term can hardly help us draw conclusions pursuant to the historical facts. If one denies the existence of civil rules in traditional China only because there was no civil code, they have obviously ignored the fact that there were civil interactions.

Popular Chinese sayings like "a verbal statement has no guarantee, and only a written statement hereby serves as proof" prove that traditional Chinese attached

R. Zhang, *Traditional Legal Culture in China*, Understanding China,
https://doi.org/10.1007/978-981-95-4697-8_5

great importance to signing a written agreement like "*Qi*." Dating back to the pre-Qin period, it was recorded that "to sign a contract (with a tyrannical state), even the oath is taken and the contract signed, it will be reversed sooner or later."[1] Besides "Fu Bie" and "Zhi Ji" (two forms of contract in ancient China), people in Han, Wei, and Jin Dynasties treated private contracts as statutes and decrees. In Han Dynasty, both the imperial edict and the order given by a superior to a subordinate had the force of law; later, the "force of law" was extended to civil contracts and Taoist incantations.[2] In Northern Wei Dynasty, the word *Qiyue* has been officially adopted in codes and records. The term "Hetong," with the same legal meaning as the one we are using now, came into being during Tang and Song Dynasties. Sayings such as "officials abide by law and commoners follow contracts" in Tang dynasty also illustrated the official recognition of the validity of contracts. Although this type of sayings no longer existed since Song and Yuan Dynasties, officially recognized contracts and private contracts were available and people revered them; hence this convention has been passed down from generation to generation.[3] The spirit of contract was fully demonstrated in ancient China, but the pertinent jurisprudential abstraction of it was rather deficient.

5.1 Changes in Contractual Practices

Contracts originated quite long ago in ancient China, which can be traced to the late primitive commune. Then developed throughout Zhou, Qin, Han, Tang, Song, Ming, and Qing Dynasties, a unique contractual legal system has been formed.

5.1.1 Incipient Contracts

In the early stage of Western Zhou Dynasty, feudal system of enfeoffment was established with land being state-owned, and the society once flourished. After the mid-Western Zhou Dynasty, vassal economies developed rapidly because of the reclamation of private land. Land, horses and cattle, and slaves served as subject matter in civil exchange. According to the historical documents, civil contracts in Western Zhou dynasty were called "Fu Bie," "Shu Qi," or "Zhi Ji." *Rites of Zhou* recorded that "*Fu Bie* is used to guarantee the performance of the debt and require the parties to conclude a contract, *Shu Qi* records the transfer of property and *Zhi Ji* functions as a contract of sale." *Shu Qi* was used as a contract to record the transfer

[1] *The Unauthorized Biography of Han Poems* Vol. 6.

[2] Wang, G. (1959). *Kwun Tong Collection Book 3*. Zhonghua Book Company. 845–846.

[3] Huo, C. (2008). The connotation and modern value of Chinese ancient spirit of contract—Reverence and respect of contract and understanding of contract system. *Journal of Jilin University*. (5).

of property that one gives and the other takes. *Fu Bie* equaled to a contract of loan and *Zhi Ji* was a contract of sale.[4] According to Zheng Xuan, *Fu Bie* was written on a bamboo slip which can be split in half.[5] Liu Xi said: *Bie*, meaning parting, with big characters written in the middle, is split in half and two halves part in the middle.[6] Zheng talked about the form of *Zhi Ji* that it was also written on a bamboo slip which was afterward split into two pieces.[7] *Zhi* and *Ji* were similar but with a slight difference. (The longer one called *Zhi* and the shorter one called *Ji*. They were used in different transactions). As for the form of *Shu Qi*, Zheng recorded that it consisted of writing on two bamboo slips, with a number of notches carved along the edges.[8] According to Liu Xi's writing, *Qi* contains the meaning of carving, to help people to recognize the number.[9]

In Qing Dynasty, Sun Dairang has made a comparison to illuminate the differences between these three forms of contract: "*Zhi Ji*, *Fu Bie*, and *Shu Qi* were three types of contracts. *Zhi Ji* refers to a bamboo slip with the same text written on both halves. The slip was split into two halves and then each party held one-half. *Fu Bie* refers to a bamboo slip with big characters written in the middle of the slip. When the slip was split into two halves, each party held one-half with half of the characters. *Shu Qi* refers to two bamboo slips with the same text written on each of them and each party held one intact slip. To sum up, for *Fu Bie*, each party held half of the text and half of the bamboo slip; for *Zhi Ji*, each party held half of the bamboo slip but all of the text and for *Shu Qi*, each party held an intact bamboo slip with complete text."[10] This custom of making contracts out of bamboo slips and inscribed wooden tablets originated in the late primitive society. According to textual research from Yuan Mei in Qing Dynasty, people did not use paper bills but a bamboo slip when buying and selling lands. They carved the price on the slip and split it into two. The buyer and the seller each held half as a proof. If they wanted to sell it later, they can simply put the two halves together for verification.[11] This original contract was essentially the same as the *Fu Bie* contract.[12]

Some unearthed bronzes also describe the contractual activities at that time. Inscriptions on bronzeware like *Nine-Year Wei Tripod*, *Wei He*, and *Peng Sheng Gui* depicted the existence and development of contract in the Western Zhou Dynasty. Take the inscription of *Ge bogui* (a type of container made in bronze), for example, it recorded the contracting time, "the first day of the first lunar month," two parties'

[4] Zheng Xuan's Notes, Jia Gongyan's Interpretation of Notes: Notes and Further Interpretation of Rites of Zhou Vol. 3, Xiaozai.

[5] Zheng Xuan's Notes: Rites of Zhou: Tian Guan: Xiaozai.

[6] Xiu, X. Explaining Names of Things: Explaining Written Contracts.

[7] Rites of Zhou: Tian Guan: Xiaozai; Sun Dairang, Justice of Rites of Zhou.

[8] Zheng Xuan's Notes: Rites of Zhou: Di Guan: Zhiren.

[9] Xiu, X. Explaining Names of Things: Explaining Written Contracts.

[10] Rites of Zhou: Tian Guan: Xiaozai; Sun Dairang, Justice of Rites of Zhou.

[11] Yuan, M. *What the Master Does Not Speak Of* Vol. 21, Cutting the Bamboo Slip.

[12] Zhang, C. (2008). *Research on the History of Contracts and Land Purchase*. Zhonghua Book Company. 40.

names Ge Bo and Peng Sheng. Ge Bo exchanged his horse for Peng Sheng's field. They split the bamboo slip in half and one held each half, which did not only serve as proof but also showed their consensus of the contract.[13] There were many analogous inscriptions on sacrificial vessels in the Western Zhou Dynasty which recorded transactions at that time. Although the contents were different, they all adopted a similar form of contract, that is, after two parties agreed with each other and the subject matter had been clearly defined, they confirmed and exchanged their goods under the supervision of an official or a third party.

5.1.2 Development of Contracts

Contracts were more widely used with the relatively rapid development of economy during the Qin and Han Dynasties, acting a critical role especially in land transaction. In the early Western Zhou Dynasty, "Land" was not always a sort of commodity, which was totally changed in the subsequent Qin and Han Dynasty. Land, house, property, and slaves entered the field of transaction as objects of civil legal relations. It diversified contract forms, giving rise to the contracts of "Buy and Sell," "Tenancy," and "Loan" and the regulation of debt guarantee. According to *The Land Contract of Lenu* recorded on Juyan Bamboo Slips of Han Dynasty, "A merchant purchases 35 *mu* (a unit of area, 1 *mu*=0.0667 ha) of land from Lenu in Changle village at the price of 900 *Qqian* (a unit of currency, copper coin)."[14] While the settlement had been completed, the amount of land was found to be insufficient. As a result, the merchant received a partial refund for the shortfall in land. Under the oversight of Chunyu Ciru, Wang Chong, and Zheng Shaoqing, a toast was shared by all parties involved in the transaction, symbolizing the finalization of the deal. The bamboo slips also revealed that Lenu sold his land to another individual, with a formal ceremony attended by witnesses to mark the event. The format of Han contracts was widely adopted during its time. Contracts were involved in the transactions of daily commodities, land, and house. In the format of Han contracts, the document typically included details such as the parties, the location, witnesses, and a set procedure of covenant.[15] During Qin and Han Dynasties, legal regulations in security of debt also appeared, including security with the material guarantee and surety bond. Meanwhile, whatever sort of security form was used, mutual consent and a third party consent should be a prerequisite. According to *Legal Questions and Answers*, if individuals from the general public were in debt, one should not forcibly take

[13] Zhang, C. (1995). *Collections of Contracts of Past Dynasties I*, Beiing: Beijing University Press.21, 26.

[14] Li, Z. (1999). Studies on traditional Chinese civil contract. *Collection of Legal History* Vol.2, Law Press·China. 70.

[15] Song, G. (2000). *Between Man and Nature: The Contract and the State in the Han Dynasty—American Scholars' Studies on Chinese Legal Tradition*, China University of Political Science and Law Press.174.

them as a hostage. If a creditor does forcibly take a debtor as a hostage, the creditor would be fined. If both the debtor and the creditor mutually agreed to the "hostage" arrangement, then both of them would be fined.[16] In the Eastern Han Dynasty, "contract" was also called "莂" (*Bie*), which was akin to "Fu Bie." Two parties each held an identical contract duplicate copy for future verification.

Ever since the Jin and Tang Dynasties, Chinese social and economic development has advanced, and the economic relationships among all the fields have become more dynamic. For example, the market in Chang'an (capital of Tang) embraced an unprecedented boom. Trades both on land and at sea developed. The establishment of inns and workshops became widespread, along with the emergence of "Feiqian," literally meaning "flying money," which was a form of early negotiable instrument similar to later money orders.[17] To adjust the development of merchandise trade relationships, civil regulations were badly needed. Contract thus became an indispensable guarantee. Contract law in the Sui and Tang Dynasties was even more complicated. Besides the contracts of "Buy and Sell," "Tenancy," and "Loan," there were also contracts of "Employment," "Deposit," and so on. The law in the Tang Dynasty stipulated that contract was the crucial legal foundation for debt liability, especially in the bulk commodity trade of land and house, slaves, and livestock. Concluding a contract was a legal procedure, and official verification was required before the contract was concluded. All land transactions shall "undergo verification by the relative authority," or "all the money would be forfeited and the disputed land would be returned to its original owner."[18] In addition, to ensure the development of cross-regional economic trade, the system of debt guarantee was developed during the Jin and Tang Dynasties. It was written in the Tang's contractual document that "if one regrets his decision, the breach of contractual agreement shall incur statutory penalties"[19]; other principles included "acceptance of collateral," "personal service as debt repayment," and "unauthorized distraint" (creditors are permitted to effectself-help repossession of debtor assets).[20] Additionally, the material evolution of contractual media from bronze and bamboo to silk and paper greatly facilitated the recording of contractual content, the third-party's guarantee, and official supervision of contracts, thus promoting the development of traditional contracts.

[16]Zhang, J. & Huai, X. (1999). *A Complete History of the Chinese Legal System Vol.7—The Legal System of the Ming Dynasty*, Law Press·China. 235.

[17]Cheng, Y., Du, H.(2007). On the fundamental characteristics and formative causes of traditional Chinese contractual legal institutions, *Journal of Inner Mongolia University* (Humanities & Social Sciences).Vol. 2.

[18]Huai, X. (1998). *The History of Chinese Law*. China University of Political Science and Law Press.183, 184.

[19]Zhang, J. (1997). *The Tradition and Modern Transition of Chinese Law*. LawPress ·China. 324.

[20]Ye, X. (1996). *History of Chinese Law*, Peking University Press, 191.

5.1.3 *Definite Formation of Contracts*

Since the Song and Yuan Dynasties, the mercantile doctrine has marked a paradigm shift in Chinese economic thought, wherein the harmonization of righteousness and profit emerged as a governing principle for both merchant communities and state officials, providing the intellectual foundation for the development of the commodity economy during the Song and Yuan Dynasties. In the late Tang Dynasty, the land policies of "*Yongye* land" (the piece of land distributed to a male that could be possessed by him permanently) and "*Koufen* land" (the piece of land distributed to a male that can only be used by him during his lifetime) were gravelly destroyed. The land annexation problem became increasingly serious, which directly led to the commercialization of land and the establishment of tenancy system in Song and Yuan Dynasties. Therefore, the civil contract that centers upon land and housing exhibits characteristics of strictness, normality, standardization, and gradual maturation. In the eighth year of Taiping's rejuvenation in the Northern Song Dynasty (983), Zhao Fu, a government official, wrote a petition about contracts. He noted that contracts were signed privately, which led to ill-defined problems and even triggered lawsuits. He proposed a uniform contract as the model format.[21] Therefore, on the basis of inheriting the civil contract of Han and Tang Dynasties, the standardized contract samples were formulated by the government. The form of contract tended to be unified, which adapted to the government's management and control. The government sold contract paper to meet the need of contract unification. At the same time, the government reduced the effectiveness of the contracts drafted by the people themselves. In the late Song Dynasty, the system of "sticking two contracts" was formed, that is, the contract drafted by the people themselves was adhered to an official contract. It not only showed the importance of agreement in civil contract but also facilitated government's supervision. The types of contracts in the Song Dynasty also varied and the classification was more detailed. There were contracts of sale, contracts of pawn, contracts of lease, contracts of loan, and contracts of guarantee. The contract of sale could also be divided into two categories. The procedures for making contracts are more standardized. It should follow the four requirements: soliciting kins and neighbors first, going to a specific state agencies to sign the contract, transferring the tax liability to the new owner, and the original owner's vacating.[22]

Contract was further developed in the Yuan Dynasty. On the basis of "sticking two contracts," the official contract paper was divided into two parts, formal contract and the root of the contract. The printing right of contract paper belonged to the Ministry of Revenue. The procedures for signing contracts were more strictly regulated in the Song Dynasty. The parties should first report to the government and

[21] Li, Z. (1999). Studies on traditional Chinese civil contract. *Collection of Legal History* Vol.2, Law Press·China. 272.

[22] Cheng, Y., Du, H. (2007). On the fundamental characteristics and formative causes of traditional Chinese contractual legal institutions, *Journal of Inner Mongolia University* (Humanities & Social Sciences). Vol. 2.

obtain its approval and then solicit the kins and neighbors and go to a specific agency to sign the contract and pay taxes. The purpose was to strengthen the government's supervision of civil contract activities.[23]

The Ming Dynasty followed the traditions of previous dynasties, and the codified civil conduct was still based on legal norms, customs, and ethics. The provisions on civil affairs in the Ming Code were more detailed than those in the previous dynasties. The system of debt in the Ming Dynasty developed greatly, especially in the evolution of contract. Although there were no specific provisions on the form of contract in the laws of the Ming Dynasty, the form of contract set by folk customs was quite standardized. Contracting parties executed agreements through standardized deed templates. The contract types of the Ming Dynasty mainly covered the following principal categories: land sale, dwelling sale, indentured pledge of sons, redemptory land pledge, dwelling mortgage, land tenancy, monetary loan, indentured service, task-based labor, vessel charter, shop lease, partnership businesses, and so on.[24]

There has also been progress in the format of contracts. In the Ming Dynasty, there were two types of contract: unilateral contract and bilateral contract. The unilateral contract was based on the trust of both parties. It was a certification issued by one party to the other party, which was a simplified form of the contract. The emergence of unilateral contract indicates that the contract could be simplified to facilitate the transaction and improve efficiency because it met the needs of the development of commodity economy. During this period, people believed in legal and effective contracts and continued to follow the folk custom of "contracts function as the law," which referred to statutory enforcement and judicial validity of contracts. Moreover, the laws of the Ming dynasty also stipulated the types and responsibilities of invalid contracts in detail.[25] The government also encourages and protects the signing and validity of contracts. Article 36 of "law of cultivating people" in the Ming dynasty stipulated: "People who lack of money or resources due to disasters or physical diseases, and has to sell the property and estates which were purchased by their father, are allowed to sign contracts of sale. Their relatives or neighbors should not take the opportunity to occupy property or food. Those who break it would be punished." This is to guarantee the autonomy of will in the signing of the real estate sale contract in accordance with law.

The contract law was gradually finalized in the late Qing Dynasty. First of all, the laws and regulations concerning contracts in the Qing dynasty widely existed in *The Great Qing Code*, *Great Qing Huidian* (the Jurisdictional Corpus on Administrative Matters Compiled during Qing), *The Rules of the Ministry of Revenue*, and *The Precedents Added to the Law of Revenue*. They also existed in the special laws which were applied to ethnic minorities, as well as the provincial laws, notices, and

[23] Li, Z. (1999). Studies on traditional Chinese civil contract, *Collection of Legal History* Vol. 2. Law Press·China. 80.

[24] Zhang, C. (1995). *Compilation and Interpretation of Contracts in Traditional China*. Peking University Press.21, 26.

[25] Zhang, J. & Huai, X. (1999). *A Complete History of the Chinese Legal System Vol.7—The Legal System of the Ming Dynasty*, Law Press·China. 243.

rules promulgated by the local offices of provinces, prefectures, and counties. Second, contracts between individuals in exchange have become quite common. In terms of land sale, house lease, indentured service, partnership business, monetary loan, and marriage, contracts were used in all of these activities as proof of civil relationship. People used contracts to embody and prove their rights. The government also recognized that "private practices were all proved by contracts. Therefore, people with contracts have jobs and those without contracts are unemployed."[26] Third, the Qing court mandated the use of official contracts for official deeds, in order to ensure the uniformity of contract formats and prevent the creation of fraudulent contracts. It was stipulated that the private contracts could not serve as evidence which should be revoked and then reproduced by using the official contract paper, and half of the contract price would be forfeited by the government. Fourth, the contract in the Qing Dynasty had a set format, which generally included the subject matter, price, remuneration, time limit, and the rights and obligations of the contractors. The sale of land, houses, slaves, and other important subject matters shall be subject to the approval of the government, pay the tax of the contract, and obtain the root of the contract with the official seal. Fifth, the contract security system was consummate. The regulations for intermediary and liability for breach of contract were very detailed. When the contract was signed, the "intermediary" who was jointly and severally liable should sign the contract to ensure the performance of the contract. The laws of the Qing Dynasty also stipulated that after the contract was signed, if one party pulled back, he should hand in half of the contract price to the government as the penalty.[27]

In conclusion, the Ming and Qing Dynasties witnessed a period of fast development of the traditional Chinese commodity economy. As an important tool for regulating legal relationships between civil and commercial parties, the contract system inherited the achievements of the previous dynasties, characterized by various forms, specific contents, strict official supervision, and multiple regulations. All of these reflected the maturity and refinement of contracts during Ming and Qing Dynasties, including the standardization of contract form, content, categories, and specifications.

[26] Ye, X. (1996). *History of Chinese Law*. Peking University Press, 131.

[27] Cheng, Y., Du, H. (2007). On the fundamental characteristics and formative causes of traditional Chinese contractual legal institutions, *Journal of Inner Mongolia University* (Humanities & Social Sciences).Vol. 2.

5.2 Contractual Customs

5.2.1 *Contract as Hard Evidence*

In the early stage, large and important contracts were engraved on Bronze vessels. The contracts could not be falsified after its execution. In the era when bamboo slips and wooden tablets were the most commonly used material for writing, people used to engrave their contracts on one bamboo slip and write a character "*Tong* (which means "the same")" on it. They split it in half and each party held one. If two pieces of "Tong" matched each other, the contract could be identified as real. Take the contract unearthed from the 53th Astana Ancient Tomb in Turpan, for example, the content of the contract begins with the right half of the "Tong" character.[28]

After the Wei and Jin Dynasties, the use of *Fu Bie* and *Zhi Ji* has fallen. Paper contracts were more common. The form of contract emerged and began to evolve. It was derived from *Shu Qi* and absorbed the advantages of *Fu Bie*. It was to put two pieces of paper side by side and write a big character "Tong" or two, "He Tong (contract)," in the middle as the verification. Each paper had half of the characters on it. Only if the characters on two papers matched each other could the contract be proved real. There were mainly two reasons why the form of *Shu Qi* was finally developed into the form of *He Tong*: the invention and widespread use of paper led to the substitution of paper for bamboo slips; it was much easier and more convenient for people to write big characters on the joint of papers as verification than to curve notches on the side of bamboo slips.[29]

Contractual bonds in later generations were also called contract. Zhao Yi, a man in Qing Dynasty, noted "Contract, also called contractual bonds, is to put two pieces of papers together, write '*He Tong*' on it as verification and each party hold one of them. It is an ancient way."[30]A similar description could also be found in the records of a literary historian Ping Buqing.[31] Contract, in Chinese, *He Tong*, has the meaning of the agreement reached by parties to the contract. "He" has the meaning of "come together" and "*Tong*" means "the same." To write "*He*" or "*He Tong*" on the contract as verification showed the consent of two parties, which was similar to *Fu Bie* and *Zhi Ji* in the Western Zhou Dynasty. That is why Chinese contract is also called *He Tong*.

After the contract is signed, the signatories must sign their names, that is, "signature as proof," using the signature as an authenticating object. However, difficulties arise when illiterates were involved. Therefore, there was the practice of "drawing a finger as a token" or "drawing a finger as verification": to sign your

[28] Chinese Cultural Relics, 1972, Vol. 1.

[29] Zhang, C. (2008). *Research on the Ground Certificate in the History of Contract.* Zhong Hua Book Company. 48.

[30] Zhao, Y. (2011). Zhao Yi's Notes on Reading Vol. 33..Shanghai Chinese Classics Publishing House.636–637.

[31] Ping, Bu. (1982). Xia Wai Jun Xie Vol. 10. Shanghai Chinese Classics Publishing House. 717.

name or draw your finger on the button of the contract. Sometimes there would be a note added to the contract: "I cannot write, so I draw my finger knuckle as verification."[32] Others had their names written by someone else and drew a cross themselves after their names as signatures. When there was no stamp available, people could press a fingerprint of their middle finger instead. These were all about proving the integrity of contract. The habit was formed at least before the Sixteen Kingdoms period (304 AD–439 AD).[33]

5.2.2 Middleman as Witness

To conclude a contract, the two parties should invite a third party to be present. The third party's name should be recorded in the contract to serve as a witness, thereby confirming the authenticity and validity of the contract. According to the "Contract of Selling the Gown" in the Western Han Dynasty (60 BC) by Jie Kuande in Guanghan County, "Officer Zhang Ziqing and Du Zhong knew the content of the contract and they were present at that time. People drank wine after the conclusion."[34] That is to say, when Jie Kuande was concluding the contract of selling the gown, two officers were on the scene as witnesses. There were different ways to record wine-drinking part in different contractual bonds, but they all meant that when the contract was signed, both parties offered wine to everyone present as a reward and each party paid half the price. The purpose was for the people present to act as witnesses, who will be needed to testify in the event of any future dispute over the contract.

After the Han and Wei Dynasties, the witnesses were given special calls, like "*Shi Ren* (contemporaries)" and "*Shu Quan* (deed writers)." During the period of Gaochang Kingdom, the appellations of witnesses at the bottom of the deeds were "*Qian Shu* (writer of the deed)," "*Shi Jian* (people who saw it at present)," and "*Lin Zuo* (people who faced to the parties)." New changes emerged in Tang Dynasty. In addition to the two parties, witnesses were required to sign at the end of the contract. They were called "Zhi Jian Ren" or "Jian Ren," people who knew and saw the process of signing the contract. The number of witnesses could be one or two or as many as six or seven.

There were also "guarantors" in the contractual bonds, the number of which could be 1–6. If the contract was about selling maids or slaves, there should be at least five guarantors. The role of the guarantor is different from that of "Zhi Jian Ren." He not only witnesses the conclusion of the contract but also guarantees that

[32] The Unearthed Documents in Turfan Vol. 2, Buying House Voucher by Zhao Huaiyuan in Gaochang County of Tangxi State, 84.

[33] Nie, X. (2009). On the legal basis of contract in ancient China, *Studies of Chinese Social and Economic History* Vol. 2.

[34] Zhang, C. (1995). *Compilation and Interpretation of Contracts in Traditional China Vol.1*. Peking University Press.P33.

the obligor will fulfill their obligations. Otherwise, the guarantor must assume joint liability of the contractual obligation. In the Qing Dynasty, the guarantors were usually referred to as "intermediary guarantors" or "middlemen." In addition to the guarantee responsibilities, they also served as introducers, so sometimes they were called "middlemen and mediators."[35]

5.2.3 Guaranty on Contract Implementation

Miscellaneous Laws in Tang Dynasty stipulated the conclusion of interest-bearing loan contract, interest prohibition, performance mode, judicial relief, pledge handling, guarantee responsibility, and so on. It also involved the judicial relief of non-interest bearing loan contract. As Volume Twenty-six of The Penal Complex of Song recorded:

If one privately lends money involving interest, the contract between creditor and debtor should be strictly enforced in privacy, and the government would not interfere in the deal. In such a contract, monthly interest must not exceed 6%, and shall not exceed the principal. If the government acts the role of creditor or the government property is involved, the accumulation of principal and interest shall temporarily be suspended. If the debt is not paid off in 50 days, interest would accrue on the rest of the principal, which shall not exceed the principal, too. If a debtor is in bankruptcy, he and all the male members in his family would take on corvee labor as the compensation of his debt. The compound interest is banned (if the lent stuff is "cereals", the interest shall not exceed the principal too). If one illegally makes the interest accrue, extort extra property taking no account of the contract, or borrow money with borrowed money, the government would interfere in the deal. The pledgee may not sell the pledge without authorization. If the pledge is not redeemed when the interest exceeds the principal, the official department would take over the pledge and sell it to offset the debt, and the rest (if there is) would be returned to the debtor. If the debtor absconds, the guarantor shall take over the debt.[36]

According to the *Miscellaneous Laws*, there were two conditions for the state's nonintervention and noninvolvement in interest-bearing loans. The first was to limit the highest interest rate, "monthly interest must not exceed 6 percent," and the second was to control the total amount of interest, "no matter how long the interest accumulates, it must not exceed the principal." That is, the total amount of interest shall not surpass the principal. The occasion was special when the government was the lender in private contracts: "If the government side acts the role of creditor or the government property is involved, the accumulation of principal and interest shall

[35] Nie, X. (2009). On the legal foundation of contract in ancient China, *Studies on Chinese Social and Economic History* Vol. 2.

[36] Dou, Y. et al. The Penal Complex of Song.

temporarily be suspended." But still, the total amount of interest must not surpass the principal.

On the relation of principal and interest, it also stipulated that lenders could not calculate interest into principal (if the lent stuff is "cereals," the interest shall not exceed the principal too). That is to say, interest could not be converted to principal to recalculate the new interest. Double-counting of interest was prohibited. At the same time, whether the loan was repaid by finance or by millet, the accumulated interest should not exceed the principal even though the time limit had expired.[37] These were the two basic requirements for the legal system of loan contract in all dynasties.

In the conclusion of the contract, the provisions of penalty for breach of contract were stated in advance and written into the contract. In Han Dynasty when bamboo slips were used, there were few written records of penalty for breach of contract. After entering Sixteen Kingdoms period when contracts were written on papers, there were records of double penalty for breach of contract. In "Zhao Bolong's contract of buying maids in 25th July, 377 AD" recorded Zhao buying an 8-year old maid by seven pieces of felt. The contract recorded that "if someone went back on his word, he should give fourteen pieces of felt to the one who abides by the contract."[38] Since this period, this pattern has become a convention in the conclusion of the contract. Sentences like this were often written in the bond deed: "two parties create contracts. After the contract is completed, each cannot go back on his word; otherwise, the one should be fined double the price and give it to the other who keeps the promise." Although this is a precautionary text, it warns the dishonest behavior in the performance of the contract. In Tang Dynasty, the penalty for breach of contracts involving money transactions was severe. For example, in the contract of "Zhang Shanxi borrowing money from Zuo Chongxi in 668 AD," Zuo lent Zhang 20 silver coins. The contract stipulated: "The monthly interest is two silver coins. By the end of each month, Zhang has to pay the interest to Zuo. If Zuo needed money, Zhang should repay the principal with interest to Zuo. Otherwise Zuo could take the equivalent property of Zhang's. If the debtor died, let his wife or children or the guarantor pay the debt. If they still refused to return money, offset the debt with half an acre of vegetable farm which must be able to produce good vegetables."[39] This was the "seizure" system by which the creditor could privately seize the property of the debtor.

[37] Huo, C. (2005). On the relationship between traditional Chinese contract and national Law—Centering on the relationship between law and loan contract in the Tang Dynasty. *Contemporary Law Review* Vol.1.

[38] St. Petersburg Branch of Oriental Institute of The Russian Academy of Sciences, Oriental Literature Department of Russian Science Press, and Shanghai Classics Publishing House edited: Dunhuang Documents collected by Soviet Union Vol.15, 2001, Shanghai Classics Publishing House, Oriental Literature Department of Russian Science Press, 212.

[39] The Unearthed Documents in Turfan Vol.3, P219.

5.2.4 Terms on Security and Exemptions

The ancient rulers highly praised the behavior of canceling private debts. For example, *Strategies of the Warring States* recorded that Feng Xuan overstepped his authority to burn bonds on behalf of Lord Mengchang of Qi to exempt debts. On the other hand, the state would also directly use the public power to issue exemptions to forgive people's private debts. Rulers usually issue exemptions when major national events occur, such as new emperor ascending the throne, changing the era name or title-conferring a prince. The exemption may involve criminal, administrative, and civil affairs.

The civil exemptions issued by the rulers not only involved public debts but also extended to private debts, which included the illegal private debts as well as legal ones. Take Emperor Zhuangzong in the Later Tang Dynasty, for example, he has issued: "The best way to govern a country is to make the people live carefree lives. The method of encouraging people should be to lower taxes so that people stopped complaining and spreading rumors. People no longer needed to be forced labors and returned to their hometown. From the time the state recovered Bianzhou, taxes, interest payments, and debts owed to the government and the private parties which the people in the city were unable to pay because of poverty, will no longer be required: nor will the taxes in surrounding area until December."[40] Emperor Shi Jingtang of the Later Jin Dynasty issued the exemption in January, 940 AD: "As the old year (938 AD) ended, we decided to discharge all the public and private debts."[41] Emperor Mingzong in the Later Tang Dynasty has issued discharges for people in several cities: "Discharge all guilty people's debts in the cities Xia, Yin, Sui, You, no matter what wrong they have done. Even though the people could not be exempted from their debts according to the previous law, he can now be exempted from all his debts. Reinstate the original local officials in these states their titles and the state will give them the money to go to their post."[42] In the Southern Song Dynasty (1189), Emperor Guangzong ascended the throne and issued: "All debts owed by the people are exempted, no matter how much or how long they have been owed." Shen Jiaben, a jurist in the Qing Dynasty, commented: "Private debts are related to people's private rights and should not be included in the exemption. Exempting private debts is definitely inappropriate. The amnesty does not involve private debts nowadays, and the laws of the Song dynasty are no longer in use."[43]

Shen's point of view was affected by the introduction of Western law and was based on the concept of inviolability of private rights. He recognized the private rights and criticized the state's discharge of people's debts as the intervention by public power which interfered with private rights. He attempted to reverse the

---

[40] Xue, J. et al. (1976). *Old History of the Five Dynasties*. Zhong Hua Book Company. 416.

[41] Xue, J. et al. (1976). *Old History of the Five Dynasties*. Zhong Hua Book Company.1037.

[42] Xue, J. et al. (1976). *Old History of the Five Dynasties*. Zhong Hua Book Company. 747.

[43] Shen, J. (1985). *Studies on Criminal Law of Ancient Dynasties*. Zhong Hua Book Company.773–774.

long-standing tradition of looking down upon private rights and advocated that public power should not be excessively involved in private rights, which was undoubtedly a historical progress.[44] However, in the traditional society with low productivity, it was also a kind of "policy of benevolence" to relieving the burden of the people according to the practical situation. The state paid all public and private debts and allowed the people to enjoy part of the dividends, which played a positive role in resolving social disputes, easing conflicts, and winning popular support.

5.3 Types and Validity of Contracts

5.3.1 Types of Contracts

5.3.1.1 Contract of Sale

Since modern times, with the introduction of the Western concept, *Qi* has gradually been replaced by contract. The category of *Qi* is broader than what the concept of "contract" covers in modern times. *Qi* and contract are actually two distinct juridical categories. *Qi* includes *Dan Qi* (unilateral contracts) and contracts. Sale of farmland and house, pawn, lease, and lending were the main contents of *Dan Qi* while contract includes property sharing, family asset management, assets exchange, partnership business, and equity sharing. *Dan Qi* is a contract which has only one copy such as private loan agreements, whereas a contract has multiple duplicates. In terms of conceptual scope, *Qi* encompasses contract as its subset. *Dan Qi* usually embodies unequal relationship, such as a covenant of personal servitude or a covenant of pawn, while a contract embodies equal relationship.[45]

Therefore, the concept of *Qi* in traditional China is broader than that of contract in the West, which ranged from contracts between private parties to contracts between public and private parties. As reflected in the contract documents in museum of *Yunnan* Province, almost all economic activities (such as buying and selling, lease, pawn, lending, taxes and corvee, supplemental payment for deficiency, refund for overpayment, gift, exchange, payment, obligatory assistance, merger, and accounting) were related to rural lands. Even in the few documents of patriarchal clan, inheritance and property distribution were mostly related to rural real estates. The objects of sales included mountain farms, ponds, housing, homestead, Feng-shui land (geomantic treasure land), storefronts, forests, toilets, livestock, and people, among which land sales are conducted most frequently. There are

[44] Huo, C. (2007). The Di She Clause (抵赦条款) institutionalized as state-mandated debt relief through imperial amnesties in the loan contracts found in Tunhuang and Turfan and the civil debt relief by the state—the conflict between the civil usury and state control in the Tang and Song Dynasties. *Journal of Gansu Institute of Political Science and Law,* Vol. 2.

[45] Yujiang. (2003). *Qiyue* and *hetong*: Forms of contract during the Qing Dynasty of China. *Social Sciences in China* Vol. 6.

many reasons for sales of real estate, such as "out of money," "management difficulties," "lack of money to file a lawsuit," "lack of money to trade," or even "lack of money to train able-bodied men," "lack of money to pay for the village self-defense force's board expenses," and so on. The identities of buyers and sellers were also complicated. Both parties of the transaction could be of the same clan or family. The transaction could also be conducted between clansmen and ancestral halls, private parties and state entities, masters and servants, or two families. Contracts of sales among the same clan are the most common.[46]

5.3.1.2 Redeemable Contract and Irredeemable Contract

Contract of sale includes foreclosure contract and redeemable contract. Contract of foreclosure, also called irredeemable contract or blocked contract, means the owner has an outright sale of the ownership of his land or other property without supplemental payment for deficiency or redemption, and the words "foreclosure contract can never be redeemed" are usually noted on it. Generally speaking, it is a one-time permanent sale contract, reflecting the transfer of the ownership of land or other property.

As opposed to foreclosure contract, a redeemable contract reserves the right of redemption for the seller. We can see the variety of this kind of contracts from the contents of redeemable contracts, including covenant of pawn, exchange contract, contract of supplemental payment, refund contract, and so on. Among them, the most typical and common form is covenant of pawn. In this kind of trade, what actually changed is only the right of use of the property, because the party can always use his real estate or title deed for land as guarantee. After repaying the pawn money within the agreed time limit, he can take the land right back. However, if the party unable to redeem his property beyond the prescribed time limit, the ownership of the property will change. The covenant of pawn will finally become a foreclosure contract.[47]

Some contracts were originally redeemable contracts, but for multiple reasons, they became irredeemable contracts. There are conventional ways to identify the conversion of contracts among the people. Take sales contract of land, for example, if the contract signed by the buyer and the seller is a "contract for assigning the right to use for long term," it is not an irredeemable contract. Take this contract for example:

Perpetual Conveyance Contract

Due to extreme impoverishment, Dianxin agrees to convey the usufructuary rights of his ancestral land to the buyer. The specific scope of the land is as follows: the border shall be Rongzhang field on the east, Runzhu field on the south, the ditch

---

[46] Wu, X. & Xu Z. (2012). Collection and Compilation of Legal Contracts and Documents in Yunnan Province Library Vol. 1 (I), preface. *People's Publishing House*. 3–4.

[47] Wu, X. & Xu, Z. (2012). *Collection and Compilation of Legal Contracts and Documents in Yunnan Library* Vol. 1 (I), preface. People's Publishing House. 3.

on the west and the Anfa field on the north. Dianxin is willing to sell the right to farmland use to Kunshan, at the price of eight thousand four hundred copper coins. The money shall be paid off on the date of conclusion of the contract. After the transaction, the buyer can use the land at will, without dissent from kins and relatives. The sale is consensual and there is no disagreement. This contract serves as the proof.

P.S. Tax payments are transferred along with the transfer of the right to farmland use.

The contract was signed in October of eleventh year of Daoguang's Reign, and thus a perpetual conveyance contract was established, sealed by Dianxin.

Witnessed by brother Changfa (seal)

Witnessed by Zhong Wenrui, and penned by Qisen (seal).[48]

The transaction above is not a foreclosure. Dianxin has only sold the right of using the farmland, but the ownership of the farmland still belonged to him, because the word "foreclosure" did not exist in the contract. Dianxin can still redeem his land after paying Kunshan 8400 copper coins. The phenomenon of "two owners of one piece of land" was very common in the transfer of land rights in Qing Dynasty. Qing Dynasty explicitly stipulated: "if the words 'pay the price differences' do not exist in a contract of foreclosure, the property cannot be redeemed. If there is no 'foreclosure' in the contract or the date of redemption is indicated, the property can be redeemed. If the seller is unable to redeem, he can entrust an intermediary to find a buyer to pay the price difference and sign another contract of foreclosure. If the buyer is unwilling to pay the price difference, he can resell the property and return the original price. If the property is sold completely with a contract of foreclosure, the seller should not find excuse (e.g. the property belongs to his relatives) or try to pick a quarrel to reduce the price. Otherwise, he should be given a heavy punishment according to the law."[49] In Dianxin's contract, there was no "foreclosure" or "additional price." It was only the right to farmland use and the duty to pay taxes to the state that has been transferred to Mao Kunshan. Mao can use the land at will, which only means he can enjoy the right to farmland use, including the harvest of farming and retransfer the right to farmland use. However, Mao did not have the ownership of the farmland. In fact, as a party to the land transaction, the buyer often does not stay at the acquisition of the right to farmland use. Although the seller hopes that his life will improve one day, so that he can redeem the land at the original price, this is not what the buyer wants. Once the seller is unable or has no hope to redeem his property, the foreclosure occurs. It is necessary to reconclude the corresponding supplementary contract on the basis of foreclosure. Therefore, the form of "contract of supplemental payment," or "supplement the contract to become a complete sale," and "eliminate the ownership credential" occurs. Concluding the

---

[48] Wang, W. (2008). *Compilation and Collation of Contract Documents in Ningbo in the Qing Dynasty*. Tianjin Ancient Books Publishing House.preface. 2–3.

[49] Examples of Qing Collected Statutes Vol. 755, Ministry of Penalty·live-sale·Homestead.

supplementary contract and eliminate the ownership credential are the final phase of the transaction from "assigning the right to use for long term" to "foreclosure."

"Contract of supplemental payment" is an institutional arrangement in the transaction from "assigning the right to use for long term" to "foreclosure" after the seller being unable to redeem or the property being transferred completely. According to the law of Qing Dynasty, "fields that are pawned can be redeemed," "If the seller is unable to redeem, he can entrust an intermediary to find a buyer to pay the price difference and sign another contract of foreclosure. If the buyer is unwilling to pay the price difference, he can resell the property and return the original price."[50] In Qing Dynasty, this kind of contract, whose main content is to obtain the bid-ask spread, is called contract of supplemental payment. When the leaser is unable to redeem his property, he can collect the difference between the rental price and the selling price, so that the relationship of selling right of using farmland becomes the relationship of selling the ownership of the farmland. After that, the leaser lost all rights to his land. Both parties should sign a contract of foreclosure or a contract of supplemental payment.[51] This strict procedural arrangement fully guarantees the rights of the seller and gives consideration to the fair interests of both parties despite the changing situation.

In order to avoid tax evasion caused by pawning property to others, some dynasties stipulated: "Those who do not pay taxes shall be given fifty lashes and handed half of the price of their fields and houses over to the government. Those who do not sign transfer formalities, shall be given forty lashes if his land was beyond five *mu* (a unit of area, 1 *mu*=0.0667 ha) and the punishment for each additional five mu of land shall be harsher, with a maximum of one hundred lashes, and all the lands shall be confiscated to the government."[52] And in the relationship of private contract, it is emphasized to sign a contract of foreclosure after finishing the supplemental payment for deficiency and complete the transfer procedure. Therefore, the "buy-out contract" or "blocked contract" which had been used since the Song Dynasty became more popular. The recognition of the separation of redeemable sale and foreclosure in the contract relationship indicates that the land sale in the Ming Dynasty has developed to a higher stage.[53]

5.3.1.3 Red Deed and White Deed

In order to protect people's legal rights and to eliminate disputes on property as well as to maintain social order, the government attaches great importance to the content and form of contracts. "In all disputes regarding land ownership, only the deeds and

---

[50] Examples of Qing Collected Statutes Vol. 160, Ministry of Revenue·Feudal Land Tax.

[51] Wang, W. (2008). *Compilation and Collation of Contract Documents in Ningbo in the Qing Dynasty*. Tianjin Ancient Books Publishing House. preface. 2–3, 5–6.

[52] The Ming Code Vol. 5, Residence Law·Homestead.

[53] Yang, G. (2009). *Research on Land Contract Documents in the Ming and Qing Dynasties (Revision)*. China Renmin University Press. Preface. 21.

contracts are considered as evidence." All these records indicate the property proof function of contract.

Unregistered private deeds (white deed 白契) and the notarized deeds (red deed 红契), marked with official vermilion seals, have different evidentiary weight in judicial practice. Unregistered private deed, literally called white deed, is the contract document signed by private parties without official procedures including registration, seal affixation, and tax payment. It mainly applies to the civil behaviors except real estate transaction, including property partition within a family, transaction, monetary loan, pawnbroking, partnership, equity sharing, indentured service, heir designation, inheritance succession, and so on. The reason why private deed can be widely used in civil affairs is that it is established by practicality, which is conventional, reasonable, and effective and can be mutually fulfilled and inherited by both parties. The government has imposed restrictions on economic behaviors such as land purchase and sale for a long time, which was mainly reflected in documents such as red deed, official deed, and contract tail.

In the Qing Dynasty, all the documents of land purchase and sales in eastern Zhejiang Province had regulated formats. This type of format was not a custom spontaneously initiated by the people but a form of document stipulated by the government. It mainly consisted of more than ten sections, such as the name of the seller, the name of the land, the area, the location of the land, the name of the buyer, the price of the land, the payment method, the rights of the buyer, the transfer of the ownership of the land, the transaction time, the intermediary, the witness, the writer of the contract, and so on.[54] In order to better clarify the property rights and to ensure the tax income of the government, the government constantly standardized the content and form of the contract as well as emphasized the evidentiary weight. *Rites of Zhou* recorded that "the concluding of *Zhi Ji* was a symbol of the termination of the proceedings." *The Enlightened Judgments* recorded that "Contract is the only evidence according to the law. In all disputes regarding land ownership, only the deeds and contracts are considered as evidence. Hence the so called "red deed" appeared.[55] Compared with white deed, red deed has stronger legal effect. There weren't many "red deeds" and "official deeds," which were both official documents, registered and recognized by the government, but there are slight differences between them. The original documents of red deeds are usually affixed with official seals, which embodies official approval, while "official deeds" used the paper printed by the government during the Republic of China, indicating the government's direct management of the civil contract behavior. "Contract tail" was always printed by the government. Generally, the contract tail was attached to the original text of the contract and affixed with the official seal. Among the documents attached with the contract tail, a foreclosure contract for sale in Tonghai in the 27th year of Jiajing's Reign in the Ming Dynasty (1548) was the earliest one found so far in Yunnan, more

[54] Wang, W. (2008). *Compilation and Collation of Contract Documents in Ningbo in the Qing Dynasty*. Tianjin Ancient Books Publishing House. preface. 4.

[55] Zhang, C. (1982). *Source and Development of Contract Forms in Ancient China. Humanities and History* Vol. 16. Zhong Hua Book Company.

than 460 years from now. The latest one existed in Yiliang documents of the 33rd year of Guangxu's Reign (1907).[56]

5.3.2 *Validity of Contracts*

5.3.2.1 Evidence in a Trial

The ownership itself has a multidimensional internal structure, which includes a vertical structure and a horizontal structure. The vertical structure is the different levels of rights coexisting within the same ownership. The horizontal structure is the different functional powers coexisting within the same ownership. The movement within the internal structure of ownership refers to the separation and combination of different levels of rights and different functional powers. Due to the absence of a comprehensive contract law, traditional China lacked theoretical development and refinement of ownership and its internal structure. However, people have achieved this separation and combination in social life through different local conventions. The contract document is material proof.[57] Since the first form of contract in traditional China (bamboo slips), it has paid attention to its function to contain and confine the relevant litigation. It has also laid emphasis on its function of testifying in the proceeding.[58] *Rites of Zhou* recorded that "the conclusion of *Zhi Ji* was a symbol of the termination of the proceedings," which refers to the prevention of litigation in a broader sense. In terms of specific operations, it also recorded that "People with debts are judged through *Pan Shu*." *Pan Shu* refers to contractual bonds. In judicial practice, cases are inadmissible without contractual bonds. When explaining the sentence "Use *Fu Bie* to *Cheng Ze*," Zheng Zhong in the Eastern Han Dynasty stated in *Rites of Zhou*: "*Cheng Ze* means loan, *Fu Bie* means contract. If there is any legal dispute over loan, the judgment will be based on the contract." It also means contracts serve as evidence for litigation. *Rites of Zhou* also recorded: "In cases of imprisonment, if the accused submits a written contract and a deposit, the case will be reviewed after three days and then heard in court." The annotation explains: "An 'imprisonment case' refers to someone being accused of a crime. The 'contract' is a written agreement now. After both parties submit the written contracts and pay the deposit, the case will be submitted to the judicial authorities for a trial after three days. This is the legal proceeding of a major case. If there is no written contract or deposit, it is equivalent to admitting guilt, and the person will lose

[56] Wu, X. Xu, Z. (2012). *Collection and Compilation of Legal Contracts and Documents in Yunnan Library* Vol. 1 (I). preface, People's Publishing House.4.

[57] Yang, G. (2009). *Research on Land Contract Documents in the Ming and Qing Dynasties* (Revision). China Renmin University Press. Preface.1–2.

[58] Huo, C. (2008). The connotation and modern value of Chinese ancient spirit of contract—Reverence and respect of contract and understanding of contract system. *Jilin University Journal Social Science Edition* Vol. 5.

the case." Therefore, if a litigant cannot provide a written contract, it is considered an admission of guilt and failure of a lawsuit.

According to *Zuo's Commentary*, when Zhao Dun started to manipulate national policies, he adopted a series of new policies including "enact administrative rules and regulations; enact criminal laws and penalties; track down fugitives; use contract to clarify the ownership of property." The last one is the practice of the "taking contract as evidence" system recorded in the *Rites of Zhou* in the Spring and Autumn Period. It is a restatement of the past system.

The law acknowledged the validity of a private deed In the Tang Dynasty and the Song Dynasty. The private contracts such as loan, sell, and employment were all bases that affirmed property rights. For example, the evidential role of contract appeared when the state confiscated the property of the sinner but with right dispute of the property. This basically followed the rules recorded in *Tiansheng Prison Officers Order* by Emperor Renzong of the Song Dynasty: When confiscating property of the prisoner, if there is a bonding relationship with others such as bailment, loan, pledge, or other contractual relations, as long as the prisoner declared at the time with a contract that can fully prove, the property should not be confiscated. The government should register the dispute over property rights for future judgment.[59]

No matter what type of contract it is, as long as it represents the expression of the parties' autonomy, it must be consciously adhered to. They are the main evidence when there is a lawsuit. For example, among more than 700 documents of the Qing dynasty found in Ningbo, all contracts were signed with legal effect. Once the contract is signed, both parties must specify their duties in accordance with the terms of the contract. The buyer has the right to "manage the planting and flower collection" or "manage and renovate the house" and meanwhile undertake the obligation of "paying taxes." After the money is paid off on the date of conclusion of the contract, the seller's duty of tax payment is transferred along with the transfer of the right to farmland use. This was a common practice for all conclusions of contracts in the Qing Dynasty. If the seller thinks the selling price is too low, he can also find an "intermediary" to negotiate together to obtain a price difference. Such "price difference" is the result of tripartite consultation, which also reflects the principle of "free consent" of the contract.[60]

5.3.2.2 Red Deed Overrides White Deed

These two kinds of contracts have a strong binding force on both parties, but the degree of legal protection is different. As a kind of certificate, the white deed is consistent with the party's Autonomy of Will. Once a dispute occurs, it can play a role of clarifying the rights and obligations of the parties concerned in a variety of

59 Tiansheng Statutes in Ming handwritten edition collected by Tianyi Pavilion Library, 2006. Zhong Hua Book Company, 338.

60 Wang, W. (2008). *Compilation and Collation of Contract Documents in Ningbo in the Qing Dynasty*. Tianjin Ancient Books Publishing House. preface. 10–11.

means of mediation. It is also recognized by the government in most cases. However, the recognition degree of the government on the white deed is greatly reduced when it comes to special contracts, especially those that are directly related to national interests such as contracts of land selling. The governments may even restrict the use of white deeds sometimes.

The "red deed" of selling farmland sealed by the government together with the official documents attached is the document with full legal effect. Except for tax payment and official management, the meaning of "red deed" showed the standardization and formatting of the conclusion of contract at that time. For parties who sign the "red deed," the focuses are the official certification of property ownership and the protection of rights.[61]

"White deed" is also the proof of property right in real life, but it is an incomplete legal text. The evidentiary validity of white deeds regarding property rights is circumscribed and potentially nullified in litigation, which may change the actual property right relationship. Under normal circumstances (e.g., neither through coercive concealment of landholdings nor by fraudulent evasion of tax obligations, shall any party evade statutory fiscal liabilities), the fulfillment of the tax contract is an indispensable procedure to conclude the land contract. Since the Yuan Dynasty, the official document attached to the end of the land purchase contract after the tax deed was called "*Qi Wei*" (contract tail). There was no fixed form of contract tail at first. In the Yuan and early Ming Dynasties, the contract tail was designed by the counties themselves. During the Zhengde Period, the Ming Court abolished the contract tail designed by local counties and issued official contract tail from the Ministry of Revenue, thus standardizing the format of the contract tail. The following is an example from Yi County in Huizhou. This may have been produced by the county itself due to its format designed before the Ministry of Revenue's format was issued. Except for some remote areas that continued to use self-designed contract tails, counties generally adopted the contract tail format issued by the Ministry of Revenue. However, the implementation was not completely consistent, and the format was also diversified.[62] For example, the format promulgated by the Provincial Administration Commission of Jiangsu province is as follows:

Qi Wei (Contract Tail)

The Ministry of Revenue has issued an order to reinstate the old practice of adopting "contract tails" to prevent private levies and falsification of contracts. Jiangnan Jiangsu Provincial Government, the Ministry of Revenue suggests: "Contract tail should be reinstated as per the old practice in private purchases of real estate after taxes are paid. These contract tails should be uniformly numbered by the Provincial Administration Commissions and then distributed to local officials who will attach them to the end of civilian contracts indicating the amount of money of the property and affixing the official seal before giving back to the people, so that

[61] Wang, X. (2013). *Millennium of Contracts: The Form and Evolution of Traditional Chinese Contracts*. Peking University Press. Preface. 5.

[62] Yang, G. (2009). *Research on Land Contract Documents in the Ming and Qing Dynasties* (Revision). China Renmin University Press. Preface. 54.

the tax money shall be fully collected and submitted." This has been decreed by the emperor: "Approved, this is the imperial order." Therefore, the Provincial Administration Commissioner shall issue contract tails to the counties and prefectures in its jurisdiction. All gentry, military personnel, and civilians who purchase land and property must submit their contracts to the authorities, pay taxes according to the price of land and property and the transaction details, including the value of the land or property, tax amount and date recorded in the contract tail. The original contract shall be affixed with the contract tail and stamped. Then the contract should be returned to the purchaser for safekeeping. If a contract is not affixed with a contract tail and is still submitted as a white contract (without tax payment) or if the contract tail does not bear the official seal, it will be charged with tax evasion and half of the property will be confiscated by the government. Should any officials or tax collectors engage in extortion or harassment, the property owner is encouraged to report it for investigation.

The contract tail shall include:

Province County Buyer's name price subject matter

Province County Seller's name

The amount of tax should be paid before the year of Qianlong's Reign to the buyer

Date submitted to the Provincial Administration Commission.[63]

In the fifteenth year of Qianlong's Reign (1750), because of many inconsistencies and complexities in the formats of contract tails issued across different provinces, the state decided to issue a unified format by the Ministry of Revenue. This format included two halves, a front half and a back half. The front half was kept by the proprietor, and the back half was sent to the provincial government for verification with the quarterly registers. Before use, the contract shall be split in half by cutting through the text, divided evenly into two parts. From then on until the end of the Qing Dynasty, all Provincial Administration Commissions issued contract tails of the same standardized format, with only slight differences in the explanatory text.[64]

It can be seen that the contract has strong judicial proof in practice. The judiciary authorities accepted cases with contract and refused those without contracts. Even if the judiciary accepted the case, the party which was unable to provide the contract will also lose the lawsuit. The contract becomes the primary evidence in the lawsuit. The national judicial organs had enforceability on voluntary agreements.

[63] Collections in resource center of Department of History, Xiamen University. The original is attached to the land sale contract. The format from Qianlong to Xuantong was the same. Quoted from Yang, G. (2009). *Research on Land Contract Documents in the Ming and Qing Dynasties* (Revision). China Renmin University Press. Preface. 58.

[64] Yang, G. (2009). *Research on Land Contract Documents in the Ming and Qing Dynasties* (Revision). China Renmin University Press. Preface. 58.

5.3.2.3 Long-Lasting Probative Force

A popular folk saying goes that a-thousand-year piece of land has 800 owners. This shows that the transfer of land rights through buying and selling is a very common and frequent practice. If the transfer of land is based on purchase and sale, there must be a contract to establish the legal relationship. During the Ming and Qing Dynasties, privileged landlords could still exploit these contracts to force purchases, a phenomenon that indeed existed on a large scale. However, the establishment of clear regulations on legal relations marked a significant historical advancement.[65]

It is a Chinese tradition to keep the covenant of faith. Once the contract is signed, the parties will involuntarily fulfill the relevant rights and obligations. The constraining force of contract has very strong continuance and permanence and will not be changed easily, especially in the sale of real estate such as land. For example, the contract documents related to "Longyuan Village" in the catalogue of "Land and Property Relationship documents" in Kunming are characterized by geographical concentration, unicity of party, and long duration of time. The time span lasts for 163 years, from the 51st year of Qianlong to the 38th year of the Republic of China (1786–1949). There are several typical cases in the contract documents of Longyuan Village: the purchase of land by Li Chun and Li Xiang brothers, the sale of land between Li Zenggui's uncles and brothers, and the multiple purchases of land by Li Xiang's nephew Li Wenzao in the same year. In Yiliang Village, for example, "land and property relationship documents" are mainly related to the surname. Among them, Yu Shouqing from Taohua Village purchased land and real estate 35 times in 20 years (from the 11th year to the 34th year of the Republic of China (1922–1945)). By the year of 1950, Yu Shouqing had as many as 50 economic activities related to land and other property. Most of the contract documents of Yi branch in Yongsheng County were activities related to real estate and land with the surnames of "Lan" and "Hai," mainly focused on the period of late Qing Dynasty and the Republic of China.[66] Another example is in eastern Zhejiang in the late Qing Dynasty; the time of land tenancy often lasted longer. However, no matter how long it is, as long as the contract did not involve foreclosure, the seller can redeem it at the original price. A typical case is Mao Rongchang selling the right to farmland use: Mao Rongchang sold his land to Mao Kunshan for 6000 copper coins in the 26th year of Daoguang (1846), and his descendants redeemed it at the original price in the ninth year of Tongzhi (1870). Mao Kunshan has leased the site for 25 years, but it can still be redeemed based on the evidence of contract,[67] which illustrated the thoroughness of contract execution in eastern Zhejiang in the late Qing Dynasty. Upon execution of a real property contract (e.g., land conveyance), the rights and obligations of the

---

[65] Yang, G.(2009). *Research on Land Contract Documents in the Ming and Qing Dynasties* (Revision). China Renmin University Press. Preface. 19.

[66] Wu, X., Xu, Z. (2012). *Collection and Compilation of Legal Contracts and Documents in Yunnan Library* Vol. 1 (I). preface. People's Publishing House. 6.

[67] Wang, W. (2008). *Compilation and Collation of Contract Documents in Ningbo in the Qing Dynasty*. Tianjin Ancient Books Publishing House. preface. 11.

parties become binding. This contractual force persists until lawful termination, reflecting the traditional principle of *pacta sunt servanda* in Chinese customary law.

5.4 Contractual Spirits and Codes

5.4.1 Contractual Spirits

The jurisprudential maturity of a nation should not be merely measured by the number of statutory output or the degree of sophistication of codification, but through its efficacy in sustaining normative social order and regulation. Similarly, the development of a civil code cannot be the only criterion for the quality of civil law. Instead, the key should be based on the establishment of civil relationships, and when disputes arise, whether there are accepted rules or solutions recognized by the parties involved. Although there was no unified civil code in traditional China, there was a long-standing tradition of contracts which played a major role in regulating and maintaining civil legal relationships. These contracts served as both the rules for civil relations as well as the basis for the settlement of civil disputes. They have also embodied and transmitted the values of integrity, free will, equality, and the spirit of harmony which have become the cornerstone of social harmony.

5.4.1.1 Honesty and Credibility

Honesty is an inherent fine tradition of our country and a national virtue that lasted for thousands of years. It is part of the ethics and morality in the Confucian philosophical system. According to *The Book of Rites*, "Honesty is the law of nature; the pursuit of honesty is the law of human beings."[68] Honesty is people's respect, pursuit, and imitation of the law of heaven and earth. It requires people to be true and nondeceptive. "Credit" is also a moral norm in Confucianism, that is, people should fulfill what they have promised. As Confucius has said, "To govern a nation of a thousand chariots, a ruler must: Observe reverent prudence in governance; Practice fiscal restraint with compassionate leadership; Mobilize labor forces seasonally,"[69] which means to govern a big country, one must be honest with the people, win their trust, and cherish their force. He demanded that people should be "trustworthy in word and resolute in deed,"[70] which means "always keep one's word." "Credit" refers to the trait of "keeping one's word" and being honest. It is defined by Confucianism as one of the "five virtues," alongside "benevolence, righteousness, propriety, and wisdom."

[68] Zheng, Kong Yingda note: Annotation of Book of Rite Vol.5, Doctrine of the Mean.

[69] The Analects of Confucius·Xue Er.

[70] The Analects of Confucius·Zi Lu.

Honesty and credibility have the same connotation. Therefore, an old saying goes: "Honesty guarantees credibility; credibility guides honesty."[71]

From the above, it is evident that people had already connected "honesty and credibility" in their efforts to educate others and discipline themselves since the Pre-Qin times. Under the influence of Confucian moral principles and ethical teachings, people became accustomed to the principle of being honest in everything and also used these values to judge the character of others. Honesty became the guiding principle for interacting with others, forming an unspoken code of conduct in daily social interactions. Contracts in traditional China were based on this moral framework and foundation maintained by the principle of honesty and credibility which formed the primary spirit to govern the interpersonal agreements. This is called the principle of good faith.

China has long had extensive and frequent practice of contract. A large number of contract documents passed so far show that China as long had contract, and there are corresponding contract awareness and concepts, as well as a specific contract culture. The structure of a hierarchical society and a state was adopted in traditional China. Distinctions of the hierarchy include political hierarchy (monarch-servant, different official positions, officials and civilians), social hierarchy (ordinary people and people of a lower social status), and family hierarchy (close and distant, superiors and inferiors, old and young). However, the hierarchical differences did not reduce contractual equality in economic life. This was because of the differences between political life, social life, family ethics life, and economic life and the differences being in officialdom, at home, and staying out. Ancient China was also a society of contract, and the contract itself was a way of life for people. In Chinese conception of contract, it was always regarded as the determination of rights and obligations; contract of creditor's rights, in particular, was a symbol of holding wealth. The Chinese concept of contract has also been highlighting the "constraint" nature of contract contents on both parties. "Constraint" here has a similar meaning with "obligationestiuris vinculum" in ancient Roman law, which literally means "a debt is a legal bond." In the spirit of the contract, Chinese people have reverence for the contract, treating contracts the same as the law, and respect for the contract, regarding contracts superior to the regulation. More fundamentally, contract was understood as an institutional arrangement. People believe that contract has the arrangements to "establish credibility," to "guarantee credibility," and to "prove credibility."[72] The word "credit and perform" is also written at the end of many contracts to indicate the parties' honest attitude and the determination to execute the promises.

[71] Zhu Zi compiles: Posthumous Papers of Chengs' Vol.25, Changqian Daoben: The importance of learning is to keep faith; the importance of keeping faith is honesty. An honest man will keep his word. Unfaithful man cannot establish himself in the society and dishonest people cannot go far in his road. The book of the four libraries of Wenyuan Pavilion.

[72] Huo, C.(2008). The connotation and modern value of Chinese ancient spirit of contract – Reverence and respect of contract and understanding of contract system. *Jilin University Journal Social Sciences Edition*.Vol. 5.

In addition to engraved and printed contracts, there are also unwritten contracts in traditional China, that is, "good faith." Phrases commonly used by peddlers, such as "genuine goods at a fair price," "neither the old nor the young will be cheated," and "gold-lettered signboards," were unwritten contracts, eliminating the need for written agreements. Private loans in the acquaintance society usually do not involve written agreements or discussions of interest. Sometimes they even eliminate interest. These practices, which transcend formal contract rules, have been summarized as "the principle of good faith" in current civil law theory. As a result, the Chinese spirit of contract is both a legal and moral principle.

5.4.1.2 Free Will

The nature of contracts is freedom. Traditional Chinese contracts naturally retain this nature likewise. From Northern Liang and Gaochang to the early and mid-Tang dynasty, the contract emphasized its free side. During this period, contracts were rife with clichés such as "sign the contract based on mutual consent." Generally, with the existence of the fact and then being expressed, there comes the contract language. And the existence of this language also indicates the existence of facts.[73]

The meaning of "和*He* (means consent or peace in Chinese)" is opposite to "compel." It is not only a simple character but a relation of will which emphasizes the freedom of will. Legist Zhang Fei in the Jin Dynasty noted: "Without consent, there is compel."[74] Freedom, by its nature, means there is no compulsion. During the Gaochang Period, "He" was more often used in conjunction with "同*Tong*" (means "the same" in Chinese)," forming the use of "和同*He Tong* (contract)." The word "He" has soon taken on the meaning of the relationship of wills between two parties. At the same time, "He" was used together with the word "可*Ke* (means can)" in other forms of contract such as loan, lease, and employment contract. This usage continued until the Tang Dynasty. However, in the Tang Dynasty, "sign the contract based on mutual consent" was more used to indicate the relations of wills between two parties, which means there was no compulsion and the wills of two parties were "He" and "Tong" (unanimous agreement). In the loan contracts of Gaochang people, under the conditions of "three owners," "four owners," "seven owners," "nine owners," and "sign contracts based on consents," the money was jointly borrowed by the debtors. However, the debtors were not guaranteed jointly. Each person is only responsible for his or her own share of debt. Therefore, it is only a variant of "sign the contract based on mutual consent" with no special meaning. In the Tang Dynasty, "sign the contract based on mutual consent" was used in all loan contracts. The meaning of words "three creditors sign the contract" in the contracts of lease was the same as the above in Gaochang period. "Sign the contract based on mutual

[73] Huo, C. & Liu, X. (2010). The nature of contract and the freedom and equality of contract in ancient China—Investigation of traditional Chinese contractual language and social history, *Gansu Social Sciences*.Vol. 2.

[74] Book of Jin, Vol. 30, Treatise on Penal Law.

consent" was actually the abbreviation expression of "sign the contract based on mutual consent by both parties." There were also expressions like "two parties peacefully leave their fingerprints as proof" and "two parties reach an agreement and sign a contract as proof." All of these have reflected the character of "He" as well as the calm and sensible atmosphere.

Although "sign the contract based on mutual consent" was always followed by "leave their fingerprints as proof," "sign the contract based on mutual consent" had its independent meaning, that is, to emphasize the freedom between two parties without the situation of coercion or intimidation. Contracts with similar words all express this meaning. In the Jin, Yuan, and Ming Dynasties, contracts of selling or pawning land and houses often had statements such as "not to reduce the debt,"[75] "to buy and sell with cash, not under duress to reduce the debt,"[76] or "this is consensual without coercion."[77] This showed that the creditor did not force the debtor to pay the debt with the land property, and the act of pawning or selling was free, which also expresses the same meaning as "sign the contract based on mutual consent." The exact words varied with changing times, but the meanings remained the same. However, we should not only focus on the revelation of experience and common sense of the form "sign the contract based on mutual consent" in the Northern Liang, Gaochang, and Tang Dynasty but also pay more attention to their consciousness. These contents which emphasized the "agreement of the will of both parties" were not dispensable but contained their practical meaning.

5.4.1.3 Equality

Equality is the prerequisite and inevitable requirement of contractual freedom. Contract and equality are also symbiotic. In the late Tang Dynasty and the five Dynasties, Song and Yuan dynasties, contracts emphasized the equality of contracts, so the phrase "two parties deliberate and decide face-to-face" was widely used, which had almost replaced the previous "sign the contract based on mutual consent." At that time, the equality of contracts mainly focused on the equality between the contracting parties. There were also certain phrases on contracts such as "to deliberate and decide by both parties face to face," "have been decided after negotiation by both parties face to face," and so on. It is the same for contract of sale, loan, lease, and employment, as well as the trusteeship diploma.

To deliberate and decide was called "平章*Ping Zhang*" in Chinese, with the emphasis on expressing opinions and deliberating with others. In those situations where discussions take place, people who attend "Ping Zhang" may be specially

---

[75] Yang, G. (1998). *Research on Land Contract Documents in the Ming and Qing Dynasties*. People's Publishing House. 30.

[76] Huang, S. (1988). *Collection of Legal Materials of the Yuan Dynasty*. Zhejiang Ancient Books Publishing House. 239, 240.

[77] Yang, G. (1998). *Research on Land Contract Documents in the Ming and Qing Dynasties*. People's Publishing House. 30.

authorized. Volume 223 of *The Taiping Imperial Encyclopedia*, in the section "Officers of State Affairs XXI—Censor-in-Chief, quotes from the *Book of Tang*: "As the Censor-in-Chief, Wang Gui often offered a counsel and was praised by Emperor Taizong. Therefore, Taizong decreed that whenever the prime ministers discussed major political affairs, a censor should be present. Since the discussing state affairs among prime ministers can be referred to as "平章大计*Ping Zhang Da Ji*" (discussing major affairs), those specially involved in such discussions would be privy to the administration of state affairs. In this sense, "Ping Zhang" not only refers to the right to speak granted to the appointee but is also used as a noun to refer to the prime minister.

Therefore, it is easy to understand why "two parties deliberate and decide (*Ping Zhang*) face-to-face" was so commonly used in the contracts of the Tang, Song, and Yuan Dynasties. They were actually the more elegant words of the face-to-face consultations between the contracting parties, which was borrowed from the "big words" used on political occasions. Sometimes it was replaced by a more informal term such as "decided after negotiation by both parties face to face." "*Ping Zhang*" was actually "discussion."

"Two parties deliberate and decide face-to-face" generally appeared at the end of the contract, followed by "no backing out." This sentence appeared in the Tang Dynasty when "Ping Zhang" was widely used. Since "sign the contract based on mutual consent" and "two parties deliberate and decide face-to-face" contain their respective meanings, why can the latter replace the former? Theoretically, the former emphasizes the freedom to reach an agreement but also includes the meaning of "face-to-face discussion." The latter one emphasizes "face-to-face discussions" to achieve mutual agreement, meaning that such discussions contain free will. That is to say they could contain each other; they could not appear in the same contract statement. Therefore, although we have discussed "sign the contract based on mutual consent" and "two parties deliberate and decide face-to-face," respectively, their common features cannot be ignored.

Ancient China was a hierarchical society. There were political hierarchy (monarch-servant, different official positions, officials and civilian), social hierarchy (ordinary people and people of a lower social status), and family hierarchy (close and distant, superiors and inferiors, old and young) according to "Five Degrees of Mourning." How could a society without basic equality, in which the colors of clothes must be worn in accordance with their respective ranks (not to mention the specifications of housing, means of transportation, marriage, and funeral) accommodate the concept of contract with equality as its nature?

Firstly, contracts are concluded between families or outside the family, which means that the hierarchy within the family may have an influence on the signing and performing of contracts but not much. The conclusion between families is carried out by the "patriarchs," such as "fathers, grandfathers, elder brothers, or uncles." Therefore, equality returns. The transaction between the two patriarchs is similar to the contract signed by the "paterfamilias" in ancient Rome, whose sons and wife also belong to him.

Secondly, contracts can also be signed between people of different official positions and between officials and the civilians. Officials could buy land and houses from the civilians (not including land granted by the state or the monarch and non-contractual expropriation) by means of officials' salary or reward, and thus bureaucratic landlords have appeared. Civilians could also buy land, houses, and slaves from fallen officials, just as described in the poem written by Liu Yuxi, "swallows which skimmed by painted eaves in bygone days, are dipping now among the humble home's doorways." Meanwhile, officials, clerks, and civilians trade as "patriarchs" required by the law.[78]

5.4.1.4 Spirit of Harmony and Union

In the traditional contract, the sentence patterns expressing the agreement of contract like "sign the contract based on mutual consent," "to reach an agreement before signing contract," and "mutual agreement" had almost become a fixed form. The sentence "reach an agreement before signing contract" was sometimes rewritten in many contracts as the word "和同*He Tong* (mutual agreement)." *Contract of Selling Land by Song in the Thirty-sixth Year of Yanchangin the Gaochang Period* recorded that "two parties deliberate together to reach an agreement and cannot go back on their words after reaching it." It indicated that "He Tong" was an expression to emphasize contractual agreement. The word "He Tong," which emphasized the agreement of contract, and "不和*Bu He* (incompatibility)," which opposed the agreement, was not only found in many contracts in the Tang Dynasty but also appeared formally in the national code. In *Tang Code with Commentaries*, "To buy servants, livestock, etc., the law requires a contract to be concluded with the agreement before the purchase," "Slaves who were trafficked or bought can be sold as long as both parties agree on their wishes," "If the two sides disagree, the party who buys or sells by force will be bastinadoed 80 times."

These provisions indicate that *The Tang Code* not only stipulated "mutual agreement," "mutual consent," "incompatibility," and other legal concepts in the code but also emphasized that the contract must be based on the agreement of both parties with the same intention.

The awareness of harmony and union pursued by the ancients still has its vitality even in modern society. People believe that the credibility or binding force should be enhanced for important events. In these related events, the "contract documents" should be signed according to the principle of equality, the spirit of traditional contract, and the awareness of harmony. For example, the following is the contract of heir concluded by the people of Anning County in Yunnan province:

The contract drafter, Chen Dingbang, designated his eldest son Chen Xiang as his successor, because grandfather died with no children. After the contract is

[78] Huo, C.&Liu, X.(2010). The Nature of Contract and the Freedom and Equality of Contract in Ancient China (cont.)—Investigation of traditional Chinese Contract Language and Social History. Gansu Social Sciences. Vol. 3.

signed today, no dispute or disagreement can arise among the parties. This contract is made by mutual consent, without coercion, etc. Oral words cannot be taken as evidence, and the contract is concluded hereby.

April 5, the twenty first year of the Republic of China (Sunday)

Contract drafter, Chen Dingbang (signature)

Kinsman, Chen Jiamo (signature)

Chen Rulin (signature)

Chen Qiren (signature)

Townsman, Xu Cui (cross)

Xu Zhou (signature)

Scrivener, Chen Wulou (signature)

The period of validity of this agreement is permanent, with this document as a proof. (written across the seam between two adjoining pages).[79]

The formal requisites of traditional Chinese contracts, such as contracting parties, kinship witnesses, community guarantors, and notarial scribes, were inherited from the traditional form of private contracts. It belongs to the type of white deed, whose binding force to relevant parties has been generally recognized by people. The traditional contract and the modern contract are well connected, realizing the spontaneous transformation. Up to now, this contractual spirit and consciousness still maintains its exuberant vitality.

5.4.2 Contracts Without Legal Codes

Montesquieu said in *The Spirit of Law*: any legal system that exists has an important relationship with the environment in which it lives. There are many factors affecting the legal characteristics, such as political system, climate, land, population, and religion. Why did not China develop "contract law" or "law of obligations" before the Han Dynasty as it did in the late Roman Republic or the early Roman Empire? Foreign scholars have concluded two reasons. Firstly, during the Han Dynasty and before, China had no professional legal class which was independent of the government (if there is one, it will cause more problems) to give a professional explanation of the relevant terminologies and contents of the agreement. As a result, there was no mechanism to promote legislation to make legal norms which covered signing and operation of civil agreements. Secondly, officials, nobles, and other ruling classes on the whole despised and doubted the merchant class. Even though they had participated in the conclusion of commercial agreements, they still thought that

[79] *The Peaceful Contract Document: Chen Dingbang's Grandfather Passed Away Without an Heir, Establishing His Eldest Son as Successor*, Wu Xiaoliang, Xu Zhengyun (ed.): Collection and Compilation of Legal Contracts and Documents in Yunnan Library, Vol. 3, Contracts of Anning: SocialRelationships: Other, 2013, People's Publishing House, 258.

it was not worthy of conducting legislative discussion and research on mercantile activities.[80]

The emergence of "contract law" or "law of obligations" did not depend on a professional legal class detached from state power, as juristic priorities shifted across historical periods. How did the privileged class in the dominant social position posture toward mercantile communities? Did they endorse or constrain the interguild agreements of collaboration and reciprocity? These constituted pivotal factors for the evolution of contract law. The paradox of elaborated contractual practices coexisting with the absence of a civil code in traditional China stemmed from diversified economic, political, and cultural reasons.

5.4.2.1 The Constraints of Economic Structure

As an integral part of the ideological sphere, law is rooted in the economic foundation and at the same time reacts on economic foundation. The structure of natural economy and smallholder peasant economy in ancient times resulted in the narrow and simple organization of market economy. It is well known that the slave society flourished in the Western Zhou Dynasty. In the ancient agricultural state, the land was owned by the state while people owned a small proportion of private real estates. Even transactions among people involving movable assets were limited. Because of its small territory, limited currency and transportation, and nascent awareness of the exchange of goods, the inscriptions do not contain much civil circulation based on contract. Therefore, what we have seen were almost contracts for sales of important goods such as land and slaves or records of disputes arising from contractual relations. Moreover, these recorded events all occurred in the middle and late Western Zhou Dynasty when private fields appeared. After the Qin and Han Dynasties, the ancient Chinese society carried out the policies of prioritizing agriculture and constraining commerce. The society discriminated against merchants, humiliated and shackled them with heavy taxes. In the Tang Dynasty, merchants were forbidden to ride horses. In the Ming Dynasty, merchants were forbidden to wear clothes made of fine yarns. Especially the overt plundering of wealthy merchants by the "royal family" in Tang, Ming, and Qing Dynasties[81] led to the suppression of the emerging commodity economy. During that period, the goods produced were for self-consumption only. The self-sufficient natural economy has long inhibited the development of civil law, including contract law. In addition, the state implemented the monopoly system of salt, wine, and iron based on the primary purpose of maintaining social order, which reduced the scope of the subject matter traded in the private market and caused the reduction of the civil legal relationship adjusted by the contract law.

---

[80] Ma, R. (2013). *The spirit of Traditional Chinese Law*. (Y. Chen, Trans.). China University of Political Science and Law Press. 205–206.

[81] Liang, Z. (1997). *Seeking Harmony in the Natural Order*. China University of Political Science and Law Press. 148.

Natural economic structure led to the suppression of traditional Chinese contracts during their evolutionary process. Consequently, traditional China's legal ecosystem lacked the necessary conditions to formulate a unified and complete civil code comparable to modern contract law that integrates theoretical principles, detailed content, and a systematic architecture.

5.4.2.2 Rules of Centralized Politics

The idea of "all under heaven are of one family" for ancient imperial rule led to emphasis on the consciousness of "coexistence of all individuals" in traditional Chinese society. It was natural for the emperor to suppress the "private" interests of his subjects in the name of protecting the interests of the "public," which was also consistent with the Confucian-Legalist paradigm of "subordinating private interests to public good." Fang Dashi from the Qing Dynasty argued: "The cases involving household affairs, marriage, land, money and debt, theft and the like are all trivial matters in the eyes of the government. But for ordinary people, these are cases related to their own interests, and are by no means trivial. Even if these are trivial matters, they are the majority in a province or a county while felony cases are the minority. If officials only pay attention to major crimes like murder or robbery, how many of such cases occur in a year?"[82] Fang Dashi's argument reached the core of the matter. Civil disputes mainly encompassed disputes over land, monetary debt, and ownership claims between private parties. Rulers believed that these matters had no direct influence on their rule, so they considered such disputes as "minor civil matters." It is said that "none are more urgent than theft and robbery in the rulers' concerns," so that the rulers need to allocate time and energy to deal with threats to their rule, such as heavy crimes and insurrections.

Traditional China had always pursued the leniency and conciseness of laws and opposed the redundancy. Rulers must delete, omit, or reduce unimportant contents such as civil and commercial affairs, so as to retain the criminal law provisions, which were crucial to maintaining their rules. There were only a few articles in the ancient code which were always concise and comprehensive. For example, *The Tang Code*, which is famous for its completeness, has only 12 chapters and 502 articles. Among which, criminal law predominated others, and there was no distinction between civil and criminal law. As a result, the legal provisions on contracts were crude. Responsibility was criminalized, scattered in cases or folk customs. No civil code was promulgated. Secondly, traditional China attached great importance to harmony and pursues nonlitigation. Confucius said: "My ability to judge cases is no different from anyone else's, but my goal is to prevent lawsuits from happening."[83] This has illustrated people's mindset and value of litigation. These concepts have led to the official supervision of civil contracts and the third party's guarantee. In

[82] Fang Dashi. Ping Ping Yan, Vol.3, Don't Neglect Trivial Matters.

[83] The Analects of Confucius: Yan Yuan.

addition to the tax administration function of the government, the intermediary played the role of witness in order to ensure the effective and successful performance of the contract, which also prevented the occurrence of litigation.

5.4.2.3 The Orientation of Cultural Concepts

Firstly, the righteousness-profit paradigm constituted the ethical logic in Confucian statecraft. The traditional Confucianism of "value justice above material gains" restricted the development of civil legal relations while affecting the formation of contract in traditional China.[84] Confucius once said: "A man of virtue understands and observes what is morally right; while a petty man only has his eyes on and goes after what brings personal gains."[85] This statement speaks of the difference between righteousness and profit, which forms the moral conflict between one another. In Confucianism, the legitimacy of an act is more important than the benefits it brings. In the aspects of orthodoxy and morality, the rulers carried out the policy of emphasizing righteousness and suppressing profits. The vigorous promotion of the policy of "prioritizing agriculture and restraining commerce" became the orthodoxy throughout this period. After the Song Dynasty, the idea of paying equal attention to both righteousness and profits began to be advocated in the field of jurisprudence. This idea was fully developed until the Ming and Qing Dynasties. However, the worship of righteousness far outweighed the pursuit of profits in the upper social class. The division of "four social strata (scholars, farmers, artisans and merchants)" and the belief that "all occupations are inferior, only study excels" coupled with the "study-for-officialdom" mentality were not conducive to the emergence of a formalized private property code which could clearly define private property.

Secondly, the assimilation of law and morality. The relationship between traditional law and morality was complicated and vague. In the Western Zhou Dynasty, the law was contained in the extensive and profound "rites." The rites and laws were initially integrated through "Zhougong's creation of rites." Rites and laws were further integrated in the Wei, Jin, and Southern and Northern Dynasties, such as the *Ba Yi* (eight privileged groups of people whose cases are to be especially deliberated) system was officially incorporated into the law. It remained the same in the Ming and Qing Dynasties. To excessively moralize and ethicize law would constrain the development of civil legal system including contracts. On the contrary, legalization of morality will also lead to the suppression and even strangulation of the technique by overdeveloped moral consciousness. Nevertheless, the "private law" purporting to safeguard civil rights and to mediate interest conflicts remained as a juristic technique,[86] and therefore the contractual legal system appeared ambiguous and crude.

---

[84] Ye, X. (1993). *History of Chinese Civil Law*, Shanghai People's Publishing House, 32.

[85] The Analects of Confucius: Li Ren.

[86] Li, G. & Chen, Y. (2001). *Research on Contractual Documents Unearthed in Dunhuang and Turpan, Papers on Commercial Law*, Law Press, 222.

Thirdly, the restriction of patriarchal concepts. According to Henry Sumner Maine, the movement of the progressive societies has hitherto been a movement from "status to contract."[87] However, in ancient China, blood ties became stronger when primitive society collapsed and the concept of family and hierarchy were irreplaceable. This was bound to be a strong constraint on the development of contract law. The free development of civil acts was constrained, and the sphere of civil law was also invaded by a large number of family rules and clan regulations. Systems like property sharing and ancestral inheritance were dominated by the ethical principle of filial piety, making individuals obey the continuation of family line. The socialized private code often gave way to the ethical family rules, because family members were not the subjects of independent economic status.

Fourthly, the narrowness of elite consciousness. The legal elites of a certain era have different missions and responsibilities. Traditional legal elites always aimed to achieve good governance and social harmony as their legislative purpose while stipulating legal rules. Therefore, the methods to maintain national stability—punishment and statecraft and the methods to foster a harmonious society—rites and morality had always been the focus of their discussions. Once conclusions were reached, they became fixed, and the ruler would forbid any change and hence the mission of the legal elites was completed. In addition to these rules, there were "trivial matters" that had little to do with the affairs of the sovereignty. Legal elites disdained spending excessive time and energy abstracting or refining these "trivial" rules. On the contrary, contracts or contractual practices were more fully manifested in the daily lives of the people and the judicial administration of local officials. Traditional China has always attached great importance to the practicability of laws but neglected abstract and normative elaboration of them. This was the common characteristic of traditional law, and the system of contracts is of no exception.

In conclusion, the existence of the contractual form and its spirit with the absence of a civil code is the result of the combined effects of the traditional political, economic, and cultural factors over thousands of years.

[87] Maine, H. S. (1997). *Ancient Law* (J. Shen, Trans.). The Commercial Press. 97.

Chapter 6
The Culture of Mediation

6.1 Antilawsuit Promotion and Inculcation

Harmony constitutes the supreme sociopolitical ideal in traditional Chinese mindset. The requirement of achieving harmony is to reduce disputes and prevent lawsuits. Confucius once said: "In hearing litigations, I am no different from others. What is necessary is to cultivate a litigation-free society."[1] Although later generations had different understandings of this saying, the ideal of cultivating a "litigation-free" society proposed by Confucius has always been a guiding principle for them. All strata in society strongly advocated "nonlitigation" and "antilawsuit," especially in the Late Qing Dynasty when the relevant systematic process was gradually institutionalized. The reasons and purposes of "antilawsuit promotion and inculcation" have been widely discussed in academic circles.[2] This chapter focuses on the diversified levels and modern value of the traditional "antilawsuit promotion and inculcation."

[1] *The Great Learning* (Chap. 42 of *the Book of Rites*).

[2] The representative works related to "antilawsuit promotion and inculcation" include *Local Government in China under the Qing* written by Qu Tongzu (Fan Zhongxin and Yan Feng, trans. Law Press, 2003), *The Counterpoint Narration of Legal Culture in Ming and Qing Dynasties* written by Xu Zhongming (Tsinghua University Press, 2007), *Right and Unredressed Injustice* written by Hiroaki Terada (Wang Yaxin, trans. Tsinghua University Press, 2012), *An Introduction to Chinese Social History of Litigation* written by Fuma Susumu (Fan Yu, trans. Institute for Arranging Classics of Law of China University of Political Science and Law, ed. *Journal of Chinese Ancient Legal Literature Studies*, 6, 2012), etc.

R. Zhang, *Traditional Legal Culture in China*, Understanding China,
https://doi.org/10.1007/978-981-95-4697-8_6

6.1.1 Official Antilawsuit Promotion and Inculcation

Many monarchs tend to exhort the people to reduce disputes through issuing imperial decrees for the purpose of improving people's loyalty and filial piety, social stability, and consolidation of power. For instance, Zhu Yuanzhang, the founder of the Ming Dynasty, enacted "Six Sacred Edicts": the people should be filial to their parents, respect their elders, unite with fellow villagers, and live together in peace, attach importance to the education of their children, and engage in their own business dutifully and lead their own lives, and do not act recklessly. These six edicts became general principles themed by harmony for the rulers of the Ming and Qing Dynasties to strengthen moral publicity and advocate "no lawsuit," and hence indoctrination of the people by rulers was gradually standardized and organized. Moreover, "antilawsuit promotion and inculcation" was systematized and concrete as the enactment of "Instructions to the People." The Instructions (Article 19) provide that each village and town shall install a copper bell with a clapper; the officials assign the elderly or the disabled to hold the bell and go the rounds in the village guided by children. They are commanded to popularize Emperor Hongwu's "Six Sacred Edicts" to all the people six times a month with the purpose to persuade people to obey the edicts and not to violate the criminal law.

In accordance with the general principles of "*Six Sacred Edicts*" and social reality, the government stipulated specific provisions on "antilawsuit promotion and inculcation" in "Instructions to the People" to inform the public. For instance (Article 23) since in some areas, many people skilled in litigation could not settle disputes in a conciliatory way, even for trifles, but directly filed a suit to the authorities of the capital, the government required the respected elders to sincerely exhort the local people, "In dealing with such trifles as marriage, farmland, brawl, and dispute, both sides should accept give-and-take and conciliation. Anyone who is subject to gross insult and considers it inexcusable should ask the respected elders for help. The elders will judge the severity of the case and impose the punishment to uphold his justice, so as to avoid the government's involvement in the lawsuit. If the stubborn subjects file the lawsuit to the local authority or overstep the local authority and appeal to higher levels of the capital instead of obeying the instructions and warning of the elders, the elders are allowed to arrest and punish them." (Article 25) "Since there is a gap between the rich and poor in the village, in case of marriage, funeral, good or ill luck, each family should help each other." (Article 28) In every season, the people have to offer sacrifices to gods or ancestors according to law, so that those who do good will be blessed and those who do evil will be punished, therefore, the people take it as a warning and dare not serve the devil. (Article 32) All the children should go to school from the beginning of the tenth lunar month to the end of the twelfth lunar month every year. (Article 33, 35) In the village, the young should respect the elderly, and the elderly should also treat them with courtesy; they care for each other, live in harmony with their clansmen and neighbors, do not violate the criminal law, and tenderly accompany their parents, wives, and children forever, in order to achieve the aim of no lawsuit in society for a long time and people's living at ease and peace. (Article 38) The common people should file a suit from lower government progressively; if not, the violators will be punished. The officers who hear these cases hereafter will severely punish those who infringe the rule. The general principle of the Indoctrination (Article 39) relates to instructing people to respect such eight virtues as filial piety, fraternal love, loyalty, trustworthiness, courtesy, righteousness, honesty, and sense of shame. It requires the officials, the respected elder (with noble character, high prestige, and outstanding ability) and Lizhang or Jiazhang (the village heads of the rural self-administration system in ancient China) to draw on the good and avoid the evil, protect their lives and families, and strictly abide by the rules, which can give full play to actual effect of the Instructions, rather than make it a mere scrap of paper. Whoever disobeys the orders will be imposed corresponding punishments. Fully taking the universality of publicity target and the operability of public behavior into account, the Instructions convey inculcation to families, society, older and younger, couples, the elders, and officials and stipulate requirements of tolerance, reading, mutual help, mutual respect, and mutual love so that it raises "antilawsuit promotion and inculcation" to the level of law popularization and fully embodies the close combination of civil spontaneity and state compulsion.

With the collapse of Ming and the rising of the Qing Dynasty, in 1652 (in the ninth year of the rule of Emperor Shunzhi), Emperor Shunzhi renamed "Six Sacred Edicts" of Zhu Yuanzhang, and adopted it entirely as the principles of inculcation for the people. Through the establishment of community compacts, Xiucai (one who passes the imperial examination at the county level) above 60 years old with outstanding virtue and achievement or the civilians of moral prestige in their sixties and seventies by public election, on the first and fifteenth day of the lunar month, were responsible for declaring the Sacred Edicts and conferring honors on the virtuous and the worthy. This was the beginning of "preaching imperial edicts" in the Qing Dynasty. In the reign period of Emperor Kangxi and Yongzheng, the activity of "anti-lawsuit promotion and inculcation" in the way of "preaching imperial edicts" was further systematized and standardized, and finally this system was formed.

In October of the ninth year of the rule of Kangxi, Kangxi issued the imperial edict to the Ministry of Rites, saying, "To realize a stable and prosperous society, we should put indoctrination first, not laws and decrees first since the laws guide the people for a while, but the indoctrination can maintain for a long time. If we only rely on laws and decrees instead of focusing on indoctrination, we will just attend to the superficial and neglect the essentials." However, the current situation had changed greatly: the moral degeneration of the society was getting worse day by day, people were arrogant and not what they were in times past, and it was not strict and fair in meting out rewards and punishments. As people were more and more skilled in schemes and intrigues, the number of litigation cases was also increasing. Kangxi was extremely worried and thought, "if those who bring a lawsuit are sentenced to death, we will pity for their ignorance; conversely, if they are forgiven, we will go against laws and principles in a diametrically opposite direction." On the horns of a dilemma, he proposed the idea of imitating the ancient emperors:

advocating benevolent rule to relax punishment and educating the people to form good morality and customs. Therefore, he put forward the following 16 guiding principles:

Highly esteem filial piety and fraternal duty to enhance human relations;
Behave generously toward the patriarchal clan to promote harmony and peace;
Cultivate peace within the neighborhood to prevent conflicts and lawsuits;
Emphasize farming and sericulture to ensure sufficient clothing and food;
Be moderate and economical to avoid wasting money and materials;
Give weight to schools and academies to honor the gentleman habits;
Wipe out heterodoxies to promote the orthodox;
Popularize knowledge of laws to warn the ignorant and obstinate;
Clarify rites and propriety to improve customs and manners;
Work diligently for the chosen vocations to establish the people's aspiration;
Instruct sons and younger brothers to keep them from wrongdoing;
Stop false accusations to safeguard the good and honest;
Warn against sheltering escaped criminals to avoid collective punishment;
Promptly and fully pay the taxes to prevent being coerced to pay them;
Join together in 10 to 100 households to prevent theft and robbery;
Be free from enmity and anger to protect life and personal safety.[3]

He required the Ministry of Rites to draw up plans for the above principles, involving how to supervise and exhort the people and how to instruct all the civil and military officials in central and local authorities. This is the famous "Sixteen Sacred Edicts." Compared with "Six Sacred Edicts" of Zhu Yuanzhang and "Placard Instructions to the People," "Sixteen Sacred Edicts" of Kangxi Emperor involves many aspects, such as family ethics, cultural cultivation, discipline and law, nonlawsuit, and so on. The core is to call on the people to abide by discipline and law and maintain social security and stability. The Edicts are highly summarized, concise, and comprehensive, being the general principles of "antilawsuit promotion and inculcation" in the Qing Dynasty. Preaching the Edicts has become an important responsibility of local officials. When recommending county magistrates, the governor-general or provincial governor should take whether these people seriously publicize "Sixteen Sacred Edicts" of Kangxi Emperor as one of the necessary conditions. If this item is not indicated in the recommendation book, the officers shall be punished by demotion.[4]

If the refined abstract meaning of "Sixteen Sacred Edicts" is to be accepted by the general public, it needs to be explained in simple and understandable words. This work was completed in the second year of Emperor Yongzheng's succession to the throne (1724). Through the article-by-article interpretation of "Sixteen Sacred Edicts," it was extended to the edicts of more than 10,000 words. *Sacred Edicts* of Emperor Kangxiis intended to widely publicize the edicts, which requires that

[3]Veritable Records of Emperor Kangxi, volume 34, article Guisi (30) written in October of the ninth year of Kangxi's reign.

[4]Veritable Records of Emperor Kangxi, volume 122, article Gengyin (27) written in October of the 24th year of the Kangxi reign.

"preach office" be set up in the densely populated places in the big villages and townships of each province, and then from the local intellectuals such as tribute and government students, one older person with high prestige shall be selected to serve as the "Yuezheng," and three or four honest and prudent persons shall be selected to be "Zhiyue." On the first and 15 days of every lunar month, they would call *Qilao*, *Lizhang* (the village heads of the rural self-administration system in ancient China) and scholars in the countryside together to read out *Sacred Edicts* of Emperor Kangxi. "They will enlighten the people and encourage the ignorant in the village to do the good." After Emperor Yongzheng, the central and local governments of the Qing Dynasty continuously issued decrees, requiring them to preach the *Sacred Edicts*. When preaching, a grand ceremony should be held, and the preaching time should reach a certain standard, in order to show that the government attaches importance to indoctrination.

About half of "Sixteen Sacred Edicts" are about legal issues, including law popularization and no litigation, such as "cultivate peace within the neighborhood to prevent conflicts and lawsuits," "popularize knowledge of laws to warn the ignorant and obstinate," "clarify rites and propriety to improve customs and manners," "instruct sons and younger brothers to keep them from wrongdoing," "stop false accusations to safeguard the good and honest," "warn against sheltering escaped criminals to avoid collective punishment," "promptly and fully pay the taxes to prevent being coerced to pay them," "join together in 10 to 100 households to prevent theft and robbery," "be free from enmity and anger to protect life and personal safety," and so on. However, the government requires people to understand the law, not in order to make them have legal awareness and good at using the law to defend their rights. Instead, the government requires that people should consciously perform their obligations under the law and should be courteous to each other and avoid resorting to the law and court in case of disputes unless absolutely compelled. "Sacred Edicts of Emperor Kangxi" is also particularly detailed in this regard.

When expounding the article "cultivate peace within the neighborhood to prevent conflicts and lawsuits," a number of quotations from *The Book of Songs* and *The Book of Changes* are cited to illustrate the importance of harmony in the village. As the saying goes, "a friend nearby is more helpful than a relative from afar." Emperor Yongzheng makes full use of the popular and understandable truth of folk proverbs to tell people that when they get along well with their neighbors, the village is in harmony, and the disputes will naturally dissolve. In order to prevent a lawsuit, the key is to eliminate the cause of the disputes. If the villagers and neighbors unite, love, and help each other, and maintain tolerance and comity, the old and the young, scholars, farmers, artisans, and merchants can coexit peacefully, and malefaction shall be constrained. As long as the subjects follow the emperor's words, cultivate honesty and integrity, and every household upholds moral cultivation, lawsuits shall be prevented and security restored, and this beneficence will extend to the descendants, fostering intercivilizational concord that will ultimately elevate to cosmic equilibrium.

When expounding the article of "popularize knowledge of law to warn the ignorant and obstinate," it is said that the laws and regulations promulgated should be analyzed in an organized, in-depth and detailed way to explain the essence of law, so that people would "be aware of law and then fear penalty; fear penalty and then abide by law," that is, on the condition that people understand law, they will be afraid of punishment; when they are aware of the provisions stipulated to punish those who overstep the local authority in order to appeal to a higher level and bring a false charge against others, they will naturally get rid of the idea of litigation. The emperor also painstakingly warned the people that the law shall be enforced based on rationality; natural equity and human sentiment are innate to the human heart; the human heart cherishes sentiment and equity, and it will not be caught by the net of law; moreover, even if one's nature is retarded and does not understand rationality and righteousness, one may still cherish himself and his family. Just imagine that once they are caught by the net of justice, they shall suffer all kinds of tortures. Instead of appealing for leniency and trying to avoid punishment, how could any external remedy compare to cleansing one's wicked heart and repenting at the still hour of night? Instead of going bankrupt and pleading for a slight reduction in their punishments, how could they escape the state code after all, and how could any external remedy compare to correcting their unrighteous conduct, cultivating more benevolent acts, and observing statutory boundaries, so that they and their families can live in security for a long time? If they do not examine their own errors, or even violate the law, their behavior will bring shame to their parents and implicate their wives and children. Neither the village nor the clan can accommodate them. Even if they obtain the emperor's grace and are exempt from punishment, they have already lost their reputation. Is not it too late to repent of their previous evils?

When expounding the article of "avoid enmity and anger and protect personal life and safety," it is said that dispelling grievances and resentments is the way to protect the whole family. If people maintain peaceful mind and eliminate hostility, bullying and rivalry will naturally subside without waiting until dangers are eliminated and disputes resolved. The best effect of relieving grievances and resentments is rural harmony and tranquility, so that people inherit their family business, serve the country, live in peace and prosperity leisurely, and live a long life together.[5] In short, people are required to maintain reasonable, change bad habits, do good deeds, reflect upon themselves, do not break the law, and protect their families. Otherwise, it will be too late to regret. If everyone can be calm and courteous in case of disputes, they can resolve the conflicts invisibly and live peacefully in a happy community.[6]

By presenting facts and reasoning, Emperor Yongzheng, from both positive and negative aspects, painstakingly asked the public to know the advantages of no lawsuit and the disadvantages of lawsuit. In order to publicize "Sacred Edicts of Kangxi" and make it sustainable, the imperial court specially assigned it as an important political task to administrative authorities at all levels, requiring that a

[5] See compilation and organization of Emperor Yongzheng: *Kangxi Emperor's Message to the People* and *Kangxi Emperor's Teaching Mottoes*, Hunan People's Publishing House, 1999, 47–82.

[6] *Sacred Edicts of the Kangxi Emperor*.Tianjin Jinhetang.

preaching group be organized to publicize the Edicts and give lectures regularly. This publicity activity lasted the longest and covered the widest in the whole publicity and inculcation of the Qing Dynasty. In the Late Qing Dynasty, some officials took the initiative to organize publicity activities. For example, in order to "correct the atmosphere and purify the hearts of the people," Ding Richang, when he served as administration commissioner of Jiangsu Province, he vigorously "respected Confucianism," commanded his subordinates to preach the Edicts, issued such various books as *Xiao Xue* (educational primers), and ordered to seriously persuade the people, so that they could be well regulated.[7] In the late Qing Dynasty, since the society was chaotic and the law of imperial court was slack, although the imperial court frequently issued decrees to strengthen the publicity of the Edicts, some local officials also figured out that this was only a pretense of the imperial court. Much said but little done, therefore, they often made verbal promises rather than actions, and the measures were difficult to achieve actual effects. In the second year of Guangxu's reign (1876), the imperial censor Wu Hong'en wrote, "The preaching of Kangxi's Sacred Edicts should be organized seriously, but recently the local officials have treated it as a mere formality, which is truly inappropriate."[8] Although the preaching activities in the Late Qing Dynasty were not as strict as those in the early times, they persisted in many places. Some provinces could not find a person who could thoroughly preach the Edicts, so they had to invite experts from other provinces to give lectures. For example, in the 15th year of the reign of Emperor Guangxu, Zhang Bi, a government student of Jiangsu Province, and Jiang Sen, a tribute student of Jiangsu Province, were invited to Anhui Province to deliver lectures because they were famous for preaching the Edicts in their villages. It is hard-won that a legal popularization campaign has lasted for a century and a half.

6.1.2 Popular Antilawsuit Promotion and Inculcation

In order to cooperate with the publicity of "Sacred Edicts of Kangxi," the local gentry also compiled catchy poems for the villagers, which are easy to remember and follow. The lyrics of the song "Be Filial to Parents" are as follows:

I urge you to be filial to your parents; do you understand the grace of your parents? They endured ten months of hardship while carrying you and spent three years nursing you without respite.

Every time you fell ill, they were even more concerned, teaching you to read and preparing you for adulthood and marriage. Is it merely for the love and toil they gave that they spend their whole lives busying themselves for you?

[7] Official Documents of Fu Wu. volume 1 and volume 2.

[8] *The Record of Donghua in the Guangxu Period*, Zhonghua Book Company, 1958, 185.

When children wish to care for their parents, it is often too late, and they can only look back in vain at what could have been. Do not let the wind and the trees bring tears to your eyes; I urge you to be filial to your parents.

The lyrics of the song "*Harmonize the Neighborhood*" are as follows:

I urge people to live in harmony with their neighbors, as kindness and unity are the foundation of a peaceful community. Remember, all under heaven are brothers, so why differentiate us from our neighbors?

Harmony has always brought good fortune, and friendly relations have been praised since ancient times. If one household has extra grain, it should be shared; if another has power, it should not be abused.

In times of trouble, help each other; if a neighbor complains, encourage them to resolve it peacefully. Fellow villagers are like close relatives, so I urge everyone to maintain harmony with their neighbors.

The lyrics of the song "*Instruct and Guide Descendants*" are as follows:

I urge people to instruct their children, as their success or failure affects the family. Like uncut jade, a child needs proper guidance; indulging them sows the seeds of trouble.

Through education and observation, cultivate the next generation to inherit and advance the skills or careers of their predecessors. Wealth may vanish, but the knowledge from books endures.

Failing to teach children is the father's fault; spoiling them is not true love. Many ruin their lives due to their parents' excessive indulgence, so I urge people to discipline their children.

The central theme of these songs is to encourage the younger generation to honor their elders, for the elders to guide their descendants, and for neighbors to live in harmony and minimize disputes.

Some of the educational primers in villages centered upon themes such as "antilawsuit" and "forbearance." From an early age, they taught the public "antilawsuit" in the form of nursery rhymes. For example, in the childhood literacy book *Tales from the Children's Knowledge Treasury* compiled by the Ming Dynasty, there is a passage with the core of "saints value no litigation."[9] Although it is a type of educational primers, it has already cited classics to praise the saints and honest officials and eulogize the society without lawsuits. In addition, such educational primers as *Extended Collections of Wise Sayings* also contain "antilawsuit" instructions to educate the masses, such as "litigious people will come to a bad end." Both *Tales from the Children's Knowledge Treasury* and *Social Wisdom* are books with comprehensive contents and great influence in Chinese traditional educational primers. There is even a saying among the people that "after reading *Extended Collections of Wise Sayings*, one can speak, and after reading *Tales from the Children's Knowledge Treasury*, one can travel around the world." By reading the relevant content on "antilawsuit" promotion, people can receive antilawsuit education from an early

---

[9] Cheng, Dengji, *Youxueqionglin: Songyu* (Tales from the Children's Knowledge Treasury: Lawsuit).

age. Its heritage value is reflected in the legal enlightenment education in traditional China. Besides, concepts such as "no lawsuit," "antilawsuit," and "shame of lawsuit," "multilawsuit," "keen on lawsuit," and "good at lawsuit" remain the topics Chinese people pay attention to today in the process of creating a harmonious society and promoting the rule of law.

There are many other educational primers with the theme on "forbearance." In Yuan Dynasty, Wu Liang collected many songs in *The Book of Forbearance*, such as the song of *No Fighting*: In moments of anger, one might impulsively resort to fists, which leads to the conviction in the court, ending up in prison, wearing shackles, and facing punishment, all while needlessly wasting money.[10] It suggests that people should learn to restrain themselves when they are in trouble. If they are impulsive to hurt people, they will be involved in a lawsuit. But the song does not address the modern distinction between personal infringement and legitimate defense. Another song called *On Forbearance* explains in more details of the advantages and disadvantages of ceasing or advancing litigation: Be patient when you can, be cautious when you must; without patience and caution, small matters can escalate into big ones. Consider those who, driven by anger, end up in lawsuits—leading to personal ruin, harm to the family, and the destruction of their homes and fortunes. Did it all begin with something so significant?[11] The above poems about exhortation and forbearance explain gains or losses of lawsuits in detail, including how to confront at court and what adverse consequences the judgment may lead to once the court decision is executed. With clear explanations, they prepare the public with enough psychological expectations and the warning effect is obvious.

In some areas, antilawsuit aphorisms are written as couplets and hung on the doorposts of *Yamen* (local magistrate's office). The goal is to enable the people intending to litigation to quickly understand that fighting a lawsuit is difficult. The couplet on the doorpost of the main gate of the county *Yamen* in Pingyao, Shanxi Province reads: Don't seek revenge, don't act out of spite, and don't be abetted by others to reach this spot. Even if you win, you waste time, effortx, and money, and ultimately harm yourself. Consider reasons, weigh emotions, and assess the situation when serving as an official. Without diligence, integrity, and caution, it is easy to commit wrongs but impossible to deceive heaven. The first line is obviously written for the people, reminding them that in case of disputes, they should exercise restraint and forbearance and should not be gullible to others' instigation and file lawsuits at every turn. Who would instigate a lawsuit? The first and foremost are the so-called "folk lawyers" who are regarded as "Songgun" (pettifogging shyster) by the government and evil "Songshi" (legal practitioner) by the public, followed by those who want to make profits from litigation. The government's reminder is very clear: even if the litigation result is successful, the party is likely to become exhausted while expending time, energy, and funds. The warning to the public is

[10] Wu, L. (2006). *Book of Forbearance: No deputes*. Faraway Press. 77.

[11] Wu, L. (2006). *Book of Forbearance: Enduring Anger and Refreshing the Heart*. Faraway Press. 43.

straightforward: had they been aware, they would not have gone down this path in the first place.

Litigation costs money and time at all times and in all countries. Chinese proverb says that "you can win a lawsuit but always lose money," and a Western proverb also says that "justice delayed is justice denied." Both especially emphasize the issue of judicial efficiency and judicial benefit, that is, even if the judicial decision is fair; however, if the decision is made too late or the judgment is executed too late, and relief of parties' rights is not implemented immediately, no definitive assertion can be made regarding the absolute fairness or partial inadequacy of justice. Of course, there are differences in the understanding of "delayed justice" between China and the West, but litigation costs money, time, and energy, which is basically the same. The traditional Chinese government admonished the public in this way, in order to persuade the public to resolve disputes before resorting to lawsuits. Once a lawsuit is filed, unexpected consequences may be caused. Therefore, the public is dissuaded from resorting to the authorities unless absolutely necessary.

6.1.3 Clan-Led Antilawsuit Promotion and Inculcation

In Chinese traditional society based on the patriarchal system, families and clans constituted the primary engine of antilitigation promotion and inculcation. Families and clans are where societal members are born and grow up. An individual is first a member of the family and clan and then a member of the society. The antilawsuit inculcation in families and clans directly affects people's behavior when they step into society. Many of the family rules and traditions require clansmen to be tolerant, to stay away from litigation, and to revere laws, especially the criminal law.

6.1.3.1 Harmony with Others

As Zhu Bolu said in the *Family Rules of the Zhu Clan* at the end of the Ming Dynasty and the beginning of the Qing Dynasty, "Don't take into court your family disputes, unpleasant endings emerge from lawsuits." The Family Rules of the Wang clan of Aotai, Bao'an, and Guangdong in the Qing Dynasty specially clarified the advantages and disadvantages of antilawsuit and multilawsuit:

Fighting among family members is inherently unfilial. Conflict within the same clan is also inhumane. Even if a dispute must be pursued, the first step should be to consult respected elders of the clan and gather at the ancestral hall to resolve it. This approach can turn major disputes into minor ones, and minor disputes into nothing. If someone insists on mistaking wrong for right, bullying the weak, heeding malicious advice, engaging in lawsuits, setting traps for others, and if they are fortunate enough to win by deceit, their conscience will still be troubled in the quiet of the night. Moreover, just as all the evil can be detected by the Qin Mirror, those who harm others will ultimately harm themselves. For those accused, if there is room for compromise, it is better to yield. A slight affront from an uncle or nephew can be endured, but the attitude of clerks and officers is hard to bear. Why allow a minor grievance to lead to the ruin of property and the destruction of family? All should respect the official intention to settle disputes and maintain public order, thereby preserving harmony within the community.

The family rules require that disputes among clansmen should be resolved within the clan first rather than reported to the officials first. After appealing to the official, it will cause a series of troubles. For the parties involved, the benefits of settling a dispute outweigh the harm caused by continuing litigation. In order to enhance the antilawsuit promotion and inculcation of the clan, the clan specially appended the master Wang Yangming's antilawsuit theory—*Yusu* (Instructions to the Commoners) to the genealogy. Wang Yangming points out that if one fights for profits and initiates lawsuits, not only will one's own life be affected, but the descendants will also be affected. The retribution of wrongs and hatred will cause endless harm.[12]

Clans focus on positively teaching clansmen to live in harmony and eliminate disputes. The genealogy of the Nie clan based in Qingjiang of Jiangxi Province quotes the ancient maxim that "litigation is an ill omen" from *the Book of Changes* in the hope that the clan "remains free from legal disputes for future generations."[13] In the family rules of the Hou clan of Nanpi, Zhili, there is also the rule of refraining from litigating against fellow clan members, which states "In the future, if disputes arise among brothers or uncles within the clan, the clan elders should organize the heads of each family to resolve the issue before it leads to a lawsuit. Disputes are easier to settle this way. If stubbornness leads to mutual harm, it weakens the entire clan. For those who persist in wrongdoing despite warnings, the clan elders should first shame them. If they still refuse to change, they should be reported to the authorities and expelled from the clan, with their names removed from the genealogy. They may be reinstated after three years if they show genuine reform."[14]

6.1.3.2 Respect the Law

One of the important goals of the compilation of the official code is to simplify the law and express complex legal relations in popular, vivid, concise, definite, and clear language, so that the public can understand the meaning of the law, and then to cultivate their awareness of consciously respecting, abiding by, applying, and protecting the law. The legal words should be able to express legal ideas that civilians and elites can like and accept. Just as Stendhal praised the *French Civil Code*

---

[12] *Genealogy of the Wang Clan of Aotai: Family Rules* in Bao' an, Guangdong.

[13] *Fourth Revision of Genealogy of the Nie Clan of Hu Zhuang: Clan Discipline* in Qingjiang, Jiangxi, Guangxu period.

[14] *Genealogy of the Hou Clan* of Nanpi, Zhili, Republic of China, the old eight of the *Ten Family Rules*, renovated in the seventh year of the Republic of China, stone printed edition, stored in the library of Nankai University.

as the "mother of art, rhetoric and law,"[15] in a country full of illiterates, it is not easy for people to read and understand the laws written in the system. Therefore, the publicity of law must find a new way to spread the law in a more oral way, which may prove better. This puts forward higher requirements for the use of legal publicity words. However, after years of supplementation, interpretation, and evolution, laws of imperial court become increasingly cumbersome and difficult for ordinary people to master and understand.

In view of the numerous laws and regulations of the imperial court, which are inconvenient to remember, some clans have written the content of the Qing Code in their genealogy, which is a simplified version of the laws and regulations, so that the clansmen can learn to chant and popularize the law. For example, in the *Genealogy of the Deng Clan* of Pingle, Guangxi in the Qing Dynasty, it quotes the poem in Su Shi's *Xiziyou* (Ridicule Ziyou, Su Shi's brother), "Reading thousands of books without studying the law leaves one with no way to assist the emperor in the rule akin to that of Yao or Shun." This sentence points out that the law code was supposed to hold as much significance as the scriptures, but currently, people mostly do not pay attention to the legal code. There are even cases that involve those who, due to trivial matters, end up facing severe punishment from which there is no escape, due to their lack of knowledge of the law. Therefore, the genealogy cites a song adapted from *The Great Qing Code*, a popular folk song, and widely publicizes it among the clans to ensure that "it prevails in every household, reflecting a widespread unity of thought and action."

This song is a concise and catchy adaptation of *The Great Qing Code*, with each line consisting of only four characters in Chinese. Its brevity and simplicity make it easy to comprehend and memorize. Here are some lyrics for your enjoyment.

Murderers sentenced to death with a deferred execution; if motivated by greed, immediate execution without pardon. Killing in a fight punished by strangulation, execution delayed for three years, without life ultimately being spared. Handling others' lawsuits for profits incurring severe penalties. Accidental killing of a bystander during a fight punished by strangulation, execution delayed, ultimately leading to death... False accusations leading to death; the accuser sentenced to strangulation, with instigators sharing the same punishment. Suing an official and appealing to higher authorities: besides the original punishment, offenders are shackled and publicly shamed. Practicing or learning witchcraft punished by strangulation and imprisonment; those involved in learning exiled. Gathering a mob of 18 people for robbery: the leader sentenced to death, the rest sent to frontier defenses. Rescuing a prisoner and causing the death of a law enforcer: the leader beheaded, accomplices strangulated. Organizing rebellion against taxes or officials: either beheaded or strangulated with no leniency. Organizing strikes or boycotts: leaders executed immediately, accomplices sentenced to strangulation. Unruly mobs causing disturbances: leaders executed with extraordinary harsh

[15] Shi, J. (2015). *The Wisdom of Codification —Portalis, Philosophy of Law and the Chinese Codification of Civil Law*. Journal of Renmin University of China. Issue 6.

penalties. Fabricating accusations or posting slanderous notices: those knowing it without reporting it sentenced to strangulation. Students using official seals to engage in lawsuits beyond their authority sentenced to severe penalties.[16]

The song is almost an abbreviation of *the Great Qing Code*. It focuses on the prevention and control of major criminal acts; covers family, ethics, and society; and includes procedural and substantive laws. There are special punitive provisions for the prevention and control of "false accusation," "fabricating words to file lawsuits," and other acts. It can be read by individuals from various walks of life, such as officials, peasants, craftsmen, intellectuals, and lawyers. It is a typical example of clan antilawsuit promotion and inculcation, showing the strong legal sense of the genealogy reviser.

6.1.3.3 Indoctrination on Forbearance

Some clans have inscribed instructions on forbearance from litigation onto stone tablets as a warning to their clansmen to avoid litigating easily. The "Song of Forbearance from Lawsuits" of the Kong clan serves as an example:

Be patient and avoid taking disputes to court; peace will come to both you and others.

Following others' instigation to go to the court costs money for the litigation and complaint.

Officers delivering summonses and orders demand money for locking you up and letting you out.

Neighbors called as witnesses need to be fed three meals a day, costing money for tea and tobacco.

The court staff is the hardest to deal with, as both trials and settlements require money.

Instigating lawsuits is inherently deceitful and greedy, costing money whether you win or lose.

Getting entangled in lawsuits leads to selling off your land and eventually your house.

There is not enough to eat and not enough to wear and both your wife and children suffer.

[16] *Genealogy of the Deng Clan* in Pingle, Guangxi, volume 2, *Song of the Great Qing Code*, Shi Xiantang edition in the 17th year of the Guangxu reign, continued in the 13th year of the Republic of China, stored in the library of Nankai University. According to historical records, the *Song of the Great Qing Code* was compiled by Gan Rulai, who lived through the period of Kangxi, Yongzheng, and Qianlong in the Qing Dynasty (1683–1739). In addition to the *Song of the Great Qing Code*, Gan also published other works such as *Complete Collection of Xun Zhai Poetry and Memorial*, *Commentary on Sacred Edicts*, *Brief Annotations on Zhou Li*, and *Record of Official Life*. See Lei Liancheng, *Collection of History and Culture in Laishui*, China Literature and History Publishing House, 2006, 437–438.

Only then do you realize the harm of lawsuits is far from trivial; cursing is in vain, and regret is useless.[17]

Throughout the song, the clan members are taught to learn forbearance and not to trust the instigators and file lawsuits in case of disputes. Since once a lawsuit is filed, no matter whether one wins or loses, there is a possibility that he will spend recklessly and his family will be destroyed. This method is similar to the imperial court's publicity of *Sacred Edicts*, but it is more accessible and memorable, which is quite representative of the antilawsuit promotion and inculcation of the traditional clans.

Some ancestral halls of clans that have been preserved to this day still contain such antilawsuit materials. For instance, the ancestral hall of the Zhang clan in Jianshui of Yunnan Province constructed during the Qianlong's reign of the Qing Dynasty has retained the Zhang clan's family motto, "a hundred forbearances." Here is the lyrics of "Zhang's Song of a Hundred Forbearances":

The song of a hundred forbearances, the song of a hundred forbearances. Forbearance is the measure of a great person, the foundation of a noble character. With forbearance, summer heat is bearable, and winter cold is endurable. With forbearance, one can find joy in poverty, and longevity in life. Without forbearance, the wealthy fall into ruin, and the prosperous suffer losses. Without forbearance, trivial matters turn into major issues; good deeds can lead to lasting regret. A lack of forbearance between father and son diminishes filial piety; a lack of forbearance between brothers undermines brotherhood; a lack of forbearance between friends breaks loyalty; a lack of forbearance between husband and wife leads to endless conflicts. Liu Ling lost his reputation because he couldn't resist alcohol; Chen Ling lost his kingdom because he couldn't resist lust; Shi Chong lost his family because he couldn't resist wealth; Xiang Yu lost his life because he couldn't resist his temper. Nowadays, all criminals are those who do not forbear to commit crimes. Of the great figures of history, who among them did not behave with forbearance?

The family motto emphasizes "forbearance" as a crucial measure against lawsuits, and with it as the main theme, they set up a family tradition: before the dispute, advocate forbearance; after the dispute, also advocate forbearance. In short, civil disputes are to be addressed through a process that emphasizes antilawsuit promotion and inculcation first, followed by persuasion and mediation, with resorting to the authorities as last.

[17] Quoted from *Wang Liyan, Careful and Prudent as a Human Being and Coordinating with Superiors and Subordinates as an Official—An Analysis of the "Twelve Precepts of Life Experience" and "Small Supplement to the First Official in Count,"* Guo Chengwei, ed. Review of Official Admonition and Research on Official Admonition Culture, China Legal Publishing House, 2000, 335.

6.1.3.4 Prohibition of Litigation

Family rules and clan disciplines generally warn people not to sue easily in case of litigation, because once involved in litigation, the consequences are hard to predict. There are many rules in the genealogy that forbid people to file lawsuits. It is stated in the Xu Clan's rules against lawsuits in Jiangxi: "Most legal disputes arise from conflicts. When a grudge is not resolved, people become increasingly hostile, leading to lawsuits that drag on for years. This leads to constant travel, humiliating oneself in court, ultimately ruining one's family and deep regret. When there are minor disputes within the clan, remember that you are of the same bloodline. Report to your elders, and they will mediate and resolve the issue. In cases of external conflicts with neighbors, the situation must be carefully assessed, avoid impulsive actions that could bring hardship to both parties. As the saying goes: 'Lawsuits never end well.' This is truly a critical warning for family life."[18] It informs the clansmen that lawsuits may lead to family destruction and humiliation, and it is still important to follow the clan rules. The rules of the Yang Clan from Qingjiang aim to quell lawsuits: "Crawling before the court is far from honorable. If it becomes absolutely unavoidable, and one must bring a case to the authorities, then in matters of trivial disputes, it is essential to listen to others who can mediate and resolve the issue. If you insist on pursuing the lawsuit to the end, it may result in misfortune. Engaging in acts of bravado and aggression is even less virtuous and should be strictly prohibited."[19] The Xiang Clan of Yiyang has a similar rule against lawsuits: "Litigation is extremely dangerous. Unless absolutely necessary, never engage in lawsuits with others. Those who take pride in litigation are on the path to ruining their family. When one endures insults without seeking legal recourse, they only suffer humiliation from a single person. However, once a lawsuit is initiated, they face humiliation from everyone. The harassment from malicious adversaries, the manipulation by ruffians, the changing testimony of witnesses, the difficulties caused by shysters, the demands of bailiffs, the cheating of clerks, the exploitation by corrupt officials, and even the mistakes made by upright judges—none of these can be avoided. The difference between enduring insults from one person and from everyone is vast. Moreover, the lawsuit will lead to neglect of one's work, mental and physical exhaustion, and fear and anxiety within the entire family. These are just a few of the many detrimental effects, and those with wisdom should be cautious."[20] It points out that if one has a dispute with another person, but choose not to litigate, he will only be humiliated by the person involved. However, if a lawsuit is filed, the one may encounter challenges throughout the whole litigation process. The reason for describing the litigation process as extremely difficult is to warn the clansmen not to do it if possible. The preface of Sheng Family Genealogy from

[18] *Genealogy of the Xu Clan of Yunxi: Clan Discipline* in Qingjiang, Jiangxi, Jiaqing period.

[19] *Third Revision of Genealogy of the Yang Clan in Yongbin Qingjiang: Clan Precepts* in Jiangxi, Qianlong period.

[20] *Continuation of Genealogy of Xiong Clan: Family Precepts* in Yiyang, Hunan.

Hanshou of Hunan province during Guangxu's Reign includes one of the *Sixteen Family Rules*: "No gathering for fights is allowed, as it may lead to injuries or even death, implicating the entire family and clan. If there is any grievance, it must first be reported to the clan for resolution. Do not listen to deceitful people who encourage litigation; immoral and illicit behavior that deteriorates public morals should be reported and collectively handled according to the law by the clan leaders to avoid future regret."[21] The *Fourth Revision of the Liu Family Genealogy* (Volume II) from Nantang of Ningxiang during the Republic of China states in its *Family Rules*: "Family members must not engage in lawsuits. All disputes must be brought to the ancestral hall for resolution by the clan. Those who bypass the clan and directly bring conflicts to the authorities will be punished."[22] It means whenever a clansman has any grievances, they must first address those issues within the clan, and lawsuits are not permitted. Only when a clansman is deemed to have committed a serious offence will the clan send him to the authorities to be punished according to the law. In summary, the clan holds the belief that winning or losing a lawsuit will not bring any benefits to them but harm the clan's reputation.

6.1.4 Religious Antilawsuit Promotion and Inculcation

Traditional China features polytheistic worship instead of monotheistic worship. In order to achieve a certain will, people can borrow some religious doctrines to assist in moral inculcation. As for foreign religions, they adhere to the principle of treating each other with tolerance and for our own use and absorb and explain them. The thought of retribution for sin is propagated with the help of religious consciousness. China's view of retribution for sin emphasizes both the present life and the afterlife. The former believes that retribution should not be in the afterlife but in the present life, such as *A Record of Strange Tales from the Imperial Examinations* and *The Treatise of the Exalted One on Response and Retribution*; the latter emphasizes "reincarnation or samsara," the eternal cycle of birth, death, and rebirth in Buddhism.[23] The hero of the Yuan drama *Zhushadan* says: "Good deeds are rewarded with good and evil deeds with evil. If the heaven did not send harsh frost, pine and cypress would be no better than common weeds; if the divine spirits did not enact retribution, accumulating virtue would be no better than accumulating evil." Most of these accounts of legal cases in literature declare that justice can only be achieved by relying on the retributive punishment. Only when the wicked are punished can the case be concluded, which is the most desirable ending for the people. Promoting mediation and moral education is an important aspect of traditional teachings to enlighten people on the principles of karma (law of cause and effect). In the religious

[21] The movable type printed version of Guanglingtang in the 27th year of the Guangxu reign.
[22] Wooden movable type printed version of Cunzhutang in the tenth year of the Republic of China.
[23] Samengwu, "*The Water Margin" and Chinese Society*, Beijing Publishing House, 2005, 57.

advocacy of reducing litigation, Buddhism preaches kindness, patience, and cause and effect, and Taoism preaches merits and faults, no desires, and withdrawal with from secular world, which are in line with the Confucian ideas of no-lawsuit, self-control, and harmonious society.

In fact, the popular publicity of antilawsuit often borrows from each other, combines secular with religious, utilitarianism with belief, and reflects the present life with the afterlife. Therefore, people can rely on what they believe and take what they need, and both the form and content are popular with the public. There is no obvious boundary between Confucianism, Buddhism, and Taoism in the "antilawsuit" promotion and the idea of "retribution for sin." Editing and distributing Instructions on Morality is the common way of antilawsuit promotion among the people. *The Book of Forbearance: Exhortations of Wang Longshu* contains a number of quotations from Buddhist and Taoist precepts. For example, the Buddha said: "Attaining the samadhi (meditative state) of non-contention is the highest achievement among humans." He also said: "Among the six perfections, forbearance is the foremost." It highlights the significance "forbearance" in Buddhism. Additionally, the Taoist text *Chao Tian Chan* (Confession) states: "Wealth and honor come from enduring humiliation." The immortal female Taoist Zi Xu Yuan Jun said: "Forgiving, forgiving, forgiving—by forgiving, countless misfortunes and disasters are eliminated; forbearance, forbearance, forbearance—debts and grievances are resolved." Immortal Taoist Sun said: "With forbearance, all evils are eliminated; with frugality, calamities do not befall you." All of these examples emphasize the importance of forbearance and forgiveness, with the belief that as long as one is able to forbear and forgive, all disputes can be resolved.

If one does not forbear and forgive, litigation may easily arise. Once litigation commences, it will be difficult to achieve favorable outcomes. Some instructions on morality attempt to quantify the positive effects of forbearance on antilawsuit. They evaluate the behavior of various parties involved in litigation and assign positive and negative points accordingly. The ultimate assessment of good or bad is dependent upon the size of the positive and negative scores. According to the Record on *Emperor Wenchang's Merits and Demerits: Holding Office*, "punishing *Songshi* (legal practitioners) and protecting one's family, reporting pettifogging shyster, and teaching stubborn people and settling disputes are each worth ten merits." Conversely, officials will "receive a penalty of one point for arbitrarily allowing lawsuits to proceed." In other words, officials are evaluated based on their ability to successfully combat lawyers, report shysters, teach stubborn people, and quell lawsuits. If they are successful, they will earn ten merits; if not, they will receive one demerit for each case. As for the intellectuals "士*Shi*," they are advised not to write complaints on behalf of others, so that litigation or false accusations can be controlled at source. The criteria for scoring are different from those of officials: "One merit is granted for refraining from writing a petition on someone's behalf. When "writing a petition on behalf of a person, it is considered ten demerits; causing people to lose their homes and even lives, plus ten times; writing a petition for false accusation, thus causing people to lose their homes, a hundred demerits." The general public holds a different standard, where "preventing a dispute or persuading the parties to make peace earns one merit, while ending a lawsuit earns ten merits." The more merits one possesses, the higher the reward and the more favorable the situation in the afterlife.[24]

The *Examples of Merits and Virtues without Costs* reveals the harmful impact of "false accusation" and "instigation of lawsuits" and demands that such acts must be severely punished. "Punishing false accusations will clear the source of litigation, resulting in fewer false accusations, and then the treacherous schemes of destroying other people's families will be eliminated. Accordingly, when those who instigate lawsuits are penalized, conflicts can be resolved, and as a result, people can live in peace and work in contentment." To achieve this, scholars should "not write false accusations or reports," while farmers should "abstain from litigation, fighting, stealing, and gambling."[25] In terms of severity, instigating lawsuits is more serious than initiating them. For example, the *Records on Merits and Demerits of Yuan Liaofan by Zen Master Yungu* stipulates that if one instigates a lawsuit, one will be penalized with thirty demerits.

The criminal law originally has the function of reward and punishment. Some instructions on morality even imitate the secular system of punishment to establish the grades of reward and punishment for lawsuits. For example, *The Record of Self-Awareness* sets forth the following guidelines: "Encouraging peace over conflict is a merit." "Persuading someone to drop a lawsuit, thereby preventing a death sentence, counts as ten merits; preventing military or prison sentences counts as five merits; preventing a flogging with the cane counts as two merits; and preventing a beating with the whip counts as a merit." Conversely, "assisting in litigation that leads to a death sentence counts as thirty demerits; causing a military or prison sentence counts as twenty demerits; resulting in a flogging with the cane counts as ten demerits; and causing a beating with the whip counts as five demerits." If someone incites a lawsuit, the punishment is even more severe: inciting a lawsuit for profit that leads to a death sentence counts as 100 demerits; causing a military or prison sentence counts as 30 demerits; and causing a beating with the whip counts as 15 demerits.[26] The imperial court enacted criminal law that permitted *chi* (beating with the light stick), *zhang* (beating with the heavy stick), *tu* (penal servitude), *liu* (exile), and *si* (execution) as punishment. The five punishments of the criminal law were vividly interpreted in the instructions on morality. The people may not know the detailed provisions of the criminal law, but in the process of worshiping Buddha, Taoism, and Confucianism, they unconsciously understand the content of the criminal law and try to avoid punishments.

Of course, if these commandments are preached by "masters" of eminent monks and Taoist priest, they will be more authoritative, classical, and persuasive, and

[24]Yuan, X. (1995). *Instructions on Morality among the People*. Shanghai Ancient Books Publishing House, 251, 238, 218–219.

[25]Li Rijing, *Examples of Merit and Virtue without Cost*, Yuan Xiaobo, (ed). *Instructions on Morality among the People*, Shanghai Ancient Books Publishing House, 1995, 160–162.

[26]*Records on Self Knowledge*, Yuan Xiaobo, ed. *Instructions on Morality among the People*, Shanghai Ancient Books Publishing House, 1995, 189–197.

there will be more believers. In a traditional society with relatively single means of communication, gathering disciples to preach scriptures can directly and quickly popularize doctrines and improve the understanding of rules. For example, Hanshandeqing, an eminent monk of the late Ming Dynasty, wrote the *Verse for Quelling Lawsuit* to tell the pros and cons of no-lawsuit and multilawsuit.

The misfortunes in my life all come from lawsuits, and my thoughts have stemmed from uncontrolled impulses. When angered by someone, I often wanted to take action, but was advised to be cautious and not act rashly. It is said that once a case is filed with the authorities, one falls prey to deceitful people. Unable to return home, one is delayed and cannot tend to the fields. His wife is driven to despair; parents are distressed with deep sorrow. Property is lost, and lives are ruined. Moreover, life is short, like a fleeting spring dream. What is the use there in flaunting power or intelligence? What purpose does revenge serve? When one speaks with empathy and reason, it naturally awakens the ignorant. If they can change their mind and turn back, this is a hidden virtue to be praised.[27]

The *Verse for Quelling Lawsuit* uses themes like family, kinship, compassion, and the value of life to discourage people from engaging in lawsuits. There is no pure preaching but full of the Buddhist compassion. The sentences rhyme and are simple and easy to understand. Religious masters or priests participate in legal education and persuasion for offenders both at home and abroad. Today, many prisons or communities in Hong Kong and Macao still pay attention to attracting religious people in the rehabilitation and psychological correction and restorative justice of offenders, which undoubtedly helps to purify the minds of offenders.

Since traditional China is not a country of monotheistic worship, the people fully enjoy freedom of belief. Few superhuman spiritual idols can unify the people's spiritual world. Confucianism, Buddhism, Taoism, etc. all have the effect of publicizing antilawsuit and encouraging people to do good deeds, which is basically consistent with the official ideal of no-lawsuit. Therefore, the three beliefs can go hand in hand in political life, social life, and spiritual life. Similarly, Catholicism and Protestantism also contain the content of "no lawsuit." For example, in the "Ten Commandments of Moses" of the *Old Testament, the Bible* tells God's people: "Honor your father and mother so that you'll live a long time in the land that GOD, your God, is giving you. No murder. No adultery. No stealing. No lies about your neighbor. No lusting after your neighbor's house—or wife or servant or maid or ox or donkey. Don't set your heart on anything that is your neighbor's."[28] In the *Luke* of the *New Testament*, Jesus explained to his disciples the conversion of weal and woe between the poor, the hungry, the weeping, the hated and reviled, and the rich, the full, the laughing, and the favored and flattered.[29] *The Bible* also requires: "It always protects, always trusts, always hopes, always perseveres" (*Corinthians*13:7). "Do

[27] *Poetry of No-lawsuit*, Yuan Xiaobo, ed. *Instructions on Morality among the People*, Shanghai Ancient Books Publishing House, 1995, 138.

[28] *Exodus* 20, *Old Testament.*

[29] *The New Testament, Luke* 6, *Blessings and Misfortunes.*

everything without grumbling or arguing" (*Philippians* 2:14). Forgive the wrongdoers, as for the wrongdoer, "the punishment inflicted on him by the majority is sufficient. Now instead, you ought to forgive and comfort him, so that he will not be overwhelmed by excessive sorrow. I urge you, therefore, to reaffirm your love for him" (*Corinthians* 2:5–8).

The *Proverbs* and the *Psalms* also contain admonitions that teach humility and forgiveness: "Better a dry crust with peace and quiet than a house full of feasting, with strife" (*Proverbs* 17: 1). "All day long he craves for more, but the righteous give without sparing" (*Proverbs* 21: 26). When someone does something wrong, and you love them, it is better to forgive rather than punish, because "the Lord is gracious and compassionate, slow to anger and rich in love" (*Psalms* 145: 8). The Bible also requires disciples to love their enemies as friends. For example, if someone strikes your left cheek, offer them the right cheek as well. Moreover, God instituted the "Judgment of Armageddon" to bring comfort to the afflicted and to warn the wrongdoers of their fate.

These doctrines also have the connotation of quasi antilawsuit to persuade people to argue less with others. In Chinese and Western cultures, the antilawsuit popularization is originally similar, but the awareness of rights in the Bible is different from Confucianism, Buddhism, and Taoism. In particular, the concept of "all beings are equal before God" is not completely consistent with traditional Chinese rites and laws. In traditional Chinese view of heavenly and ethical order, there are natural differences in the status of each person, and social order is often set by heavenly and ethical order.

6.1.5 Antilawsuit Promotion and Inculcation and Transfer of Rights

In traditional China, antilawsuit promotion and inculcation is all round. Keeping restraint and tolerant and eliminating disputes and lawsuits can be often regarded as good personal virtues or family traditions from generation to generation. Its main purpose is that tolerance can reduce disputes, thus reducing litigation, so that ultimately social order can be harmonious and stable. This is not only the ideal governance model of successive governments but also the ideal life of most people. "Kongrong giving away bigger pears" in the Three Kingdoms Period is a vivid story in educational primers. Zhang Ying, the Minister of Defense in the Qing Dynasty, wrote a family letter to persuade the family in Tongcheng to take the initiative to step back when they built their house—"the family letter travelling 1000 *li* (unit of length, 1 *li*= 1/2 kilometer) is only for the sake of the wall, but I suggest yielding three *chi*(unit of length, 1 *chi*=1/3 meter); today the Great Wall is standing firm, and yet the First Emperor of Qin Dynasty died long ago." The reason why the story and letter can be eulogized widely by future generations is that it extols humility and tolerance, which is in line with the basic etiquette for interacting with others.

There is no absolute equality in the world. Even before God, it is impossible to realize the ideal that "everyone is equal," let alone before a judge. Although judicature is the "last line of defense" to guard social justice, and courts and judges seem to be the patrons of this "line of defense," in fact, judicature is not absolutely fair, and judgments of judges may not be completely reliable; otherwise there will not be several "trial levels," even US federal justice Posner admitted, "decisions of the Supreme Court are ultimate, not because they are right, but because they are ultimate." The same reasoning: if there is another "super court," many final judgments of the Supreme Court may also be overturned.[30]

Since modern times, science has been flourishing and pragmatism has prevailed. After the May Fourth Movement, the status and role of traditional Confucianism, Buddhism, and Taoism have gradually declined, and various emerging "doctrines" or "schools" have taken their place. Under the guidance of many "doctrines," the people have readjusted their lifestyles, directly causing the politicization and utilitarianism of spiritual beliefs.

Although publicity and education cannot be directly linked to "antilawsuit promotion and inculcation," it cannot be denied that they have played a positive role in guiding people to be kind to others, live in harmony, help each other, and maintain restraint and humility. The combination of rites and law, as well as integration of virtue and punishment, is the basic strategy of governing the country in traditional China. To maintain the harmony and stability of social order, we should first prevent or reduce social disputes to the greatest extent. "Settling disputes and eliminating lawsuits" becomes the main external embodiment of the function of rites and laws, and "antilawsuit" publicity and inculcation naturally become the preferred method to achieve "settling disputes and eliminating lawsuits." As a result, the state, the people, clans, and religions have been the main fields of "antilawsuit" promotion and inculcation, which integrates moral education and law popularization into one. The laws and regulations in a variety of forms have become catchy "jokes" of antilawsuit promotion, deeply rooted in the hearts of the people.

As the ancients said, "the saint values no lawsuit," and "enjoys the ideal life in peace without disputes and lawsuits," that is, to settle disputes and live in peace. The purpose for the state to formulate rites and laws is to purify the hearts of the people, enrich customs, and conform to human feelings. Portalis, a jurist who participated in the formulation of *French Civil Code*, says, "we must not forget that law is established for people, not people for the law; the law must adapt to characteristics, habits and conditions of the target people."[31] Voltaire also says, "law and custom are not contradictory. If the custom is good, the law will be useless."[32] Apart from instrumental preaching and publicity, the education of kindness and tolerance based on the traditional Chinese social structure and social life has played an important

[30] Xiong, B. (2014). The saw of Posner, *Reading*, (9).

[31] Shi, J. (2015). The wisdom of codification—Portalis, philosophy of law and the Chinese codification of civil law, *Journal of Renmin University of China*, (6).

[32] Voltaire. (2008). *Philosophical Dictionary* (J. Xu, Trans.). Beijing Publishing House, 143.

role in settling disputes and reducing litigation, which not only reduces the costs of the parties but also saves limited judicial resources of the country. It has delivered more positive energy to the country, the government, the society, and the people.

Overemphasis on forbearance and antilawsuit promotion will certainly restrain the individual rights and interests and weaken the awareness of the rule of law; however, too much emphasis on individual rights and interests may also harm overall rights and interests. In many cases, the individual transfers part of his private rights, and it can maintain the integrity of the overall rights and interests; the integrity of overall rights and interests may benefit more individuals and help to maintain the maximum balance between the individual and the overall. Up to now, it is still worth learning from.

6.2 Township Mediation

Mediation complements antilawsuit promotion and inculcation. The purpose of antilawsuit promotion is to prevent disputes, but in case a dispute arises, mediation is the preferred means of resolution over a lawsuit. It serves as a bridge between antilawsuit and lawsuit, with a long-standing history in China. With its low litigation costs, flexibility of methods, and simplicity of proceedings, mediation gained widespread popularity among the public as a means of resolving disputes. Over time, it became one of the most commonly used methods of disputes resolution, playing a significant and positive role in improving the stability and growth of ancient Chinese society. The mediation system was effective in ancient China and continues to thrive in modern times as a valuable tool in resolving social disputes. This represents a major contribution of traditional China to the human judicial civilization.

According to the identity of the mediator, traditional mediation in China involves various forms such as self-mediation, township mediation, clan-led mediation, and government mediation.

6.2.1 Self-Mediation

This is a mediation method in which disputing parties invite neighbors, relatives, friends, elders, or individuals with prestige in their local community to persuade, intercede, and mediate, thereby resolving conflicts. The process is free from fixed procedures or the blackmail of *Chaiyi* (*Yamen* runners) and is flexible and simple in nature, making it particularly popular among the people. For instance, in the Han Dynasty, two clans in Luoyang had an ongoing feud for several years. Despite repeated interventions by the government, the disputes remained unresolved. Ultimately, Guo Jie, a chivalrous expert, stepped in and persuaded the clans to reconcile. His public-spirited and kindhearted nature earned him the title "the man who saves lives without boasting about his own merits."

In the event of a civil dispute, individuals with acknowledged prestige in rural areas are often asked to mediate. These individuals have lived in the area for a long time and possess abilities, qualifications, and personalities that the surrounding people recognize. Because of the recognition of the mediators, there is usually no need to sign a mediation agreement when resolving ordinary disputes. People generally agree with the authority and fairness of the mediation, and there is little opposition to the mediation outcome. Everyone is thoroughly satisfied. As is described in Shen Congwen's *Border Town*: "The man in charge of the docks was one Shunshun… he had acquired eight boats that plied the river, a wife, and two sons. This untrammeled and free-spending fellow, able though he was in business, liked to store up friends and give out money. Shunshun was always there for those in need, so he never became greatly rich like the tung oil merchants. His walk was uneven, but his character and judgments were straightforward, right down the middle. Things were fairly simple out on the river; everything was decided by customary practice. Which boat was at fault in a collision, which boat had harmed another's property—usually there was an established way to decide it. But to apply all these customary laws they needed an elder of tested virtue. On an autumn day some years before, the old boss of the riverfront had passed away. Shunshun took his place. He was only fifty at the time, but he was so astute, upright, and even-tempered, so free of greed and venality, that no objections were heard on account of his youth." Although Shunshun is not yet "an elder of tested virtue," his character has earned him respect among the local people, who turn to him for assistance with both minor and major matters.

For more serious disputes, such as those involving real estate and minor injuries, it is usually necessary to sign a mediation agreement. For example, in Anning County, Yunnan, people involved in verbal or physical disputes would go through mediation and then signed an agreement:

The contract signatories, Xie Dengqi and Xie Denggui, residents of Huolong Village in Dongjie, have been involved in a dispute and fight over water usage. This matter has now been reported to the local elders for mediation. From now on, they must resolve issues through mediation and are not allowed to resort to violence. If anyone initiates violence, they will be fined 10,000 coins, which will be handed over to the local office as public funds. Regarding water usage, according to tradition, it will be divided among all users, with one ration for one person and ten people sharing it equally. For those with water storage ponds, water can only be stored when there is an excess; if there is no excess, water cannot be stored. The two parties, whose fields are adjacent, must not use this matter as an excuse to create further disputes. If anyone does so, they will also be fined 10,000 coins. This agreement is made voluntarily by both parties, without coercion. To ensure it is followed, this contract is kept as evidence.

November 10th, the third year of Emperor Xianfeng's reign.[33]

The villagers asked mediation from the village elders to address conflicts over water release. Both parties accepted the outcome of the mediation, effectively resolving the irrigation conflict. To ensure the legitimacy and permanence of the outcome, the parties and the mediator signed the agreement, which was publicly disclosed.

The rural society is made up of acquaintances who are familiar with each other. Successive dynasties have advocated antilawsuit inculcation. In an acquaintance society, legal action is often viewed as unsympathetic, and filing a lawsuit would put aside all considerations of individual's feelings, thus despised in the village. Furthermore, neighbors consider any conflict leading to lawsuit as a matter of dishonor in this area. Villagers who have disputes should initially resort to persuasion and mediation. If a lawsuit is imminent, they will also make every effort to prevent it. During the Yuan Dynasty, a system called "Gao Lan" existed, which focused on resolving disputes through nonlawsuit means (the system of withdrawing complaints and promoting reconciliation). The *Statutes of the Yuan Dynasty: Ministry of Justice: Lawsuit* has a specific subheading and provision on *Tiantugaolan*, which outlines the Gaolan system in terms of a case and the central government's instructions regarding the case. The case records that Wang Cheng and Qi Ama of Fengqiu County, Bianliang Road, disputed a field of about 19 acres. Before the government intervened, a knowledgeable figure named Zheng Zhi facilitated a resolution between the parties. They reached a private agreement through voluntary negotiations, dividing the disputed fields between them. From then on, neither party could break the agreement. If either party breached the agreement, they would be subject to a caning of up to 87 strikes. All land would be allocated to the party that abided by the agreement, and they could not be appealed to the government. *Xingsheng* (Province), *Libu* (the Ministry of Rites), and *Zhongshusheng* (the Secretariat) all provided affirmative instructions on this private agreement. The unanimous opinion was "In cases of household, marriage, land, and private debt, if a mediator negotiates and reaches an agreement, it should be considered final and not subject to further appeal. The government may not accept the case in such cases."[34]

The popular superstition of "punishment by the government" also caused villagers to prevent lawsuits. According to *The Exposure of the Official World*, when the country gentleman Wang's servant quarreled with Zhao Wen's family, Wang was so angry that he wanted to take the servant to the local magistrate. However, Zhao Wen's father stopped him and gave the following reason: "If a person who has been punished by the government becomes a ghost after his death, he will not be allowed

---

[33] Wu, X. & Xu, Z. (2013). *Anning Contract: Social Relations: Others* and *Anning Mediation of Contracts for Verbal Disputes and Fights*. volume 3 of *Compilation of Contract Documents for Yunnan Museum Collection*. People's Publishing House. 276.

[34] See volume 53 of Statutes of the Yuan Dynasty, volume 15 of Ministry of Justice, and volume 3 of *Gaolan: Tiantugaolan*, Zhonghua Book Company and Tianjin Ancient Books Publishing House, 2011, 1789–1790.

to reincarnate for eternity, won't this ruin him?"[35] This superstition deepened people's fear of lawsuits, and they not only tried to keep themselves away from the lawsuits but also hoped that people they knew would not get involved in lawsuits so easily.

The villagers typically take the lead in avoiding litigation through various means such as persuading, convincing, and admonishing, presenting the facts and analyzing benefits and drawbacks so that both sides can reach a mutual understanding. More formally, the involved parties may sign a memorandum of understanding in the form of a contract to serve as evidence. For instance, during the Qing Dynasty, the resolution of grass-roots social conflicts in the southern county of Sichuan involved a method known as "*Lan Liu*" (interception of disputes), which survived a lot of "contracts for intercepted disputes." In the *Archives of Nanbu County*, 53 contracts for intercepting the dispute have been preserved. These contracts involve a variety of disputes, including two families fighting for the scope of the cemetery; the head of a family addicted to alcohol and domestic violence which intensified family conflicts; the ambiguous communication of the younger brother and his elder brother's wife leading the elder brother's resentment to filing a lawsuit; and cutting down the temple trees and the unequal distribution of the spoils. Villagers and clansmen intervened to intercept the parties to avoid litigation, and after mediation, both sides signed a contract. At the end of the contract, it is mostly written, "In order to avoid unexpected troubles, both parties should sign this contract in public and promise not to file any future lawsuit, hereby leaving this as a proof," and "From the date of signing the contract, both parties shall live in harmony and shall not make mischief. If anyone violates the etiquette and law and commits any further mistakes, the clansmen will report it to the local government for punishment!"[36] In these contracts, mediation is not considered the final solution for settling disputes. Instead, it is explicitly stated that violation of the mediation agreement may result in government punishments. It enhances the credibility and warning of the mediation agreements and allows the parties to acknowledge it psychologically.

Certainly, mediation primarily centers on providing positive guidance, emphasizing persuasion and reconciliation. For instance, during the Jiaqing period of the Qing Dynasty, in Baodi County, Shuntian Prefecture, a land dispute arose between Zhang, the widow of the Sun family, and Sun Wenjiang, the cousin of her deceased husband. A local "Jiansheng" (a student enrolled by Guozijian, the Imperial Academy) and five villagers intervened to mediate, ultimately leading Sun Wenjiang to recognize their familial connection and take the initiative to compromise. He reestablished an agreement with Zhang, saying that in the future, they would each keep their own family land and live together in harmony. It is apparent that such

[35] Li Baojia, Chap. 1 of *The Exposure of the Official World.*An Aspiration for Fame: The Scholar Admonishes Unruly Children on Composition, and the Gentry Encourage the Younger Generation.

[36] Wu, P. (2014). *The Archives of Nanbu County: Contracts for Intercepting the Party in the Settlement of Social Disputes at the Grass-Roots Level in the Border Areas of the Qing Dynasty*, Wang Shirong et al. eds. *Historical Experiences of Legal Governance at the Border Areas in the Successive Dynasties of China II.*Law Press.111–116.

disputes frequently arise among neighbors, relatives, and friends. Therefore, local individuals with prestige and impartiality intervene to "alleviate dissatisfaction of the weaker party, mitigate the arrogance of the stronger party", balance the situation between the stronger and weaker sides, and ultimately "reach a reconciliation and peaceful coexistence."[37]

6.2.2 Township Mediation

In early ancient China, township mediation is semiofficial where official designees who are not part of the government's official staff handled civil disputes. The role of these mediators is more prominent in the autonomous organizations of villages, and the mediation serves as a crucial prelitigation procedure, with the nature of quasijudicial proceedings.

The mediation system in traditional China was systematically recorded as early as the Zhou dynasty. The Rites of Zhou defines "Liuxiang Liusui" (six interior districts, six exterior districts), which are grassroots self-governance units listed in order, five *Jia* (households) as *Bi* (neighborhood), with *Bizhang* as the neighborhood head; five *Bi* as *Lü* (village), with *Lüxu* as the village assistant; four *Lü* as *Zu* (precinct), with *Zushi* as the precinct commander; five *Zu* as *Dang* (ward), with *Dangzheng* as the ward rectifier; five *Dang* as *Zhou* (township), with *Zhouzhang* as the township head; and five *Zhou* as *Xiang* (interior district), with *Xiang Dafu* as the interior district grand master. In addition to *Zhang*, *Xu*, *Shi*, *Zheng*, and *Dafu*, there are also *Bishi*, *Zanzhang*, *Lizai*,*Linzhang*, etc., all of who are in charge of the township governance in the early times. *Guanzi* also outlines the "dynasty rule" and "township rule." Since the Zhou Dynasty, China has had a township organization. Among the recorded official titles in the *The Rites of Zhou: Terrestrial Offices*, "Tiaoren" is an official with expertise in mediation. His role is "to investigate the people's difficulties with the goal of resolving conflicts and promoting harmony."[38] During the Spring and Autumn and Warring States Periods, officials who specialize in mediating revenge cases are also referred to as "Tiaoren." During the State of Qin, the Shiwu system (the household registration system) was established after the Shang Yang reform.

During the Qin and Han Dynasties, *Xiang* (village) was established under *Xian* (county), with *Youzhi*, *Sanlao*, and *Sefu* as petty officials with ranks in the district authorities, responsible for moral education and dispute mediation. If the mediation failed, they could report to the county office. "Ten *Li* (hamlet) as *Ting* (neighborhood), with *Tingzhang* as neighborhood head; ten *Ting* as *Xiang* (township), with *Sanlao* (three elders), *Sefu* (collector), and *Youjiao* (patroller)." *Sefu* oversees

[37] Wang, Huizu, *Zhisong*, Xu Dong, volume 17 of *Mulingshu*, *XingmingI* (Book of the Governor and the Magistrate: Law and Order).

[38] Sun, Y. (1987). *Annotation of the Zhouli*. Zhonghua Book Company. 38.

litigation and mediates disputes and judges right and wrong by means of questioning. The Eastern Han Dynasty continued the system of "*Likui* (village heads) and *Shiwu* (the household registration system)," to distinguish between good and evil. The mediation procedure was also increasingly standardized. In the Han Dynasty, first, the judicial organ accepting the lawsuit wrote a *Yuanshu* (court report or transcript) on the basis of the plaintiff's complaint and sent the *Yuanshu* to the court of the county or head of the garrison where the defendant was located, and then the county court or head of the garrison delivered the *Yuanshu* to *Sefu* or *Houzhang* (observation official) of the grassroots level to be responsible for questioning and mediating the dispute. During the period of the Three Kingdoms, the Jin Dynasty, and the Northern and Southern Dynasties, the township governance system was continually strengthened, and civil disputes were resolved through mediation to "uphold justice and reduce litigation" so that the number of disputes was "more than 10 times less than before, and all areas were stabilized and harmonized."[39]

The Tang Dynasty implemented the system of *Xiangbao*, in which civil lawsuits were first mediated by *Lizheng*, *Cunzheng*, and *Fangzheng*, and disputes that could not be resolved would be referred to the county and the prefecture. Before the mid-Tang Dynasty, township mediation was effective, with "all levels in contact with each other" and "each performing their own duties," thereby "fostering harmonious relations between officials and commoners." This contributed to creating a peaceful and content community. However, at the end of the Tang Dynasty, the township governance collapsed and the dynasty declined.[40] Despite minor distinctions among the *Dubao* system in the Song Dynasty, the *Shezhang* system in the Yuan Dynasty, the *Lijia* system in the Ming Dynasty, and the *Baojia* system in the Qing Dynasty, they are all national grassroots autonomous organizations. *Baozhang*, *Lizheng*, and *Xiangzhang* are responsible for rent and tax collection, military payment distribution, and civil dispute mediation.

The Ming and Qing Dynasties are considered the most mature period of the traditional township mediation system. Emperor Taizu of Ming ordered local officials to select fair and impartial elders to deal with disputes in the townships. Disputes over household, marriage, land, housing, and fight were to be resolved through negotiation between the elders and *Lixu*. Only in serious cases should these disputes be reported to the government; otherwise they would be considered "overstepping the local authority and appeal to a higher level."[41] Both *the Ming Code* and *the Great Qing Code* maintain the clause of instructing elders to handle litigation in the townships, authorizing village elders to adjust "trivial matters"[42] related to family relations and real estate. It is even stipulated that civil disputes that had not been mediated by the township could not be subject to judicial proceedings. Even if a

---

[39] Weishu, Shihuozhi VII (Book of the Northern Wei: Treatise on Food and Commodities).

[40] *Collation and Annotation of Rizhilu (Part 1)*, Yuelu Publishing House, 2011, 364.

[41] Volume 232 of Veritable Records of Emperor Taizu of Ming, Renwu article in April of the 27th year of the Hongwu reign, and see *Collation and Annotation of Rizhilu*, Yuelu Publishing House, 2011, 36–364.

[42] The Great Qing Code: Ministry of Justice: Miscellaneous Offences.

lawsuit has been filed with the government, it must be returned to the township for mediation and adjudication. If the mediation is reasonable, no further lawsuit shall be filed. However, if other disputes cannot be resolved by the local elders, they should be submitted to the prefectural and county governors. "Sixteen Sacred Edicts of Emperor Kangxi" and *Sacred Edicts of Emperor Kangxi* in the Qing Dynasty also emphasize the importance of mediation as the primary means of handling "trivial matters" and minor injury cases.

How are the scope and operation mode of the elders and neighborhood head in mediating disputes put into practice? In this regard, the most clear and specific provisions are found in the *Instructions to the People*. During the early Ming Dynasty, the system of Mediation by the Elders was implemented with the *Shenmingting* (Pavilions for Explicating Clarity, the pavilion for the public moralization and precaution against evildoing) in the township to publicize the *Instructions to the People* issued by the Ministry of Revenue, which stipulates: "All minor matters such as household, marriage, land, fight, and altercation shall be determined by the elders and *Lijia* of the township. Serious issues, such as robbery, theft, fraud, and homicide, must be reported to the relevant government. After the issuance of this order, officials who dared to violate it shall be punished with capital punishment. If the people dare to violate it, the whole family shall be exiled." Obviously, which can be reported directly to the government, which must be determined by the elders and *Lijia* before reporting to the government, there are general provisions. The Ming government made mediation a prelitigation procedure, and no lawsuit could be filed without mediation of the *Shenmingting*. *The Instructions to the People* was posted at the *Shenmingting* (Pavilions for Explicating Clarity) or *Jingshanting* (Pavilions for Extolling Goodness, the pavilion for commending virtuous behavior in the community) in front of the local office, as well as in areas where the public frequently passed by or gathered.

The government has refined specifications for the powers, responsibilities, rights, and duties of the elders and *Lijiazhang*, as well as members of the township, involved in dispute resolution. These specifications include the proceedings for resolving disputes among villagers (Article 1), the powers and responsibilities of the elders and *Lijia* (Article 2), the establishment and maintenance of their authority (Article 3), the punishment for their faults (Articles 7, 8, and 9), the association between mediation and official justice (Article 10), the credibility of mediation in disputes (Article 12), the prevention of abuse of power by the elders and *Lijia* (Articles 13 and 14), and the responsibility of the elders and *Lijia* to punish evil and promote good (Articles 16, 17, and 18). According to *the Instructions to the People*, except for some major criminal cases, for civil cases and minor criminal cases, the elders and *Lijia* are responsible for mediating in advance, including the persuasion and punishment of the involved parties. Only if they are unable to resolve the dispute, should they report the case to the government. Similarly, if anyone of the township reports a case directly to the government, bypassing the elders or *Lijia*, the government will return the case to the original township for the elders or *Lijia* to handle in the first place. The law of the government safeguards the authority of the elders and *Lijia* in mediation, ensuring comprehensive implementation and protection of township mediations. The model of township mediation during the early Ming Dynasty was further developed in the middle and late stages. The "Xiangyue" system was widely introduced, with each *Li*里 as a *Yue*约, setting up tablets inscribed with "Shengyu" (emperor's edicts) and "deities and law." The people of the village were assembled once a half-month to preach the sacred edicts and mediate disputes, with the officials keeping a record. If the parties agreed to reconciliation, they would record them in the register for compromise. Those who disagreed may resort to the government. In the middle and late periods of the Ming Dynasty, the township mediation was ineffective. For instance, during the reigns of Emperor Xuanzong and Emperor Yingzong, the collapse of the Shenmingting and Jingshanting in many places resulted in disruption of township mediation. Furthermore, "trivial matters that would have traditionally been handled by the elders and *Lijia* were instead reported directly to the government, leading to a significant increase in lawsuits."[43] The township mediation system of the Ming Dynasty was refined by the Qing Dynasty, with emphasis on a mediation policy centered on preaching the "Sixteen Sacred Edicts of Emperor Kangxi" and *Sacred Edicts of Emperor Kangxi* to prevent lawsuits. Since the Republic of China, township mediation has persisted in rural society.

The *Instructions to the People* frequently mentions the subjects of mediation as "the elders" and "Lijia." In this context, "the elders" does not exclusively refer to the oldest individuals but rather encompasses multiple aspects including competence, character, reputation, qualifications, etc. The term "Lijia" refers to head of "Li" and "Jia." Mediators include not only these two types of people but also "Liangzhang" and others. Moreover, the names of grassroots organizations differ across regions and times. In addition to "the elders" and "Lijia," from the Ming and Qing dynasties to the Republic of China, such individuals as *Xiangyue*, *Qimin*, *Gongzheng*, *Yuezhang*, *Yuelin*, *Zuzheng*, *Xiangzhang*, *Baozhang*, *Cunzhang*, *Shezhang*, *Xiangshen*, *Huizhang*, etc. play a crucial role as township mediators. They are either purely elected by the people or officially recognized or authorized. The former primarily act as mediators, whereas the latter serve as both mediators and adjudicators, with a quasijudicial nature. For instance, in the Qing dynasty, the system of *Zuzheng* emerged during the Yongzheng's reign and persisted throughout the Qianlong's reign but was finally abolished after considerable deliberation. Nevertheless, in certain areas, the system was still practiced during the Jiaqing and Daoguang periods as well as some subsequent periods. In this system, the clan nominates candidates, selecting "an individual of outstanding integrity who is respected by the entire clan,"[44] but the candidate also needed official recognition. *Zuzheng* is responsible for addressing the undesirables within the clan and delivering them to the ancestral hall for education or to the government for questioning. Additionally, they will act as mediators in resolving various conflicts; honor the loyal, the filial, and the just; and encourage the good and the virtuous. It is important to note that they are not government officials nor are they managers of ancestral halls of the clan. However,

[43] *Collation and Annotation of Rizhilu (Part1)*, 364.

[44] Volume 23 of General Examination on Documents of Qing Dynasty: Corvée.

they play a significant role in mediating between the government and the commoners, with functions similar to the *Baojia* and *Xiangyue*,[45] which are part of the township mediation.

The practice of mediation in traditional China is diverse but grounded in the fundamental principle of the patriarchal society where "courtesy and virtue are of utmost importance," with its roots in the traditions of "keeping relatives and friends close" and "respecting the superior." The government has favored the township mediation for two main reasons. Firstly, the prestige of the *Baozheng* and *Lizheng* in the township can gain the consent of both parties involved in the dispute. Secondly, they possess knowledge of local customs and conditions, which is helpful for the investigation and resolution of disputes. Mediation therefore appears to be a reasonable measure based on the consideration of the background of the civil disputes.

6.3 Clan-Led Mediation

6.3.1 Mediation as a Priority in Dispute Solution

Clan-led mediation refers to the resolution of disputes within a clan by the clan chief in accordance with clan rules and regulations. As early as the Zhou Dynasty, there were cases of "Zongzi" mediating disputes in the inscriptions of bells and tripods. In ancient China, most of the clansmen with the same family name often gathered and lived together in the same village to foster synergistic relationships and protect shared interests under the Confucian principle—"a man commended by his relatives for filial piety and by his fellow villagers for deference to the elders." These clustered clans would elect a senior, prestigious individual as the clan chief and establish a set of norms to serve as the clan's code of conduct. The clan chief has the power to govern the clan and the obligation to maintain order within the clan for the state. The *Yanyi Yimou Lu* (Plans and support for the coming generations) of the Song Dynasty recorded the rules of the Qiu clan in Zhaozhou: "There is a kind of bamboo plates called "Zhubi" passed down from generation to generation, with which the patriarch punishes the guilty." Similarly, *the Genealogy of the Zang Clan of Zhejiang Province* in the Kangxi period of the Qing Dynasty stipulated "anyone who becomes a thief or slave and corrupts ethical customs will be expelled from the entire clan." It is because the clan rules and village regulations, guided by Confucian ritual norms, played an important role of "complementary to the inadequacy of the official law, for the protection of the good people." It was the complementarity between family law and state law that made the rulers of successive dynasties

---

[45] Qianlong period, volume 25 of the Great Qing Code: Ministry of Justice: Bandits and Robbers: "If there are any criminals, their neighborhood heads must report them. If they cover up or conceal the crime out of favoritism, they will be punished according to the same laws as the Baojia system." See Feng Erkang, *National Law, Family Law, Indoctrination—Taking the Qing Dynasty as an Example*, Nanjing University Law Review, Fall 2006.

recognize the power of the clan and gladly leave disputes within the clan to the patriarch to resolve.

During the Ming and Qing dynasties, the government strongly advocated the right to "self-government" for clans and county gentlemen. *The Sixteen Sacred Edicts* of the Kangxi Emperor emphasized the importance of "cultivating peace within the neighborhood to prevent quarrels and lawsuits" along with "promptly and fully paying taxes" and "eliminating thieves and robbers." *The Great Qing Code* stipulated that minor offenders and women offenders could be sent to their clans to be disciplined and admonished. As for civil disputes, especially involving marriage and inheritance, most of them were referred to the clans for resolution, where "the entire clan would hold a public discussion on the matter." The genealogy of the clan usually contains the provisions for mediating conflicts within the clan.

Disputes are inevitable, but the key is what priority should be given to resolving them. The genealogy stipulates that general disputes should not be reported to the government but to the ancestral hall, where the clan chief convenes the two parties to mediate, that is, "to distinguish right from wrong in front of the ancestral tablets." The principle of handling disputes is "to determine right and wrong on the basis of superiority and inferiority, and complicated facts."[46] It is the same as the patriarchal clan law of the state, which imposes "different punishments for the same crime," protects the superior, and suppresses the inferior. Since the purpose is to distinguish between right and wrong, no partiality is allowed on the basis of a person's status—"Those from the affluent and powerful classes aligned themselves with one side, while those from the poor and sparsely populated groups aligned themselves with another."[47] *The Genealogy of the Ren Clan of Yixing Xiaoli* in Jiangsu Province states: "If someone of low status or of a young age files a lawsuit directly, instead of going through the ancestral hall, he will receive a punishment of 40 strokes with the cane. If someone of high status commits an offense, he will receive a punishment of 20 strokes with the cane, and if the offender is a senior, his son will be punished on his behalf. The clan chief will investigate the facts of the case and punish the offender together." *The genealogy of the Shao clan of Huayang* in Jixi, Anhui Province records:

Being wronged by others is indeed difficult to tolerate, but one must report it to the relatives and have it resolved through mediation in the ancestral hall. If one impulsively pursues litigation, both parties may resort to endless efforts, leading to ruin and regret beyond remedy. Only in cases of grave offenses such as vengeance for the death of a parent, desecration of ancestral graves, or serious moral transgressions should one pursue justice with full effort. All the rest should be resolved with leniency and reason. When bringing a case to the ancestral hall, a fee of three

[46] *Genealogy of the Zhuang Clan of Piling*, volume 11, *Commandments.*

[47] *Genealogy of the Yang Clan of Jimo: Family Commandments.*

Yuan should be paid for the communal meal expenses of the assembly, and no further gratitude is required.[48]

The clan rules stress that the resolution of disputes, apart from those involving vengeance for the death of a parent, desecration of ancestral graves, or serious moral transgressions, must be resolved within the clan in accordance with the clan rules and that litigation should not be allowed easily. The genealogy of the Hu clan of Shexian Weichuan also mentions: "In large and complex families, disputes and conflicts are inevitable. However, one should not resort to litigation easily. Instead, it is important to first report the issue to the respected elders or family heads, who will thoroughly investigate the situation, fairly discern right from wrong, persuade the just party to show tolerance, and the guilty party to admit fault. The goal is to mediate and resolve the conflict to end the dispute. In order to resolve family disputes, both sentiment and reason must be considered; nevertheless, local authorities only strictly apply laws. If the issue can be resolved peacefully and fairly, then it should just end there. However, if one resorts to malicious litigation, it will only lead to the ruin of the family, resulting in irreparable regret."[49] The clan rules grant the clan the power to handle internal disputes.

The clan chief possesses the highest authority and greater responsibility, directly relating to the governance of the clan. The genealogy generally grants the chief full authority and responsibility for dealing with disputes within the clan, defines their rights and duties, and requires the clansmen to absolutely obey the authority of the clan chief. For instance, in *The Genealogical Rules of the Li Clan: Family Precepts* of Jiaohe county in Zhili Province, in addition to the 15 family precepts, there are also 15 genealogical rules, one-third of which are related to the authority, responsibility, rights, and obligations of the clan chief. "A clan chief should be appointed to manage the affairs of the entire clan. The appointed clan chief must be upright and of impeccable character, with a calm and fair temperament, to earn the respect of others and effectively handle matters. The clan chief is responsible for enforcing discipline among clan members, who must strictly adhere to the family rules and lead by example to properly guide the younger generation. If the chief behaves improperly or violates the rules, the entire clan will gather to publicly discuss the wrongdoing. If there is any sign of repentance, a light punishment may be administered as a warning for the future; otherwise, the chief's name will be permanently removed from the position, and they will never be allowed to serve again. If one clan chief is dismissed, a replacement must be selected immediately through public discussions, electing someone who is honest and upright, to avoid leaving the position vacant and thereby hindering public affairs. The clan chief must not use their

[48] Volume 1 of *Genealogy of the Shao Clan of Huayang* in Jixi during the Guangxu period, *Newly Added Regulations of Ancestral Hall*, compiled by Shao Junpei from Jixi, published in Xuluntang in the 33rd year of Guangxu.

[49] Volume 2 of *Genealogy of the Hu clan of Weichuan* in Shexian during the Republic of China, *Regulations*, in the second year of Daoguang's Reign, in the auspicious summer month of the year of Renwu, the descendants respectfully record and publish this. Thread bound movable type edition in the fourth year of the Republic of China.

position for improper purposes or handle matters unjustly, which could lead to disorder within the clan. Any clan member who violates the family rules will be subject to a public discussion and punished according to the severity of their offense, ensuring fair and impartial judgment without personal bias, so as to maintain the trust of the people." If the individual holds the title of "clan chief," he is qualified to supervise and manage the affairs of the entire clan. It is vital that the clan chief should enhance his moral integrity and maintain impartiality in his judgments to successfully assume the significant responsibilities. Otherwise, the entire clan can reelect a new chief by public election.

6.3.2 Punishment on Misconducts by Family Rules

Anyone who violates the clan rules shall be punished in accordance with family regulations. Even if the plaintiff is justified, he must first be punished for the mistake of not seeking mediation in the ancestral hall before reporting to the government. For example, the Wang Clan of Wujin District will punish such clansmen by requiring them to kneel in front of the ancestor's tablet and hosting a feast to make amends[50]; if the defendant defies the authority of the ancestral hall and fails to appear for mediation, they will be punished for the offence of resistance and subsequently subjected to a determination of right or wrong; if the two parties are willing to report the case to the *Yamen*, both will face punishments; if a younger individual takes legal action against an elder, the punishment will be even more severe. The clan adjudicates matters of right and wrong according to family rules, and those who fail to abide by the sanctions are subject to investigation and punishment by the government and in serious cases are cut off from the clan. Minor civil disputes cannot be reported to the government in accordance with state code, and it is permitted by the government to minimize administrative expenses. The primary components of clan justice are as follows.

6.3.2.1 Admonitory Prohibition

The behaviors prohibited in the family rules and disciplines include those prohibited within the clan, as well as national laws and regulations. While there exist some differences and concurrences between them, the overall concepts are fundamentally similar, that is, emphasizing loyalty, filial piety and virtue, and abiding by national laws and family rules. The primary form of prohibition is through admonition. For instance, the Genealogy of the Lang Clan of Hebei Province outlines 12 prohibitions in the Family Rules of the Lang Clan on heresy, prodigality, cruelty, extravagance, slander, nonsense, jealousy, inferiority, disrespect, arrogance, alcoholism,

---

[50] Volume 1 of *Genealogy of the Wang Clan of Jinling*: *Ordinary Rules*.

and debt. The genealogy emphasizes that these rules are "written based on the wishes of their ancestors" and that it is mandatory for the clan members to "follow and correct them."

The *Genealogical Rules of the Li Clan* of Jiaohe county in Zhili province stipulates 15 family rules: (1) no drunkenness and cursing, (2) no teasing of younger brothers and their sisters-in-law, (3) no acting as a *Yamen* runner, (4) no bullying of neighbors by virtue of the clan's greatness, (5) no discussing the rights and wrongs of the clansmen with those of other surnames, (6) no helping friends and relatives to file lawsuits with the clansmen, (7) no shirking of responsibilities for any major events such as weddings or funerals of fellow clansmen, (8) no gambling or visiting prostitutes, and (9) no children entering teahouses and bars. (10) In the event that a member of the clan who is a widow, widower, orphan, or pauper cannot afford a burial coffin, the entire clan will collectively organize the funeral; (11) no one is allowed to befriend a prodigal; (12) no one is allowed to learn how to shave head or trim feet; (13) no one is allowed to marry a slave; (14) no one is allowed to be an actor or a piper; and (15) no one is allowed to let oxen, donkeys, or horses trample the fields and seedlings, which is detrimental to the agricultural industry.[51]

At the first volume of *the Genealogy of Sheng Clan* of Hanshou, Hunan Province, during Guangxu's Reign, there are 16 family rules. These rules address specific actions such as offending their superiors, delaying or resisting payment of money and grain, marriages between individuals from different social classes, gambling or visiting prostitutes, causing lawsuits and provocations, and destroying the graves of ancestors. These actions are prohibited by national law and discouraged by family rules. Engaging in menial labor, associating with individuals of poor moral character, using a different surname to disrupt the clan genealogy, and using the strength of the strong to bully the weak are forbidden by the clan rules and disciplines.[52]

6.3.2.2 General Punishment

Since disputes cannot be easily reported to the local authorities, clans are responsible for devising their own systems of punishment and creating corresponding clan regulations. The punishment system encompasses various methods, including economic, spiritual, physical, and expulsion from the clan. Economic sanctions like monetary fines, compulsory feasting, and penitential theater are commonly used; physical punishments such as corporal punishment and flogging are also adopted; spiritual tortures such as public bondage display, kneeling, and humiliation are also inflicted; ritual feasting suspension, ancestral hall exclusion, and genealogical expulsion are executed eventually so as to remove the deviants and to maintain the reputation of the clan.

[51] Seven revisions were made in the eighth year of the Republic of China.

[52] See the movable type printed version of Guanglingtang in the 27th year of the Guangxu reign.

In general, for minor violations of the family rules and discipline, the clan mainly imposes economic punishments, while more serious cases are punished by caning. For example, the Genealogy of the Ren Clan of Xiaoli Village in Yixing, Jiangsu Province, stipulates individuals who fail to participate in rituals according to the regulations will be subject to a fine, the amount of which is determined by the severity of the violation. On the day of the ancestral sacrificial rites, the drum is beaten once, signaling all officials in charge to assemble. After the second drumbeat, all sacrificial items must be prepared. With the third drumbeat, the officials arrive to begin the ceremony. Those who arrive late are fined one coin as the penalty; those who fail to attend without a valid reason are fined three coins; officials who have been assigned duties but do not attend the ceremony are fined five coins. Anyone who shows disrespect during the ceremony is fined three coins; those who disrupt the order or cause noise are fined two coins. All tables, benches, bowls, dishes, and other utensils belonging to the ancestral hall must not be removed. Unauthorized borrowing or lending of these items results in a fine of one tael of silver. For more serious offenses, additional punishments may be imposed, such as the following: anyone found stealing from family fields, gardens, or mountains will be punished with 30 strokes; those whose family members are caught committing the same offense will receive 40 strokes. Women entering temples to burn incense are fined two taels of silver, and those who leave the village to watch operas are fined one tael of silver, with their fathers, brothers, or husbands held responsible. Additionally, burning incense may result in a punishment of 20 strokes, and watching operas may result in ten strokes. Clan members who refuse to pay taxes to the ancestral hall are tied to the hall's gate for public display during the two annual ceremonies until the taxes are fully paid. All clansmen are equal before the clan rules, and no partiality is allowed when applying the family disciplines. "Anyone who shows partiality will be questioned by the entire clan, superiors and inferiors, elders, and children."[53]

In addition to the worship of ancestors and spirits, the ancestral hall serves to discipline the descendants, and in administering clan justice, it acts like a *Yamen*, a symbol of the clan's public authority, and clan disputes must be resolved in public at the ancestral hall. In the second volume of the Liu Clan Genealogy from Nantang, Ningxiang of Hunan province, fourth revised during the Republic of China, the family rules stipulate: If brothers are hostile to each other and treat each other as enemies over disputes regarding inheritance, they shall be taken to the ancestral hall for adjudication and punishment. Those who sell their daughters as concubines are required to redeem them, and the responsible household will be punished in the ancestral hall; those who knowingly allow it without reporting will be held accountable. Marrying a wife is primarily for continuing the family line; if someone marries off a divorced wife without cause, except due to poverty or hardship, they shall be punished in the ancestral hall. If a widow wishes to remain chaste even in poverty, she should be supported. If her parents or brothers force her to remarry, she may seek protection in the ancestral hall, where the family will be punished accordingly.

[53] *Genealogy of the Ren Clan of Xiaoli Yixing* in Jiangsu, *Clan Rules (Part 2).*

The entire above are related to property disputes, marriages, and inheritance of family lineage among clansmen. Certain actions are subject to forms of punishment including fines, corporal punishment, and even public humiliation, which makes it difficult for them to maintain their dignity among the clansmen. In the Li Clan Genealogy from Jiahe, Zhili, the family precepts state: "All clan members must treat each other with courtesy, as this reflects the dignity of a noble family. Those who dare to disrespect their elders or speak frivolously to them shall be severely punished. If an elder fails to conduct properly and instead mocks or scolds their juniors, they shall not only provide incense and candles but also kneel at the entrance of the ancestral hall as a form of public humiliation. Any clan member who fails to honor family rules and insults the fellow clansmen shall face punishment. They shall knock on each family's door regardless of rank or status and perform compulsory door-to-door Kowtow as communal deterrence."

6.3.2.3 Lynching

The imperial court prohibited civilians from carrying out the death penalty, with few exceptions during the Yongzheng period when the clan was granted the authority to execute outlaws. However, the imperial court soon withdrew this power to prevent rampant lynchings and challenges to national authority. Nevertheless, there have been repeated instances of clansmen being lynched. The *Genealogical Rules of the Li Clan: Family Precepts* of Jiaohe county in Zhili province stipulates: "if anyone violates the law, corrupts morals, commits theft, arson, or other evil deeds, the entire clan has the right to execute the clan member through public discussion without obstruction from his families." The clan's authority to execute members within the clan is clearly stated in the genealogy. In the chapter of *Customs and Rites of Gazetteer of Nanxi County* from Sichuan province (Volume 4), it is recorded in this region, "If there was a rebellious son in the village, the clan would gather to impose punishment on him, which included burial alive or drowning, with extreme cruelty and no pity. This practice, carried on for a long time, was upheld as a customary belief. Thus, for the extremely poor and thieves who engaged in illegal acts, such severe consequences were regarded as natural as the matters of supporting the living and burying the dead."[54] This shows the cruel situation in lynchings of clansmen.

Some family rules provide for the execution of clansmen for the following reasons: in traditional societies, clans possess a high degree of autonomy; with the saying "the heaven is high and the emperor is far away," if the clansmen do not report to the government, it is very difficult for officials to investigate the clan's illegal acts in a timely manner; in addition, such violations are usually deemed disgraceful to the clan, diminishing the family's prestige, therefore, in accordance with the principle of "not publicizing the shame of the family," the punishment is carried out under the family rules, ensuring that the negative effects are restricted to the clan.

[54] Bashu Publishing House, 1937, 615.

The imperial court expected the clans to assume the responsibilities of educating, disciplining, and governing their members. However, it did not want the clans to become so powerful that family rules would override national law and supplant the imperial court in executing the death penalty. The attitude of the imperial court toward the clan's power to impose the death penalty varied over time. Sometimes it was appropriately decentralized; however, most of the time, the imperial court withdrew this power. In any case, it consistently kept a high level of vigilance, and when detecting a tendency to overstep the national law, it promptly issued prohibitive orders. For instance, during the early Qianlong period, the clans in some areas of Jiangxi often formulated their own rules and lynched their clansmen, resulting in conflicts between family rules and national law. The Qianlong Emperor issued a special order to the Premier Minister in Affairs to ban such actions. He mentioned that the phenomenon of lynching clan members was primarily a result of the negligence of the local officials to indoctrination. If serious crimes and lawlessness occurred, the clansmen should be subjected to official punishment. The ordinary people did not have the right to take the place of the official and murder others. It was clearly intended to uphold the authority of the national judiciary and the gravity of the law, in order to prevent family rules from overriding national law. It was decreed that "civil and military officials of the province should strictly prohibit such actions in accordance with the law, and if anyone fails to comply with this order and commit further offenses, they should be immediately arrested and severely punished, with no leniency."[55]

Due to the slow evolution of the social structure, the custom of lynching clan members still existed in several rural communities during the Republican period. The patriarch of the family and the clan served as the final "judge" and possessed the power to make the final decision on members who breached the clan rules. For instance, there was a father of the Zhang clan and his daughter living in Henan province. The daughter had an affair with a young carpenter from a different village, which was discovered on the spot by a member of the Zhang clan, and this case was handed over to the ancestral hall. The patriarch held a public hearing at night and concluded that the daughter's wrongdoings had tarnished the clan's reputation for generations. Ultimately, he decided to have the father hang his daughter to grant preservation of corporeal integrity for reincarnation as a human. It was still considered a lenient sentence.[56] From the perspective of national law, what the Zhang clan chief did undoubtedly violated the national law. However, as it belonged to the Zhang clan's internal affairs, if the neighbors did not report, and the judicial supervision was not strictly enforced, the case would be closed. As for the neighbors, the Zhang clan's decision did not surprise them, and they chose not to meddle with it. The recurrent practice of executing clan members who violated clan rules as demonstrated by the Zhang clan was prevalent in rural areas during the late Qing Dynasty and early Republican period. The cruelty of these executions surpassed statutory penal standards.

---

[55] Veritable Records of Emperor Qianlong of the Qing Dynasty, volume 18, written in May, The 43th article, the first year of the Qianlong's Reign.

[56] Wang, J. (2001). *Thus Passes All That Was*. China Youth Publishing House. 17.

6.3.3 *Compatibility Between Clan-Led Settlement and Government Adjudication*

6.3.3.1 Competition and Cooperation Between Clan Justice and National Justice

Clansmen who violate prohibitive norms of the clan are subject to family rules. The line between family rules and national law is sometimes unclear. Clan justice takes precedence over national justice for violations of family rules, and the punishment of clan justice is sometimes more severe than that of national law. However, there are many competitions and cooperations between the two systems. Take the family rules of the Kuang clan in Xiangxiang, Hunan Province, as an example. Most of the unlawful crimes involved in the family rules align with the regulations outlined in the Great Qing Code, including regulations as regards to ethical and filial conduct, marriage, funerary, and sacrificial practices. For example, "if one sells the daughter to a servant's son as a wife, he dishonors not only the ancestors but also fellow clansmen; he shall be punished with one hundred strokes of the cane according to the law," which shows that family rules are consistent with national law. There are also some penalties that exceed the limits of national law, and the clan imposed its own stricter penalties, including "expulsion from the border, confiscation of property by the ancestral hall," and the doctrine of collective household liability holds lineage heads accountable through joint and several liability for negligence and dereliction of duty.[57]

If family rules fail to regulate certain acts, clansmen can report to the official authorities for support. In accordance with the law, many illegal acts can only be punished by state authorities, and clans should take the initiative to report them to the officials for investigation and punishment. Many clans have addressed it appropriately, drawing up family rules discreetly to avoid overstepping national law. They handle the relationship between national law and family rules appropriately to maintain a proper degree of judicial power without abusing it and violating the national law, thus successfully realizing an institutional interface between the family rules and national law.

6.3.3.2 Consequences for Not Complying with the Punishment Imposed by the Family Rules

Many family rules and regulations stipulate that if the punished individuals refuse to comply with the family rules after the application of disciplinary measures, the clan will resort to the local authorities for further adjudication. *The Genealogy of the Ren Clan of Yixing Xiaoli* in Jiangsu Province is very detailed in terms of the

[57]Volume 1 of *Continuation of Genealogy of the Kuang Clan* in Xiangxiang, Hunan Province, *Family Rules*, published by Jieyitang, in the eighth year of the Daoguang's reign.

matters to be reported to the local authorities for further adjudication. For example, various places have applied strict prohibitions regarding grave sites, stating, "Those who resist and refuse to comply shall be handed over to the authorities for adjudication." It further stipulates: "Being unfilial to parents and disrespectful to the elders, dissolute family life, theft, or becoming slaves are the most serious offenses within the clan. If someone is unfortunately guilty of such acts, they shall be expelled from the clan and forbidden from entering the ancestral hall, with the case reported to the authorities for due punishment. Within the clan, apart from the cases of the expelled ones being unfilial to parents and disrespectful to the elders, those juniors who disrespect or oppress the seniors receive various punishments: for severe cases, forty strokes and a fine of three taels of silver with a recorded offense; for lighter cases, thirty strokes and a fine of one tael of silver with a recorded offense. Those who resist and refuse to comply shall be handed over to the authorities for due punishment. Gamblers shall receive thirty strokes and have their offense recorded, and those who host gambling activities shall be tied to the gate of the ancestral hall for three days, receive fifty strokes, and have their offense recorded. Anyone who reports stolen goods will be publicly rewarded with two taels of silver; if the offender resists, the clan chief and elders shall jointly report the case to the authorities for adjudication." In the second volume of the Liu Clan Genealogy from Nantang, Ningxiang of Hunan province, fourth revised during the Republic of China, the family rules stipulate: "If juniors insult seniors, punishment will be determined based on their relationship to the senior within the ancestral hall. Those who forcibly bury the dead in the ancestral mountain or encroach upon ancestral graves shall be ordered to exhume the body, offer prayers of atonement, and face punishment within the ancestral hall. If they refuse to comply, they will be reported to the authorities." Some clans have stipulated through the stone tablet prohibitions that those who refuse to obey the clan rules will be subject to national law. "Everyone must adhere to the family rules and be respectful and obedient to their parents. Any disobedience or defiance of the family rules will result in punishment by the authorities, and no leniency will be given."[58] The provisions above share the common feature that clan justice is indispensable, and only in cases of disobedience are offenders sent to the local authorities for punishment. There is no need to consider whether clan justice is just and whether the claims of clan members are reasonable. Within the clan, their family rules and regulations are regarded as "good rules" that must not be violated.

[58] Tan, D. et al. (2001). *Collection of Stele Inscriptions in Guangdong*. Guangdong Higher Education Press. 704.

6.3.3.3 Consequences for Those Who Do Not Repent After the Punishment Imposed by the Family Rules

After the implementation of clan justice, punished clansmen may initially agree to comply with the ruling yet disregard it afterward and go their own ways. If it is difficult for clan justice to make the clansmen correct their behaviors, the clan will send the offenders to the government to force the offenders to correct their words and behaviors by public authority. In Huang Clan's Revised Genealogy from Lingan of Jiangxi province during Daoguang's Reign, the family rules state: "If one does not adhere to the common practices of the four social classes, violates the principles of filial piety and brotherly respect, engages in adultery, theft, or disrupts ethics, bringing shame to ancestors and deteriorating the family, they shall be subject to punishment. If they remain unrepentant, their cases shall be handed over to the authorities for severe investigation, have their genealogy removed, and be denounced as a warning to others." In the second volume of the Liu Clan Genealogy from Nantang, Ningxiang of Hunan province, fourth revised during the Republic of China, the family rules stipulate: "A son who is unfilial to his parents or a daughter-in-law who is disrespectful to her parents-in-law shall be brought to the ancestral hall by their uncles and elders for severe punishment. If unrepentant, they shall be handed over to the authorities and permanently expelled from the clan. If there are unworthy descendants who are lazy and fall into criminal behavior, they shall be brought to the ancestral hall for severe punishment. If unrepentant, they shall be handed over to the authorities and not be allowed to remain in the clan. Those who learn illegal practices, become gang members, or act violently shall be brought to the ancestral hall for severe punishment. If unrepentant, they shall be handed over to the authorities and expelled from the clan."[59] In the first volume of the Genealogy of Sheng Clan of Hanshou, Hunan Province, during Guangxu's Reign, there are 16 family rules that state: "Descendants are admonished not to use wealth to oppress the poor, strength to bully the weak, the majorities to overpower the minorities, indulge in laziness, or engage in deception and intimidation. All illegal acts, including spreading rumors and committing fraud, must be reported to the clan for immediate rectification. Offenders shall be given a chance to reform, but if they persist, they shall be handed over to the authorities for adjudication."[60] After reporting to the authorities, the clan cannot intervene in their handling of the reported cases. However, once the cases are submitted to the authorities, the concerned clan members will lose their rights within the clan. Correspondingly, clan penalties will also be aggravated, including expulsion from the clan and genealogical exclusion.

The *Genealogy of the Ren Clan of Yixing Xiaoli* in Jiangsu Province states that anyone who is unfilial or unfaithful, or a thief or a slave, "will be prohibited from entering the ancestral hall, and will be sent to the official for punishment." The *Twelve Rules of the Old Genealogical Family Rules*, volume 4 of the *Genealogy of*

[59] Wooden movable type printed version of Cunzhutang in the tenth year of the Republic of China.

[60] The movable type printed version of Guanglingtang in the 27th year of the Guangxu reign.

the Zhu Clan of Zijiang in Guizhou in the Republic of China period, stipulates: if any member of the clan fails to follow the teachings of their family, often gets into trouble and repeatedly engages in prostitution and gambling, the patriarch, clan chief, and impartial elders will discipline and punish them. The member will be given an opportunity to amend their ways. However, if they fail to do so and lack loyalty to the clan, they will be sent to the authorities for punishment. If anyone ignores the shame of being a prostitute or thief, they will be turned over to the government for punishment, and the clan will remove their family names from the clan genealogy.[61]

6.3.3.4 Consequences for Those Who Go Beyond the Jurisdiction of Family Rules

Some clans take the initiative to send to the local authorities for adjudication or assistance the wrongdoers who go beyond the limits of punishment imposed by family rules. The family rules of the Liang An Gao clan in Jixi clearly state that: "National law includes five types of punishment, whereas family rules only provide two measures: corporal punishment with a stick and expulsion. If an offense goes beyond these, it falls outside the jurisdiction of family rules and must be handled by the national law... Therefore, family rules are limited to corporal punishment and expulsion; if the crime exceeds these limits, it must be handed over to the authorities for proper legal action, and no private execution is permitted."[62] Penalties that are outside the jurisdiction of family rules should not be implemented within the clan. The clans should report them to the officials to show respect for national law.

The common feature of the above situations is that family rules and national law are complementary, and clan justice takes precedence over national justice. However, the efficacy of family rules in governing and disciplining clan members is not omnipotent, and once the family rules is out of control, if they do not resort to national law, the interests of the entire clan will be affected by a few lawless people, and they may even be sanctioned by national law. It is stipulated in the Rules of the Longzhi Hall Charity Estate of the Zou Clan in Changshu: "The charity land is rented out, relying on the tenants' labor to support our clan members, so they should be treated with some favor. For tenants who pay the full rent each year, a reward of 3,000 grains of white rice per *Dan* (a unit of dry measure for grain, 1 *Dan*=28 Kilos in Qing Dynasty) will be given. If there is any slight arrear, they should be immediately reported to the authorities for investigation without leniency."[63] The tenants of farmsteads and fields may be the members of the same clan or different clans, and

---

[61] Revised by Zhu Qiqian, typography printed in the 24th year of the Republic of China, stored in the library of Nankai University.

[62] Compiled by Gao Fuhao, volume 11 of *Genealogy of the Gao Clan of Liang'An: Family Law* in Jixi, movable type edition in the third year of Guangxu.

[63] *Regulations of Charitable Estate of Longzhitang of the Zou Clan in Changshu*, Daoguang and Xianfeng periods, Suzhou Museum of Inscribed Stone Tablets, Wang Guoping and Tang Lixing,

in the event of delayed rent or refusal to pay, the former can be dealt with directly within the clan in accordance with clan rules, while the latter have to resort to the officials. Many honors of the clan, such as the chastity archway and the tablet of loyalty, filial piety, chastity, and righteousness, had to be operated by local authorities and bestowed by the imperial court, thus expanding the clan's regional influence. The seamless integration of family rules and national laws is mutually beneficial for both the clan and the country, where national laws and civil rules are highly consistent.

Before any disputes arise, traditional Chinese clans restrain lawsuits and encourage members to exercise restraint and tolerance and respect the law to avoid litigation. Such behavior is highly valued as desirable personal traits and family traditions of the clan. The basic principle is that tolerance reduces conflict, thereby reducing litigation and promoting a harmonious and stable social order. It is both the ideal mode of governance pursued by successive governments and the state of life desired by most of people. After the dispute has arisen, mediation is regarded as the preferred means of resolution, thus maintaining the unity of the clan and the order of acquaintance society. The clan plays the function of mediating disputes, to reduce the burden of national justice, lower the cost of justice for the people, and save national judicial resources.

The clan punishes the members for misbehavior in public ancestral halls according to clan rules, which serves to prevent crime and uphold social order. If a clan member does not submit to the punishment of the family rules, they are sent to the authorities for investigation and punishment. It can obtain timely support from the authorities and realize the natural interface between clan justice and national justice, where the national law and the civil rules become highly compatible.

6.4 Mediation by the Government

6.4.1 Mediation of "Trivial Matters"

The resolution of civil disputes at the township level is usually referred to as out-of-court mediation, in which many mediation bodies are involved without reporting to officials. If the disputes cannot be resolved, it is inevitable to resort to the government for further mediation, which is referred to as mediation in litigation. Flogging, caning cases, and "Xigu" (trivial matters) cases are adjudicated by the county magistrates. The final decisions of these cases can be made by the chief official at the local level. The number of lawsuits often serves as a crucial measure of the local security. Legal proceedings are simple, and the court remains serene, which is advocated by the government and applauded by the public. Litigation documents in the

---

ed. *Collection of Stele Inscriptions in the Social History of Suzhou Since the Ming and Qing Dynasties*, Suzhou University Press, 1988, 230–235.

judicial archives of the government are mostly filed documents that have been processed in accordance with a specific official procedure. Many disputes reported to the government are often resolved through mediation by the government in advance and therefore do not need to be reported for review or filing. Mediation is the preferred method for grassroots officials to deal with disputes.

Mediation by the government is generally utilized for civil disputes that are more contentious and difficult to resolve through civil mediation. *The Rites of Zhou: Terrestrial Offices* includes a position known as "Tiaoren," who acts as a mediator responsible for "investigating the people's difficulties with the goal of resolving conflicts and promoting harmony." From the point of view of the subjects involved, mediation is commonly employed in disputes between relatives. On the one hand, it is because officials tend to prefer mediation to litigation in such cases. Local officials, out of the need to promote indoctrination and family ethics, believe that the litigation between relatives is not worthwhile because of the loss. Once a verdict is delivered, no matter what the result is, it may harm the kinship and ethical principles. Therefore, "if the people are involved in lawsuits between relatives, the officials urge them to withdraw the lawsuits by emphasizing the importance of the moral order."[64] On the other hand, the people have lived for generations under patriarchal law, valuing family bonds and respecting ethical principles. Even if the lawsuits are filed with the government, they do not completely disregard the family ties and ethics, making it easier for officials to convince them to comply with ethical principles. This psychological foundation results in a higher successful rate in resolving antilawsuit cases involving relatives. From the content of the litigation, most antilawsuit cases involve economic disputes or cases related to economic interests, and even the litigations between relatives are not an exception. The rise of such cases reflects the diversification of economic interests and people's attachment to their "rights" as a result of abundant economic activities. They are no longer afraid to fight for their right but dare to boldly defend their own interests, even if they have to resort to litigation between relatives. Since economic disputes are "trivial matters" heard by the county magistrates, the state has no time to deal with them. There is often a lack of legal foundation for such cases, leading to the absolute discretion of county magistrates.

The reason why the government first mediates civil disputes is not only because the government advocates the rule by rites but also because the escalation of disputes will break the order of acquaintance society, which is not conducive to harmony and stability. Therefore, the government generally adopts a conciliatory approach to civil disputes. The county magistrates often believe that multiple lawsuits represent a corrupt culture and lack of education, which is a negative social atmosphere. If litigation cases are heard arbitrarily and not controlled, it may lead to the obsession with litigation among the people, allowing *Songshi* (legal practitioners) and other individuals obsessed with litigation to run rampant. Since the county

[64] Hu, Wenbing. *The Mirror for Judging Cases.* volume 1, *Crimes against: Propriety: Settling Deputes between Kinship Relatives.*

magistrates hold the title of "parental officials," they are tasked with persuading and educating those within their jurisdiction. Their role embodies a loving parental caring for children who are experiencing conflicts. When hearing civil cases, they generally do not base their rulings solely on whether the parties' behavior is legal or not but also consider factors beyond the case including moral principles, ethics, and neighborhood relations. They do not make determinations of right and wrong but encourage the parties to reflect on their own actions, make concessions to reach a settlement, and achieve a permanent resolution of the case. Compared with the win-or-lose litigation ruled by law, mediation allows for greater flexibility and prioritizes the balance of interests between all parties involved.

Mediation in lawsuits requires officials with high qualifications. In order to achieve effective antilawsuit promotion, county magistrates must carefully observe the situation and persuade the parties involved to willingly withdraw their lawsuits, which is an arduous and demanding task. The officials have used various means to set up heavy defenses for lawsuits, causing fear of lawsuits among the public and discouraging the parties from proceeding with a lawsuit unless they are in a serious conflict or influenced by litigation enthusiasts. In this way, still adhere to the lawsuit, the depth of the conflict between the parties to the conflict, the determination of litigation, can be imagined. Therefore, impartial officials with high qualifications are necessary to effectively mediate and facilitate the withdrawal of lawsuits in deputes. It is essential to avoid mediocre and corrupt officials and instead rely on honest and competent officials to handle such deputes. Judicial officials may act based on their own experience and different targets to achieve resolution with flexibility.

6.4.2 Persuasion on Compliance

First, there is the general persuasion, which involves officials informing individuals of ethics, explaining the importance of the situation, and quoting from classics to clarify the truth and prevent misunderstandings. Confucius was skilled at this practice. According to the record, "Confucius served as the head of the Minister of Justice of the state of Lu. During a legal dispute between a father and son, Confucius imprisoned the son for three months without hearing the case. Eventually, the father requested the case to be dropped, and then Confucius accepted and released his son,"[65] thus preserving their familial bond. "In the early years of the Kaihuang period of the Sui Dynasty, Liu Kuang served as the magistrate of Pingxiang County and rode alone to his office. When the people sued each other, he provided moral guidance rather than employing punishment; as a result, the litigants felt ashamed and voluntarily withdrew their lawsuits, and the dispute was settled. During his seven years in office, the customs and morals of the people became more

[65] School Sayings of Confucius.

straightforward, interpersonal relationships were more amicable, there was no inmate in the county jail, litigation was nonexistent, and the courtyard of the *Yamen* was overgrown with dry grass, having remained unoccupied for an extended period."[66] Liu Kuang resolved conflicts through promoting moral principles, leading to a decrease in legal cases, unused prisons, and serene courts. When Zhao Yu, a judicial official of the Ming Dynasty, served as the governor of Songjiang, he would advice the parties to go home and reconsider filing a lawsuit in case of litigation. Critics at the time compared Zhao Yu with another famous official, Fong Zhong, and regarded the latter as more competent, while recognizing Zhao Yu as simply a good official. It is believed that Zhao Yu excelled at mediation while Fong Zhong had a talent for decision-making and was reputed to be "decisive in dealing with difficult problems."[67] The purpose of Zhao Yu's request for both parties to "come tomorrow" was not to dismiss the lawsuit but to give them more time to calm down and consider their situations, thus facilitating a resolution through mediation.

6.4.3 Moral Persuasion

The officials personally persuade individuals, some even detailing their own experiences, in order to emphasize the value of familial love and encourage a voluntary withdrawal of cases. For instance, in the Yongzheng period of the Qing Dynasty, Weng Yunbiao served as the magistrate of Wuling County. "He tried a case involving two brothers fighting over a field. During the trial, he sat in the field and suddenly covered his face, crying. The parties were surprised and asked him what was wrong. He said, 'In the past, my brothers and I relied on each other. However, after moving to Wuling, I couldn't see my brother anymore. Upon seeing you brothers, I am reminded of him, so I am very sad.' Before the words were finished, the parties were also moved to tears. Eventually, they reconciled and divided the fields equally." Using his personal feelings of yearning for his relatives, Weng motivated the brothers involved in the lawsuit to value their kinship and withdraw their case voluntarily. Another two families have been feuding for decades over a piece of land in the lake. Despite numerous attempts to persuade them, Weng Yunbiao's efforts proved fruitless, and he stood in the rain and said, "You are not afraid of the heavy punishments suffered by generations over a piece of land. What harm would it cause if I suffered a little bit?" The two families were moved and personally delimited the boundary, resulting in the settlement of the lawsuit.[68] When Lu Longqi of the Qing Dynasty heard a case regarding a property dispute between brothers, "he did not decide about the distribution of the property or distinguish between right and wrong. Instead, he

[66] Volume 25 of *Book of Sui*, Chap. 20 of *Treatises*, *Criminal Law*.

[67] Volume 99 of *Veritable Records of Emperor Yingzong Rui of Ming*, December of the seventh year of the Zhengtong reign.

[68] Hu, Wenbing. *The Mirror for Judging Cases*. volume 6, *Various Crimes(Part 2): Settling Dispute over Lands*.

had the two brothers shout each other's names. Before the fiftieth time each other's names were called, they were already in tears and withdrew their lawsuit voluntarily."[69] He adopted mediation methods similar to those of Weng Yunbiao, successfully reducing lawsuits through an affective dispute resolution. Most officials believed that with respect to lawsuits, "if persuaded with genuine empathy and told what is at stake, the parties will feel ashamed and voluntarily withdraw their lawsuits."[70] Some officials blamed themselves immediately after receiving the lawsuit, making the parties repent and withdraw the lawsuit. For example, when Xu Jing served as the governor of Guiyang, two brothers filed a lawsuit over monetary disputes. Xu Jing believed his own incompetence in promoting education and culture caused the lawsuit, and he resigned, which made the brothers repent and withdraw the lawsuit.[71]

During the Kangxi and Qianlong periods of the Qing Dynasty, there was an official named Lan Dingyuan, who was widely praised by the people. He compiled the documents of the cases he decided when he was the magistrate of Puning County and Chaoyang County into *The LuzhouGong'an*. He was lauded for "his decisiveness and accuracy in adjudicating cases like Bao Zheng, an honest and upright official. When faced with difficult cases with ambiguous facts, he calmly and carefully examined the evidence using his unique method."[72] His achievements made him a positive model among the bureaucrats of the Qing Dynasty, and his methods of governance and trial were also imitated by other officials of the time and future generations.[73] For example, the case of "brothers' land litigation" in *the LuzhouGong'an* is not only a typical case that Lan Dingyuan handled with great success but also a type of mediation that was appreciated by the rulers of the Qing Dynasty. After the successful mediation, the magistrate documented his thoughts:

If this case is decided according to the usual method, each brother will be beaten 30 strokes and the fields will be divided equally, and then the case will be closed. I employed a euphemistic approach to instruct them, resulting in them automatically admitting their faults and making mutual concessions. Therefore, the brothers and

---

[69] Lu, L. *Interpretation of Lu Jiashu: A Wonderful Judgment of Brothers' Property Dispute.*

[70] Zhang, Y. *Advice for the Government: Advice for Governing the People*.volume 1. *Hearing* (Part 3): *Eliminating Litigation.*

[71] Hu, Wenbing. *The Mirror for Judging Cases.* volume 1. *Crimes against Propriety: Brothers' Litigation for Propriety.*

[72] Lan, D. (1995). *Complete Biography of Lan.* proofread by Guo Yanan. Ethnic Publishing House. preface.

[73] Liu Heng, a native of the Qing Dynasty, said: "Later, while serving in Guangdong, I came across the casebook "Cases of Luzhou" by Prefect Lan Dingyuan of Zhangpu, who had previously served as the magistrate of Chaoyang County. He compiled difficult and complex cases that he had adjudicated into this work, also known as "New Book of Wisdom." The book is highly effective in resolving hidden crimes. I frequently read it, finding it quite enlightening, and I believe it should be widely available by now."—Liu Heng: *Questions and Answers from a Sichuan Official: Books to Read Beyond Laws and Regulations.*

sisters-in-law are cordial and supportive. Such a process should be the norm, thereby ensuring that officials are deemed effective.[74]

The issue of this case centered upon the ownership of seven acres of field that was inherited by both parties from their father. Lan Dingyuan did not make a judicial determination of the probative force of the evidence presented by the two parties. If the two pieces of evidence were both true and of probative force, the judgment would be based on fairness; if they contradicted each other, the judgment would be based on the testamentary priority principle. As a result, Lan Dingyuan "resolved the dispute by moral education," deviating from the contemporary fact-finding and rule-application principles. Lan Dingyuan never focused on the legal ownership of the field; instead, he used indoctrination and intimidation to persuade both parties to "confess their mistakes" and make concessions.

Although the actual effect was satisfactory for all parties involved, this nonjudicial approach did not align with the principle of procedural justice in terms of the modern concept of the rule of law. Determining the legal ownership of the fields was not Lan Dingyuan's primary goal. Throughout the process, he did not reference any of the relevant laws and regulations but solely relied on vernacular rationality and other nonlegal norms. The subjects involved in this case went beyond the triangular pattern formed by the two parties and the judge, and in terms of social effect, the emergence of these subjects appeared to be reasonable, but none of them were legal litigants. Lan Dingyuan assumed the dual role of "official" and "father," embodying both the county magistrate's public authority and the father's parental authority, coupled with emotional reasoning; therefore, both parties were inculcated to cease litigation. Lan Dingyuan played a significant role in intimidation and promotion of mediation through the arbitrary punishment on the parties, so that the authoritative mediation was equipped with coercive undertones. However, a mediation case lacking "legitimacy" has not only caused the presiding official to be proud of his decision but also become a precedent for future officials to mediate cases of "trivial matters" in the same way. The reason why Lan Dingyuan believed that the handling of this case was the most satisfactory experience in his life was that if the court evidence provided by the two sides were recognized, the two brothers should receive equal penalty and the fields should be equally divided. This was a simple and easy solution that demonstrated fairness but could result in long-term discord between the two brothers and their respective families, as well as conflicts between neighbors. Therefore, through tactful persuasion and patient mediation, the two parties voluntarily withdrew the case, avoiding the negative outcomes and maintaining the normal interpersonal relationships in the rural society, which could be comparable to the traditional "three dynasties of virtuous rule" (three dynasties refer to the Xia, Shang, and Zhou Dynasties).

[74] Lan Dingyuan: *Cases of Lu Zhou: Brothers' Litigation for Fields*.

6.4.4 Solution to Problems

Some officials generously assist the parties in resolving life difficulties and coordinate disputes of the interests to facilitate lawsuit settlements. For instance, during the Cao-Wei period, Zhang Changnian served as governor of Runan, where there was a case of the Liu brothers disputing over the distribution of their family property. Due to family poverty, they owned only one cattle and found it difficult to divide. Consequently, they filed a lawsuit in the court. Zhang Changnian expressed empathy and suggested, "As you possess only one cattle, it is challenging to resolve the dispute. If there are two cattle, there will be no lawsuit." He immediately gave one of his own cattle to the Liu brothers. "The entire prefecture was moved by the governor's mediation, and thus they treated politely each other with respect and avoided lawsuits."[75]

Outside the Shakya Mani Hall of Lingyin Temple in Hangzhou, there is a pair of couplets: "Ancient sites of Chonghu Mountain have witnessed many renowned figures; the most memorable are Bai Juyi's poems and Su Dongpo's judgments. The auspicious connection of incense lingers, inviting visitors to this place; do not waste the opportunity to enjoy the autumn Osmanthus fragrans and the ten miles of lotus flowers." "Bai Fu" and "Su Gong" refer to Bai Juyi and Su Shi, respectively. Su Shi, during his service as the Controller-general in Hangzhou, received public recognition for his competence in resolving cases. In fact, many of these disputes were resolved through mediation. For example, Su Shi provided the parties of the lawsuit with his writings and paintings, which they sold for money, clearing their debts and settling the disputes. It was fortunate for the parties to meet such a judge. When Wang Yu served as the governor of Huainan during the Ming Dynasty, "the people were unable to pay their debts, which triggered legal disputes between the father-in-law and son-in-law or between two brothers." Wang Yu said: "Why should we hurt the affection for the sake of money?" He paid the debt on behalf of the people and advised them to get along with each other.[76]

6.4.5 Persuasion by Moral Duties and Reasoning

Only when officials are knowledgeable in literature and capable of persuasive communication can they effectively cite the classics in their judgments and find reasonable solutions that are in line with reasoning and human feelings in different situations, ultimately leading the parties to accept mediation and withdraw their lawsuits. There are four cases of litigation between husband and wife in *The Mirror*

---

[75] Hu, Wenbing. *The Mirror for Judging Cases*. volume 5.*Various Crimes: Giving Cattle to Settle Disputes*.

[76] Hu, Wenbing. *The Mirror for Judging Cases*. volume 1. *Crimes against Propriety: Family Property Depute*.

for Judging Cases. Three of the four cases were caused by husbands suspecting infidelity due to their wives' unusual pregnancies. One woman had been pregnant for up to 2 years, while another gave birth after only 5 months of marriage. The husbands reported the cases to officials, believing their wives had adulterous affairs with someone else. The officials cited the classics in their judgment, explaining that it was normal for women to give birth to children after 5 months of pregnancy up to decades and that some even experience miraculous births, so there was no need to make a big fuss about it. Among them, the official document of mediation in the *Two Years of Pregnancy* is the most typical: "it is common for a woman to give birth in the ninth or tenth month of pregnancy. There are also many unique cases of births with infants living long and healthy lives despite being born prematurely in the seventh month."[77] The official explained that throughout the history, unnatural pregnancies and births were common and that the sons of unnatural births often achieved great successes later. The official convinced the woman's husband to withdraw his complaint with delight, ultimately leading to a reconciliation. It shows the importance of the official's extensive knowledge in persuading the parties.

Another marital lawsuit arose from the husband's suspicion of his wife's infidelity. Han, a woman in Jiangning, was betrothed to the son of Li Xiucai (one who passed the imperial examination at the county level) in the same city. One day, she was blown by the wind to a place 30 miles away and later returned. Li Xiucai did not believe that wind could carry people so far away and suspected that Han had an adulterous affair with someone else. He reported to the government and demanded to terminate the marriage. The magistrate of Jiangning, Yuan Mei, who was knowledgeable and talented, asked them, "In ancient times, winds blew people 2000 miles away, did you know that?" When Xiucai did not believe him, Yuan Mei took out the *Lingchuan Ji* of Hao Jing in the Yuan Dynasty and said: "Hao Jing was a loyal official, would he lie? The woman who was blown 2000 miles away by the wind married the prime minister. I'm afraid your son won't be lucky enough to be a prime minister." After hearing Yuan Mei's words, Xiucai was delighted, and "the marital bond between the two families remained unchanged." The author concludes: "Therefore, those who deal with lawsuits need to have wide experience and extensive knowledge."[78] Here Yuan Mei not only considered the status of the litigant as a "Xiucai" and used the example of a loyal official but also utilized people's desire for the prosperity of their descendants to persuade them, demonstrating his remarkable literati qualities.

According to modern scientific principles, it is difficult to justify the above reasons for mediation. However, in the absence of scientific knowledge among the public, it may be an alternative manifestation of substantive justice for a judicial officer, with profound humanistic skills and superior mediation wisdom, to heal the rift between relatives and save a family from possible collapse.

---

[77] Hu, Wenbing. *The Mirror for Judging Cases*. volume 1. *Crimes against Propriety: Two Years of Pregnancy.*

[78] Hu, Wenbing. *The Mirror for Judging Cases*. volume 1.*Crimes against Propriety: with Ancient and Modern Learning.*

In addition to the mediation mentioned above, there are alternative forms of mediation, such as "nongovernmental mediation with official approval." County magistrates will draw general conclusions based on case facts while settling disputes and then send the cases back to mediators and request that the outcome of the mediation should be reported to the government, if the case is trivial or if it is deemed a matter of familial relations that are unworthy of summons or should not be handled openly. The specific methods of "nongovernmental mediation with official approval" include county magistrates order the clans to mediate the cases in the townships; and they also order the gentry and community heads to mediate.[79] In addition, the officials often prefer extrajudicial adjudication and occasionally consult suitable unofficial mediators for cases. If out-of-court mediation proves ineffective and the dispute is reported to the government, the parties will be considered recalcitrant, and the case will suffer serious prejudice. When the official has difficulties in reaching a judgment at trial, he will mediate at the trial of first instance and even in the process of the appeal. In fact, many judgments are considered as a process of reconciliation in nature.[80]

6.5 The Effectiveness of Mediation

In traditional Chinese society, from an official perspective, mediation and antilawsuit promotion contribute to stabilizing social order and promoting ethical indoctrination. These measures can maximize the effect of social governance at minimal cost. However, from the viewpoint of the vast rural community, people prefer to accept mediation and stay away from lawsuits as much as possible due to their practical interests, rather than based on the evaluation of the litigation value or the pursuit of abstract personal rights.

6.5.1 Saving Judicial Resources

The traditional Chinese bureaucracy operates as a centralized unitary system. Although all levels of government have specialized judicial institutions and judicial officials, and there is a certain judicial division of labor, such as the Ministry of Penalty, the *Dalisi* (the Court of Judicial Review), the Censorate (*Duchayuan*) in the central department, and locally appointed *Tixing Anchashi* (the Provincial Surveillance Commissioner), this division of labor is relative, as the final judicial power of "five punishments" lies with the chief executive at all levels of

[79] Chunyang.(2009). *Research on the Mediation System of Civil Disputes in Late Qing Rural Society*. Peking University Press. 163–165.

[80] Ke En, (2001). *Mediation in China on the Eve of Modernization*. quote from Qiang Shigong, ed. *Mediation, Legality, and Modernity: Mediation in China*, China Legal Publishing House. 104.

government. As far as the administrative team is concerned, from the emperor to the governor-general, provincial governor, and county officials, it appears to be a hierarchical power structure in place, with one person governing the country, one person governing the government, and one person governing the *Yamen*. Taxpayers are responsible for funding only one single unit of administrative expenses. In recent times, there has been an increase in the number of state authority institutes, which has resulted in taxpayers facing multiple administrative expenses.

However, it will inevitably result in a shortage of judicial resources, particularly at the grassroots level. It can be inferred that the county magistrates are in charge of almost all affairs except military; such affairs as land, tax, water, official governance, education, public and private entertainment, and public security are decided and implemented by one person, and maintaining social security is just one of many duties assigned to county magistrates. It is crucial to note that group crimes such as theft pose a significant threat to social security. Therefore, the local administrators must prioritize preventing and controlling theft and burglary. The judicial function is part of the function of social security, in which murder trials is the priority. As murder cases inevitably involve the possibility of the death penalty, they must go through a reporting and review procedure and the ultimate decision of the final trial rests with the emperor. Basic level administrators are responsible for personally exploring the scene of criminal cases, conducting examinations of corpses, collecting witness testimony, and detaining suspects involved in the cases. Compared to criminal cases, civil cases of "Xigu" are relatively insignificant, which refer to disputes over households, marriage, land, inheritance, and so on, without posing a serious threat to public order. Unless there are fatalities or severe injuries, such cases are not required to be reported or reviewed. The grassroots officials do not worry about the time limit for trials, and even in cases of injustice, individuals seldom overstep the local authority and appeal to higher levels and even to the emperor. The law of the Qing Dynasty has special requirements for appeals, and "Xigu" cases generally cannot be appealed to higher levels. It also stipulates that related *Yamen* in the capital city is not authorized to accept "Xigu" cases regarding imperial appeals. The county *Yamen* functions as one-person ruling court presided over by county magistrate. Alternatively, the entire county is subject to one official "judge," in charge of investigation, filing, prosecution, and trial. Despite the assistance of such judicial assistants as Zuoer, Zazhi, Muliao, and Xuli, the magistrate assumes all responsibilities including court hearings and final reviews of documents. Any lawsuit, regardless of its severity, is subject to a standard trial, which requires significant time and efforts to handle efficiently. Therefore, it is evident that the judicial resources are limited, and grassroots administrators do not prioritize "Xigu" cases.

The traditional mediation system is based on the Confucian idea of "no lawsuit" as a value orientation, and successive governments have often associated the number of lawsuits with the performance of officials, which led to the official promotion of fewer lawsuits and the official demotion of more lawsuits. Therefore, the county magistrates resort to various strategies to mediate civil disputes and even some criminal disputes to avoid lawsuits.

The imperial court also fully recognizes the limited resources of the country and the abundant quasijudicial resources of the people. It fully mobilizes the power of the people, including the elders, community heads, clan chiefs, village regulation, and gentry, allowing them to mediate disputes. The imperial court assesses officials' judicial performance with a focus on social effects, rather than judicial impartiality, that is, whether cases are settled in a timely manner without a backlog of cases. No importance is attached to the means adopted and whether the legal procedures are fully followed.

For instance, during the Qing Dynasty, Emperor Xianfeng summoned Zhang Jixin, a 60-year-old local official, and inquired about inspecting the counties. Zhang replied, "The counties are easy to inspect: if there are no pending criminal cases, no shortfall in the land and miscellaneous taxes, and no litigation, then the official is efficient."[81] The promotion of the government and the instruction and influence of the officials further inculcate the ideas of "shame of lawsuit" and "meaningless lawsuit" into the public consciousness, so that the people generally agree that "lawsuits should be discouraged" and that it is a disgrace to be involved in lawsuits and those who file lawsuits are considered to be an enemy. The government vigorously promotes antilawsuit publicity prior to any disputes arising; during dispute mediation, it cedes part of the judicial power of the state to give mediators encouragement and support; after mediation, the government agrees to handle unresolved disputes, utilizing the public power of the state to ultimately close the case and resolve the dispute.

6.5.2 Lowering the Cost of Litigation

One significant reason why people in rural community choose mediation to resolve disputes is that litigation proves to be too expensive. Litigation costs include economic costs and reputation costs. In the traditional judicial system, people participating in litigation face several economic, personal, and psychological challenges, including undignified and degrading proceedings, "grudges," and "dishonorable reputation" caused by lawsuits, extortion by officials and *Songshi*, begging others in a lowly manner (covert bribery), etc.[82] The most important of these is the economic cost.

The people think that the cost of litigation is too high to afford. Both the antilawsuit strategy and the multilawsuit strategy arise from the parties' personal interests. If the costs of mediation are lower than the fees of litigation, and the benefits outweigh the outcomes of litigation, the parties will undoubtedly choose mediation. Otherwise, they will file lawsuits.

---

[81] Zhang, J. (1981). *The Record of the Officialdom in Daoxian*, Zhonghua Book Company.260.

[82] Fan, Z. (2001). *The Basic Spirit of Chinese Legal Tradition*. Shandong People's Publishing House. 246.

Civil disputes arising from trivial matters such as household, marriage, land, and debt can quickly escalate involving the interests of many parties and incurring high costs once reported to the government, and all levels will claim some of the benefits of these "trivial matters," so that the parties involved in civil disputes have to shrink back from difficulties. They need to pay someone to write the complaint. Since there is only one court and one judge in a county, litigation can only be filed at the county *Yamen*. Moreover, transportation arrangements are inconvenient, and they must bear their own expenses for travel, lodging, and meals. Due to the lack of information and the provision of "Wuxian" (stopping lawsuits during the busy farming season) in the county, the parties do not know the exact information of the court hearings, so they have to go back and forth, which is time-consuming and costly. In addition, lawsuits are often put on hold or delayed when the county magistrates have important matters to deal with. For example, when Zhao Yu served as governor of Songjiang in the Ming Dynasty, he was afraid of multi-lawsuit. When the litigants arrived, he always said, "Come tomorrow." Amused, people began spreading a rumor that "the governor of Songjiang would come tomorrow." And after a night, the litigants either calmed down or were persuaded, leading them to abandon their lawsuits.[83] This method of "delaying" effectively resolved many disputes. It is assumed that Zhao was too busy with other official business to deal with civil disputes; however, it cannot be ruled out that he deliberately eased the parties' inclination to file lawsuits. Furthermore, there are additional expenses incurred to grease the wheels (i.e. making informal payments to officials at each stage or level of the litigation), etc.

In ancient China, the government did not impose a statutory fee for hearing cases. However, the emperor and those officials who claimed to "love the people like their own children" openly charged common people who complained about their grievances and asked for justice a fee for adjudication, which was considered to be undignified.[84] Wang Huizu, a famous official of the Qing Dynasty, summarized his experience as *Muliao* (aides and staff):

The proverb says: "The six doors of *Yamen* are open, but if you just have a case without money, don't enter." This does not imply that the officials are necessarily corrupt or that the clerks are inherently dishonest. Once a case is filed, the procedure starts with payments to the bailiffs who come to your home, for food and gifts; for transportation to the city, there are travel expenses; when the hearing date is set, there are fees to be given to the lawyers, witnesses, and concerned friends and relatives, all taken from the accuser. If the hearing date is changed, the expenses must be paid again. Besides these, there are various informal payments to the clerks, each with different names. The saying goes, "In the mountains, rely on the mountains; by the water, rely on the water" (to live by surrounding circumstances). The law cannot

[83] Hu, Wenbing. *The Mirror for Judging Cases*. volume 5. *Various Crimes (Part 1): Come Tomorrow*.

[84] Fang, L. (1999). Research on civil litigation charges. *Chinese Social Sciences*. (3).

prohibit these, such as the extorted bribes which are beyond the reach of official regulations.[85]

Wang Huizu, as a Muliao, recognizes the challenges involved in litigation. Many of the costs are not charged by the authorities, and the additional costs are not prohibited by law, which often burden the parties.

Resorting to the government is not only a time-consuming, expensive, and uncertain process, but it can also result in feelings of shame and anguish. Litigation often carries a personal stigma in the eyes of the public, and it is also distasteful to present private problems to uninformed third parties. Additionally, those who pursue legal action are frequently subjected to embarrassment by the subordinates of the judge. There is a risk that one or more parties will be unlawfully imprisoned before the hearings and during the appeal process. During the trial, both parties and witnesses are subjected to torture and kneel in the courtroom. Ultimately, the future relationship between the litigants and their families, and possibly even their clans, neighboring villages, or guilds, will remain uneasy due to the outcome of the lawsuit. Considering these factors, it is understandable that lawsuits are not the preferred way for people to resolve disputes.[86] The uncertainty of the outcome and the degrading process in litigation has somewhat limited the rights of litigation for the people. To minimize the associated risk, people have tended to opt for mediation. The ancient Chinese people did not hate or hold contempt for lawsuit; instead, their attitude was "fear" of it. The ancient Chinese possessed a deeper and more secretive consciousness for lawsuit, which can be appropriately called "fear of lawsuit." It is based on the weighing of these interests that the people are usually unwilling to litigate easily and prefer to settle disputes through mediation.

The government's excessive restrictions on the litigation right of the parties involved have made it very difficult for ordinary people to resolve disputes through litigation. Claiming the litigation right of the parties is limited by time, evidence, procedures, and the litigation qualification of the parties. Individuals with limited capacity to act, such as women, the elderly, children, and the disabled, face comparable restrictions on their litigation rights. There are also limitations on the lawsuits in civil disputes, for example, "no more than three witnesses are permitted for minor matters such as household, marriage, and land," and "no one is permitted to sue for marriage without a matchmaker's agreement or a letter of appointment; for land without a grain number, a receipt, or a deed; or for debts without a note or a contract." The litigation rights of the illiterate people should also be restricted and so on. Resolving disputes through litigation is challenging for the people, and when

[85] Wang, H. (1997). To Observe the Civil Situation, Handbook for Subordinate Officials. Liu Junwen and Tian Tao, eds., *Collections of Official Exhortative Books* (Photocopy). Huangshan Publishing House.

[86] Ke,En, (2001).*Mediation in China on the Eve of Modernization*, quote from Qiang Shigong, (ed.), *Mediation, Legality, and Modernity: Mediation in China*.China Legal Publishing House. 104.

faced with numerous civil disputes, they have to opt for mediation as a means of settling disputes.[87]

6.5.3 Promoting Social Harmony

According to Confucianism, the legal system is not the ultimate aim of civilization or the most effective method of governance but rather a regrettable necessity, in line with the Western proverb stating that the law is to some extent a necessary evil. The fewer the laws, the more visible the virtue. It is the ruler who is "strict with oneself and tolerant with others"[88] is to be praised. As stated in *the Zuo Zhuan*, "When a state is about to fall, it will certainly make more laws." Du Yuankai's interpretation of *the Zuo Zhuan* states that "when the law is in good order, people will obey the law; but when the law is corrupt, the law will obey people." Gu Yanwu argues that "legal regulations should not be abolished by rulers, not for the purpose of governing the country, but rather to rectify the hearts of the people and harmonize their customs."[89] Thus, even if grievances exist, it is always inappropriate for people to resort to litigation and deal with governmental offices. The act of litigation can cause disruption to the natural harmony of human affairs. Therefore, even if individuals have grievances, it is always unseemly to report them to *Yamen*. Lawsuits disturb the inherent balance of human affairs.

The reliance of law on the support of power is not always endorsed by Confucianism. Rather, it is believed that most disputes can be resolved by moral persuasion first, and only when persuasion proves ineffective can they be resolved by the power of the monarch. In other words, litigation makes people litigious and shameless, focusing only on their own interests to the detriment of society. The Confucian values prioritize the regulation of social order and preservation of the community, rather than individual interests. The concepts of order, responsibility, hierarchy, and harmony are at the core of the dominant social norm—"rite." Rite is a pattern of behavior based on an individual's status and a specific social situation. Among these concepts, harmony is the most significant. When harmony is disrupted, mediation is preferred to defense in the court for resolution. Confucianism has always emphasized the importance of self-discipline and self-reflection and to get along with others, even if they are treated unjustly, by improving their behavior and abandoning litigation, thus settling disputes. Engaging in litigation implies that one is unsympathetic, unforgiving, and inconsiderate, resulting in a loss of moral character. Therefore, the Confucians advocate mediation and despise litigation.

---

[87] Chun, Y. (2008). Grounds for Choosing Mediation to Resolve Civil Disputes in Qing Dynasty. *Application of Law*. (3).

[88] *The Analects of Confucius: Yong Ye.*

[89] Gu, Y.(2011). *Collation and Annotation of Rizhilu (Part 1)*. volume 11. *Legal System*. Zhang Jinghua's annotations. Yuelu Book Company. 373–374.

On the other hand, Confucianism focuses on the protection of status differences in a hierarchically organized society. The "rite" strictly regulates patterns of behavior in the family and society that are appropriate to a person's age and rank. In contrast, Legalism attempts to establish legal rules that applies equally to all, regardless of social and economic status, but was ineffective and unsustainable. Confucian morality exhibits a sense of impersonality, with rite appropriate for all people in the same social role. However, the classification of social relationships is extremely rich, and the behavioral norms that dominate each type of relationship are based on the status of the individual within a highly detailed social hierarchy. These norms are extremely diverse and require those involved in dispute mediation to be careful about the social context in which the dispute takes place, to accurately determine the roles of the parties, to be clear about how the case relates to its past and its future, and to find the best mediation solution.

For the people, since neighbors cannot get away from each other, publicly exposing conflicts will easily damage the existing harmony and unity of the interpersonal, interfamily, interethnic relations. As the folk proverb: "denouncing a person can generate three generations of enmity." Instead of litigating in the court, it is preferable to resolve conflicts through mediation among the people. The traditional rural society in China is a typical acquaintance society, with low population mobility and a strong connection between land and human. If an individual persists in assigning fault and responsibility and pursues legal action to defend their rights, they may win the case; however, they risk permanently damaging their social connections. That is why numerous clan rules impose penalties on those who engage in litigation to promote harmony and stability in interpersonal, interfamily, and interclan relations. Therefore, people always take litigation as a precaution, put patience first, and resort to mediation, which is the instinctive choice of dispute resolution in the society of etiquette and acquaintance.

"No lawsuits" is the ideal state of governance permanently pursued by traditional Chinese rulers, and the initial approach to achieving it is mediation. Although the major schools of thought, such as Confucianism, Buddhism, and Taoism, vary in their strategies for ruling the country, they all pursue a similar ideal social model with a state of "no disputes" and "no lawsuits." They believe that if individuals fulfill their responsibilities and live in harmony with each other, the ruler will be able to govern with inaction to maintain a harmonious society.

6.5.4 The Continuation of Mediation

Mediation, as "the most culturally representative form of mainstream justice in the Chinese legal system,"[90] is considered "an important resource of traditional Chinese legal culture." "Comparative jurists view it as a fundamental symbol of the division of the Far Eastern legal system and the Chinese legal system."[91]

The sustainability of mediation varies depending on the time and location. For instance, civil power dominated township mediation, and many of the mediation policies in the early period of the dynasty were well applied due to their semiofficial recognition, while there was a risk of laxity during the middle and late dynasty. This was the case with township mediation in the middle and late Ming Dynasty, as reflected by a local official during the Xuande period:

During the Hongwu period, "Declaration" and "Commendation" pavilions were established in all towns and villages across the country. The deeds of the people, whether good or bad, were recorded there to encourage virtuous behavior and deter wrongdoing. Matters such as household disputes, land issues, and fights were resolved by the village elders in these pavilions. However, many of these pavilions have been obsolete, and the recording of good and bad deeds has ceased. Minor disputes are no longer settled by village elders but are instead taken directly to higher authorities, leading to an increase in legal cases and litigation.

The collapse of the *Shenmingting* in rural areas and the weakening of the township mediation resulted in a significant rise in the number of lawsuits. The imperial court would also make necessary adjustments based on the situation, for example, in the Jingtai period of the Ming Dynasty, an edict was issued to penalize individuals who were idle and failed to perform their duties in accordance with *the Instructions to the People*. During the Tianshun period, it was stipulated that for those thieves who were repeatedly punished by the government but not reformed, the government would write the words "Thief's House" on their doors; the words could be removed only after the offenders had been guaranteed by the elders, their relatives, and neighbors that they had reformed.[92] The government of the Qing Dynasty also encouraged and supported civil mediation to ensure its continued vitality.

During the Republic of China, although the modern legal system was basically established, the civil society still retained most of the mediation system. For instance, the "family council" empowered families to handle family disputes, which served as a legal procedure. In *The Civil Law of the Republic of China: Family Law*, the Chapter "Family Council" clearly defines the composition of the council and its

[90] Hu, X. (2005). *Interpretation on Historical Science of Law*. China University of Political Science and Law Press. 311.

[91] Fan,Y. (2000). *Research on Alternative Dispute Resolution*. Renmin University of China Press. 65.

[92] Gu,Y. Records of Daily in Knowledge. volume 11.Position of Xiangting.

functions.[93] In the case of kinship disputes, if a family member refuses to obey the resolutions of family council, he may complain to the court within 3 months, and if the resolution of family council has not been adopted, the court may dismiss the claim.[94] The statutory effectiveness of family mediation has been enhanced through legislation.

In the revolutionary base areas under the leadership of the Communist Party of China, the mediation system was revolutionized. The methods and principles of mediation were comprehensively renewed, with the prominent birth of "Ma Xiwu Adjudicative Model" and a set of mediation methods for adjudicating cases through the mass line. These mediation experiences laid the basic foundational for the civil litigation model established after the founding of the People's Republic of China, which was later developed into a judicial system. It aimed to establish a civil judicial system of litigation and mediation with Chinese characteristics, based on the core principle of "following the mass line."

The prevalence of mediation in traditional China is based on the closed smallholder economy and cognatic kinship networks, the ethical order of rites, and the model of rural autonomy. Mediation requires three essential conditions: first, the scarcity of judicial resources; secondly, the abundance of mediation resources; and thirdly, the positive social effects. Over time, Chinese society has experienced great changes in various aspects, including shifts in attitude toward conflicts, the evolution of the acquaintance society, and the stranger society. It is unrealistic and unnecessary to expect modern society to fully adopt the traditional model of mediation. However, the values of patience, humility, tolerance, and understanding, as well as goodwill toward others promoted by the mediation system, can be integrated into modern judicial concepts and systems. After all, Portalis asserted: "Laws are instituted for mankind, not mankind for laws; legislation must conform to the national character, customary practices, and social conditions of those it governs." It is acknowledged that the law does not encompass all aspects of life and a flawless law is not existent. Mediation plays an instrumental role in fostering harmonious justice and unifying legal and social effects. However, excessive reliance on mediation undermines the fairness and gravity of justice and reduces the predictability of the law, inhibits the evolving public awareness of legal rights, and fosters a culture of private settlements. This may lead to many negative consequences that warrant caution and prevention.

---

[93] Chapter 7 "Family Council", Article 1129–1137.

[94] Archives of the Supreme Court in the Collection of the Second Historical Archives of China, File No.16, Case No.69, Maintenance Fees, see Yu Shang Zi No.2962 of 1938.

Chapter 7
The Culture of Justice

What are the defining features of China's traditional judicial system? Scholars hold differing views. For example, instructive mediation played a key role in cases adjudicated by county magistrates, where the commonsense of fairness and equilibrium were deemed intrinsic. Given the need for legal stability and predictability, judges typically rendered decisions in accordance with established statutes. Judiciary decisions are based on principles of fairness, righteousness, neutrality, appropriateness, and harmony, with the ideal of establishing a harmonious society. When centralization of power was strengthened, less litigation arose and more mediation occurred, but when centralization of power waned, there was more litigation and less mediation. The judicial system of traditional China bore similarities with the Islamic Qadi system, characterized by patriarchal authority in the administration of justice. Judges needed to strike a balance between heavenly principles, human emotions, and national laws.[1] In general, to understand the traditional judicial culture of China, we need to observe the judicial professionals, judicial principles, judicial ideals, and judicial disorders comprehensively. Certainly, the mediation culture introduced in Chap. 6 is also an integral aspect of the judicial culture.

[1] These opinions could be found in the following books: Principles of Chinese Family Law by Shiga Shuzo (Law Press, 2003 Version), Rights and Injustice by Hiroaki Terada (Tsinghua University Press, 2012 Version), Laws, Society and Culture of the Qing Dynasty: the Expression and Practice of Civil Code by Huang Zongzhi (Shanghai Bookstore Publishing House, 2007 Version), An Introduction to the History of Chinese Litigation by Fu Majin [the Sixth Volume of Chinese Ancient China by Zhang Weiren (Morden Law Science, volume 5, 2006)], Between Nothing to Say and Something to Talk—Review of Zhang Weiren's The Judiciary and Jurisprudence of Traditional China by Gao Hongjun (Political and Legal Forum, Volume 3, 2006), Emotions, Diligent Officials and Judicial Practice during the Ming and Qing Dynasties by Xu Zhongming (Shanghai Sanlian Bookstore, 2009 Version), and so on.

R. Zhang, *Traditional Legal Culture in China*, Understanding China,
https://doi.org/10.1007/978-981-95-4697-8_7

7.1 People Involved in Adjudication

The judicial activities of legal professionals were necessary for applying textual laws to social reality, thereby transforming "static laws" into "dynamic laws." Throughout different historical periods, political systems, and social structures, the influence of legal professionals on the legal system varies. In traditional society, individuals had more influence on laws, whereas in the modern era, their influence diminished. The individuals' impact on the rule of law may be more prominent in a highly centralized government system but less significant in a dualistic or pluralistic system of government. Regardless of the situation, people's influence did exist, to various degrees. In traditional China, emperors, scholar-officials, jurists, officials, *Mufu* (private advisors), petty officials, *Songshi* (legal practitioners), gentries, elders, and heads of clans were all legal professionals. However, unlike modern legal professionals, they could not easily interchange roles with each other because they did not share the same professionalism, such as professional knowledge, mind-sets, skills, beliefs, and ethics. Besides, in most cases, there was even friction among them. In the modern era, only civil servants engaged in judicial activities are referred to as judges, while other legal professionals are considered participants in the "legal professional community." However, due to the complexity and distinctiveness of the judicial professionals in traditional China, not only judges but also other supporting personnel, such as *Mufu* (private advisors), heads of clans, and gentries, among others, were recognized by the government to undertake part of the judicial functions. Others like *Songshi* (legal practitioners), who were banned by the government, still had a direct or indirect influence on judicial outcomes. Both supporting personnel and *Songshi* (legal practitioners) were categorized as "quasijudicial officers." In the following section, we will discuss three categories of legal professionals: judicial officers (including emperors), legal advisers, and legal practitioners who had a great influence on adjudication and explore their roles, functions, and influences on the development of China's legal system.

7.1.1 The Group of Monarchs

In the traditional society of China, monarchs, heads of national administrations, wielded immense power in administration, legislation, judiciary, economy, and military affairs. Without written laws, imperial announcements, oaths, plans, admonitions, and ordinances held the same weight as laws, and the emperor possessed absolute power to punish those who disobeyed his commands. After the formation of written laws, an emperor's mandates, decisions, instructions, edicts, great announcements, sacred edicts, and wide-reaching admonitions also functioned as laws. Even though the throne changed hands many times, the fundamental laws remained unchanged. From *Canon of Laws* by Li Kui to the *Great Qin Code*, *Nine Chapter Law* in the Han Dynasty, the *Kaihuang Code* in the Sui Dynasty, the *Tang*

Code in the Tang Dynasty, the *Penal Code in the Song Dynasty*, and codes in the Ming and Qing Dynasties, each was built upon and modified from the preceding one. To some extent, it demonstrates that emperors of all dynasties respected legal tradition, including not only the laws of their ancestors but also the legal systems of previous dynasties.

Unified jurisdiction and administration were among the primary factors contributing to judicial corruption in traditional China. Monarchs, situated at the pinnacle of national administration, held vast authority in administration, legislation, and economic and military affairs. It can be inferred from the imperial announcements, oaths, ordinances, admonitions, and decrees issued by past monarchs that they possessed absolute authority to punish those who defied their directives. Following the establishment of written laws, expert judicial officials were appointed. But monarchs were undoubtedly the final decision-makers in all major cases. For example, Emperor Qin Shihuang personally presided over cases, "He recorded case information personally, conducted trials during the day and read documents at night, handling everything by himself. The documents he reviewed in a single day weighed approximately one *Dan* (1 *Dan* equals 61.58 Jin, 30.79 kg in the Qin Dynasty)."[2] During the Sui and Tang Dynasties, death penalty cases must be resubmitted to emperors. During the Song Dynasty, emperors made final decisions on punishment personally. In the Ming and Qing Dynasties, at joint adjudications for capital cases, emperors held the authority to determine death penalties by marking criminals' names with red ink. All these reflected the emperors' final say in settlements of major cases.

In certain dynasties, almost all emperors dominated or engaged in the judicial process. Taking the Song Dynasty as an example, Emperor Taizu of Song, Zhao Kuangyin, the founding emperor, often reviewed cases in person and emphasized that punishment should be severe yet not excessive. During his reign, he appointed personnel for the Censorate, the Court of Judicature, and Revision with great prudence. Emperor Taizong of Song, Zhao Guangyi, usually adjudicated cases himself, if there were any catches in cases of the capital city. Each time, he could find some clues. No matter how bad the weather was, he would review cases personally. Emperor Zhenzong of Song, Zhao Heng, kind and lenient, prudent in the infliction of punishment, believed that judicial officials must not be nominated at will. After reviewing the record of prison, he noticed that over 800 people across the nation were sentenced to the death penalty, and hence he felt sad and resumed the system of capital case resubmission hereafter. Emperor Renzong of Song, Zhao Zhen, characterized by modesty, was especially prudent in the infliction of punishment. Emperor Yingzong of Song, Zhao Xu, made nearly no change to the previous statutes and ordinances for his short reign. Hence officers were adjusted to the previous legal system. Emperor Shenzong of Song, Zhao Xiang, actively sought equitable judgments in criminal cases. Emperor Gaozong of Song, Zhao Gou, was gentle and merciful; when he ruled a case, he pardoned the accused instead of abusing the

[2] Book of Han: Penal Code.

penalty. Emperor Xiaozong of Song, Zhao Shen, was dedicated to supervising criminal cases. At the end of each year, he went to prisons to inspect prisoners. Requiring officials to prepare case files a few days in advance, he would decide those cases personally later. If there were any amendments to laws and regulations, he also took part in the modification. Emperor Ningzong of Song, Zhaokuo, overused detention and penalties at the early stage of his rule but later became more prudent in the infliction of punishment, and finally the number of prisoners under sentence of death substantially dropped. Emperor Lizong of Song, Zhao Tao, who hailed from a common family without political pedigree, clearly knew the disadvantages of abusing penalty. As soon as he came to the throne, he required leniency in punishment and wrote the Article on Interrogation and Punishment to alert incumbent officials. Every year, during the Great Heat (from July 23 to August 7), he inspected prisoners himself. Almost all emperors in the Song Dynasty displayed a high degree of legal proficiency and judicial acumen and kept in line with the judicial philosophy of the founding monarch of the Song Dynasty. However, the exception was Emperor Huizong of Song, Zhao Jie, who indulged in entertainment and extravagance. Under his administration, Cai Jing and Wang Fu (treacherous court officials) caused chaos in the administration of justice by cheating the emperor to seek personal interest.[3] All in all, traditional emperors were not only the supreme legislator but also the final decision-makers.

Since the power of emperors was not subject to any other checks and balances, their backgrounds, trial experiences, knowledge, qualities, beliefs, and personalities significantly influenced the administration of justice. A wise monarch might have a positive influence on the judicial system, while a muddle-headed monarch or a puppet monarch was harmful to it. A purported saint and wise monarch was able to deter his officials from corruption if he was diligent in political affairs, competent in ruling the nation and his officials, prudent in judicial decisions, and could abide by laws and try cases in person. Emperors such as Qin Shihuang, Emperor Gaozu of Han, Emperor Wu of Han, Emperor Taizong of Tang, Wu Zetian, Emperor Taizu of Song, Emperor Taizu of Ming, and Emperor Yongzheng all could rule by law. Emperors who were incompetent and fatuous often failed to control the judiciary. They recklessly delegated their ultimate authority over justice to their trusted advisors or placed excessive reliance on junior judicial officials, resulting in the inevitable corruption of the judicial system.

[3]Volumes 190, 200, 201 in History of Song Dynasty, and Volumes 152, 153, 154 in Treaties, and Volumes 1, 2, 3 in Penal Law.

7.1.2 The Group of Judges

In the early stage of traditional China, a clear division existed between the judiciary and administration. For example, in the Zhou Dynasty, there were Grand Masters in charge of six interior districts and Grand Masters in charge of six exterior districts; all of them were subordinated to Ministers of Civilian Affairs and were responsible for edicts and injunctions of interior and exterior districts, respectively. While servicemen of interior districts, exterior districts, and counties were subordinated to *Da Sikou* (Minister of Justice), they were responsible for criminal cases at interior districts, exterior districts, and counties, respectively. In other words, administrative officials and judicial officials had distinct roles that operated independently of each other. "Such a system of separated judiciary and administration was similar to the Western judicial system in the modern era" commented by Shen Jiaben (an official and jurist in the late Qing Dynasty). However, during the later period of traditional China, the "fusion of administration and judiciary turned into a trend." Over time, the relationship between the administration and the judiciary became tighter. Hence, officers at all levels were all-rounders, competent both in administration and judiciary. As for the personnel involved in the judiciary, they were roughly categorized as legal decision-makers, supervisors, political advisors, bailiffs, runners, and subordinate corpse examiners. Due to the absence of specialized training, most of them were nonprofessionals. Nevertheless, various adaptations and adjustments were made in different dynasties.

Before the Spring and Autumn Period, judicial talents were trained by the government. During the Spring and Autumn Period and Warring States Period, judicial talents were trained in private schools, as exemplified by figures like Deng Xi. During the Qin Dynasty, administrative officials also administered justice and shouldered the responsibility of promulgating laws. But during the Han dynasty, it was Confucian scholars, such as Dong Zhongshu, who were trained in national institutions and took part in judicial activities. After the Han Dynasty, despite the apparent decline of Legalism and the rise of Confucianism, laws continued to be an integral part of social life. There were full-time judicial workers, such as prison officers. Many judicial experts had previously served as administrative officials, such as Zhao Yu. According to *Biographies of Cruel Officials* in *Records of the Grand Historian*, Zhao Yu accumulated feats when he worked as a petty prison official, and then he was gradually promoted to Chief Prosecutor. The emperor recognized his competence, appointing him as Grand Counselor of the Palace. Together with Zhang Tang, they enacted laws that required officials to monitor each other, leading to increased stringency in the laws of the Han Dynasty. Zhao Yu was promoted from petty prison officer to Chief Prosecutor and Grand Counselor of the Palace owing to his rich experience accumulated when he served as a petty prison official. Another famous cruel official was Zhang Tang. He also had a great talent for adjudication since he was young, and he was promoted to Chamberlain for Law Enforcement eventually. The biography of him in the *Records of the Grand Historian* depicted a vivid story: "Zhang Tang's father was a Governor of the County of

Chang'an. Once his father went out and left the young boy to mind the house. When the father came back and found that meat was lost, he was so angry that he reprimanded the boy. After that, the boy dug a hole and found the thief rats and the remnants of missing meat. He charged the rats and interrogated them with torture after carrying out interrogations multiple times, recording the interrogation process, and reporting the ruling in a document. Finally, the rats and the remnants of meat were taken to a moot court where the case was decided. His father was surprised by the young man's written judgment which resembled the work of experienced prison officials. Hence, the father guided his son to read more judicial documents. After his father died, Zhang Tang assumed the role of County Governor of Chang'an." The story tells us when Zhang Tang was wrongfully accused of eating the missing meat, he caught and tried rats (the thieves), and wrote a detailed paper of judgment to prove his innocence, from which his father noticed that the boy was a born judge and cultivated him in this regard. All these behaviors at least proved that Zhang Tang might often witness the process of trial when his father served as the Governor of the County of Chang'an. Zhang Tang started as a judge and was promoted to Prosecutor, Grand Counselor of the Palace, and Chamberlain for Law Enforcement step by step. Finally, he was promoted to Chief Prosecutor which was among the Nine Ministers.

"Chamberlain for Law Enforcement" and "Grand Judicial Reviewer" were Chief Grand Justices between the Qin, Han, and Jin Dynasties. In the early Cao-Wei period, under the Chamberlain for Law Enforcement, there were erudite professors for law who specialized in imparting legal knowledge to improve the judicial level of judicial officials. During the Northern Qi Dynasty, the "Chamberlain for Law Enforcement" turned into the "Grand Judicial Reviewer" which became the highest judiciary ministry. There were multiple levels of officials affiliated with it. The number of erudite professors for law (*Lü Boshi*) increased from one to four, expanding the judicial department. The highest administrative department was the Department of State Affairs (renamed *Shangshusheng* later), which was followed by six ministries, including ministries specialized in judiciary, administration, and prisons. The local judicial system was integrated with the administration in general. Depending on the severity, cases were either decided by local governments or transferred to higher judicial levels, ultimately reaching the aforementioned Chamberlain for Law Enforcement or Grand Judicial Reviewer.

After the Sui and Tang Dynasties, the judicial institution of the central government was gradually composed of three ministries, namely, the Ministry of Justice, the Court of Judicial Review, and the Censorate. Generally, the Ministry of Justice was in charge of trials and judicial administration. The Court of Judicial Review was responsible for reviewing cases. And the Censorate's duty was supervision. To hear and try complicated major cases in the capital, a joint adjudication by three ministries was formed which was composed of chief officials of the three ministries. For complex cases outside the capital, the joint adjudication by the three ministers was formed of vice ministers or lower-ranking staff from the three ministries, known as "commissioners of the three offices." Since the Sui and Tang Dynasties, the Ministry of Justice, the Court of Judicial Review, and the Censorate (named "duchayuan" after the Ming Dynasty) basically formed the supreme judicial system of the central government. During the Ming and Qing Dynasties, in the joint adjudication of death penalties, the number of trial officers increased from three to nine, which meant that a grand joint adjudication was formed by chief officials of the nine ministries of the central government to try capital cases.

The judicial affairs of local governments from counties to provinces were managed by chief administrative officials in counties and provinces. Although there were specialized judicial officials, such as judicial commissioners or the provincial surveillance commission, all of them were not directly controlled by monarchs. For example, during the Song and Ming Dynasties, such judicial officials were controlled by regional chief administrative officials, and during the Qing Dynasty, serious criminal cases heard by the provincial surveillance commissions should be reported by Governor-generals or Governors to the central government and wait for monarchs to make final judgments. As for civil cases and minor criminal cases in which the losing party would be punished by flogging with heavy or light bamboo, Prefects and County Magistrates were authorized to preside over and adjudicate these cases independently. The judicial function was only one of the administrative functions of Prefect and County Magistrates; in other words, the judicial and administrative functions were integrated in prefectures and counties.

After the Sui and Tang Dynasties, the cultivation of legal talents changed constantly. During the Qin and Han Dynasties, scholars, who mastered laws, were the main source of officials. After over 300 years of transition, in the Sui and Tang Dynasties, law experts were selected through the Chinese Imperial Examination System which officially covered legal knowledge. Since then, the training of legal talents became specialized and nationwide. In the Song Dynasty, more attention was paid to the selection of legal talents. For example, Emperor Shenzong of Song started the study of law and set up the official position called "erudite professors for law" (*LüBoshi*) who were examined on the legal knowledge and the ability of adjudication, and in the Southern Song Dynasty, a specialized judicial examination was introduced.[4] Undoubtedly, with the advocacy from governments, people would pay more attention to legal knowledge. Su Shi, a scholar in Northern Song Dynasty, once highlighted the importance of learning law in his poem, "if an official had read numerous books except books on law, he can't assist an emperor in becoming as saintly as *Yao* and *Shun*." As the central government attached importance to laws, the whole society would follow it. Just as Shen Jiaben, a legal scholar in Qing Dynasty, said, "When the government set up a new position, scholars across the country would learn something relevant to the profession for a promotion; when the emperor considered something important, everyone believed it was important; when the emperor oversaw something, all the civilians would follow suit. I haven't heard of a situation where an emperor failed to attach importance to the study of law; however, all his civilians valued it." Due to the lack of officials of Erudite professors

[4]Notions of the History of Song Dynasty: Penal Code, edited by Shanghai Academy of Social Science Institution of Law, Qunzhong Press, 1982 Version, Pages 16–17.

for laws, the study of law waned during the Yuan Dynasty. Although the central government repeatedly instructed civilians to study law, nothing came of it. Following the trend of the Yuan Dynasty, the government of the Ming Dynasty directly abolished this position. Luckily, there was a provision in the *Ming Code* that all officials and civilians should study laws. Although the position of Erudite professors for law was vacant, laws and decrees continued to be studied in the Ming Dynasty.[5]

However, on account of the trend that officials were selected through imperial exams on "eight-legged essays" in the Ming and Qing Dynasties, the number of scholars who devoted themselves to Confucian thought and knowledge increased sharply; fewer people studied laws and governments neglected professional legal education. To acquire legal knowledge, officials mainly depended on reading books such as *Book of Governors and the Magistrates, Admonitions to State Officials and Sacred Edicts of Emperor Kangxi*, etc. After taking office, the officials were not required to learn legal skills and practical knowledge, leading to the prevalence of irrational judicial activities. During that period, the personal likes, dislikes, character, temperament, and morality of officials decisively influenced trial outcomes. If an official diligently focused on self-improvement through study, he could make right judgments on his own. If an official was lazy, irrational, and reckless, he could not make the right judgment, acting impetuously and subjectively. In order to complete their superiors' tasks and at the same time fulfill their judicial obligations, the officials, who were at the end of their wits, had to seek help from others such as *Mufu* (a Chinese private advising organ) and petty officials. Members of *Mufu* learned from their forefathers or teachers, instead of specialized legal institutions. The petty officials were a mixed bag. Some of them caused trouble due to misunderstandings and arbitrary legal judgments.

Compared with the traditional judicial team, the major feature of the modern judicial team is the separation between administration and judiciary. Since then, a truly independent judicial team emerged, which was mainly composed of judges and prosecutors. In the early twentieth century, the Chinese judicial system became independent gradually in the process of abolishing extraterritorial jurisdiction and striving for judicial independence. For the abolishment of extraterritoriality, laws were amended during the late Qing Dynasty, facilitating the transformation from traditional to modern laws and guiding China's legal system toward modernization. From 1906 to 1928, grassroots judges were called *Tuishi* (the former Chinese name of judges). Since 1928, they have been mostly called "Faguan" commonly. The title of procurators, however, never changed.

[5] Shen, J. (1985). Articles of Jiyi, Volume 1, On Erudite professors for law. Studies on Penal Law of Previous Dynasties. Vol. 4. Zhonghua Book Company. 2060.

7.1.3 The Group of Private Advisors

7.1.3.1 The Emergence of Private Advisors

In traditional China, administrators could not take full charge of legal affairs. From the Qin-Han Period to the Sui-Tang Period, both administrative officials and petty officials could manage part of legal matters. From then until the Ming and Qing Dynasties, the judiciary affairs were dominated by petty officials, as administrative officials had limited knowledge of laws. Owing to the situation that the Chinese Imperial Examination focused on Confucian classics instead of legal practice, traditional scholars, who became governmental officials, only read Confucian classics instead of books on laws. With the duty of handling legal affairs and collecting taxes and grains, petty officials, as officials serving in the government, had to learn laws in practice and use the practical experience they gained in work. Even if they had no prior knowledge of laws before entering government offices, they had to learn the judicial knowledge for their work and more importantly for their living. Over time, after mastering the laws of government offices, they became experts in administration and grasped the power of their offices. Because administrative officials had no capacity for administration and petty officials could not be abolished or controlled, it was the best way for the administrative officials to hire someone capable of dealing with administrative duties and controlling those petty officials. Consequently, the role of private advisors emerged.

Resulting of the fierce competition in the Chinese Imperial Examination, even when someone passed the examination, they only got an admission ticket to become a candidate for an official position, and they might wait many years for a chance to become an official. As a candidate without an official salary, he must earn a living through other methods. For most candidates and scholars who did not pass the examination, except those from wealthy families, working as private advisors was the best way to earn a living. On the one hand, private advisors were well-paid enough to support their families. On the other hand, they could learn how to work as officials, laying the foundation for passing the imperial examination and gaining scholarly honors and official ranks. Furthermore, scholars in the traditional society followed the tenet that "To be a scholar is to be at the top of society." This belief made scholars unable to secure official posts become reluctant to engage in agriculture, industry, commerce, and other professions. Instead, they often chose to work as private advisors for livelihood and continued study.

Shiye (private advisors), also commonly known as private assistants in governments, emerged in the Ming Dynasty and became widespread in the Qing Dynasty. In ancient times, when a general was engaged in battle away from home, he had no fixed abode. Therefore, *Mu* (tents) waw erected as *Fu* (mansions), collectively referred to as *Mufu*.[6] The ancillary staff working in *Mufu* were called *Muliao* (private advisors), *Muyou* (private friends), and *Mubin* (private guests). They were

[6] Zhang, Y. (2001). *Miscellany of Shaoxing Culture*. Zhonghua Book Company. 268.

important helpers to chief officials; therefore, runners and henchmen in feudal government offices, respectfully, called officials "lords" and called private advisors "masters." *Shiye* (private advisors) were employed by chief officers of local governments to help them handle judicial, accounting, and clerical affairs. Although they were only helpers without official posts, they were the guests of the chief officers and enjoyed an equal status with the chief officers. Those advisors earned their name as "guests of the lord."

During the Ming and Qing Dynasties, private advisors were talented scholars proficient in judiciary, accounting, and clerical work and were employed by officials at all levels for assistance. Without any official titles, they only assisted their officials by giving advice, drafting documents, dealing with cases, and running errands. In the Ming and Qing Dynasties, private advisors, who played an important role in judicial practice in local communities, became widespread. In the Qing Dynasty, officials at all levels, especially officials in prefectures and counties, often hired private advisors to deal with cases and political affairs. Commonly, there were different kinds of private advisors responsible for different tasks, such as dealing with judicial affairs, dealing with tax affairs, drafting documents, and making registration. At that period, there was a saying that "Governmental offices couldn't operate without private advisors." Nearly all criminal and civil cases were handled by private advisors specialized in judicial affairs, who could be regarded as "judicial officials without the title of judges." Their activities influenced not only the chief officials' political achievements but also had practical legal effects on society. Many private advisors could exert their efforts to help chief officials properly handle cases, to keep the society peaceful and stable, and meanwhile to create political achievements for the chief officials and accumulate their own political capital for promotion to higher positions.

Because private advisors were territory-specific, those aspiring to specialize in judicial or fiscal affairs needed to learn from more experienced advisors. Among the groups of private advisors from various regions and interpersonal networks, the most famous came from Shaoxing City (a city in Zhejiang province). Why did they stand out? A scholar once quoted a saying that "Shaoxing City was famous for its wine and private advisors who were experts in judicial and fiscal affairs." There were private advisors specialized in criminal cases or civil cases, who were called "private advisors from Shaoxing City." When the Song government retreated to the south of the Yangtze River, books on laws and regulations of the central government were relocated to Shaoxing City. Over the next 700 years, local people studied these valuable texts, leading to a situation where virtually no governmental office across the country functioned properly without some personnel from Shaoxing City.[7] Zhou Zuoren mentioned in his book "So-called *Shaoxing Shiye* (private advisors from Shaoxing City) refers to private advisors who are specialized in dealing with judicial affairs; other types of private advisors are not included."[8] Li Boyuan also wrote

[7] Jiang, M. (1967). *New Trend*, Biographies Press. 111–112.

[8] Zhou, Z. (1988). *Collected Articles by Zhitang after 1949*. Yuelu Press. 34.

in his *Modern Times* that "There was a hereditary career in Shaoxing City, which was called private advisor… It was surprising that those legal secretaries who were specified in judicial affairs all came from Shaoxing City. Hence a clique was formed that outsiders could not join."[9] In fact, not all late-imperial private advisors were from Shaoxing City. However, since many private advisors originated from Shaoxing City and frequently recommended each other, a conventional perception emerged that if a private advisor was skilled in judicial affairs, they were likely to be considered a "private advisor from Shaoxing City." This nickname became a professional trademark unexpectedly.

7.1.3.2 Duties of Private Advisors

The private advisors specified in judicial affairs were assistants in judicial activities, who were power holders without titles, so they had to give full play to their specific talents and at the same time avoid exceeding their power cap, focusing on their own work as well. The judicial duties of private advisors specified in judicial affairs were as follows.

Their first duty was to draft reports. At the beginning of trials, they needed to check the forms of pleadings and the condition of accusers. "After chief officials approved the drafted reports, these reports should be transcribed and published." Hence, the orders of chief officials were based on the drafts written by their private advisors. And there was another condition that the private advisors had made final judgments, while the chief officials still had no idea about the cases. It led to a situation where final decisions were made by private advisors, while chief officials merely endorsed these judgments without review.[10]

The second duty was to hear cases and settle lawsuits. After the drafts were permitted, the private advisors specified in judicial affairs needed to prepare for trials, determine the date of trials, and summon the defendants. If necessary, they also needed to summon witnesses and collect evidence, in accordance with laws. At trials, the private advisors specified in judicial affairs were not allowed to appear in the *Yamen* courtroom, and there was even no seat for them. Although they did not appear in trials, private advisors specified in judicial affairs still influenced trials by reviewing depositions after trials or hearing behind the scenes. Usually, the private advisors specified in judicial affairs would propose their insights in discussions with chief officials after following orders from them. However, when it came to the convictions and punishments, these private advisors were the true decision-makers.

The third duty was to draft judicial records, including final judgments, case briefs, instructions, and detailed reports addressed to superiors. The detailed reports addressed to superiors included reports on the process of the trials and reports on the

[9] Li, B. *A Brief History of Enlightenment*, Chapter 30.

[10] Gao, H. (2000). *Researches on Private Advisors Specialized in Law in the Qing Dynasty*. China University of Political Science Press. 43.

retrials and the final judgment. In order to avoid unnecessary problems, some specific skills were needed when the private advisors wrote detailed reports addressed to their superiors.[11]

When participating in local judicial activities, private advisors specified in judicial affairs gave full play to their talents, which was necessary for public security and social stability. As assistants to chief officials in trying cases, they must bear the corresponding responsibilities. After adjudicating cases on behalf of county magistrates, these legal secretaries were also required to draft judicial comments bearing their unofficial personal seals. Unlike standard name seals, theirs were inscribed with aspirational mottos rather than personal names. If their judicial comments contained clerical errors or subsequent modifications, they were required to affix this special seal. This served to confirm that the drafters assumed full responsibility for any mistakes or amendments, while also authenticating the date, the county magistrates' names, and the private legal advisors' seals. Generally, private advisors did not disclose their true names in documents, but the seals on the drafts could tell which private advisors made these reviews. The inscriptions on these seals reflected the professional interests and priorities of individual private advisors. Some seals were inscribed with judicial principles, such as "observe the law," "make decisions based on consultation," and "think twice before making final judgments"; some were meant to encourage private advisors themselves, like "How can we satisfy all? Yet may our hearts stay clear," "diligence, prudence, candor"; some were meant to mock at themselves, such as "bureaucratic exhaustion"; some did not contain any special meaning, like "Modoujian" (Admonition on Verbal Prudence)."[12] To maintain case continuity amid prolonged adjudication periods and frequent turnover of chief magistrates, successive private advisors were required to maintain detailed judicial records.

7.1.3.3 The Situation and Reputation of Private Advisors

Private advisors often felt they merely served as cat's paws and did not get any sense of achievement in their work. Indeed, private advisors' duty was to help others. Therefore, whether they helped officials with administration or helped officials in ruling subjects, their work was to assist chief officials. From the aspect of assisting others, there was nothing special for private advisors in the Qing Dynasty. However, these private advisors often experienced a strong sense of disappointment due to the contradiction between their personal values and the reality of their situation, feeling underestimated and lacking opportunities for promotion. As officials at all levels had no power to grant titles to their secretaries, private advisors were always deemed as their masters' "guests" or "friends," who were merely recruited for assistance.

---

[11] Guo, R. (1996). Government, private advisors and scholars—Researches on "private advisors from Shaoxing City," *China Social Science Press*, 138.

[12] Tian, T., Xu, C.& Wang, H. (2004). Introduction of Lawsuit files at Huangyan by Wang Hongzhi, *Lawsuits and Research Reports at Huangyan*. Volume 1. Law Press. 67–68.

During the Qing Dynasty, although some people proposed to turn private advisors into regular officials, the government never permitted any of them to attain formal official status. Becoming a private advisor often meant a career dead end for scholars.[13] Gong Weizhai, a private advisor from Shaoxing City, once remarked "The uneducated in poverty were forced to become thieves, and the unsuccessful scholars in poverty were forced to serve as private advisors." Though radical, this comment reflected a harsh reality: scholars became private advisors out of poverty and often ended up poorer."[14] The stark contrast between the uneducated and scholars, as well as between thieves and private advisors, highlighted the plight of private advisors. Only those who had experienced this could truly understand the severe pain, indicating that private advisors' roles were neither as lucrative for gray income nor as promising as many had once believed. This situation clearly showed the status and the work of private advisors determined their prospects. As chief officials were promoted, their private advisors often felt a sense of sorrow, as they themselves were unable to transition into official positions.[15]

As a result of working in obscurity, private advisors were looked down upon by many nobles. And some private advisors belittled themselves, by overly showcasing their literary ability and thereby destroying their reputation. Although private advisors specialized in judicial affairs acted as "legal professionals" to assist all kinds of cases, playing an important role in the local judiciary, they usually handle cases according to previous cases or theories in classics, apart from laws and regulations. This approach fostered a tendency toward prioritizing relationships and inflexibility.

A huge gap can be found in moral quality among different private advisors specialized in judicial affairs. Quite a few pernicious and cunning private advisors specialized in judicial affairs tarnished others' reputations. However, many dedicated and impartial private advisors assisted governments in policymaking and became officials' true friends. Through their great efforts, they could pass the Chinese Imperial Examination and be promoted to administrative officials. Some penned admonitions to state officials, achieving enduring renown. For example, Wang Huizu, a famous private advisor, became a county magistrate in Ningyuan County, Hunan Province, after serving other officials for 34 years. There were serious tax arrears, numerous unsettled lawsuits, and barbarous vagrants. He improved the local security greatly by catching the most aggressive offenders and driving out their henchmen. Wang Rucheng, from Shanyin County, redressed many unjust cases and rehabilitated innocent people when he worked as a private advisor for Chen Qingxie, a governor in Shandong province. The relevant files were mounted on

[13] Li, Q. (1995). *China's Private Advisors*. The Commercial Press. 135–148.

[14] Letters from Xuehong Pavilion, Argumentative Essay, in reply to Zhou Fanxing by Gong Weizhai.

[15] Feng, E. (2012). *Researches on the Historical Records of Biographies at the Qing Dynasty*. Yuelu Press. 216–226. Based on the Letters from Qiushui Pavilion written by Xu Simei (Jia Cun), who was born at Shaoxing City in the Qing Dynasty, Feng Erkang complied the Biography of Xu Simei which records the work experience, living situation, and psychological status of Xu Simei and described the general situation of private secretaries.

cloth as a standard for future generations.[16] The books he wrote, such as *Records of My Dreams in Ailment*, *On Governance*, and *Advice on How to Assist a Chief Official in Governance*, were regarded as models of admonitions to state officials. Fan Zengxiang, who later became a chief official, was promoted from the role of private advisor due to his diligence and exemplary conduct. His books, *Political Book by Fan Shan* and *Critics on Trying Cases*, were praised by his mentors and peers: "Although numerous policy books have been written throughout history, his are the only ones that are rational, realistic, and appealing to both scholarly and general audiences." Many impartial private advisors forged genuine friendships with their administrative officials, contributing to the development of a generation of distinguished officials. For example, Tian Wenjing, a governor of Henan province in the Qing Dynasty, was praised by the Emperor Yongzheng for his exceptional administration of his region. However, a folk tale suggests that all his reports to the throne were ghostwritten by a private advisor surnamed Wu, and Tian Wenjing did not review these reports himself. Allegedly, Emperor Yongzheng once acknowledged Wu's contribution in a remark, "I'm fine. And how about Mr. Wu?" This anecdote illustrates the significant influence of private advisors.[17]

7.1.3.4 The Fadeout of Private Advisors

As society evolved, private advisors specialized in judicial affairs also faced ups and downs. During the mid and late Qing Dynasty, the society gradually got out of hand, and the ethos among private advisors deteriorated to the point where long-standing issues became deeply entrenched. In response, some visionary figures attempted to reform the system of private advisors. For example, after Zhang Zhidong was inaugurated as a Viceroy of Huguang, the first change he made was to reform the system of private advisors by dismissing the employed private advisors. In his office, only tutors were permitted to be called "old masters," and the General Clerical Office was set up to replace private advisors specialized in judicial affairs and private advisors specialized in tax affairs. The clerical commissioner was akin to the previous private advisors specialized in clerical affairs, responsible for drafting documents in Zhang Zhidong's private advising office. However, this reform was more than just a change in titles: previously, private advisors were seen as masters' friends, able to share their advice freely. Postreform, they became subordinates in a hierarchy where they were required to obey their superiors' orders. While private advisors were once considered equals, a hierarchy among them was now established. Private advisors used to be cordially invited to offices, but now they were formally delegated for assistance. Private advisors used to be private assistants, but now they were formal officials. Private advisors used to be titular, but now they were expected to bear

[16] Zhang, Y. (2006). *Miscellany of Shaoxing Culture*, Zhonghua Book Company. 276.

[17] Chen, T. (1975). Stories between Private Advisors Specialized in Judicial Affairs and Private Advisors Specialized in Tax Affairs and Me by by Cai Shenzhi et al. *Stories about Prefectures and County Magistrates in the Qing Dynasty*. Chinese Literature and History Press. 50.

official responsibility. All in all, their nature of work saw changes and so did their status. The actions of clerical secretaries became subject to their chief officials' directives. Zhang Zhidong was the actual dominator. In Zhang Zhidong's private advising office, private advisors were not allowed to participate in political affairs, transforming them into mere guests discussing casual matters. Because of the advocacy from Zhang Zhidong, the governments at all levels followed in his footsteps, changing the title of private advisors specialized in judicial affairs into section chief or secretary. Later, similar reforms were implemented in other provinces. Therefore, Liu Chengyu, a modern politician, poignantly observed, "The business of private advisors from the Shaoxing City was entirely eradicated by Zhang Zhidong."[18]

In the late Qing Dynasty, emulating some Western countries, the government adopted Constitutional Monarchy, advocating for judicial independence, which entailed that litigation would be exclusively heard by courts. As a result, schools of political science and law were established to cultivate judicial officials in all provinces with the status of legal private advisors gradually on the wane. During the period of the Republic of China, the appearance of new intellectuals fundamentally undermined the political status of private advisors specialized in judicial affairs. Private advisors specialized in judicial affairs finally faded into insignificance. Many private advisors from Shaoxing City with expertise soon became Section Chiefs. Particularly following the 1911 Revolution, reforms in the system of state officials required county-level governments to restructure, resulting in co-located administrative offices led by Section Chiefs instead of private advisors. At the same time, the judiciary became independent. In other words, courts were specialized in hearing lawsuits. There was a Supreme Court in the capital Beijing, higher courts in all provinces, and district courts in all counties. Besides, schools of political science and law, crash law courses, and cultivating academies were set up one after another in all the provinces. After graduation, students were delegated to administrative offices, which led to the rapid wane of private advisors. Furthermore, these schools of political science and law offered courses in finance, economy, statistics, and accounting, among others. When these students graduated, they replaced a large part of private advisors. Since then, although private advisors specialized in judicial affairs and private advisors specialized in tax affairs were recognized by the government as legal professionals, they still faded in history.

[18] Liu Chengyu, *Miscellaneous Memories from the Shizai Studio; The Abolishment of Private advisors by Zhang Zhidong*; Wang, Zhenzhong. (1997). *Private Advisors from Shaoxing City*, Fujian People's Publishing House, 180–181.

7.1.4 The Group of Nonofficial Legal Practitioners

7.1.4.1 *Songshi* (Legal Practitioners)

In ancient China, individuals akin to lawyers did not enjoy formal titles. These professionals were commonly named *Songshi* (legal practitioners); thus they might be referred to as "informal lawyers." Private advisors were different from legal practitioners. Private advisors commonly referred to as private advisors specialized in judicial affairs and were recruited by Prefects and County Magistrates. They earned their salaries by assisting their masters—chief officials at all levels—to deal with lawsuits. However, legal practitioners earned their salary by representing their clients in lawsuits. Although not officially recognized, they possessed knowledge of laws. They were different from shysters who lacked legal knowledge but sought unjust benefits by inciting disputes and instigating lawsuits. However, private advisors were often conflated with shysters.

Since the Spring and Autumn Period, informal lawyers or legal practitioners appeared, exemplified by figures like Deng Xi, who was born in Zheng Country. In the Ming and Qing Dynasties, legal practitioners were extremely active in villages and towns. Normally, forks were unwilling to go to court. But for legal practitioners, the only worry was no case for them to get in on. Because common people who lived in poverty were mostly uneducated and nearly knew nothing about laws and policies of nations, they were hesitant to engage in legal proceedings. If they had to be engaged in cases, they still needed to seek help from legal practitioners who were literate, familiar with laws and policies, skillful at writing complaints, and clear about the key to winning or losing a lawsuit and connecting with some officials. Hence, although they cannot appear in court, they were able to give advice to their clients. Indeed, many legal practitioners endeavored to solve problems, resolve disputes, and seek justice for ordinary people. For example, during the Qing Dynasty, under Emperor Yongzheng's rule, a legal practitioner from Songjiang County, named Wu Moqian, proficient in laws and policies, gained prominence. The legal practitioner was popular among folks and the government did not interfere with his work.[19]

In both traditional and modern societies, a persuasive complaint can significantly influence the direction of a case and shape the judge's attitude toward it. To propose causes of action most beneficial to their clients, agents often made appropriate modifications to case circumstances, sometimes even resorting to exaggeration. In traditional society where legal practitioners were not officially recognized, the skill of writing complaints may even directly affect the progression of cases. Whether local officials paid attention to a particular complaint among many cases largely depended on the reputation of the employed legal practitioner and how they described the case's circumstances.

[19] Xu, K. (1984). *Collected Anecdotes and Trifles of the Qing Dynasty*. Vol 3. Zhonghua Book Company. 1047.

Although scholars often use the phrase "no lies, no complaints" to describe legal practitioners' written complaints in traditional China, the "lies" mentioned here were actually a strategic part of the litigation skills employed by these practitioners. The important role of legal practitioners can be seen from a righteous lawyer, Shi Zhibo, depicted in Chapter 24 of the novel *Strange Cases of Nine Murders* in the Qing Dynasty. In two lawsuits featured in this novel, it is shown that without the assistance of Shi Zhibo, the legal practitioner, the plaintiff Liang Tian would have been at a loss on how to proceed.[20] It was a special condition that common people's lawsuits entirely relied on the help of legal practitioners which made the social requirement on legal practitioners stricter. If legal practitioners assumed the responsibility of upholding justice, focusing on helping disadvantaged groups, advocating for good, and mitigating evil, ordinary people could greatly benefit from their services. From this perspective, legal practitioners, a distinctive professional cohort, were the de facto the operational backbone of the judicial system. Their behind-the-scenes involvement in litigation contributed to ensuring judicial fairness and preventing injustices to a certain extent.

Although legal practitioners were never formally recognized in terms of political status by the government, there was a high societal demand for their services. As a result, even legal practitioners who were relatively lesser-known could be well paid. It was difficult to calculate the exact income of legal practitioners, and it can only be deduced from some records. According to a historical archive, "people from Suzhou (a city in Eastern China) were particularly litigious, resulting in a dense concentration of legal practitioners there."[21] Given these circumstances, it is evident that legal practitioners enjoyed a lucrative career and could be considered part of the high-income group. Their income was nothing more than fees charged from their clients. Just as the saying goes, poor people were unable to afford lawsuits, which made the common people discouraged from filing lawsuits. This situation meant that even those willing to pay a high price found it difficult to hire a legal practitioner. But it was also not easy for the wealthy to file lawsuits. Even if they win their lawsuits, they still need to spend large sums of money. For example, in the book *Strange Cases of Nine Murders*, even if the rich Liang family received help from Shi Zhibo, an excellent legal practitioner, they did not win their lawsuit in the long term. If an individual was too poor to afford a legal practitioner and consequently unable to secure their assistance, winning a lawsuit became significantly more challenging.[22]

The role of a legal practitioner was unique in that, although often despised by ordinary people, they were still heavily relied upon. As legal practitioners cannot

---

[20] Wu, J. *Strange Cases of Nine Murders*, Chapters 24–25.

[21] Xu F. (1995). Huadangge Congtan, Volume Three, "Zhu Yingju", Zhou Guangpei. (Ed.) *Short Sketches and Fictions of the Ming and Qing Dynasties: Collection of Novels of Past Dynasties*, Volume 11, Hebei Education Press, 191–192.

[22] Huo, C. (2006). Litigating Lawsuits, Desiring for Wealth and Hindering Rule of Law: Legal practitioners in the Mind of Governments of the Qing Dynasty, Newspaper Printed by Renmin University of China. Jurisprudence: Historical Science of Law. Volume 4.

achieve moral satisfaction, they naturally seek compensation in economy to obtain their mental balance. This kind of mentality made many legal practitioners indulge in seeking fortune. Economic incentives motivated legal practitioners to manipulate judicial proceedings through their expertise, intentionally distorting case facts to influence sentencing outcomes, either mitigating or aggravating penalties, which ultimately determined the defendants' fates. This judicial discretion was described in the proverb: "With but a stroke of their brush, legal practitioners wield the power over life and death."

7.1.4.2 Status of *Songshi* (Legal Practitioners)

The social status of legal practitioners in traditional China was relatively awkward. As the unluckiest legal group, they suffered from all kinds of taunts, criticism, and suppression but never enjoyed normal treatment since the day of their appearance. Deng Xi could be regarded as the ancestor of modern lawyers, who were favored by the public. However, he was decapitated because politicians worried that his criticism of the government might agitate common people and influence social stability. Luckily, the government absorbed the *Penal Law on Bamboo*, written by Deng Xi secretly, and formed the earliest statute law, a significant achievement attributable to him. After him, informal lawyers were not so lucky whose reputations became worse and situations became more difficult. During the Ming and Qing Dynasties, legal practitioners were despised, and their reputation was tarnished. For example, in folk dramas, the roles of legal practitioners from Shaoxing City were normally played by amusing clowns who told gags in the dialect of Shaoxing City. In the dialect of the Southern Jiangsu province, there was a nickname for legal practitioners meaning they were bad guys who only gave bad advice. The government explicitly labeled them as shysters and ruffians.[23] So why did the legal practitioners possess such a low social status? The main reasons include the following:

The first reason was legal prohibition. These informal lawyers were very petty and were called shysters. When they handled cases, they risked committing crimes and even faced the possibility of execution. Official laws banned legal practitioners from taking part in lawsuits. In the Tang and Song Dynasties, there were crimes of "exaggerating circumstances in making a written statement for a person" and "instigating a person to make a false accusation in court." *The Great Qing Code* prescribed that any legal practitioners who abetted anyone to file lawsuits shall be punished according to law; if anyone filed false lawsuits, he shall be sentenced to military exile to frontier regions (such as Yunnan, Guizhou, Guangzhou, or Guangxi Provinces); any superior officials failed to oversee legal practitioners shall be severely punished according to regulations; if there was any coverup, local officials shall be arrested as lawbreakers and be sentenced by Ministry of Personnel; any

[23] Bao, T. (1999). *Reminiscences from the Residence of Chuanying Building: Sequel: Stories on Lawyers in Shanghai*. Shanxi Education Press/Shanxi Ancient Book Press. 727.

books on legal practitioners which taught people how to make up stories in lawsuits, such as *Jingtianlei*, *Xiang Jiao*, *A New Book on Laws*, *XingtaiQinjing*, etc., shall be banned and destroyed. Anyone who published the aforementioned books shall be sentenced in line with the crime of publishing pornographic novels and shall be beaten with 100 strokes of heavy bamboo and sent to exile for 3000 *li*. Anyone who sold the aforementioned books shall be sentenced to 3 years of penal servitude and 100 strokes of the heavy bamboo. Anyone who bought the aforementioned books shall be beaten with 100 strokes of heavy bamboo. Anyone who hid the aforementioned books whose punishment shall be reduced by one degree compared with the publisher.[24]

The issue of legal practitioners even garnered the attention of emperors. For example, Emperor Yongzheng criticized legal practitioners in the twelfth maxim "Hold back false accusations to safeguard the good and honest" of the *Sixteen Maxims of Emperor Yongzheng* which is amplified instructions on the *Sacred Edicts of Emperor Kangxi*. Notably, these seemingly minor legal practitioners drew criticism from the emperor himself, being condemned as malevolent individuals who harmed people and undermined the law.

The second reason was the suppression from governments. In judicial practice, officials at all levels tried their best to crack down on legal practitioners. Certain local officials, known for their "uprightness," gained notoriety for their harsh measures against legal practitioners, with some even citing their effective suppression as a political achievement. For example, Liu Heng, a county magistrate in the Qing Dynasty, summarized a set of experiences regarding restrictions on legal practitioners. His methods were so cruel that legal practitioners faced daytime inspections, nighttime arrests, and both mental and physical abuse. In his jurisdiction, legal practitioners were in an abyss of suffering without any chance to work.[25]

Even in the late Qing Dynasty, when massive revisions in laws were about to begin, officials at all levels still fought against legal practitioners. For example, in the story of *Xiao Baicai and Yang Naiwu*, one of the "four most astonishing cases" of the Qing Dynasty, Yang Naiwu was such an intellectual snob who was found meddling in villagers' lawsuits that he offended a county magistrate called Liu Xitong. After he was involved in a murder case, the county magistrate took the chance to torture him who had to confess to false charges and nearly died. Upon the redresses of these wrongs and his subsequent release, he resumed his previous activities. Later, he was arrested by the Prefect Magistrate of Hangzhou and sent to a labor camp for reformation.[26]

Thirdly, many legal practitioners tarnished their reputations through their actions. Certain legal practitioners engaged in profoundly unethical conduct, exhibiting a range of professional misconduct including but not limited to disseminating false information, fabricating evidence, trafficking in stolen goods, tampering with crime

[24] The Great Qing Code, Volume 30, Instigating Actions.

[25] Dull Words from a Dull Petty Official by Liu Heng.

[26] May 25, 1897, Shanghai News, No. 8657, XihuYuchang.

scenes, instigating frivolous litigation, and colluding with local officials to extort civilians. Numerous other stories illustrated their misconduct. One legal practitioner infamously wrote a supposed complaint in "human blood," which was actually pig blood. In a case where a son knocked out his father's front teeth, a legal practitioner distorted the truth, falsely claiming that the father's teeth fell out because he bit his son's finger. In a suicide case, a legal practitioner changed the clothes of a corpse and strangulated the corpse many times to produce fake evidence of murder against an innocent person. When a father sued his unfilial and wicked son, a legal practitioner fabricated that it was because the father coveted his beautiful daughter-in-law. Such stories went viral among people. The pervasive misconduct of these profit-driven and ethically compromised individuals significantly eroded the public trust in the legal profession, ultimately provoking widespread societal condemnation.[27]

Fourthly, the orthodox scholars despised legal practitioners. Before the Tang and Song Dynasties, mainstream society still valued legal knowledge, and scholars proficient in law could ascend to higher societal ranks. Since the Ming and Qing Dynasties, the Chinese Imperial Examination focused on Confucian classics. During that period, all scholars devoted their lives to studying Confucian thoughts and hoped to succeed in the Chinese Imperial Examination while no one cared about law, which became the least popular course. Orthodox scholars believed that only those who failed the Chinese Imperial Examination and were deemed morally inferior would resort to working as low-end private advisors. Not only did they look down upon private advisors, but they also wrote fabricated plots in literary works to smear legal practitioners. In the works of orthodox scholars, almost all legal practitioners were typically portrayed as villainous characters meeting tragic fates.[28] Other scholars cursed legal practitioners by searching for bad stories.[29] There were many such stories, which were intended to demonize legal practitioners and warn people not to be legal practitioners and not to seek help from legal practitioners when they faced lawsuits.

In fact, except for some unethical legal practitioners, to some extent, many others earnestly endeavored to safeguard the rights and interests of their clients. And many legal practitioners pursued justice for their clients and disclosed the corruption in governments. Legal practitioners even had their own set of ethical guidelines. For example, in the Qing Dynasty, there was a tenet that legal practitioners should not engage in three kinds of cases: cases without justified reasons, murder cases, and cases filed by litigious people.[30] Under traditional laws, unrelated people were not

---

[27] Collected Anecdotes and Trifles of the Qing Dynasty, Volume 3, Lawsuits: Tricks of Legal practitioners, Zhonghua Book Company, 1984 Version, 1191–1995.

[28] Shen, Q. (1998). *Satirical Legal Parables* (chapter 5) Statement of Legal practitioners in Lawsuits, Shanxi People's Press. 96; Qian, Yong. Fuyuan Conghua: The Legal Scribes.

[29] Xu, K. (1984). Collected Anecdotes and Trifles of the Qing Dynasty. Volume 3. Lawsuits: Tricks of Legal practitioners. Zhonghua Book Company. 1192–1193.

[30] Xu, K.(1984) Collected Anecdotes and Trifles of the Qing Dynasty. Volume 3. Lawsuits: Three Kinds of Cases that Legal practitioners would not Engage in, Zhonghua Book Company. 1190.

allowed to represent plaintiffs in lawsuits. Hence, legal practitioners could not appear in court and were only allowed to advise their clients how to debate in court behind the scenes. Although this may be seen as instigating lawsuits, legal practitioners who provided legal enlightenment to people who knew nothing about laws were the basic group to popularize law.

7.1.4.3 The Transition from *Songshi* (Legal Practitioners) to Lawyers

Lawyers of modern China first appeared in courts of concessions in the late Qing Dynasty. In the early years of the Republic of China, organizations of lawyers emerged in developed Eastern China, such as Suzhou, Shanghai, and Hangzhou. They represented clients in court and registered as lawyers. For example, Wu Tingfang, the then Minister of Justice, once carried out the defense system in some specific trials. At the beginning of the Republic of China, in the case against Yao Rongze, Wu Tingfang debated with Chen Qimei, a Chinese revolutionary activist and a Commander of the Military in Shanghai, about whether the case should be settled by the judicial official or the military government. As a legal elite, Wu Tingfang stuck to laws and insisted the judicial independence. However, he paid a heavy price for this such as the deterioration of the relationship between revolutionary activists.[31] Wu Tingfang and other pioneers in the lawyer group set a good example for their successors. In March 1912, experts drafted the *Law on Lawyer* and submitted it to Yuan Shikai, the provisional president. Sun Yat-sen pointed out that "the lawyer system is closely interwoven with judicial independence and is widely used in other developed countries." He forwarded the draft to the Legislative Affairs Bureau for review, paving the way for the Senate to vote on it. Although the draft was not implemented, it was a good start for the form and implementation of the Law on Lawyers and the improvement of the lawyer system.

In the early stages of the Republic of China, the government began to issue Lawyer's licenses to qualified lawyers which meant Chinese lawyers were legally recognized. Since then, lawyers took part in political and social activities such as promoting human rights and striving for judicial sovereignty, where they showed their great presence and sense of responsibility. Compared with *Songshi* (legal practitioners), Chinese lawyers transitioned from operating in a quasilegal status to a fully legal professional since the late Qing Dynasty, with their previously undercover work becoming public. They not only made a living through their job but also bore the responsibility to protect human rights, promote democracy and the rule of law, strive for national independence, etc. Generally, the entire society came to respect lawyers, recognizing their crucial role in the transition from a traditional society to a modern society.

[31] Shen, Y. (1976). *Collected Writings of Zhi Yong: Source Material on the History of Modern China*. Vol. 66. Taiwan Wenhai Press. (I) 50–69, (II) 68–80.

7.2 Judicial Principles

The question of whether the judiciary in traditional China made judgments based on rationality or evidence warrants a separate discussion. From the perspective of formal rationality, judicial standards were characterized by objectivity and determinacy. The codes of traditional China, especially the penal law codes, were unique in the global legal frameworks. They were complete, systematic, and successive, showing the seriousness and objectiveness of laws. It can be seen from the *Canon of Laws*, *Qin Code*, *Han Code*, *Cao and Wei Code*, *Jin Code*, *North Qi Code*, *Tang Code*, *Great Ming Code*, *Great Qing Code*, etc. that the penal law of traditional Chinas gradually became more and more formal and systematic after inheritance and development. It was hard to define a unified judicial principle of traditional China in the specific judicial process due the diversity of time, space, conditions of cases, levels of the trial, temperaments of judges, etc. However, it is definite that the balance between heavenly principles, human emotions, and national laws is of the highest ideal of judicial practice, which could be regarded as the kingly way principle of jurisprudence. The unification of rationality and experience is the basic principle of the judiciary in traditional China. In details, these principles include ruling by law, abiding by procedures, justice by experience, examination of evidence, and practices in different seasons and times. All of them will be elaborated in the following sections, and Chap. 6 can be referred to for more information on "Priority of Mediation."

7.2.1 Ruling by Law

Both in China and abroad, fulfilling equity and justice is the ultimate goal of the judiciary. In the West, there was a statue of "Lady Justice" representing fairness and justice, with a balance in her left hand and a sword in her right hand. Nevertheless, she was blindfolded, with the standard of justice in her heart, she discerned evil from good, punished the cruel, and protected the innocent. Coincidentally, in traditional China, there was a Minister of Law, named Gao Yao under the administration of Emperor Shun. According to legend, he was the creator of Chinese law and the first "Chief Justice" in China. In rendering judicial decisions, his celestial Xiezhi (獬豸), a legendary creature symbolizing juridical discernment would instinctively strike the guilty party. This imagery is embedded in the archaic Chinese character for law "灋" ("法"), where the Xiezhi radical (廌) explicitly embodies the concept of an ordeal. The text Huainanzi: Craft of the Ruler by Liu An recorded that "although Gao Yao could not speak, he was rational and never abused punishment," and "he looked like a peeled melon."[32] Despite his unsightly appearance and muteness, distinct from "Lady Justice," both of them could uphold justice and eliminate

[32] Xunzi: Contra Physiognomy.

disputes according to the standard in their hearts. There was another legend about Gao Yao that he created the first prison by drawing on earth. Gao Yao could be regarded as a representative of judges in traditional China. As time went on, he gradually became the symbol of the judiciary of traditional China. He was respected as the God of judiciary and Prison so that judges, bailiffs, and prisoners needed to worship him regularly.[33]

Since the formation of written law, the principle of judgment according to law kept developing, becoming a universal value. This principle of traditional China was at the forefront of the global judicial culture. Many codes set strict requirements on judges' judicial behavior. The principle of judgment according to laws was the priority, which required judges to make judgments according to statutes, ordinances, regulations, specifications, precedents, etc. In ancient China, it was stipulated in the *Book of Documents* that in the process of making judgments,[34] the situation of cases must be investigated thoroughly, the judgment must comply with the penal law of traditional China, and the whole process must be under strict supervision. There was a similar provision in the *Tang Code*, "All sentences of crimes must cite a formal provision of statutes, ordinances, regulations, specifications. Any offender shall be punished by thirty flogging." In all cases, if an imperial decree or imperial edict for sentencing was only a makeshift but not a formal regulation, it may not be cited analogically later. If it was improperly cited and caused the punishment to be decreased or increased, a penalty would be imposed on the official.[35]

Any increase or decrease in conviction rates was strictly prohibited. For example, it was stipulated in the *Tang Code* that if officials deliberately made wrong judgments such as returning an acquittal to the guilty, sentencing innocent people, convicting people who commit a misdemeanor of a felony, and convicting people who commit a felony of a misdemeanor, by intentionally adding to or subtracting from the circumstances sufficiently to change the punishment, by sentencing prisoners after hearing that there will be an amnesty, or by hinting the prisoner to make false testimony, they shall be punished.[36] There were similar regulations in the Qing Dynasty. Whenever an official intentionally decreased or increased a person's penalty, whether it was a complete acquittal or a complete conviction, sentence on the basis of the whole penalty. If an official intensified a light punishment or lessened a severe one, they were to be sentenced based on the extent of the increase or decrease. If such alterations led to a death sentence, the punishment would be based on the death penalty. If a penalty was mistakenly increased, the penalty for intentional increase should be reduced by three degrees in each case. If there was a mistaken decrease, in each case, the penalty was reduced intentionally by five degrees. The

[33] Book of the Later Han: Biography of Fan Pang, Book of Documents ·Book of Punishments by Lü.

[34] Tang Code: Judgment and Prison, Article "Citation of the Code, the Statutes, the Regulations, and the Ordinances in Sentencing."

[35] Tang Code: Judgment and Prison, Article "Sentencing in Accord with an Imperial Decree or Imperial Edict."

[36] Tang Code: Judgment and Prison, Article "An Official Who Decreases or Increases a Person's Punishment."

penalty for chief officers should be reduced by one degree compared to clerks and similarly for assistant officials. If a prisoner was not allowed to be released but was released and was apprehended again, in each case, the penalty was reduced by one degree.[37]

Owing to the strict requirement for judgment according to law, many judges consciously complied with laws. Zhang Shizhi of the Han Dynasty became historically renowned for his adherence to legal judgment. According to the historical record, Zhang Shizhi was nominated as a "Chief Justice" (Chamberlain for Law Enforcement) by Emperor Wen of Han. Later, as Emperor Wen of Han was passing the Zhong Wei Bridge, a person unexpectedly emerged from under the bridge, startling the emperor's escort. The emperor commanded cavalries to catch him and ordered Zhang Shizhi to adjudicate the case. The person confessed that he was a newcomer to Chang'an City, and when he heard that the escort of the emperor would pass by and no one was permitted to go through the bridge, he had to hide underneath it. After waiting for a long time, he believed the emperor's carriage had passed. But as he crept out, the carriage was approaching, forcing him to flee. Zhang Shizhi submitted a judgment to the emperor and said, "The person should be fined for passing in a restricted zone." Emperor Wen of Han swore, "He startled my horse. Luckily, it was docile. If it was hot-tempered, the carriage would run out of control and I would be hurt. How could you just impose a fine on him?" Zhang Shizhi answered, "Laws are binding for both emperor and normal people and should not tilt to anyone. If punishments are arbitrarily increased, public trust in the law will diminish. Your Majesty, it would have been easy to impose a harsher punishment initially. But now the case is in the charge of the Chamberlain for Law Enforcement, who is the model of justice. If the Chamberlain for Law Enforcement makes any mistake, all law executors would increase or decrease punishment randomly. Then how would the common people react? I hope you think twice, your Majesty." After a long period, Emperor Wen of Han admitted, "Your judgment is right." There was another similar case where a person was caught stealing a sacrifice, a jade ring, from the royal ancestral temple. Emperor Wen of Han huffed, "It's too outrageous! He even dared to steal the late emperor's sacrifice! He deserves death! I entrusted this case to you, expecting you to sentence his entire family. But you treated the case as a misdemeanor, which deviated from my ordinary intention to worship ancestors." Zhang Shizhi took off his cap and kowtowed to the emperor to make an apology, "According to law, such punishment is the strictest. If anyone committed the same crime, he should be judged on the basis of the severity of crime. If someone's entire family were exterminated just because one person stole a sacrifice in the royal ancestral temple. Then if an innocent individual digs earth on Changling Mausoleum, the tomb of Emperor Gaozu, how would you punish him, your Majesty?" The

[37] The Great Qing Code: Judgments and Prisoners, Article "An Official Who Decreases or Increases Penalties."

Emperor Wen of Han shared the story with Empress Dowager and she also stood by Zhang Shizhi. Hence the Emperor approved the judgment of Zhang Shizhi.[38]

Hundreds of years later, judges still cited the judgments made by Zhang Shizhi who stuck to rule of law. For example, under the rule of Emperor An of Eastern Jin, Liu Yi, a general, was shot by an arrow when he went out. The arrow was from Chen Man, an official at Junling County, who was meant to hunt birds. Although the general was not seriously wounded, Chen Man was executed in public. He Chengtian advised, "Judgment should be made according to the truth. If there is any doubt, the suspect shall be acquitted. In the past, someone startled the carriage of Emperor Wen of Han, however, Zhang Shizhi only fined him for a misdemeanor. Why? Since he did not intend to hurt anyone, his punishment should not be increased. At present, Chen Man was meant to hunt birds instead of hurting anyone. In accordance with laws, one should be sentenced to three years in prison, if he injured other people for negligence, let alone the fact that the person was not physically hurt."[39] All cases above are models of rule of law.

Apart from the central government, Emperor Wen of Han also paid attention to the nomination of local officials. Hence, many upright and honest officials, later lauded in historical accounts, distinguished themselves among their peers. For example, Liu Xingben was a county magistrate in Daxing County who was so incorruptible and impartial that no magnate or dignitary dared to bribe him. On account of his clear and strict administration, both officials and subjects missed him.[40] Local officials taking the lead to work without corruption was also the basic guarantee to improve judicial efficiency and reduce lawsuits.

In ancient Greece, there was the story of Socrates sacrificing himself to uphold the authority of law, although some argued the law in question was unjust. For thousands of years, numerous legal professionals were touched by this story. In Chinese history, there was a similar story. Li Li sacrificed himself to safeguard the credibility of judiciary after he made a wrong judgment and killed someone by mistake. As a judge of Duke Wen of Jin, he imprisoned himself and sentenced himself to death for the purpose of safeguarding the credibility of laws after he realized that he made a wrong judgment and killed an innocent person. Duke Wen of Jin said, "That is the fault of your subordinate, instead of yours." Li Li replied, "Although I am a leader, I didn't share my superiority with my subordinates. Although I earned more salary, I never shared any benefit with my subordinates. How could I shrug off my responsibility to them, when I found an innocent person was killed for my wrong judgment?" He refused the pardon from Duke Wen of Jin. Duke Wen of Jin said, "You think you are guilty. Am I guilty too?" Li Li said, "It is specified that if a judge makes a wrong judgment, he should be punished and if he kills an innocent person, he should pay with his life. You appointed me as a judge because you believe I am prudent and capable of deciding hard cases. Now, as I made a wrong judgment and

[38] Book of Han: Biography of Zhang Shizhi.

[39] Comprehensive Statutes: Notes I, Volume 160.

[40] History of Sui, Volume 25, Treatise, No. 20, Penal Law.

killed an innocent person, I should be sentenced to death." Li Li refused the amnesty order from Duke Wen of Jin and committed suicide by slitting his throat with his sword. Later generations usually praised judges who tried cases according to law for they were upright, impartial, and not afraid of power. A lot of them became model judges.

7.2.2 Abiding by the Procedures

There were strict requirements in the judicial process of traditional China. From evidence collection to retrial and reexamination, from the form of judicial records to the standard of punishment shall follow a set of regulations. If relevant regulations were violated, judges needed to pay the corresponding penalty.

The traditional Chinese adjudication hierarchy comprised five graduated sanctions: beating with the light stick, beating with the heavy stick, penal servitude, exile, and capital punishment. The final adjudicative authority of the five sanctions was stipulated by relevant law in details based on the severity of the cases. For example, in the Ming and Qing Dynasties, Prefects and County Magistrates had the authority to make final decisions in cases where the defendants would be beaten with the light stick or the heavy stick. Prefectures and Provinces Magistrates had the authority to make final decisions in cases in which the defendants would be punished with penal servitude or exile. And if the defendants in cases were sentenced to death penalty, the Ministry of Justice would participate in joint adjudication for those capital cases first and then submit them to emperors for review. Due process within the traditional judiciary was especially evident in the trial procedures for criminal cases, particularly those involving death penalty. From the judgments of different dynasties, it is not difficult to find out how precise relevant judicial procedure could be. To illustrate this, let us examine how criminals sentenced to the death penalty were processed in the Qing Dynasty, based on a copy of a routine memorial specifying the trial procedure for a death penalty case during the Jiaqing Period.

Source of the case: Local constables accompanied the relatives of the parties to the local magistrate's office to report the case. Except for criminal cases discovered by Prefects and County Magistrates in inspections, most criminal cases were reported to them by people in charge of villages, such as local constables, community liaison officers, security group heads, security heads, tithing heads, village heads, and so on.

The responsibility of Prefects and County Magistrates: Once Prefects and County Magistrates received reported cases, they must lead subordinate corpse examiners to crime scenes immediately. Subordinate corpse examiners carried out autopsies publicly in accordance with laws and completed autopsy reports. Normally subordinate corpse examiners needed to move corpses to open and bright space first. Then they would examine corpses publicly, report injuries of corpses in a loud voice, and fill in information about the injuries of corpses. All these processes were mandatory. The reports to higher officials included documents on autopsy, arrest and detention of murderers (in murder cases), inquest on the related person, oral confession of people involved in cases, and other witnesses and real evidence. Prefects and Magistrates would collect and file relevant documents and then submit them to judicial offices at the provincial level for final judgment.

Judicial authority at the provincial level: Homicide cases must go through preliminary trial and be sentenced in the provincial office except for special cases or in extraordinary periods. Judges at provincial judiciary were called the first provincial surveillance commission, whose job was to make preliminary judgments on the basis of files submitted by Prefects and County Magistrates. In accordance with the criminal code, death row prisoners were normally sentenced to "deferred strangulation" or "deferred decapitation." After preliminary trials, officials at the provincial level must make reports to Governor-generals and Provincial Governors, waiting for their permission. Then, Governor-generals and Provincial Governors needed to complete documentation and classification of the cases per Autumn Assizes procedures and then submitted them to the Grand Secretariat and Ministry of Justice by the Transmission Office on schedule. As for the death penalty cases within the jurisdiction of the capital tried by the Ministry of Justice, the Ministry of Justice needed to document them and submit them directly to the Grand Secretariat.

Joint adjudication of death penalties: The joint adjudication system was improved gradually after the Sui and Tang Dynasties. The joint adjudication by three ministries in the Tang Dynasty was a relatively normative collegial panel system. In the Ming and Qing Dynasties, the joint adjudication by the nine ministers gradually formed. The joint adjudication by the nine ministers was the largest collegial panel across the nation, which was composed of the nine chief officials at nine ministries—the Ministry of Personnel, the Ministry of Revenue, the Ministry of Rites, the Ministry of War, the Ministry of Justice, the Ministry of Works, the Court of Judicial Review, the Censorate, and the Office of Transmission and other chief officers of their departments. The collegiate panel conducted centralized case adjudication during two statutory judicial seasons around the solar terms of Beginning of Autumn and Frost Descent, as codified in the Qing Code's judicial calendar. There were four types of judgment: confirmed execution, deferred retrial, commiserable mitigation, and filial piety-based sentence suspension.

Tick to confirm execution in red ink by emperors: The joint adjudication by the nine ministers was not the final step for judgment. The decision of the collegial panel must be checked by the three judicial ministries (Ministry of Justice, Court of Judicial Review, Censorate) and other offices, and then it would be submitted to the emperors for the final decision. In the final review, emperors would make marks by criminals' names with brushes dipped in vermillion to show that these criminals should be executed. If criminals' names were not marked, their sentences would be suspended. If criminals were excusable or had the aged to care for, they would not be sentenced to the death penalty. After emperors made the final reviews, the Grand Secretariat would pass the documents to the Supervising Censors of Law who would transcribe the documents to the lower governments for execution. Offenders in the capital shall be executed at a market gate, while offenders outside would be executed by local officials when orders from the central government were delivered.

In a case, Emperor Jiaqing annotated in red ink at the final review, "Despite the previous sentence of decapitation, Qiu Sangou shall be put on reprieve and he shall be executed at autumn."[41]

Till then, the trial of a murder case came to an end. All judicial processes must strictly comply with legal procedures. For example, every detail of the judicial records submitted by the local governments must be precisely and correctly recorded. The title, cause, process, and result of the case should be accurate. The judgments that they drew up shall be exact and definite. For example, the scars in the cases which were classified as "killing during a fight" included wounds caused by chopping, pinning, stabbing, beating, strangulating, kneeling, kicking, treading, biting, snagging, smashing, falling over, scalding and so on. The cases of fornication were categorized as "fornication with consent, fornication with seduction, fornication with force, fornication brought about by trick, sodomy, fornication with a young girl of twelve or below, group rape, facilitating and tolerating the wife or concubine engaging in fornication with another, fornication with a pregnant woman, fornication between relatives, falsely accusing the father-in-law of fornication, a slave or hired servant who engaged in fornication with the wife of the household head, fornication with a wife or daughter of someone in the area to which one is posted, those who were in mourning, or Buddhist or Taoist priests who fornicated, persons of honorable and base condition who fornicated with each other, an official or clerk who slept with a prostitute, to buy a person of honorable condition as a prostitute, and so on."[42] These details must be recorded accurately because they determined the final sentences. Therefore, from the autopsy to the following judicial activities, every step must follow rational, precise, standard procedures; otherwise, the related officials would be punished in accordance with statutes and ordinances. The official anthology of precedents, *Quintessential Judgments, Enlightened Judgments of Famous Judges*; the routine memorials of criminal cases, *Compilation of Criminal Cases* and *Newly Compiled Collection of Re-judged Cases*; or the official document, *Notices of Autumn Execution*, all embody the character of the rational judiciary.

Other penal judicial procedures were clearly stipulated. For example, in order to obtain an oral confession, torture could be used. But the tools, objects, and extent of torture were clearly regulated by the penal codes of all dynasties to prevent illegal abuse of torture. In this way, major criminal cases were handled in line with the principles of objectivity, justice, and rationality.

[41] Du, J. (2008). *Selected Compilation of Historical Materials about Society in the Routine Memorials to the Ministry of Justice during the Jiaqing Reign, Qing Dynasty*. Vol. 1. Tianjin Ancient Book Press. 74–75.

[42] Shen, J. Notices of Autumn Execution: Titles of Documents.

7.2.3 *Justice by Experience*

There is a basic requirement for judgments in Chinese judicial circles, "Take facts as the basis and laws as the criteria." Some scholars think the concept of "facts" is too general and there are substantial divergences of opinions on finding facts. The so-called facts may not be the facts recognized by law or the "facts" with judicial credibility. Hence the sentence should be changed to "Take legal facts as the basis and laws as the criteria."

Criminal cases, in which the convicts would be sentenced to being beaten with light or heavy sticks, and civil cases that happened outside the capital, were heard by Prefects and County Magistrates whose decisions were final. Although some of these cases were judged in accordance with the law, most of these cases were judged on the basis of judicial experiences. The character of litigation via patriarchal instruction was extremely obvious in trials of local government. Such descriptions normally appeared in case reports of Prefects and County Magistrates and unofficial history. This kind of judicial experience was mainly about the process of obtaining evidence rather than trials.

In several Chinese dynasties, trial and judgment functions were separated. A notable example is the Song Dynasty's "separation of Ju and Yan" (鞫讞分司), where fact-finding and application of law were two distinct processes, similar to the common law system, in which juries determine facts while judges apply the law. However, in most dynasties, lower-level judicial officials acted as generalists, handling investigations, case filings, verdicts, and even sentence executions. Their duties combined the functions of modern police, prosecutors, and courts; yet unlike today's collaborative case-handling system, they operated without clear division of labor.

In traditional China, good judicial officials, especially judicial officials at the basic level, who went down in history and earned a reputation, were not appraised for they could judge according to law, apply the law correctly, or explain the law appropriately but for he was skilled at collecting evidence and accurately and promptly identifying the guilty. As long as he caught the offender in time and got evidence like witnesses, physical evidence, confession, and so on, the case could be resolved at any time. From this perspective, if someone wanted to be a good judicial official, he must be a good detector first, to whom the experience was paramount.

In ancient times, sovereigns tended to claim divine selection, just as the *Book of Documents* recorded, "the Xia Dynasty and Yin Dynasty enjoyed the favoring decree of Heaven."[43] They also asserted that their legislation and judiciary came from Heaven's will, which was legal and orthodox. These laid the foundation for the trend toward mysticism in the law of ancient China. Such mysticism was also embodied in the method of trial, determining the irrational inclination of trial in ancient China. In other words, without strict procedures of litigation, trials in ancient China mainly depended on judges' subjective opinions. Most of such judgments

[43] Book of Documents: Zhao Gao.

were based on the perception of facts; therefore, each judge was different in the identification of the truth and falsehood of the case and the degree of influence of the facts. How could such trials be credible to normal people? Hence, mysticism was born at the right moment. In order to make most people trust their judgments, sovereigns needed to find some convincing explanation to support their judgments which resulted in the emergence of "Bing Chuan," a mythical animal. This creature, believed to possess the ability to discern right from wrong, became a symbol of justice, fairness, and truth. And judges claimed to be representatives of such a mythical animal, asserting that it guided them to make fair judgments. Apart from *Bing Chuan*, other mythical stories such as "judgments made by mythical animals" and "the Heaven sent Swallow down to give birth to the sire of *Shang*" echoed the mysticism. This phenomenon in the development of Chinese law somewhat paralleled certain aspects of the development of Western jurisprudence.

The ancient Western world also witnessed mysticism in judiciary, such as ordeal by water, ordeal by fire, and ordeal by ingestion. Throughout history, both in the East and the West, mysticism has been a persistent theme, never completely fading away. Although the trial by the mythical animals in legend was superstitious, it represented a technique employed by astute judges who leveraged people's devout worship of deities to identify criminals. Judgments of God were common in records of later generations, particularly in unofficial records. "A thief found by a bell" was one of these stories. In this story, Chen Shugu was in charge of Pu City, Jian Prefecture, where a rich household filed a lawsuit to the government for they lost some belongings. Despite apprehending several suspects, the true thief could not be identified. Chen Shugu tricked the suspects into believing that a bell in an old temple possessed magical properties that could identify the true thief. Later, Chen Shugu sent people to fetch the bell and enshrined it in a cabinet. And then he led the suspects to stand facing the bell and told them, "The bell will only ring if touched by a thief." Chen Shugu solemnly guided the suspects to pray to the bell. Afterward, he enclosed the bell within curtains and covertly ordered it to be coated with ink. After a long time, these suspects were ordered to touch the bell. After inspection, Chen Shugu found that all suspects' hands were ink-stained, except one man. The man with clean hands should be the real thief, who did not dare to touch the bell because he worried it would ring. After interrogation, he conceded.[44] The main issue of this case was the evidence law system. Although this method was unscientific and incredible, it demonstrated how judges in ancient China utilized suspects' fear of divine judgment to collect evidence and make judicial decisions.

The case, "Injustice Told by a Raven to Wei Daoheng," in the ancient casebook—*Detailed Reports on Complicated Legal Cases*—recorded a similar story. When Wei Daoheng, the chief official of the Ministry of Justice, visited Huguang for amnesty on behalf of the central government, he had a dream about a rabbit wearing a cap, which he interpreted as a sign of an unresolved injustice. With the guidance of a raven in the on-site inspection, he found a victim's corpse, and then he ascertained

[44] Shen, K. Dream Pool Essays, Volume 13.

the homicide case and rehabilitated the innocent.[45] There was another widespread story. At a late night, Yan Zhi's father was murdered. Shi Shilun, an official, fabricated that God would leave a mark on the murderer's back. He commanded five suspects, dressed in trousers only, to stay in a dim room, lining up beside a wall. When the room turned bright, the guy with the black mark on his back was the most suspicious. After interrogation, the speculation was confirmed. It turned out that as Shi Shilun coated the wall with ash in advance, the murderer got stained with ash because he worried about the touch from God and leaned against the wall. Meanwhile, innocent people were confident enough to just stand still and remained untainted.

It was unimportant whether the case was judged by Shi Shilun or not. The significant aspect is that the prevalence of such stories in various records and among folklore suggests the existence of a group of legal experts adept in detection and skilled at inferring offenders' intentions and logically deducing case details. The *Kun* opera "Fifteen Strings of Cash Coins," adapted from a folk story, narrated a murder-for-profit case. During an incognito visit, Kuang Zhong, the magistrate of Suzhou Prefecture, found Lou Ashu weird. Disguising as a fortune teller, he took refuge in a temple at night where he tricked Lou by claiming that a deity had appeared in his dream, thereby coaxing a confession from Lou. At last, he arrested Lou, tried him, and exonerated Xiong Youlan and Su Rongjuan who were convicted of murderers in error by a magistrate. Finally, the truth was revealed and the innocent people were vindicated. The case was resolved through Zhong's wisdom and diligence, not divine intervention. Based on rational inspections, he caught the real murderer in the name of God. Without thorough scrutiny, many injustices that appeared to be supported by irrefutable evidence would have remained uncorrected.

Commonly, as long as people had a basic knowledge of modern science and technology, they would not believe that gods, ghosts, or beasts could make judgments. However, in eras characterized by lower levels of civilization, widespread illiteracy, undeveloped technology, and the absence of modern media, some unconventional detective methods could yield unexpected results. Ji Yun, a scholar in the Qing Dynasty, thoroughly analyzed the essence of such detection and judgment. He believed that the truth of cases could be discovered through careful research and analysis, but it was unreliable to blindly rely on dreams and guesses because invoking gods and dreams were just methods to intimidate the gullible into confession.[46] As a scholar with extraordinary intelligence, Ji Yun would not be bewitched by the fabricated myth. Nevertheless, it was common for uneducated villagers to be intimidated or to feel a guilty conscience under such circumstances.

For judicial officials at the first trial, superb detective ability was the precondition to becoming fair judges. As the superstitious methods to seek evidence were abolished, a set of skills and experience in detection and examination appeared in the judicial development of traditional China. As early as the Western Zhou Dynasty,

---

[45] Detailed Reports on Complicated Legal Cases: The Injustice Told by A Raven to Wei Daoheng.

[46] Ji, Yun. Notes of Yuewei Caotang. Volume 4. Notes Made During Retreat at Liyang. IV.

there was a 五听 *Wutin* (five-observation) system: observation of the "verbal consistency,", "respiratory patterns," "facial microexpressions," "auditory responsiveness," and "eye movements" of suspects, respectively. Undoubtedly, it was a great breakthrough in traditional judicial psychology. Even to this day, the five types of observation are still useful when police officers investigate cases and interrogate suspects. Therefore, the "five-observation" method has not been outdated.

7.2.4 Examination of Evidences

Since the birth of *Collected Cases of Injustice Rectified*, a book written by Song Ci in the Song Dynasty, traditional forensic science reached a historic height. During the Yuan, Ming, and Qing Dynasties, this book was not only collated and annotated but also was applied in practice continuously, becoming the standard of forensic tests. The catalog of this book is listed below.

Book I: Regulations, General remarks on inquests (Part one and Part two), Difficult and complicated diseases (Part one)

Book II: Difficult and complicated diseases (Part two), The first inquest, Further inquest, Examination of corpses, Examination of female corpses, Examination of kids and fetus, Decomposition of bodies at different seasons, Washing and preparing the body, Examination of a corpse which has not been buried, Examination after temporary burial, Examination of decomposed corpses, Examination without corpses, Sudden death

Book III: Examination of bones, On the bones and veins of the human body, Suicide by strangulation, Strangulation with violence passed off as suicide, Death from drowning

Book IV: Wounds inflicted by the hand, foot, and weapons generally, Suicide with weapons, Wounds inflicted by wooden or mental weapons, stones, etc., Dismemberment, Cauterization, Death from scalding, Accidental poisoning, Diseases, Death inflicted by acupuncture, Statement of the dying

Book V: Death during interrogation, Death from blows, Falling from a height, Crushed to death, Choking or gagging, Prodding, Trampling by a horse or cattle, Running over by a carriage, Being struck by lightning, Being bit by tigers, Wounds from snakes or insects, Death from drunkenness and repletion, Death during consensual sex, Bodies at the curb, bodies sent to the tomb, Checking the bodies in the neighboring counties, Prescription to avoid death, Prescription to save the dying, Checking the conditions of corpses

Later, such work was assumed by the forensic experts, *Wuzuo* (corpse examiners), empowered by law. They were required to arrive at the crime scene alongside Prefects and County Magistrates to conduct corpse examinations and uncover the truth. Whether the inquest was timely and correct was concerned with the accuracy of evidence. And the accuracy of evidence determined whether cases could be adjudicated fairly. Many Prefects and county magistrates had abundant experience in this, who not only read professional publications such as *Collected Cases of Injustice Rectified* but also summarized and recorded their experiences in judicial practices which later became popular "official admonitions." In the Qing Dynasty books like *An Unreliable Treatise*, written by Pan Yueshan, and the *Blessing Book*, written by Huang Liuhong, thoroughly recorded detective skills, which were popular among officials. The famous private advisor Wang Huizu gave instructions to chief officials in his *Views on Learning Governance* that in the investigation of homicide cases inspections must be taken seriously, which included "inspection on wounds of the living must be taken rashly; confessions of homicide cases should be obtained promptly; inspections should be made as soon as possible; subordinate corpse examiners should make inspections in person; inspections should be taken at the scene and follow the guidance of *Collected Cases of Injustice Rectified* which was the most persuasive; inspection should be detailed and prudent, etc." In another book, *Medicinal Words for Assisting Governance*, he also pointed out that "the decrease and increase of punishment of homicide cases depended on the situation of cases… In the examination, subordinate corpse examiners must verify whether the murders' confession was consistent with the crime scene. Only in this way, judgments could be irrefutable."[47]

Although subordinate corpse examiners were trivial in offices in feudal government offices, they were able to affect the progression of lawsuits. Their primary duty was to assist administrative chief officials and follow their orders, while forensic tests were their secondary responsibility. After all, only the judgment of local officials determined the outcomes of cases. Some officials made unfair judgments which resulted in wrong or false convictions, for they were inexperienced or did not take supervision seriously. In the famous case "*Yang Naiwu and Xiaobaicai*" in the late Qing Dynasty, Liu Xitong, a county official, was so credulous that he believed the false autopsy report that the husband of Xiao Baicai died from poison. Under severe torture, Yang Naiwu and Xiao Baicai were coerced into confessing to the false charge of conspiring to poison Xiao Baicai's husband. After many setbacks, the case was retried 3 years later, with the help of many people. The injustice was rectified when a more experienced subordinate corpse examiner reexamined the body and refuted the erroneous conclusion of death by poisoning. However, the case remained skeptical on the ground that the redress was made only on the basis of a report from the subordinate corpse examiners. There were some doubts such as whether the opinion of subordinate corpse examiners serving in the Criminal Department was more authoritative than that of the County subordinate corpse examiners, whether the result was accurate after the body had been buried in soil for 3 years, and whether the traditional forensic task was capable to find the chronic toxicity. Some judicial officials dissented that not all poisoning death could be discovered. For instance, deaths from gradual, long-term exposure to a slowly increasing dosage of poison could elude detection by traditional silver needle

[47] Wang, H. Medicinal Words for Assisting Governance: How to Examine Homicide Cases.

testing.[48] Another instance was the practice of using blood tests to identify relatives. The *Collected Cases of Injustice Rectified* recorded that two testers were kindred if their blood coagulated when they dripped two droplets of blood, respectively, in a bowl of water. In addition, there was a practice of dripping blood on a bone to identify relatives. In the test, a tester needed to drip one or two droplets of blood on a skeleton. If his blood could infiltrate into the bone, he was kin to the deceased. Otherwise, they were unrelated.[49] Such forensic tests were queried before. In the Qing Dynasty, Ji Yun once doubted that "Biography of Former Sages in Runan County" of the Han Dynasty recorded that Cheng Ye dropped blood on a bone to find his brother. However, an elder official once told me it was normal for relatives' blood to merge. But if the test happened in winter or the container is chilled on ice, or salt and vinegar were added to the water, even blood from relatives will not merge. Therefore, the test of dripping blood is unreliable.[50] Since the Han Dynasty, the practice of using blood tests to determine kinship has been recorded. It was only effective in normal situations for many limits on the test. The weather and the elements in a container would affect the result. Even in normal situations, there were many coincidences that could influence the accuracy of tests and absolute accuracy cannot be guaranteed. Therefore, the validity of these tests in light of modern anatomy and pharmacology merits further consideration.

Since the forming of the modern judicial system in the late Qing Dynasty, the judicial function gradually separated from the administrative function. As the trial and inquest became two different processes, detection and inquest became the duty of police and subordinate corpse examiners, and judges became more and more professional. In 1909, Shen Bingkun, the provincial administration commissioner of Yunnan Province, reported to the central government on the reformation of subordinate corpse examiners in Yunnan. In Yunnan Province, subordinate corpse examiners were renamed "Wushu," and academies of inquest were founded to train them. Upon graduation, the first batch of trainees received diplomas and returned to serve in their original offices. After the proposal of the Ministry of Justice was approved by the central government, the "Teaching and Learning Department of Inquest," an affiliate of the Academy of Inquest, was set up, and subordinate corpse examiners and "Wushu" were renamed "Official for Inquest." After the graduation of the second batch of learners, the academies of inquest ceased. After the establishment of the Department of Judgment, the "Teaching and Learning Department of Inquest" was set up to affiliate with it.[51] The insignificant "subordinate corpse examiners" in tradition were renamed the "Official for Inquest" which was a relatively decent job among judicial groups in modern times.

---

[48] Liu, T. Yicilu. Volume 2.

[49] Anonymity: The New Thundercracker, Volume 6, No Wrongs—Dripping Blood on the Bone to Identify Relatives, Valuable Judicial Documents of all Dynasties, Book 11, The Collection of Eight Secret Books on Legal Practitioners of the Ming and Qing Dynasties, Volume 1, Social Sciences Academic Press, 2012, 364.

[50] Ji, Yun. Notes of Yuewei Caotang. Volume 11. Huaixi Magzine. I.

[51] Political Record of Xuantong Era of the Great Qing Dynasty. Volume 24. 1909 (10). Article 54.

In the early Republic of China, with the introduction of Western medicine, new majors such as physiology, anatomy, and other new courses became a trend. On November 22, 1913, the Ministry for National Politics launched *Rules on Dissection*. In 1915, the traditional course on body examination was replaced[52] by the course on anatomy, physiology, forensic medicine, physics, math, criminal law, jurisprudence, criminal law, field experiment, histology, hygiene, inorganic chemistry, algebra, pathology, drug identification, dissection, forensic chemistry, psychiatry, bacteriology, geometry, foreign languages, etc.[53] Hence the corpse-examining course based on *Collected Cases of Injustice Rectified* became outdated. In 1925, in order to enhance local judiciary capability, the Adjudication Bureau and Procuratorate of Zhejiang Province delegated schools of medicine to establish a special course on forensics and cultivate forensic experts.[54] Henceforth, the Officials for Inquest transformed into "forensic doctors" who were specialists differentiated from judges and medical doctors. Forensic doctors' attitude to the corpse was contrary to clinicians. "The approach of forensic doctors to corpses contrasted with that of clinicians. Forensic doctors investigated the cause of death and clarified all aspects of the deceased. Despite living people may deceive, a silent corpse cannot. Through thorough examination and dissection, the corpse itself revealed the cause of death. Thus, the role of forensic doctors was to listen to the dead. Although they could not treat living patients, forensic doctors played a crucial role in upholding the rights of the deceased by attentively analyzing their remains."[55] Since then, the inquest function of traditional judicial officials was transferred to professional forensic doctors, which led to an ultimate change of the theme of judgment in accordance with experiences. As the judicial officials of traditional China enjoyed more experience in detection, examination, arrest, trial, and execution, the judiciary was fairer, and wrong or false cases could be avoided to a large extent.

However, avoiding false justice was never easy on the basis of modern anatomy, physiology, or pharmacology, let alone traditional corpse-examining skills. The advent of DNA technology marked a revolutionary leap in forensic science. The application of DNA technology proved that many innocent people who never committed felonies were punished wrongly, and a large number of cases cited invalid or inappropriate evidence.[56] Hence, in long-term legal history, the

---

[52] The Ministry of Justice orders the Fengtian High Supervision Department to Transform Higher Forensic Hospital for Cultivating Examination Talents. Compilation of Government Report. 1915(15). 110.

[53] Statute of the Fengtian Higher Forensic Doctor Institution. Compilation of Government Report. 1915(15). 140–144.

[54] Zhejiang Province Appeal to Set Up a Special Course on Forensics. Law Review. 1925. No. 87. Page 9.

[55] You do not yet know about the living, how can you know about the dead?—Stories on Forensic Doctors by Masahiko Ueno, translated by Wang Wenting, the Peking University Press, 2014, Page 9.

[56] False Justice: Eight Myths that Convict the Innocent by Jim Petro, Nancy Petro, translated by Yuan Ningning, etc., the Peking University Press, 2012, "Preface," 1.

judicial officials with the special status of traditional China paid high attention to the examination of evidence and heard cases with prudence, showing their judicial professionalism.

7.2.5 Practices in Different Seasons and Times

7.2.5.1 Seasonal Litigation

As agriculture was the priority of traditional China, the self-reliant natural economy was its major economic form. The agricultural output influenced both the basic living needs of common people and the national taxation. And the living standard of people determined the long-term stability of policy and domination. During the peace period, almost all activities of China were agriculture-centered. Consequently, agricultural practices also exerted a significant influence on policies and the judiciary. Most of the Chinese territory was seated in a temperature zone, characterized by sowing seeds in spring, growing crops in summer, and harvesting in fall. The agricultural activities during this period were crucial in determining the annual yield. While once there were trials or penalty executions, people needed to detain suspects and summon witnesses, which not only wasted rural labor but also distracted officials from the management of agricultural affairs, damaging agricultural productivity. On the ground that agricultural activities in autumn and winter were relatively slack, the penalty execution in fall and winter was less burdensome to rural labor and less harmful to agricultural productivity. All in all, under such circumstances, the execution in fall and winter met the needs of agricultural activities during busy farming seasons.

When dealing with lawsuits, governments also considered whether such activities would damage agricultural productivity and save labor force or not. For instance, the execution of death penalties was scheduled to avoid conflicting with the natural order, such as the 24 solar terms in traditional China, which guided agricultural activities. In this case, it was stipulated in the Tang Dynasty that it was not allowed to report emperors about carrying out executions on days of great sacrifices; on days of abstinence; on the 1st and 15th days of each lunar month, during the 1st quarter of the month; on the 24 annual "solar terms"; on days when the rain had not yet cleared, when the nights were not yet bright, during the months and on the days when it was prohibited to butcher animals; and on rest days.[57] Apart from this, when officials accepted cases or made judgments, they should consider the farming calendar. In the Tang and Song Dynasties, the *Wuxian Provision*, a provision on trial emerged, which suspended civil lawsuits during the busy farming seasons to ensure production. *Wu* referred to agricultural activities. *Xian* referred to the period of restriction. More specifically, the period between the 1st day of the 2nd month of the Chinese lunar calendar and the 30th day of the 9th month of the Chinese lunar

[57] Old History of the Tang Dynasty. Volume 50. Treatise No. 30. Penal Law.

calendar was called the "beginning of *Wu*." During this period, civil lawsuits on houses, debts, and rents were suspended. After the 1st day of the 10th month of the Chinese lunar calendar, officials were allowed to settle these civil lawsuits, which was called the "end of *Wu*." Under the ruling of Emperor Kangxi, there was a statute on suspending lawsuits during the busy farming season. It was stipulated on the ground that the farming calendar was between the 1st day of the 4th month of the Chinese lunar calendar and the 30th day of the 7th month of the Chinese lunar calendar; during that period, all civil lawsuits on house, marriage, and land were suspended, except felonies such as treason, robbery, murder, corruption, and felonies with concrete evidence. This meant that only in the slack season civil lawsuits on house, marriage, and land could be settled.[58] The available time for civil cases per month was 6–9 days. After eliminating other vocations, the total time for civil cases was only around 40–50 days a year. Besides, accepting civil lawsuits within the 4 months of the farming calendar became a misdeed of officials. Obviously, this statute was set to conform to the seasons. By relieving people's burden of lawsuits in the farming calendar, they could concentrate on farming production.

The statute of suspending lawsuits during the busy farming seasons covered civil cases on houses, marriages, and lands and minor criminal cases, except major criminal cases. In traditional China, there were many restrictions on the time to file lawsuits. The appearance of the statute on suspending lawsuits in busy farming seasons reflected the application of the ruling classes' policy of focusing on agriculture and respecting the natural seasons and showed the influence of traditional ethics and morality.

Normally, the time limits of cases in the central governments were determined by emperors. For example, at the beginning of the Song Dynasty, the time limits of trials were written in the imperial instructions, in which cases were classified into major, medium, small, and minimal levels in accordance with the severity of crimes. The time limits, more specifically, were "40 days for major cases, 20 days for medium cases, 10 days for small cases, and no more than 3 days for minimal cases. If there was any delay, officials should explain why they went beyond the time limit." If cases were over 40 days overdue, they would be submitted to higher officials for judgment. The Court of Judicial Review also set time limits for trials, "major cases must be settled within 25 days, medium ones within 20 days, and small cases within 10 days." In addition, there were time limits for judicial review for the Supreme Court of Judicial Review. "Major cases were limited within 5 days, medium ones were limited within 10 days, and small ones were limited within 5 days." Such time limits were similar to deadlines in modern criminal procedure law, and the time limits of the past were even shorter. However, the classification standards among major, medium, and small cases were unclear. Until the Yuanyou Era of the Emperor Zhezong of Song, the Ministry of Justice and the Court of Judicial Review made relevant regulations on distinctions between major, medium, and

[58] Wu, T. Notes of The Great Qing Code. Volume 30. Criminal Lawsuits. Attachments of Article "Inadmissible Cases."

small cases. "In trials, the sum involved in the major cases was more than 20,000 *wen* (copper coins). The sum involved in the medium case was between 10,000 and 20,000 *wen*. The sum involved in the small cases was less than 10,000 *wen*." At the same time, the time limit of trials was specified with more details. The time limits for major cases, medium cases, and small cases were 12 days, 9 days, and 4 days, respectively. In the inner capital city and eight districts of the outer capital city, major cases, medium cases, and small cases must be settled within 30 days, 15 days, and 3 days, respectively. The time limit of impeachment for the Ministry of Surveillance and the Ministry of Justice was 10 days, and the deadline for the Three Departments and the Bureau of Military Affairs was reduced to 5 days, respectively. The time limit could be extended by 5 days at most if there were any accidents. For difficult cases handled by governments, major cases shall be solved within 35 days, medium cases within 25 days, and small cases within 10 days. For cases that happened in the inner capital city and eight districts of the outer capital city, time limits for major cases, medium cases, and small cases were 30, 15, and 10 days. The total time limit of impeachment for the Ministry of surveillance and the Ministry of Justice was 30 days. Within every 10 days, 7 days were allocated for making judgments and 3 days for case discussions.[59] The regulation on the time limit was set up by authorities on the basis of the relationship between people's livelihood, details of cases, and the judiciary.

Local officials could determine when to "accept complaints" in accordance with their local situations. For example, some officials prescribed that cases could be accepted on days related to three and eight; some tried cases on days related to three, six, and nine; and others chose days related to five and ten to try cases. But no one tries cases on days related to four and seven, because these days were deemed inauspicious. Such complaints were normal cases. Major cases such as robbery and murder should be handled without any delay, which did not need follow the date of "accepting complaints."[60] Besides, punishment should not be carried out on holidays arranged by countries and on days around great ceremonies. For example, it was stipulated in the Qing Dynasty that both criminal and civil cases should not be accepted on happy festivals in the 1st, 6th, or 10th months and on 7 days around the Chinese New Year; 3 days around the Lantern Festival, 1 day on the Dragon Boat Festival, Mid-Autumn Festival, and Double Ninth Festival; 7 days around the Birth Day of Emperor; days of great sacrifices and abstinence; the 8th day of the 4th month of the lunar calendar[61]; the 1st and 2nd day of every month; and so on. In the 1st month, the 6th month, and on 10 days before the winter solstice, all criminals who had been sentenced to immediate execution and felons who had been sentenced to death in autumn assizes and court assizes would not be executed.

[59] Tuotuo. History of Song. Volume 199. Treatises 152. Penal Law. No. 1.

[60] Bo, H. (2003). Six Abusements of the Judiciary in Prefectures and Counties in the Ming and Qing Dynasties. Research of the History of the Qing Dynasty. (1).

[61] Laws and Precedents of the Great Qing. Volume 37. Judgments and Prisoners. Await the Reply to a Petition to the Emperor in the Case of those Condemned to Death.

Officials made inquisition by torture, but there were many regulations on when officials could use torture. In the Ming Dynasty, trial by torture was forbidden between the Start of Spring and the Autumnal Equinox. Besides, on specific days of each month, such as the 1st, 8th, 14th, 15th, 18th, 23rd, 24th, 28th, 29th, and 30th day, 10 days in total, no torture should be used. Any official who made inquisition by torture in such months or dates shall be investigated and impeached.[62]

Although the central government did not set a unified standard on when would trial by torture be prohibited, most diligent and upright officials could restrain themselves and enact punishment rules that were suitable to their jurisdictions. Such officials would become law-abiding and competent. Apart from some specific dates, many officials also made rules by themselves. "No torture shall be used on the anniversary of the Birth of Emperor, the anniversary of the Death of Emperor or Queen, the New Year's Day, and the 1st and the 15th day of each lunar month. If there was a gale, snowstorm, rainstorm, or thunderstorm, no torture shall be used. If a person needed to scoot, he shall not be tortured. If a person was furious, or drunken, he shall not be tortured. If the fact was unclear, the suspects shall not be tortured. If a person was fettered, he should not be tortured. If a person went through a period of mourning, he shall not be tortured. Pregnant women, the old, the disabled, and kids shall not be tortured. If a person was about to go on a long journey, he shall not be tortured."[63] Different officials had different standards. As such standards were not compulsory, officials abided by them at will. But it was undoubted that seasonal litigation and auspicious timing constituted an undisputed judicial consensus among the officials.[64]

7.2.5.2 Execution in Autumn and Winter

The belief that "man should live in harmony with heaven," "follow the course of heaven," and *Yin-yang* and Five Elements theory were widespread in traditional China. Humans respected and even worshipped "heaven." When people faced a setback or impasse, they usually exclaimed "Oh, my Heaven!" or "Heaven!," while Western people tended to burst out "Jesus!" or "Oh, my God." When coping with social affairs, Chinese people were accustomed to correlating them with natural phenomena and arranging social affairs in accordance with natural order. The same went for the judiciary. Punishments were correlated with natural phenomena and seasons, and judicial activities were arranged in accordance with the course of nature. Owing to these, the major judicial principle of "granting awards in spring and summer and punishing criminals in autumn and winter" appeared.

[62] Collected Regulations of the Ming Dynasty. Volume 177. The Ministry of Justice. Judgments.

[63] Huang, L. Blessing Book, Volume 11, The Ministry of Justice: Reduction of Punishment in Summer Assizes.

[64] Bo, H. (2003). Six Abusements of the Judiciary in Prefectures and Counties in the Ming and Qing Dynasties. Research of the History of the Qing Dynasty. (1).

As early as in the Western Zhou Dynasty, the tradition of "punishing criminals in autumn and winter" emerged. In the *Rites of Zhou*, judiciary officers in charge of punishment were named "autumn officers." The reason why in spring and summer officials grant amnesty for criminals and in autumn and winter officials executed the death penalty was to follow the course of nature (Planting in spring. Growing in summer. Harvesting in autumn. Storing in winter). Cruel punishments were exclusively administered during stern autumn and winter seasons, which synchronized judicial severity with cosmic rhythms. To conclude, it was a simple analogy: in autumn and winter, everything lay dormant. Hence, carrying out punishments in autumn and winter will not influence the growth of animals and plants. In other words, it will not defy the natural order.

The *yin-yang* and five elements theories also influenced the policy of execution. It was believed that, in spring and summer, the *yang* energy was ascending, during which everything flourished again and lives were the most vigorous. Carrying out executions in this period was inauspicious, and it was seen as a defiance of nature. As everything waned in autumn and winter, it was suitable to carry out executions. Hence, executions should conform to seasons. Just as the Chapter *Seasons* in *Guanzi* recorded: "Penalty and benevolence should conform to four seasons. If they abide by seasons the blessing would happen, otherwise, disasters would befall."[65] When it came to punishments and seasons people in the Han Dynasty believed that "It is normal for everything to be prosperous in spring, and sapless in autumn. If any plants wither in spring or any plants flourish in autumn, disasters would take place." It was concluded that emperors should grant rewards in spring and summer, and carry out executions in autumn and winter. As to the aim, "hearing cases and carrying out executions in winter became the proper way."[66] The depiction in the *Book of Han·Penal Code* was clearer: "Penalties and punishments were used to simulate the deterrent of nature. And rewards and benevolence emulated the nourishment of nature." Only when execution was suitable to seasons, people could reap benefits; otherwise, it would lead to adverse consequences. Carrying out executions in autumn and winter would produce welfare and became the most utilitarian support for the execution system. It was also a safeguard to apply this system.

In ancient China, different dynasties had different regulations on whether death penalties should be carried out in autumn or winter or in which month of autumn or winter. Only in the Qin Dynasty, death penalties could be carried out at any time, which led to later generations' criticism of it. *Book of the Later Han· Biography of Chenchong* criticized that "the administration of the Qin Dynasty was savage because it carried out penalties at four seasons." Before the Spring and Autumn Period and the Warring State Period, executions were carried out in autumn. Just as *Book of Rites·Monthly Ordinances* recorded, "In the seventh month, punish those who are criminal and pass sentence in accordance with laws. The airs between

[65] Guanzi, Chapter Four Seasons.

[66] Book of Rites: Monthly Ordinances.

heaven and earth become severe, and indulgence should not be allowed." It was believed that execution could be carried out in autumn.

After the Han Dynasty, executions were carried out in September, October, and November of the Chinese Lunar Calendar. At the beginning of the Han Dynasty, the execution system in autumn and winter of the Western Zhou Dynasty was restored. When formulating *Nine Chapter Law*, Xiao He regulated that "executions shall be carried out in September of the Chinese Lunar Calendar and avoid February of the Chinese Lunar Calendar."[67] It meant that the system of execution in autumn and winter has been implemented since the beginning of the Han Dynasty. During the reign of Emperor Wu of Han, under the advocacy of Confucianism which was led by Dong Zhongshu, especially after the combination of the *yin-yang* theory, the system of execution in autumn and winter became more theoretical and systematic.

In the Tang Dynasty, there was a rule that execution of death penalty was forbidden between the Beginning of Spring and the Autumn Equinox. It was stipulated in the *Tang Code*, "All officials sentencing death penalties between the Beginning of Spring and the Autumn Equinox shall be punished by one year of penal servitude. Even punishment for crimes that need not wait for the correct season to be administered may not be carried out during a month when the slaughter of animals is prohibited, or on days when killing is forbidden. The punishment is sixty blows with heavy sticks in each case. Even if the official waits for the correct season, but there are violations, the punishment is increased two degrees." The *Old History of the Tang Dynasty·Penal Code* also recorded, "No death penalty shall be carried out between the Beginning of Spring and the Autumn Equinox." In the Tang Dynasty, death penalty was normally executed in winter because it was the season when every living being was withered and people were not busy with farming. Executions at this period complied with the requirement of arable culture.

In the Song and Yuan Dynasties, the system was carried on as before. On the ground that, death penalty cases must be reported to emperors for permission, and the execution of death penalty cases was normally carried out in autumn and winter, the tradition that both retrial and review of local and central governments should happen in autumn formed. However, the Yuan Dynasty did not strictly follow the regulation of execution in autumn and winter.

In the Ming Dynasty, the specific timeline of execution was between the Autumn Equinox and the Beginning of Spring, and criminals of court assizes should be executed between the Frost's Descent and the Winter Solstice. The Autumn Equinox is the beginning of autumn, during which death penalty cases and immediate-execution cases could be tried but not executed.

The Qing Dynasty carried forward the "summer assize" system which originated from the Ming Dynasty. It was recorded that "In the 10th year of Kang Xi's reign, it was stipulated that each year from the 10th day after the Grain Buds to the day before the Beginning of Autumn, the punishment of criminals who were sentenced to death penalty, military exile, life exile would be mitigated. In the 43rd year of the

[67] Book of Han. Volume 23. Treatises No. 3. Penal Law.

Kang Xi's reign, the Ministry of Justice was ordered to suspend the practice." At the beginning of the reign of Emperor Yongzheng, this practice was resumed. During the reign of Emperor Qianlong, punishments underwent systematic mitigation, and sentences of beating with light sticks and heavy sticks were commuted by 20%. Cangues were gradually abolished while other penalties remained unaltered. The specific period of autumn-and-winter execution started from the Beginning of Autumn to the Winter Solstice each year. The Qing government ruled that the autumn-and-winter execution should start after the Autumn Equinox. If the Autumn Equinox was in the 6th month of the Chinese lunar calendar, the execution shall be carried out after the 6th month. If solar terms which should be covered in the 6th month of the Chinese lunar calendar happened to be in the 5th month, no execution could be carried out in the 5th month of the Chinese lunar calendar. Therefore, in the Qing Dynasty, June covered both the dates of the month and the solar terms within the month.

7.3 Ideals of Adjudication

7.3.1 Ruling of Cases by Classic Doctrines

The integration of rites into law represented a significant incorporation of ethics into legal practices. After the Han Dynasty, this trend became stronger. The Han Confucians, represented by Dong Zhongshu, adapted to the situation and applied the rite and concepts embodied in *Three Fundamental Bonds, and the Five Constant Virtues*, into judicial practice, among which the most outstanding attempt was making legal judgment by citing Confucian classics. Making legal judgment by reference to classics also named "citing Confucian classics in judgment," "making conviction on the basis of the cause of a case," "making conviction on the basis of the motive of a crime," "making judgment on the basis of *Spring and Autumn Annals*," and so on. Making a conviction on the basis of criminal motive was to clarify the causes of cases and investigate the criminal motive, which emphasized whether the motive was kind or evil and whether the emotion was appropriate or inappropriate. If the motive conformed to the beliefs of *Spring and Autumn Annals*, it was virtuous; otherwise, it was evil. Although the entire *Judgments by the Spring and Autumn Annals*, a casebook compiled by Dong Zhongshu, was lost, from a few remaining cases, we can notice that the principle of making judgments on the basis of the *Spring and Autumn Annals* was accepted by officials of that era.

Case one: In this case, an adoptive father harbored his guilty son. At that time, there was no such principle that when father and son concealed each other, they were not guilty. According to the regulation of *Qin Code*, if anyone harbored a criminal, he was guilty. Besides, laws did not recognize the adoptive father and son enjoying the same rights and obligations as the biological father and son. At the beginning of the Han Dynasty, there was no difference from the Qin Dynasty in this aspect. But this thought was contrary to Confucian ethics. Confucius proposed that a son should mourn his father for 3 years since there were ties of family and foster relationships between them. In this case, Dong Zhongshu returned an acquittal on the basis of the principle that "father and son could conceal each other" in *Spring and Autumn Annals.*

Case two: In this case, a son accidentally injured his father. In the past, if a son injured his father, he would be sentenced to death penalty, because such an offense was a felony. According to the mood and motive of the suspect, Dong Zhongshu made the judgment that his behavior was accidental rather than deliberate. Hence the son should not be sentenced to death.

Case three: The case referred to the remarrying of widows. It was specified in law that when a husband died and was not buried, his wife was not allowed to remarry. If a woman remarried without permission, she would be sentenced to death. However, Dong Zhongshu thought this was inappropriate and listed several reasons. Firstly, according to the *Spring and Autumn Annals*, if a husband was dead and his wife had no kids, she could remarry. Secondly, the woman in the case was meek, chaste, and filial. As her husband had disappeared at sea, heads of the clan arranged the remarriage; in other words, she upheld chastity and refrained from remarrying without proper authorization. Therefore, the woman should not be guilty.

The sentences of the cases above were more lenient than provisions of statutes. Legal principles originated from the philosophy in *Spring and Autumn Annals*, and it was the start for the Han Confucians to transform penalty laws on the basis of *Spring and Autumn Annals*. By introducing rites into law, people added a softener to the rigid and cruel criminal law and injected human emotions into judicial practice in the Han Dynasty. In the following thousands of years, many judicial principles derived from this, including "Ba Yi" (eight privileged groups of people whose cases are to be especially deliberated), conviction according to five degrees of mourning, caution and leniency in penalization, indulgence to offenders for preserving the lineage or indulgence to offenders for parental or grandparental support, etc. This led to the trend of the combination of rites and laws, morality, and punishment.

7.3.2 Leniency on Revenge by Relatives

The fusion of ethics and laws, the merge of rites and laws, and the combination of morality and punishment were important characteristics of traditional legal practice in China, particularly of criminal law. These characteristics emerged from judicial practices, where human emotions were gradually incorporated into legal proceedings and eventually became an accepted norm

In the Tang Dynasty, during the reign of Empress Wu Zetian, there was a man named Xu Yuanqing whose father was killed by Zhao Shiyun, a Subprefect. When Zhao Shiyun was promoted to Chang'an City, Xu followed him and worked there secretly. Once he had a chance, he killed Zhao Shiyun for revenge and then confessed his crime to authorities. This case caused quite a stir. Some people thought the son should be executed. The other believed that he should be treated leniently. ChenZiang proposed his opinion that "if the man was not executed, rules and laws were disregarded. Hence, he must be executed. But, the ancient ethics provided that the feud over the father's death was intolerant. Since Xu Yuanqing was determined to revenge without the fear of the death penalty, he was quite filial and should be honored. Therefore, after Xu Yuanqing was executed, a monument should be erected on his tomb." Chen's opinion prevailed.[68] The settlement of this case embodied the combination of law, morality, and penalty of traditional law. As Confucianism gradually became popular, virtues such as filial piety, code of brotherhood, and chastity earned praise from the whole society. National organs, on the one hand, should assure the authority of law; on the other hand, they must tactfully balance heavenly principles and human emotions.

Blood feud was a traditional custom of clan societies. With Confucianism's growing influence, society gradually recognized blood feuds. It was deemed rational and legal to a large extent. *Book of Rites*:*Qu Li* recorded, "With regard to the personal enemy who killed one's father, this is his sworn enemy; with regard to the personal enemy who killed his brother, one should bring his weapon with him in order to seek an opportunity to revenge; with regard to the enemy who killed his friend, one should not live in the same state with him." These described that the murder of someone's father or brother was intolerable. Although the blood feud belonged to private remedies, it gained acceptance in public opinion, judiciary, and legislation. Even ordinary people felt satisfied when blood feud carriers killed their sworn enemies. "If a murderer was not convicted, the victim's family member would take revenge. If a murderer was convicted, the victim's family would not reconcile themselves to the situation. Even sissy men or tender women, who were lamenting and angry, would pluck up the courage to revenge."[69] In official history, there were many records that people took revenge for their seniors such as *Book of the Later Han*, Volume 53; *Biography of Shen Tupan*; *Book of the Later Han·Biography of Heroic Women*; *Imperial Reader of the Taiping Era*, Volume 481; *Chronicle of the Kingdom of Wei*, Volume 24; *Biography of Han Ji*; *History of the Southern Dynasties; and Biography of Zhang Jingren*. In literature, revenge was also a hot topic. Revenge for blood feud was praised in poems such as *Jingweipia* by Caozhi and *A Courage Women Living on the East Coast by Libai*, novels such as *New Stories at the Great Tang Dynasty*, *Biography of Xie Xiaoe*, *Rustic Talks from the East of Qi· Revenge by Wang Gongyan*, *Water Margin*, *Strange Stories from a Chinese Studio*, etc.

In judicial practice, in the Tang Dynasty, Liang Yue, a dweller of Fuping County, surrendered himself after avenging his father's murder by killing Qin Guo. Emperor Xianzong of Tang commanded, "Killing murderers for revenge was recorded in

[68] Liu, X. Old History of the Tang Dynasty. Volume 190 (2). Biographies No. 140.

[69] Qu, T. (2003). *Chinese Law and Chinese Society*. Zhonghua Book Company. 83.

classics. He was not afraid of death and confessed his sin voluntarily to officials. Since he took revenge for instinct and did not demand to live dishonorably, his penalty should be reduced."[70] Considering that he instinctively revenged for his father and turned himself in, he was absolved from the death penalty and should be sentenced to 100 blows with light sticks and life exile to Xun Prefecture. It was stipulated in the *History of Song Dynasty: Penal Code*, If someone revenged for his child, he should be forgiven. However, in specific cases, officials should consider the family affection and make some adjustments. Under the reign of Emperor Renzong of Song, Liu Yu's father was beaten to death by Wang De who was exempted from punishment for he was granted amnesty by chance. In order to take revenge, Liu Yu killed Wang De privately. Such misdeed violated the national law, but Emperor Renzong of Song thought it was righteous and only punished Liu Yu with beating with heavy sticks and banishment. Under the reign of Emperor Shenzong of Song, at Qing Perfect, Wang Yun's father was beaten to death. But he was too young to revenge. When he grew up, he decapitated the murderer. After mourning for his father with the murderer's head, he turned himself in. In accordance with laws, he should be sentenced to decapitation. However, the emperor spared his death penalty and sentenced him to life exile to Lin Prefecture for he revenged for his father and turned himself in.[71] The behavior of revenge was illegal, while the corresponding penalty was always reduced for "emotional state," "fraternal bonds," "motive," and so on. There was a buffer between laws which was objective and harsh and emotions which were subjective and soft. It was recorded, "Revenge is human nature. If someone doesn't want to retaliate against his enemy, he is impersonal…"[72] Anyone who didn't revenge for their kin would be criticized as impersonal, brutal, and indifferent. This criticism may evoke the courage of the revengers to retaliate against enemies. The revengers could earn the admiration of the whole world, and their fame might be recorded in history.

After the Han Dynasty, murder for revenge was under strict regulation. However, this regulation was only targeted at normal revengeful murder. Once filial sons or daughters revenged for their blood relatives, officials would offer leniency to them, exonerate them of blame by all means, or honor their behavior. In such a judicial process, human emotions and heavenly principles outweighed laws. Besides, the legislation left leeway for this. In other words, making a private settlement with a murderer who killed the elderly was prohibited. For example, in the 17th chapter—*Violence and Robbery* of *Tang Code*—"All cases of a person who makes a private settlement with someone who has killed that person's paternal grandparents or parents are punished by life exile at a distance of 2,000 *li*. If the victim was a relative within the second degree of mourning, the punishment is two and one-half years of penal servitude. If the victim was a relative of the third degree of mourning or less, the punishment is progressively reduced one degree…" The legal basis was "virtues

[70] Old History of the Tang Dynasty. Volume 50, Treatises. Chapter 30. Penal Law.

[71] History of Song. Volume 200. Treatises. Chapter 153. Penal Law. Chapter 2.

[72] Comprehensive Investigations Based on Literary and Documentary Sources. Volume 166.

and rites as the foundation of governance, punishments as its tool. Like night and day, the *yang* of spring and the *yin* of autumn, they are mutually dependent to bring completeness."[73] The statutes of the Ming and Qing Dynasties all prohibited relatives from private settlements with murderers and the right to revenge was controlled by the country. Although blood feud was limited under the statutes of the Qing Dynasty, excusable reasons of crimes would be taken into account. The punishment might be reduced depending on the circumstances of murder. "In a case where paternal grandparents or parents were killed by another who escaped from official capture, if the victims' children or sons' children killed the murderer, they would receive 100 strokes of the heavy bamboo. In a case where the murderer was arrested or fled back to his hometown after amnesty or banishment, if the victims' children or sons' children killed him, they would receive 100 strokes of the heavy bamboo and be exiled at a distance of 3,000 *li*."[74]

In the modern era, although blood feud was strictly forbidden, when human emotions conflicted with laws, human emotions still made a difference. On November 13, 1935, there was a thrilling case in Tianjin: Shi Jianqiao, a woman, assassinated Sun Chuanfang, a warlord, to revenge for her father and then confessed with relief. With the support and pressure of the whole society, the government absolved Shi Jianqiao, after she had been detained for 11 months. And the defendant became populous for her legendary experience of killing the enemy who murdered her father after holding the motive for 10 years. The public believed that her aspiration was praisable and sympathetic and her motive was pitiable and excusable. The absolution of the government should be deemed as complying with the public will and the common sense of justice.

7.3.3 Reduction of Punishment for Crimes Involving Protection of Family Members

Blood feud was a premeditated intentional homicide. Killing people for "saving relatives in a hurry" was a crime of negligence that happened in a condition of urgency, to which the corresponding penalty could be reduced.

Normally, the so-called saving people in a hurry meant a person manslaughter others in an emergency to protect his grandparents or parents when he saw his grandparents or parents being beaten or fighting with others. His penalty could be mitigated and he need not pay with his life for the killings. It was stipulated that "In every case in which grandparents or parents are struck by another, and a child or son's child immediately aid them and returns the blows. If the offender is not injured

[73] Tang Code. Administrative Regulations.

[74] Laws and Precedents of the Great Qing. Volume 28. Laws Relating to the Board of Punishments. Affrays and Blows. When the Father or Paternal Grandfather Are Struck by Another. The Great Qing Code. Volume 26.

to the extent of fracture, then there is no penalty. If there is fracture or above, then reduce the penalty by three degrees compared with the penalty of ordinary affray." "In a homicide case in which grandparents, parents, or husband are struck by another. In an extreme emergency, if a child, son's child or wife beats the offender to death, officials should report the condition in a memorial and wait for the final decision made by the emperor."[75] If a child rushed to protect his parents from attack and harmed the offender who had beaten his parents, the child was pardonable because his behavior embodied filial duty. Children could be punished when they encroached on their parents' power, and they could enjoy commutation or they could be absolved when they safeguard their parents' rights.

For example, during the Qing Dynasty, in autumn assizes, there were four kinds of judgments (confirmed execution, deferred retrial, commiserable mitigation, and filial piety-based sentence suspension), which meant the sentence was negotiable. "Saving relatives in an emergency" belonged to mitigation because of moral reasons. As long as a person killed or injured others to protect his lineal elders, his punishment could be mitigated.[76] On the contrary, if a senior relative was assaulted or murdered, and the junior relative failed to provide adequate or immediate assistance, the latter would be punished one degree more severely than under the statute on Failure to Intervene and Rescue, that is, 1 year of penal servitude. For instance, in a case involving a commoner named *Yu Rui* from *Zhili* province, who injured his paternal uncle while rescuing his father, the provincial magistrate initially adjudicated the case under the statute on junior relatives assaulting seniors, given the hierarchical nature of familial relations. However, the Ministry of Justice, upon reviewing the case by imperial instruction, ruled that the situation of *Yu Rui*'s case differed from ordinary cases of nephews assaulting uncles and thus granted him a mitigated sentence. This decision affirmed that the uncle-nephew relationship is subordinate to the father-son relationship.

[75] Laws and Precedents of the Great Qing, Volume 28, Laws Relating to the Board of Punishments, Affrays and Blows, When the Father or Paternal Grandfather Are Struck by Another. When the father or paternal grandfather were struck by someone in the clan, if the criminal struck or even killed others in order to save his father or paternal grandfather, his penalty would be reduced. It is the communication for saving family in emergency. The Great Qing Code, Volume 28, Laws Relating to the Board of Punishments, Affrays and Blows, Striking Superior or Elder Relatives of the Second Degree.

[76] Essentials on the Autumn Assizes, Volume 1; Cases at the Qianlong Era, Volume 1, Fumingan, the thirteen year of the Kangxi Era, Conspectus of penal cases, Book 3 (including the following cases) "beating one couple to death for saving father", "beating two men to death and one of them is the murderer of one's father". Beijing Historical Book Press, 2004 Version.

7.3.4 Saving the Criminal for Parental Support

Being unfilial had been deemed a felony in traditional law. In laws after the Northern Qi Dynasty, it was listed among the "ten felonies" or "ten abominations" and could not be absolved. In the legal practice of later generations, the statute of this crime was constantly being refined which became rather detailed till the Qing Dynasty. Bringing lawsuits against or cursing one's paternal grandparents or one's parents was considered lack of filial piety. The offense of lacking filial piety encompassed various acts, including neglecting one's duty to care for parents when they established a separate household registration or divided family property from the household head, arranging one's own marriage, engaging in entertainment, or removing mourning garments during the prescribed mourning period for a parent, failing to observe mourning rites upon hearing the death of paternal grandparents or parents, and falsely declaring the death of paternal grandparents or parents. The corresponding rules on "violating the orders of one's paternal grandparents or parents" and "a deficiency in supplying one's paternal grandparents and parents" amounted to nine articles. In every case where a child or son's child violated the orders of his paternal grandparents or parents, or where there was a deficiency in supplying paternal grandparents and parents, he would be sentenced to 100 strokes of the heavy stick. When a child offended his parents or grandparents repeatedly, he would be sentenced to exile to remote southwest China if he was of Han ethnicity, and he would be sent to Heilongjiang Province for penal servitude if he was Manchu. When parents suicided for their children were too poor to support them, the children shall be beaten with 100 strokes of the heavy stick and sent to exile for 3000 *li*. Thieves or murderers shall be sentenced to be hanged immediately if their parents were weighed down with sorrow and chose to suicide or were killed deliberately by avengers. When children or grandchildren broke national laws, if their parents or grandparents connived in the crimes at first and suicided later for fear of punishment, the children or grandchildren shall be sentenced to military exile to Yunnan, Guizhou, Guangzhou, or Guangxi Provinces. If grandparents or parents were beaten or killed deliberately, their children or grandchildren should be sentenced to postponed hanging. If grandparents or parents instructed their children or grandparents to steal or murder and then they suicide for fear of punishment when the crimes were discovered, the children and grandparents should be sentenced to 3 years of penal servitude and 100 strokes of heavy stick. If parents or grandparents were deliberately killed by revengers, their children or grandchildren should be sentenced to exile to a distance of 3000 *li* and 100 strokes of the heavy stick. In cases where children or grandchildren committed crimes which should be sentenced to death penalty or murdered others deliberately, they should be punished immediately according to their charges, if their crimes were uncovered and their parents or grandparents suicided. In the later seven cases, grandparents or parents died because of their unfilial children or grandchildren, the children or grandchildren shall be sentenced to felonies. While sons were expected to be filial, fathers were to exercise leniency; while younger brothers were respectful to their elders, elder brothers were to demonstrate fraternal kindness. Even when fathers or elder brothers infringed on the interests of their sons or younger brothers, the law still prescribed punishment for such transgressions, albeit lighter. This legal practice reinforced the ethical principle that paternal and fraternal authority should be tempered with benevolence.[77]

The "system of filial piety-based sentence suspension" was a system applied to safeguard filial duty. It meant that when direct relatives of criminals were too old to live alone, they should be supported by their children, but if there was no adult man in their families and the crimes the criminal committed did not belong to ten abominations, officials could report the situation to emperors. The emperors would decide whether the punishments should be reduced or not. For instance, criminals would be free from exile, and their penal servitude during imprisonment could be suspended. This aimed to leave criminals to take care of their lineal elders, and only when the old passed away, they would be executed. *The History of Wei: Chapter of Criminal Law* recorded, "If a condemned criminal's grandparents or parents were over 70 years old and had no adult son and grandson or close relatives to serve them, the condition should be set forth in a report to emperors. With the favor of emperors, the punishment of life exile would be replaced by beating with light sticks in order to keep criminals at home to serve their relatives. When their relatives passed away, the criminal would be exiled again and would not be granted amnesty anymore."[78]

This regulation embodied the concept of filial duty. After the system of filial piety-based sentence suspension was enacted in the Northern Wei Dynasty, it was passed down and became more and more systematic. The *Tang Code* provided: "All cases involving those who commit crimes punished by death penalty other than the ten abominations, where their paternal grandparents or parents were aged or infirm and needed care and the family had no adult relative within the second degree of mourning, may send up a petition for pardon."[79] It meant that if the only son of a family committed a capital offense, officials could plead the government to be lenient and suspend his punishment. The Statutes of the Ming Dynasty stipulated: "For any prisoners under sentence of death and not included in a general amnesty, if their grandparents or parents are old and need services from others and there are no younger brothers in the family, the cases should be reported to emperors for final decision. If a criminal is sentenced to exile or penal servitude in imprisonment, he would be punished by 100 blows of heavy stick and other penalties would be delayed for he needs to remain at home and serve lineal elders. In other words, only when criminals' parents are old, ill, disabled and lack other sons, criminals who should be punished with military exile and penal servitude in imprisonment are permitted to remain at home to serve their parents." The *Great Qing Code* provided, "For those under a death sentence without younger brothers, if their parents or grandparents are

[77] Laws and Precedents of the Great Qing, Volume 4, Ten Abominations, Volume 30, Criminal Law, Lawsuits, Violating the Orders of One's Paternal Grandparents or Parents; Shen Xintian: Mingfa Zhizhang, Volume 1, Homicide Cases Committed by One's Child or Grandchild, issued in the Daoguang Era.

[78] History of Wei, Volume 121, Treatises, Chapter 16, Punishment.

[79] Tang Code, Names and General Rule.

over 70 years old, or their mothersare over 50 years old and live in widowhood for over 20 years, the related judicial official could plead emperors to show compassion to the criminals and spare their death penalty. They could remain at home and care for their family."[80] The scope of "permitting culprits to support lineal elders" expanded and relative policies were loosened. For example, if a criminal's parents or grandparents were over 70 years old, seriously ill, or disabled, he could remain at home to support his family. If a criminal was 16 years old or above and he had no younger brothers, then there was no difference between this case and that of the only son. The provisions kept changing and whether there were any people to care for parents or grandparents became the prerequisite, which did not stick precisely to the legal instruments.[81]

The system of permitting culprits to support lineal elders in the Qing Dynasty tried to balance the rights between parents of offenders and parents of victims. For example, in the 2nd year of the Yongzheng era, when the Ministry of Justice reviewed a case and decided whether Li Fangyi, the criminal who thrust Guo Dingguo to death, should be permitted to remain at home and support his lineal elders, Yongzheng wrote in an imperial edict that "Although the murderer meets the standard of the system of remaining at home to support lineal elders, officials should check whether the victim's parents are still alive and whether the victim is the only son. If the victim's parents are old and he is the only son, once he is killed no one could care for his parents. However, the murderer could be free from death penalty and care for his parents. This is cruel and irrational." In the 5th year of the Qianlong era, when amending codes, officials added "when the victim is the only son and no one could support the victim's relatives. The murderer could not be exempt from punishment and he could not remain at home to serve his parents."[82]

In the Qing Dynasty, apart from the condition that offenders could remain at home to care for their parents if their parents were old or sick, there was a new statute that if the only son of a widow committed crimes, the son could remain at home to care for his mother. After the death of one's father, his mother became the only parent in the home; hence she enjoyed the privilege of the father. When the only son committed a crime, he could be absolved for he needed to care for his widowed mother. The absolution of an offender required that the crime should be unintentional (e.g., accidental or playful harm rather than a fight), that he be the family's only son, and that his widowed mother be either over 50 years old or widowed for

---

[80] Laws and Precedents of the Great Qing, Volume 4, Names and General Rules, Indulgence to offenders by permitting them to care for their parents or grandparents; Commentaries made by Lu Yu; Commentaries on The Great Qing Code, Names and General Rules, Indulgence to offenders by permitting them to care for their parents or grandparents, Anhui Fuwen Press, 1875 Version.

[81] Commentaries on The Great Qing Code, Volume 4, Names and General Rules, Persons Convicted of Offences Who are Permitted to Remain to Care for Relatives, Page 240; Administrative Code of the Qing Dynasty of the Guangxu Era, Volume 724, Ministry of Justice, Names and General Rules, Indulgence to offenders by permitting them to care for their parents or grandparents.

[82] Commentaries on the Great Qing Code, Volume 4, Names and General Rules, Indulgence to offenders by permitting them to care for their parents or grandparents, Page 243.

at least 20 years, as long as the victim was not an only son. If these conditions were met, the offender could receive a suspended sentence to care for his mother, which was subject to imperial approval.

If criminals were not filial, even if they were eligible to remain at home and serve their families, they could not do so. Du Xueliang, an only son, worked in a dockyard that was far away from his hometown. As he killed his elder clan brother, he was sentenced to decapitation. Although the criminal's parents were under 70 years old, the criminal was the only son in the family. It seemed that he could be absolved to support his family. However, Emperor Qianlong vetoed that judgment and expressed his opinion in a sacred edict, "In the future, convicts could remain at home to support their relatives only when officials ascertain that criminals commit crimes at their birth places. If convicts committed crimes far from home, they were deemed unfilial for neglecting their familial duties. Even if the situations technically complied with the law, they should not remain at home to support their families."[83] The system was used to safeguard the Paternal Patriarchal System, but the convicts who did not serve their parents at home violated the Confucian philosophy of "While his parents are alive, a son should not travel far." Since the son was so unfilial that he neglected his familial duties, he should not be permitted to remain at home to support his family. The inconsistency between human emotions and laws was the reason why the emperor vetoed the filial piety-based sentence suspension.

The sentence suspension to convicts by permitting them to carry on their family line was a derivation of the filial piety-based sentence suspension. In a case, a man killed his elder brother and there was no other man in his family; if the younger brother was sentenced to death penalty, the lineage of this household would be terminated. In order to prevent the household from being extinct, the convict would be absolved from death penalty.[84] In the third year of the Kangxi's reign, Guan Congfu and Guan Congzhou committed crimes together, and they were sentenced to military exile according to the law. In consideration of the situation, their mother, whose family name was Wang, was old enough, and there was no one in the family who could take care of her; Guan Congfu, the elder brother, was released to remain at home to support his family, and Guan Congzhou, the younger brother, was sentenced to military exile. In the fifth year of the Qianlong's reign, it was stipulated that when biological brothers were convicted, one of them would be absolved to remain at home and support his family. The one saved from punishment should be the elder brother, in order to follow the lineal primogeniture system.[85]

---

[83] The Veritable Record of the Emperor Gao of Qing Dynasty, Volume 428, December of the seventeen year of Qianlong, Article 29.

[84] Origins of The Great Qing Code, Names and General Rules 5, Indulgence to offenders by permitting them to care for their parents or grandparents.

[85] Commentaries on The Great Qing Code, Volume 4, Names and General Rules, Indulgence to offenders by permitting them to care for their parents or grandparents, Page 240; Administrative Code of the Qing Dynasty of the Guangxu Era, Volume 724, Ministry of Justice, Names and General Rules, Indulgence to offenders by permitting them to care for their parents or grandparents.

Morality served as both the foundational of legal codes and the standard for judicial decisions. In this framework, law existed fundamentally to uphold moral principles. Consequently, the moral emphasis on legal compliance was rationally justified. In judicial practice, magistrates based their rulings not only on contemporary statutes but also on assessments of the moral character of the involved parties. Human emotions or rites became the logical premise of judgment. Therefore, there were theories like "enforcing law according to the cause of a case" and "making conviction on the basis of the cause of a case." The text of judgment in *Pure and Bright Collection of Verdicts by Eminent Masters* included sentences such as "considering the human emotions when making a judgment," "balancing human emotions and laws" and "those who gain illegally would feel uneasy," etc. Human emotions were intertwined with laws. Judicial officials could use them flexibly. When used properly, the common sense could take effect and satisfy the emotions of human beings. For example, when Hai Rui, an official in the Ming Dynasty, dealt with complicated cases, he always followed the principle of "When there is anything suspicious in litigation. it is preferable to wrong the younger brother rather than the elder brother; to wrong nephews rather than uncles; to wrong the rich rather than the poor; to wrong the cunning and stubborn rather than the simple and honest."[86] Ethics, filial duty, strength, weakness, poverty, wealth, and so on all constituted factors in making convictions in accordance with the cause of a case. Wise judicial officials could make a compromise between heavenly principle, human emotions, and national laws; pursue specific justice in legal practice, such as neutrality, righteousness, fairness, and appropriateness; deal with cases "justifiably, rationally, thoroughly, and properly"[87]; cultivate the people's virtues of benevolence, righteousness, courtesy, wisdom, faith, loyalty, filial piety, fraternal respect, sincerity, kindness, love, kindness, etc.; and care for human nature, comfort people, and shape the order of rule of rites through laws so as to build a harmonious and stable society.

7.3.5 The Combination of Emotion, Reasoning, and Law

The judicial ideal of traditional China could be summarized as a combination of human emotions, heavenly principles, and national laws. In Pingyao County, Shanxi Province, a couplet on both sides at the *Yamen* gates, warned: "Be a rational, lenient, flexible and diligent official. The lazy, corrupt, and negligent who practice evil cannot deceive Heaven." Obviously, this was used to remind local officials that they were unable to deceive heaven; therefore, they must be rational, lenient, flexible, diligent, upright, and prudent when they try cases. The back walls of many *Yamen*

[86] Collected Work of Hairui, Articles on revolutions, Zhonghua Book Company, 1987 Version.

[87] Zhang, W. (2011). Images and Symbols of Justice in China and the West. The Editor-in-chief of Chinese Legal History Society and "Institute of History and Philosophy, Academia Sinica". Study of Legal History. (20).

halls were hung with inscribed plaques bearing "heavenly principle," "national laws," and "human emotions." When Prefects and County Magistrates worked there, they could see the plaques as they looked up and gradually inculcated them in mind. To officials, all lawsuits were related to these three phrases. Just as Zhang Wuwei wrote in his *Wei Neng XinJi*, "Folk lawsuits are different in details. However, these matters were nothing more than houses, marriage, land, murder, robbery, and battle," and the situation was nothing more than grievance or defraud. "People who hear cases should make judgments in accordance with laws and heavenly principles after detecting facts of cases."[88] Human emotions and facts of cases and law were common collocations in official historical records. For example, in *History of Song Dynasty: Penal Code*, the term of "human emotions" appeared 14 times, which usually referred to human sentiments and common senses. For instance, "Since the Kaibao Era, most of those who committed capital crimes could be spared the death penalty as long as their crimes were not particularly serious" and "In every Prefect, no commutation would be granted to murderers and robbers since their behaviors deserved no mercy." The term "facts of cases and law" appeared five times in *History of Song Dynasty: Penal Code*, such as "Criminals' penalty could be increased or decreased on the basis of the facts of cases. It was stipulated that when laws were not applied to the facts of cases, officials should submit them to the emperors for the final decision. Eventually, officials only petition for penal increases but never petition for penal decreases. Hence criminals are prone to be punished rather than to be absolved, which goes against the aim of the prudent application of laws. Since then, officials were obligated to maintain equilibrium between human emotions and national laws. Failure to uphold this balance would result in disciplinary sanctions." All the above examples emphasized that in judicial practice, officials should strive for a balance between human emotions, heavenly principle, and national laws and properly handle civil and criminal cases, which was the ideal state expected by the government.

The meanings of the Chinese character *qing* include details of cases (or facts), kinship (or affection between family members), emotions (or motives), and so on. In the judiciary, when human emotions, heavenly principles, and national laws were mixed together, normally, human emotions referred to kinship and sentiments. In the criminal judiciary, it meant taking kinship and criminal motives into full consideration when making convictions and sentences. After assessing criminals' identity and motives in a given legal structure, officials shall appropriately adjust the standard of convictions and sentences. The theory of "making judgment on the basis of *Spring and Autumn Annals* " (citing Confucian classics in judgment) of Dong Zhongshu, in the Han Dynasty, called for making judgments according to the causes of cases (also known as making judgments according to the original motives). Within this framework, the concepts of "sentiments" and "minds" were fundamentally related to emotions and motives. Motives were usually provoked by emotions, which were deeply rooted in kinship affections. Such kinship affections were based

[88] Zhang, W. *Wei Neng Xin Ji*. Volume 1. General Introduction.

on ethical norms which could extend to shape social relationships. Social relationships in turn influenced value systems that ultimately determined the legitimacy of the regime.

Traditional Chinese society operated within a rigid framework of feudal ethics, where Confucian ethical code permeated all strata of the society. These rules fettered males and females from free relationships and marriage. Doctrines such as "physical contact between genders is prohibited," "the Three Cardinal Guides (ruler guides subject, father guides son and husband guides wife), and Five Constant Virtues (benevolence, righteousness, propriety, knowledge, and sincerity)," and "keep the natural law and abolish human desire" were seen as constraints on human emotions. Most conservative officials were guardians and promoters of feudal ethics, rites, etc. Although many feudal ethics and rites were strictly stipulated in text, compromise always appeared in real practice. In different periods, the functions of feudal ethics and rites were different. Furthermore, not all officials rigidly adhered to these ethical norms with a strict demeanor when adjudicating cases involving relationships. Instead, they frequently set aside strict doctrines and delivered judgments that balanced rationality and humanity. It was recorded in *Court Documents at Wu Regin* that Peng De'mo, a County Magistrate at Suzhou in the late Qing Dynasty, often made full use of the right of discretion when he tried cases. With the combination of the administrative principle of Confucianism with the leniency of Buddhism, he flexibly broke through limitations and satisfied everyone, making many classic judgments that complied with humanity and rationality.[89] Peng served as a County Magistrate during the reigns of Emperor Xianfeng and Emperor Tongzhi, a period marked by a weaker centralized government and a less stringent adherence to feudal ethics and rites. Consequently, Peng's judicial approach has been historically noted. In Peng's adjudications, the guiding principle was that ethics and rites should align with human emotions rather than restrict them. Peng believed that "human emotions" encompassed human desires, the freedom of life choices, and interpersonal equity. Obviously, his judicial judgments exhibited characteristics of humanism of modern judiciary. Due to his talent, his judgments were replete with literary quotations, making them not only legal precedents but also elegant proses.

Prefect Qiao "Mismatched" the Couples in *Stories to Awaken the World* was another widespread case in which human emotions, heavenly principles, and national laws were perfectly balanced. In the traditional society where children were expected to follow the commands of their parents and the recommendations of match-makers, Qiao made a seemingly "misguided" judgment by deliberately pairing affectionate couples whose families had forced them apart. This judgment represented a remarkable convergence of human emotions, heavenly principles, and Confucian rites. Even novelists praised this judgment as "a temporary mismatch creating eternal virtue." While literary accounts may contain fabricated plots, the enduring popularity of the judgment nonetheless reflected people's expectation for

[89] Peng, Demo. Judicial Documents in the Wu Region.

a legal system that valued affection, compassion, and the fulfillment of all the parties involved.

Heavenly principles were not merely illusions; rather, they were principles of daily life grounded in natural law, ethical relationships, and living habits recognized and adhered to by the majority. National laws referred to the legal framework established by the state. There was no fixed hierarchy among heavenly principle, national laws, and human emotions. Their relevance and status were not static but constantly evolving, often complementing one another in practice. In judicial practice, the ideal was to balance heavenly principle, national laws, and human emotions and make fair, lawful, and reasonable judgments. This approach necessitated the precondition that everyone, from Prefects and County Magistrates to emperors, should fully consider the motives, identities, emotions, and circumstances of the involved parties and employ flexible judgments to facilitate the evolution and refinement of written statutes through their judicial decisions.

7.4 Disorder in Justice

Judicial equity is permanently dynamic. There had been no absolute equity in judiciary. The only problem is the extent of judicial inequity instead of the existence of judicial inequity. Every dynasty kept alert to judicial inequity and took relevant measures to minimize it. However, due to the historical limitations, such inequity had never been uprooted. People had been trying to explore a prescription that could address both symptomatic manifestations and systemic root causes.

7.4.1 Misconducts in Adjudication

A series of judicial principles evolved over time through the judicial practices of various dynasties in traditional China. Among judicial values, adherence to the principle of "harmony between humans and heaven" was essential. For instance, the system of execution in autumn and winter prescribed when to file cases and the time limits of trials. Officials were expected to integrate ethics with laws, consider commonsense notions of justice and ethics, and align these with heavenly principles and legal statutes, as seen in practices like "conviction according to the five degrees of mourning" and "convictions based on the original motive." Officials should be prudent in punishment, such as adopting the五听*Wutin* (five-observation) system (observation of the "verbal consistency," "respiratory patterns," "facial microexpressions," "auditory responsiveness," and "eye movements" of suspects), implementing "the tripartite inquest system" (consultations with nobility, officials, and commoners), applying the resubmission system of death penalty cases (Three Resubmissions System in the Sui Dynasty and Five Resubmissions System in the Tang Dynasty), and implementing the "joint adjudication system" (joint adjudications, court assizes, summer assizes, and so on in the Ming and Qing Dynasties) in order to prevent or reduce wrongful convictions. Except for actions prohibited by law, the government guided judicial officials by commending and praising upright officials and setting examples of judicial impartiality. The imperial judicial system partially decentralized its authority by empowering local communities to develop customary mediation practices. At the subcounty level, village elders, local gentry, and clan leaders routinely resolved disputes which simultaneously reduced litigation costs for villagers and alleviated the caseload pressure on magistrates. Mediation not only served as a vital supplement to the formal judiciary but also established the historical foundation for China's modern people's mediation system. During certain historical periods, these preventive dispute-resolution mechanisms demonstrated significant effectiveness in maintaining social stability.

Rulers at all dynasties were on high alert to guard against judicial injustice; therefore, they issued prohibitions and took punitive measures constantly. As early as the Shang and Zhou Dynasties, there were "three misconducts and ten punishments"[90] which were imposed on administrative officials and "five judicial abuses"[91] (viz., the abuse of power, personal vendettas, female solicitation, bribery, or lobbying) which were imposed on judicial officials. It was stipulated in *Qin Code: Questions and Answers to Legal Matters*, "embezzling governmental fund is equal to stealing"; officials bore the responsibility of education of law and if folks committed crimes for inadequate education on law, officials should bear the criminal responsibility; judicial officials should learn legal knowledge, and they were divided into "virtuous officials" and "evil officials" according to whether they had "a good knowledge of laws." *Qin Code: Yushu* recorded, "Virtuous officials know laws and decrees, hence they can do everything. Honest and loyal officials could serve emperors. Evil officials who are unfamiliar with laws and corrupted can't serve emperors." In the Han Dynasty, it was provided that "any officials who pervert justice for bribe shall be sentenced to public execution."[92] The *Tang Code* summarized "six illicit goods" in economic crimes. "There are six types of original goods mentioned in the Code. These are: robbery by force, burglar, taking bribes and subverting the law, taking bribes without subverting the law, taking goods and articles in the area under one's supervision, and taking illicit goods through malfeasance."[93] Taking bribes and subverting the law, taking bribes without subverting the law, taking goods and articles in the area under one's supervision, and taking illicit goods through malfeasance were related to judicial behaviors. The Ming Dynasty punished corrupted officials by flaying their skins and stuffing them with straw in order to frighten officials who took bribes by misusing laws. People were allowed to appeal to higher officials by bypassing their direct rulers, such as "appealing to the

[90] Book of Documents: History of Shang: Yi Xun.

[91] Book of Documents: History of Zhou: Book of Punishments by Lü.

[92] History of Jin, Volume 30, Treatises, Chapter 20, Penal Law.

[93] Tang Code, Volume 11, Where Robbery Is Committed or Robbers Are Harbored in the Area under an Official's Control.

central judicial organ for redress" in the Han Dynasty, the "accusation letter box" in Cities of the Tang Dynasty, the "drum for redress" in the Song Dynasty and "appeal redress in the capital city," and "intercepting officials' carriages to complain grievances" in the Qing Dynasty, which increased the remedy channel for parties. There were strict statutes on punishing judicial injustice in *Ming Code*, *Great Announcements of the Ming Dynasty*, and *The Great Qing Code*.

A series of policies and regulations formed in traditional China played an important role in restraining judicial inequity and improving official works. So far, such measures are still useful. The prevention of judicial injustice was regarded as a major mission in past dynasties; however, judicial injustice still emerged repeatedly. Although there were deep reasons, to some extent, they were natural attachments to the traditional political system.

7.4.2 Weak Surveillance

The judicial injustice of traditional China mainly resulted from the combination of judicial power and administrative authority, and judicial activities were administratized. Emperors, the supreme class in national administration, enjoyed the authority of administration, legislation, jurisdiction, economy, and military all together. In the oaths, admonitions, announcements, and plans issued by emperors of ancient China, it can be found that they had the absolute right to punish subjects who disobeyed their orders. After the forming of written laws, there were relatively professional judicial officials in countries. However, undoubtedly, emperors were the final decision-makers of all major cases. Qin Shihuang decided cases in person. In the Song Dynasty, emperors "settled lawsuits personally." In the Ming and Qing Dynasties, there were "joint adjudications for capital cases." All of these reflected that emperors had the final say on major cases. Since there was no counterbalance to emperors' power, their knowledge, qualities, and personalities were closely related to judicial justice. If an emperor was a so-called saint and wise emperor, he was diligent in political affairs and prudent in judicial decisions, able to abide by the law and try cases in person, and capable of deterring his officials from judicial injustice. Emperors such as Qin Shihuang, Emperor Wu of Han, Emperor Taizong of Tang, Emperor Taizu of Ming, Emperor Yongzheng, and so on could be regarded as emperors who had the ability to rule by law.

Emperors, free from restraint on power, were initiators of judicial inequity. They were both legislators and destroyers of law. They were both judiciaries and betrayers of normal judicial procedure. They were able to impose extra punishment beyond legal restrictions or shrug off their judicial power and let crooked officials abuse the power to persecute people. Emperors who were bossy and extravagant often used their judicial power to satisfy their own desires or persecute their people. Tyrants like Emperor Zhou of Shang, the Second Emperor of Qin, the Martial Emperor of the Jin Dynasty, Emperor Yang of the Sui Dynasty, and so on were typical. Shiftless emperors such as Emperor Gaozong of Song, Emperor Yingzong of

Ming, and Emperor Wanli, who were slack in policies, overlooked their judicial power, and let crooked officials take bribes and pervert laws. Even diligent and innovative emperors who took strong action against judicial inequity such as Qin Shihuang and Wu Zetian once tarnished jurisdiction. Out of personal spite, Qin Shihuang burned Confucian books. In order to wipe out political rivals, Wu Zetian mainly relied on cruel officials. In order to strengthen imperial power, Zhu Yuanzhang created the Embroidered-Uniform Guard, which was a malicious start for secret agents participating in judicial affairs. Emperors in the Ming and Qing Dynasties overused literary inquisitions in which innocent people were implicated. All of these seriously injured the authority of standard laws and penalties.

On account of the centralization of power by emperors, judicial authority became intertwined with administrative power. This led to a blurred definition of judicial authority, rendering it incapable of independent action. The vertical leadership hierarchy in traditional China's bureaucracy meant that politically, officials were obliged to please emperors rather than serve the needs of the civilians. "What pleases the higher echelons is even more favored by the lower ones." The hierarchical relationship between the sovereign and the minister extended to all levels of bureaucracy resulting in the condition that lower officials obeyed every order of the higher, while often neglecting the needs of those below them. Officials were mainly supervised by higher organizations rather than horizontal organizations. The vertical supervision was far less efficient than horizontal supervision. Consequently, when officials at any level abused their power, it became challenging to curb such behaviors effectively.

The vertical system of executive power was also applied to all levels of judicial officials. Executive power lacked supervision and checks, as did judicial power. As long as officials who were concurrently in charge of judicial affairs pleased their leaders, they did not need to worry about supervision even if they abused their power and made judgments arbitrarily. The couplet "petty officials grovel before their superiors with endless kowtows, while commoners surrender the fruits of their life's labor to the county magistrate's coffers" described a vivid situation that all judicial officials fawned on superiors and oppressed inferiors. There were officials who scrupulously abided by the tenet "If an official does not care about his people, he'd better resign his seat and sell sweet potato at home." But they only relied on their limited power and sympathy for folks, rather than laws and judicial procedures that were used to safeguard social justice. Governments also tried to supervise judicial officials by setting up some systems, such as supervision systems which had a long history in China. However, the effect of such supervision depended on the central power of emperors.

7.4.3 Irrationalities in Adjudication

In traditional China, officials were all-round talents who shall obtain the knowledge on administration, judiciary, and military affairs. As for the judicial subjects, they were roughly composed of people who engaged in trials and supervision or worked as legal decision-makers, supervisors, political advisors, bailiffs, runners, and *Songshi* (legal practitioners). Due to the absence of specialized training, most of them were nonprofessionals. Before the Spring and Autumn Period, judicial talents were trained by governments. During the Spring and Autumn Period and Warring States Period, "judicial talents" were trained in private schools, such as Deng Xi. In the Qin Dynasty, "administrative officials also performed judicial functions." The cultivation of judicial talents was the duty of the government, and officials shouldered the responsibility of promulgating laws. During the Han Dynasty, "scholars became officials" which meant that Confucian scholars, such as Dong Zhongshu, who had studied at national institutions, participated in judicial proceedings. After the Han Dynasty, despite the apparent decline of Legalism and the rise of Confucianism, laws remained an integral part of social life. Confucianism and Legalism struck an excellent balance. During the Wei and Jin Dynasties, specialized legal education was still absent, and executive officials, like Ruan Ji and Chen Zhonggong, continued to concurrently handle judicial matters. After the Sui and Tang Dynasties, certain improvements were made. Experts in law were selected in the Chinese Imperial Examination System in which legal knowledge was officially covered. Since then, the training of legal talents began to be specialized and nationwide. The Song Dynasty saw increased emphasis on the selection of legal talents. For instance, Emperor Shenzong of Song initiated legal studies and established the position of "Erudites of Law," who received assessment on their legal knowledge and case adjudication skills. In the Southern Song Dynasty, specialized judicial examinations were introduced.[94] Undoubtedly, with the advocacy from governments, society would pay high attention to legal knowledge. Sushi, a scholar in North Song Dynasty, once highlighted the importance of learning laws in his poem, "if an official had read numerous books except books on law, he would be unable to assist an emperor to be a saint as *Yao* and *Shun*." As Shen Jiaben, a legal scholar in the Qing Dynasty, observed, "When the emperor established a new official post, scholars nationwide would diligently master the required knowledge to secure advancement. What the emperor deemed significant became the empire's priority; where his attention lay, the people's focus followed. Never in history has it occurred that the sovereign neglected legal studies while his subjects held them in high esteem." The scarcity of Erudites of Law during the Yuan Dynasty led to a decline in legal studies. Despite repeated directives from the central government encouraging the study of law, these efforts were largely fruitless. Following the trend of the Yuan Dynasty, the government of the Ming Dynasty directly abolished this position.

---

[94] Commentaries on History of Song: Penal Code compiled by Shanghai Academy of Social Sciences Institute of Law, Civilian Press, 1982, Pages 16–17.

Fortunately, there was a provision in the *Ming Code* that all officials and civilians should study law. While the Ming Dynasty did not maintain the institutionalized position of Erudites of Law as seen in earlier dynasties, the study of legal codes and imperial edicts nevertheless persisted as an essential component of official education.[95]

However, with the institutionalization of the imperial examination system's focus on "eight-legged essays" during the Ming and Qing Dynasties, the number of scholars who devoted their lives to Confucian orthodoxy increased sharply; the number of scholars specialized in law declined and the government neglected the professional education on law. To acquire legal knowledge, officials mainly depended on reading books such as *Decrees on Populace Governance, Admonitions to State Officials and Sacred Edicts of Emperor Kangxi*, etc. After taking office, the officials were not obligated to acquire legal skills and practical knowledge, which made irrational judicial activities a common phenomenon. During that period, the personal preferences, characters, temperaments, and morality of officials significantly influenced trial outcomes. If an official diligently concentrated on studying law to improve himself, he could make the right judgments on his own. An official who demonstrated indolence, irrationality, and recklessness in his duties would inevitably make flawed judicial decisions, whose unsettled cases piled up. Ni Wangzhong, who worked as a County Magistrate in Zhu Ji county in the Qing Dynasty, witnessed officials who "read case reports once they get off their carriages. But one-tenth to two-tenths of lawsuits filed ten years ago were unsolved, half of the lawsuits filed three or four years ago were unsolved."[96] In response to their superiors' directives, officials must fulfill their judicial duties. When they were unable to solve cases, they had to seek help from others such as private advisors and petty officials. Private advisors learned legal knowledge from their forefathers or teachers, instead of specialized social institutions.

As administrators entrusted clerical work to their private advisors who were good at writing articles, they were inevitably manipulated and judicial injustice then emerged. For example, in a malicious accusation against Yang Naiwu in the late Qing Dynasty, Zhang Lunxiang, a private advisor, bribed the owner of a pharmacy to perjure. In order to help Liu Xitong, the county magistrate, make falsification and backstab Yang, the owner told a lie that it was Yang who bought arsenic to murder the victim. Private advisors were also called "masters who only save four kinds of people," which meant they only saved the living rather than the dead (as the deceased had gone, revenge for the victim meant nothing more than killing one more person), saved officials other than civilians (redressing a civilian's grievances risked the future of the accused official, while failure meant mere military exile for the civilian), saved senior officials rather than petty officials (superior officials' cases were complex to be settled with grave consequences and more people were involved in

[95] Shen, J. (1985). Articles of Jiyi. Volume 1. On erudite professors for law. Studies on Penal Law of Previous Dynasties. Volume 4. Zhonghua Book Company 2060.

[96] Ni Wangzhong. Educating the People of Zhuji. Selected Records: Preface.

the cases. Inferior officials' cases were easy to be settled because the crimes were less serious and fewer people were involved in these cases), and saved experienced officials rather than new officials (there would be more loss for experienced officials when they left their posts, while new officials still had more time and opportunities).[97] In the Qing Dynasty, the story that a private advisor who fabricated the fact by changing "the murderer killed the victim with a knife" into "the suspect accidentally killed the victim by tossing a knife" was widespread. It was not only an example of covering up the crime of the murderer but also a typical case of disregarding human life.[98] Unscrupulous officials could take advantage of loopholes in administration to persecute civilians. Proverbs like "even if an official's integrity is as pure as water, his subordinate officials may be as slick as grease" and "even upright officials could not avoid cunning petty officials" were satires on unscrupulous officials who exploited their power to bully people and pursued personal gains through deception. Inefficiencies in the judiciary allowed petty officials to mediate dishonestly between parties for their own interests, to the detriment of civilians.[99] "An indecisive magistrate's incompetence left lawsuits unresolved for months, paralyzing local productivity as citizens abandoned livelihoods to pursue justice. This failure enriched corrupt petty officials and private legal advisors who exploited the chaos. While right and wrong remained undetermined, countless families faced ruin." The Late Qing witnessed unprecedented growth in the study of law, and it became a prominent school of thought, which meant that there was a shortage of professional legal talents in society.

7.4.4 Collection of Evidence in Interrogation by Torture

Inquisitorial trials prevailed in traditional China since there was a lack of legal surveillance organizations, defense lawyers, and juries.

One of the important principles of the trial system was that no conviction can be made without the confession of the defendant. It was stipulated in *Tang Code* that "If the accused does not confess after enduring the full torture, he shall be released on bail." The statutes of the Ming Dynasty and Qing Dynasty also provided that "conviction must be based on confessions made by the accused" and "conviction requires confessions from the accused." Since confession was the basis of conviction, inquisition by torture was inevitable.

The aftermath of extorting confession by torture in the inquisition included: firstly, related parties and the people who were entrusted to defend the parties were prohibited from pleading not guilty and they were beaten to confess which damaged procedural justice and always led to miscarriages of justice. For example, in *History*

---

[97] Ji, Yun. Notes of Yuewei Caotang. Volume 18, Masters Who Only Save Four Kinds of People.

[98] Li, Q. (1995). Chinese Private Advisor. The Commercial Press. 117.

[99] Sun Dinglie. SixizhaiJueshi: Preface.

of the Song Dynasty: Heroic Women, a woman, whose family name was Zhang, was blackened by others but she did not confess. In order to force her to confess, officials threw her mother into a pit surrounded by fire and filled water in it. In the Yuan Dynasty, when officials tried Dou E, they forced the filial woman to confess by punishing her mother-in-law. In the Qing Dynasty, Yang Naiwu and Xiao Baicai were also tortured into confession. Secondly, when inquisition by torture prevailed, punishment became the tool of political combat, which infringed on victims' human rights. When victims regained social standing, they often pursued justice with heightened intensity. This shift precipitated a transformation in legal functions, diminishing their institutional authority. Treacherous officials, such as Zhou Xing and Lai Junchen in the Tang Dynasty and Liu Jin and Wei Zhongxian in the Ming Dynasty, all used cruel torture to damage their opponents. However, later they were revenged in more brutal ways by the victims' colleagues. Thirdly, tortures beyond the law were widespread, which made law more frightening. Most civilians were afraid of it and did not dare to be engaged in lawsuits. Therefore, the law became less popularized and cannot truly establish its authority.

In history, most indiscriminate punishment was closely related to the inquisition by tortures used by tyrants and cruel officials; therefore, authorities were prudent in the abuse of penalties, and they tried to control and correct this. *Book of Rites: Monthly Ordinances* recorded, "In the second month of Chinese Lunar Calendar, officials should not indiscriminately torture criminals and should not accept lawsuits." The term "torture" in this context refers to the practice of extracting confessions through physical punishment. Since crimes would influence national security, social stability, and emperors' rule, penal codes were highly developed, and criminal lawsuits were given paramount importance in the traditional Chinese legal system. The enforcement of penal law mainly depended on penalties. In different dynasties, the standards of penal law were different. Some dynasties, such as the Qin Dynasty, followed the severe-penalty doctrine, where even culprits who committed misdemeanors would be sentenced to severe penalties. Some dynasties, such as the early period of the Han Dynasty and the Tang Dynasty, were prudent in punishment, where penalties would be mitigated. Some dynasties, such as the Ming Dynasty, indoctrinate people by punishments, and penal laws were given priority. But themes of penal laws were invariably revenge, intimidation, and suppression. Moreover, penal laws were mainly used to safeguard hierarchy and consolidate monarchy. In trials, officials did not respect the principle that crime and punishment must be judged based on laws; instead, they strictly enforced the presumption of guilt. Many punishments were very inhuman and ignored personal rights and human dignity, among which the inquisition by tortures was the most typical.

Since the Qin Dynasty, the traditional inquisition system, usually by torture, has become more and more standardized and institutionalized. *Qin Code* included relevant regulations of inquisition by torture which was regarded as the worst thing to do. If parties repeatedly changed their confessions or had no way of defending themselves, they would be tortured in accordance with laws, and their confessions would be recorded in files. Then the Han Dynasty followed the inquisition system of the Qin Dynasty. According to *Biography of Du Zhou* in *Book of Han*, in the process of inquisitions, the officials compelled the prisoners to plead guilty in accordance with the bill of indictment. If the accused pleaded not guilty, they would be beaten with canes until they pleaded guilty. Lu Wenshu, who was born in the Western Han Dynasty, once criticized that "what confession could not be obtained after the charged were subjected to fierce beating by canes and rods? The pain was almost more than any prisoners could bear, then they would cook up falsehoods and plead guilty. Officials took advantage of this by fabricating charges and forcing prisoners to plead guilty." In the Southern Liang Dynasty, a torture was created to punish prisoners who did not plead guilty. In details, criminals would be starved for 3 days, and then only two *sheng* (around 400 ml) of porridge, offered by their family members, was allowed for them. If the prisoners were women, old people, or kids, porridge was allowed after 150 *ke* (around 1 and a half days). This torture would stop after 1000 *ke* (around 10 days). Torture by standing on a soil pile was used in the Southern Chen Dynasty, which meant "if prisoners did not confess, after being beaten with 20 whips and 30 flogs, they would be forced to wear fetters and stand on a soil pile that was only room for two feet. Every day the punishment took 7 *ke* (around a quarter to two hours). They would be whipped one time within seven days. If a prisoner could endure 150 beatings with heavy sticks, he would be free from the death penalty." The inquisition by torture in the North Wei Dynasty was crueler. Judges and County and Prefecture Magistrates "were not allowed to reduce the penalties for excusable criminals. Criminals needed to wear heavy cangues and heavy stones were hung on their necks. They were inflicted with severe injuries and strong jailors would beat them repeatedly. When the criminals could not endure torture anymore, they had to confess to false accusations. Officials believed this method was good."[100] All in all, the inquisition system in the Jin and North and South Dynasties was on a malicious trend in development.

The provisions in the *Tang Code* "judicial torture should not exceed a total of three times" and "except beating with heavy sticks no other methods could be used to punish the accused" effectively suppressed the torture used by cruel officials. However, torture was still used. Under the reign of Wu Zetian, cruel officials such as Zhou Xing and Lai Juncheng imposed cruel torture, including pouring vinegar into criminals' noses and placing criminals in grilled jars from which the idiom "invite someone into a jar" originated. Historical records from the Chuigong era (685–688 CE during Wu Zeitian's reign) document that "all whose families were broken by criminal prosecution had endured inquisition by torture."[101] At the beginning of the Song Dynasty, inquisition by torture was once strictly restricted, but judicial officials still abused cruel torture. *History of Song—Penal Code* depicted the inquisition by torture under the reign of the Emperor Lizong of Song. "Beating hands or feet with sticks" was named "dropping of sticks"; strangulation using ropes was named "neck crusher"; constricting the skull with rope-wound wood was named "head hoop"; and forcing kneeling prisoners to endure turnkeys jumping on

[100] History of Wei. Chapter 16. Penalty 7.

[101] Old History of the Tang Dynasty. Volume 50. Treatises. Chapter 30. Penal Law.

their cudgel-pressed legs with hands bound behind their backs was named "leg crusher."

In the Yuan Dynasty, rulers imposed many restrictions on the system of inquisition by torture. It was stipulated that cruel tortures should not be used in all cases. If felons needed to be interrogated by punishment, official assistants should hold meetings to decide whether torture could be used. However, this regulation was only a useless scrap of paper. Many officials abused torture and killed innocent subjects regardless of law. At the beginning of the Ming Dynasty, although there were regulations that prohibited illegal judicial torture, inquisition by torture was ubiquitous. For instance, secret judicial organs employed various tortures despite nominal restrictions. In the Kangxi Era of the Qing Dynasty, instruments of torture such as iron shackles, cudgels, leg crushers, head hoops, branding irons, and so on were officially prohibited. However, in felonies such as homicide and robbery cases, if a male suspect refused truthful testimony, he shall endure leg-crushing, and if a female suspect refused truthful testimony, she shall suffer finger-pressing. Apart from physical torture, there was mental abuse, which forced parties to confess by beating their relatives.[102] Tortures were countless. At the end of the Qing Dynasty, in order to push forward legal reform, the government issued the *The Great Qing Current Penal Code*, which abolished the system of inquisition by torture. However, in fact, this code was not implemented.

Although it was stipulated that inquisition should be carried out in accordance with laws, torture should not be abused. However, illegal punishment could be seen in every dynasty. Usually, the founder of every dynasty observed laws, while their descendants abused torture, or their descendants were benevolent at first but brutal at the end, or their descendants were strict at the implementation of torture at first but misused punishment at the end. For example, at the beginning of the Sui Dynasty, when Yang Jian inherited the throne from the Northern Zhou Dynasty, he enacted *Kaihuang Code*. He made an edict in person that "Laws enacted by different emperors should be adapted to times as every dynasty has different backgrounds. The punishment of hanging could lead to death. The punishment of decapitation was believed to annihilate the offender's corporeal form. These are the most severe expression of penalties. However, exemplary punishments such as "public display of severed heads" and "dismemberment by chariots" are unacceptable. These punishments failed to serve as crime deterrents, only to expose the cruelty of law to commoners."[103] He acted as a benevolent emperor by abolishing such barbaric penalties as "public display of severed heads" and "dismemberment." However, not for long, his cruel nature was revealed. In trivial cases such as "four people stole one bucket together or three people stole one melon together," offenders would be executed immediately.[104] Compared with *Kaihuang Code*, which was issued under the

[102] Lü, B. & Meng, X. (1995). *Complaints and Judgments of Traditional China*. The Commercial Press, International Co., Ltd. 95–98.

[103] History of Sui. Volume 25. Treatises. Chapter 20. Penal Law.

[104] History of Sui. Volume 25. Treatises. Chapter 20. Penal Law.

reign of the Emperor Wen of Sui, *Daye Code* which was launched when the Emperor Yang of Sui ascended the throne was less strict, and it even abolished many provisions that were already not strict in *Kaihuang Code*. However, as the mild code was put into force, it did not stabilize society as expected. Instead, it intensified conflicts between different social classes. Hence the Emperor Yang of Sui urged more strict penalties. He ordered that, across the whole country, thieves would be guillotined regardless of the gravity of the offense. In the 9th year of the Daye Era, he made another edict that "For any thief, the personal property in his house shall be confiscated." Later cruel penalties such as dismemberment by chariots, public display of severed heads, extermination of nine kinship clans, and so on were resumed. Since the Emperor Yang of Sui destroyed the legal system and abused penalties, officials across the country "executed or spared individuals at their own discretion" and "did not obey rules and regulations anymore." Consequently, widespread popular discontent and resistance erupted, severely destabilizing the social order, which culminated in the overthrow of the Sui Dynasty and the assassination of Emperor Yang. Such policy inconsistencies had greatly reduced legal institutions to instruments of arbitrary punishment. During Wu Zetian's reign, she often employed ruthless officials who extrajudicially abused punitive measures to purge political opponents while maintaining constant surveillance. These practices significantly intensified societal tensions throughout her rule.

7.4.5 Absence of Public Credibility

All legal systems are fundamentally shaped by their culture, social structures, and collective mentalities. Undoubtedly, these three factors also significantly influenced the judicial system of traditional China.

From the perspective of culture, Confucianism and Legalism emphasized hierarchy and centralization of authority, advocated governments' authority, and repressed private rights, so that, in judicial practice, governments could infringe on private rights without facing institutional checks or social censure. Buddhism called on people to endure suffering, keep ascetic in their lifetime, and enjoy bliss in their next life. While Taoist philosophy emphasized moral self-cultivation, its tendency toward social disengagement made it ineffective in protecting private rights.

Traditional China depended on an agricultural economy characterized by self-sufficiency for a long time where agriculture was bound to patriarchal political structures, resulting in a society that was insular and closed-off. Private rights were systematically suppressed while the state power expanded boundlessly through the combination of agricultural economy, autocratic rule, and patriarchal hierarchy. The prevailing doctrine that "the commoners should obey laws without comprehending them" fostered a culture of rule by men rather than rule of law. This system operated through strictly vertical administration where officials at each level were accountable solely to superiors while suppressing subordinates with virtually no horizontal checks. The combination of judicial and executive powers in magistrate roles systematically nullified any meaningful separation of authority and the judicial power could not find its place. Consequently, the traditional ruling structure inevitably manifested what Lord Acton famously termed "All power tends to corrupt, and absolute power corrupts absolutely."

After the birth of law in traditional China, it was employed with characteristics of violent suppression. It was believed that laws were related to penalties, suppression, slaughter, and military affairs which were deemed inauspicious. The "Treatises on Criminal Law" in official dynastic histories have effectively become historical narratives centered on penal codes; therefore, the legal history of China was always misinterpreted as a history of penal law. Except for "evil *Songshi* (legal practitioners)" and "shysters" who were keen on filing lawsuits and exaggerating trivial matters, most people were afraid of lawsuits. In traditional Chinese litigation, ordinary people had to "battle through lawsuits," a phrase that vividly reflected the judicial reality: plaintiffs risked corporal punishment upon filing cases, while bribery became essential to curry favor with officials. Tragedies such as "A single vermilion judgment in court draws thousands of drops of tears outside" forced people to shrink back and lose hope in legal remedy. Popular maxims such as "*Yamen* gates face south; none enter without silver, though reason they may bear," "Win the lawsuit, lose a fortune," "Dog dung tastes bitter; lawsuits prove harder," "Avoid litigation lifelong, and pawnshops never need entering," and "All lawsuits end in misfortune" manifested people's skepticism on judiciary. The so-called aspiration for legal remedy was at best a psychological dependence on "imperial edicts," "saintly emperors," and "celestial justice," reinforcing cultural mindsets such as "saintly emperors," "celestial justice," "no lawsuits," "avoiding lawsuits," and "refraining from disputes."

Chinese people value "being kind to others," "harmony is precious," "the golden mean," "comity first," and so on, which are deemed as the golden signboard of China, "a country of etiquettes." These basic social principles have enduring ethical value. However, when such values are advocated in isolation, they risk fostering social apathy, manifesting behaviors such as "sweeping snow from one's own doorstep while ignoring the frost on neighbors' roofs," "avoiding trouble at all costs," "indifferent bystanderism," and "shrinking from mutual aid." This type of mentality not only fails to encourage resistance against social injustice but actively breeds systemic judicial inequities.

The degree of judicial injustice not only reflects the strength of social control of a state or a government and the speed of the process of rule of law but also reflects the public mentality that affects social changes. After the late Qing Dynasty, in order to satisfy the need for social modernization, and abolish consular jurisdiction, China began to push forward judicial modernization by promulgating new-style legal codes, establishing new-style courts, setting up judicial and procuratorial offices that supervised each other, establishing new-style institutions, sending students abroad for legal training and cultivating modern legal talents, introducing the Western attorney system and the adversarial trial procedures, experimenting with the checks and balance system through tripartite and pentapartite power divisions so as to pursue de facto judicial independence, etc. All of these were beneficial and effective to prevent judicial injustice. However, judicial injustice still existed. For example, during the period of the Beiyang Government, which was generally recognized by later generations as having a relatively independent judiciary, the factors bred judicial injustice included inconsistent application of laws, military intervention in trials, insufficient judicial funds, and police or military organs usurping judicial power.[105] During the period of the Nanjing Nationalist government, although the modern code system marked by the "Six Codes" was basically complete, judicial injustice was still serious in judicial practice, which became a social phenomenon criticized by both home and abroad. During the late period of the Nanjing Nationalist Government, as economic collapse and policy chaos escalated, the judicial equilibrium disintegrated, the judicial machine paralyzed, and public trust in law evaporated. This institutional breakdown accelerated societal destabilization.[106] After 1949, the rule of law advanced in fits and starts, with China's judicial system gradually evolving through sustained institutional innovation.

[105] Report of Investigation Committee, Law Review, supplement 182, published on December 26, 1926, Page 112; Wu Xianglin, Concrete Plans to Improve China's Judicial System, China Legal Science, New Volume 1, Omnibus No. 5, 6, Cheng Chung Book Store, 1937, Page 68.

[106] Zhang, R. (2005). Judicial Corruption and Social: 1928–1949, Social Science Academic Press. 438–439.

Index

R. Zhang, *Traditional Legal Culture in China*, Understanding China,
https://doi.org/10.1007/978-981-95-4697-8

The manufacturer's authorised representative in the EU is Springer Nature Customer Service Centre GmbH, Europaplatz 3, 69115 Heidelberg, Germany. If you have any concerns regarding our products, please contact ProductSafety@springernature.com

Printed and bound by CPI Group (UK) Ltd, Croydon, CR0 4YY
21/09/2026
02220014-0002